Lecture Notes in Computer Science   8232

Commenced Publication in 1973
Founding and Former Series Editors:
Gerhard Goos, Juris Hartmanis, and Jan van Leeuwen

Zhenan Sun   Shiguang Shan
Gongping Yang   Jie Zhou
Yunhong Wang   Yilong Yin (Eds.)

Biometric Recognition

8th Chinese Conference, CCBR 2013
Jinan, China, November 16-17, 2013
Proceedings

 Springer

Volume Editors

Zhenan Sun
Chinese Academy of Sciences
Institute of Automation, National
Laboratory of Pattern Recognition
Beijing, China
E-mail: znsun@nlpr.ia.ac.cn

Shiguang Shan
Chinese Academy of Sciences
Institute of Computing Technology
Beijing, China
E-mail: sgshan@ict.ac.cn

Gongping Yang
Shandong University, School of
Computer Science and Technology
Jinan, China
E-mail: gpyang@sdu.edu.cn

Jie Zhou
Tsinghua University
Software Engineering Institute
Beijing, China
E-mail: jzhou@tsinghua.edu.cn

Yunhong Wang
Beihang University, School of
Computer Science and Engineering
Beijing, China
E-mail: yhwang@buaa.edu.cn

Yilong Yin
Shandong University, School of
Computer Science and Technology
Jinan, China
E-mail: ylyin@sdu.edu.cn

ISSN 0302-9743
ISBN 978-3-319-02960-3
DOI 10.1007/978-3-319-02961-0

e-ISSN 1611-3349
e-ISBN 978-3-319-02961-0

Springer Cham Heidelberg New York Dordrecht London
Library of Congress Control Number: 2013951158
CR Subject Classification (1998): I.4, I.5, I.2.10, F.2.2, I.3.5, K.6.5
LNCS Sublibrary: SL 6
Image Processing, Computer Vision, Pattern Recognition, and Graphics

Typesetting: Camera-ready by author, data conversion by Scientific Publishing Services, Chennai, India

Printed on acid-free paper

Springer is part of Springer Science+Business Media (www.springer.com)

Preface

Chinese citizens have been required to register their fingerprints when applying for ID cards since January 2013. It is expected that biometric technology will be widely deployed in China for both public and personal security concerns. China is the country with the largest population in the world, which means that China is also the largest potential market of biometrics with a rapid national economy growth. However, it is also a great challenge to develop a user-friendly, accurate, efficient, robust and secure biometric system to identify 1.3 billion Chinese subjects. Current biometric systems are limited in performance and cannot meet the requirements of the rapidly increasing security applications. Therefore, great efforts are still needed to solve the core problems in biometric sensors, algorithms, and systems.

Biometric recognition has attracted a large number of researchers in China, and Chinese researchers have played an important role in the international biometrics community. Therefore, it is necessary to organize an annual conference to bring together leading biometrics researchers and system designers in China to promote the research and development of reliable and practical solutions for biometric authentication. The Chinese Conference on Biometric Recognition (CCBR) has been successfully held in Beijing, Hangzhou, Xi'an, and Guangzhou for seven times since 2000. The 8th Chinese Conference on Biometric Recognition (CCBR 2013) was held in Jinan, during November 16-17, 2013. This volume of conference proceedings contains 57 papers selected from among 100 submissions; all papers were carefully reviewed by three reviewers on average. The papers address the problems in face, fingerprint and palmprint, vein, iris and ocular, and behavior biometrics as well as other related topics. The novel ideas on biometric sensor algorithms presented in these papers are expected to promote R&D in biometric systems and new research directions.

We would like to express our gratitude to all the contributors, reviewers, and Program Committee and Organizing Committee members, who made this conference successful. We also wish to acknowledge the support of the Chinese Association for Artificial Intelligence, Springer-Verlag, the Chinese Academy of Sciences' Institute of Automation, and Shandong University for sponsoring this conference. Special thanks are due to Qing Zhang, Xiaoming Xi, Zhen Yu, Xianjing Meng, Lu Yang, Rongyang Xiao, and Xiaowei Yan for their hard work in organizing the conference.

November 2013

Zhenan Sun
Shiguang Shan
Gongping Yang
Jie Zhou
Yunhong Wang
Yilong Yin

Organization

Advisors

Tieniu Tan	Institute of Automation, Chinese Academy of Sciences
Jie Tian	Institute of Automation, Chinese Academy of Sciences
Jingyu Yang	Nanjing University of Science and Technology, China
Xilin Chen	Institute of Computing Technology, Chinese Academy of Sciences
Jianhuang Lai	Sun Yat-sen University, China

General Chairs

Jie Zhou	Tsinghua University, China
Yunhong Wang	Beihang University, China
Yilong Yin	Shandong University, China

Program Chairs

Zhenan Sun	Institute of Automation, Chinese Academy of Sciences
Shiguang Shan	Institute of Computing Technology, Chinese Academy of Sciences
Gongping Yang	Shandong University, China

Program Committee

Chengjun Liu	New Jersey Institute of Technology, USA
Karthik Nandakumar	I2R, Singapore
Kim, Jai-Hie	Yonsei University, Republic of Korea
Zhongmin Cai	Xi'an Jiaotong University, China
Caikou Chen	Yangzhou University, China
Fanglin Chen	National University of Defense Technology, China
Wensheng Chen	Shenzhen University, China
Xi Chen	Kunming University of Science and Technology, China
Zhen Cui	Huaqiao University, China
Weihong Deng	Beijing University of Posts and Telecommunications, China

Xiaoqing Ding   Tsinghua University, China
Fuqing Duan   Beijing Normal University, China
Yuchun Fang   Shanghai University, China
Jianjiang Feng   Tsinghua University, China
Jufu Feng   Peking University, China
Ran He   Institute of Automation, Chinese Academy
                             of Sciences
Yuqing He   Beijing Institute of Technology, China
Zhenyu He   Harbin Institute of Technology Shenzhen
                             Graduate School, China
Qingyang Hong   Xiamen University, China
Dewen Hu   National University of Defense Technology,
                             China
Haifeng Hu   Sun Yat-sen University, China
Wei Jia   Institute of Nuclear Energy Safety Technology,
                             Chinese Academy of Sciences, China
Changlong Jin   Shandong University (Weihai), China
Wenxiong Kang   South China University of Technology, China
Wei Li   Fudan University, China
Wenxin Li   Peking University, China
Ziqing Li   Institute of Automation, Chinese Academy
                             of Sciences
Heng Liu   Southwest University of Science and
                             Technology, China
Qingshan Liu   Nanjing University of Information Science and
                             Technology, China
Yuanning Liu   Jilin University, China
Zhi Liu   Shandong University, China
Chaoyang Lu   Xidian University, China
Yuan Mei   Nanjing University of Information Science and
                             Technology, China
Zhichun MU   University of Science and Technology Beijing,
                             China
Gang Pan   Zhejiang University, China
Hong Pan   Southeast University, China
Dongmei Sun   Beijing Jiaotong University, China
Taizhe Tan   Guangdong University of Technology, China
Kejun Wang   Harbin Engineering University, China
Kuanquan Wang   Harbin Institute of Technology, China
Zengfu Wang   Institue of Intelligent Machines (IIM), CAS,
                             China
Lifang Wu   Beijing University of Technology, China
Xiangqian Wu   Harbin Institute of Technology, China
Xiaohua Xie   Shenzhen Institute of Advanced Technology
                             (SIAT), CAS, China

Yuli Xue	Beihang University, China
Jinfeng Yang	Civil Aviation University of China, China
Jucheng Yang	Tianjin University of Science and Technology, China
Xin Yang	Institute of Automation, Chinese Academy of Sciences
Yingchun Yang	Zhejiang University, China
Yuxiang Yang	Xi'an University of Technology, China
Xueyi Ye	Hangzhou Dianzi University, China
Shiqi Yu	Shenzhen University, China
Weiqi Yuan	Shenyang University of Technology, China
Cairong Zhao	Tongji University, China
Qijun Zhao	Sichuan University, China
Xiaosi Zhan	Zhejiang International Studies University, China
Baochang Zhang	Beihang University, China
Lei Zhang	The Hong Kong Polytechnic University, China
Shengping Zhang	Harbin Institute of Technology at Weihai, China
Yongliang Zhang	Zhejiang University of Technology, China
Zhaoxiang Zhang	Beihang University, China
Huicheng Zheng	Sun Yat-sen University, China
Weishi Zheng	Sun Yat-sen University, China
Dexing Zhong	Xi'an Jiaotong University, China
En Zhu	National University of Defense Technology, China

Organizing Committee Chair

Qing Zhang	Shandong University, China

Organizing Committee

Xiaoming Xi	Shandong University, China
Zhen Yu	Shandong University, China
Xianjing Meng	Shandong University, China
Lu Yang	Shandong University, China
Rongyang Xiao	Shandong University, China
Xiaowei Yan	Shandong University, China

Table of Contents

Part I: Face

Part II: Fingerprint and Palmprint

Part III: Vein Biometrics

Part IV: Iris and Ocular Biometrics

Part V: Behavioral Biometrics

Part VI: Others

Normalization for Unconstrained Pose-Invariant 3D Face Recognition

Xun Gong[1,2], Jun Luo[3], and Zehua Fu[1]

[1] School of Information Science and Technology,
South West Jiaotong University,
Chengdu 600031, P.R. China
[2] ChongqingKey Laboratory of Computational Intelligence,
Chongqing 400065, P.R. China
xgong@home.swjtu.edu.cn
[3] Sichuan Academy of Medical Sciences &Sichuan Provincial People's Hospital,
Chengdu 600072, P.R. China

Abstract. This paper presents a framework for 3D face representation, including pose and depth image normalization. Different than a 2D image, a 3D face itself contains sufficient discriminant information. We propose to map the original 3D coordinates to a depth image using a specific resolution, hence, we can remain the original information in 3D space. 1) Posture correction, we propose 2 simple but effective methods to standardize a face model that is appropriate to handle in following steps; 2) create depth image which remain original measurement information. Tests on a large 3D face dataset containing 2700 3D faces from 450 subjects show that, the proposed normalization provides higher recognition accuracies over other representations.

Keywords: 3D face recognition, depth image, pose correction, normalization.

1 Introduction

Boston Marathon bombing events, in 2013, has drawn a lot of public attention to automatic face recognition problem again. A.K. Jain et al. [1] have conducted a case study on automated face recognition under unconstrained condition using the two Boston Marathon bombing suspects. Results indicate that there is still a room for processing images under unconstrained scenes.

With the rapid development and dropping cost of 3D data acquisition devices, 3D face data, which represents faces as 3D point sets or range data, can be captured more quickly and accurately. The use of 3D information in face recognition has attracted great attention and various techniques have been presented in recent years [2-4]. Since 3D face data contain explicit 3D geometry, more clues can be used to handle the variations of face pose and expression.

Even though 3D data potentially benefit to face recognition (FR), many 3D face recognition algorithms in the literature still suffer from the intrinsic complexity in representing and processing 3D facial data. 3D data bring challenges for data

Z. Sun et al. (Eds.): CCBR 2013, LNCS 8232, pp. 1–8, 2013.

preprocessing, like spike removing, hole filling, pose correction and feature representation. The motivation of this paper is to propose a practical 3D face pose normalization method. And what's more, we argue that 3D face itself contains abundant discriminant information. The question is that how to find a good 3D data representation manner. The main contributions are: (1) we propose 2 effective pose correction methods for an arbitrary 3D face obtained by a 3D data acquisition device; (2) create a depth image which can keep original measurement information.

2   3D Face Posture Normalization

For any practical 3D face recognition systems, posture normalization is always an indispensable step, which can also be called as pose correction. In this paper, we propose 2 pose normalization methods, self-dependent pose correction, shorted as SD, and generalized iterative closest point pose correction (GICP).

2.1   Self-dependent Pose Correction

The key step of the proposed correction method SD is carried out by finding a synthesized plane that is parallel to the face plane (as shown in Fig. 1(a)). Then, rectify the plane to make it perpendicular to the direction of Z-axis. In that way, the angle of yaw (around Y-axis) and pitch (around X-axis) can be correctly compensated. At last the roll angle (around Z-axis) can be easily corrected by the connecting line between two pupils or the center line of the mouth, see Fig. 1 for more details.

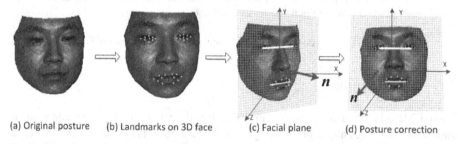

(a) Original posture   (b) Landmarks on 3D face   (c) Facial plane   (d) Posture correction

Fig. 1. Main idea of SD pose correction. Cyan grid in (c) and (d) illustrates the virtual face plane, normal direction of which is denoted by the arrow n. And the connecting lines between two eyes and mouth denote the auxiliary line used for roll angle correction.

Current commercial 3D scanners can generate a 3D point cloud and a registered 2D texture image simultaneously, just as published by some 3D databases like Texas 3DFR[5] and BU_3DFE[6]. Since the texture channel and the 3D points correspond well, 2D information can assist to find the face regions and key features. Chang et al. [7] applied a skin detection method on the texture channel to help 3D facial region extraction. Wang et al. [8] preform 3D facial region cropping with the help of the texture channel. For feature extraction, we also apply the method ASM work on the texture image, as shown in Fig. 1(b). The steps of SD are described as follows:

1)   3D Facial landmarks detection. At first, the face and its characteristic points ("landmarks") on 2D texture image are located through the approach presented in [9], namely, the extended Active Shape Model (STASM) algorithm which is widely used in academic area [10, 11]. The algorithm locates 76 interest points. The precision of the location procedure depends on the amount of face distortion. However, as aforementioned, those key feature points are only used for fitting the face plane, so our system has tolerance of inaccuracy in extend. Once obtain the 2D landmarks on the texture, 3D landmarks V_{76} on 3D face can be obtained according to their corresponding relationship.

2)   Face plane Σ_f fitting. Points on eyes and mouth can be generally seen as placed on the same virtual plane. So we choose the landmarks on two eyes and mouth, 32 points in total (see Fig. 1(b)), to synthesize the facial plane. Those 32 points denote as V_f. Excluding landmarks around the facial contour because those points are always more inaccurate than V_f. A plane can be defined as

$$ax + by + cz + d = 0 \tag{1}$$

With V_f, parameters $[a,b,c,d]$ in (1) can be approximated by using least square method, thus Σ_f is determined.

3)   Pose correction. With Σ_f and its normal n, the pitch and yaw angles can be easily obtained by compute the angle between n and Y-axis and Z-axis, respectively. By calculating the angel α_1 between X axis and connecting line of two pupils, the angel α_2 between X-axis and connecting line of two mouth corners, then, the roll angle is straightforward by average α_1 and α_2. Correction example is shown in Fig. 1(d).

2.2   Generalized Iterative Closest Point Pose Rectification

Iterative Closest Point (ICP) [12] is an effective tool for 3D model registration. But its defects are also well known, like time consuming. For ICP, how to find the matching point pairs is always the key problem, which influent the final result significantly. Another common technique, named as Generalized Procrustes Analysis (GPA) [13], is frequently used for aligning a group of 2D shapes. However, in the problem of 3D model registration, scale in GPA is not needed.

Inspired by GPA, we propose a novel generalized ICP, denoted as GICP, for pose correction problem, which is summarized in Algorithms 1.

Algorithm 1. Generalized ICP
Input: A set of n 3D faces $F = \{ f_1, ..., f_n \}$

Procedure:
1)   Similar to the SD, 76 landmarks are extracted by STASM, and then the 3D landmarks are obtained for each 3D face in F. All of the 3D landmarks are concatenated as a vector s_i, which represents the shape of each face f_i:

$$s_j = \left(x_1, y_1, z_1, \ldots x_j, y_j, z_j, \ldots x_{76}, y_{76}, z_{76} \right), \quad 1 \le j \le 76 , \tag{2}$$

where, $v_j = \left(x_j, y_j, z_j \right)$ is the j-th landmark.

2) Removing the translational component for each shape by subtracting the mean of all landmarks (i.e., $v_j \leftarrow v_j - (1/76)\sum_{j=1}^{76} v_j$).

3) Choose the 1st shape s_1 as the reference, i.e., $s_r \leftarrow s_1$.

4) As relationship between s_r and s_i ($1 \le i \le n$) is known, compute translational and rotational matrix R_i, T_i of s_i by ICP. Update each $s_i = R_i \cdot s_i + T_i$.

5) Update the reference shape by $s_r = (1/n)\sum_{i=1}^{n} s_i$.

6) Compute the difference e between previous reference shape s_r and updated s_r', if $e = |s_r - s_r|_2$ larger than a given threshold ε then repeat step 4 and 5, or goto step 7.

7) Compute the final average shape $\bar{s} = (1/n)\sum_{i=1}^{n} s_i$.

8) Using ICP once again to compute the final translational matrix R_i and rotational matrix T_i for each shape s_i, which are used to adjust each face f_i.

Output: The corrected 3D faces $F' = \{ f_1', \ldots, f_n' \}$ and average shape $\bar{s}$.

It's worth to mention that, with the average shape $\bar{s}$, a new input 3D face can be quickly corrected by the simple ICP with one step after landmarks annotated. For a novel input, GICP can be run as quickly as SD method dose without any iteration.

3   Depth Image Normalization

For a 3D face, a fast and effective way to use 3D information is to create a depth image [2]. And in our experiments, depth image is effective enough for FR if created correctly. If not, the depth image will introduce errors in matching. From examples shown in the second column of Fig. 2(b), we can see that the top face is apparently smaller than the bottom one, which will cause miss matching, due to normalization. The main concern of this section is to find a right way to align depth images.

A common approach alignment in 2D uses the centers of the two eyes. The face is geometrically normalized using the eye locations to (i) scale the face so the inter-pupillary distance (IPD) between eyes is l pixels, and (ii) crop the face to $m*n$ pixels.

We argue that IPD based alignment method is ill-suited for depth image. There are two apparent defects to normalize the depth image by IPD:

(1) Different persons have different IPDs, normalize the depth image by IPD will inevitably cause loss of the original metrics contained in 3D data.
(2) In terms of current technology, the same to 2D face recognition, pupil detection is sensitive to illumination or other factors.

We propose to map the original coordinates (X, Y directions) to a 2D space with fixed resolutions, e.g., 0.5mm per pixel. Since the original measurement data is remained, we denote this image as measurement depth image (MDI). As shown in Fig. 2, IPD based depth image (shorted as IDI) and MDI have different appearances. As for IDI, the results are sensitive to the accuracy of pupils' location, which is always effected by illumination, see Fig. 2(b), e.g., reflection of glass may cause pupil detection fail. For MDI, however, we just put the nose tip to the center of the image, and the final image need not to scale to a specified resolution. In this way, MDI remain the real dimension of one subject. Then we crop it to a predetermined size.

In general, the position of nose tip is easy to obtain by finding the vertex with the largest Z value. Note that this method sometimes may fail to find the actual nose tip due to the burrs, which can be easily wiped off by a filter. So it is still the most significant geometrical feature in 3D space that is widely used in 3D FR area. Even we can develop more sophisticated method to find nose tip, but this is not the main concern of this paper. One can refer more detail from the references [4, 8].

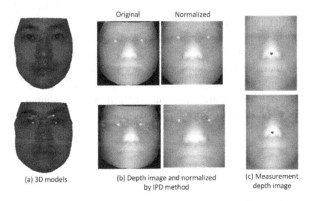

(a) 3D models   (b) Depth image and normalized   (c) Measurement
                            by IPD method   depth image

Fig. 2. Depth image normalized by two different manners. The yellow points in (b) denotes the pupils detected automatically. The red points in (c) are the nose tips.

4   Experiments and Discussion

4.1   3D Face Database

This section carries out experiments to validate our normalization method. At first, we create a 3D face database that consists of 450 persons with 6 models per subject.

Fig. 3. Capture system and one captured 3D face model with different views

The capture system setup is shown in Fig. 3 (a) and, the 3D face example obtained is shown in Fig. 3 (b). Our database consists of 450 persons due that some faces are not correctly segmented in the post-processing. Each person in the database has 6 models, including 5 different poses (frontal, up, down, left and right) and one model with random expression & lighting condition.

4.2   Evaluation of Posture Correction

This paper has proposed 2 kinds of posture correction methods in section 2, i.e., SD and GICP. As we known, without a special system to measure the actual pose of the face obtained, it's hard to assess the accuracy of correction results. We propose here to consider the pose evaluation as a texture matching problem. Local correlation matching (LCM) [10] is used as the similarity measurement. Matching function value closer to 1 once the two images are similar enough. After pose correction, 3D face model is mapped to a 64*64 depth image at first, and then we use LCM to measure the similarity between each pair of depth images of one person. Both SD and GICP methods are tested for all persons in the database, the result is illustrated in Fig. 4, where (a) is the average similarity of every person measured by LCM and (b) is its variance. It's clear that these two approaches are performing basically very similar. What's more important, the average similarity, for both methods, is larger than 0.98 and variance is less than 10^{-3}, which is summarized in Table 1. On conclusion can be drawn that both SD and GICP are appropriate for posture normalization.

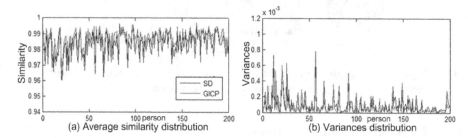

Fig. 4. Comparison the similarity and variance of depth image by 3D models after corrected by SD and GICP, respectively. Only 300 persons are shown in order to see the details more clearly.

Table 1. Average similarity and variance of data in Fig. 4

Methods	Average similarity	Average variance
SD	0.9835	**1.5704e-004**
GICP	**0.9863**	2.4624e-004

4.3   Evaluation of Two Depth Image in FR

In this part, we will illustrate the advantage of measurement depth image (MDI) over IPD based depth image (IDI). In our tests, Local Binary Patterns (LBP), Linear Discriminant Analysis (LDA), and Support Vector Machines (SVM) and their combinations are used: LBP+LDA(LL), LBP+SVM(LS), and LBP+LDA+SVM(LLS).

At first, we compare 3 different methods to normalize the depth image: (1) IPD based depth image (IDI) with automatic pupil detection [14], denoted as IDI-A; (2) IPD based depth image (IDI) with manually selected pupil positions, denoted as IDI-M; (3) measurement depth image (MDI). Since the 2nd type of depth image need tedious manually annotation works, we just choose 100 persons in the test. Even in this case, we have to annotate 600 (100*6) images manually in total. Rank-1 recognition accuracy by LS and LLS are compared in Table 2 and Table 3. As we can see that MDI performs significantly better than the other two depth image.

Table 2. Recognition results of 3 different normalized depth images. FR method: LS

Depth image	Number of images per subject in training set				
	1	2	3	4	5
IDI-A	73.20%	90.50%	93.33%	91.00%	84.00%
IDI-M	72.80%	93.00%	97.67%	98.00%	97.00%
MDI	**81.60%**	**96.75%**	**99.00%**	**99.50%**	**99.00%**

Table 3. Recognition results of 3 different normalized depth images. FR method: LLS

Depth image	Number of images per subject in training set				
	1	2	3	4	5
IDI-A	93.00%	92.50%	94.67%	91.50%	84.00%
IDI-M	95.40%	96.75%	97.67%	98.00%	95.00%
MDI	**98.80%**	**99.25%**	**99.00%**	**98.50%**	**99.00%**

Performance of different FR methods is compared in Fig. 5, as we can see that LLS outperforms the other two methods. Bu LS achieves nearly the same accuracy when more than 1 images for training. Based on SVM theory, it can be easily understood that SVM could not get a valid hyper-plane for classification with a single training sample for each class. As the training number grows, LL performs as well as LLS.

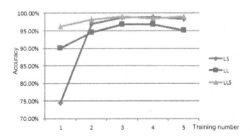

Fig. 5. Comparison of 3 FR method using MDI

5 Conclusions

This work is motivated by fact that 3D data capture system is capable to capture actual space coordinate. A 3D face itself contains sufficient discriminant information.

The main objective of this work is to demonstrate the potential of take full advantage of 3D data in face recognition. Without any feature alignment, FR accuracies using our depth images really exceed the accuracy using other normalized depth image.

In conclusion, this paper proves that even depth image could represent the 3D face information well if it is created in a right way.

Acknowledgments. The authors wish to thank Jiawei Sun for his constructive comments. This work is partially supported by the National Natural Science Foundation of China(61202191), the Fundamental Research Funds for the Central Universities(SWJTU12CX095), and Chongqing Key Laboratory of Computational Intelligence(CQ-LCI-2013-06).

References

1. Klontz, J.C., Jain, A.K.: A Case Study on Unconstrained Facial Recognition Using the Boston Marathon Bombings Suspects 2013, pp. 1–8 (2013)
2. Wang, Y., Liu, J., Tang, X.: Robust 3D Face Recognition by Local Shape Difference Boosting. IEEE T Pattern Anal, 32, 1858-1870 (2010)
3. Guo, Z., Zhang, Y., Xia, Y., Lin, Z., Fan, Y., Feng, D.D.: Multi-pose 3D face recognition based on 2D sparse representation. J. Vis. Commun. Image R 24, 117–126 (2012)
4. Mohammadzade, H., Hatzinakos, D.: Iterative Closest Normal Point for 3D Face Recognition. IEEE Transactions on Pattern Analysis and Machine Intelligence 35(2), 381–397 (2013)
5. Gupta, S., Castleman, K.R., Markey, M.K., Bovik, A.C.: Texas 3D Face Recognition Database. In: Proc. 2010 IEEE Southwest Symposium on Image Analysis Interpretation (SSIAI), TX 2010, Austin, pp. 97–100 (2010)
6. Yin, L., Wei, X., Sun, Y., Wang, J., Rosato, M.J.: A 3D Facial Expression Database For Facial Behavior Research, pp. 211–216 (2006)
7. Chang, K., Bowyer, K.W., Flynn, P.: Multiple Nose Region Matching for 3D Face Recognition under Varying Facial Expression. IEEE Trans. Pattern Analysis and Machine Intelligence 28(10), 1695–1700 (2006)
8. Wang, Y., Liu, J., Tang, X.: Robust 3D Face Recognition by Local Shape Difference Boosting. IEEE T Pattern Anal. 32, 1858–1870 (2010)
9. Milborrow, S., Nicolls, F.: Locating Facial Features with an Extended Active Shape Model. In: Forsyth, D., Torr, P., Zisserman, A. (eds.) ECCV 2008, Part IV. LNCS, vol. 5305, pp. 504–513. Springer, Heidelberg (2008)
10. De Marsico, M., Nappi, M., Riccio, D., Wechsler, H.: Robust Face Recognition for Uncontrolled Pose and Illumination Changes. IEEE Transactions on Systems, Man, and Cybernetics: Systems 43(1), 149–163 (2013)
11. Bonnen, K., Klare, B.F., Jain, A.K.: Component-Based Representation in Automated Face Recognition. IEEE Transactions on Information Forensics and Security 8(1), 239–253 (2013)
12. Besl, P.J., McKay, N.D.: A Method for Registration of 3-D Shapes. IEEE Trans. Pattern Anal. Mach. Intell. 14, 239–256 (1992)
13. Gower, J.C.: Generalized procrustes analysis. Psychometrika 40(1), 33–51 (1975)
14. Valenti, R., Gevers, T.: Accurate Eye Center Location through Invariant Isocentric Patterns. IEEE T Pattern Anal. 34, 1785–1798 (2012)

An Improved Adaptive Weighted LTP Algorithm for Face Recognition Based on Single Training Sample

Rong Huang[1], Lian Zhu[1], Wankou Yang[1], Baochang Zhang[2], and Changyin Sun[1]

[1]School of Automation, Southeast University, Nanjing 210096, China
[2] School of Automation Science and Electrical Engineering,
Beihang University, Beijing 100191, China
{hranny,zhulianseu}@163.com, wankou.yang@yahoo.com,
bczhang@buaa.edu.cn, cysun@seu.edu.cn

Abstract. For the single training sample per person (SSPP) problem, this paper proposes an adaptive weighted LTP algorithm with a novel weighted method involving the standard deviation of the sub-images' feature histogram. First, LTP operator is used to extract texture feature and then feature images are split into sub images. Then, standard deviation is used to compute the adaptive weighted fusion of features. Finally, the nearest classifier is adopted for recognition. The experiments on the ORL and Yale face databases demonstrate the effectiveness of the proposed method.

Keywords: face recognition, Adaptive weighted LTP, single training sample.

1 Introduction

Extracting effective features is a key problem in face recognition, and the feature quality determines the recognition rate. Brunelli and Poggio[1] think that the main face recognition technology and methods can be classified into two broad categories: methods based on geometric features and methods based on template matching.Some representative algorithms such as Principal Component Analysis (PCA) [2], *Linear Discriminant Analysis* (LDA) [3], *Local Feature Analysis* (LFA) [4] *et al.* Many face recognition algorithms/systems have been developed in the last decade and excellent performances have also been reported when there is a sufficient number of representative training samples .In many real-life applications such as passport identification, only one well-controlled frontal sample image is available for training. Under this situation, the performance of existing algorithms will degrade dramatically or may not even be implemented [5]. Faced with SSPP problem, the recognition rate of the available face recognition algorithms will suffer a dramatic decline.

In this paper, to improve the SSPP recognition rate, we apply the adaptive weight to *Local Ternary Patterns* (LTP) [6] which is derived from *Local Binary Patterns* (LBP) [7]. The paper is organized as follows: In Section 2, the LTP representation is introduced. Section 3 presents the concept and the main idea of our proposed approach.

Z. Sun et al. (Eds.): CCBR 2013, LNCS 8232, pp. 9–15, 2013.

In Section 4, we apply the new method in face recognition to ORL and Yale databases and compare the recognition rate with LBP (weight=1.0) and LTP (weight=1.0). Finally, we summarize this paper in Section 5.

2   Local Ternary Pattern

LBP was originally used in texture classification [7]. In 2004, it was applied to face recognition and *Uniform Patterns* [6] was defined. However, as the threshold is the central value of 3×3- neighborhood, the LBP descriptor tends to be sensitive to noise, especially in uniform image regions. It is necessary to improve the robustness of the existing descriptors in these areas. Then the generalization of LBP, Local Ternary Pattern (LTP), is proposed to improve the robustness to noise. In LTP, graylevels in a zone of width ±*t* around i_c are quantized to zero, ones above this are quantized to +1and ones below it to −1, the indicator $p(u)$ is replaced by a 3-valued function:

$$p(i,\ i_c,t) = \begin{cases} +1 & i \geq i_c + t \\ 0 & |i - i_c| < t \\ -1 & i \leq i_c - t. \end{cases} \tag{1}$$

Here *t* is a user-specified. The encoding process of LTP is shown in Fig. 1(set *t*=5).

Then, we separate the LTP code into two code patterns, we call them positive pattern and negative pattern as is illustrated in Fig.2. We can treat the LTP operator as two LBP operators and separately compute their histograms and similarity metrics, combining them only at the end of the computation.

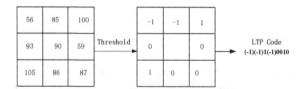

Fig. 1. The basic LTP operator

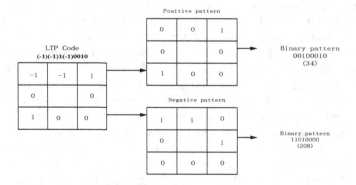

Fig. 2. Splitting a LTP code into positive pattern and negative patterns

3   Face Feature Extraction Based on Adaptive-Weighted LTP

3.1   Face Description with LTP

In this paper, first, we use the LTP operator to extract the texture feature of the face image (a) shown in Fig.3, and we will get one positive eigenface *(a1)* and one negative eigenface *(b1)*. Second, dividing the eigenface into m×m sub blocks, for each sub block we get its positive histogram and negative histogram, and then concatenate the positive and negative histogram of the sub blocks, at last all histograms of the sub blocks are concatenated into a global histogram that represents both the statistics of the facial micro-patterns and their spatial locations, This procedure can be described as follows (here *m=3*):

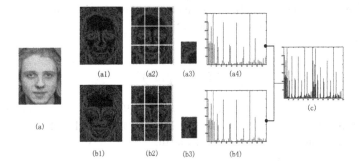

Fig. 3. (a) is an original image from ORL face database. *(a1)* and *(b1)* are respectively the LTP positive and negative engenface. *(a2)* and *(b2)* are the partition processes. *(a3)* and *(b3)* are the *kth* sub image, the histograms *(a4)and(b4)* of the two sub images are concatenated to be one regional histogram*(c)*, and the regional histograms are concatenated to the final spatially enhanced histogram.

3.2   Adaptive Weighted Fusion

T. Ahonen *et al.* introduced an LBP based method for face recognition [7] that divides the face into a regular grid of cells and histograms the uniform LBP's within each cell, finally using nearest neighbor classification in the $\chi 2$ histogram distance for recognition:

$$\chi 2(S, M) = \sum_i \frac{(S_i - M_i)^2}{S_i + M_i}.$$ (3)

Here *S,M* are two image descriptors (histogram vectors). When face images are divided into regions, some regions contains more information, so it's better to set a weight for each region based on the importance of the information it contains. The weighted $\chi 2$ statistic becomes:

$$\chi 2(S, M) = \sum_{i,j} w_j \frac{(S_i - M_i)^2}{S_i + M_i} \tag{4}$$

Where w_j indicates the weight of the regions. The earlier researches on LBP or LTP face recognition are almost based on self-define weight .Some define the default weight=1.0, others set different weights to different blocks manually[7], but it is sometimes a little complex to manually change the weight as the number of the blocks change .

In this paper, we proposed a novel adaptive weighted LTP. It is a generalization of the adaptive weighted LBP. Zhao et $al.$ [8] proposed that in the statistic, variance is a typical statistics used to estimate the divergent degree of a random variable. Here, we use the standard deviation (SD) to estimate the classification quality of the sub images, it is also the optimal choice of the weight.

For every sub image, SD is defined as follows:

$$\delta = \sqrt{\frac{1}{N} \sum_{i=1}^{N} (d(S_i^k, s^k))^2}. \tag{5}$$

Where, N represents the total sample number, $d(S_i^k, s^k)$ denotes the measure distance of the kth sub image of two images, s^k is the kth sub images of all samples'average sub image, k=1, 2, 3...m× m. The $\chi 2$ histogram distance of two histograms is described as:

$$\chi 2(h^1, h^2) = \sum_i \frac{(h_i^1 - h_i^2)^2}{h_i^1 + h_i^2}. \tag{6}$$

In this condition, the SD formula (5) should be

$$\delta = \sqrt{\frac{1}{N} \sum_{i=1}^{N} (\chi^2(h_i^k, h^k))^2} \tag{7}$$

Where, h_i^k represents the kth sub image's histogram vector of the image S_i, h^k is the histogram vector of   the kth sub image that belongs to the average image of all sample images. We set the SD calculated by formula (7) as the weight of each sub image. In theory, the weighted method can effectively improve the recognition rate.

4   Experiments and Results

To verify the effectiveness of the adaptive weighted algorithm, we operate the experiment on the ORL and Yale face database respectively.

In face recognition, shadow, shade, dark light, highlight caused by illumination changes can make recognition rate dropped substantially, therefore we need to adopt the method of preprocess to adjust the face image. In this paper, we use the Gamma Correction to preprocess the image. Process the images by a nonlinear transform:

$$I \rightarrow \log (I)' \; \gamma \in [0, 1]$$ (8)

In ORL, there are 40 persons, everyone have ten different images. There are variations in facial expression (open/closed eyes, smiling/non-smiling.), facial details (glasses/no glasses) and scale (variation of up to about 10 %).

In the experiment, each training sample set is composed of a single sample per person. Each person selects the kth $(k=1,2,...,10)$ image for training, the rest for testing. We choose ten group training sample sets for experiments, and have the average recognition rate as the recognition rate. The recognition result on ORL database is shown in the following Table 1 and Table2.

From Table 1 and Table 2, we can conclude that the method based on Adaptive-weighted LTP do better than other methods, especially the original face recognition based on LBP.

Additionally, to gain knowledge about the robustness of our method against slight variation of facial expression, illumination condition and occlusions, we tested our approach on the Yale database. Table 3 shows the average recognition rate of the experiment on different training sample set with different partition.

Table 1. The recognition rate of LBP, LTP, LTP(Adaptive-weighted), m=3

3*3	LBP(weight=1.0)	LTP(weight=1.0)	LTP(Adaptive-weighted)
K=1	0.766667	0.802778	0.827778
K=2	0.719444	0.800000	0.808333
K=3	0.702778	0.802778	0.822222
K=4	0.763889	0.808333	0.827778
K=5	0.719444	0.744444	0.761111
K=6	0.705556	0.758333	0.766667
K=7	0.691667	0.788889	0.798889
K=8	0.722222	0.800000	0.811111
K=9	0.705556	0.750000	0.777778
K=10	0.758333	0.786111	0.796111
average	0.725556	0.784167	0.807778

Table 2. The recognition rate of LBP, LTP, LTP(Adaptive-weighted), m=4

4*4	LBP(weight=1.0)	LTP(weight=1.0)	LTP(Adaptive-weighted)
K=1	0.766667	0.797222	0.800000
K=2	0.744444	0.772222	0.775000
K=3	0.716667	0.763889	0.769444
K=4	0.736111	0.775000	0.777778
K=5	0.744444	0.738889	0.744444
K=6	0.688889	0.736111	0.738889
K=7	0.713889	0.725000	0.752778
K=8	0.722222	0.758333	0.772222
K=9	0.747222	0.777778	0.802778
K=10	0.769444	0.758333	0.777778
average	0.735000	0.760278	0.770278

Table 3. The average recognition rate of LBP(weight=1.0), LTP(weight=1.0), LTP(Adaptive weighted), where ,m=3,4

	LBP(weight=1.0)	LTP(weight=1.0)	LTP(Adaptive-weighted)
3*3(average)	0.673333	0.692121	0.705051
4*4(average)	0.716970	0.802424	0.826263

The recognition rates in Yale face database show that face recognition based on Adaptive weighted LTP really works better than that based on LBP (weight=1.0), LTP(weight=1.0). The experiment in different face databases suggests that this method has a better robustness.

5 Conclusion

For the SSPP problem in the field of face recognition, we have proposed a novel face recognition method based on adaptive weighted LTP, we make use of the standard deviation to complete the adaptive weighted fusion of the features. This method not only takes advantage of the local texture feature, but also efficiently fuses the feature of each region. It covers the deficit of the existing weighted method and increases the recognition rate in some degree. But the recognition rate of SSPP is still not so ideal, we should do more research in this field.

Acknowledgments. This work is supported in part by NSF of China (61005008, 61375001, 60903065, 61039003 and 61272052), in part by the Ph.D. Programs Foundation of Ministry of Education of China, under Grant 20091102120001, in part by the Fundamental Research Funds for the Central Universities, and by the Program for New Century Excellent Talents in University of Ministry of Education of China.

References

1. Brunelli, R., Poggio, T.: Face recognition: face versus templates. IEEE Trans. on Pattern Analysis and Machine Intelligence 15(10), 1042–1052 (1993)
2. Turk, M., Pentland, A.: Eigenfaces for recognition. Journal of Cognitive Neuroscience 3, 71–86 (1991)
3. Etemad, K., Chellappa, R.: Discriminant analysis for recognition of human face images. Journal of the Optical Society of America 14, 1724–1733 (1997)
4. Penev, P.S., Atiek, J.J.: Local Feature Analysis: A General Statistical Theory for Object Representation. Network: Computation in Neural Systems 7(3), 477–500 (1996)
5. Huang, J., Yuen, P.C., Chen, W.S., Lai, J.H.: Component-based Subspace LDA Method for Face Recognition with One Training Sample. Optical Engineering 44(5), 057002 (2005)
6. Tan, X., Triggs, B.: Enhanced local texture feature sets for face recognition under difficult lighting conditions. In: Zhou, S.K., Zhao, W., Tang, X., Gong, S. (eds.) AMFG 2007. LNCS, vol. 4778, pp. 168–182. Springer, Heidelberg (2007)
7. Ahonen, T., Hadid, A., Pietikainen, M.: Face recognition with local binary patterns. In: Pajdla, T., Matas, J(G.) (eds.) ECCV 2004. LNCS, vol. 3021, pp. 469–481. Springer, Heidelberg (2004)
8. Zhao, R., Fang, B., Wen, J.: Face recognition with single training sample per person based on adaptive weighted LBP. Computer Engineering and Application (31) (2012)

Robust Face Recognition
Based on Spatially-Weighted Sparse Coding

Peipei Zhang, Huicheng Zheng, and Chun Yang

School of Information Science and Technology, Sun Yat-sen University
135 West Xingang Road, 510275 Guangzhou, China
zhenghch@mail.sysu.edu.cn

Abstract. Recently sparse representation has been widely used in face recognition. It has been shown that under maximum likelihood estimation of the sparse coding problem, robustness of face representation and recognition can be improved. In this paper, we propose to weight spatial locations based on their discriminabilities in sparse coding for robust face recognition. More specifically, we estimate the weights at image locations based on a class-specific discriminative scheme, so as to highlight locations in face images that are important for classification. Furthermore, since neighboring locations in face images are often strongly correlated, spatial weights are smoothed to enforce similar values at adjacent locations. Extensive experiments on benchmark face databases demonstrate that our method is very effective in dealing with face occlusion, corruption, lighting and expression changes, etc.

Keywords: Face recognition, sparse coding, spatial weighting.

1 Introduction

Face recognition has been a long-lasting and challenging research topic in computer vision and biometrics [1,2,3]. Many methods have been exploited for face recognition in the past decades, such as eigenfaces [4], Fisherfaces [5], locality preserving projection (LPP) [7], neighborhood preserving embedding (NPE) [10], marginal Fisher analysis (MFA) [15], local discriminant embedding (LDE) [16] and support vector machine (SVM) [6]. Recently, Wright *et al.* [21] employed sparse representation for robust face recognition and achieved impressive performance. Many new methods [8,9,11,18] have been proposed by following this track.

When sufficient training samples are available in each class, a test sample is expected to be best represented as a sparse linear combination of training samples from the same class. The sparse coding problem is often formulated as

$$\min_{\boldsymbol{\alpha}} \|\boldsymbol{y} - \boldsymbol{D}\boldsymbol{\alpha}\|_2^2 \quad s.t. \quad \|\boldsymbol{\alpha}\|_1 \leq \varepsilon, \tag{1}$$

where $\boldsymbol{D}$ is a dictionary of coding atoms often corresponding to training samples, $\boldsymbol{y}$ is the test sample to be represented by using $\boldsymbol{D}$, $\boldsymbol{\alpha}$ is a vector containing coding

Z. Sun et al. (Eds.): CCBR 2013, LNCS 8232, pp. 16–25, 2013.

coefficients of y over D, and $\varepsilon > 0$ is a user-defined constant to enforce sparsity of the coding vector α. Therefore, Eq. (1) represents a sparsity-constrained least square estimation problem [17], where $\min_{\alpha} \|y - D\alpha\|_2^2$ is an l_2-norm fidelity term and $\|\alpha\|_1 \leq \varepsilon$ is an l_1-norm sparsity constraint.

It is known that the coding residual $e = y - D\alpha$ is assumed to follow a Gaussian distribution when the l_2-norm is adopted in the fidelity term [18]. On the other hand, when the l_1-norm is used in the fidelity term instead, the coding residual is assumed to follow a Laplacian distribution, which is believed to be more robust to outliers. Wright et $al.$ propose to use training face images as the dictionary, and a test image is represented as a linear combination of sparse items in the dictionary via l_1-norm minimization [13]. However, both the Gaussian and Laplacian assumptions of the distribution of the residual e may not be appropriate when the face images are subject to complex variations, such as occlusions, corruptions, or expression variations. Yang et $al.$ [18] proposed the robust sparse coding (RSC) to improve the robustness and effectiveness of sparse coding for face recognition. In RSC, elements of the coding residual are assumed to be independent with some probability density function not necessarily Gaussian or Laplacian. The maximum likelihood estimation principle is utilized to robustly represent the given signal with sparse regression coefficients. To the end, they transformed the optimization problem into an iteratively-reweighted sparse coding problem. The sparse coding model in Eq. (1) is replaced by

$$\min_{\alpha} \| M^{\frac{1}{2}}(y - D\alpha)\|_2^2 \quad s.t. \quad \|\alpha\|_1 \leq \varepsilon, \tag{2}$$

where M is a diagonal matrix of weights assigned to pixels of the query image y. For pixels corresponding to outliers (such as occlusion, corruption) and therefore with large residuals, the related elements in M will be adaptively suppressed to reduce their impacts on the regression estimation and improve the robustness to outliers.

However, the RSC ignores the fact that different spatial locations in a face image may have distinct discriminabilities. Motivated by the above observation, we propose to incorporate the discriminability of pixel locations into the sparse coding procedure. Locations (such as mouth, eyes) which may have important contributions to face recognition are expected to be assigned high weight values, and less important areas are given lower weight values. Such weight values are determined through class-specific supervised training. In addition, since adjacent locations in face images are often strongly correlated, we introduce spatially-smoothing constraints to ensure that adjacent image locations exhibit similar weight values. The experimental results show that the proposed method can significantly improve the robustness and effectiveness of sparsity-based face representation and recognition with respect to complex variations including occlusions, corruptions, and expressions.

The rest of this paper is organized as follows. The model of spatially-weighted sparse coding is presented in Section 2. Section 3 presents the overall structure of our algorithm. Experimental results are presented in Section 4. Finally, Section 5 concludes our paper.

2   Spatially-Weighted Sparse Coding

2.1   The Spatial Weighting Strategy

From Eq. (2), we can see that in the RSC approach, the sparse coding is actually weighted pixel-wise. Elements at the diagonal of M correspond to weights resulting from outlier detection, which tend to have small values for pixels corresponding to outliers. However, different locations in a face image may have distinct discriminabilities. Therefore, we propose to incorporate the spatial importance distribution into the sparse coding scheme. More specifically, the training samples D and a specific testing sample y are spatially weighted as follows,

$$\Omega = WD, \tag{3}$$
$$\Gamma = Wy, \tag{4}$$

where W is a diagonal matrix to be learned discriminatively. The i-th diagonal coefficient in W encodes the contribution of the i-th image location. This weighting matrix will be used in sparse coding to incorporate discriminabilities of different pixel locations.

We propose to generate the spatial importance weighting matrix W by following a class-specific discriminative strategy. A practical choice is the linear discriminant analysis (LDA) [12], which is used to find an optimal direction (represented as a weight vector) in terms of discrimination. More specifically, the weighting matrix W is determined by maximizing the between-class scatter while minimizing the within-class scatter of the training samples, namely

$$w^* = \arg\max_w \frac{w^T S_B w}{w^T S_W w} \tag{5}$$

where w is a projection vector and $W = diag(w^*)$, which is a diagonal matrix whose elements correspond to components in w. S_B and S_W are, respectively, the between-class scatter matrix and the within-class scatter matrix of training samples defined as follows,

$$S_B = \sum_{k=1}^{C} n_k (m_k - m)(m_k - m)^T \tag{6}$$

$$S_W = \sum_{k=1}^{C} \sum_{x \in X_k} (x - m_k)(x - m_k)^T \tag{7}$$

where C is the number of classes, X_k is the set of samples in class k, m_k is the mean image of class X_k, n_k is the number of samples in class X_k, m is the mean image of all training samples.

2.2   Spatial Correlation of Weight Coefficients

The spatial correlation between nearby pixel locations in face images suggests the real degree of freedom in the weighting vector w should be less. In this paper, we adopt the approach in [22] and introduce a simple constraint that enforces similar values for components of w corresponding to neighboring image locations. More specifically, we implement a cost function [22]

$$\sum_{i,j}(w_i - w_j)^2 s_{ij}, \tag{8}$$

where w_i and w_j are the i-th and j-th components of w, respectively. s_{ij} are elements of a similarity matrix S and given by

$$s_{ij} = \exp(-\frac{\|l_i - l_j\|_2^2}{2\sigma^2}), \tag{9}$$

where l_i and l_j are the spatial coordinates of the i-th and j-th pixel locations, respectively. σ controls the strength of smoothing and is fixed as 0.5 in our experiments. Minimizing Eq. (8) imposes heavy costs for neighboring elements of w with large gap. In fact,

$$\sum_{i,j}(w_i - w_j)^2 s_{ij} = 2w^T L w \tag{10}$$

where L is a Laplacian matrix defined as $L = C - S$, with C being a diagonal matrix whose diagonal entries are sums of columns (or rows) of the matrix S, i.e. $C_{ii} = \sum_j s_{ij}$.

We would like to solve the maximization problem in Eq. (5) while minimizing Eq. (10). Therefore, these two objective functions are combined as follows,

$$w^* = \arg\max_w \frac{w^T S_B w}{w^T S_W w + \gamma w^T L w} \tag{11}$$

$$= \arg\max_w \frac{w^T S_B w}{w^T \widetilde{S}_W w} \tag{12}$$

where $\widetilde{S}_W = S_W + \gamma L$, γ is a regularization parameter in $[0,1]$. The solution w^* is the eigenvector corresponding to the largest eigenvalue of the generalized eigen-problem:

$$S_B w = \lambda \widetilde{S}_W w. \tag{13}$$

In the RSC, coding residuals at various locations are assumed to be uncorrelated. However, this assumption is often invalid in practice, as analyzed previously. Therefore, we also propose to enforce smoothness of M. More specifically, denoting by v the weight vector formed by diagonal elements of the matrix M in Eq. (2), i.e. $M = diag(v)$, we propose to smooth v by using the Gaussian kernel matrix S as follows,

$$\phi = Sv. \tag{14}$$

Therefore, adjacent elements of ϕ tend to have similar values, i.e. neighboring locations in the image tend to have similar weight values corresponding to the outlier detections.

3   The Algorithm of Spatially-Weighted Sparse Coding

As discussed in Section 2, compared to the RSC, we consider the spatial importance distribution of face images and correlation of nearby spatial locations in sparse coding. The proposed spatially-weighted sparse coding algorithm is a modification of the RSC [18] and can be summarized as follows.

Input
y: l_2-normalized input test image
D: Dictionary with l_2-normalized columns
Output
α: Sparse code
Procedure

1. Solve the spatial weight vector w^* based on Eq. (13). Then $W = diag(w^*)$.
2. The dictionary D and test sample y are spatially weighted as:

$$\Omega = WD,$$

$$\Gamma = Wy.$$

3. Start from $t = 1$, compute the residual $e^{(t)} = y - y_{rec}^{(t)}$, where $y_{rec}^{(1)}$ is initialized as the mean image of all training images.
4. Estimate weights $v_i^{(t)}$ corresponding to outlier detection by using RSC [18], i.e.

$$v_i^{(t)} = \frac{\exp(\mu^{(t)}\delta^{(t)} - \mu^{(t)}(e_i^{(t)})^2)}{1 + \exp(\mu^{(t)}\delta^{(t)} - \mu^{(t)}(e_i^{(t)})^2)}$$

   where μ and δ are two positive scalars controlling the decreasing rate and the location of demarcation point of the function, respectively.
5. Smooth the weights $v_i^{(t)}$:

$$\phi^{(t)} = Sv^{(t)}.$$

6. Compute the current sparse coding vector:

$$\alpha^* = \arg\min_{\alpha} \| M^{\frac{1}{2}}(\Gamma - \Omega\alpha)\|_2^2 \quad s.t. \quad \|\alpha\|_1 \le \varepsilon$$

   where M is a diagonal matrix with $M_{ii}^{(t)} = \phi_i^{(t)}$.
7. Update the sparse coding vector:

$$\alpha^{(t)} = \alpha^{(t-1)} + \lambda^{(t)}(\alpha^* - \alpha^{(t-1)}),$$

   where the step size $0 < \lambda^{(t)} < 1$ and $\alpha^{(1)} = \alpha^*$.

8. Compute the reconstructed sample:

$$y_{rec}^{(t+1)} = D\alpha^{(t)}$$

and let $t = t + 1$.

9. Go back to Step 3 until $\frac{\|M^{(t)} - M^{(t-1)}\|_2}{\|M^{(t-1)}\|_2} < \xi$ (where ξ is a small positive scalar), or until a certain number of iterations is reached.

4 Experimental Results

This section presents the experimental results of our methods compared to related state-of-the-art methods in the literature by using benchmark datasets. In Section 4.1, we test our method for face recognition without occlusion on the AR [14] database, and in Section 4.2, we show the robustness and effectiveness of our method in face recognition under complex variations such as corruption and occlusion etc., on the Extended Yale B [19,20] and AR [14] databases. The main parameters have been set according to [18].

4.1 Face Recognition without Occlusion

Our method is first evaluated on face images with illumination or expression variations, but no occlusion, on the AR database [14]. As in [18], we choose face images of 50 males and 50 females from the AR dataset with only illumination and expression variations. For each subject, 7 images from Session 1(2) are chosen for training(testing). All the images were cropped to 42×30. The comparison of our method to SRC and RSC is given in Table 1. We can see that the accuracy of our method is better than the SRC, and comparable to the RSC, which represents state-of-the-art performance on this dataset.

4.2 Face Recognition with Occlusion

In this subsection, we run extensive tests to verify the robustness and effectiveness of our method to different kinds of occlusions including random pixel corruption, random block occlusion, and real disguise.

1) Face recognition with pixel corruption: The Extended Yale B database is used for this purpose. In accordance to the experiments in [18,21], 717 images with normal-to-moderate lighting conditions from Subset 1 and Subset 2 were used of for training, and 453 images with more extreme lighting conditions from

Table 1. Face recognition rates on the AR database

Algorithms	SRC [21]	RSC [18]	Ours
Recognition rate	94.10%	**96.85%**	96.14%

Subset 3 were used for testing. All the images were resized to 96 × 84. For each testing image, we used random values within [0,255] to replace a certain percentage of pixels in the image to simulate pixel corruption. Locations of the corrupted pixels are random and unknown to the algorithm.

Figure 1 plots the recognition rates of the SRC, the RSC, and our method under various percentages (0% – 90%) of corrupted pixels. We can see that all three methods report an almost perfect accuracy when the percentage of corruption is between 0% – 60%. When 80% of pixels are corrupted, our method can still classify all the test images correctly, while the RSC has a recognition rate of 98.9%, and the SRC only has a recognition rate of 37.5%. The recognition rates of the SRC, the RSC and our method are, respectively, 7.1%, 42.1%, 46.3% when 90% of the pixels are corrupted.

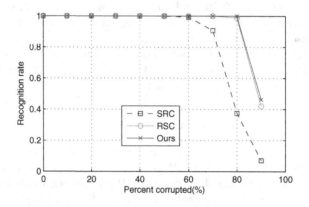

Fig. 1. The recognition accuracies of our approach, the SRC, and the RSC under various percentages of random pixel corruption

2) Face recognition with block occlusion: To test the robustness of our method to artificial block occlusion, we randomly chose a square block in each test image and replaced it with an irrelevant image. As in [18,21], Subset 1 and Subset 2 of Extended Yale B were used for training and Subset 3 for testing. All the images were cropped to 96 × 84. The results of the SRC, the Gabor-SRC (GSRC) [8], the RSC, and our method are shown in Table 2. Again we can see that when the block occlusion is 40%, the recognition rate of our method is still 100%. When half of the image is occluded, our method achieves a recognition rate of 87.1%, over 3% higher than that of the RSC, comparable to that of the GSRC, while the SRC only achieves a rate of 65.3%.

3) Face recognition with real face disguise: In the experiment on real face disguise, we used a subset from the AR database consisting of 2,599 images from 50 males and 50 females, which amount to about 26 samples per subject. As in [18], we carried out two tests. All the images were resized to 42 × 30.

In the first test, we chose 799 images of non-occluded frontal views with various facial expressions (refer to Fig. 2 (a) for some examples) from Sessions 1 and 2

Table 2. The recognition rates under different levels of block occlusion

Occlusion	0%	10%	20%	30%	40%	50%
SRC [21]	1	1	0.998	0.985	0.903	0.653
GSRC [8]	1	1	1	0.998	0.965	**0.874**
RSC [18]	1	1	1	0.998	0.969	0.839
Ours	1	1	1	1	1	0.871

Table 3. Recognition rates of the SRC, the GSRC, the RSC, and our method on the AR database with occlusion of real disguise

Algorithms	SRC [21]	GSRC [8]	RSC [18]	**Ours**
Sunglasses	87.0%	93%	99%	**100%**
Scarf	59.5%	79%	97%	**100%**

for training (about 8 samples per subject), while two separate sets of 200 images with neutral expression for testing (1 sample per subject and per session). In the first set, face images of the subjects are partly occluded by sunglasses (refer to Fig.2 (b) for some examples). The second set consists of images of the subjects wearing scarfs (refer to Fig.2 (c) for some examples). Table 3 lists the results of the SRC, the GSRC, the RSC, and our method. It can be seen that even with sunglasses or scarfs, the recognition rate of our method is 100%. Compared to all the other methods, our method can significantly improve the robustness of face recognition to real disguise.

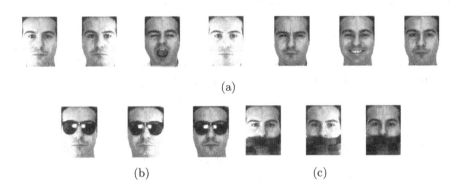

(a)

(b)   (c)

Fig. 2. A subject in the AR database. (a) Training samples with various facial expressions and illumination changes without occlusion. (b) Testing samples with sunglasses, the expression is neutral. (c) Testing samples with scarf, the expression is neutral.

In the second test, we chose 400 images of non-occluded frontal views with neutral expression and various illuminations from Session 1 for training (4 samples per subject), while four separate sets of 300 images with various illuminations for testing (3 samples per subject with sunglasses or scarf for each of Sessions 1 and

Table 4. Recognition rates of the RSC, the SRC, and our method on the AR database with sunglasses (sg-x) or scarf (sc-x) in Session x

Algorithms	sg-1	sc-1	sg-2	sc-2
SRC [21]	89.3%	32.3%	57.3%	12.7%
GSRC [8]	87.3%	85%	45%	66%
RSC [18]	94.7%	91.0%	80.3%	72.7%
Ours	**98.33%**	**95.33%**	**87.67%**	**82.33%**

2). Compared to the first test, the number of training samples is much less. Table 4 shows the results of the SRC, the GSRC, the RSC, and our method. We can see that our method achieves the best results in all the cases. On faces occluded by sunglasses/scarf from Session 1, our method achieves a recognition rate of 98.33%/95.33%, at least 4% higher than that of the RSC. On faces occluded by sunglasses/scarf from Session 2, our method achieves a recognition rate of 87.67%/82.33%, about 7%/10% higher than that of the RSC. Compared to the SRC or the GSRC, the improvements brought by our method are even more significant. The results verified that robust face recognition can be obtained by considering the spatial distribution of discriminabilities and correlation of image locations in sparse coding.

5   Conclusion

In this paper, we propose to incorporate a discriminatively-trained spatial importance distribution model into a previous robust sparse coding approach for face recognition. This idea is motivated by the observation that different locations in a face image may have different levels of contributions to face recognition. More specifically, the importance distribution at pixel locations are regarded as a weight vector and trained discriminatively based on face image of all classes. Furthermore, we propose to smooth the weights to take spatial correlation of image locations into account. To verify the performance of the proposed method, we carry out a number of experiments on benchmark datasets for face recognition under various conditions, including variations of illumination and expression, as well as random pixel corruption or block occlusion, and real disguise. The extensive experimental results verified that our method is very robust against occlusion, corruption, and real disguise for face recognition.

Acknowledgements. This work is supported by National Natural Science Foundation of China (No. 61172141) and Key Projects in the National Science & Technology Pillar Program during the 12th Five-Year Plan Period (No. 2012BAK16B06).

References

1. Zhao, W.Y., Chellppa, R., Phillips, P.J., Rosenfeld, A.: Face recognition: A literature survey. ACM Computing Survey 35(4), 399–458 (2003)
2. Su, Y., Shan, S., Chen, X.L., Gao, W.: Hierarchical ensemble of global and local classifiers for face recognition. IEEE Trans. IP 18(8), 1885–1896 (2009)
3. Zhang, W.C., Shan, S., Gao, W., Chen, X.L.: Local Gabor binary pattern histogram sequence (LGBPHS): A novel non-statistical model for face representation and recognition. In: ICCV, pp. 786–791 (2005)
4. Turk, M., Pentland, A.: Eigenfaces for recognition. J. Cognitive Neuroscience 3(1), 71–86 (1991)
5. Belhumeur, P.N., Hespanha, J.P., Kriengman, D.J.: Eigenfaces vs. Fisherfaces: Recognition using class specific linear projection. IEEE Trans. PAMI 19, 711–720 (1997)
6. Heisele, B., Ho, P., Poggio, T.: Face recognition with support vector machine: Global versus component-based approach. In: ICCV, pp. 688–694 (2001)
7. He, X., Niyogi, P.: Locality preserving projections. In: NIPS (2003)
8. Yang, M., Zhang, L.: Gabor feature based sparse representation for face recognition with Gabor occlusion dictionar. In: Daniilidis, K., Maragos, P., Paragios, N. (eds.) ECCV 2010, Part VI. LNCS, vol. 6316, pp. 448–461. Springer, Heidelberg (2010)
9. Zhang, L., Zhu, P., Hu, Q., Zhang, D.: A linear subspace learning approach via sparse coding. In: ICCV, pp. 755–761 (2011)
10. He, X., Cai, D., Yan, S., Zhang, H.-J.: Neighborhood preserving embedding. In: ICCV, pp. 1208–1213 (2005)
11. Yang, M., Zhang, L., Feng, X., Zhang, D.: Fisher discrimination dictionary learning for sparse representation. In: ICCV, pp. 543–550 (2011)
12. Duda, R.O., Hart, P.E., Stork, D.G.: Pattern classification, 2nd edn. Wiley Interscience, Hoboken (2000)
13. Wright, J., Ma, Y.: Dense error correction via l_1-norm minimization. IEEE Trans. IT 56(7), 3540–3560 (2010)
14. Martinez, A., Benavente, R.: The AR face database. Technical Report 24, CVC (1998)
15. Yan, S., Xu, D., Zhang, B., Zhang, H.-J., Yang, Q., Lin, S.: Graph embedding and extension: A general framework for dimensionality reduction. IEEE Trans. PAMI 29(1), 40–51 (2007)
16. Chen, H.-T., Chang, H.-W., Liu, T.-L.: Local discriminant embedding and its variants. In: CVPR, pp. 846–853 (2005)
17. Tibshirani, R.: Regression shrinkage and selection via the lasso. Journal of the Royal Statistical Society B 58(1), 267–288 (1996)
18. Yang, M., Zhang, L., Yang, J., Zhang, D.: Robust sparse coding for face recognition. In: CVPR, pp. 625–632 (2011)
19. Georghiades, A., Belhumeur, P., Kriegman, D.: From few to many: Illumination cone models for face recognition under variable lighting and pose. IEEE Trans. PAMI 23(6), 643–660 (2001)
20. Lee, K., Ho, J., Kriegman, D.: Acquiring linear subspaces for face recognition under variable lighting. IEEE Trans. PAMI 27(5), 684–698 (2005)
21. Wright, J., Yang, A., Ganesh, A., Sastry, S., Ma, Y.: Robust face recognition via sparse representation. IEEE Trans. PAMI 31(2), 210–227 (2009)
22. Feng, J., Ni, B., Tian, Q., Yan, S.: Geometric l_p-norm feature pooling for image classification. In: CVPR, pp. 2697–2703 (2011)

Non-negative Sparse Representation
Based on Block NMF for Face Recognition

Meng Chen, Wen-Sheng Chen*, Bo Chen, and Binbin Pan

College of Mathematics and Computational Science, Shenzhen University
Shenzhen 518060, China
chenws@szu.edu.cn

Abstract. This paper attempts to utilize the basis images of block non-negative matrix factorization (BNMF) to serve as the sparse learning dictionary, which is more suitable for non-negative sparse representation (NSR) because they have non-negative compatibility. Based on BNMF-basis-image dictionary, the NSR features of query facial images can be learnt directly by solving l_1-regularized least square problems. The NSR-feature based algorithm is then developed and successfully applied to face recognition. Subsequently, to further enhance the discriminant power of NSR method, this paper also proposes a feature fusion approach via combining NSR-feature with BNMF-feature. The proposed algorithms are tested on ORL and FERET face databases. Experimental results show that the proposed NSR+BNMF method greatly outperforms two single-feature based methods, namely NSR method and BNMF method.

Keywords: Face Recognition, Non-negative Sparse Representation, Block Non-negative Matrix Factorization.

1 Introduction

Non-negative matrix factorization (NMF) [1][2] is a popular machine learning algorithm for part-based feature extraction and plays an important role in face recognition. NMF aims to conduct non-negative matrix decomposition on the training image matrix V such that $V \approx WH$, where $W(\geq 0)$ and $H(\geq 0)$ are called the basis image matrix and the coefficient matrix respectively. The local non-negative image features are modeled and contained in W as column vectors. All facial images can be represented by the NMF basis images with dense non-negative coefficients. To obtain sparse representation and improve the performance of traditional NMF method, we previously proposed a block non-negative matrix factorization (BNMF) [3] approach for face recognition. The basic idea of BNMF is firstly to perform NMF algorithm on training image matrix of each individual and then to combine corresponding non-negative basis image matrices or coefficient matrices to obtain the whole non-negative matrix

---

* Corresponding author.

Z. Sun et al. (Eds.): CCBR 2013, LNCS 8232, pp. 26–33, 2013.

decomposition. BNMF is actually a supervised method and has low computational cost. More importantly, BNMF has non-negative sparse coefficient matrix and the coefficient column vectors between different classes are orthogonal.

Non-negative sparse representation (NSR) is a promising feature representation method for face recognition. The main task of NSR needs to address an optimization problem, namely l_0 norm regularization and non-negative-least-squares minimization problem. Unfortunately, the l_0 regularized least squares minimization is an NP-hard problem, where l_0-norm denotes the number of nonzero entries in a vector. Along with recent breakthrough in the sparse signal theory [4]-[6], non-negative sparse representation based face recognition methods [7][8] can avoid directly tackling the l_0-minimization NP-hard problem, which can be equivalently replaced by its closest convex function l_1-norm minimization when the solution is sufficiently sparse.

In NSR algorithms, different learning dictionaries can yield different NSR results. This paper will model the NSR dictionary using BNMF method. In detail, the supervised basis images of BNMF are chosen as the NSR learning dictionary. It is quite suitable for non-negative sparse representation because of their non-negative compatibility. For the training facial images, their NSR features under BNMF-dictionary can be obtained by dealing with l_1-regularized least square minimization problems using the truncated Newton interior-point method [9]. We firstly develop an NSR-feature based face recognition algorithm and then propose a feature fusion approach via combining NSR-feature with BNMF-feature. Two publicly available face databases, namely ORL face database and FERET database, are selected for evaluations. Compared with two single-feature based methods, namely NSR method and BNMF method, experimental results show that the proposed NSR+BNMF feature fusion method has the best performance.

The rest of this paper is organized as follows. Section 2 briefly introduces the related works. In section 3, our two methods, namely NSR-feature method and NSR+BNMF method, are proposed. Section 4 reports the experimental results. Finally, Section 5 draws the conclusions.

2   Review of Related Work

This section will give a brief review of some related works. Details are as follows.

2.1   NMF

NMF aims to seek two non-negative matrices W and H such that:

$$V_{m \times n} \approx W_{m \times r} H_{r \times n},$$
(1)

where matrix V is also an non-negative matrix generated by total n training images. Each column of W is called basis image, and H is the coefficient feature matrix. The divergence between V and WH is defined as:

$$F(W, H) = \sum_{ij} \left(V_{ij} \log \frac{V_{ij}}{(WH)_{ij}} - V_{ij} + (WH)_{ij} \right).$$
(2)

NMF is equivalent to the following optimization problem:

$$\min_{W,H} F(W, H), \text{ subject to } W \geq 0, H \geq 0, \sum_i W_{i,k} = 1, \forall k. \tag{3}$$

Above problem (3) can be solved using the following iterative formulae, which converge to a local minimum:

$$W_{ij} \leftarrow W_{ij} \sum_k \frac{V_{ik}}{(WH)_{ik}} H_{jk}, \; W_{ij} \leftarrow \frac{W_{ij}}{\sum_k W_{kj}}, \; H_{ij} \leftarrow H_{ij} \sum_k W_{ki} \frac{V_{kj}}{(WH)_{kj}}.$$

2.2   BNMF

The basic idea of BNMF is to perform NMF on c small matrices $V^{(i)} \in R^{m \times n_0}$ $(i = 1, 2, \cdots, c)$, namely

$$(V^{(i)})_{m \times n_0} \overset{NMF}{\approx} (W^{(i)})_{m \times r_0} (H^{(i)})_{r_0 \times n_0}, \tag{4}$$

where $V^{(i)}$ consists of n_0 training images from the ith class, and c is the number of classes. The total number of training images is $n = cn_0$. Therefore, we can obtain the following block non-negative matrix factorization from (4):

$$V_{m \times n} \overset{BNMF}{\approx} W_{m \times r} H_{r \times n}, \tag{5}$$

where $r = cr_0$, $n = cn_0$, $V_{m \times n} = [V^{(1)} V^{(2)} \cdots V^{(c)}]$, $W_{m \times n} = [W^{(1)} W^{(2)} \cdots W^{(c)}]$ and $H_{r \times n} = diag(H^{(1)}, H^{(2)}, \cdots, H^{(c)})$.

Here the basis image matrix W will be used in this paper as NSR dictionary.

2.3   Non-negative Sparse Representation

For a testing facial image vector $y \in R^m$, we seek its sparsest non-negative representation $s \in R^n$ according to a non-negative dictionary $W \in R^{m \times n}$. This leads to solving an optimization problem of the form

$$\min_s \|y - Ws\|_2^2 + \lambda \|s\|_0, \; s \geq 0, \; \lambda \geq 0. \tag{6}$$

Here notation $\| \cdot \|_0$ signifies the number of non-zero elements in a vector and λ is a regularization parameter. However, above l_0-norm least squares problem (6) is very hard to tackle since it is an NP-hard problem[4]-[6]. Fortunately, if the solution s is sufficiently sparse, then the regularization term $\|s\|_0$ can be equivalently replaced by $\|s\|_1$ such that the problem (6) becomes convex. So, we can solve the following l_1-regularized least squares problem to obtain an non-negative sparse solution:

$$\min_s \|y - Ws\|_2^2 + \lambda \|s\|_1, \; s \geq 0, \; \lambda \geq 0. \tag{7}$$

3   The Proposed Method

This section will give our two BNMF based NSR face recognition approaches. The details are as follows.

3.1   The Proposed NSR Algorithm

Assume c is the number of class and $V^{(i)}$ is a matrix formed by the training images from class i ($i = 1, 2, \cdots, c$). Non-negative matrix V is generated by all training samples, namely $V = [V^{(1)}, V^{(2)}, \cdots, V^{(c)}]$. By (4) and (5), we can obtain the BNMF of V and choose basis image matrix $W = [W^{(1)}, W^{(2)}, \cdots, W^{(c)}]$ as the non-negative learning dictionary. For a query vector y, we can get its non-negative sparse solution s by solving the l_1-regularized least squares problem (7). It yields that $y \approx Ws = \sum_{i=1}^{c} W_i s_i$, where $s = [s_1^T, s_2^T, \cdots, s_c^T]^T$ and s_i is the sparse coding coefficient associated with W_i. We will assign the testing sample y to the lth class if $\|s_l\|$ is maximal.

Hence, our NSR algorithm is designed as follows.

Step 1: Given the initial values of parameters r_0 and λ. Perform NMF on $V^{(i)}$, $i = 1, 2, \cdots, c$. we have

$$(V^{(i)})_{m \times n_0} \overset{NMF}{\approx} (W^{(i)})_{m \times r_0} (H^{(i)})_{r_0 \times n_0}.$$

Step 2: Generate the sparse learning dictionary W as $W = [W^{(1)}, W^{(2)}, \cdots, W^{(c)}]$.

Step 3: For every testing image y, solving the following l_1-minimization problem and obtain its non-negative sparse feature vector s:

$$\min_{s} \|y - Ws\|_2^2 + \lambda \|s\|_1, s \geq 0, \lambda \geq 0.$$

Step 4: Rewrite s as $s = [s_1^T, s_2^T, \cdots, s_c^T]^T$, where s_i is the sparse coding coefficient vector associated with W_i.

Step 5: If $l = \arg\max_i\{\|s_i\|_1\}$, then the query image y is assigned to the lth class.

3.2   The Proposed NSR Plus BNMF Method

This subsection will present a feature fusion face recognition algorithm called NSR+BNMF method. Details of NSR+BNMF algorithm is designed below.

Step 1: Given the initial values of parameters r_0, t and λ. Perform NMF on $V^{(i)}$, $i = 1, 2, \cdots, c$. we have

$$(V^{(i)})_{m \times n_0} \overset{NMF}{\approx} (W^{(i)})_{m \times r_0} (H^{(i)})_{r_0 \times n_0}.$$

Step 2: Get the sparse learning dictionary W as $W = [W^{(1)}, W^{(2)}, \cdots, W^{(c)}]$ and calculate its Moore-Penrose pseudo inverse of W^{+}.

Step 3: Compute the class center vectors m_i from $V^{(i)}$, $i = 1, 2, \cdots, c$.

Step 4: For every testing image y, solving the following l_1-minimization problem and obtain its non-negative sparse feature vector s from (7). Rewrite s as $s = [s_1^T, s_2^T, \cdots, s_c^T]^T$, where s_i is the sparse coding coefficient vector associated with W_i.

Step 5: Calculate $d_i = (1 - t) * \|W^+(y - m_i)\|_2 - t * \|s_i\|_1$, where $0 < t < 1$.

Step 6: Identity(y)=$\arg \min_i \{d_i\}$.

---

4   Experimental Results

This section will evaluate the performance of the proposed methods for face recognition. In all experiments, the values of parameters are given as $r_0 = 30$, $t = 0.2$ and $\lambda = 0.01$.

4.1   Face Databases

In our experiments, the ORL database and FERET database are selected for the evaluations. The ORL database contains 400 images of 40 persons and each person consists of 10 images with different facial expressions (open or closed eyes, smiling or not smiling), small variations in scales and orientations. The resolution of each image is 112x92, and with 256 gray levels per pixel. Image variations of one person in ORL database are shown in Figure 1.

For FERET database, we select 120 people, 6 images from each person. The resolution of each facial is also 112x92. The six images are extracted from four different sets, namely Fa, Fb, Fc and duplicate. Fa and Fb are sets of images taken with the same cameras on the same day but with different facial expressions. Fc is a set of image taken with different cameras on the same day. Duplicate is a set of images taken around 6-12 months after the day of taking Fa and Fb photos. Images from two individuals are shown in Figure 2.

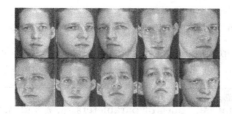

Fig. 1. Images of one person from ORL database

Fig. 2. Images of two persons from FERET database

4.2   Comparisons on ORL Database

The experimental setting on ORL database is as follows. We randomly selected $n(n = 2, 3, \cdots, 9)$ images from each individual for training and the rest $(10 - n)$ images are for testing. The experiments are repeated 10 times and average accuracies are then calculated. The average accuracies are recorded and tabulated in Table 1 and plotted in Figure 3 (left). TN in table 1 means the numbers of training samples.

It can be seen that the recognition accuracy of our NSR+BNMF method increases from 92.19% with 2 training images to 99.50% with 9 training images. The accuracies of BNMF and NSR increase from 80.84% and 86.69% with TN=2 to 96.00% and 98.50% with TN=9 respectively. Experimental results show that our NSR method outperforms BNMF method, while our NSR+BNMF method have the best performance on ORL database.

Table 1. Recognition rates on ORL database

TN	2	3	4	5	6	7	8	9
BNMF	80.84%	87.64%	92.33%	92.95%	95.06%	95.75%	95.63%	96.00%
NSR	86.69%	92.86%	95.04%	97.15%	98.19%	98.50%	98.13%	98.50%
NSR + BNMF	**92.19%**	**96.11%**	**97.13%**	**98.50%**	**99.25%**	**99.08%**	**99.13%**	**99.50%**

4.3   Comparisons on FERET Database

The experimental setting for the FERET database is similar with that of ORL database. As the number of images for each person is 6, the number of training images is ranged from 2 to 5. The experiments are repeated 10 times and the average accuracy is then calculated. The average accuracies are recorded and tabulated in Table 2 and plotted in Figure 3 (right) respectively. When 2 training images used for testing, the recognition rate of our NSR+BNMF method is 83.06%, while the accuracies of BNMF and NSR are 75.60% and 73.44% respectively. The performance for each method is improved when the number of training images increases. When the number of training images is equal to 5, the accuracy for our NSR+BNMF method is increased to 94.83%, while the accuracies of BNMF and NSR ascend to 90.58% and 88.83% respectively. It can be seen that the proposed NSR+BNMF method also outperforms other two methods on FERET database.

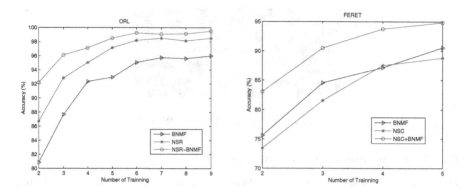

Fig. 3. Recognition rate on ORL face database (left) and FERET face database (right)

Table 2. Recognition rates on FERET database

TN	2	3	4	5
BNMF	75.60%	84.56%	87.17%	90.58%
NSR	73.44%	81.56%	87.54%	88.83%
NSR+BNMF	**83.06%**	**90.50%**	**93.75%**	**94.83%**

5   Conclusions

In order to get a compatible non-negative sparse learning dictionary, this paper proposed to use BNMF method to generate the suitable dictionary and then developed a BNMF dictionary based NSR face recognition algorithm. The non-negative sparse feature of a testing facial image can be obtained by solving l_1-regularized least square problem. Our NSR method achieves good performance and outperforms BNMF method on ORL database. But the proposed NSR method is not robust to facial illumination variations. To further enhance the discriminant power of NSR method, we also proposed a feature fusion approach via combining NSR-feature with BNMF-feature. Experimental results have shown that the proposed NSR+BNMF method gives superior performance.

Acknowledgements. This paper is partially supported by NSFC (61272252) and the Science and Technology Planning Project of Shenzhen City (JC201105130447A, JCYJ201303261111024546). We would like to thank Olivetti Research Laboratory and Amy Research Laboratory for providing the face image databases.

References

1. Lee, D.D., Seung, H.S.: Algorithms for non-negative matrix factorization. Proc. NIPS 13, 556–562 (2001)
2. Lee, D.D., Seung, H.S.: Learning the parts of objects by non-negative matrix factorization. Nature 401, 788–791 (1999)

3. Chen, W.S., Pan, B.B., Fang, B., Li, M., Tang, J.: Incremental Nonnegative Matrix Factorization for Face Recognition. Mathematical Problems in Engineering 2008, Article ID 410674, 17 pages (2008), doi:10.1155/2008/410674

4. Donoho, D., Tanner, J.: Sparse non-negative solution of underdetermined linear equations by linear programming. Proc. Nat. Acad. Sci. 102(27), 9446–9451 (2005)

5. Donoho, D.: For most large underdetermined systems of linear equations the minimal $l1$-norm solution is also the sparsest solution. Comm. Pure and Applied Math. 59(6), 797–829 (2006)

6. Bruckstein, A.M., Elad, M., Zibulevsky, M.: On the uniqueness of non-negative sparse solutions to underdetermined systems of equations. IEEE Trans. Inf. Theory 54(11), 4813–4820 (2008)

7. He, R., Zheng, W.S., Hu, B.G., Kong, X.W.: Two-Stage Non-negative Sparse Representation for Large-Scale Face Recognition. IEEE Transactions on Neural networks and Learning Systems 24(1), 35–46 (2013)

8. Wright, J., Yang, A.Y., Ganesh, A., Sadtry, S.S., Ma, Y.: Robust Face Recognition via Sparse Representation. IEEE Transactions on Pattern Analysis Machine Intelligence 30(2) (2009)

9. Kim, S.J., Koh, K., Lustig, M., Boyd, S., Gorinevsky, D.: A method for large-scale l_1-regularized least squares. IEEE Journal on Selected Topics in Signal Processing 1(4), 606–617 (2007)

An Illumination Invariant Face Recognition Scheme to Combining Normalized Structural Descriptor with Single Scale Retinex

Lifang Wu[*], Peng Zhou, and Xiao Xu

School of Electronic Information and Control Engineering, Beijing University of Technology,
Beijing, China, 100124
lfwu@bjut.edu.cn, {king_zhoupeng,xuxiao}@emails.bjut.edu.cn

Abstract. Illumination variation is still a challenging issue to address in face recognition. Retinex scheme is effective to face images under small illumination variation, but its performance drop when illumination variation is large. We further analyze the normalized images under large illumination variation and we find that the illumination variation has not been removed thoroughly in these images. Structural similarity is one of image similarity metrics similar to human perception. From SSIM, we extract the structure related component and name it as Normalized Structure Descriptor. It is clear that NSD is robust to illumination variation. We propose a scheme to combining Normalized Structural Descriptor with Single Scale Retinex. In our scheme NSD is extracted from the normalized image from SSR. And the face recognition is performed by the similarity of NSD. The experimental results on the Yale Face Database B and Extended Yale Face Database B show that our approach has performance comparable to state-of-the-art approaches.

Keywords: Face Recognition, illumination Variation, Normalized Structural Descriptor (NSD), Single Scale Retinex (SSR).

1   Introduction

Existing face recognition (FR) systems have obtained satisfactory performances in controlled environment. However, some factors in uncontrolled environment have great impacts on the performances of FR systems. Among the factors, illumination variation is one of the most challenging issues to address in face recognition. It has been proven that in face recognition, differences caused by illumination variations are more significant than differences between individuals [1]. Both the face recognition vendor test (FRVT) 2002 [2] and FRVT 2006 [3] have revealed that large variations in illumination can seriously affect the performance of techniques for face recognition.

Recently, numerous different approaches have been proposed to deal with illumination variation. Basically, these methods can be classified into three main categories: (1) illumination normalization, (2) illumination modeling, (3) illumination invariant feature extraction. In the first category, face images under illumination variation are normalized to face images under normal illumination. The typical

Z. Sun et al. (Eds.): CCBR 2013, LNCS 8232, pp. 34–42, 2013.

algorithms include Histogram Equalization (HE) [4], Logarithmic Transform and Gamma Correction. The illumination conditions of the processed image have not been considered in these algorithms and it is difficult to obtain the satisfactory results with them. The second category uses the assumption of certain surface reflectance properties, such as Lambertian surface, to construct images under different illumination conditions. Basri and Jacobs in [5] proved that the images of a convex Lambertian object obtained under different illumination conditions can be well approximated by a 9D linear subspace. Georghiades et al. [6] showed that the illumination cones of human faces can be approximated well by low dimensional linear subspaces. Therefore, the set of face images in   xed pose but under different illumination conditions can be efficiently represented using an illumination cone. Lee et al. [7] showed that the linear subspaces could be directly generated using real nine images captured under a particular set of illumination conditions. These methods can model the illumination variations quite well. However, the main disadvantage of them is that a lot of training samples are required, which makes it not practical for real applications.

The third category tried to find the illumination invariant representation of face images under varying illumination conditions. Numerous approaches have been proposed to solve illumination problems. Local binary pattern (LBP) [8]. DCT [9] More recently, self-quotient image (SQI) [10] has been proposed with impressive improvement of performance for illumination problem. SQI employs the weighed Gaussian filter in which the convolution region is divided into two sub-regions with respect to a threshold, and separate values of weights are applied in each sub-region. Logarithmic total variation (LTV) [11] proposed by Chen et al improved SQI by utilizing the edge-preserving capability of the total variation model. Inspired by the weber's law, Wang et al. [12] proposed a novel illumination insensitive representation (Weber-face) of face images under varying illuminations via a ratio between local intensity variation and the background. Hou et al. [13] use relative gradients (RG) to restore an illumination compensated image by solving a Possion equation. Zhang et al. [14] proposed Gradient-faces which is more robust to different illumination thanks to no need to estimate reflectance R. Gradient-faces extracts illumination insensitive measure in certain scale while high frequency details are important to classification, so it has also less edge-preserving ability.

The Retinex theory motivated by Land [15] is proposed to extract the reflectance component $R(x, y)$ from the image $I(x, y)$ by the illumination-reflectance model. Based on Retinex theory, Jobson [16] proposed Single Scale Retinex (SSR) to remove the illumination variation in face image. But it is effective for image under small illumination variation. Seok Lai Park [17] proposed an iterative scheme to removing the illumination variation more effectively. The iteration causes heavy computational complexity and it is time consuming.

Structural similarity (SSIM) [18] is one of image similarity metrics similar to human perception. From SSIM, We extract the structure related component and name it as Normalized Structure Descriptor. It is clear that NSD is robust to illumination variation.

Motivated by above, we propose a scheme to combining Normalized Structural Descriptor (NSD) with Single Scale Retinex (SSR-NSD) for illumination invariant face recognition. We first get the normalized face images from SSR, which has removed most of illumination variation. we further extract NSD from the normalized images. NSD is robust to illumination variation. it complement the defect of SSR, which can not remove the illumination variation thoroughly if the illumination variation is large. Face recognition is implemented by the similarity between NSDs. Experimental results on Yale Face Database B [6] and Extended Yale Face Database B [6] show that our approach is fast and has the performance comparable to state-of-the-art approaches.

2   The Single Scale Retinex

How robust is the Single Scale Retinex algorithm to illumination variation on face images? We test it using Yale Face Database B. The example face images from subset 1-5, the normalized images and their histogram are shown in Fig.1.

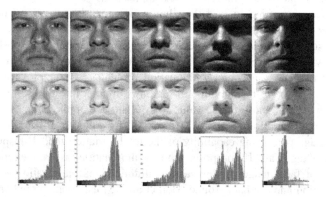

Fig. 1. The example face images , the normalized images from SSR and the histograms

From Fig. 1, the normalized images from subset1~subset3 are good, while those from subset 4 and 5 still include the clear shadow. Furthermore, their histograms are much different from that of subset 1-3. Therefore, we could say that the Single Scale Retinex could reduce most of illumination variation. It leave little illumination variation for the face images under large illumination variation. To this problem, we need introduce further post-process.

3   The Proposed Approach

3.1   The Framework of the Proposed Approach

We first extract the reflectance component R(x,y) by Retinex scheme [16]. Then we reduce the noise by smoothing linear filter. Finally we extract the normalized structural descriptor (NSD) and face recognition is implemented by the similarity of NSDs.

The scheme to SSR-NSD

Input: an aligned face image I

Output: SSR-NSDs of I

1: Extract the reflectance component R from face image using SSR scheme

2: Reduce the noise of R by smoothing, and we get normalized image S.

3: The S is divided into sub-images of size 5*5, the Normalized Structural Descriptor is extracted from each sub-image. The descriptors for all the sub-images are integrated into SSR-NSDs of image I.

3.2   Extract the Normalized Structural Descriptor (NSD)

At the beginning of this section, we analyze characteristics of Structural similarity (SSIM). SSIM is proposed to measure the similarity between image q and t. The measurement from SSIM is much similar to human perception. The traditional SSIM is the product of illumination contrast function L, the contrast contrast function C and structural contrast function S. the component L is related to the average illumination. And the component C is related to the variation of illumination. S is related to the structure. Therefore, we could say that the component S is possibly robust to illumination variation. We further analyze the component S [18].

$$s = \frac{c_{qt} + C}{\sigma_q \sigma_t + C} \tag{1}$$

Where c_q and c_t are the variance of image q and t respectively. c_{qt} is the correlation covariance of image q and t, as shown in Equation (2).

$$\sigma_{qt} = \frac{1}{N-1} \sum_{i=1}^{N} (q_i - \mu_q)(t_i - \mu_t) \tag{2}$$

Where N is the total number of pixels in image q and t. q_i and t_i are the i th pixel in image q and t respectively. μ_q and μ_t are the average of the corresponding image.

where the constant C is included to avoid instability when $c_q c_t$ is very close to zero Therefore, we could say that C is neglectable in theory. By combining Equation (1) and (2), we get Equation (3)

$$s = \frac{\frac{1}{N-1}\sum_{i=1}^{N}(q_i - \mu_q)(t_i - \mu_t)}{\sigma_q \sigma_t}$$

$$= \frac{1}{N-1}\sum_{i=1}^{N}\frac{(q_i - \mu_q)}{\sigma_q}\frac{(t_i - \mu_t)}{\sigma_t}$$

$$= \frac{1}{N-1}\sum_{i=1}^{N}NSD_{qi} \times NSD_{ti}$$

(3)

In Equation (3), S is the summary of product of two similar components, each of which is from the corresponding image. We name the component as Normalized Structural Descriptor (NSD). In a sub-image, the NSD is represented as follows:

$$NSD(x, y) = \frac{(f(x, y) - \mu_f)}{\sigma_f}, (x, y) \in W_{x,y}$$

(4)

Where, $W_{x,y}$ is the sub-image of size 5*5. $f(x, y)$ is the pixel in $W_{x,y}$, μ_f and c_f are the average and variance of the pixels in the sub-images $W_{x,y}$ respectively.

4   Experiments

4.1   Experiment Setting

We test our approach on the Yale Face Database B [6] and Extended Yale Face Database B [6]. These databases are the most commonly used databases for face recognition across illumination variation, so it is best for comparison with state-of-the-art approaches. We compare our approach with HE [4], LBP[8], DCT [9], SQI [10], LTV [11], WF [12], RG [13], GF [14], SSR [16], LRM [19] and NSD. The results of these approach except SSR are obtained from the corresponding reference. The results of SSR are obtained from our experiment.

The Yale B database contains 5760 face images of 10 subjects under 64 different illumination conditions for 9 poses per subject. The Extended Yale Face Database B contains 16128 images of 28 human subjects under 64 different illumination conditions for 9 poses per subject. Because we focus on the issue of illumination variation, only frontal face images are used in this experiment. All images are cropped and resized to 180*180.

The images are divided into 5 subsets based on the angle between the light direction and the camera axis. Subset 1 (0 to 12 degree), subset 2 (13 to 25 degree), subset 3 (26 to 50degree), subset 4 (51 to 77 degree), subset 5 (above 78 degree). Fig. 2 shows some sample images of the first subject in different subsets.

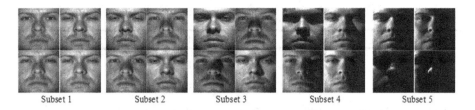

| Subset 1 | Subset 2 | Subset 3 | Subset 4 | Subset 5 |

Fig. 2. Sample images of the first subject in five subsets

4.2   Comparison of Single Scale Retinex and SSR-NSD

We compare the image from SSR and SSR-NSD, as show in Fig. 3. The images from SSR-NSD look more similar to each other than that from SSR. Furthermore, the SSR-NSDs from different subjects are different. Therefore, we could say that the SSR-NSD further reduces the illumination variation and it preserves the inter-class discrimination.

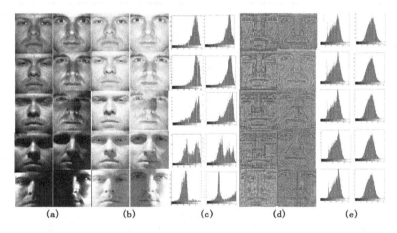

| (a) | (b) | (c) | (d) | (e) |

Fig. 3. Comparison of SSR and SSR-NSD (a) the original five face images of two subjects, (b) the normalized images from SSR, (c) the histogram of (b), (d) the image from SSR-NSD, (e)the histogram of (d)

4.3   Comparison of Face Recognition Performance

In the first experiment, the neutral light sources ("A+000E+00") are chosen as the gallery and all the other frontal images in subsets 1-5 are probes. Face recognition is performed with the nearest neighbor classifier measured with the NSD. The comparison results in Yale face database and Extend Yale face database are shown in Table 1 and Table 2 respectively.

Table 1. The comparison results on Yale Face Database B (neutral light sources as gallery)

Methods	subset 1	subset 2	subset 3	subset 4	subset 5	average
HE	100.0	99.2	73.3	42.1	43.2	71.56
RG	100.0	100.0	94.2	59.3	39.5	78.6
LTV	100.0	100.0	75.8	72.1	79.8	85.54
SSR	100.0	100.0	92.86	87.5	91.5	94.372
NSD	100.0	100.0	91.43	84.17	90.53	93.226
Ours	100.0	100.0	97.1	92.5	96.8	97.28

Table 2. The comparison results on Extended Yale Face Database B (neutral light sources as gallery)

Methods	subset 1	subset 2	subset 3	subset 4	subset 5	average
HE	97.81	92.76	36.18	10.90	13.42	50.214
SQI	88.60	100.0	85.75	87.97	81.20	88.704
LTV	87.28	99.78	66.67	45.49	44.32	68.708
WF	79.39	99.78	75.88	77.07	74.38	81.3
GF	94.74	100.0	83.33	75.94	74.65	85.732
SSR	91.23	100.0	81.95	78.48	81.16	86.564
NSD	90.35	100.0	79.89	76.32	79.75	85.262
Ours	96.0	100.0	84.38	78.90	87.79	89.414

Both Table 1 and Table 2 show that HE and LTV have good performance for face image in subset 1 and 2. And RG is good for subset 1-3, our approach gets 100% recognition rate for subset 1 and 2, and we get over 90% recognition rate for other three subsets. The averaging recognition rate is 97.28%. Our approach is better than Single Scale Retinex (SSR) and Normalized Structural Descriptor (NSD) .

In the second experiment, the face images in subset 1 are chosen as the gallery, and all the other frontal images in subsets 2-5 are probes. The comparison results in two face databases are shown in Table 3 and 4 respectively.

Because more face images are included in the gallery, our approach got 100% recognition for all the four subsets in Yale face database B and we get near 100% recognition rate in Extend Yale face database. It is also better than the compared schemes.

In summary, our approach outperforms LTV, LBP, HE, SQI, DCT and LRM. But we get a little better performance than SSR and NSD.

Table 3. The comparison results on Yale Face Database B (subset 1 as gallery)

Methods	subset 2	subset 3	subset 4	subset 5	average
HE	100.0	81.4	47.1	38.6	66.775
SQI	100.0	96.7	80.7	84.7	90.525
LTV	100.0	100.0	98.5	100.0	99.625
GF	100.0	100.0	99.3	100.0	99.825
SSR	100.0	98.3	98.3	100.0	99.15
NSD	100.0	100	98.33	99.47	99.45
Ours	100.0	100.0	100.0	100.0	100

Table 4. The comparison results on Extended Yale Face Database B (subset 1 as gallery)

Methods	subset 2	subset 3	subset 4	Subset 5	average
DCT	100.0	89.5	89.2	87.4	91.525
LTV	100.0	85.9	85.9	85.4	89.3
LBP	100.0	98.0	77.6	35.6	77.8
LRM	100.0	88.8	92.4	92.4	93.4
SSR	100.0	99.81	98.68	98.31	99.2
NSD	100.0	98.87	96.71	97.23	98.328
Ours	100.0	100.0	99.8	98.9	99.675

5   Conclusion

Face recognition across illumination is a challenging problem. Although there are some competitive approaches, practical approaches still are needed. We propose an illumination invariant face recognition scheme to combining Normalized Structural Descriptor (NSD) with Single Scale Retinex (SSR-NSD). The compared experimental results on Yale Face Database B and Extended Yale Face Database B show that our approach has performance comparable to the state-of-the-art approaches.

References

1. Adini, Y., Moses, Y., Ullman, S.: Face recognition: The problem of compensating for changes in illumination direction. IEEE Trans. Pattern Anal. Mach. Intell. 19(7), 721–732 (1997)

2. Phillips, P.J., Grother, P., Micheals, R.J., Blackburn, D.M., Tabassi, E., Bone, J.M.: FRVT 2002: Evaluation Report Mar, http://www.frvt.org/FRVT2002/
3. Phillips, P.J., Scruggs, W.T., Toole, A.J.O., Flynn, P.J., Bowyer, K.W., Schott, C.L., Sharpe, M.: FRVT 2006 and ICE 2006 large-scale results. In: National Institute of Standards and Technology, NISTIR., vol. 7408 (2007)
4. Pizer, S.M., Amburn, E.P.: Ada ptive histogram equalization and its variations. Comput. Vis. Graph. Image Process 39(3), 355–368 (1987)
5. Basri, R., Jacobs, D.W.: Lambertian reflectance and linear subspaces. IEEE Trans. Pattern Anal. Mach. Intell. 25(2), 218–233 (2003)
6. Georghiades, A.S., Belhumeur, P.N., Kriegman, D.J.: From few to many: illummation cone models for face recognition under variable lighting and pose. IEEE Trans. Pattern Anal. 23(6), 643–660 (2001)
7. Lee, K.C., Ho, J., Kriegman, D.: Nine points of lights: Acquiring subspaces for face recognition under variable lighting. In: Proc. IEEE Conf. CVPR (2001)
8. Ahonen, T., Hadid, A., Pietikainen, M.: Face description with local binary patterns: application to face recognition. IEEE Trans. Pattern Anal. Mach. Intell. 28(12), 2037–2041 (2006)
9. Chen, W., Er, M.J., Wu, S.: Illumination compensation and normalization for robust face recognition using discrete cosine transform in logarithm domain. IEEE Transactions on Systems, Man, and Cybernetics, Part B: Cybernetics 36, 458–466 (2006)
10. Wang, H., Li, S.Z., Wang, Y.: Face recognition under varying lighting conditions using self quotient image. In: Proc. Conf. Autom. Face Gesture Recognit., Seoul, pp. 819–824 (2004)
11. Chen, T., Zhou, X.S., Comaniciu, D., Huang, T.S.: Total variation models for variable lighting face recognition. IEEE Trans. Pattern Anal. Mach. Intell. 28(9), 1519–1524 (2006)
12. Wang, B., Li, W., Yang, W., Liao, Q.: Illumination Normalization Based on We-ber's Law With Application to Face Recognition. IEEE Trans. on SP Letters 18(8), 462–465 (2011)
13. Hou, Z., Yau, W.: Relative gradients for image lighting correction. In: ICASSP, pp. 549–556 (2010)
14. Zhang, T., Tang, Y., Fang, B., Shang, Z., Liu, X.: Face recognition under varying illumination using gradient faces. IEEE Trans. on IP 18(11), 2599–2606 (2009)
15. Land, E.H., McCann, J.J.: Lightness and Retinex Theory. J. Opt. Soc. Am. 61(1), 1–11 (1971)
16. Jobson, D.J., Rahman, Z., Woodell, G.A.: Properties and performance of a center/surround Retinex. IEEE Trans. Image Process. 6(3), 451–462 (1997)
17. Park, Y.K., Park, S.L., Kim, J.K.: Retinex method based on adaptive smoothing for illumination invariant face recognition. Journal Signal Processing Archive 88(8), 1929–1945 (2008)
18. Wang, Z., Bovik, A.C., Sheikh, H.R.: Image quality assessment: From error visibility to structural similarity. IEEE Transactions on Image Processing 13(4), 600–612 (2004)
19. Lian, Z., Er, M.J., Li, J.: A Novel Local Illumination Normalization Approach for Face Recognition. In: 8th International Symposium on Neural Networks, pp. 350–355 (2011)

Shape Constraint and Multi-feature Fusion Particle Filter for Facial Feature Point Tracking

Tao Zhao, Xun Gong*, Tianrui Li, Xinjiang Li, and Wei Xiong

School of Information Science and Technology,
Southwest Jiaotong University, Chengdu, 610031, China
njtcjkzl123@gmail.com, {xgong,trli}@swjtu.edu.cn,
{lxjbb777,xionw12345}@163.com

Abstract. The traditional active shape model (ASM) and optical flow tracking methods are mainly used in the near frontal face or little changes on the face. However, they may easily fail to work, when there exists a change of face posture, expression or shelter. This paper presents a particle filter facial feature point tracking method that based on color and texture features and a shape constraint model. As the nostrils feature point area usually has non-rigid changes in the whole tracking, we extract the color and texture features of the area as the observation model. Then the rest feature points take it as a reference and build a geometric shape constraint model for tracking in real-time. If the tracking error exceeds the threshold value, we restart ASM searching and update the observation model so that each of the feature points can be tracked accurately. Experimental results demonstrate the effectiveness and accuracy of the proposed method.

Keywords: Facial Feature Point Tracking, ASM, Particle Filter, Shape Constraint Model, Color and Texture Features.

1   Introduction

In recent years, real-time and robust facial feature point tracking in computer vision is still a challenging task. It is widely used in various fields of human-computer interaction. For example, facial expression recognition, facial expression imitation, and 3D face modeling. They all need precise tracking results to use for further data analysis. So far, the facial feature point tracking faces many challenges, e.g., the change of face posture, expression and illumination as well as short occlusion.

To solve these problems, early researchers often use the principal adaboost algorithm to detect the face at first, and then track the facial points by the deformable template [1] and active appearance model (AAM) matching method [2]. Although these methods can accurately conduct face contour tracking, but the real-time is not satisfactory. Huang *et al.* [3] proposed a combination of random forest and linear discriminate analysis (LDA) pose estimation algorithm for tracking the facial feature

---

* Corresponding author.

Z. Sun et al. (Eds.): CCBR 2013, LNCS 8232, pp. 43–50, 2013.

points, and then used the online appearance model (OAM) [4] and incremental principal component analysis (PCA) [5] to update the AAM texture model. This method efficiently solves the change of illumination, expression and poses during tracking. Cui *et al.* [6] proposed to use Lucas-Kanade optical flow algorithm [7] to align the human face based on the traditional AAM. Although this method is real-time, but cannot effectively solve the posture change or temporary occlusion, and is not robust for real applications.

Recently, some scholars began to use the particle filter [8] to perform facial feature point tracking. Yun *et al.* [9] proposed a multi-differential evolution particle filter Markov model and color of the kernel-based correlation analysis method. But its error is large and its time complexity is also high. David *et al.* [10] proposed a low-dimensional subspace incremental learning representation method. It effectively adapted the online target model changing, which mainly includes two important features for the model update: updating sample mean and joining a forgetting factor. The method effectively improved the tracking performance. It performed well in dealing with the variation of pose, illumination and expression.

This paper presents a particle filter feature point tracking method that based on color and texture features and a shape constraint model. First, we use the ASM to locate the facial feature points automatically. According to the nostrils feature point area usually has non-rigid changes during tracking, we extract the color and gradient texture features of this area as the observation model. The rest feature points take the nostrils area as a reference and build a shape constraint model for real-time tracking.

The rest of this paper is organized as follows. Section 2 describes our facial feature point tracking algorithm in detail. In Section 3, experiment results are presented to demonstrate the effectiveness and accuracy of the proposed method. In Section 4, the conclusion and future work are outlined.

2   The Proposed Algorithm

Video usually has so much information. If we use only a single feature as the observation model, it is easily fail to track. So we need to use the multiple features fusion to represent it. In this paper, we select the color histogram and direction gradient texture features to represent the observation model.

2.1   Color Histogram Feature

Color features are usually used as the basic feature for target tracking. Because there exists a strict correlation among the various components in the *RGB* color space, we transform the *RGB* color space into the *HSV* color space. *H* component represents the color hue. After we get the *H* component, we calculate the *H* component color histogram and normalize it.

At time t, all particles $X_t = \{x_t^i, w_t^i, i = 1, 2, \cdots, N\}$ use the previous position of former particles at time t-1 as the center, and calculate their corresponding target models for the candidate region. Thus we get N candidate normalized histograms. Then we use the Bhattacharyya distance formulation to measure the similarity between each candidate region of the normalized H_c and the target color histogram H_0.

$$D_c(H_c, H_0) = \sqrt{1 - \frac{\sqrt{\sum_{i=1}^{N} H_c(i) H_0(i)}}{\sqrt{\sum_{i=1}^{N} H_c(i) \sum_{i=1}^{N} H_0(i)}}} \qquad (1)$$

where i is the number of histogram box, and $D_c(H_c, H_0)$ represents the similarity between each candidate normalized color histogram and the target color histogram.

2.2   The Amplitude and Direction Gradient Texture Feature

The amplitude and direction gradient texture information of each pixel of the nose feature point area are calculated by the gradient of the texture with the weighted magnitude and direction. For the similarity of the gradient texture feature, we use the Euclidean distance to measure it between each candidate area and the model area.

$$D_T[p(X_t), q] = \sum_{i=0}^{m} \sqrt{(TEXTURE_{xy}^i - q_{MODEL}^i)^2} \qquad (2)$$

where $D_T[p(X_t), q]$ represents the gradient texture similarity between each candidate area and the model area at X_t, q_{MODEL}^i is the direction gradient texture feature in the model area and m devotes pixel numbers.

2.3   Dynamic Model

The state of particle is defined as $X = [x, y, dx, dy]$, where x, y specifies the center of the target area, and dx, dy indicates the offset of the x and y directions. The dynamic model usually is represented by a first order autoregressive process model.

$$X_t^{(n)} = X_{t-1}^{(n)} + N_{t-1}^{(n)} \qquad (3)$$

where $N_{t-1}^{(n)}$ is a noise matrix at time t-1. It can be obtained by the random number generator or the empirical distribution and training.

2.4   Observation Model

The observation model of each particle is represented by the color histogram and direction gradient texture features in this paper. The color likelihood measurement is given by

$$p_c(z_t \mid x_t^i) = \exp(-20 D_c(H_c, H_0)) \qquad (4)$$

where $p_c(z_t \mid x_t^i)$ refers to the probability of color histogram between each candidate area and the target area at time t. If the value is large, it means that area is the particles most likely concentrated. The texture likelihood measurement is defined as follows:

$$p_T(z_t \mid x_t^i) = \exp(-10D_T[p(X_t),q]) \tag{5}$$

where $p_T(z_t \mid x_t^i)$ refers to the probability of the normalized direction gradient texture between each candidate area and the target area under X_t at time t. If the value is large, it means that area is the particles most likely concentrated. Thus, the weighted multiple features likelihood measurement can be obtained by combing the color histogram and direction gradient texture feature measurements at time t:

$$p(z_t \mid x_t) = \alpha p_c(z_t \mid x_t^i) + \beta p_T(z_t \mid x_t^i) \tag{6}$$

where $\alpha + \beta = 1$. Let the importance density function be $q(X_t \mid X_{t-1},z_t) = p(X_t \mid X_{t-1})$, Then, the update of each particle weighted value is given as follows:

$$w_t^{(i)} = w_{t-1}^{(i)}[\alpha p_c(z_t \mid x_t^i) + \beta p_T(z_t \mid x_t^i)] \tag{7}$$

According to the dynamic model $X_t^{(i)}$ and the observation model $w_t^{(i)}$, we can obtain the state position of each particle as follows:

$$E(X_t) = \sum_{i=0}^{N-1} w_t^{(i)} X_t^{(i)} \tag{8}$$

2.5   Shape Constraint Model

Our method focuses on using color histogram and direction gradient texture features to track the nostrils feature point area. The rest key feature points take the area as a reference and build a geometric shape constraint model for tracking [11]. Our geometric shape constraint model is defined as follows (see Fig. 1).

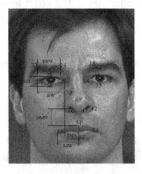

Fig. 1. Shape constraint model

This paper mainly uses the eyes, eyebrows, nostrils, mouth, and other key feature points to build the shape constraint model as shown in Fig. 1. These key feature points includes: Eight eyes points: right eye 27, 28, 29, 30 and left eye 32, 33, 34, 35; Four eyebrows points: left eyebrow 16, 18 and right eyebrow 22, 24; Nostrils points 46, 47;

Four mouth points 48, 51, 54, 57. The shape constraint condition of each feature point is defined as follows:

(1) The shape constraint of the eyes and eyebrows

$$\frac{2}{3} \times EW \le Width(x(29) - x(27)) \le \frac{4}{3} \times EW \;;\quad Height(x(29) - x(27)) \le \frac{1}{3} \times EH \;;$$

$$\frac{2}{3} \times EBW \le Width(x(24) - x(22)) \le \frac{4}{3} \times EBW \;;\quad Width(\frac{x(29) + x(34)}{2} - \frac{x(46) + x(47)}{2}) \le \frac{1}{2} EMW \;;$$

$$W(\frac{x(29) + x(27)}{2}) - \frac{1}{4} \times EW \le Width(x(30)) \le W(\frac{x(29) + x(27)}{2}) + \frac{1}{4} \times EW \;;$$

$$Height(x(24)) \le Height(x(28)) \le Height(x(30)) \;;$$

$$Height(\frac{x(29) + x(27)}{2}) \le Height(x(30)) \le Height(\frac{x(29) + x(27)}{2}) + EH \;.$$

(2) The shape constraint of the mouth

$$Width(x(46)) \le Width(x(51)) \le Width(x(47)) \;;\quad Height(x(51)) \ge Height(\frac{x(46) + x(47)}{2}) + \frac{1}{2} \times HMN \;;$$

$$Height(x(51)) \ge Height(\frac{x(46) + x(47)}{2}) + \frac{1}{2} \times HMN \;;\quad Width(x(46)) \le Width(x(57)) \le Width(x(47)) \;;$$

$$Height(x(57)) \ge Height(x(51)) \;;\qquad\qquad Height(x(57)) \ge Height(x(51)) \;;$$

$$Width(x(51)) - 2 \times MW \le Width(x(48)) \le Width(x(51)) - \frac{1}{2} \times MW \;;\quad Height(x(48)) \ge Height(x(51)) \;;$$

$$Width(x(51)) + \frac{1}{2} \times MW \le Width(x(54)) \le Width(x(51)) + 2 \times MW \;;\quad Height(x(54)) \ge Height(x(51)) \;.$$

2.6   Summary of the Tracking Algorithm

(1) Use the Viola Jones to detect the human face position in the first frame.
(2) Use ASM algorithm to locate the facial feature points in the first frame automatically.
(3) Initialize the color histogram and direction gradient texture parameters and the particle filter numbers.
(4) Move to next frame. According to the dynamic model (Formula (3)), find the nostrils target area, and then calculate the color histogram and direction gradient texture features of the area according to Formulae (4) and (5), at last calculate the similarity of the whole observation model (Formula(6)).
(5) Update the weight value according to Formula (7) and normalize it, use Formula (8) to decide the particles state position at time t.
(6) In the particle filter tracking, start the shape constraint model. If the track fails, or the distance between rest feature points and nose reference point exceeds the threshold value, restart ASM searching and update the observation model.
(7) Go to step (4) until video ends.

2.7   The Flowchart of the Tracking Algorithm

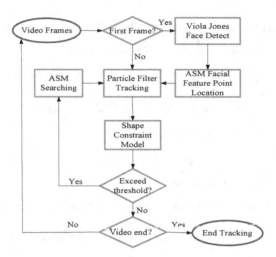

Fig. 2. Flowchart of facial feature tracking system

3   Experimental Results

The proposed facial feature tracking algorithm is implemented in Visual Studio 2008 and OpenCV 2.1 environment on a Windows platform with Intel Core 2 CPU 2.7GHz. To evaluate the effectiveness of our algorithm, we record a video for experiment by ourselves. Its resolution is 320×240 pixels and contains 580 frame numbers. The video frame rate is 30 frames per second. This video includes facial posture, expression, shelter and other complex changes. In the experiment, the target area is based on the center coordinates of feature point 67. The x and y coordinate difference of points 42 and 38 are the area's width and height, respectively. The particle number is 100. We compare our Shape Constrained Color and Texture Particle Filter Tracking (SCCT-PF) with Optical Flow Tracking (OF), and Color and Texture Particle Filter Tracking (CT-PF) [8]. Fig. 3 shows that OF is easy to fail tracking. If continue tracking, the feature points will easily drift away. CT-PF [8] used the particle filter based on color and texture to track. Though it is not easy to drift, the tracking accuracy is not satisfactory for each feature point. But if we use two features and shape constraint model to track, every point can be tracked accurately. Fig. 4 shows some tracking results by using SCCT-PF.

Finally, we compare the Root Mean Square Error (RMSE) for the three tracking methods. The average error rate of OF is 15.4944 and CT-PF method is 12.3697, but SCCT-PF is only 4.5677, which shows that the RMSE of our method is the lowest and the accuracy of tracking is the best. Fig. 5 shows the varying tendency of the three tracking methods. It can be seen, the RMSE of our method is significantly lower than the other two methods. Thus, in the particle filter tracking framework, building a geometric shape constraint model is also important to extract the color and texture features as the tracking information. It can well improve the accuracy of facial feature point tracking.

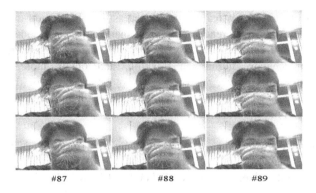

Fig. 3. Feature point tracking results under varying shelter (row 1: OF; row 2: CT-PF; row3: SCCT-PF)

Fig. 4. Tracking Results of SCCT-PF (frames 1, 69, 103, 139, 164, 287, 402, 503, from left to right and up to down)

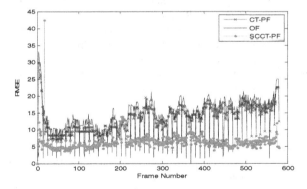

Fig. 5. RMSE Comparison among three tracking methods

4   Conclusion

This paper presented a particle filter facial feature point tracking method that based on color and texture features and a shape constraint model. We extracted the color and texture features of the nostrils feature point area as the observation model. The rest feature points took it as a reference and built a shape constraint model for real-time tracking. This method can well improve the performance when shelter, posture and facial expression change during the tracking, and obtain more accurate and satisfactory results. Our further work focuses on the selection of the observation model and the improvement of the dynamic model with other features. Also, the update of the model needs further improvement.

Acknowledgments. This work is supported by the National Natural Science Foundation of China (Nos. 61202191, 61175047) and the Fundamental Research Funds for the Central Universities (Nos. SWJTU11ZT08, SWJTU12CX095).

References

1. Gallo, O., Manduchi, R.: Reading 1D barcodes with mobile phones using deformable templates. IEEE Transactions on Pattern Analysis and Machine Intelligence 33, 1834–1843 (2011)
2. Zhou, M., Liang, L., Sun, J., Wang, Y.: AAM based face tracking with temporal matching and face segmentation. In: 2010 IEEE Conference on Computer Vision and Pattern Recognition (CVPR), pp. 701–708 (2010)
3. Huang, C., Ding, X., Fang, C.: A robust and efficient facial feature tracking algorithm. Acta Automatic Sinica 38, 788–796 (2012)
4. Wang, P., Qiao, H.: Online appearance model learning and generation for adaptive visual tracking. IEEE Transactions on Circuits and Systems for Video Technology 21, 156–169 (2011)
5. Yang, H., Song, Z., Chen, R.: An improved unscented particle filter for visual hand tracking. In: 2010 3rd International Congress on Image and Signal Processing (CISP), vol. 1, pp. 427–431 (2010)
6. Cui, Y., Jin, Z.: Facial feature points tracking based on AAM with optical flow constrained initialization. J. Pattern Recognition Research, 72–79 (2012)
7. Kalyan, T., Malathi, M.: Architectural implementation of high speed optical flow computation based on Lucas-Kanade algorithm. In: 2011 3rd International Conference on Electronics Computer Technology (ICECT), vol. 4, pp. 192–195 (2011)
8. Tian, H., Chen, Y.Q., Shen, T.Z.: Face tracking using multiple facial features based on particle filter. In: 2010 2nd International Asia Conference on Informatics in Control, Automation and Robotics (CAR), vol. 3, pp. 72–75 (2010)
9. Yun, T., Guan, L.: Fiducial point tracking for facial expression using multiple particle filters with kernel correlation analysis. In: 2010 17th IEEE International Conference on Image Processing (ICIP), pp. 373–376 (2010)
10. Ross, D.A., Lim, J., Lin, R., Yang, M.: Incremental learning for robust visual tracking. International Journal Computer Vision 77, 125–141 (2008)
11. Fazli, S., Afrouzian, R., Seyedarabi, H.: Fiducial facial points tracking using particle filter and geometric features. In: 2010 17th IEEE International Conference on Image Processing (ICIP), pp. 396–400 (2010)

Robust Marginal Fisher Analysis

Shuxian Yi, Caikou Chen, Juanjuan Cui, and Yu Ding

College of Information Engineering, Yangzhou Univeristy
yzcck@126.com

Abstract. Nonlinear dimensionality reduction and face classifier selection are two key issues of face recognition. In this paper, an efficient face recognition algorithm named Robust Marginal Fisher Analysis (RMFA) is proposed, which uses the recent advances on rank minimization. Marginal Fisher Analysis (MFA) is a supervised manifold learning method who perseveres the local manifold information. However, one major shortcoming of MFA is its brittleness with respect to grossly corrupted or outlying observations. So the main idea of RMFA is as follows. First, the high-dimensional face images are mapped into lower-dimensional discriminating feature space by low-rank matrix recovery (LR), which determines a low-rank data matrix from corrupted input data. Then try to obtain a set of projection axes that maximize the ratio of between-class scatter $\mathbf{S}_b$ against within-class scatter $\mathbf{S}_w$ by using MFA. Several experiments are used to illustrate the benefit and robustness of RMFA.

Keywords: Low-rank Decomposition, Marginal Fisher Analysis, Robust, Classification.

1 Introduction

Face recognition (FR) has attracted the attention of researchers for more than two decades due to its widespread applications in many fields. However, in the real world, image data often lies in a high-dimensional space, ranging from several hundreds to thousands. Thus, it is necessary to transform the data from high-dimensional space to a low-dimensional one for alleviating the curse of dimensionality. As a result, numerous face recognition algorithms have been proposed. Among them, Principal Components Analysis (PCA) and Linear Discriminant Analysis (LDA) are two well-known feature extraction and dimensionality reduction methods for face recognition [14]. However, they fail to discover the intrinsic structure of face data which is more important than the global Euclidean structure[15]. To discover the intrinsic manifold structure of the face data, Kernel method and Manifold learning were proposed.

In 2000, the idea of manifold learning was first been proposed in *Science* [3], and became a hotspot in information science field due to its important significant in theory and application. Several nonlinear dimensional reduction algorithms (including ISOMAP[2], LLE[3], LE[4] and MFA[1]) were recently developed. Among these

Z. Sun et al. (Eds.): CCBR 2013, LNCS 8232, pp. 51–61, 2013.

algorithms, Marginal Fisher Analysis(MFA) has gained significant popularity due to its solid theory foundation and generalization performance[13]. MFA aims to preserve the within-class neighborhood relationship and dissociating the sub-manifolds for different classes. It is based on the graph embedding framework and explicitly considers the internal geometry structure and class label information. Although MFA seems to be more efficient than other manifold learning algorithms for face recognition, its performance and applicability are limited by a lack of robustness to sparse errors with large magnitudes for FisherFaces.

In many applications like face recognition and computer vision, gross errors are ubiquitous, where some measurements may be arbitrarily corrupted (e.g., due to occlusion or sensor failure) or simply irrelevant to the structure we tend to identify. The performance will be degraded when using such corrupted images for training. Thus, several approaches on solving this problem have been explored in the literature including robust PCA and low-rank matrix recovery (LR). Among them, low-rank matrix recovery can be solved in polynomial time and has been shown to provide promising results [5].

Motivated by recent progress in low-rank matrix decomposition and MFA, we propose a more effective method, called Robust Marginal Fisher Analysis (RMFA) in this paper. The main idea of RMFA is that the LR constraint can decompose the original corrupted training data matrix $\mathbf{X}$ into the low rank matrix $\mathbf{A}$ and sparse error matrix $\mathbf{E}$. Thus, a noise-free data matrix $\mathbf{A}$ has been obtained. By adding the low-rank constraint, we use the noise-free data matrix $\mathbf{A}$ for training, which can lead RMFA have more robustness and discriminating power compared with traditional classification algorithms. The extensive experimental results in the paper will demonstrate the effectiveness of RMFA.

2   Related Works

In this section, we will introduce two related Marginal Fisher Analysis and Low-rank matrix decomposition.

2.1   Marginal Fisher Analysis

Marginal Fisher Analysis (MFA) is a kind of manifold learning algorithm which is an effective tool for nonlinear problem. The main idea of MFA is to construct two graphs according to the neighborhood relationship of samples, then formulate the criterion of cohesion among intra-class samples and separation among inter-class samples according the two graphs.

MFA mainly contains two graphs (intrinsic graph and penalty graph), shown in Fig.1. Owning to taking the labels of training samples into consideration, a criterion function has been formulated to find a projection that maximizes the ratio of between-class scatter $\mathbf{S}_b$ against within-class scatter $\mathbf{S}_w$. That is to say MFA tend to obtain a set of projection axes to preserve the within-class neighborhood relationship while dissociating the sub-manifolds for different classes. The criterion function can be defined as:

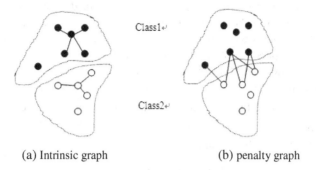

| (a) Intrinsic graph | (b) penalty graph |

Fig. 1. Intrinsic graph and penalty graph. (a) is the intrinsic graph, which is used to connect the k_1 neighborhoods for each samples in the same class and describe the tightness within the class. (b) is the penalty graph, which is used to connect the k_2 neighborhoods (boundary points) for each sample in different classes and describe the separability.

$$J_{MFA}(\mathbf{w}) = \arg\max_{\mathbf{w}} \frac{\mathbf{W}^T \mathbf{S}_b \mathbf{W}}{\mathbf{W}^T \mathbf{S}_w \mathbf{W}} \tag{1}$$

2.2 Robust PCA and Low Rank Matrix Recovery

In many engineering problems, the input matrixes are often corrupted by gross errors or outliers, some of the matrix data could even be missing, or only a set of measurements of the matrix is accessible rather than its entries directly. Due to this problem,

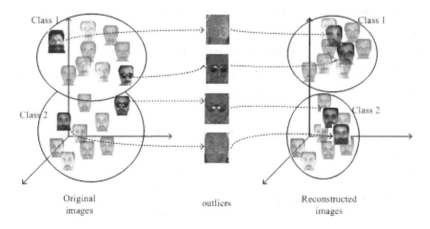

Fig. 2. Decompose the original corrupted by outliers into low-rank matrix and associated sparse error. There are nine images for both of the classes with different expression and noise. Obviously, there is no distinct boundary in original images between the two classes, after decomposition, the two classes gather in their own district.

Low-rank matrix recovery (LR) is used to correct corrupted or missing data. Thus, we intend seeking to recover the true matrix **A** from **X**. Low-rank matrix recovery (LR) is a technique to decompose a data matrix **X** into **A** + **E**, where **A** is a low-rank matrix and **E** is the associated sparse error. In other words, LR is used to remove the outliers or corruptions and project only the noise-free images [7]. As shown in Fig.2

Assume the input data matrix $\mathbf{X} \in \mathbb{R}^{d \times n}$, LR minimizes the rank of matrix **A** while reducing $\|\mathbf{E}\|_0$ to derive the low-rank approximation of **X**. Since the aforementioned optimization problem is NP-hard, Candes *et al.* [6] solve the problem by transforming the objective function as following:

$$\min_{\mathbf{A},\mathbf{E}} \|\mathbf{A}\|_* + \lambda \|\mathbf{E}\|_1$$
$$\text{s.t.} \quad \mathbf{X} = \mathbf{A} + \mathbf{E}$$

(2)

where $\|\cdot\|_*$ denotes the nuclear norm of the matrix (i.e., the sum of the singular values of the matrix), and $\|\cdot\|_1$ represents the l_1-norm, (i.e. the sum of the absolute values of entries in the matrix).

3   Robust Marginal Fisher Analysis

3.1   Objective Function

Let $\mathbf{X} = \{\mathbf{x}_1, \mathbf{x}_2, \cdots, \mathbf{x}_n\}$ be a matrix containing nd-dimensional samples and belonging to c classes, possibly corrupted by outliers. $\mathbf{x}_i \in R^d, i = 1, \cdots, m$, and **w** donates the projection, $\mathbf{y}_i = \mathbf{w}^T \mathbf{x}_i (i = 1, \cdots, m)$. Formally, $\mathbf{X} = \mathbf{A} + \mathbf{E}$, where **A** is the underlying noise-free low-rank component and **E** contains the outliers. In the traditional Marginal Fisher Analysis (MFA), one usually uses the original data directly from **X** as training set. The noise-free component **A** is unknown, so Fisherfaces constructed by **X** is a biased estimation. Our RMFA solved this problem by factorizing **X** into **A** plus **E** (using (2)) and then using the noise-free matrix **A** to construct the Fisherfaces.

The most common method for solving this convex relaxation version called augmented Lagrange multipliers (ALM) [8], which has been applied due to its computational efficiency. Thus the objection function can equivalent to:

$$L(\mathbf{A},\mathbf{E},\Gamma,\mu) = \|\mathbf{A}\|_* + \lambda \|\mathbf{E}\|_1 + \langle \Gamma, \mathbf{X} - \mathbf{A} - \mathbf{E} \rangle + \frac{\mu}{2} \|\mathbf{X} - \mathbf{A} - \mathbf{E}\|_F^2$$

(3)

Using the noise-free samples for training and then construct the Intrinsic Graph and Penalty Graph. The Within-class scatter matrix $\mathbf{S}_w$ can be defined as:

$$\mathbf{S}_w = \sum_i \sum_{i \in N_{k_1}^+(j) \text{ or } j \in N_{k_1}^+(i)} \left\| \mathbf{w}^T \mathbf{a}_i - \mathbf{w}^T \mathbf{a}_j \right\|^2 = 2\mathbf{w}^T \mathbf{A}(\mathbf{D} - \mathbf{W})\mathbf{A}^T \mathbf{w}$$

$$\mathbf{W}_{ij} = \begin{cases} 1, & \text{when } i \in N_{k_1}^+(j) \text{ or } j \in N_{k_1}^+(i) \\ 0, & \text{otherwise} \end{cases}$$

(4)

Where $N_{k_1}^+(i)$ denotes the sample set of k_1 neighbor points of $\mathbf{x}_i$ within the class, $\mathbf{D}$ is a Diagonal matrix, and $\mathbf{D}_{ii} = \sum_j \mathbf{W}_{ij}$. The Between-class scatter can be defined as:

$$\mathbf{S}_b = \sum_i \sum_{(i,j) \in P_{k_2}(c_i) \text{ or} (i,j) \in P_{k_2}(c_j)} \left\| \mathbf{w}^T \mathbf{a}_i - \mathbf{w}^T \mathbf{a}_j \right\|^2 = 2\mathbf{w}^T \mathbf{A}(\mathbf{D}^b - \mathbf{W}^b)\mathbf{A}^T \mathbf{w}$$

$$\mathbf{W}_{ij}^P = \begin{cases} 1, & \text{when } (i,j) \in P_{k_2}(c_i) \text{ or } (i,j) \in P_{k_2}(c_j) \\ 0, & \text{otherwise} \end{cases}$$

(5)

Where $P_{k_2}(c_i)$ denotes the sample set of k_2 neighbor points of $\mathbf{x}_i$ between the classes, $\mathbf{D}^P$ is a Diagonal matrix, and $\mathbf{D}_{ii}^b = \sum_j \mathbf{W}_{ij}^b$.

Thus, the criterion function can be defined as:

$$J_{RMFA}(\mathbf{w}) = \arg \max_{\mathbf{w}} \frac{\mathbf{w}^T \mathbf{A}(\mathbf{D}^b - \mathbf{W}^b)\mathbf{A}^T \mathbf{w}}{\mathbf{w}^T \mathbf{A}(\mathbf{D} - \mathbf{W})\mathbf{A}^T \mathbf{w}}$$

(6)

Where $N_{k_1}^+(i)$ denotes the sample set of k_1 neighbor points of $\mathbf{x}_i$ within the class, $\mathbf{D}$ is a Diagonal matrix, and $\mathbf{D}_{ii} = \sum_j \mathbf{W}_{ij}$.

The objective function can be solved by Lagrangian method and transform the equation to $\mathbf{S}_b^L \mathbf{v} = \lambda \mathbf{S}_w^L \mathbf{v}$. In order to avoid $\mathbf{S}_w^L$ to be singular.

3.2   Algorithm Process

The detailed algorithmic procedure of robust MFA is stated in Algorithm 1.

Algorithm 1. ALM algorithm for solving Robust Marginal Fisher Analysis

---

1:    **input:** training data $\mathbf{X} = [\mathbf{x}_1, \ldots, \mathbf{x}_n]$, the parameters λ

2:    Reduce the dimension of original images using PCA.

5:    Low-Rank decompose: $\mathbf{X} = \mathbf{A} + \mathbf{E}$

6:    Construct Intrinsic Graph   and Penalty Graph:

$$W_{ij}^{\,w} = \begin{cases} 1 & if \mathbf{a}_i \in N_{K_w}\left(\mathbf{x}_j\right) or \mathbf{a}_j \in N_{K_w}\left(\mathbf{x}_i\right) \\ 0 & otherwise \end{cases} ,$$

$$W_{ij}^{\,b} = \begin{cases} 1 & if \mathbf{a}_i \in P_{K_b}\left(\mathbf{a}_j\right) or \mathbf{x}_j \in P_{K_b}\left(\mathbf{a}_i\right) \\ 0 & otherwise \end{cases}$$

7:    Construct Within-class scatter matrix $\mathbf{S}_w$ and between-class scatter matrix $\mathbf{S}_b$:

$$\mathbf{S}_w = \mathbf{A}(\mathbf{D}^w - \mathbf{W}^w)\mathbf{A}^T, \mathbf{S}_b = \mathbf{A}(\mathbf{D}^b - \mathbf{W}^b)\mathbf{A}^T$$

8:    solving the generalized characteristic equation: $\mathbf{S}_b^L \mathbf{v} = \lambda \mathbf{S}_w^L \mathbf{v}$

10: **output: v**

---

4   Experiments

In this section, the proposed method was applied for pose estimation and face recognition and tested on two well-known face image databases (AR and extended Yale B).

We compare our RMFA method against classical methods on pose estimation and face recognition. In order to evaluate the robustness of the proposed method, we applied it to problems with intrinsic noises and outliers to different extents. The first experiment illustrates the ability of RMFA to remove in-subspace outliers in AR and Extended Yale B databases. The second experiment reports the comparisons of our RLDAMFA against PCA and RPCA, MFA and UDP on the same two databases.

(a) Faces in AR database

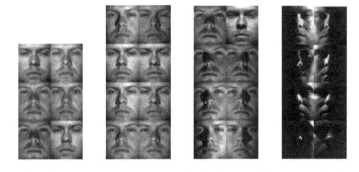

(b) Faces in Extended Yale B database

Fig. 3. AR and extended Yale B database for object recognition and action classification. (a) be the samples taken from AR database. (b) be the samples taken from extended Yale B database.

4.1   Experiments on the AR Face Database

AR database [9] consists of over 4,000 color frontal face images of 126 subjects (70 men and 56 women). Each subject contains 26 images which are separated in two sessions and each session contains 13 images (three images with sunglasses, another three with scarves, and the remaining seven simply with illumination and expressions variations). We cropped the face portion of each image manually and then resized it to $50 \times 40 = 2000$ pixels (see Fig.3 (a)). We separate the experiment into two parts: (1) we choose several images without occlusion for training; (2) we choose both images with and without occlusion for training.

4.2   Images without Occlusion

In this experiment, we choose the first 7 clean images from the first session for training, and the corresponding clean images in session 2 for testing. Thus, the total number of training and testing samples is both 840. The result shown in Fig.4.

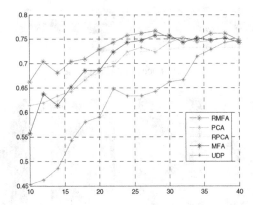

Fig. 4. The performance of different methods while training samples were noise-free

In this experiment, RMFA is slightly better than other algorithms due to using the noise-free training samples. In order to reveal the advantage of our method, we experiment the method with corrupted training samples in the next sections.

4.1.2   Images with Occlusion

In this experiment, we test the performance on AR database under varying occlusions due to sunglasses and scarf. And compare RMFA with PCA, RPCA, MFA and UDP in recognition. We selected corrupted images due to the occlusion of expressions which occlude about 20%, sunglasses which cover nearly 30% and scarf which cover nearly 50% of the faces. (1) Seven clean images and three images with sunglasses in session 1 for training and the remaining images for testing; (2) Seven clean images and three images with scarf in session 1 for training and the remaining images for testing; (3) Seven clean images and two different occluded images (one images with glasses an one images with scarf) in session 1 for training and the remaining images for testing. The results shown in Table.1 and Fig.5

Table 1. The best recognition results under cases with occlusions

	RMFA	PCA	RPCA	MFA	UDP
Sunglasses	0.7833	0.7167	0.71	0.7233	0.7467
Scarf	0.7333	0.68	0.68	0.7	0.7
Sunglasses +Scarf	0.7	0.6423	0.6397	0.6846	0.6333

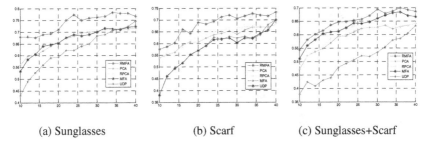

(a) Sunglasses   (b) Scarf   (c) Sunglasses+Scarf

Fig. 5. The performance of different methods while training samples were disturbed by sunglasses and scarves

When 20%, 30%, 50% of the images are corrupted, MFA and UDP can both perform better than traditional discriminate methods. The most important reason is that manifold methods preserved the intrinsic structure of images. However, they ignore the occlusion included in the images, thus our RMFA has a big advantage in separating noise from corrupted images. And we can see RMFA reaches 78.33%, 73.33% and 70%, which are higher than other similar methods while MFA reaches 74.6%, 70% and 63.33%. In other words, our method improves the MFA by 3% to 7%. In next subsection, we will illustrate the ability of RMFA in head pose estimation under different lighting conditions.

4.3   Experiments on the Extended Yale B Database

extended Yale B database [10] consists of 2,414 frontal face images of 38 subjects (around 59-64 images for each person) from Yale Database B and C. The size of cropped and normalized face images is $192 \times 168 = 32256$ pixels. According to the angle the light source direction makes with the camera axis, the images from each pose were divided into 4 subsets: subset1 ($\leq 12°$), subset2 ($\leq 25°$), subset3 ($\leq 50°$), subset4 ($\leq 77°$), shown in Fig.3 (b).

In order to indicate the effectiveness of our method, we experiment further on Extended Yale B database. In this experiment, we choose randomly 20 images for training and the remaining images for testing. And we also compare our method against PCA, RPCA MFA and UDP for discrimination (results shown in Fig.6).

In both experiments, our method outperforms all other associated methods for pose estimation as shown in Fig.6(a) and face recognition as shown in Fig.6(b). Comparing the two methods (in Fig.6(a)) of MFA and RMFA, they both perform well, but MFA fails in preserving more personal features, while LRLDA obtains noise-free images and keeps main features at the utmost in the same time. In Fig.6(b), MFA performs much better than PCA, RPCA and UDP in recognition, and reach 70%. But RMFA achieves 80% which due to the noise-free samples for training. In other words, our method improves MFA by about 10%. Thus, we confirm the useful of our RMFA especially when alleviates the problem of severe illustration variations even such noise is presented in both training and testing samples.

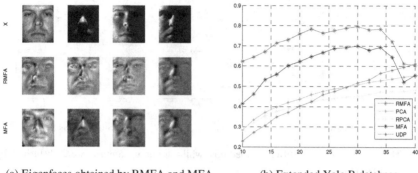

(a) Eigenfaces obtained by RMFA and MFA   (b) Extended Yale B database

Fig. 6. The performance of different methods while training samples were disturbed by no occlusions

According to the experiments we demonstrated above, RMFA has been proved to be an effective tool for pose estimation, classification and discrimination. Thus, we successfully confirm the effectiveness and robustness of our proposed method.

5   Conclusion

The paper proposed a Robust Marginal Fisher Analysis (RMFA) that is robust to corruptions in the input data. By introducing the low-rank constraint into the traditional Marginal Fisher Analysis (MFA), we can get a set of noise-free images and obtain a projection subspace for classification. The experiments on AR and Extended Yale B databases have demonstrate the effectiveness and robustness of our method in discrimination and classification.

References

1. Yang, J., Zhang, D.: Globally maximizing, locally minimizing: unsupervised discriminant projection with applications to face and palm Biometrics[C]. IEEE Transaction on Pattern Anal Machine Intell. 29(4), 650–664 (2007)
2. Tenenbaum, J.B., de Silva, V., Langford, J.C.: A Global Geometric Framework for Nonlinear Dimensionality Reduction. Science 290, 2319–2323 (2000)
3. Roweis, S.T., Saul, L.K.: Nonlinear Dimensionality Reduction by Locally Linear Embedding. Science 290, 2323–2326 (2000)
4. Belkin, M., Niyogi, P.: Laplacian Eigenmaps and Spectral Techniques for Embedding and Clustering. In: Advances in Neural Information Processing Systems, vol. 14, pp. 586–691. MIT Press (2001)
5. Candès, E.J., Li, X., Ma, Y., Wright, J.: Robust Principal Component Analysis. Journal of the ACM (3) (2010)
6. Candès, E.J., Li, X., Ma, Y., Wright, J.: Robust Principal Component Analysis. Journal of the ACM (3) (2010)

7. Huang, D., Cabral, R., De la Torre, F.: Robust Regression
8. Hotelling, H.: Analysis of a complex of statistical variables into principal components. Journal of Educational Psychologh 24(6), 417–441 (1933)
9. Martinez, A., Benavente, R.: The AR face database. CVC Technical Report, 24 (1998)
10. Chen, Y.D., Jalali, A., Sanghavi, S., Caramanis, C.: Low-rank Matrix Recovery from Error and Erasures.
11. Fisher, R.A.: The Statistical Utilization of Multiple Measurements. Annals of Eugenics 8, 376–386 (1938)
12. Fukunaga, K.: Introduction to Statistical Pattern Recognition, 2nd edn. Academic Press (1990)
13. Yan, S., Xu, D., Zhang, B., Zhang, H.-J., Yang, Q., Lin, S.: Graph embedding and extensions: a general framework for dimensionality reduction. IEEE Transactions on Pattern Analysis and Machine Intelligence 29, 40–51 (2007)
14. Duda, R.O., Hart, P.E., Stork, D.G.: Pattern Classification, 2nd edn. WileyInterscience, Hoboken (2000)
15. He, X., Yan, S., Hu, Y., Niyogi, P., Zhang, H.-J.: Face recognition using Laplacianfaces. IEEE Transactions on Pattern analysis and Machine Intelligence 27, 328–340 (2005)

Face Recognition Based on Adaptive Soft Histogram Local Binary Patterns

Huixing Ye[1], Roland Hu[1,*], Huimin Yu[1], and Robert Ian Damper[2]

[1] Department of Information Science and Electronic Engineering, Zhejiang University, China
[2] Department of Electronics and Computer Science, University of Southampton, United Kingdom
{yehuix,haoji_hu,yhm2005}@zju.edu.cn,
rid@ecs.soton.ac.uk

Abstract. In this paper we propose the adaptive soft histogram local binary pattern (ASLBP) for face recognition. ASLBP is an extension of the soft histogram local binary pattern (SLBP). Different from the local binary pattern (LBP) and its variants, ASLBP is based on adaptively learning the soft margin of decision boundaries with the aim to improve recognition accuracy. Experiments on the CMU-PIE database show that ASLBP outperforms LBP and SLBP. Although ASLBP is designed to increase the performance of SLBP, the proposed learning process can be generalized to other LBP variants.

Keywords: local binary pattern (LBP), soft histogram local binary pattern (SLBP), face recognition.

1 Introduction

As proposed by Pietikäinen *et al.* [1], the local binary pattern (LBP) has been widely implemented in computer vision and pattern recognition. The advantage of LBP lies in a low computational complexity and low sensitivity to changes in illumination, so that it has been used in several applications such as face recognition [2], texture classification [3] and medical imaging [4], etc.

The calculation of the LBP descriptors depends on the gray level difference between a pixel and its local neighborhood placed on a circle of radius R, thus this calculation is sensitive to local noise that tends to modify gray level values. Because of this, several variants of LBP have been proposed to deal with the issue of noise sensitivity.

One variant of LBP is the local triplet pattern [5], in which the gray level difference between the center pixel and the neighboring pixel is encoded into a triplet code. Local triplet pattern is less sensitive to noise because small pixel differences are encoded into a separate state. To reduce the dimensionality of local triplet pattern, Tan and Triggs [6] proposed the local ternary pattern (LTP), which split

---

* Corresponding author.

Z. Sun et al. (Eds.): CCBR 2013, LNCS 8232, pp. 62–70, 2013.

the local triplet pattern into two binary codes: a positive LBP and a negative LBP, so that the number of histogram bins decreases from 3^P to $2 * 2^P$ (P is the number of neighborhood pixels around the central pixel). A similar work was proposed by Nanni *et al.* [4], where they use a quinary code instead of trinary code and split it into four binary codes instead of two.

Another variant is to use soft histogram boundaries to replace the hard decision boundary of LBP. Ahonen and Pietikäinen proposed the soft histogram local binary pattern (SLBP) [2], in which the thresholding function of LBP was replaced by two fuzzy membership functions which are piecewise linear in a thresholding range. Another similar work was proposed by Barcelo *et al.* [7], where the difference was that they used LTP instead of LBP, thus the number of fuzzy functions become three rather than two. Ren *et al.* [8] also proposed a relaxed local ternary pattern (RLTP) which aims to split LBP into 2^N patterns, where N is the number of fuzzy bits of LBP.

One problem of the above methods is that the descriptors are designed arbitrarily, thus their performances are not optimal for specific applications. In this paper, we propose another LBP variant which is called Adaptive Soft Histogram Local Binary Pattern (ASLBP) based on training the margin of SLBP with the aim of improving recognition accuracy. Although this method is an extension of SLBP, the learning process can be generalized to other LBP variants.

This paper is organized as follows: In Section 2, we review the LBP and SLBP approaches; Then we clarify the ASLBP method in Section 3; Experimental results are shown in Section 4 and finally conclusions are drawn in Section 5.

2   Review of LBP and SLBP

The LBP operator selects a local neighborhood around each pixel of an image, and then thresholds the P neighboring gray values with respect to the center pixel and concatenates the result into binary bits. Formally, the LBP label associated with a center pixel (x_c, y_c) is represented as:

$$LBP_{P,R}(x_c, y_c) = \sum_{p=0}^{P-1} f_1(i_p - i_c)2^P \qquad (1)$$

Here i_c is the gray value of the center pixel (x_c, y_c), i_p is the gray value of its neighbors, P is the number of neighbors, R is the radius of the neighborhood, and $f_1(z)$ is the thresholding function.

$$f_1(z) = \begin{cases} 1 & z \geq 0 \\ 0 & z < 0 \end{cases} \qquad (2)$$

If any neighbor does not fall exactly onto a pixel position, the value of that neighbor is estimated using bilinear interpolation of pixel values around it. Finally the histogram is represented by accumulation of these labels:

$$H_{LBP}(i) = \sum_{x,y} \delta\{i, LBP_{P,R}(x, y)\}, \ i = 0 \sim 2^P - 1 \qquad (3)$$

The original LBP is sensitive to noise because the thresholding function (2) generates a hard decision boundary. To increase its noise robustness, Ahonen and Pietikäinen proposed SLBP [2], in which $f_1(z)$ is replaced by a soft thresholding function.

$$f_{1(SLBP)}(z) = \begin{cases} 0 & z < -d \\ 0.5 + \frac{0.5z}{d} & -d \le z \le d \\ 1 & z > d \end{cases} \tag{4}$$

In Fig. 1(a), $f_{1(SLBP)}(z)$ is shown together with its dual form $f_{0(SLBP)}(z) = 1 - f_{1(SLBP)}(z)$.

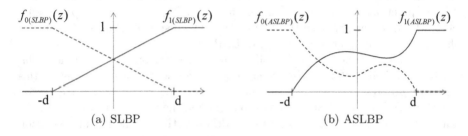

(a) SLBP   (b) ASLBP

Fig. 1. The soft thresholding functions for (a) SLBP; and (b) ASLBP

In SLBP, the contribution of a single pixel (x_c, y_c) has been scattered to all bins by $f_{0(SLBP)}(z)$ and $f_{1(SLBP)}(z)$:

$$SLBP(x,y,i) = \prod_{p=0}^{P-1} \left[b_p(i) f_{1(SLBP)}(i_c - i_p) + (1 - b_p(i)) f_{0(SLBP)}(i_c - i_p) \right] \tag{5}$$

where $b_p(i) \in \{0,1\}$ denotes the numerical value of the pth bit of binary representation of the ith bin. The complete histogram is computed by summing up the contributions of all pixels in the image:

$$H_{SLBP}(i) = \sum_{x,y} SLBP(x,y,i), \ i = 0 \sim 2^P - 1 \tag{6}$$

3   Adaptive Soft Histogram Local Binary Patterns

Different from previous LBP variants, we propose the ASLBP with the aim of adaptively learning the thresholding functions to obtain better recognition accuracy on the training data. Similar to [2], we define soft histogram function $f_{1(ASLBP)}(z)$, which follows three constraints:

1. $f_{1(ASLBP)}(z) = 0$ when $z \le -d$;
2. $f_{1(ASLBP)}(z) = 1$ when $z \ge d$;
3. $0 \le f_{1(ASLBP)}(z) \le 1$ when $-d < z < d$;

Fig. 1(b) illustrates the soft thresholding function $f_{1(ASLBP)}(z)$ and its dual form $f_{0(ASLBP)}(z) = 1 - f_{1(ASLBP)}(z)$. Compared with Fig. 1(a), we can see that $f_{1(ASLBP)}(z)$ can take any shape that satisfies the above constraints. Then we discretize $f_{1(ASLBP)}(z)$ by only taking its integer values.

$$f_{1(ASLBP)}(z) = \begin{cases} 1 & \text{round}(z) \geq d \\ p[\text{round}(z)] & -d+1 \leq \text{round}(z) \leq d-1 \\ 0 & \text{round}(z) \leq -d \end{cases} \quad (7)$$

where $0 \leq p[n] \leq 1$ is a discrete function which only has values on $n = \{-d+1, -d+2, ..., d-2, d-1\}$. We further define the vector P as the combination of all $p[n]$'s.

$$P = [p[-d+1], p[-d+2], ..., p[d-2], p[d-1]]^T$$

Similar to (5), the histogram of ASLBP is calculated as:

$$ASLBP(x, y, i) = \prod_{p=0}^{P-1} \left[b_p(i) f_{1(ASLBP)}(i_c - i_p) + (1 - b_p(i)) f_{0(ASLBP)}(i_c - i_p) \right]$$
$$(8)$$

$$H_{ASLBP}(i) = \sum_{x,y} ASLBP(x, y, i), \ i = 0 \sim 2^P - 1 \quad (9)$$

Suppose that a training dataset consists of N images. By (7), (8) and (9), we can obtain their histograms $H_1, H_2, ..., H_N$. Following [9], we use the Chi square distance to measure the similarity of each two histograms:

$$Dist(H_i, H_j) = \sum_{k=1}^{2^P-1} \frac{(H_{i,k} - H_{j,k})^2}{H_{i,k} + H_{j,k}} \quad (10)$$

Face recognition is based on a nearest neighbor classifier. The histogram of a testing image H is assigned to the class that minimizes the Chi square distance in Eqn. (10):

$$i = \arg\min_{k \in \{1,2,...,K\}} Dist(H, H_k) \quad (11)$$
$$\text{decide } H \in \omega_k, \text{if } H_i \in \omega_k$$

An ideal approach of selecting P is to minimize the empirical classification error rate on the training dataset, but this would bring two problems: firstly, Eqn. (11) is not differentiable on P, which would make the minimization problem intractable; secondly, directly minimizing the classification error rate may generate overfitting problems on testing data.

Because of this, we alternatively minimize a differentiable energy function of P. We can see that all distance values calculated by Eqn. (10) can be divided into two sets: D_{sim} and D_{diff}.

$$D_{sim} = \{Dist(H_i, H_j) \mid H_i \text{ and } H_j \text{ are from the same class.}\} \quad (12)$$
$$D_{diff} = \{Dist(H_i, H_j) \mid H_i \text{ and } H_j \text{ are from different classes.}\}$$

where D_{sim} consists of distance values generated from images in the same class, while D_{diff} consists of distance values from images in different classes. The mean and variance of each set is calculated as:

$$\overline{d_{sim}} = \frac{1}{\#\{D_{sim}\}} \sum_{d_i \in D_{sim}} d_i \tag{13}$$

$$\sigma^2_{sim} = \frac{1}{\#\{D_{sim}\}} \sum_{d_i \in D_{sim}} (d_i - \overline{d_{sim}})^2$$

$$\overline{d_{diff}} = \frac{1}{\#\{D_{diff}\}} \sum_{d_i \in D_{diff}} d_i \tag{14}$$

$$\sigma^2_{diff} = \frac{1}{\#\{D_{diff}\}} \sum_{d_i \in D_{diff}} (d_i - \overline{d_{diff}})^2$$

where $\#\{D_{sim}\}$ and $\#\{D_{diff}\}$ represent the number of elements in D_{sim} and D_{diff}. Finally, the energy function to be minimized is given by:

$$E(P) = \frac{\sigma^2_{sim} + \sigma^2_{diff}}{(\overline{d_{diff}} - \overline{d_{sim}})^2} \tag{15}$$

Our goal is to find suitable P to minimize $E(P)$. Although quite complicated, $E(P)$ is a differentiable function of P because Eqn. (8), (9), (10), (13), (14) and (15) are all differentiable functions.

The idea of our approach is similar to linear discriminant analysis (LDA), which minimizes the ratio of within-class variances to between-class variances. In this paper, we modify the gradient descent method to obtain the local minimum of $E(P)$. The optimization process is described in Algorithm 1. The main idea is to find the gradient descent direction of $E(P)$ and minimize the function along this direction. Here α is a parameter to control the convergence speed.

4   Experimental Results

We carry out experiments on the CMU-PIE database, which is a standard database for face recognition [10]. The database contains over $40,000$ facial images of 68 subjects, across 13 difference pose, under 43 different illumination conditions, and with 4 different expressions. We choose the 'illumination' set for our experiments, which contains 1407 face images of 67 subjects (21 images each). Fig. 2 shows the 21 images of one subject as an example.

We choose three images with neutral lighting to train ASLBP (Image ID: $07, 08, 09$), and test the recognition performance for the other 18 images, so there are 201 images for training and $1,206$ images for testing. All images are pre-processed by Gamma correction, difference of Gaussian filtering and contrast equalization. The images are normalized to $147 * 126$ pixels, and then divided

---

Algorithm 1 Gradient descent minimization of E

Input: objective function $E(P)$, step size α, iteration number $k = -1$.
Output: optimal P^* which minimizes $E(P)$.
1: initialize $P = P_0$.
2: compute $E(P_0)$.
3: **repeat**
4:     $k \leftarrow k + 1$
5:     compute $P_{k+1} = P_k - \alpha \frac{\nabla E(P_k)}{\|\nabla E(P_k)\|}$;
6:     **for** $n = -d + 1 : d - 1$ **do**
7:         **if** $p_{k+1}[n] < 0$ **then**
8:             $p_{k+1}[n] = 0$;
9:         **else if** $p_{k+1}[n] > 1$ **then**
10:            $p_{k+1}[n] = 1$;
11:        **end if**
12:    **end for**
13:    compute $E(P_{k+1})$.
14: **until** $E(P_{k+1}) > E(P_k)$
15: **return** $P^* = P_k$

Fig. 2. Face images in the CMU-PIE database

into $7 * 7 = 49$ blocks with equal size ($21 * 18$ pixels for each block). $LBP_{8,2}$, $SLBP_{8,2}$ and $ASLBP_{8,2}$ are computed for each pixel. The whole histogram is obtained by concatenating histograms of the 49 blocks together.

To test robustness against noise, the images are normalized in the range of $(0, 1)$, and then applying additive uniform noise in the range of $(-\sigma/2, \sigma/2)$. Figure 3(a) to (c) shows the classification error rates of LBP, SLBP and ASLBP on the testing dataset when $\sigma = 0$ (No noise added), 0.1 and 0.15, respectively. For ASLBP, the P is initialized by the values of SLBP as shown in Eqn. (4).

It can be observed that in most situations ASLBP outperforms LBP and SLBP, with the only exception that when $\sigma = 0.15$ and $d = 1$, SLBP generates classification error rates of 12.5% compared with 14.3% for ASLBP. This is because when d is small, the number of parameters to be optimized is also small, it is possible that the optimization process gets stuck at some 'bad' local minimums. However, the lowest classification error rates in Fig. 3(a) to (c) are obtained by ASLBP with $d = 4, 2, 8$ respectively, which validates the superiority of the proposed approach.

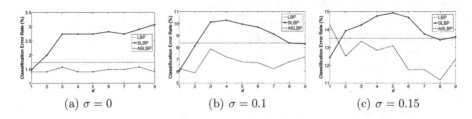

Fig. 3. Classification error rates of LBP, SLBP and ASLBP by varying d when (a) $\sigma = 0$; (b) $\sigma = 0.1$; (c) $\sigma = 0.15$

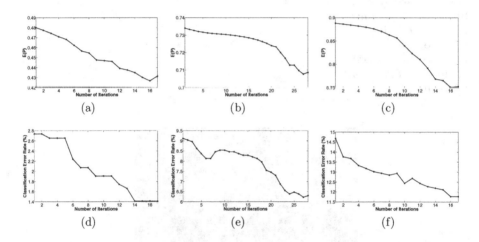

Fig. 4. The energy function $E(P)$ and classification error rate versus number of iterations. (a) Energy function $E(P)$ when $\sigma = 0, d = 5$; (b) $E(P)$ when $\sigma = 0.1, d = 7$; (c) $E(P)$ when $\sigma = 0.15, d = 6$; (d) Classification error rate when $\sigma = 0, d = 5$; (e) Classification error rate when $\sigma = 0.1, d = 7$; (f) Classification error rate when $\sigma = 0.15, d = 6$.

Fig. 4 shows that minimization of $E(P)$ corresponds to classification error rate reduction on the testing data. We choose three situations where $(\sigma = 0, d = 5)$, $(\sigma = 0.1, d = 7)$, and $(\sigma = 0.15, d = 6)$ because the number of iterations takes big values in these situations. It can be observed that generally minimization of energy functions corresponds to decrease of classification error rates.

Because only the local minimum of $E(P)$ is obtained, the performance of ASLBP is sensitive to the initial value of P. Fig. 5 shows the minimization process by two different initializations on P when setting $\sigma = 0.15$ and $d = 9$. In Fig. 5(a), energy minimization takes place by initializing P as the SLBP values. More specifically, $P = [0, 0.056, 0.112, 0.167, 0.222, 0.278, 0.334, 0.389, 0.444, 0.5,$ $0.556, 0.611, 0.667, 0.722, 0.778, 0.833, 0.889, 0.944, 1]^T$. The shape of $f_{1(ASLBP)}(z)$ after optimization is shown in Fig. 5(b). The corresponding classification error rate is 12.35%. In Fig. 5(c), the energy function is obtained when P is initialized as

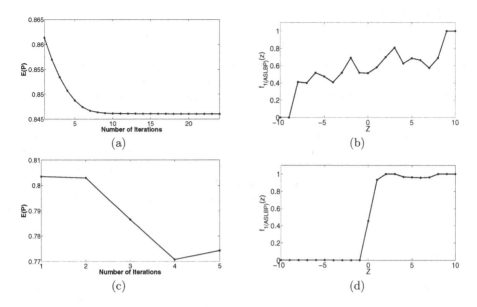

Fig. 5. $E(P)$ and $f_{1(ASLBP)}(z)$ when taking different initializations. (a) $E(P)$ when initializing P by the SLBP values; (b) $f_{1(ASLBP)}(z)$ corresponding to (a); (c) $E(P)$ by initializing P as another value; (d) $f_{1(ASLBP)}(z)$ corresponding to (c).

$[0, 0.1, 0.1, 0.1, 0.1, 0.1, 0.1, 0.1, 0.1, 0.5, 0.9, 0.9, 0.9, 0.9, 0.9, 0.9, 0.9, 0.9, 1]^T$. The shape of $f_{1(ASLBP)}(z)$ in this situation is shown in Fig. 5(d). The corresponding classification error rate in this situation is 14.34%.

These two initializations have brought to very different shapes of $f_{1(ASLBP)}(z)$ and 2% error rate difference, which indicates the importance of selecting initialization values. We suggest to initialize P with the SLBP values because from our experiments, this initialization can generate good results in most situations. One of our future directions is to research on how to find the global minimum or sub-optimal local minimums of the energy function $E(P)$.

Our experiments are carried out on Matlab with Intel(R) core(TM) i3-2100 CPU@3.10Ghz and 2.00G RAM. The running time of LBP and SLBP are 118 and 356 seconds respectively, which includes the feature extraction and recognition processes on testing images. The testing time of ASLBP is the same as SLBP because both share the same testing procedure, except that the vector P is trained for ASLBP while it is predefined for SLBP. However, the training process of ASLBP is more time-consuming. Based on Algorithm 1, the training time $T_{training}$ can be modeled by the following equation:

$$T_{training} = 2NT_0d \tag{16}$$

where N is the number of iterations, d is the parameter as shown in (4) and T_0 is the time to calculate gradients for all training images ($T_0 = 50$ seconds for these 201 training images).

5 Conclusions

In this paper, we have proposed the ASLBP approach for face recognition, which is based on adaptively learning the soft margin of decision boundaries with the aim to improve recognition accuracy. Experiments on the CMU-PIE database show that ASLBP outperforms LBP and SLBP in most situations.

Acknowledgmentss. This work is supported by the National Science Foundation of China (Grant No. 61202400), the National Research Foundation for the Doctoral Program of Higher Education of China (Grant No. 20110101120053), the Fundamental Research Funds for the Central Universities (Grant No. 2011FZA5003) and the National Science Foundation of Zhejiang Province (Grant No. LQ12F02014).

References

1. Ojala, T., Pietikäinen, M., Harwood, D.: A comparative study of texture measures with classification based on feature distributions. Pattern Recognition 29(1), 51–59 (1996)
2. Ahonen, T., Pietikäinen, M.: Soft histograms for local binary patterns. In: Proceedings of the Finnish Signal Processing Symposium, FINSIG 2007, Oulu, Finland, pp. 1–4 (2007)
3. Pietikäinen, M., Nurmela, T., Mäenpää, T., Turtinen, M.: View-based recognition of real-world textures. Pattern Recognition 37(2), 313–323 (2004)
4. Nanni, L., Lumini, A., Brahnam, S.: Local binary patterns variants as texture descriptors for medical image analysis. Artificial Intelligence in Medicine 49, 117–125 (2010)
5. He, D., Cercone, N.: Local triplet pattern for content-based image retrieval. In: Kamel, M., Campilho, A. (eds.) ICIAR 2009. LNCS, vol. 5627, pp. 229–238. Springer, Heidelberg (2009)
6. Tan, X., Triggs, B.: Enhanced local texture feature sets for face recognition under difficult lighting conditions. IEEE Transactions on Image Processing 19(6), 1635–1649 (2010)
7. Barcelo, A., Montseny, E., Sobrevilla, P.: Fuzzy texture unit and fuzzy texture spectrum for texture characterization. Fuzzy Sets and Systems 158, 239–252 (2007)
8. Ren, J., Jiang, X., Yuan, J.: Relaxed local ternary pattern for face recognition. In: Proceedings of the International Conference on Image Processing, ICIP 2013, Melbourne, Australia (2013)
9. Ahonen, T., Hadid, A., Pietikäinen, M.: Face description with local binary patterns: Application to face recognition. IEEE Transactions on Pattern Analysis and Machine Intelligence 28(12), 2037–2041 (2006)
10. Sim, T., Baker, S., Bsat, M.: The CMU pose, illumination and expression (PIE) database. In: Proceedings of the International Conference on Automatic Face and Gesture Recognition FG 2002, Washington, DC, pp. 46–51 (2002)

Complete Pose Binary SIFT for Face Recognition with Pose Variation

Lifang Wu[1,*], Peng Zhou[1], Yaxi Hou[1], Hangming Cao[1],
Xiaojing Ma[1], and Xiuzhen Zhang[2]

[1] School of Electronic Information and Control Engineering,
Beijing University of Technology, Beijing, China, 100124
[2] School of CS&IT, RMIT University, GPO Box 2476, Melbourne, VIC 3001, Australia
lfwu@bjut.edu.cn, {king_zhoupeng,houyaxi,caohanming,
maxiaojing}@emails.bjut.edu.cn,
xiuzhen.Zhang@rmit.edu.au

Abstract. Some pose invariant face recognition approaches require preprocessing such as face alignment or landmark fitting, which is another unresolved problem. SIFT based face recognition schemes could resolve the problem of constrained pose variation without such preprocessing. we find that the sift descriptors are robust to off-plane rotation within 25 degree and in-plane rotation. Furthermore, we propose complete pose binary SIFT (CPBS) to address the issue of arbitrary pose variation. First, five face images with poses of frontal view, rotation left/right 45 and 90 degree respectively are selected as gallery images of a subject. Then the binary descriptors of these images are pooled together as CPBS of the subject. Face recognition is finished by hamming distance between the probe face image and the CPBS. Experimental results on the CMU-PIE and FERET face databases show that our approach has performance comparable to state-of-the-art approaches, while not requiring face alignment or landmark fitting.

Keywords: Face Recognition, Pose Variation, Complete Pose Binary SIFT.

1 Introduction

Face recognition has been one of the most active research topics in computer vision and pattern recognition for almost four decades. The applications of face recognition can be found in telecommunication, law enforcement, biometrics and surveillance. Although there have been some early successes in automatic face recognition. High accuracy can be achieved under a controlled imaging condition, which means frontal faces with indoor lightings and normal expressions. In fact, the performance of most existing face recognition systems drops significantly when there are variations in pose, illumination and expression, thus the problem of face recognition is still far from being completely solved, especially in uncontrolled environments.

Pose variation is one of the bottlenecks in automatic face recognition. The major difficulty of the pose problem is that the variations in facial appearance induced by a

Z. Sun et al. (Eds.): CCBR 2013, LNCS 8232, pp. 71–80, 2013.

pose are even larger than that caused by different identity. It leads to a special phenomenon that the distance between two faces of different persons under a similar viewpoint is smaller than that of the same person under different view points [1].

The approaches dealing with pose variation can be generally divided into two categories. The first one is to generate the face image of a new pose similar to the probe (or gallery) face image from gallery (or probe) face images [1-9], so that the face images of same pose could be compared. The problem of these approaches is that the usable information is limited, therefore, the face model is generally utilized [2,3,5]. Prince et al. [4] proposed a linear statistical model, tied factor analysis model, to describe pose variations, Their underlying assumption is that all face images of a single person in different poses can be generated from the same vector in identity space by performing identity-independent (but pose-dependent) linear transformations. Blanz and Vetter [7] proposed 3D morphable model which was built using PCA on 3D facial shapes and textures that are obtained from a set of 3D face scans and the 3D face is reconstructed by fitting the model to the input 2D image. The 3D pose normalization algorithm proposed by Asthana et al. [5] uses the pose-dependent correspondences between 2D landmark points and 3D model vertices in order to synthesize the frontal view. Li [1] proposed a bias-variance balanced regressor based face recognition method. They used Ridge regression to estimate coefficients of a linear combination of a subject's face image in terms of training subject's images in the same pose and comparing the coefficients using normalized correlation. The drawback of these methods is the dependence on the fitting of landmarks. Huang et al.[8] train view-specific neural networks using eigenfaces to handle any view in a certain viewing angle range (out of plane rotation of left 30 degrees through right 30 degrees). Abhishek Sharma et al [9]. proposed discriminant multiple coupled latent subspace framework to implement pose-invariant face recognition, but they need four fiducial points for alignment.

The second type of approaches is to extract pose invariant features (usually local features) from face image. The commonly used features are ASM[10], AAM parameters [11], Elastic Bunch Graph Matching [12], local binary patterns (LBP) [13] and so on. However these approaches require locating the local regions accurately, which are usually the semantic regions such as eyes, nose, mouths. But it is difficult to locate the semantic regions accurately because there is a gap between the semantic features and low-level features. The other problem is that how robust these local features are to pose variation. Zhang [14] found that LBP can tolerate small pose variations and achieve perfect recognition rates when the rotations are less than 15 degree. Rama Chellappa et al. [15] extracted a pose-invariant feature using the spherical harmonic representation of the face texture-mapped onto a 2D sphere for video-based face recognition in camera networks. They measured the similarity between feature sets from different videos in a Reduced Kernel Hilbert Space.

In comparison, locating the key points based on low-level features is easier and more reliable. Scale-invariant feature transform (SIFT) [16] is detected by the local extreme point and SIFT descriptor consists of statistics of gradient histogram. Therefore, we could say that there is a stable connection between the SIFT descriptor and the pixel value. Furthermore, the gradient histogram is aligned to the dominant orientation, it makes SIFT descriptor invariant to rotation. The blurring of each scale images is consistent with a target from near to far imaging on retina, and therefore the

SIFT descriptor is scale invariant. Furthermore, Yu and Morel [17] proposed the improved ASIFT algorithm by using a new parameter(transition tilt) to measure the large affine distortion. The ASIFT descriptor is affine invariant. Facial pose variation is related to rotation or affine transformation. Many researchers applied SIFT to face recognition with occlusion or pose variation [18-25]. Some researchers presented the SIFT points as a graph, and the face recognition problem is modeled as a graph matching process [18,19]. Other researchers implemented face recognition by computing the similarity of SIFT descriptors [20-22]. Luo et al.[23] proposed to ensemble a K-means clustering scheme to construct the sub-regions automatically based on the locations of SIFT features in training samples. Wu et al.[24] proposed a novel face authentication approach based ASIFT and SSIM. The ASIFT descriptor was used to match the gallery and probe face images, and a mean SSIM (MSSIM) at all pairs of matched points was computed for authentication. Liao [25] proposed to construct a large gallery dictionary of multi key-point descriptors (MKD) by pooling all the SIFT descriptors. For a probe face image, the SIFT descriptors were extracted. Its identity was determined by the multi-task sparse representation based classification algorithm. The gallery face images are randomly selected in [25].

Facial pose variation includes in-plane rotation and off-plane rotation. We analyze how robust SIFT is to pose variation by experiments. We find that the SIFT descriptor is robust to in-plane variation. We further compare the matched pairs for the face images with horizontal rotation from -90 to +90 degree on the CMU-PIE database. We find that there are more matched pairs in the face images with neighboring poses, while the number of matched pairs drops significantly with the pose variation increases. Generally we find that the SIFT descriptor is robust to off-plane rotation within 25 degree.

To address the issue of arbitrary pose variation, we propose the complete pose binary SIFT (CPBS) for face recognition across poses. We first extract the SIFT points in five face images with pose of front view, rotation left/right 45 degree, and rotation left/right 90 degree. In order to reduce the data we utilize the binary SIFT descriptors instead of the original SIFT descriptors. Then we pool all the binary SIFT descriptors of the same subject as the complete pose binary SIFT (CPBS). For a probe face image, we can determine its identity by the similarity between it and the CPBSs. Experimental results on CMU-PIE and FERET face databases show that our approach has good performance for face images with pose variation.

2   Robustness of SIFT Descriptors to Pose Variation

How robust is the SIFT descriptor to pose variation? Facial pose variation includes in-plane rotation and off-plane rotation. From the property of SIFT descriptors, we infer that it should be robust to in-plane rotation, which is shown in Fig. 1. In Fig. 1, there are many matched pairs between the face images with in-plane rotation of over 45 degree.

We further analyze the robustness of SIFT descriptors to off-plane rotation by experiments . We count the matching pairs between the face images with off-plane rotations of -90 degree through +90 degree with space of almost 25 degree . The number of matching pairs between two face images of different poses is shown in Fig.2.

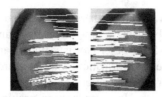

Fig. 1. The matched SIFT points in face images with in-plane rotation

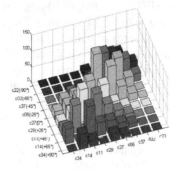

Fig. 2. The number of matching pairs between the face images with horizontal rotation from -90 degree to 90 degree

From Fig. 2 we can see that there are more matched pairs between the face images with neighboring pose than those whose poses are not neighboring to each other. Furthermore, the number of matching pairs drops significantly with the pose difference increases. The poses difference between neighboring poses are smaller than or equal to 25 degree. In other words, if the pose difference is smaller than or equal to 25 degree of horizontal rotation, the number of matching pairs is big enough. However, the number of matching pairs drops significantly with pose difference increases. The false matching pairs are very little because the RANSAC algorithm [26] is utilized at the final step.

We further analyze how the Euclidean distance varies with pose variation for the samples as in Fig. 3. We compute the Euclidean distance between two SIFT descriptors, which are from the same points (such as eye corners, mouth corners and so on) of different face images of the same subject. Fig. 3 shows how the average Euclidean distance varies as pose difference increases. It is clear that the Euclidean distance increases quickly as the pose difference increases. It means that the same points have more different appearance with the pose difference increases.

To summarize the above, the SIFT descriptors from face images are not robust to arbitrary pose variation, however, they are robust to face images with in-plane rotation or off-plane rotation of 25 degree. Therefore, if we select the face images whose horizontal rotation angle difference is about 50 degrees (such as front view, rotation left/right 45 degrees, and rotation left/right 90 degrees) as gallery face images, these face images can cover the pose variation with rotation left/right 90 degrees and up/down 25 degrees.

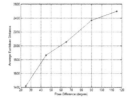

Fig. 3. Variation of the Distance between two SIFT points as pose difference

3   The Proposed Approach

3.1   The Framework of the Proposed Approach

For each subject, we extract the SIFT descriptors of the face images with five poses. The number of SIFT points in a face image is about 3000, and the total number of SIFT points in five face images is about 15000. Each SIFT descriptor can be represented as a 128 dimensional vector. Under the assumption of one byte per vector component, the total data for a subject is about 8,000,000 bytes. It is very large. Therefore, it is necessary to reduce the data of SIFT descriptors. Binary SIFT is proposed by Zhou [27], they showed that the binary SIFT descriptor preserves the quality of vector comparison on the original SIFT descriptor. Inspired by Zhou [27], we further extract the binary SIFT descriptors instead of the original SIFT descriptors in this paper, so that the data is reduced while the performance is preserved.

For each subject, we get their face images of five poses as shown in Fig. 4. The SIFT descriptors are extracted firstly from the five face images. Then the binary SIFT descriptors are obtained. Next, the final complete pose binary SIFT (CPBS) descriptors of the subject are obtained by pooling all of the binary SIFT descriptors together.

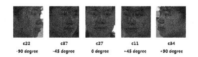

Fig. 4. Gallery face images of five poses

For a probe face image, the similarity between it and the CPBS of each subject is measured. Face recognition is implemented by the similarity.

3.2   The Complete Pose Binary SIFT (CPBS)

To allow for arbitrary pose face recognition, we construct the complete pose binary SIFT. In each face image, the SIFT points are extracted using the Affine SIFT extractors [17], so that more SIFT points can be obtained. For each subject S in the gallery, we get K_s SIFT points, which are denoted as $D_{S1}, D_{S2}, \ldots, D_{SK_s}$, from five images corresponding to five poses (front view, rotation left/right 45 degree and rotation left/right 90 degree). Then we generate the binary SIFT descriptor from the original SIFT descriptor.

Given the ith SIFT descriptor $D_{si} = (f_{i1}, f_{i2}, \cdots, f_{i128})^T \in R^{128}$, we convert it to the binary vector $B_{si} = (b_{i,1}, b_{i,2}, \cdots, b_{i,128})^T$ by Equation (1):

$$b_{i,j} = \begin{cases} 1 & \text{if} \quad f_{i,j} > \tilde{f}_i \\ 0 & \text{if} \quad f_{i,j} \leq \tilde{f}_i \end{cases} \quad (j = 1,2,\cdots,128) \tag{1}$$

Where $\tilde{f}_i$ is the median value of the vector D_{si}.

Then the binary descriptors from the subject s form the complete pose binary SIFT (CPBS) of size $128 \times K_s$ bits. The gallery for all the N subjects is represented as

$$\begin{aligned} GB &= \{CPBS_1, CPBS_2, \ldots, CPBS_N\} \\ &= \{B_{11}, B_{12}, \ldots, B_{1K_1}, B_{21}, B_{22}, \ldots, B_{2K_2}, \ldots, B_{N1}, B_{N2}, \ldots, B_{NK_N}\} \end{aligned} \tag{2}$$

By now, each subject is represented as a complete pose binary SIFT(CPBS), which is a set of binary vectors. The face recognition can be achieved by measuring the similarity between a probe face image and the CPBS of each subject.

3.3   The Similarity Based on Hamming Distance

Assume that k binary descriptors can be extracted from a probe face image. The probe face is represented as k binary descriptors.

$$Y = \{B_{y1}, B_{y2}, \ldots, B_{yk}\} \tag{3}$$

We can measure the similarity between the probe face image and the CPBS of a subject as follows:

$$Sim(Y, CPBS_i) = \sum_{m=1}^{k} SGN(\min_{j=1}^{K_i} dis_H(B_{ym}, B_{ij})) \tag{4}$$

where

$$dis_H(x, y) = x \oplus y \tag{5}$$

$$SGN(x) = \begin{cases} 1, x \leq T \\ 0, x > T \end{cases} \tag{6}$$

Both x and y are binary vectors and $dis_H(x, y)$ is the Hamming distance between x and y. T is the threshold, in this paper, T=28 is determined by experiments.

Then we determine the identity of the probe face image by the maximum similarity.

$$R_{class}(Y) = \max_{i=1}^{N} Sim(Y, CPBS_i) \tag{7}$$

4   Experiments

We test our approach on the FERET [28] and CMU-PIE [29] face databases. These databases are the most commonly used databases for face recognition across pose variation, so it is best for comparison with previous approaches. The face images of size 80*80 are cropped without face alignment or landmark fitting, as shown in Fig. 5 and Fig. 7.

The FERET face database includes 200 individuals. Each individual has face images with 9 pose variations. Fig. 5 shows the face images of the same individual.

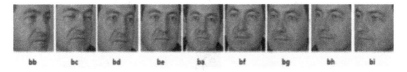

Fig. 5. Example face images from FERET

Face images of three poses bc(-40 degree), ba(0 degree) and bh(+40 degree)   are selected as gallery face images. The complete pose binary sift (CPBS) of the subject is obtained from these three face images. Each of the remaining images is used as a probe face image. We compare our approach with Blanz and Vetter's approach [7] and Li's approach with holistic or local features [1]. The results are shown in Fig.6.

From Fig. 6, our approach get over 90% recognition rate for all of the face poses, which is much higher than Li's approach with holistic features. Furthermore, our approach get over 95% recognition rate when the pose variation under ±25 degree which is a little lower than Li's approach [1]. But our approach get good performance than Li's approach with pose of rotation left/right 60 degree. The performance of our approach is a little lower than that of Blanz's [7] in almost all the poses except rotation +60 degree. We get 100% recognition rate with pose of rotation left/right 40 degree because they are selected as gallery data. On average, our approach get 94.3% recognition rate without gallery face images. It is a little lower than the average recognition rate (94.5 %) of Li's approach, And it is lower by 1.5% than that of Blanz's approach. However, both Blanz's and Li's approaches require fitting of landmarks and Li's approach assumes that the pose of the probe face images is known.

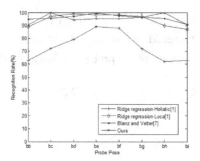

Fig. 6. Performance comparison with Li's approaches on the FERET database

The CMU-PIE face database includes 68 individuals. Each individual has face images with 13 pose variations. Fig. 7 shows the face images of the same individual. Similarly, Face images of five poses (C22 (-90 degree), C37(-45 degree), C27(0 degree), C11(+45 degree) and C34(+90 degree)) are selected as gallery face images. Each of the remaining images is used as a probe face image.

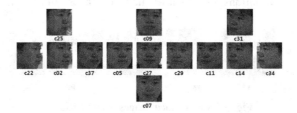

Fig. 7. Example face images from CMU-PIE

We compare our approach with some state-of-the-art approaches on the CMU-PIE database. the experimental results are shown in Table 1. It is clear that our approach is better than Shahdi's approach [30]. Our approach has almost the same performance as Asthana's [5] and Ho's [6] approaches within 25 degree, but their approach can't handle large pose variation. Wang's and Li's approaches are a little better than ours for face images with small rotation angles, but the recognition rate of our approach is much higher than their approach with large pose variation. Furthermore, Li's approach requires fitting of landmarks and estimating the face pose. While Wang's approach requires training pose classifier and the varieties of LDA projection matrices.

Table 1. Recognition Rates Of Different Approaches On The CMU-PIE Database

	C25	C02	C05	C07	C09	C29	C14	C31	Average
Asthana[5]	-	-	100%	98.5%	100%	100%	-	-	-
Ho[6]	-	-	100%	98.5%	100%	100%	-	-	-
Wang[4]	-	68%	100%	100%	100%	100%	76%	-	-
Shahdi[30]	76%	94%	97%	97%	97%	88%	82%	82%	89.125%
Li[1]	≈90%	100%	100%	100%	100%	100%	≈82%	≈70%	92.75%
Ours	98.5%	98.5%	98.5%	100%	100%	100%	80.6%	91.0%	95.89%

5   Conclusion

Face recognition across poses is a challenging problem. Although there are some competitive approaches, practical approaches are still needed. We propose complete pose binary sift for face recognition across poses. By analyzing the robustness of sift descriptors to face pose, we estimate that SIFT descriptors are robust to in-plane rotation and off-plane rotation within 25 degree. To deal with pose variation of large range, we extract the complete pose binary sift (CPBS) for each subject Face recognition is done by measuring the similarity between the probe face image and the CPBS. The experimental results on CMU-PIE and FERET face databases show that our approach is comparable to the state-of-the-art approaches. Furthermore, our approach does not require any preprocessing such as face alignment or fitting of landmarks, and therefore it is more practical.

The proposed scheme is robust to pose variation. But the gallery data is large because We just combine the binary sift descriptors together from all the gallery face images of the same subject. Our further research will focus on reducing the gallery data by sparsity or other effective algorithms. And in the future, we should also make sure if there is local minimum problem in the proposed scheme.

References

1. Li, A., Shan, S., Gao, W.: Coupled Bias Variance Trade off for Cross-Pose Face Recognition. IEEE Transactions on Image Processing 21(1), 305–315 (2012)
2. González-Jiménez, D., Alba-Castro, J.L.: Toward pose invariant 2-D face recognition through point distribution models and facial symmetry. IEEE Transactions on Information Forensics and Security (2007)
3. Prince, S.J.D., Warrell, J., Elder, J.H., Felisberti, F.M.: Tied factor analysis for face recognition across large pose differences. IEEE Trans. Pattern Anal. Mach. Intell 30(6), 970–984 (2008)
4. Wang, Z., Ding, X., Fang, C.: Pose Adaptive LDA Based Face Recognition. In: ICPR, pp. 1–4 (2008)
5. Asthana, A., Marks, T., Jones, M., Tieu, K.: Fully automatic pose-invariant face recognition via 3D pose normalization. In: Proc. Int. Conf. Comput., pp. 937–944 (2011)
6. Ho, H.T., Chellappa, R.: Pose-Invariant Face Recognition Using Markov Random Fields. IEEE Transactions on Image Processing 22(4), 1573–1584 (2013)
7. Blanz, V., Vetter, T.: Face recognition based on fitting a 3D morphable model. IEEE Trans. Pattern Anal. Mach. Intell. 25(9), 1063–1074 (2003)
8. Huang, F.J., Zhou, Z.-H., Zhang, H.-J., Chen, T.: Pose invariant face recognition. In: Proceedings of the 4th IEEE ICAFGR, pp. 245–250 (2000)
9. Sharma, A., Haj, M.A., Choi, J., Davis, L.S., Jacobs, D.W.: Robust pose invariant face recognition using coupled latent space discriminant analysis. Computer Vision and Image Understanding, 1095–1110 (2012)
10. Cootes, T.F., Cooper, D., Taylor, C.J., Graham, J.: Active shape models-their training and application. Compute Vision Image Understanding 61(1), 38–59 (1995)
11. Cootes, T.F., Edwards, G.J., Taylor, C.J.: Active appearance models. IEEE Trans. Pattern Anal. Mach. Intell. 23(6), 681–685 (2001)

12. Wiskott, L., Fellous, J.M., Kruger, N., von der Malsburg, C.: Face recognition by elastic bunch graph matching. IEEE Trans. Pattern Anal. Mach. Intell. 19(7), 775–779 (1997)
13. Ahonen, T., Hadid, A., Pietikainen, M.: Face description with local binary patterns: application to face recognition. IEEE Trans. Pattern Anal. Mach. Intell. 28(12), 2037–2041 (2006)
14. Zhang, X., Gao, Y.: Face Recognition Across Pose: A Review. Pattern Recognition 42, 2876–2896 (2009)
15. Du, M., Sankaranarayanan, A.C., Chellappa, R.: Pose-Invariant Face Recognition from Multi-View Videos. IEEE Transactions on Image Processing (2012)
16. Lowe, D.G.: Distinctive image features from scale-invariant keypoints. International Journal of Computer Vision 60, 91–110 (2004)
17. Yu, G., Morel, J.-M.: A fully affine invariant image comparison method. In: ICASSP, pp. 1597–1600 (2009)
18. Bicego, M., Lagorio, A., Grosso, E., Tistarelli, M.: On the use of SIFT features for face authentication. In: Proc. Of IEEE Int Workshop on Biometrics, in Association with CVPR, pp. 35–41 (2006)
19. Kisku, D.R., Rattani, A., Grosso, E., Tistarelli, M.: Face Identification by SIFT-based Complete Graph Topology. In: IEEE Workshop on Automatic Identification Advanced Technologies, pp. 63–68 (2007)
20. Geng, C., Jiang, X.: SIFT features for face recognition. In: Computer Science and Information Technology, pp. 598–602 (2009)
21. Liu, T., Kim, S.-H., Lee, H.-S., Kim, H.-H.: Face Recognition base on a New Design of Classifier with SIFT keypoints. In: Intelligent Computing and Intelligent Systems, pp. 366–370 (2009)
22. Rosenberger, C., Brun, L.: Similarity-based matching for face authentication. In: International Conference on Pattern Recognition (ICPR), pp. 1–4 (2008)
23. Luo, J., Ma, Y., Takikawa, E., Lao, S.H., Kawade, M., Lu, B.L.: Person-specific SIFT features for face recognition. In: ICASSP, pp. 563–566 (2007)
24. Wu, L., Zhou, P., Liu, S., Zhang, X., Trucco, E.: A Face Authentication Scheme Based on Affine-SIFT (ASIFT) and Structural Similarity (SSIM). In: Zheng, W.-S., Sun, Z., Wang, Y., Chen, X., Yuen, P.C., Lai, J. (eds.) CCBR 2012. LNCS, vol. 7701, pp. 25–32. Springer, Heidelberg (2012)
25. Liao, S., Jain, A.: Partial Face Recognition: An Alignment Free Approach. In: Proc. 2011 IEEE International Joint Conference on Biometrics, pp. 1–8 (2011)
26. Fischler, M.A., Bolles, R.C.: Random sample consensus:A paradigm for model fitting with applications to image analysis and automated cartography. Commun. ACM 24(6), 381–395 (1981)
27. Wang, W., Li, H., Wang, M., Lu, Y., Tian, Q.: Binary SIFT: Towards Efficient Feature Matching Verification for Image Search. In: ICIMCS (2012)
28. Phillips, P., Moon, H., Rizvi, S., Rauss, P.: The FERET Evaluation Methodology for Face Recognition Algorithms. In: IEEE PAMI, pp. 1090–1104 (2000)
29. Sim, T., Baker, S.: The CMU Pose, Illumination Expression Database. IEEE PAMI 25(12), 1615–1618 (2003)
30. Shahdi, S.O., AbuBakar, S.A.R.: Varying Pose Face Recognition Using Combination of Discrete Cosine & Wavelet Transforms. In: International Conference on Intelligent and Advanced Systems, pp. 642–647 (2012)

Coupled Kernel Fisher Discriminative Analysis for Low-Resolution Face Recognition

Xiaoying Wang[1], Le Liu[2], and Haifeng Hu[1,*]

[1] School of Information Science and Technology, Sun Yat-sen University, Guangzhou
wangxiaoy05@163.com, huhaif@mail.sysu.edu.cn
[2] Supercomputer Office, Sun Yat-sen University, Guangzhou
Liule2@mail.sysu.edu.cn

Abstract. In this paper, we propose a novel approach called coupled kernel fisher discriminative analysis (CKFDA) based on simultaneous discriminant analysis (SDA) for LR face recognition. Firstly, the high-resolution (HR) and low-resolution (LR) training samples are respectively mapped into two different high-dimensional feature spaces by using kernel functions. Then CKFDA learns two mappings from the kernel images to a common subspace where discrimination property is maximized. Finally, similarity measure is used for classification. Experiments are conducted on publicly available databases to demonstrate the efficacy of our algorithm.

Keywords: face recognition, kernel, linear discriminative analysis.

1 Introduction

Face recognition has attracted considerable attention, and the results on FRVT 2006 and ICE 2006 Large-Scale [1] indicate the fact that current face recognition systems almost perform perfectly on high-resolution frontal images. However, in realistic situation, face recognition systems are confronted with many great challenges, especially the low resolution problem. It is also shown in [1] that such low resolution can seriously degrade the performance of most face recognition systems. This is because the LR face images contain very limited information and many discriminative details have been lost.

Many approaches have been proposed to deal with the low-resolution problem. Most of these methods [2], [3] are based on some applications of super-resolution (SR) algorithms to reconstruct a high resolution version of the low resolution face image. Actually, these methods utilize a SR preprocessing as the first step. And the recovered high-resolution face images are used for the second step for classification. Baker and Kanade [4] propose face hallucination to infer the HR face image from an input LR one based on face priors. Chang et al. [5] propose a method based on locality linear embedding [6] which has fairly good performance. However, one of the major drawbacks of SR algorithms is time-consuming and not suitable for real-time applications.

Z. Sun et al. (Eds.): CCBR 2013, LNCS 8232, pp. 81–88, 2013.

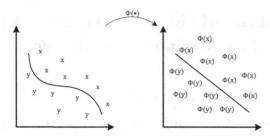

Fig. 1. Mapping non-linearly distributed data to linearly distributed data in the feature space via using the kernel function ϕ

Recently, some works without explicit SR have been proposed in the face recognition community. Li et al. [8] propose coupled mappings method for LR face recognition, which projects the images with different resolutions into a common lower dimensional space which favors the task of classification, however, the performance are seriously dependent to the locality affinities. Zhou et al. [9] propose simultaneous discriminant analysis (SDA) which learns a couple of mappings from LR and HR face images respectively to a common subspace, where the mappings function is designed on the idea of the classical discriminative analysis [10].

In this paper, we propose a novel face recognition approach CKFDA based on SDA to overcome the limitation. We learn a coupled kernel fisher discriminative analysis method to map the LR and HR face images onto a common subspace and implement the classification step in the new space. Our method can achieve better effectiveness and accuracy, which will be demonstrated in the experiments.

The rest of this paper is organized as follows. Section 2 presents our CKFDA for classification. Section 3 demonstrates experiment results on the public available databases. In section 4, we conclude the paper.

2   Coupled Kernel Fisher Discriminative Analysis

2.1   CKFDA and Kernel Methods

Actually, the key of CKFDA is the application of kernel methods. As we all know, kernel methods are effective algorithms for pattern analysis, and they can be used to solve nonlinear problems by mapping the complex distributed data from the original space into a high-dimensional feature space [11] where the data is linearly separable, which can be described in Fig.1.

In this paper, we propose to map respectively the HR and LR data onto two different high-dimensional feature spaces V and W via using kernel functions. Then the samples become more linearly separable, which is useful for classification.

2.2   The Proposed Algorithm

In this work, CKFDA is introduced in detail for LR face recognition. The training set in the original HR and LR feature spaces is expressed as $H = [h_1, h_2, \cdots, h_{N_t}]$ and $L = [l_1, l_2, \cdots, l_{N_t}]$, respectively.

First of all, the HR and LR data are mapped respectively onto two different high-dimensional feature spaces V and W by using kernel functions ϕ and φ.

$$\phi : \Re^M \to V, \ \boldsymbol{x} \mapsto \phi(\boldsymbol{x}) \tag{1}$$

$$\varphi : \Re^m \to W, \ \boldsymbol{x} \mapsto \varphi(\boldsymbol{x}) \tag{2}$$

where $\Re^M$ means the original HR input data space, and $\Re^m$ means the original LR input data space. Then the two kernel matrices K_H and K_L are constructed as:

$$K_H(i,j) = < \phi(\boldsymbol{h}_i), \phi(\boldsymbol{h}_j) >, \ K_L(i,j) = < \varphi(\boldsymbol{l}_i), \varphi(\boldsymbol{l}_j) >$$

Therefore, the two kernel matrices K_H and K_L correspond to the original HR and LR face images, respectively. The aim of CKFDA is to project the data $\phi(H)$ and $\varphi(L)$ into a unified feature space $\Re^d$ including H' and L' by using P_H and P_L, and then carry out classification. Let

$$H = [\boldsymbol{h}_1, \boldsymbol{h}_2, \cdots, \boldsymbol{h}_{N_t}] \to \phi(H) = [\phi(\boldsymbol{h}_1), \phi(\boldsymbol{h}_2), \cdots, \phi(\boldsymbol{h}_{N_t})]$$
$$\to H' = [\boldsymbol{h}'_1, \boldsymbol{h}'_2, \cdots, \boldsymbol{h}'_{N_t}]$$

$$L = [\boldsymbol{l}_1, \boldsymbol{l}_2, \cdots, \boldsymbol{l}_{N_t}] \to \varphi(L) = [\varphi(\boldsymbol{l}_1), \varphi(\boldsymbol{l}_2), \cdots, \varphi(\boldsymbol{l}_{N_t})] \to L' = [\boldsymbol{l}'_1, \boldsymbol{l}'_2, \cdots, \boldsymbol{l}'_{N_t}]$$

Denote the mean of the ith class samples in the common space by

$$\boldsymbol{\mu}'_i = \frac{1}{2N_i} (\sum_{j=1}^{N_i} \boldsymbol{h}'^i_j + \sum_{j-1}^{N_i} \boldsymbol{l}'^i_j) = 0.5 P_H^T \boldsymbol{\mu}^\phi_{H_i} + 0.5 P_L^T \boldsymbol{\mu}^\varphi_{L_i} \tag{3}$$

where N_i denotes the number of samples in the ith class of LR or HR face subsets, $\boldsymbol{h}'^i_j$ and $\boldsymbol{l}'^i_j$ respectively denote the jth sample of the ith class of H' and L', and $\boldsymbol{\mu}^\phi_{H_i}$ and $\boldsymbol{\mu}^\varphi_{L_i}$ are the means of the ith class of $\phi(H)$ and $\varphi(L)$, respectively. The total mean matrix of all samples in the unified space is expressed as

$$\boldsymbol{\mu}' = \frac{1}{2N_t} (\sum_{j=1}^{N_t} \boldsymbol{h}'_j + \sum_{j=1}^{N_t} \boldsymbol{l}'_j) = 0.5 P_H^T \boldsymbol{\mu}^\phi_H + 0.5 P_L^T \boldsymbol{\mu}^\varphi_L \tag{4}$$

among which, $\boldsymbol{\mu}^\phi_H$ and $\boldsymbol{\mu}^\phi_L$ represent respectively the mean of $\phi(H)$ and $\varphi(L)$.

The within-class scatter is defined as

$$J_{w_i} = \sum_{j=1}^{N_i} (\boldsymbol{h}'_j - \boldsymbol{\mu}'_i)^2 + \sum_{j=1}^{N_i} (\boldsymbol{l}'_j - \boldsymbol{\mu}'_i)^2$$
$$= [P_H^T \ P_L^T] \begin{bmatrix} W_{HH}^i & W_{HL}^i \\ W_{LH}^i & W_{LL}^i \end{bmatrix} \begin{bmatrix} P_H \\ P_L \end{bmatrix} \tag{5}$$
$$= P^T W^i P$$

where $P = \begin{bmatrix} P_H \\ P_L \end{bmatrix}$. The sub-matrices of matrix W^i are

$$W_{HH}^i = \sum_{j=1}^{N_i} (\phi(h_j^i) - 0.5\boldsymbol{\mu}_{H_i}^\phi)(\phi(h_j^i) - 0.5\boldsymbol{\mu}_{H_i}^\phi)^T + 0.25 N_i \boldsymbol{\mu}_{H_i}^\phi (\boldsymbol{\mu}_{H_i}^\phi)^T$$

$$W_{HL}^i = -0.5 N_i \boldsymbol{\mu}_{H_i}^\phi (\boldsymbol{\mu}_{L_i}^\varphi)^T$$

$$W_{LH}^i = -0.5 N_i \boldsymbol{\mu}_{L_i}^\varphi (\boldsymbol{\mu}_{H_i}^\phi)^T \tag{6}$$

$$W_{LL}^i = \sum_{j=1}^{N_i} (\varphi(l_j^i) - 0.5\boldsymbol{\mu}_{L_i}^\varphi)(\varphi(l_j^i) - 0.5\boldsymbol{\mu}_{L_i}^\varphi)^T + 0.25 N_i \boldsymbol{\mu}_{L_i}^\varphi (\boldsymbol{\mu}_{L_i}^\varphi)^T$$

Let $Z = \begin{bmatrix} \phi(H) & 0 \\ 0 & \varphi(L) \end{bmatrix}$, by using dual representation, the projections in P can be expressed as linear combinations of the feature Z, i.e., $P = ZU$. Therefore, The within-class scatter J_{w_i} in (5) becomes

$$J_{w_i} = U^T Z^T W^i Z U \tag{7}$$

Then we can obtain the total within-class scatter matrix in the way:

$$J_w(U) = \frac{1}{2N_t} \sum_{i=1}^{C} J_{w_i} = U^T (\frac{1}{2N_t} \sum_{i=1}^{C} Z^T W^i Z) U = U^T S_w U \tag{8}$$

where C is the number of classes in samples, $S_w = \frac{1}{2N_t} \sum_{i=1}^{C} Z^T W^i Z$ is the counterpart of within-class scatter matrix in discriminant analysis[10].

In the similar way, the between-class scatter matrix is given by

$$J_b(U) = \frac{1}{2N_t} \sum_{i=1}^{C} 2N_i(\boldsymbol{\mu}_i' - \boldsymbol{\mu}') = \frac{1}{N_t} \sum_{i=1}^{C} N_i(\boldsymbol{\mu}_i' - \boldsymbol{\mu}')$$
$$= U^T Z^T B Z U \tag{9}$$
$$= U^T S_b U$$

B is block matrix, i.e., $Z = \begin{bmatrix} B_{HH} & B_{HL} \\ B_{LH} & B_{LL} \end{bmatrix}$, where

$$B_{HH} = \frac{1}{4N_t} \sum_{i=1}^{C} N_i(\boldsymbol{\mu}_{H_i}^\phi - \boldsymbol{\mu}_H^\phi)(\boldsymbol{\mu}_{H_i}^\phi - \boldsymbol{\mu}_H^\phi)^T$$

$$B_{HL} = \frac{1}{4N_t} \sum_{i=1}^{C} N_i(\boldsymbol{\mu}_{H_i}^\phi - \boldsymbol{\mu}_H^\phi)(\boldsymbol{\mu}_{L_i}^\varphi - \boldsymbol{\mu}_L^\varphi)^T$$

$$B_{LH} = \frac{1}{4N_t} \sum_{i=1}^{C} N_i(\boldsymbol{\mu}_{L_i}^\varphi - \boldsymbol{\mu}_L^\varphi)(\boldsymbol{\mu}_{H_i}^\phi - \boldsymbol{\mu}_H^\phi)^T$$

$$B_{HH} = \frac{1}{4N_t} \sum_{i=1}^{C} N_i(\boldsymbol{\mu}_{L_i}^\varphi - \boldsymbol{\mu}_L^\varphi)(\boldsymbol{\mu}_{L_i}^\varphi - \boldsymbol{\mu}_L^\varphi)^T$$

Thus $S_b = Z^T B Z$ can be regarded as the counterpart of the between-class scatter matrix by comparing with LDA [10].

Finally, we can get the optional projection U^* of our CKFDA by maximizing

$$J(U) = \frac{J_b(U)}{J_w(U)} = \frac{U^T S_b U}{U^T S_w U} \qquad (10)$$

where the solution to the optimization function with respect to U could be given by the first d largest generalized eigenvectors $\boldsymbol{u}$ of $S_b \boldsymbol{u} = \lambda S_w \boldsymbol{u}$. In addition, since S_w is not always invertible, we need perform a regularization operation, i.e., $S_w + \zeta I$. ζ is a small positive value which is smaller than the smallest nonzero eigenvalue.

Naturally, the optional projection $U^* = \begin{bmatrix} U_H^* \\ U_L^* \end{bmatrix}$ is used for recognition. $G = [\boldsymbol{g}_1, \boldsymbol{g}_2, \cdots, \boldsymbol{g}_N]$ is assumed as a enrolled gallery set, and transform G into the common feature space $\Re^d$ by $G' = P_H^T \phi(G) = U_H^{*T} \phi^T(H)\phi(G)$. For a test sample l_t, transform it into the common space $\Re^d$ by $l_t' = P_L^T \varphi(l_t) = U_L^{*T} \varphi^T(L)\varphi(l_t)$. So that we can infer the class label of l_t by the nearest neighbor classifier in the common feature space.

3   Experimental Results

3.1   Databases Description

To evaluate the classification performance of our CKFDA method, we compare it with SDA, HR-PCA/LDA (using the HR query images), CLPM, CM [8] methods on the FERET database [12] and PIE database [13].

The FERET database is a well-known facial images set, where the images bear with many differences in lighting, expression and facial details. And the PIE database contains images of 68 subjects. The images are taken in different illumination conditions, pose, and expression.

For the FERET database, the training set has 1002 frontal face images from 429 persons. The standard gallery (1196 images) and the probe set "fafb"(1195 images) are used in test stage. The HR face images with size of 72×72 pixels are aligned with the positions of two eyes. The LR images with 12×12 pixels are acquired by smoothing and down-sampling their corresponding HR ones.

In the PIE database, we randomly select 10 images of each subject for training, and the rest 10 images of each subject are used for testing. All the selected images are in the same pose which is approximately frontal. The HR face images(64×64)and the LR images (12×12) are preprocessed in the similar way.

3.2   Results and Analysis

The recognition rate curves on FERET database with different feature dimensions of different algorithms are plotted in Fig.2(a). From the figure, CKFDA with 96 features achieves the highest recognition rate, e.g. 94.6%. However, the highest recognition rates achieved respectively by the compared approaches are: SDA 92.3% with 67 features, HR-PCA 67% with 140 features, HR-LDA 90.6% with 100 features, CLPM

90.2% with 79 features, CM 77.4% with 140 features. The CLPM, HR-LDA and CKFDA methods achieve relatively high and stable recognition rates, whereas the performance of CKFDA is consistently better than all the compared algorithms. The results also indicate that the proposed algorithm provides more discriminative information than SDA. Note that the cubic kernel function is adopted for our CKFDA algorithm.

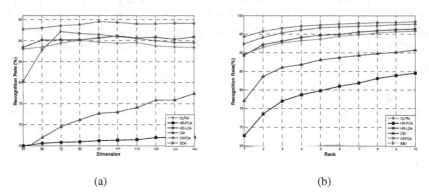

(a)   (b)

Fig. 2. Experimental results on FERET database. (a) Recognition results of different dimensions. (b) Cumulative recognition results.

According to the optional dimension, the cumulative recognition results on FERET database of the different methods are plotted in Fig. 2(b). From the figure, the rank k means that a test image is regarded as correctly recognized if at least one of the k neighbors from the gallery shares the same class with the test image. As is shown by Fig.2(b), our algorithm still stays superior to all the compared algorithms.

The experimental results on PIE database are shown in Fig.3. As we can see, our algorithm is more excellent than other algorithms except HR-LDA (using the HR query images). The highest recognition rate of the CKFDA is 95.6%, which shows the effectiveness of the proposed method.

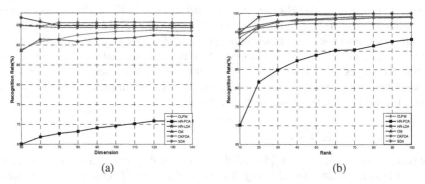

(a)   (b)

Fig. 3. Experimental results on PIE database. (a) Recognition results of different dimensions. (b) Cumulative recognition results.

Due to exploiting the kernel method, the running speed of CKFDA is faster than the SDA method. Thus it is suitable for real-time applications, which is illustrated in Table 1.

Table 1. Comparison CPU time for each method

Method	CLPM	HR - PCA	HR - LDA	CM	CKFDA	SDA
Time(sec)	29.198	22.149	16.102	36.687	46.363	1372.9

4   Conclusion

In this paper, we proposed a coupled kernel fisher discriminative analysis method for LR face recognition without any SR preprocessing. CKFDA aims to map the original HR and LR data into two high-dimensional feature spaces and learn two mappings from the kernel images into the common feature space. By using the nonlinear mapping function, CKFDA provides more discriminative information; meanwhile, it enhances greatly the computational efficiency for the non-linearly distributed data. The experiments using nonlinear kernel functions on the standard databases demonstrate the effective improvement in recognition accuracy.

Acknowledgments. This work is supported by NSFC under Grant 60802069 and Grant 61273270, by the Fundamental Research Funds for the Central Universities of China, and by the Key Projects in the National Science \& Technology Pillar Program during the 12th Five-Year Plan Period under Contract 2012BAK16B06.

References

1. Phillips, P.J., Scruggs, W.T., O'Toole, A.J., Flynn, P.J., Bowyer, K.W., Schott, C.L., Sharpe, M.: FRVT 2006 and ICE 2006 Large-Scale Results. In: NISTIR (2007)
2. Yang, J.C., Wright, J., Huang, T., Ma, Y.: Image super-resolution via sparse representation. IEEE Trains. Image Processing 19(11), 2861–2873 (2010)
3. Protter, M., Elad, M.: Super-resolution with probabilistic motion estimation. IEEE Trans. Image Processing 18(8), 1899–1904 (2009)
4. Baker, S., Kanade, T.: Hallucinating faces. In: Proc. Int. Conf. Automatic Face and Gesture Recog., pp. 83–88 (2000)
5. Chang, H., Yeung, D., Xiong, Y.: Super-resolution through neighbor embedding. In: Proc. IEEE CVPR, pp. 275–282 (2004)
6. Roweis, S., Saul, L.: Nonlinear dimensionality reduction by locality linear embedding. Science 290, 2323–2326 (2000)
7. Phillips, P.J., Flynn, P.J., Scruggs, T., Bowyer, K.W., Chang, J., Hoffman, K., Marques, J., Min, J., Worek, W.: Overview of the face recognition grand challenge. In: CVPR, pp. 947–954 (2005)
8. Li, B., Chang, H., Shan, S.G., Chen, X.L.: Low-resolution face recognition via coupled locality preserving mappings. IEEE Signal Processing Letters 17(1), 20–23 (2010)
9. Zhou, C.T., Zhang, Z.W., Yi, D., Lei, Z., Li, S.Z.: Low-Resolution Face Recognition via Simultaneous Discriminant Analysis. In: IJCB, pp. 1–6 (2011)

10. Belhumeur, P., Hespanha, J., Kriegman, D.: Eigenfaces vs. fisherfaces: Recognition using class specific linear projection. IEEE Transactions on Pattern Analysis and Machine Intelligence 19(7), 711–720 (1997)
11. Scholkopf, B., Smola, A., Muller, K.: Nonlinear component analysis as a kernel eigenvalue problem. Neural Comput. 10(5), 1299–1319 (1998)
12. Philips, P.J., Moon, H., Rizvi, S.A., Rauss, P.J.: The FERET evaluation methodology for face-recognition algorithms. IEEE Trans. Pattern Anal. Mach. Intell. 22(10), 1090–1104 (2000)
13. Sim, T., Baker, S., Bsat, M.: The CMU pose, illumination, and expression database. IEEE Transactions on Pattern Analysis and Machine Intelligence 25(1), 1615–1618 (2003)

A Simplified Active Shape Model
for Speeding-Up Facial Features Detection

Wei Jiang[1], Yuchun Fang[1,*], and Yonghua Zhu[1,2]

[1] School of Computer Engineering and Science, Shanghai University,
200444 Shanghai, China
[2] Computing Center, Shanghai University,200444 Shanghai, China
ycfang@shu.edu.cn

Abstract. Facial feature detection is a well-studied field. Efficient facial feature detection is significant in face analysis based applications, especially on mobile devices. Balance between accuracy and time efficiency is a practical problem in real time applications. This paper aims at proposing a real-time and accurate algorithm for facial feature detection. It is based on the assumption that classifiers may improve performance by limiting searching region. We propose a simplified Active Shape Model (ASM) to speed up such searching process. To ensure accuracy, several facial feature detectors are compared, such as the Adaboost classifiers with the Haar-feature, and the random forest classifiers. Since the simplified ASM provides a good constraint to different facial features, the detected results are promoted as well. We also design multiple experiments to verify our hypothesis by varying searching region. Experiments on MBGC databases prove the effect of the proposed simplified ASM model (sASM).

Keywords: Facial Feature Detection, Adaboost, ASM, Random Forest.

1 Introduction

Applications and researches pay more and more attention to facial feature detection. Such as face recognition, control devices for disabled people, face retrieval, and human-computer interaction. Facial feature detection tends to be the fundamental task in facial applications. Automatic face recognition technology is increasingly demanded. As a necessary step in automatic face recognition [1], face registration works in real-time is significant. And accuracy of face registration significantly influences accuracy of face recognition. Face registration needs the information of detected facial features. Even more extraordinary, facial features detection can directly be used for recognition tasks [2] to obtain better performance.

It has been a long time that facial features detection became a main step in facial expression analysis [3]. Until recent years, facial features are still the keys for facial expression recognition [4], [5], [6], [7]. On the other side, expressions and poses can be used for facial features detection. Sangineto proposed such a creative way [8]. And from 3D images, facial features occupy an important position for facial expression analysis [9] and face transformation [10].

Z. Sun et al. (Eds.): CCBR 2013, LNCS 8232, pp. 89–96, 2013.

As Dibeklioglu mentioned [11], facial features detection usually goes after face detection. With face detected, local models built for facial feature points obtain better effect. Based on this, facial feature detection algorithms are often classified with different principles. Hamouz believed that there are three kinds of algorithms for face detection [12]. The first one is image-based method. From this type, target is globally presented with high-dimensional features. While detecting, sliding window is often utilized to search in different scales [19]. Another example is using random forest for facial features detection [17], [18]. The second one is called feature-based method. From these methods, target consists of components, which are decided with prior knowledge or saliency of facial features. The last one is warping method, such as ASM [15]. The strategy is based on global feature or local feature.

Based on how many features to be used, Valenti also classified the algorithms into three types while detecting eyes [13], i.e. model-based methods, feature-based and hybrid methods. Most model-based methods adopt global features, which perform accurate and robust. Feature-based methods utilize local features. Locality makes feature-based methods not as stable as model-based methods, and often sensitive to noise. Hybrid methods combine advantages of the former two kinds of algorithms.

In this paper, we propose a hybrid strategy to detect facial features fast based on our previous work [14], [19]. The classifier-based methods, model-based methods and prior-knowledge are combined to find a better balance between accuracy and speed. These three strategies can be distinguished by statistical sufficiency. Normally classifier-based methods perform more robust, they rely on sufficient features and obtain sufficient statistic information. In this paper, we train two most famous classifiers such as RF and Adaboost. Model-based methods are faster with less features, but they are less accurate. In this paper, we propose a simplified ASM model which serves to control both precision and speed. Prior-knowledge based methods are fastest but less stable than the other two methods. They incline to be invalid when target changes such as pose variation of face. However, when combined with the other two methods, a real-time and accurate facial feature detection algorithm can be realized. Experiments on MBGC database prove the above assumption.

2   Facial Feature Detection with Simplified ASM

The proposed facial feature detection algorithm is illustrated in Fig. 1. It combines a simplified ASM with facial feature classifiers and takes advantages of both ASM and facial feature detector (Detector-sASM). Average shape model is used to detect an initial shape. Initial shape leads to a coarse detection. And facial feature detector further provides detail adjustment. What's more, we restrain the result from detectors with average shape model.

2.1   Learning Average Shape Model

The shape model consists of facial feature points. Training average shape model is aligning training shapes and averaging aligned shapes. Just as the shape model of ASM, we also learn a simplified average shape model as in [14].

We construct a shape for each face image. Each shape is a sort of ordered facial feature points. Basically, points in shape are divided into two classes. The first class is stable points. Relatively, the second one is unstable points. Stable points vary less than unstable points as expression, pose and illumination changes, such as eyes' center and nose's center. On the contrary, mouth's center is an unstable point. Stable points' detection are usually more accurate.

Shapes aligned with stable points are more reliable than the ones aligned with unstable points. While training, we normalize shapes with stable points. Shape normalization is realized through rotation, scaling and translation until input shape S_i is as close as possible to average shape $\bar{S}$, denoted as $\|S_i - \bar{S}\| < \varepsilon$. And S_i is added to the shape group to recalculate average shape $\bar{S}$.

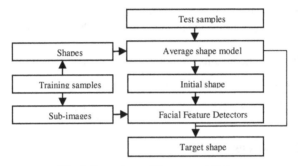

Fig. 1. Procedure of Detector-sASM

2.2   Speed up Facial Feature Detection

The algorithm of facial feature detection with the simplified ASM contains three steps. Firstly, detect an initial shape with average shape model. Secondly, detect with detectors under limited space. At last, constrain the result with average shape model.

The faster initial shape locates, the better. We locate initial shape as [14]. The eyes are more salient. And eye detection is more accurate. So we detect two eyes first. Shape alignment requires two points at least. We align average shape with detected eyes. Eyes' centers are stable points. So the aligned shape is relatively reliable. We map average shape model to the detected eyes and get an initial shape.

False-alarm
Input: points
   ①   Generate all possible shapes with detected points.
   ②   Align shapes to average shape model with stable points.
   ③   Calculate the best shape with $\arg\min \|S_i - \bar{S}\|$.
Output: S_i

Fig. 2. Procedure to deal with false-alarm situation

After coarse detection, every facial feature gets an initial position. For higher accuracy, we generate a searching region for each facial feature. We detect the facial feature with a facial feature detector. Within the limited searching region, we detect assigned facial feature with corresponding detector. With initial shape, the searching regions become much smaller. Sliding window is used on different scales.

In consideration to false-alarm and invalidation, we make a further restriction with average shape model. The procedures are summarized in Fig. 2 and Fig. 3. Repeat the adjustment step and restriction step until the result is stable.

Invalidation
Input: points
    ①   If the number stable points is less than two, the detected eyes in initial shape are treated as stable points.
    ②   Align shapes to average shape model with stable points. And get the shape S.
    ③   Replace the invalidated points with corresponding points in S.
Output: S

Fig. 3. Procedure to deal with invalidation situation

3   Facial Features Detectors

To validate proposed speeding-up model, we apply it on both RF [14], [16], [17], [18] and Adaboost [19], [20]. Adaboost and RF are benchmarks for facial features detection because of their high accuracy. With them, our algorithms can obtain high accuracy.

Adaboost for facial feature detection is a benchmark algorithm [20]. It is still very popular in face recognition systems. Adaboost classifier boosts weak classifiers. And the weak classifiers come from Haar features. It finds the optimal cut-off points and connects them as the optimal dividing line. But Adaboost detects with sliding window. So it is time consuming. We also train Adaboost for major facial feature such as eyes and mouth [19]. Since facial feature detection are performed after face detection, the negative samples are also obtained from facial regions outside of the detected facial feature. Irrelevant negative samples are ignored due to such context restraints. This makes classifiers more correlative. With boosted weak classifiers, we obtain a strong classifier for each facial feature. The strong classifiers can ensure the accuracy. We define Adaboost-sASM as combination Adaboost with simplified ASM.

RF is famous for its accuracy. For facial feature detection, there are several kinds of RFs, such as [17], [18]. We use RF as Ding [17] proposed. The feature used in RF [14] is kind of similar with Haar feature. The former one is difference between gray values of two points, and Haar feature is difference between gray values of two areas. Point-feature is more sensitive to noise than area-feature. The positive samples are the same as those in Adaboost. But the negative ones are image patches near corresponding facial feature point. Every feature is a weak classifier. And a classifier constructs a node. We construct a binary tree with nodes. And a forest consists of trees. With this procedure, weak classifiers construct a strong classifier.

Detectors like RF and Adaboost searches with sliding window. Searching region influences time efficiency directly. With initial shape from ASM we generate a limited searching region for every facial feature. The size of searching region is decided with experience experiments in Section 4. Reducing searching region is not only valuable for speeding up the search, but also benefit to accuracy. For detectors like Adaboost, false-alarm and invalidation may happen, constraints with average shape model can lead to more precise detection.

4   Experiments

We test our method on Collection B of MBGC database [21]. Collection B of MBGC contains 33,247 images with pose, expression and illumination variations. The former 22,164 images are used as training samples. The left ones are test samples. The images are normalized that distances between eyes are 60 pixels. Both time efficiency and accuracy are calculated. We compare time efficiency and accuracy with benchmark algorithms such an RF, Adaboost, ASM, RF-ASM and Adaboost-sASM.

Relative error $e = \|P_s - P_c\| / d$ is used to measure accuracy of the algorithm, where P_s stands for the detected point, P_c is the ground truth and d means the distance between two eyes. Normally, it is acceptable when $e \le 25\%$. We test the algorithms under four different relative errors. Results on time efficiency and results on accuracy are performed as Fig. 4.

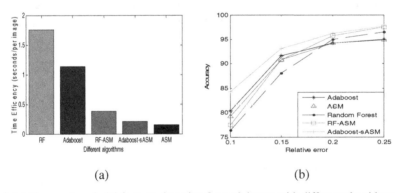

(a)   (b)

Fig. 4. (a) Time cost on facial features detection for each image with different algorithms. From left to right, the algorithms are RF, Adaboost, RF-ASM, Adaboost-sASM and ASM. (b) Result of accuracy on Collection B of MBGC. Relative error varies from 10% to 25%.

Adaboost-sASM and RF-ASM are almost as fast as ASM. On average, Adaboost-sASM costs 0.210 second per image. Adaboost costs 1.759 seconds per image. Adaboost-sASM is much faster than Adaboost. The same as RF-ASM (0.386 seconds per image) to RF (1.759 seconds per image). The fastest is ASM (0.156 seconds per image).

Adaboost-sASM obtains an accuracy of 84.3% under relative error 10%, and 93.1% under relative error 15%. Within acceptable relative error, its accuracy reaches 97.7%. Under a sound relative error, its accuracy is higher than that of others, even more accurate than Adaboost. And RF-ASM obtains higher accuracy than RF and ASM. What's more, it is more accurate than RF-ASM. This owes to Adaboost classifier. Adaboost is more stable than RF. High accuracy from Adaboost makes Adaboost-sASM higher on accuracy.

To further explore the contributions of searching region, we specially design tests under different searching region with typical points. We test the relatively stable points and unstable points. We select eye centers as stable points, and mouth center as unstable point. Results with the Adaboost detector are shown in Fig. 6 and Fig. 7.

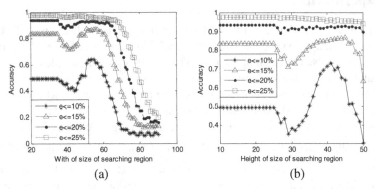

(a)   (b)

Fig. 5. (a) Accuracy of Mouth center under different width of searching region. In this Fig, the height of searching region is 55 pixels. The width varies from 10 to 90 pixels with a step of 1. (b) Accuracy of mouth's center under different height of searching region. In this Fig, the width searching region is 50 pixels. The height varies from 10 to 50 pixels with a step of 1.

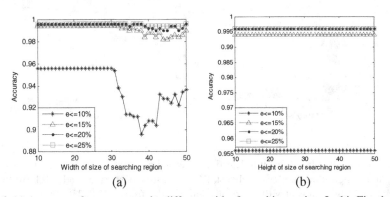

(a)   (b)

Fig. 6. (a) Accuracy of eye center under different with of searching region. In this Fig, the height of searching region is 50. The width varies from 10 to 50 with a step of 1. (b) Accuracy of eye center under different height of searching region. In this Fig, the width of searching region is 30. The height varies from 10 to 50 with a step of 1.

From Fig. 6 and Fig.7, accuracy keeps stable when searching region is smaller than fixed size. Accuracy reduces when searching is larger than fixed space. Between the two fixed points, accuracy varies as searching region varies. Its average accuracy is higher. And it reaches the maximum value around a certain point.

There are two critical points for the searching region. The first one is the boundary between ASM and Adaboost-sASM. If the searching region is smaller than the critical point, Adaboost-sASM performs more close to ASM. The second one is the boundary between Adaboost-sASM and Adaboost. If the searching region is larger than the second critical point, it performs more close to Adaboost. With searching region limited between the two critical points, it takes both advantages of ASM and Adaboost. Under this condition, it obtains good accuracy and high time efficiency.

Although, stable points perform not so obviously. They still perform this kind of tendency. For stable point, accuracy is hardly influenced by varying searching region. For unstable point, accuracy goes bottom while searching region get widest. This means when searching region is large enough, facial feature classifiers such as Adaboost has nearly no contribution. And while the searching region is small, the accuracy is decided by ASM. So it is stable in front portion of the curve.

Comparison experiments between stable points and unstable points indicates that unstable points are more sensitive to varying searching region. Stable point varies little. So varying searching region influences stable point little. Unstable point varies easily. Limiting space is good for its accuracy. For this reason, we can set different searching region for different point.

5   Conclusions

In this paper, we propose and prove an assumption that detectors can obtain better time efficiency and accuracy. Based on the assumption, we propose a kind of accurate and efficient algorithms. We combine fast search strategy with accurate facial feature detectors. We build average shape model as the fast search strategy. Average shape model lessens searching region. It makes detectors efficient. Average shape model provides a further shape constraint. The constraint makes detectors more accurate. Experiments with varying searching regions prove our assumption. Experiments on Collection B of MBGC show the proposed methods are precise and fast. The effect varies as the size of searching region changes. We can obtain the optimal effect within an interval. Comparisons between stable points and unstable points demonstrate that stable points and unstable points should be treated separately. Searching region should be different while stability of facial feature points are different.

Acknowledgments. The work is funded by the National Natural Science Foundation of China (No.61170155), the Shanghai Leading Academic Discipline Project (No.J50103) and the Innovation Project of Shanghai University (A.10-5-3-09-001).

References

1. Zhao, W., Chellappa, R., Phillips, P.J., Rosenfeld, A.: Face recognition: A literature survey. Acm Computing Surveys (CSUR) 35, 399–458 (2003)
2. Yang, X., Su, G., Chen, J., Su, N., Ren, X.: Large scale identity deduplication using face recognition based on facial feature points. In: Sun, Z., Lai, J., Chen, X., Tan, T. (eds.) CCBR 2011. LNCS, vol. 7098, pp. 25–32. Springer, Heidelberg (2011)

3. Ekman, P., Friesen, W.V., Hager, J.C.: Facial action coding system (FACS). A technique for the measurement of facial action. Consulting, Palo Alto (1978)
4. Yang, P., Liu, Q., Metaxas, D.N.: Boosting coded dynamic features for facial action units and facial expression recognition. In: IEEE Conference on Computer Vision and Pattern Recognition, CVPR 2007, pp. 1–6 (2007)
5. Tulyakov, S., Slowe, T., Zhang, Z., Govindaraju, V.: Facial expression biometrics using tracker displacement features. In: IEEE Conference on Computer Vision and Pattern Recognition, CVPR 2007, pp. 1–5 (2007)
6. Yang, P., Liu, Q., Cui, X., Metaxas, D.N.: Facial expression recognition using encoded dynamic features. In: IEEE Conference on Computer Vision and Pattern Recognition, CVPR 2008, pp. 1–8 (2008)
7. Yang, P., Liu, Q., Metaxas, D.N.: Exploring facial expressions with compositional features. 2010 IEEE Conference on Computer Vision and Pattern Recognition (CVPR), 2638–2644 (2010)
8. Sangineto, E.: Pose and expression independent facial landmark localization using dense-SURF and the Hausdorff distance (2013)
9. Sumarsono, A.R., Suwardi, I.S.: Facial expression control of 3-dimensional face model using facial feature extraction. In: 2011 International Conference on Electrical Engineering and Informatics (ICEEI), pp. 1–5 (2011)
10. Blanz, V., Vetter, T.: A morphable model for the synthesis of 3D faces. In: Proceedings of the 26th Annual Conference on Computer Graphics and Interactive Techniques, pp. 187–194 (1999)
11. Dibeklioglu, H., Salah, A.A., Gevers, T.: A statistical method for 2-d facial landmarking. IEEE Transactions on Image Processing 21, 844–858 (2012)
12. Hamouz, M., Kittler, J., Kamarainen, J.-K., Paalanen, P., Kalviainen, H., Matas, J.: Feature-based affine-invariant localization of faces. IEEE Transactions on Pattern Analysis and Machine Intelligence 27, 1490–1495 (2005)
13. Valenti, R., Gevers, T.: Accurate eye center location through invariant isocentric patterns. IEEE Transactions on Pattern Analysis and Machine Intelligence 34, 1785–1798 (2012)
14. Jiang, W., Fang, Y., Zhou, Z., Tan, Y.: Active Shape Model with random forest for facial features detection. In: 2012 21st International Conference on Pattern Recognition (ICPR), pp. 593–596 (2012)
15. Cootes, T.F., Taylor, C.J., Cooper, D.H., Graham, J.: Active shape models-their training and application. Computer Vision and Image Understanding 61, 38–59 (1995)
16. Breiman, L.: Random forests. Machine Learning 45, 5–32 (2001)
17. Wang, L., Ding, X., Fang, C.: Accurate localization of facial feature points based on random forest classifier. Journal of Tsinghua University (Science and Technology) 4, 021 (2009)
18. Dantone, M., Gall, J., Fanelli, G., Van Gool, L.: Real-time facial feature detection using conditional regression forests. In: 2012 IEEE Conference on Computer Vision and Pattern Recognition (CVPR), pp. 2578–2585 (2012)
19. Chi, Q., Zhu, Y.-H., Fang, Y.-C.: Framework for video-based facial features tracking and detecting. Computer Engineering and Design 32, 3819–3823 (2011)
20. Viola, P., Jones, M.: Rapid object detection using a boosted cascade of simple features. In: Proceedings of the 2001 IEEE Computer Society Conference on, Computer Vision and Pattern Recognition, CVPR 2001, vol. 1, pp. I-511–I-518 (2001)
21. Flynn, P.J., Bowyer, K.W., Phillips, P.J.: Assessment of time dependency in face recognition: An initial study. In: Kittler, J., Nixon, M.S. (eds.) AVBPA 2003. LNCS, vol. 2688, pp. 44–51. Springer, Heidelberg (2003)

A Method for Efficient
and Robust Facial Features Localization

Yuanxing Zhao[*] and Xianliang Wang

Beijing Hisign Technology Co. Ltd.
{zhaoyuanxing,wangxianliang}@hisign.com.cn

Abstract. We present a fast and robust algorithm for face alignment. There are three key contributions. The first is the introduction of a new shape indexed feature called multi-resolution wrapped features (MRWF), which is robust to scale and poses variation, and can be calculated very efficiently. The second is a new gradient boosting method based on a mixture re-sampling strategy, which allows the model to resistant to imbalance of training samples. The third contribution is a method for localizing facial feature points of an unknown image in a new iterative manner, which makes the algorithm robust to initial location. Extensive experiments over images with obvious pose, expression and illumination changes have shown the accuracy and efficiency of our method.

Keywords: face alignment, multi-resolution wrapped features, shape indexed feature, gradient boosting.

1   Introduction

Face alignment plays an important role in many face related applications such as head pose estimation, facial expression analysis and face recognition. These requirements are still challenging when face images are taken under extreme poses, illuminations, expressions, and partial occlusions. Generally, there are 3 steps to fulfill face alignment: modeling texture, modeling shape and localizing in a new image.

Modeling texture is to build a texture model compact and robust to extreme environment. Such methods can be generally divided into two categories: local texture model [1-6] and global texture model [7-12]. For the first category, a model is built for each landmark and the decision is made based on local regions. The best approach to build the model is to learn from the training set. For example in [1] a covariance matrix is trained by the difference of pixels normal to the boundary. It is suitable for the points placed on the strongest edge in the locality. When the points represent a weaker edge or some other image structure, some complex models is used, such as gentle boosting and Haar features [3], random forest and point pair features [2], random forest and Gabor [5], Supervised Descent Method and SIFT [6]. Their advantage over competitors is robust to global changes, such as illumination and poses variation.

---

[*] Corresponding author.

Z. Sun et al. (Eds.): CCBR 2013, LNCS 8232, pp. 97–104, 2013.
© Springer International Publishing Switzerland 2013

However, when applying local model to face alignment, a main problem arises: local feature's discrimination is not enough, so some unwished regions similar to the facial point might be found. In global texture model, [7-10] wrapped all pixels into a mean texture model to reduce the poses and expressions influences. In [11], the texture information over the entire face is utilized by a deep convolutional network to locate each landmark. In [12], the shape indexed features are extracted according to landmarks' location. Compared with local texture model, global texture model is more discriminative, but easier to be affected by some global changes, such as poses and expressions.

Modeling shape is a kind of method to describe the shape's variation. Earlier works can be classified into two categories: parametric model and nonparametric model. For parametric method, the model's flexibility is often heuristically determined and suboptimal because of using a fixed shape model. Principal component analysis is often used in face alignment [1-4, 7-10]. Some other nonlinear models are also used such as mixture of Gaussians [13] and kernel principal component analysis [14]. In recent years, there has been a shift towards methods based on nonparametric, such as [6, 12, 15] which is a linear combination of all training shapes and generalize better to untrained situations.

Localizing in a new image needs some strategies to improve the models' accuracy during localizing. In many situations, high accuracy cannot be reached by only one time localizing. Some methods are used to improve the accuracy, such as iterative methods [1,7, 13] and multiple initializations [12]. For iterative methods, a single model is run several times in a sequence until convergence, and in multiple initializations methods, the method is initialized on several locations and the distribution of multiple results indicates the confidence of estimation.

In this paper, firstly a new global texture model is built by multi-resolution wrapped features (MRWF) and re-sampling gradient boosting. MRWF is a new shape indexed feature, which is robust to the variation of poses and scales, and can be calculated more efficiently than shape indexed feature proposed in [12]. Re-sampling gradient boosting is a new gradient boosting, which is robust to imbalance of training samples. Then, a nonparametric model is used to describe the variations of shape. At last, a new iterative method is used to improve the accuracy.

The rest of this paper is organized as follows. Section 2 describes the framework of our algorithm. Section 3 presents some experiments compared with previous works. Section 4 is devoted to discussions and conclusions.

2   Framework of the Proposed Method

In this section, we introduce our face alignment algorithm. Firstly, MRFW is introduced. Then, a new gradient boosting method based on re-sampling is proposed to improve the accuracy for unknown images. Lastly, our localizing strategy is described.

2.1   Multi-resolution Wrapped Features

Indexed feature is first proposed in [17]. [12] proposes a shape indexed feature used in the field of face alignment, which is a pixel pair feature and the pixel is indexed relative to the currently estimated shape rather than the original image coordinates. This feature achieves better geometric invariance and faster convergence in boosted learning. But this feature is only robust to some simple affine variation, such as scale and rotation. This paper proposed features resist not only to affine variation but also to complex shape variation.

The procedure of feature extraction is shown in Fig. 1. To generating a feature, firstly, the Delaunay triangles are calculated from the landmark points of the mean shape, and a triangle is selected randomly. Then a point located in the triangle is selected. Lastly, a scale is random selected from some predefined scale ranges. When a new image is inputted with its current landmark location, the Delaunay triangles are calculated and new landmark points are generated according to the same procedure as the training process. Some examples of such features are shown in Fig. 2, which show the same features of different individuals. This is the basic feature of our algorithm and we called it multi-resolution particle wrapped features (MRPWF), because the features are calculated in different samples with the same scale and triangle, and have the same location in the wrapped global texture model. Thanks to Delaunary triangulation, MRPWF is robust to shape variation, however, it is not discriminative enough. So we use the difference between two MRPWF as a feature to describe the texture, such feature is called multi-resolution wrapped features (MRWF).

As the feature extraction process is not only dependent on the current shape's angle and scale, but also dependent on shape's variation, MRWF is more robust to shape variation compared with features in [12]. Besides, MRWF can be calculated very efficiently by using integral image [18], and there is no need to calculate transform matrix from the current shape to the mean shape as shown in [12], which makes it calculation more efficiently than [12].

1.	**Generate a feature**
2.	**Input:** Mean shape $\bar{S}$, scale ranges $\{ 1, 2, 3 \}$.
3.	Calculate Delaunay triangles from the landmark points of $\bar{S}$, and denote the triangles as $\{V_t, t = 1,2, ..., N\}$, where N is the number of triangles.
4.	Random select a triangle V_t.
5.	Defined f() that $(x, y) = f(\bar{S}[V_t])$, modeling the relationship between the selected triangle and sampling location (x, y).
6.	Random select a scales, s in scale ranges.
7.	MRPWF $= \{ V_t, f(), s \}$.
8.	**Calculate a feature**
9.	**Input:** Image I, currently shape S, V_t, MRPWF $= \{ V_t, f(), s \}$.
10.	Get the triangle $S[V_t]$ in shape S.
11.	Get the sampling location $(x, y) = f(S[V_t])$.
12.	Get the rect $= \{ (x - s, y - s), (x + s, y + s) \}$, which is the scope of sampling.
13.	feature $= I(rect) / (s * 2 + 1)^2$, which is the average of pixel in the rectangle.

Fig. 1. The procedure of feature extraction

Fig. 2. The theory of our multi-resolution particle wrapped features

2.2   Re-sampling Gradient Boosting

In this section we use MRWF to train a model of re-sampling gradient boosting. Gradient boosting is first proposed in [19], and has been successfully used in face alignment previously [9, 12]. However, in real situations, collecting and labeling faces with frontal pose is much easier than collecting and labeling faces with non-frontal poses, so generally there are more frontal samples than non-frontal samples, which results in imbalance of training samples. The imbalance of training samples can greatly influence the performance of gradient boosting and other classifiers, such as decision trees[16]. To alleviate the influence of imbalance of training samples, we propose a new gradient boosting. The intuitive idea is that non-frontal faces with few training samples have higher residual and less probability, and get higher weights in the next iteration.

To begin with, we briefly introduce the gradient boosting regression used in [12]. [12] uses boosted regression to combine T weak regressors R_t. Given a face image and an initial face shape S^0, each regressor computes a shape increment dS to decrease the residual of the shape. In each iteration a weak regressor R_t is selected based on (1).

$$R_t = \arg \min_R \sum_{i=1}^N \|r_i - R(I_i, S_i^t)\| \tag{1}$$

Where r_i is current residual for the ith sample, and some shape indexed features are extracted from image I_i based on current estimated shape S_i, then a weak regressor is trained by these features to reduce training residual greatly. After obtained the regressor the residual and shape of a sample is update by (2). The regressors $(R_1, ... R_t, ... R_T)$ are sequentially learnt until the training residual no longer decreases.

$$\begin{aligned} r_{i+1} &= r_i - R_t(I_i, S_i^t) \\ S_{i+1} &= S_i + R_t(I_i, S_i^t) \end{aligned} \tag{2}$$

In this paper, a re-sampling strategy is used in each iteration to assign a weight to each training sample, and the weight of each training sample is calculated based on its residual. Specifically, the weight $w(r)$ is defined as (4).

$$R_t = \arg \min_R \sum_{i=1}^N w(r_i) * \|r_i - R(I_i, S_i)\| \tag{3}$$

$$w(r) = \frac{1}{p(r)} * f(r) \tag{4}$$

where $p(r)$ is the probability of r all over the training set, estimated by Parzen estimator. The distribution of weighted residual is a uniform distribution, and the weight is the reciprocal of the probability. $f(r)$ is a monotone increasing function of residual, in this paper we use a power function. In order to speed up the training process, we normalize $w(r)$ to be in the range [0, 999], and force some sample weights to 0, which will be discarded in the next round of training process. Fig 3 shows our re-sampling gradient boosting.

2.3 Localizing Strategy

In localizing step, due to great variation of face images, using a single model may not get satisfactory result, so we proposed a specially designed localizing strategy in this section. We found the initial position of face landmarks is important to accurate face alignment, and use the same model to alignment face several times can greatly improve the locating accuracy. At the first locating step, the initial shape is initialized by the mean shape, then run the model and get the updated shape, and in subsequent step, the shape is re-initialized by the output of the previous updated shape normalized by a statistical shape model [1], and run the model repeatedly. The iteration is repeated until convergence. At each iteration the location result is more accurate than previous one, as show in Fig. 4. The left image is the initial shape, and after 6 iterations we get the ideal results.

Input: Data(I_i, S_i) for i=1…N, and stopping threshold α
1. $InitS_i^0$
2.   For t = 1 to T do
3.   Training regressor: $R_t = \arg\min_R \sum_{i=1}^N w(r_i) * \|r_i - R(I_i, S_i)\|$
4.   Update residual and shape: $\begin{aligned}r_{i+1} &= r_i - R_t(I_i, S_i^t)\\ S_{i+1} &= S_i + R_t(I_i, S_i^t)\end{aligned}$
5.   If $\sum_{i=1}^N r_i < \alpha$
6.   End for
7.   Output $R = (R_1, … R_t, … R_T)$

Fig. 3. Re-sampling Gradient Boosting

Fig. 4. Localizing result in iteration

3   Experiments

This section is divided into two parts. The first part compares our approach with previous works. The second part validates the proposed approach. In all experiments we use re-sampling 3 iterations strategy. Here we build the face alignment model by 88 landmarks defined by [2]. The accuracy is measured by (5), which is the point to point error, between the face alignment results P_a and manually labeled ground-truth P_m, is normalized by the distance between left and right eye d_e.

$$e = \sum_{i=1}^{88} \|P_a - P_m\|_2 / (88 * d_e) \qquad (5)$$

For clarity, we briefly introduce the two datasets used in the experiments. They present different challenges, due to image variations.

Set A is the same as [2], which consists of 2000 near frontal images, created by [2]. It includes Yale, FRGC and JAFFE, and the images are divided into two sets, 1500 images are used in training and 500 images in test. See [2] for detailed description of this database.

Set B is similar to [12]. [12] randomly selects 4002 images for training and 2469 images for testing in LFW [20] which includes many pose variation. Because we do not know which images are used for training and which for testing by them, we randomly selected 3700 images for training and 2500 images for testing. Also note that the number of landmark points is 88, which is also different from their 87 landmarks.

3.1   Comparisons with Previous Works

Comparison with[1] and[2]

To verify our algorithm, we compare our method with [1] and [2] in set A and B. Some results are shown in Fig. 5, the accurate is shown in Fig. 6. and table 1. Comparison in Fig. 6 shows that the location accurate rate by our method is better than [1] and [2], especially in set B, which proves that our method is more robust to pose variation than [1] and [2]. In addition, the speed of our method is less than 12 ms (4ms * 3 iteration), on a PC with i3, 1.2 Hz, CPU, which is also faster than [1] and [2].

Comparisons with [12]

The error is measured by RMSE same as [12]. The result is shown in table 2. Experiment shows that our algorithm is better than [12].

3.2   Algorithm Validation and Discussions

We verify the effectiveness of the different components of the proposed approaches. The experiment is based on Set B (LFW dataset), as used in above experiment. The error rate is shown in Fig. 8, experiments show that iteration and re-sampling strategy can improve the accurate largely.

4   Discussion and Conclusion

We have presented an approach for localizing facial feature in face images. There are three key contributions. The first is a new shape indexed feature called multi-resolution wrapped features (MRWF), which is robust to pose and affine variation, and can be calculated very efficiently. The second is a new gradient boosting method based on a mixture re-sampling strategy which can improve the accuracy largely. The third contribution is a method for fitting to an unknown image with an iterative way, which makes the algorithm robust to initial location. Extensive experiments show that our approach is both accurate and efficient.

Fig. 5. Select result in test set defined in [2]

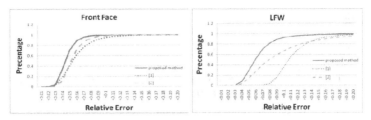

Fig. 6. Comparisons with [1] and [2]

Table 1. Relative error and speed of three face alignment algorithm

		Timing	<0.05	<0.1	<0.15	<0.20
Set	Proposed Method	12.3ms	0.71	0.99	0.99	0.99
A	Method in[1]	20.2 ms	0.40	0.94	0.99	0.99
	Method in[2]	73.2 ms	0.44	0.98	0.99	0.99
Set	Proposed Method	11.5 ms	0.28	0.92	0.97	0.98
B	Method in[1]	19.3 ms	0	0.18	0.70	0.88
	Method in[2]	70.8 ms	0.13	0.67	0.87	0.95

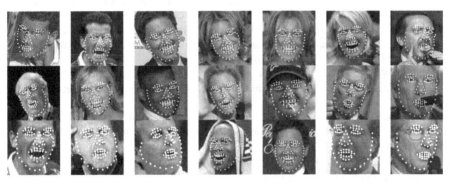

Fig. 7. Selected results in LFW

Table 2. Percentages of test images with RMSE

	<5 pix	<7.5 pix	<1 pix
Proposed Method	88.7	96.68	98.57
Method in [12]	86.1	95.2	98.2

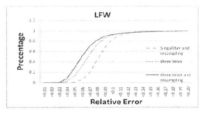

Fig. 8. Algorithm validation

References

1. Cootes, T.F., Taylor, C.J., Cooper, D.H., Graham, J.: Active shape models-their training and application. Computer Vision and Image Understanding 61, 38–59 (1995)
2. Wang, L., Ding, X., Fang, C.: A Novel Method for Robust and automatic Facial Features Localization. Acta Automatica Sinic 35, 10–16 (2009)
3. Cristinacce, D., Cootes, T.F.: Boosted Regression Active Shape Models. In: BMVC, pp. 1–10 (1998)
4. Cristinacce, D., Cootes, T.: Automatic feature localisation with constrained local models. Pattern Recognition 41, 3054–3067 (2008)
5. Dantone, M., Gall, J., Fanelli, G., Van Gool, L.: Real-time facial feature detection using conditional regression forests. In: 2012 IEEE Conference on Computer Vision and Pattern Recognition (CVPR), pp. 2578–2585. IEEE (2012)
6. Xiong, X., De la Torre, F.: Supervised Descent Method and its Applications to Face Alignment. In: CVPR (2013)
7. Cootes, T.F., Edwards, G.J., Taylor, C.J.: Active appearance models. IEEE Transactions on Pattern Analysis and Machine Intelligence 23, 681–685 (2001)
8. Sauer, P., Cootes, T., Taylor, C.: Accurate regression procedures for active appearance models. In: Hoey, J., McKenna, S., Trucco, E. (eds.) Proceedings of the British Machine Vision Conference, pp. 30.31–30.11 (2011)
9. Tresadern, P.A., Sauer, P., Cootes, T.F.: Additive update predictors in active appearance models. In: British Machine Vision Conference, p. 4, Citeseer (2010)
10. Kahraman, F., Kurt, B., Gokmen, M.: Robust face alignment for illumination and pose invariant face recognition. In: IEEE Conference on Computer Vision and Pattern Recognition, CVPR 2007, pp. 1–7. IEEE (2007)
11. Sun, Y., Wang, X., Tang, X.: Deep Convolutional Network Cascade for Facial Point Detection. In: 2013 IEEE Conference on Computer Vision and Pattern Recognition, CVPR (2013)
12. Cao, X., Wei, Y., Wen, F., Sun, J.: Face Alignment by Explicit Shape Regression. In: 2012 IEEE Conference on Computer Vision and Pattern Recognition (CVPR), pp. 2887–2894. IEEE (2012)
13. Cootes, T.F., Taylor, C.J.: A mixture model for representing shape variation. Image and Vision Computing 17, 567–573 (1999)
14. Romdhani, S., Gong, S., Psarrou, A.: A Multi-View Nonlinear Active Shape Model Using Kernel PCA. In: BMVC, pp. 483–492 (1999)
15. Belhumeur, P.N., Jacobs, D.W., Kriegman, D.J., Kumar, N.: Localizing parts of faces using a consensus of exemplars. In: 2011 IEEE Conference on Computer Vision and Pattern Recognition (CVPR), pp. 545–552. IEEE (2011)
16. Japkowicz, N., Stephen, S.: The class imbalance problem: A systematic study. Intelligent Data Analysis 6, 429–449 (2002)
17. Dollár, P., Welinder, P., Perona, P.: Cascaded pose regression. In: 2010 IEEE Conference on Computer Vision and Pattern Recognition (CVPR), pp. 1078–1085. IEEE (2010)
18. Viola, P., Jones, M.J.: Robust real-time face detection. International Journal of Computer Vision 57, 137–154 (2004)
19. Friedman, J.H.: Greedy function approximation: a gradient boosting machine (English summary). Ann. Statist 29, 1189–1232 (2001)
20. Huang, G.B., Mattar, M., Berg, T.: Learned-Miller, Labeled faces in the wild: A database for studying face recognition in unconstrained environments (2007)

Low-Rank Constrained Linear Discriminant Analysis

Shuxian Yi, Caikou Chen, and Juanjuan Cui

College of Information Engineering, Yangzhou Univerisity
yzcck@126.com

Abstract. Traditional linear discriminant analysis is very sensitive to largely corrupted data. To address this problem, based on the recent success of low-rank matrix recovery, the paper proposes a novel low-rank constrained linear discriminant analysis (LRLDA) algorithm for head pose estimation and face recognition. By adding the low-rank constraint in our method, LRLDA can obtain more robustness and discriminating power compared with traditional LDA algorithms. The extensive experimental results demonstrate the effectiveness of LRLDA.

Keywords: Low-rank recovery, Linear Discriminant Analysis, Image Classification.

1   Introduction

Linear Discriminant Analysis (LDA) [1, 2] is a widely used and successful technique for face recognition, which can obtain an effective representation that linearly transforms the high dimensional raw data space into a low dimensional feature space where the data is as well separated as possible under the assumption that the data classes are Gaussian distributed. LDA also enjoys a number of optimality properties when the training data are clean or even only mildly corrupted by small noise, and can be stably and efficiently. However, one major shortcoming of LDA is its brittleness with respect to grossly corrupted or outlying observations. Thus, its performance and applicability are limited by a lack of robustness to sparse errors with large magnitudes. Gross errors are ubiquitous in many applications like face recognition and computer vision, where some measurements may be arbitrarily corrupted (e.g., due to occlusion (scarf, gauze mask, or sunglass) or sensor failure) or simply irrelevant to the structure we are trying to identify. When using such corrupted images for training, the learned LDA-subspace might overfit the extreme noise of occlusion instead of modeling the faithful face subspace structure, and thus the resulted classification performance will be degraded.

Recently, sparse representation-based classifier (SRC) [3] has shown to be powerful method for face recognition. It regards each test image as a sparse linear combination of the training samples by solving an l1-minimization problem. However, SRC might not generalize well if training images are corrupted. More recently, using low-rank matrix recovery for denoising has attracted much attention. Low-rank matrix recovery, which determines a low-rank data matrix from corrupted input data, has been successfully applied to applications including salient object

Z. Sun et al. (Eds.): CCBR 2013, LNCS 8232, pp. 105–114, 2013.

detection [4], segmentation and grouping [7], background subtraction [5], and tracking [6].

Motivated by recent progress in low-rank matrix decomposition, this paper proposes a novel robust LDA technique, named low-rank constrained linear discriminant analysis (LRLDA), which can find robust and discriminant subspace representations from the data containing sparse errors with large magnitudes. The central idea of LRLDA is that the low-rank constraint can be used to decompose the original training data matrix $\mathbf{X}$ with large sparse errors into the low rank matrix $\mathbf{A}$ and sparse error matrix $\mathbf{E}$. The obtained clean matrix $\mathbf{A}$ is used to perform LDA-subspace. By adding the low-rank constraint, LRLDA can have more robustness and discriminating power compared with traditional LDA algorithms. The extensive experimental results in the paper will demonstrate the effectiveness of LRLDA.

2   Related Works

2.1   Linear Discriminant Analysis

Let the input data matrix is $\mathbf{X} \in \mathbb{R}^{d \times n}$, containing nd-dimensional samples and belonging to c classes. LDA creates a linear combination of these which yields the largest mean differences between between-class $\mathbf{S}_b$ scatter and within-class scatter $\mathbf{S}_w$.

$$\mathbf{S}_b = \sum_{i=1}^{c} P(\mathbf{x}_i)(\mathbf{m}_i - \mathbf{m}_0)(\mathbf{m}_i - \mathbf{m}_0)^{\mathrm{T}} \tag{1}$$

$$\mathbf{S}_w = \sum_{i=1}^{c} P(\mathbf{x}_i) E\{(\mathbf{X} - \mathbf{m}_0)(\mathbf{X} - \mathbf{m}_0)^{\mathrm{T}} / \mathbf{x}_i\} \tag{2}$$

$$\mathbf{S}_t = \mathbf{S}_b + \mathbf{S}_w = E\{(\mathbf{X} - \mathbf{m}_0)(\mathbf{X} - \mathbf{m}_0)^{\mathrm{T}}\} \tag{3}$$

$P(\mathbf{x}_i)$ denotes priori probability of training sample belonging to ith class. $\mathbf{m}_i = E\{\mathbf{X} / \omega_i\}$ denotes the mean value of samples belonging to ith class. $\mathbf{m}_0 = E\{\mathbf{X}\}$ denotes the mean value of all training samples. Then Fisher criterion function is defined as

$$J_j(\mathbf{w}) = \mathrm{Tr}((\mathbf{W}^{\mathrm{T}} \mathbf{S}_w \mathbf{W})^{-1} \mathbf{W}^{\mathrm{T}} \mathbf{S}_b \mathbf{W}) \tag{4}$$

where $\mathbf{W} \in \mathbb{R}^{d \times k}$ is the projection matrix. In [8], author provided a simpler derivation of the relation between regression and LDA. He described the problem as:

$$E(\mathbf{A}, \mathbf{B}) = \left\| \mathbf{G}^{\mathrm{T}} \mathbf{G}^{-\frac{1}{2}} (\mathbf{G}^{\mathrm{T}} - \mathbf{B} \mathbf{A}^{\mathrm{T}} \mathbf{X}) \right\| \tag{5}$$

where $\mathbf{G}$ denotes the indicator matrix. The LS regression problem minimizes $\arg \min_{\mathbf{T}} \|\mathbf{D} - \mathbf{T}\mathbf{X}\|_{\mathrm{F}}^2$, $\mathbf{D} \in \mathbb{R}^{t \times d}$ be a high-dimensional data set, $\mathbf{T} \in \mathbb{R}^{t \times d}$ be the regression matrix, $\mathbf{T} = \mathbf{B}\mathbf{A}^{\mathrm{T}}$ as the outer product of two matrices of rank k, where $\mathbf{A} \in \mathbb{R}^{d \times k}$ and $\mathbf{B} \in \mathbb{R}^{t \times k}$,similar to [9][11]. In this case, $\mathbf{A}$ is equivalent to the maximization of

$$E(\mathbf{A}) \propto \mathrm{Tr}((\mathbf{A}^T \underbrace{\mathbf{D}\mathbf{D}^T \mathbf{A}}_{\mathbf{S}_t})^{-1} \mathbf{A}^T \underbrace{\mathbf{D}\mathbf{G}(\mathbf{G}^T \mathbf{G})^{-1} \mathbf{G}^T \mathbf{D}^T \mathbf{A}}_{\mathbf{S}_b})$$

(6)

2.2 Low-Rank Matrix Recovery

In many engineering problems, the entries of the matrix are often arbitrarily corrupted due to occlusion (scarf, gauze mask, or sunglass), some of the entries could even be missing. Due to these problems, Low-rank structure is used to either approximate a general matrix, or to correct for corrupted or missing data. Low-rank matrix recovery (LR) is a technique to decompose a data matrix $\mathbf{X}$ into $\mathbf{A} + \mathbf{E}$, where $\mathbf{A}$ is a low-rank matrix and $\mathbf{E}$ is the associated sparse error..

LR minimizes the rank of matrix $\mathbf{A}$ while reducing $\|\mathbf{E}\|_0$ to derive the low-rank approximation of $\mathbf{X}$. Since the aforementioned optimization problem is NP-hard, Candes *et al.* [10] solve the problem by transforming the objective function as following:

$$\min_{\mathbf{A},\mathbf{E}} \|\mathbf{A}\|_* + \lambda \|\mathbf{E}\|_1$$

s.t. $\mathbf{X} = \mathbf{A} + \mathbf{E}$

(7)

where $\|\cdot\|_*$ denotes the nuclear norm of the matrix (i.e., the sum of the singular values of the matrix), and $\|\cdot\|_1$ represents the l_1-norm, (i.e. the sum of the absolute values of entries in the matrix).

3   Low-Rank Constrained Linear Discriminant Analysis

3.1 Objective Function

Let $\mathbf{X} \in \mathbb{R}^{d \times n}$ and $\mathbf{X} = \mathbf{A} + \mathbf{E}$, where $\mathbf{A}$ is the underlying noise-free low-rank component and $\mathbf{E}$ contains the outliers. In the traditional LDA, one usually uses the original data directly from $\mathbf{X}$ as training set, so Fisherfaces constructed by $\mathbf{X}$ is a biased estimation. Our LRLDA construct the Fisherfaces using $\mathbf{A}$. Thus, the optimization problem of LRLDA can be written as

$$\min_{\mathbf{H},\mathbf{K},\mathbf{A},\mathbf{E}} \left\| (\mathbf{Y}^T \mathbf{Y})^{-\frac{1}{2}} (\mathbf{Y}^T - \mathbf{H}\mathbf{K}^T \mathbf{A}) \right\|_F^2 + \|\mathbf{A}\|_* + \lambda \|\mathbf{E}\|_1$$

s.t. $\mathbf{X} = \mathbf{A} + \mathbf{E}$

(8)

where $\mathbf{Y} \in \mathbb{R}^{n \times c}$ is a binary indicator matrix such that $\sum_j y_{ij} = 1$, $y_{ij} \in \{0,1\}$ and $y_{ij} = 1$ if x_i belongs to class j, otherwise $y_{ij} = 0$. $\lambda \geq 0$ is positive weighting parameter.

Using Augmented Lagrange Multiplier (ALM), the objective (8) can be rewritten as:

$$\min_{\mathbf{H},\mathbf{K},\mathbf{A},\mathbf{E}} \left\| (\mathbf{Y}^T\mathbf{Y})^{-\frac{1}{2}}(\mathbf{Y}^T - \mathbf{H}\mathbf{K}^T\mathbf{A}) \right\|_F^2 + \|\mathbf{A}\|_* + \lambda\|\mathbf{E}\|_1 + \langle\mathbf{\Gamma}, \mathbf{X} - \mathbf{A} - \mathbf{E}\rangle + \frac{\mu}{2}\|\mathbf{X} - \mathbf{A} - \mathbf{E}\|_F^2 \quad (9)$$

Where $\mathbf{\Gamma} \in \mathbb{R}^{d\times n}$ is Lagrange multiplier matrix, μ is the penalty parameter, $\|\cdot\|_F$ is Frobenius norm.

3.2   Optimization of Formulation

The solution variables $\mathbf{H}$, $\mathbf{K}$, $\mathbf{A}$ and $\mathbf{E}$ of LRLDA are solved by the following subproblems:

$$\mathbf{K}^{k+1} = \arg\min_{\mathbf{K}} L(\mathbf{A}, \mathbf{K}^{(k)}, \mathbf{E}, \mathbf{H}, \mathbf{\Gamma}); \quad (10)$$

$$\mathbf{H}^{k+1} = \arg\min_{\mathbf{K}} L(\mathbf{A}, \mathbf{K}, \mathbf{E}, \mathbf{H}^{(k)}, \mathbf{\Gamma}); \quad (11)$$

$$\mathbf{A}^{k+1} = \arg\min_{\mathbf{K}} L(\mathbf{A}^{(k)}, \mathbf{K}, \mathbf{E}, \mathbf{H}, \mathbf{\Gamma}); \quad (12)$$

$$\mathbf{E}^{k+1} = \arg\min_{\mathbf{K}} L(\mathbf{A}, \mathbf{K}, \mathbf{E}^{(k)}, \mathbf{H}, \mathbf{\Gamma}); \quad (13)$$

$$\mathbf{\Gamma}^{k+1} = \arg\min_{\mathbf{K}} L(\mathbf{A}, \mathbf{K}, \mathbf{E}, \mathbf{H}, \mathbf{\Gamma}^{(k)}); \quad (14)$$

where k denotes the index of iterations.

3.2.1   Updating Regression Matrix H and K
In this subsection, we discuss the solution of subproblem (10) and (11) while fixing $\mathbf{A}$ and $\mathbf{E}$

$$E(\mathbf{H},\mathbf{K}) = \left\| (\mathbf{Y}^T\mathbf{Y})^{-\frac{1}{2}}(\mathbf{Y}^T - \mathbf{H}\mathbf{K}^T\mathbf{A}) \right\|_F^2 \quad (15)$$

Let $(\mathbf{Y}^T\mathbf{Y})^{-\frac{1}{2}} = \mathbf{W}$, then :

$$E(\mathbf{H},\mathbf{K}) = \left\| \mathbf{W}(\mathbf{Y}^T - \mathbf{H}\mathbf{K}^T\mathbf{A}) \right\|_F^2 = \text{Tr}(\mathbf{Y}\mathbf{W}^T\mathbf{W}\mathbf{Y}) - 2\text{Tr}(\mathbf{Y}\mathbf{W}^T\mathbf{W}\mathbf{H}\mathbf{K}^T\mathbf{A}) + \text{Tr}(\mathbf{A}^T\mathbf{K}\mathbf{H}^T\mathbf{W}^T\mathbf{W}\mathbf{H}\mathbf{K}^T\mathbf{A}) \quad (16)$$

The necessary conditions in $\mathbf{H}$ and $\mathbf{K}$ for the minimum of (16) are

$$\frac{\partial E}{\partial \mathbf{H}} = 2\mathbf{W}^T\mathbf{W}\mathbf{H}\mathbf{K}^T\mathbf{A}\mathbf{A}^T\mathbf{K} - 2\mathbf{W}^T\mathbf{W}\mathbf{Y}^T\mathbf{A}^T\mathbf{K} = 0 \quad (17)$$

$$\frac{\partial E}{\partial \mathbf{K}} = 2\mathbf{A}\mathbf{A}^T\mathbf{K}\mathbf{H}^T\mathbf{W}^T\mathbf{W}\mathbf{H} - 2\mathbf{A}\mathbf{Y}\mathbf{W}^T\mathbf{W}\mathbf{H} = 0 \quad (18)$$

where $\langle\mathbf{P},\mathbf{Q}\rangle = \text{tr}(\mathbf{P}\mathbf{Q}^T)$ is trace of matrix multiplication between $\mathbf{P}$ and $\mathbf{Q}$. Assuming that $\mathbf{K}^T\mathbf{A}\mathbf{A}^T\mathbf{K}$ is invertible and substituting the optimal $\mathbf{H} = \mathbf{Y}^T\mathbf{A}^T\mathbf{K}(\mathbf{K}^T\mathbf{A}\mathbf{A}^T\mathbf{K})^{-1}$ derived from (18) into (15), minimizing $E(\mathbf{K})$. $\mathbf{K}$ is equivalent to the maximization of:

$$\mathbf{K}^{k+1} = \mathrm{Tr}(\mathbf{K}^T \mathbf{A}^k (\mathbf{A}^k)^T \mathbf{K})^{-1} (\mathbf{K}^T \mathbf{A}^k \mathbf{Y} \mathbf{W}^T \mathbf{W} \mathbf{Y}^T (\mathbf{A}^k)^T \mathbf{K}) \tag{19}$$

Assuming that $\mathbf{H}^T \mathbf{W}^T \mathbf{W} \mathbf{H}$ and $\mathbf{A} \mathbf{A}^T$ is invertible and substituting the optimal $\mathbf{K} = (\mathbf{A} \mathbf{A}^T)^{-1} \mathbf{W}^T \mathbf{W} \mathbf{H} \mathbf{K}^T \mathbf{A} \mathbf{A}^T \mathbf{K} (\mathbf{H}^T \mathbf{W}^T \mathbf{W} \mathbf{H})^{-1}$ derived from (17) into (15), minimizing $E(\mathbf{H})$. $\mathbf{H}$ is equivalent to the maximization of:

$$\mathbf{H}^{k+1} = \mathrm{Tr}((\mathbf{H}^T \mathbf{W}^T \mathbf{W} \mathbf{H})^{-1} \mathbf{H}^T \mathbf{W}^T \mathbf{W} \mathbf{Y}^T (\mathbf{A}^k)^T (\mathbf{A}^k (\mathbf{A}^k)^T)^{-1} \mathbf{A}^k \mathbf{Y} \mathbf{W}^T \mathbf{W} \mathbf{H}) \tag{20}$$

3.2.2   Updating Low-Rank Matrix A

In this subsection, we discuss the solution of subproblem (12) while fixing $\mathbf{H}$, $\mathbf{K}$ and $\mathbf{E}$

$$L(\mathbf{A}) \propto \|\mathbf{A}\|_* + \left\|\mathbf{W}(\mathbf{Y}^T - \mathbf{H} \mathbf{K}^T \mathbf{A})\right\|_F^2 + \langle \mathbf{\Gamma}, \mathbf{X} - \mathbf{A} - \mathbf{E} \rangle + \frac{\mu}{2} \|\mathbf{X} - \mathbf{A} - \mathbf{E}\|_F^2 \tag{21}$$

$$F(\mathbf{A}) = \left\|\mathbf{W}(\mathbf{Y}^T - \mathbf{H} \mathbf{K}^T \mathbf{A})\right\|_F^2 + \langle \mathbf{\Gamma}, \mathbf{X} - \mathbf{A} - \mathbf{E} \rangle + \frac{\mu}{2} \|\mathbf{X} - \mathbf{A} - \mathbf{E}\|_F^2 \tag{22}$$

The partial derivative of (22)   :

$$\frac{\partial F(\mathbf{A})}{\partial \mathbf{A}} = 2 \mathbf{K} \mathbf{H}^T \mathbf{W}^T (\mathbf{W} \mathbf{H} \mathbf{K}^T \mathbf{A} - \mathbf{W} \mathbf{Y}^T) - \mathbf{\Gamma} - \mu(\mathbf{X} - \mathbf{A} - \mathbf{E}) = 0 \tag{23}$$

$$\mathbf{A}^{k+1} = [2 \mathbf{K}^k \mathbf{H}^{(k)T} \mathbf{W}^T \mathbf{W} \mathbf{H}^k \mathbf{K}^{(k)T} + \mu \mathbf{I}_d]^{-1} [2 \mathbf{K}^k \mathbf{H}^{(k)T} \mathbf{W}^T \mathbf{W} \mathbf{Y}^T + \mathbf{\Gamma}^k + \mu(\mathbf{X} - \mathbf{E}^k)] \tag{24}$$

3.2.3   Updating Sparse Error Matrix E

In this subsection, we discuss the solution of subproblem (13) while fixing $\mathbf{H}$, $\mathbf{K}$ and $\mathbf{A}$

$$L(\mathbf{E}) \propto \lambda \|\mathbf{E}\|_1 + \langle \mathbf{\Gamma}, \mathbf{X} - \mathbf{A} - \mathbf{E} \rangle + \frac{\mu}{2} \|\mathbf{X} - \mathbf{A} - \mathbf{E}\|_F^2 \tag{25}$$

which can be rewritten in an equivalent problem as

$$L(\mathbf{E}) \propto \lambda \|\mathbf{E}\|_1 + \frac{\mu}{2} \left\|\mathbf{X} - \mathbf{A} - \mathbf{E} + \frac{1}{\mu} \mathbf{\Gamma}\right\|_F^2 \tag{26}$$

using the shrinkage operator $S_b(a) = \mathrm{sgn}(a) \max(|a| - b, 0)$, the subgradient of (26) provides a closed-form solution for $\mathbf{E}$ as

$$\mathbf{E}^{k+1} = \mathbf{S}_{\frac{\lambda}{\mu}} (\mathbf{X} - \mathbf{A}^k + \frac{\mathbf{\Gamma}^k}{\mu}) \tag{27}$$

3.2.4   Updating Lagrange Multiplier Matrix Γ

The Lagrange multiplier matrix is updated by

$$\mathbf{\Gamma}^{k+1} = \mathbf{\Gamma}^k + \mu(\mathbf{X} - \mathbf{A} - \mathbf{E}) \tag{28}$$

The penalty variables μ is updated by

$$\mu^{k+1} = \rho \mu^k \tag{29}$$

where $\rho > 1$ is a constant. Larger ρ imposes in stronger regularization on data decomposition $\mathbf{X} = \mathbf{A} + \mathbf{E}$, and lead to faster convergence, but may result in poor estimation of regression and vise versa. In our experiments, we choose $\rho = 1.01$.

The detailed algorithmic procedure of robust LDA is stated in Algorithm 1.

Algorithm 1. ALM algorithm for solving Robust Laplacian Sparse Coding

1: **input:** training data $\mathbf{X} = [\mathbf{x}_1, \ldots, \mathbf{x}_n]$, the parameters λ

2: **initial:** initialize $\mathbf{A}^0 = \mathbf{X}$ and $\mathbf{E}^0 = \mathbf{X} - \mathbf{A}^0$,

$$\text{Lagrange Multiplier Initialization: } \boldsymbol{\Gamma}^0 = \frac{\mathbf{X}}{\|\mathbf{X}\|_2}, \ \mu^0 = \frac{dn}{4}\|\mathbf{X}\|_1$$

3: **repeat**

4:    Update $\mathbf{K}$: $\mathbf{K}^{k+1} = \text{Tr}(\mathbf{K}^T\mathbf{A}^k(\mathbf{A}^k)^T\mathbf{K})^{-1}(\mathbf{K}^T\mathbf{A}^k\mathbf{YW}^T\mathbf{WY}^T(\mathbf{A}^k)^T\mathbf{K})$

5:    Update $\mathbf{H}$: $\mathbf{H}^{k+1} = \text{Tr}((\mathbf{H}^T\mathbf{W}^T\mathbf{WH})^{-1}\mathbf{H}^T\mathbf{W}^T\mathbf{WY}^T(\mathbf{A}^k)^T(\mathbf{A}^k(\mathbf{A}^k)^T)^{-1}\mathbf{A}^k\mathbf{YW}^T\mathbf{WH})$

6:    Update $\mathbf{A}$: $\mathbf{A}^{k+1} = [2\mathbf{K}^k\mathbf{H}^{(k)T}\mathbf{W}^T\mathbf{WH}^k\mathbf{K}^{(k)T} + \mu\mathbf{I}_d]^{-1}[2\mathbf{K}^k\mathbf{H}^{(k)T}\mathbf{W}^T\mathbf{WY}^T + \boldsymbol{\Gamma}^k + \mu(\mathbf{X} - \mathbf{E}^k)]$

7:    Update $\mathbf{E}$: $\mathbf{E}^{k+1} = \mathbf{S}_{\frac{\lambda}{\mu}}(\mathbf{X} - \mathbf{A}^k + \frac{\boldsymbol{\Gamma}^k}{\mu})$

8:    Update $\boldsymbol{\Gamma}$: $\boldsymbol{\Gamma}^{k+1} = \boldsymbol{\Gamma}^k + \mu(\mathbf{X} - \mathbf{A} - \mathbf{E})$

9: **until** $\dfrac{\|\mathbf{X} - \mathbf{A}^k - \mathbf{E}^k\|_F}{\|\mathbf{X}\|_F} \le 10^{-8}$ **or** $\dfrac{\|\mathbf{Y}^T - \mathbf{H}^k(\mathbf{K}^k)^T\mathbf{A}^k\|_F}{\|\mathbf{X}\|_F} \le 10^{-8}$

10: **output:** H, K, A, E

---

4   Experiments

This section compares our LRLDA method against classical methods on pose estimation and face recognition. In order to evaluate the robustness of the proposed method, we applied it to problems with intrinsic noises and outliers to different extents.

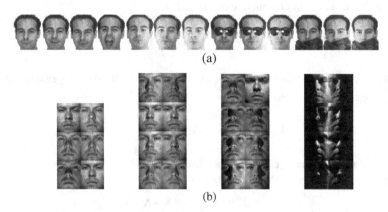

(a)

(b)

Fig. 1. (a)The samples taken from AR database. (b) The samples taken from extended Yale B database.

4.1   Experiment for Head Pose Estimation

This section illustrates the benefit of LRLDA in the problem of head pose estimation from corrupted images under different conditions (expression, occlusion and light).

AR database [13] consists of 126 subjects (70 men and 56 women). Each subject contains 26 images which are separated in two sessions and each session contains 13 images (three images with sunglasses, another three with scarves, and the remaining seven simply with illumination and expressions variations). The face portion of each image are with $50 \times 40 = 2000$ pixels (see Fig.1 (a)).

extended Yale B database [14] consists of 2,414 frontal face images of 38 subjects (around 59-64 images for each person). According to the angle the light source direction makes with the camera axis, the images from each pose were divided into 4 subsets : subset1($\leq 12°$), subset2($\leq 25°$), subset3($\leq 50°$), subset4($\leq 77°$) , shown in Fig.1 (b).

4.1.1   Experiment on AR Database

We choose the first session (13 images for each class) from 60 classes for samples to experiment. We selecte corrupted images due to the occlusion of expressions which occludes about 20%, sunglasses which covers nearly 30% and scarf which covers nearly 50% of the face. Similarly, the selected images include three clean images with different expressions, one image with sunglass and one with scarf.

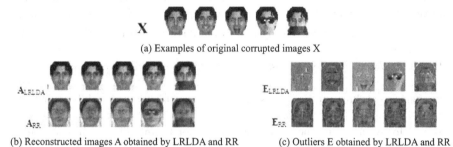

(a) Examples of original corrupted images X

(b) Reconstructed images A obtained by LRLDA and RR   (c) Outliers E obtained by LRLDA and RR

Fig. 2. Decomposition of input images X in (a) by LRLDA and RR. The images are corrupted by different occlusions, such as expression, sunglass and scarf.

We have compared our method with Robust Regression [12]. As we can learn from Fig.2, when 0%, 20%, 30%, 50% of the images are corrupted, LRLDA performed much better than RR, especially when image ate blocked by sunglass. The two methods both performed well in head pose estimation, but RR failed in certain circumstances, while LRLDA can be applied in almost all conditions.

4.1.2   Experiment on Extended Yale B Database

We randomly choose 10 images from each subject and resize the images into $100 \times 88 = 8800$ pixels. Let $\mathbf{X} \in \mathbb{R}^{8800 \times 380}$ and the labels are gathered in the matrix $\mathbf{Y} \in \mathbb{R}^{1 \times 380}$.

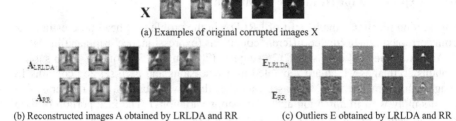

(a) Examples of original corrupted images X

(b) Reconstructed images A obtained by LRLDA and RR   (c) Outliers E obtained by LRLDA and RR

Fig. 3. Decomposition of input images X in (a) by LRLDA and RR

Similar to previous work, the images are corrupted about 0%, 50% and over 90% separately. The results clearly demonstrated that our method performed better than RR, especially when the images are corrupted seriously. Fig.3 visualized the decomposition done by LRLDA and RR for the same input images. Both of the two experiments presented before illustrated that LRLDA preserves much more personal facial details in **A** than RR and reduces interference of different kinds of noise.

4.2   Experiment for Recognition

The advantages of LRLDA mainly come from its ability of decomposition, which automatically extracting salient features from corrupted data ($\mathbf{X} = \mathbf{A}_{RLDA} + \mathbf{E}_{RLDA}$). We compare LRLDA against related algorithms on classification on AR and Extended Yale B database.

In AR database, we first choose (1)seven clean images and three images with sunglasses in session 1 for training and the remaining images for testing; (2)seven clean images and three images with scarf in session 1 for training and the remaining images for testing; (3)seven clean images and two different occluded images in session 1 for training and the remaining images for testing. (The results shown in Table.1). Then we choose all images in session 1 for training and the remaining images for testing for comparing the performance against PCA, LDA, RPCA and RR (The results shown in Fig.5 (a)). In Extended Yale B database, we choose randomly 20 images for training and the remaining images for testing. In this experiment, we also compare our method against PCA, LDA, RPCA and RR for face recognition (results shown in Fig.5(b)).

Table 1. The recognition results under cases with occlusions

	LRLD	PCA	LDA	RPCA	RR
Sunglasses	0.76	0.7167	0.7433	0.6967	0.76
Scarf	0.7464	0.68	0.7306	0.6633	0.7246
Sunglasses	0.7141	0.6423	0.6668	0.6410	0.6675

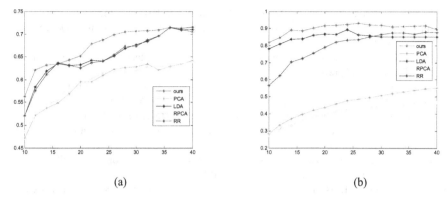

(a)	(b)

Fig. 4. The average recognition rates in (a)AR database and (b) Extended Yale B database

It's clearly that in Table.1 and Fig.4 (a), our method achieved 76%, 74.64% and 71.41% for the occlusion from sunglasses (30% occlusion), scarf (50% occlusion) and both sunglasses and scarf (90% occlusion). Due to the presence of occlusion and disguise, the associated performance (using the corrupted images for training directly) is degraded. But it is obviously that LRLDA outperforms all other methods. Fig.4(b) better illustrates the superiority of our algorithm. Using RR and LDA, which are the most relevant methods to ours, RR obtains 88.52% and LDA obtains 89.95%, while LRLDA achieve 93.18%,. In other words, we improve the method of RR by about 4% to 5% and improve LDA by about 3% to 4%. Thus, we confirm the use of our LRLDA especially when alleviates the problem of severe illustration variations even such noise is presented in both training and testing samples.

LRLDA has been proved to be an effective tool for head pose estimation and face recognition. It obtains noise-free data from corrupted images and finds the faithful LDA-subspace for classification and discrimination. Thus, we successfully confirm the effectiveness about robustness of LRLDA.

5   Conclusion

The paper proposed a robust LDA method, which is robust to data with large corruptions. By introducing the low-rank constraint into the traditional Linear Discriminant Analysis (LDA), we can get a set of noise-free images, and the obtained clean data can be used to find the faithful LDA-subspace for the final classification. The experiments on several databases have demonstrated the effectiveness and robustness of LRLDA.

References

1. Fukunaga, K.: Introduction to statistical pattern recognition, 2nd edn. Academic Press (1990)
2. Belhumeur, P.N., Hespanha, J.P., Kriegman, D.J.: Eigenfaces vs. Fisherfaces: Recognition Using Class Specific Linear Projection. IEEE Transactions on Pattern Analysis And Machine Intelligence 19(7), 711–720 (1997)

3. Wright, J., Yang, A., Ganesh, A., Sastry, S., Ma, Y.: Robust face recognition via sparse representation. IEEE Transactions on Pattern Analysis And Machine Intelligence 31(2), 210–227 (2009)
4. Shen, X., Wu, Y.: A unified approach to salient object detection via low rank matrix recovery. In: CVPR (2012)
5. Zhang, T., Ghanem, B., Liu, S., Ahuja, N.: Low-rank sparse learning for robust visual tracking. In: Fitzgibbon, A., Lazebnik, S., Perona, P., Sato, Y., Schmid, C. (eds.) ECCV 2012, Part VI. LNCS, vol. 7577, pp. 470–484. Springer, Heidelberg (2012)
6. Zhang, Z., Matsushita, Y., Ma, Y.: Camera calibration with lens distortion from low-rank textures. In: CVPR (2011)
7. Lee, J., Shi, B., Matsushita, Y., Kweon, I., Ikeuchi, K.: Radiometric calibration by transform invariant low-rank structure. In: CVPR (2011)
8. la Torre, F.D.: A Least-Squares Framework for Component Analysis. IEEE Transactions on Pattern Analysis And Machine Intelligence 34(6), 1041–1055 (2012)
9. Diamantaras, K.I.: Principal Component Neural Networks (Theory and Applications). John Wiley & Sons (1996)
10. Candès, E.J., Li, X., Ma, Y., Wright, J.: Robust Principal Component Analysis? Journal of ACM 58(1), 1–37 (2009)
11. Schar, L.: The SVD and reduced rank signal processing. Signal Processing 25(2), 113–133 (2002)
12. Huang, D., Cabral, R.S., De la Torre, F.: Robust Regression. In: Fitzgibbon, A., Lazebnik, S., Perona, P., Sato, Y., Schmid, C. (eds.) ECCV 2012, Part IV. LNCS, vol. 7575, pp. 616–630. Springer, Heidelberg (2012)
13. Martinez, A., Benavente, R.: The AR face database, CVC Technical Report, 24 (1998)
14. Chen, Y.D., Jalali, A., Sanghavi, S., Caramanis, C.: Low-rank Matrix Recovery from Error and Erasures. In: 2011 IEEE International Symposium on Information Theory, St. Petersburg, Russia, July 31 - August 5 (2011)

Kernelized Laplacian Collaborative Representation Based Classifier for Face Recognition

Juanjuan Cui, Caikou Chen, Shuxian Yi, and Yu Ding

College of Information Engineering, Yangzhou University
yzcck@126.com

Abstract. A recently proposed sparse representation based classifier, called collaborative representation based classification with regularized least square (CRC_RLS), has attracted notable attention. The extensive experiments demonstrate that the CRC_RLS technique has less complexity than traditional sparse representation based classifier (SRC) but results in better classification performance. However, the existing SRC-like approaches fail to consider the manifold structure of the data space. It has been shown that the manifold information of the data is important for discrimination. The paper presents a more effective classification scheme, termed kernelized laplacian collaborative representation based classifier (KLCRC) for face recognition. KLCRC explicitly take into account the nonlinear distribution and local manifold structure of the data. The extensive experimental results over several standard face databases have demonstrated the effectiveness of the proposed algorithm.

Keywords: kernel, Laplacian matrix, sparse representation, face recognition.

1 Introduction

Face recognition has been an active research topic in pattern recognition and computer vision areas in the past decades. Simultaneously, a great number of successful algorithms have been proposed for face representation and classification [1]. Recently, sparse representation based classification method (SRC) has aroused interests and been widely used for face recognition. Wright *et al.* [2] presented a sparse representation-based classification (SRC) method for robust face recognition. The main idea behind SRC is that a given test sample is represented as a sparse linear combination of all training samples while the sparse nonzero coefficients should concentrate on the training samples with the same class label as the test sample. After Wright's pioneering work, numerous sparsity-based classification methods have been proposed in recent years. Gao *et al.* [3] presented the kernel sparse representation, while Yang and Zhang [4] used the Gabor features for SRC with a learned Gabor occlusion dictionary to reduce the computational cost. Yang *et al.* [5] gave an insight into SRC and provided some theoretical supports for its effectiveness.

Unfortunately, while SRC achieves impressive results, its working mechanism has not been revealed and the effectiveness. Most importantly, the effectiveness of the l_1-norm-based sparsity constraint that improves the face recognition performance has

Z. Sun et al. (Eds.): CCBR 2013, LNCS 8232, pp. 115–121, 2013.

been called into question recently. Zhang et al. [6] argued that the collaborative representation based classification with regularized least square plays a more important role than the l_1-norm-based sparsity constraint and proposed an l_2-norm-based collaborative representation classifier (CRC), which is computationally more efficient than SRC.

Over the past years, nonlinear feature representations have aroused considerable interest in the fields of pattern recognition. Two most representative ones are kernel methods and manifold learning respectively. The popular algorithms for kernel methods include support vector machines (SVMs) [7], kernel principal component analysis (KPCA) [8], and kernel Fisher discriminant analysis (KFD) [9]. The core of kernel methods is the kernel trick, which maps the non-linear separable features into high dimensional feature space where features from the same class are easier grouped together and linear separable. It has been shown that face images lie in a low dimensional manifold. In order to capture the underlying manifold structure of data, many manifold learning methods have been proposed, including locally linear embedding (LLE) [11], ISOMAP [10], and Laplacian Eigenmap [12]. All manifold learning algorithms share the idea of locality preserving, that is, the nearby points are likely to have similar representations (embeddings). It has been demonstrated that learning performance can be significantly enhanced if the locality information is exploited. Motivated by recent progress in sparse coding, manifold learning and kernel methods, in this paper we propose a novel algorithm, called kernelized laplacian collaborative representation based classifier (KLCRC). KLCRC explicitly integrates nonlinear distribution and local manifold structure of the data into the objective function of CRC. The extensive experimental results over several standard face databases have demonstrated the effectiveness of the proposed algorithm.

2   The CRC with Regularized Least Square (CRC_RLS) Algorithm

Let $\mathbf{X} \in \Re^{m \times n}$ denote the dataset of the ith class, and each column of $\mathbf{X}_i$ is a sample of class i, Suppose that there are K classes of subjects, and let $\mathbf{X} = [\mathbf{X}_1, \mathbf{X}_2, \cdots, \mathbf{X}_K]$. For a given testing sample $\mathbf{y} \in \Re^m$, one can represent it as $\mathbf{y} = \mathbf{X}\alpha$, where $\alpha = [\alpha_1; \alpha_2; \ldots; \alpha_K]$ and α_i is the coding vector associated with class i. We take all the training samples as the dictionary, and then given a test sample $\mathbf{y}$, we represent it in the dictionary, i.e. $\mathbf{y} = \mathbf{X}\alpha$. If $\mathbf{y}$ is from the ith class, usually $\mathbf{y} = \mathbf{X}_i\alpha_i$ holds well.

The steps of the CRC_RLS algorithm are summarized in the following [8].

Step 1 Normalize the columns of X to have unit l_2-norm.

Step 2 Code y over X by regularized least square

$$\tilde{\beta} = \arg\min_{\beta} \{\|\mathbf{y} - \mathbf{X}\beta\|_2^2 + \lambda \|\beta\|_2^2\} \tag{1}$$

$$\tilde{\beta} = \mathbf{P}\mathbf{y} \tag{2}$$

where λ is the regularized parameter and $\mathbf{P} = (\mathbf{X}^{\mathrm{T}}\mathbf{X} + \lambda\mathbf{I})^{-1}\mathbf{X}^{\mathrm{T}}$.

Step 3 Compute the regularized residuals

$$r_i = \left\| \mathbf{y} - \mathbf{X}_i\boldsymbol{\beta}_i \right\|_2 / \left\| \tilde{\boldsymbol{\beta}}_i \right\|_2 \tag{3}$$

Step 4 Compute the class label of y as

$$k = \arg\min_i r_i \tag{4}$$

3   Kernelized Laplacian CRC_RLS

3.1   Kernelization

When the data are nonlinearly separable in the input space, we may consider to nonlinearly mapping the data into a feature space, where the data becomes linearly separable. This makes it possible to directly use some linear classification methods in the feature space. In practice, however, it is still difficult to do so because the high (or even infinite) dimensionality of feature space makes the computation of inner products very time-consuming (or impossible). Fortunately, kernel trick can be introduced to tackle this problem. The inner products in the feature space can be computed efficiently using a predefined *kernel function* of data in the input space.

Definition 1 (kernel function) A kernel k is a function that for all $\mathbf{u}, \mathbf{v} \in \Omega$ satisfies

$$\mathbf{k}(\mathbf{u}, \mathbf{v}) = \phi(\mathbf{u}) \cdot \phi(\mathbf{v})$$

where Φ is a mapping from the input space Ω to the feature space Φ, i.e.,

$$\phi : \mathbf{u} \mapsto \phi(\mathbf{u}) \in \Phi$$

Suppose we have a set of K-class data $\mathbf{X} = [\mathbf{X}_1, \mathbf{X}_2, ..., \mathbf{X}_K]$ where $\mathbf{X}_i \in \Re^{m \times n}$ denote the dataset of the ith class, and a kernel function k. Let the kernelized dataset as $\mathbf{F} = [\phi(\mathbf{X}_1), \phi(\mathbf{X}_2), ..., \phi(\mathbf{X}_K)]$ where $\phi(\mathbf{X}_i) = [\phi(\mathbf{x}_{i1}), \phi(\mathbf{x}_{i2}), ..., \phi(\mathbf{x}_{in_i})]$. We can reformulate the objective function of CRC_RLS in the feature space induced by the kernel function k and get the following optimization function:

$$\tilde{\boldsymbol{\beta}} = \arg\min_{\boldsymbol{\beta}} \{ \left\| \phi(\mathbf{y}) - \phi(\mathbf{X})\boldsymbol{\beta} \right\|_2^2 + \lambda \left\| \boldsymbol{\beta} \right\|_2^2 \} \tag{5}$$

3.2   Locality Regularization

SRC has shown its effectiveness and robustness in face classification. However, the local information among data may lose during sparse representation process. Recent work has shown that the relationship among data is important for classification, such as the underlying manifold structure. To better characterize the locality of data, we explicitly introduce a regularization term into the optimization problem (5) to preserve the consistence of sparse codes for the similarity between training samples and testing sample. Given a set of n data samples $\mathbf{X} = \{\mathbf{x}_1, \mathbf{x}_2, ..., \mathbf{x}_n\}$ and a given testing sample y, we canalculate its k-nearest neighbors of $\mathbf{y}$ in $\mathbf{X}$ and form a similarity vector $\mathbf{w}$. If $\mathbf{x}_i$ is among the k-nearest neighbors of $\mathbf{y}, \mathbf{w}_i = 1$, otherwise, $\mathbf{w}_i = 0$. Consider the problem of mapping the k-nearest neighborhood between a testing sample and training samples to the sparse representations, a reasonable criterion for choosing a "good" map is to minimize the following objective function

$$\sum_{i=1}^{n} \|\phi(\mathbf{X})\boldsymbol{\beta} - \phi(\mathbf{x}_i)\|^2 \, \mathbf{w}_i \qquad (6)$$

By incorporating the k-nearest neighborhood (6) into the objective function (5), we can get the new objective function:

$$\tilde{\boldsymbol{\beta}} = \arg\min_{\boldsymbol{\beta}} \{\|\phi(\mathbf{y}) - \phi(\mathbf{X})\boldsymbol{\beta}\|_2^2 + \lambda \|\boldsymbol{\beta}\|_2^2 + \gamma \sum_i \|\phi(\mathbf{X})\boldsymbol{\beta} - \phi(\mathbf{x}_i)\|^2 \, \mathbf{w}_i\} \qquad (7)$$

where γ is the regularization parameter.

The optimization problem can be rewritten as the following equation:

$$\begin{aligned}
\varepsilon(\boldsymbol{\beta}) &= \|\phi(\mathbf{y}) - \phi(\mathbf{X})\boldsymbol{\beta}\|_2^2 + \lambda \|\boldsymbol{\beta}\|_2^2 + \gamma \sum_i \|\phi(\mathbf{X})\boldsymbol{\beta} - \phi(\mathbf{x}_i)\|_2^2 \, \mathbf{w}_i \\
&= \phi\left(\mathbf{y}^{\mathrm{T}}\right)\phi(\mathbf{y}) - 2\left(\phi(\mathbf{X})\boldsymbol{\beta}\right)^{\mathrm{T}} \phi(\mathbf{y}) + \left(\phi(\mathbf{X})\boldsymbol{\beta}\right)^{\mathrm{T}}\left(\phi(\mathbf{X})\phi\right) + \gamma\boldsymbol{\beta}^{\mathrm{T}}\boldsymbol{\beta} \\
&+ \gamma\left(\phi(\mathbf{X})\boldsymbol{\beta}\right)^{\mathrm{T}}\left(\phi(\mathbf{X})\boldsymbol{\beta}\right)\sum_i \mathbf{w}_i - 2\gamma\left(\phi(\mathbf{X})\boldsymbol{\beta}\right)^{\mathrm{T}} \sum_i \phi(\mathbf{x}_i)\mathbf{w}_i + \gamma\sum_i \phi\left(\mathbf{x}_i^{\mathrm{T}}\right)\phi(\mathbf{x}_i)\mathbf{w}_i
\end{aligned} \qquad (8)$$

Requiring the gradient of function (8) vanish gives the following equation:

$$\begin{aligned}
\frac{\partial(\varepsilon(\boldsymbol{\beta}))}{\partial(\boldsymbol{\beta})} &= \phi(\mathbf{X}^{\mathrm{T}})\phi(\mathbf{X})\boldsymbol{\beta} + \lambda\boldsymbol{\beta} + \gamma\phi(\mathbf{X}^{\mathrm{T}})\phi(\mathbf{X})\left(\sum_i \mathbf{w}_i\right)\boldsymbol{\beta} \\
&- \phi(\mathbf{X}^{\mathrm{T}})\phi(\mathbf{y}) - \gamma\phi(\mathbf{X}^{\mathrm{T}})\phi(\mathbf{X})\mathbf{w} = 0
\end{aligned} \qquad (9)$$

Finally, we compute the representation coefficient vector by

$$\boldsymbol{\beta} = \left[\phi\left(\mathbf{X}^{\mathrm{T}}\right)\phi(\mathbf{X}) + \lambda\mathbf{1} + \gamma\left(\sum_i \mathbf{w}_i\right)\phi\left(\mathbf{X}^{\mathrm{T}}\right)\phi(\mathbf{X})\right]^{-1} \left[\phi\left(\mathbf{X}^{\mathrm{T}}\right)\phi(\mathbf{y}) + \gamma\phi\left(\mathbf{X}^{\mathrm{T}}\right)\phi(\mathbf{X})\mathbf{w}\right] \qquad (10)$$

$$\boldsymbol{\beta} = \left[\mathbf{K}(1 + \gamma h) + \lambda\mathbf{1}\right]^{-1} \left[k(\mathbf{y}) + \gamma\mathbf{K}\mathbf{w}\right] \qquad (11)$$

where $h = \sum_i \mathbf{w}_i$ is the degree of the i th sample and I denotes the matrix with all entries equal to 1.

4   Experimental Results and Analysis

In this section, we evaluate our method on two databases: ORL and FERET. In our objective function, there are two parameters: γ and λ. Generally, they are fixed at 0.1

or 0.01. The Gaussian kernel function is   chosen as $k(i,j) = \exp\left(-\dfrac{\|\mathbf{x}_i - \mathbf{x}_j\|^2}{2\sigma^2}\right)$, and

σ^2 was set to the square of Frobenious norm of the covariance matrix of training samples. In the experiment, the training sample set is used to construct the kernel space and then represent all the testing samples. It was also claimed that the Nearest Subspace (NS) classifier is employed which represents testing sample by the training samples of each class.

4.1   Experiment on ORL Database

The ORL database includes 400 face images taken from 40 subjects, with each subject providing 10 face images. For some subjects, the images were taken at different times, with varying lighting, facial details (glasses or no glasses). On ORL, we use 5 images of each subject as the training samples randomly and took the remaining images as the testing samples. We use PCA to reduce the dimension of images to 100 .

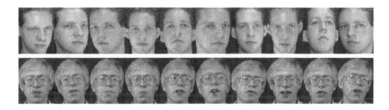

Fig. 1. Some face images of a subject of the ORL database

In the experiment, We used PCA to reduce the dimension of each image to 100 and compare KLCRC and kernelized laplacian nearest subspace (KLNS) with NS, CRC_RLS, laplacian nearest subspace (LNS), laplacian collaborative representation based classifier (LCRC) by using different training sample set, and the results are listed in Fig.2. The curve shows the average recognition accuracy and the histogram show the variance of different method. Clearly, KLNS gets the best recognition accuracy and minimum variance, and KLNS is the second one.

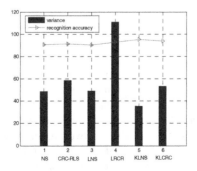

Fig. 2. The average recognition accuracy and the variance of different method

4.2   Experiment on FERET Database

The FERET face contains 1400 gray face images of 200 subjects, including varying postures, genders, lighting condition, shooting directions and race. The face portion of each image is manually cropped and the normalized to 80×80 pixels.

Fig. 3. Some face images of a subject of the FERET database

The comparison of recognition rate with different dimension is given in Fig.4. For each subject, the 3 images in front are used for training with the other 4 images are used for testing. We can see that KLCRC and KLNS which achieve 73.4% and 75.4% respectively are both the best two methods, and at least 6%~7% higher than other methods. Table 1 show the recognition rate of different training number. We can see when the training number is 5, the recognition rate is becoming decreasing.

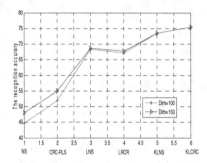

Fig. 4. The average recognition rate of different dimensions

Table 1. The recognition rate of different number of the training sample

Train number	2	3	4	5
KLCRC (%)	55.0	75.4	79.2	55.2

5   Conclusion

In this paper, we propose a novel framework of sparse coding for face recognition. In order to keep the relationship between similar samples, we add the locality preserving constraint in the objective function. By mapping the non-linear features into a higher dimensional feature space, we make the features of different categories linearly separable. Then we implement our method to two-phase, the experiment results show the great advantage compare with state-of-the-art method. But the proposed method does not perform well in original space; our future work is to find a better code to make it has a good performance in original space.

References

1. Zhao, W., Chellappa, R., Rosenfeld, A., Phillips, P.J.: Face recognition: A literature survey. ACM Comput. Surv. 35(4), 399–458 (2003)
2. Wright, J., Yang, A.Y., Ganesh, A., Sastry, S.S., Ma, Y.: Robust face recognition via sparse representation. IEEE PAMI 31(2), 210–227 (2009)
3. Gao, S., Tsang, I.W.-H., Chia, L.-T.: Kernel Sparse Representation for Image Classification and Face Recognition. In: Daniilidis, K., Maragos, P., Paragios, N. (eds.) ECCV 2010, Part IV. LNCS, vol. 6314, pp. 1–14. Springer, Heidelberg (2010)
4. Yang, M., Zhang, L.: Gabor Feature based Sparse Representation for Face Recognition with Gabor Occlusion Dictionary. In: Daniilidis, K., Maragos, P., Paragios, N. (eds.) ECCV 2010, Part VI. LNCS, vol. 6316, pp. 448–461. Springer, Heidelberg (2010)
5. Yang, J., Zhang, L., Xu, Y., Yang, J.Y.: Beyond sparsity: The role of L1-optimizer in pattern classification. Pattern Recognit. 45(3), 1104–1118 (2012)
6. Zhang, L., Yang, M., Feng, X.C.: Sparse representation or collaborative representation: Which helps face recognition? In: Proc. IEEE Int. Conf. Comput. Vis., pp. 471–478 (November 2011)
7. Vapnik, V.: The Nature of Statistical Learning Theory. Springer, New York (1995)
8. Mika, S., Ratsch, G., Weston, J., Scholkopf, B., Muller, K.R.: Fisher discriminant analysis with kernels. In: Proceedings of IEEE International Workshop on Neural Networks for Signal Processing IX, pp. 41–48 (1999)
9. Tenenbaum, J., Silva, V., Langford, J.: A global geometric framework for nonlinear dimensionality reduction. Science 290(5500), 2319–2323 (2000)
10. Roweis, S., Saul, L.: Nonlinear dimensionality reduction by locally linear embedding. Science 290(5500), 2323–2326 (2000)
11. Belkin, M., Niyogi, P.: Laplacian eigenmaps and spectral techniques for embedding and clustering. Adv. Neural Inf. Process. Syst. 15, 585–592 (2002)
12. Hadsell, R., Chopra, S., LeCun, Y.: Dimensionality reduction by learning an invariant mapping. In: Proc. IEEE Comput. Soc. Conf. Comput. Vis. Pattern Recognit., pp. 1735–1742 (2006)

LPQ Based Static and Dynamic Modeling of Facial Expressions in 3D Videos

Qingkai Zhen[1], Di Huang[1*], Yunhong Wang[1], and Liming Chen[2]

[1] Laboratory of Intelligent Recognition and Image Processing,
Beijing Key Laboratory of Digital Media
School of Computer Science and Engineering, Beihang University, Beijing, China
buaazqk@cse.buaa.edu.cn, {dhuang,yhwang}@buaa.edu.cn
[2] Ecole Centrale de Lyon, LIRIS UMR5205, F-69134, Lyon, France
liming.chen@ec-lyon.fr

Abstract. Automatic Facial Expression Recognition (FER) is one of the most active topics in the domain of computer vision and pattern recognition. In this paper, we focus on discrete facial expression recognition by using 4D data (i.e. 3D range image sequences), and present a novel method to address such an issue. The Local Phase Quantisation from Three Orthogonal Planes (LPQ-TOP) descriptor is applied to extract both the static and dynamic clues conveyed in facial expressions. On the one hand, it locally captures the shape attributes in each 3D face model (facial range image). On the other hand, it detects the latent temporal information and represents dynamic changes occurred in facial muscle actions. The SVM classifier is finally used to predict the expression type. The experiments are carried out on the BU-4DFE database, and the achieved results demonstrate the effectiveness of the proposed method.

Keywords: 4D Facial Expression Recognition, LPQ-TOP.

1 Introduction

Automatic recognition of human facial expression has interested many researchers since it plays a key role in various applications such as Human Computer Interaction (HCI), tired detection, facial animation, psychological studies as well as virtual reality [1]. Facial expressions are generated by facial muscle contractions which result in temporary facial deformations in both facial geometry and texture [2]. In the past few decades, the main focus of expression analysis has been on the 2D domain (i.e. images and videos), while these techniques have achieved remarkable performance, illumination and pose variations are still big challenges. The 3D data, on the other hand, are inherently information-rich by nature and considered to be more effective to deal with the above challenges. Recent years have witnessed the progress within this filed, which allows us to analyze facial behaviors at a detailed level. With more recent advance in 3D

---

* Corresponding author.

Z. Sun et al. (Eds.): CCBR 2013, LNCS 8232, pp. 122–129, 2013.

image sensing, 4D data (3D range image sequences) are available, and they not only accurately describe the facial geometry property, but also convey a wealth of timing information. Recently, increasing attentions have been received in the area of 4D FER for the publicity of the BU-4DFE database [3].

4D FER generally involves in two critical issues, i. e. geometry representation in single 3D face model as well as dynamics encoding in 3D face model sequences. For the former one, similar to the approaches proposed for static 3D facial expression recognition, it is important to describe the shape attributes on facial surfaces. The techniques in the literature can be roughly categorized into two main classes: feature based and model based. Feature based ones generally concentrate on the extraction of expression sensitive geometry features from 3D face models, while model based ones make use of a generic model based on which common expressions can be indicated by measuring the feature vector composed by the parameters of shape deformation achieved in the fitting phase. For the latter, compared to the studies which describe expressions using static 2D facial images [4] and 3D face models [5], video based methods tend to better represent expressions especially the subtle ones like anger and disgust, since from 3D videos, dynamic features can be obtained, which are critical to model the changes in facial expressions formed by periodical muscular movements [6].

This paper concentrates on discrete facial expression recognition by using 4D data (i.e. 3D range image sequences), and proposes a novel approach to solve this problem. The Local Phase Quantisation from Three Orthogonal Planes (LPQ-TOP) descriptor is introduced to extract both the static and dynamic clues of facial expressions. On the one hand, it locally captures the shape attributes in each 3D face model. On the other hand, it detects the latent temporal information and represents dynamic changes occurred in facial muscular actions. The widely-used SVM classifier is finally used to predict the expression type. The experiments are conducted on the BU-4DFE database, and the achieved results illustrate the effectiveness of the proposed method.

The remainder of the paper is organized as follows: Section 2 briefly reviews recent development in this domain. We then describe the proposed method in Section 3 and analyze the experimental results in Section 4. In Section 5 we conclude the paper.

2   Related Work

There have been extensive investigations on solving the problem of 3D Facial Expression Recognition (FER). As indicated in [2] [7], most existing research merely focuses on 3D static images while 3D videos are believed to be of more information and critical for expression recognition. In order to construct a spatio-temporal descriptor, Yin et al. [5] introduced a tracking model to estimate motion trajectories and proposed a facial expression label map (FELM) based tracking approach. In their research, the FELM vector and the motion vector were concatenated to form the descriptor of facial expressions that become the input to a linear LDA classifier.

Sun et al. [8] used an Active Appearance Model (AMM) to track feature points in frames of the 2D texture video and retrieve their corresponding 3D positions. The authors further employed Radial Basis Function (RBF) to adapt all meshes of the video with the first mesh and each vertex of the 3D mesh in the video was characterized by its primitive geometric surface features (e. g. convex peaks and concave pits) [9]. An optimal discriminative feature space was then constructed for every mesh using Linear Discriminant Analysis (LDA). For classification, Hidden Markov Models (HMM) was applied in training data of the statistical information and the temporal dynamics, and the Bayesian decision rule was finally adopted to classify query sequences.

Sandbach et al. [10] modeled a facial expression sequence with the state of neutral, onset, apex, and offset. They first made use of an iterative closed point algorithm (ICP) to align all 3D meshes with the first mesh. Then Free-Form Deformations (FFDs) were used to capture the motion between frames before a quad-tree decomposition was applied to extract the features. The features were then collected using a variant of the boosting scheme and HMMs were employed to model the temporal dynamics of the complete expression sequence.

Le et al. [11] introduced an approach based on facial level curves for 3D face expression recognition. They compared the curves across frames using Chamfer distances to extract spatio-temporal features for 4D FER. For classification, an HMM-based decision boundary focus classification algorithm was used.

Fang et al. [1] proposed a robust approach for registering 4D data and used a variant of local binary patterns on three orthogonal planes (LBP-TOP) for feature extraction. They presented a registration framework that preserves the temporal coherence of 4D data and incorporated it into an automatic 4D facial expression recognition pipeline leveraging the annotated deformable face model approach [12].

Munawar et al. [13] improved the work by presenting a fully automatic system which exploits the dynamic of 3D video. Local video-patches of variable lengths were extracted from different locations of the training videos and represented as points on the Grass-mannian manifold. An efficient spectral clustering based algorithm was used to separately cluster points for each of the six expression classes. The system was invariant to the temporal length of the video sequences and it did not make any assumptions about the presence of all four segments nor their temporal order in a video.

3   LPQ Based 4D FER Approach

3.1   Data Processing

The videos of the BU-4DFE are captured from a real-time 3D scanner and each mesh with shoulder up level remained, the resolution and size of each mesh of a given 3D video vary from frame to frame. Preprocessing is essential since there are always unavoidable spike nose and missing data in some areas of the mesh surface. In our experiments, the 3D face models are displayed in the form of range images, with a resolution of 256×256. The x, y, z coordinates of each 3D face model are stored in three matrices respectively. All the mesh sequences are preprocessed using the toolbox [14], for removing spikes and filling holes. Then an Iterative Closest Points (ICP) based algorithm is employed to correct pose variations.

3.2   Local Phase Quantization

The Local Phase Quantization (LPQ) operator is a local descriptor which was originally proposed for texture classification and proves robust to image blurring [15]. The descriptor uses local phase information extracted by a short-term Fourier transform (STFT) computed over a rectangular M-by-M neighborhood N_x at each pixel position x of the image $f(x)$ defined as follows

$$F(u, x) = \sum_{y \in N_x} f(x - y)e^{-2\pi j u^T y} = w_u^T f_x \qquad (1)$$

where w_u is the basis vector of 2-D DFT at frequency u, and f_x is the vector containing all M^2 samples from N_x. The STFT is efficiently evaluated for all image position $x \in \{x_1, ..., x_N\}$ using simply 1-D convolutions for the rows and columns successively. The local Fourier coefficients are computed at four frequency points: $u_1 = [a, 0]^T$, $u_2 = [0, a]^T$, $u_3 = [a, a]^T$, and $u_4 = [a, -a]^T$, where a is a sufficiently small scalar. For each pixel position these coefficients result in a vecotr $F_x = [F(u_1, x), F(u_2, x), F(u_3, x), F(u_4, x)]$. The phase information in the Fourier coefficients is recorded by examining the signs of the real and imaginary parts of each components in F_x, achieved by using a simple scalar quantiser

$$q_j = \begin{cases} 1 & \text{if } g_j \geq 0 \\ 0 & \text{otherwise} \end{cases} \qquad (2)$$

where $q_j(x)$ is the jth component of the vector $G_x = [Re\{F_x\}, Im\{F_x\}]$. The resulting eight bit binary coefficients $q_j(x)$ are represented as integers by using binary coding:

$$f_{LPQ(x)} = \sum_{j=1}^{8} q_j 2^{j-1} \qquad (3)$$

As a result, a histogram of these values from all the positions is composed by constructing a 256-dimensional feature vector. Histograms discard all information regarding the spatial arrangement of the patterns. Similar to Local Binary Patterns (LBP), we think that LPQ encodes local shape attributes of 3D facial surfaces when it is applied to 3D face analysis. We thus divide the face region into m local regions, from which LPQ histograms are extracted and then concatenated into a single feature histogram (see Fig. 1). An image divided into $m \times n$ blocks thus produces a feature vector with the dimension of $256 \times m \times n$.

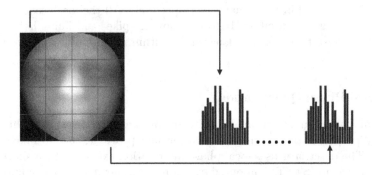

Fig. 1. Illustration of LPQ based 3D face representation

3.3   LPQ-TOP

To extend the LPQ descriptor to the temporal domain, the basic LPQ feature is extracted independently from three sets of orthogonal planes: XY, XT and YT, considering only the co-occurrence statistics in these three directions, and stacking them into a single histogram [16] (see Fig. 2). The XY plane provides the spatial domain information while the XT and YT planes provide temporal information. This method results in $256 \times 3 = 768$ bins per space-time volume. Note that features are extracted from all possible XY, XT and YT planes (See Fig. 3). One important parameter for the LPQ descriptor is the neighborhood size N_x. It is not reasonable to use the same rectangular neighborhood size of the spatial plane and the two temporal planes,and it should be experimentally fixed.

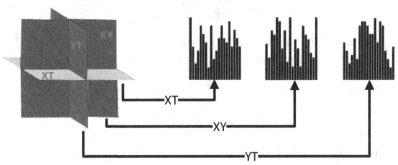

Fig. 2. Concatenated histogram from three planes.

4   Experimental Results

The proposed method was tested on the BU-4DFE database [3] which contains 606 dynamic 3D sequences from 101 subjects. Each subject performs the six prototypical expressions (i.e. anger, disgust, fear, happiness, sadness and surprise).

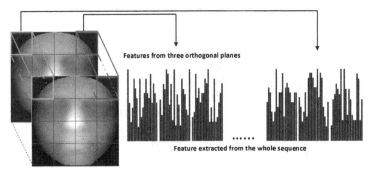

Fig. 3. The concatenation of feature vectors, each of which is extracted from a block to represent the whole sequence.

Although in the database description, the authors state that each sequence contains expression performed gradually from neutral appearance, low intensity, high intensity, back to low intensity and neutral appearance, but this statement does not hold for some sequences [1]. In [1], the authors identified and removed the videos containing corrupted meshes and the videos with obvious discontinuity, and the LBP-TOP descriptor was used to extract features from the 507 sequences of 100 subjects. The author tested six expressions and a average performance of 74.63% is achieved by using the SVM classifier.

In our experiments, the LPQ-TOP descriptor is used to encode both the static facial shape attributes and the spatio-temporal changes occurred in facial expressions, and the proposed method is evaluated using the same protocol as in [1] for fair comparison, especially to highlight the advantages of LPQ-TOP over LBP-TOP in 4D FER. In order to avoid the inconsistency of data used in experiments, we extract the LBP-TOP features ourselves with the help of [17]. It should be noted that we perform 10-fold cross validation in SVM based classification with a Radius Basis Function (RBF) kernel. To reduce gender bias, the subjects are selected independently from females and males. Furthermore, we ensure that no subjects appear in both the training and testing sets. Table 1 and Table 2 show their performance, and from them we can see that the proposed LPQ-TOP based method is much more effective than the LBP-TOP based one [1] for 4D FER. It outperforms [1] in classifying all the six expressions and thereby in the average accuracy.

To the best of our knowledge, the topic of 4D FER is relatively new and there are only few methods in the literature that directly tackle dynamic 3D FER on the BU-4DFE database with explicit experiment protocols. Sun and Yin [9] achieved a better classification performance (90.4%) when considering all the six expressions, but they manually selected 60 subjects and used a set of 6-frame subsequences from each expression sequence. Le et al. [11] selected 60 subjects and evaluated the proposed method only on three expressions, i.e. happiness, sadness, and surprise. Sandbach et al. [10] chose a subset of the subjects manually and test only on the happy, sad and surprise expressions.

Table 1. Confusion matrix obtained by using the LBP-TOP feature

%	AN	DI	FE	HA	SA	SU
AN	**61.3**	8.0	5.8	2.0	21.7	1.2
DI	11.6	**65.8**	13	3.2	1.6	4.8
FE	4.7	13.3	**59.6**	11.4	1.1	9.9
HA	1.0	2.9	10.0	**84.9**	0.1	1.1
SA	17.6	0.6	4.1	0.1	**76.4**	1.2
SU	0	4.6	8.7	3.2	3.5	**80.0**
Average:			**71.33**			

Table 2. Confusion matrix obtained by using the LPQ-TOP feature

%	AN	DI	FE	HA	SA	SU
AN	**62.5**	5.4	12.5	0.2	14.5	4.9
DI	1.9	**77.5**	11.3	2.4	4.7	2.2
FE	2.5	5	**65.0**	7.5	5.0	15.0
HA	0.7	1.8	10.5	**85.0**	1.2	0.8
SA	11.6	1.1	2.5	1.9	**82.5**	0.4
SU	0	2.5	11	2.9	1.1	**82.5**
Average:			**75.83**			

5 Conclusion

In this paper, we present a novel method to address 4D facial expression recognition. The LQP-TOP descriptor is applied to extract both the static and dynamic clues in facial expressions. It can not only captures the shape attributes in each 3D face model but also detects the latent temporal information and represents dynamic changes occurred in facial actions. The experiments are carried out on the BU-4DFE database, and the achieved results demonstrate the effectiveness of the proposed method.

Acknowledgments. This work was supported in part by the National Basic Research Program of China under grant 2010CB327902; the National Natural Science Foundation of China (No. 61202237 and No. 61061130560); the joint project by the LIA 2MCSI laboratory between the group of Ecoles Centrales and Beihang University; and the Fundamental Research Funds for the Central Universities.

References

1. Fang, T., Zhao, X., Shah, S.K., Kakadiaris, I.A.: 4d facial expression recognition. In: ICCV Workshops, pp. 1594–1601 (2011)
2. Fang, T., Zhao, X., Ocegueda, O., Shah, S.K., Kakadiaris, I.A.: 3d facial expression recognition: A perspective on promises and challenges. In: FG, pp. 603–610 (2011)

3. Yin, L., Chen, X., Sun, Y., Worm, T., Reale, M.: A high-resolution 3d dynamic facial expression database. In: FG, pp. 1–6 (2008)
4. Padgett, C., Cottrell, G.W., Adolphs, R.: Categorical perception in facial emotion classification. In: Proceedings of the 18th Annual Conference of the Cognitive Science Society, pp. 249–253. Erlbaum (1996)
5. Yin, L., Wei, X., Longo, P., Bhuvanesh, A.: Analyzing facial expressions using intensity-variant 3d data for human computer interaction. ICPR (1), 1248–1251 (2006)
6. Zeng, Z., Pantic, M., Roisman, G.I., Huang, T.S.: A survey of affect recognition methods: audio, visual and spontaneous expressions. In: Proceedings of the 9th International Conference on Multimodal Interfaces, ICMI 2007, pp. 126–133 (2007)
7. Sandbach, G., Zafeiriou, S., Pantic, M., Yin, L.: Static and dynamic 3d facial expression recognition: A comprehensive survey. Image Vision Comput. 30(10), 683–697 (2012)
8. Sun, Y., Reale, M., Yin, L.: Recognizing partial facial action units based on 3d dynamic range data for facial expression recognition. In: FG, pp. 1–8 (2008)
9. Sun, Y., Yin, L.: Facial expression recognition based on 3D dynamic range model sequences. In: Forsyth, D., Torr, P., Zisserman, A. (eds.) ECCV 2008, Part II. LNCS, vol. 5303, pp. 58–71. Springer, Heidelberg (2008)
10. Sandbach, G., Zafeiriou, S., Pantic, M., Rueckert, D.: A dynamic approach to the recognition of 3d facial expressions and their temporal models. In: FG, pp. 406–413 (2011)
11. Le, V., Tang, H., Huang, T.S.: Expression recognition from 3d dynamic faces using robust spatio-temporal shape features. In: FG, pp. 414–421. IEEE (2011)
12. Kakadiaris, I.A., Passalis, G., Toderici, G., Murtuza, M.N., Lu, Y., Karampatziakis, N., Theoharis, T.: Three-dimensional face recognition in the presence of facial expressions: An annotated deformable model approach. IEEE Trans. Pattern Anal. Mach. Intell. 29(4), 640–649 (2007)
13. Hayat, M., Bennamoun, M., El-Sallam, A.A.: Clustering of video-patches on grassmannian manifold for facial expression recognition from 3d videos. In: WACV, pp. 83–88 (2013)
14. Szeptycki, P., Ardabilian, M., Chen, L.: A coarse-to-fine curvature analysis-based rotationinvariant 3D face landmarking. In: International Conference on Biometrics: Theory, Applications and Systems (September 2009)
15. Ojansivu, V., Heikkilä, J.: Blur insensitive texture classification using local phase quantization. In: Elmoataz, A., Lezoray, O., Nouboud, F., Mammass, D. (eds.) ICISP 2008 2008. LNCS, vol. 5099, pp. 236–243. Springer, Heidelberg (2008)
16. Jiang, B., Valstar, M.F., Martinez, B., Pantic, M.: Dynamic appearance descriptor approach to facial actions temporal modelling. IEEE Transactions of Systems, Man and Cybernetics – Part B (accepted 2013)
17. http://www.cse.oulu.fi/CMV/Downloads/LBPMatlab

Kernel Collaborative Representation with Regularized Least Square for Face Recognition

Zhenyu Wang[1], Wankou Yang[1], Jun Yin[2], and Changyin Sun[1]

[1] School of Autmation, Southeast University, Nanjing 210096, China
[2] College of Information Engineering, Shanghai Maritime University, Shanghai 201306, China
wangzhenyujia@163.com, wankou.yang@yahoo.com, cysun@seu.edu.cn

Abstract. Sparse representation based classification (SRC) has received much attention in computer vision and pattern recognition. SRC is very slow since it needs optimize an objective function with L1-Norm. SRC consists of two parts: collaborative representation and L1-norm constrain. Based on SRC, collaborative representation based classification with regularized least square (CRC_RLS) is prosed. CRC_RLS is a linear method in nature. There are many variations of illumination, expression and gesture in face images. So face recognition is a nonlinear case. Here we propose a kernel collaborative representation based classification with regularized least square (Kernel CRC_RLS, KCRC_RLS) by implicitly mapping the sample into high-dimensional space via kernel tricks. The experimental results on FERET face database demonstrate that Kernel CRC_RLS is effective in classification, leading to promising performance.

Keywords: Face Recognition, Kernel, Collaborative Representation.

1 Introduction

Human faces contain important information, such as gender, race, mood, and age. In the area of human-computer interaction, there are both commercial and security interests to develop a reliable gender classification system from a good or low quality images [1-3].

In face and pattern recognition, classification is an indispensable step and classifier design is one of the most popular technologies. A great deal of work has been made to design classifiers in the past several decades [4-12]. The nearest neighbor (1-NN) classifier is one of the most widely used classifiers due to its simplicity and effectiveness. As a generalization of 1-NN classifier, kernel NN classifier was presented subsequently [6]. In recent years, with the popularity of manifold learning, the NN-based classification methods arouse considerable research interests and a number of improved variants of the NN classifier have been developed [7-12].

Recently, sparse representation is a hot research topic in computer vision and pattern recognition. It is widely applied to image super-resolution [13], motion segmentation [14], supervised denoising [15] and sparse reconstruction [16]. Wright gave a sparse representation based classification (SRC) [17] and successfully applied it

Z. Sun et al. (Eds.): CCBR 2013, LNCS 8232, pp. 130–137, 2013.

for face recognition. In SRC, a testing sample is coded by sparse linear combination of all the training samples and classified into the class with minimum sparse reconstruction error. The working mechanism of SRC and found that it was the collaborative representation, but not the L1-norm sparsity, that plays the essential role for classification in SRC [18]. A collaborative representation based classification with regularized least square (CRC_RLS) scheme for image recognition was proposed in [18], which has significantly less complexity than SRC but leads to very competitive classification performance. CRC_RLS is a linear method in nature and cannot handle samples with complex nonlinear variations.

CRC_RLS may fail to deliver good performance when samples (e.g. face images) are subject to complex nonlinear changes due to large pose, expression or illumination variations, as it is a linear method in nature. Kernel methods [19-21] have been widely used to overcome the limitation of some linear feature extraction and classification because Kernel methods can discover the nonlinear structure of the images. Here, we propose a kernel collaborative representative based classification with regularized least square algorithm for image recognition (Kernel, KCRC_RLS). For KCRC_RLS, samples are first mapped into a high dimensional space and then CRC_RLS is performed in the transformation space. We prove that KCRC_RLS in the high dimensional space can be formulated in terms of the inner products, while the inner products could be computed by kernel function.

2   CRC_RLS

L. Zhang et al. pointed that it was collaborative representation, but not the L1-norm sparse constraint, that truly improved the face recognition performance. In SRC L1-norm is used to regularize the solution, but it is not necessary to use L1-norm constraint. L2-norm can be used to regularize the solution and can get competitive performance with less computation complexity. Consequently they present a collaborative representation based classification with regularized least square (CRC_RLS) algorithm for face recognition.

Denote by $X_i = [x_{i,1}, x_{i,2}, \cdots, x_{i,n_i}] \in R^{m \times n_i}$ the set of training samples of the ith class, where $x_{i,j}(j=1,2,\ldots,ni)$ is a m-dimensional vector stretched by the jth training samples of the ith class. For a testing sample $y_0 \in R^m$ from this class, intuitively, y_0 could be well approximated by linear combination of the sample within X_i, i.e, $y_0 = \sum_{j=1}^{n_i} x_{i,j} \cdot w_{i,j} = X_i w_i$, $w_i = [w_{i,1}, w_{i,2}, \cdots, w_{i,n_i}]^T$ is the coefficient. Suppose we have c classes, and let $X = [X_1, X_2, \cdots, X_c]$ be the total training samples set and $n=n_1+n_2+\ldots+n_c$, then the linear representation of y0 can be written in terms of all training samples as $y_0 = Xw_0$, where $w_0 = [w_1; \cdots; w_i; \cdots; w_c] = [0, \cdots, 0, w_{i,1}, w_{i,2}, \cdots, w_{i,n_i}, 0, \cdots, 0]^T$. The objective function of the collaborative representation with regularized least square is as follows:

$$w = \arg\min \left\{ \|y - Xw\|_2^2 + \lambda \|w\|_2^2 \right\} \tag{1}$$

where λ is the regularized parameter. The former in Eq.(1) is the collaborative represent part and the later in Eq (1) is least square (L2 norm) constraint instead of L1 norm sparsity constraint. The regularization has two constraints: First, it makes the least square solution stable; Second, it also introduces a certain amount of sparsity to the solution w, yet this sparsity is much weaker than that by L1-norm. The solution of the collaborative representation with regularized least square is

$$\hat{w} = \left(X^T X + \lambda I \right)^{-1} X^T y. \tag{2}$$

The CRC_RLS algorithm is shown in Algorithm 2. More details about CRC_RLS can be found in [18].

3   Our Proposed Method

CRC_RLS is a linear method in nature, and it is inadequate to represent the nonlinear space like many linear methods. As we know, kernel approach can change the distribution of samples by mapping samples into a high dimensional feature space. This change possibly has two merits if an appropriate kernel function is selected. On the one hand, some linear inseparable samples in the original feature space become linear separable in the high dimensional feature space. On the other hand, a test sample can be represented as the linear combination of the training samples from the same class as itself more accurately in the high dimensional feature space than original. In this section, we will extend the CRC_RLS algorithm to the nonlinear case via the kernel tricks. An initial motivation of Kernel CRC_RLS (KCRC_RLS) is to perform CRC_RLS in the feature space F (Actually, it is reasonable to view F as Hilbert space).

Given a nonlinear mapping ϕ, the original data space χ is mapped into a higher dimensional feature space F:

$$\begin{aligned} \phi &: \chi \to F \\ x &\mapsto \phi(x) \end{aligned} \tag{3}$$

Denote by $\Phi = \left[\phi(x_{1,1}), \phi(x_{1,2}), \cdots, \phi(x_{c,n_c}) \right]$ the mapped samples from the original feature space.

In the high dimensional feature space F, to collaboratively represent the query sample $\phi(y)$ over the whole training samples $\Phi = \left[\phi(x_{1,1}), \phi(x_{1,2}), \cdots, \phi(x_{c,n_c}) \right]$, but with very low computation burden, we propose the objective function of KCRC_RLS as follows:

$$w = \arg \min \left\{ \| \phi(y) - \Phi w \|_2^2 + \lambda \| w \|_2^2 \right\} \tag{4}$$

where λ is the regularized parameter.

The solution of KCRC_RLS in Eq.(4) can easily and analytically derived as:

$$\hat{w} = \left(\Phi^T \Phi + \lambda I \right)^{-1} \Phi^T \cdot \phi(y) \tag{5}$$

In the high dimensional feature space, the inter product of samples can be computed via kernel function. For any two samples $\phi(x_i)$, $\phi(x_j)$, we have $\phi(x_i)^T \phi(x_j) = (\phi(x_i) \cdot \phi(x_j)) = k(x_i, x_j)$, where k is a kernel function. Then

$$\Phi^T \Phi = \left[\phi(x_{1,1}), \phi(x_{1,2}), \cdots, \phi(x_{c,n_c})\right]^T \cdot \left[\phi(x_{1,1}), \phi(x_{1,2}), \cdots, \phi(x_{c,n_c})\right]$$

$$= \begin{bmatrix} k(x_{1,1}, x_{1,1}) & k(x_{1,1}, x_{1,2}) & \cdots & k(x_{1,1}, x_{c,n_c}) \\ k(x_{1,2}, x_{1,1}) & k(x_{1,2}, x_{1,2}) & \cdots & k(x_{1,2}, x_{c,n_c}) \\ \vdots & \vdots & \ddots & \cdots \\ k(x_{c,n_c}, x_{1,1}) & k(x_{c,n_c}, x_{1,2}) & \cdots & k(x_{c,n_c}, x_{c,n_c}) \end{bmatrix} \tag{6}$$

$$\Phi^T \cdot \phi(y) = \left[\phi(x_{1,1}), \phi(x_{1,2}), \cdots, \phi(x_{c,n_c})\right]^T \cdot \phi(y)$$

$$= \begin{bmatrix} k(x_{1,1}, y) \\ k(x_{1,2}, y) \\ \vdots \\ k(x_{c,n_c}, y) \end{bmatrix} \tag{7}$$

When the kernel function is given, $\Phi^T \Phi$ and $\Phi^T \phi(y)$ can be obtained and $\hat{w}$ is calculated. We also use the class specific residual $\left\| \phi(y) - \Phi_i \cdot \hat{w_i} \right\|_2 / \left\| \hat{w_i} \right\|$ for classification, where $\Phi_i = \left[\phi(x_{i,1}), \phi(x_{i,2}), \cdots, \phi(x_{i,n_i})\right]$ and $\hat{w_i}$ is the coefficient vector associated with class i.

$$\left\| \phi(y) - \Phi_i \hat{w_i} \right\|_2$$

$$= \sqrt{\left(\phi(y) - \Phi_i \hat{w_i}\right)^T \cdot \left(\phi(y) - \Phi_i \hat{w_i}\right)}$$

$$= \sqrt{(\phi(y))^T \cdot \phi(y) + \left(\Phi_i \cdot \hat{w_i}\right)^T \cdot \Phi_i \cdot \hat{w_i} - 2(\phi(y))^T \cdot \Phi_i \cdot \hat{w_i}} \tag{8}$$

$$= \sqrt{k(y, y) + \hat{w_i}^T \Phi_i^T \cdot \Phi_i \cdot \hat{w_i} - 2(\phi(y))^T \cdot \Phi_i \cdot \hat{w_i}}$$

where

$$\Phi_i^T \Phi_i$$
$$= \left[\phi(x_{i,1}), \phi(x_{i,2}), \cdots, \phi(x_{i,n_i})\right]^T \cdot \left[\phi(x_{i,1}), \phi(x_{i,2}), \cdots, \phi(x_{i,n_i})\right]$$
$$= \begin{bmatrix} k(x_{i,1}, x_{i,1}) & k(x_{i,1}, x_{i,2}) & \cdots & k(x_{i,1}, x_{i,n_i}) \\ k(x_{i,2}, x_{i,1}) & k(x_{i,2}, x_{i,2}) & \cdots & k(x_{i,2}, x_{i,n_i}) \\ \vdots & \vdots & \ddots & \vdots \\ k(x_{i,n_i}, x_{i,1}) & k(x_{i,n_i}, x_{i,2}) & \cdots & k(x_{i,n_i}, x_{i,n_i}) \end{bmatrix}$$

$$(\phi(y))^T \Phi_i$$
$$= (\phi(y))^T \cdot \left[\phi(x_{i,1}), \phi(x_{i,2}), \cdots, \phi(x_{i,n_i})\right].$$
$$= \left[k(y, x_{i,1}), k(y, x_{i,2}), \cdots, k(y, x_{i,n_i})\right]$$

The KCRC_RLS algorithm is summarized in Algorithm 3.

Algorithm 3. The KCR_RLS algorithm
1. (Code) Code $\phi(y)$ over Φ by Eq.(6)(7)(8).
2. (Classification) Computer the regularized residuals ri(y): $r_i(y) = \left\| \phi(y) - \Phi_i \widehat{w_i} \right\|_2 / \left\| \widehat{w_i} \right\|_2$, for $i=1,...,c$.
3. Output that $\text{label}(y_0) = \arg\min_i r_i(y_0)$.

4   Experiments

The FERET face database is used to evaluate the performance of the proposed KCRC_RLS, CRC_RLS, the k nearest neighbor (kNN), minimum (class mean) distance (MD), the local mean based nearest neighbor classifier (LM-NN), LRC, and SRC, and Kernel Nearest Neighbor (KernelNN). Kernel SRC is very slow and not be evaluated here. Here the experiments are multi-class problem. Two kernel functions are applied here. One is Gaussian kernel $k(x,y) = \exp\left(-\|x-y\|^2/t\right)$, the other is polynomial kernel $k(x,y) = \left(1 + x^T y\right)^d$. In the PCA stage, we preserve nearly 95% image entry to select the principal components. Since Kernel Nearest Neighbor with Gaussian kernel is equivalent to NN, only polynomial kernel is used in KernelNN. The parameters d, t and λ are set by grid search. All the experiments are performed on the laptop with P8600 CPU and 2G RAM under the Matlab 2010a programming environment.

The FERET face image database is a result of the FERET program, which was sponsored by the US Department of Defense through the DARPA Program [24,25]. It has become a standard database for testing and evaluating state-of-the-art face recognition algorithms.

The proposed algorithm was tested on a subset of the FERET database. This subset includes 1,400 images of 200 individuals (each individual has seven images). This subset has variations of facial expression, illumination, and pose. In our experiment, the facial portion of each original image was automatically cropped based on the location of eyes and the cropped images were resized to 40 by 40 pixels. Some example images of one person are shown in Fig. 1.

Fig. 1. Images of one person in FERET

In the first experiment, we use the first 6 images of each class to form the training set, and the remaining 1 image of each class to form the validating set. So there are 1200 training samples and 200 testing samples. We compare the performance of the competing methods on pixel intensity features, PCA features. For intensity features, all images are downsampled to 10*10. For PCA features, we keep 250-dimensional. The maximum average recognition rates over all possible parameters, e.g. the number of nearest neighbors, the regularized parameters in SRC and CRC_RLS, and the kernel parameters in KCRC_RLS, are shown in Table 1. We can find that: 1) KCRC_RLS has the best results and significantly improves the recognition rates. 2) KCRC_RLS with Gaussian kernel improves the recognition rates with 16.5%, 10% and 1% over CRC_RLS respectively. 3) KCRC_RLS improves the recognition rates with 7.5%, 20.5% and 5.5% over SRC respectively. 4) kNN and LM-NN have the same maximum recognition rates with the same nearest neighbors number k=1. We further perform experiments by 10-run tests. In each run, we randomly choose 6 images from each class for training, and the remaining images for test. Based on the optimal parameters we obtained on the first experiment, the average recognition rates and standard deviations are shown in Table 2. When kNN and LM-NN both choose the nearest neighbor number k=1, kNN is equal to LM-NN in nature. So we don't do experiments with LM-NN. The curve of recognition rates versus different training sets is shown in Fig.2. The average classification time is shown in Table 3. The speed of KCRC_RLS is slower than CRC_RLS, but still much faster than SRC. KCRC_RLS shows a good and robust performance.

Table 1. The recognition rates of competing methods on FERET database

Method	Pixel	PCA
*k*NN	0.2700 *(k=1)*	0.3900 *(k=1)*
MD	0.1150	0.1350
LM-NN	0.2700 *(k=1)*	0.3900 *(k=1)*
LRC	0.5000	0.3250
SRC	0.5450 ($\lambda = 2^{-4}$)	0.5450 ($\lambda = 2^{-2}$)
CRC_RLS	0.4550 ($\lambda = 2^{-4}$)	0.6500 ($\lambda = 2^{-3}$)
KernelNN	0.5800($d = 2^{-7}$)	0.3900($d = 2^{0}$)
KCRC_RLS(P)	**0.6000**($\lambda = 2^{1}$, $d = 2^{1}$)	**0.6400**($\lambda = 2^{8}$, $d = 2^{0}$)
KCRC_RLS(G)	**0.6200**($\lambda = 2^{-31}$, $t = 2^{7}$)	**0.7500**($\lambda = 2^{-17}$, $t = 2^{10}$)

Table 2. The average recognition rates of competing methods on FERET database

Method	Pixel	PCA
*k*NN	0.6880(0.1569)	0.6950(0.1175)
MD	0.5005(0.1524)	0.5975(0.1794)
LM-NN	0.9095(0.1495)	0.8440(0.1897)
LRC	0.8785(0.1224)	0.8590(0.1162)
SRC	0.7890(0.1420)	0.7755(0.0486)
CRC_RLS	0.7940(0.0851)	0.6950(0.1175)
KernelNN	**0.9065**(0.1209)	0.7890(0.0593)
KCRC_RLS(P)	**0.9165**(0.1162)	**0.8885**(0.0581)
KCRC_RLS(G)	0.6880(0.1569)	0.6950(0.1175)

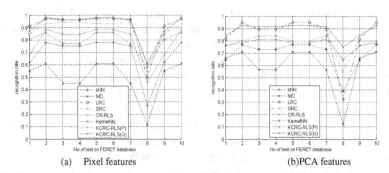

(a)   Pixel features   (b)PCA features

Fig. 2. The recognition rates of various classification methods on FERET database

Table 3. Average time on FERET database

Method	Pixel	PCA
kNN	0.4203(0.0137)	0.5658(0.0208)
MD	1.4281(0.0771)	1.7936(0.0430)
LM-NN	3.3594(0.0557)	4.4328(0.1034)
LRC	148.3264(16.3319)	146.8781(5.5698)
SRC	0.8078(0.0276)	0.8486(0.0440)
CRC_RLS	0.5096(0.0109)	0.5322(0.0168)
KernelNN	5.8532(0.1034)	5.8454(0.0237)
KCRC_RLS(P)	6.4138(0.5272)	5.9922(0.0213)
KCRC_RLS(G)	0.4203(0.0137)	0.5658(0.0208)

5   Conclusions

CRC_RLS is a new method induced by Sparse representation based classification and has been successfully applied in face recognition. Being intrinsically linear, classification based on CRC_RLS may fail to handle the data from a nonlinear structure space. Using the kernel tricks that are often used in SVM, we extend the CRC_RLS method to kernel space where we can measure the nonlinear similarity, named kernel CRC_RLS (KCRC_RLS). Experiments on face recognition on FERET face database show the effectiveness of KCRC_RLS algorithm.

Acknowledgments. This work is supported by NSF of China (61005008, 61375001).

References

1. Albert, A.M., Ricanek, K., Patterson, E.: A review of the literature on the aging adult skull and face: Implications for forensic science research and applications. Forensic Science International 172, 1–9 (2007)
2. Makinen, E., Raisamo, R.: Evaluation of gender classification methods with automatically detected and aligned face. IEEE Trans. Pattern Anal. Mach Intell 30(3), 541–547 (2008)
3. Bekios-Calfa, J., Buenaposada, J.M., Baumela, L.: Revisiting linear discriminant techniques in gender recognition. IEEE Trans. Pattern Anal. Mach Intell. 33(4), 858–864 (2011)

4. Kotsiantis, S.B.: Supervised machine learning: a review of classification techniques. Informatica 31, 249–268 (2007)
5. Cover, T.M., Hart, P.E.: Nearest neighbor pattern classification. IEEE Transactions on Information Theory 13(1), 21–27 (1967)
6. Yu, K., Ji, L., Zhang, X.: Kernel nearest-neighbor algorithm. Neural Processing Letters 15, 147–156 (2002)
7. Li, S.Z., Lu, J.: Face recognition using the nearest feature line method. IEEE Transactions on Neural Network 10(2), 439–443 (1999)
8. Zheng, W., Zhao, L., Zou, C.: Locally nearest neighbour classifiers for pattern recognition. Pattern Recognition 37(6), 1307–1309 (2004)
9. Lou, Z., Jin, Z.: Novel adaptive nearest neighbour classifiers based on hit-distance. In: Proceedings of the 18th International Conference on Pattern Recognition (ICPR 2006), August 20-24, vol. 3, pp. 87–90 (2006)
10. Gao, Q., Wang, Z.: Center-based nearest neighbor classifier. Pattern Recognition 40(1), 346–349 (2007)
11. Shen, F., Hasegawa, O.: A fast nearest neighbor classifier based on self-organizing incremental neural network. Neural Networks 21(10), 1537–1547 (2008)
12. Mitani, Y., Hamamoto, Y.: A local mean-based nonparametric classifier. Pattern Recognition Letters 27(10), 1151–1159 (2006)
13. Yang, J., Wright, J., Huang, T., Ma, Y.: Image super-resolution as sparse representation of raw patches. In: CVPR 2008 (2008)
14. Rao, S., Tron, R., Vidal, R., Ma, Y.: Motion segmentation via robust subspace separation in the presence of outlying, incomplete, and corrupted trajectories. In: CVPR 2008 (2008)
15. Mairal, J., Sapiro, G., Elad, M.: Learning multiscale sparse representations for image and video restoration. SIAM MMS 7(1), 214–241 (2008)
16. Wright, S.J., Nowak, R.D., Figuelredo, M.A.T.: Sparse reconstruction by separable approximation. In: IEEE International Conference on Acoustics, Speech and Signal Processing, pp. 3373–3376 (2008)
17. Wright, J., Yang, A., Sastry, S., Ma, Y.: Robust face recognition via sparse representation. IEEE Transactions on Pattern Analysis and Machine Intelligence 31(2), 210–227 (2009)
18. Zhang, L., Yang, M., Feng, X.: Sparse representation or collaborative representation: which helps face recognition. In: ICCV 2011 (2011)
19. Muller, K.-R., Mika, S., Ratsch, G., Tsuda, K., Scholkopf, B.: An introduction to kernel-based learning algorithms. IEEE Trans. Neural Networks 12(2), 181–201 (2001)
20. Mika, S., Ratsch, G., Weston, J., Scholkopf, B., Mullers, K.R.: Fisher discriminant analysis with kernels. In: Proc. IEEE Int'l Workshop Neural Networks for Signal Processing IX, vol. 199, pp. 41–48 (1999)
21. Yang, J., Frangi, A.F., Yang, J.Y., Zhang, D.: KPCA plus LDA: a complete kernel Fisher discriminant frame work for feature extraction and recognition. IEEE Trans. Pattern Analysis and Machine Intelligence 27(2), 230–244 (2005)
22. Phillips, P.J., Moon, H., Rizvi, S.A., Rauss, P.J.: The FERET evaluation methodology for face recognition algorithms. IEEE Transactions on Pattern Analysis and Machine Intelligence 22(10), 1090–1104 (2000)
23. Phillips, P.J.: The facial recognition technology (FERET) database (2004), http://www.itl.nist.gov/iad/humanid/feret/feret_master.html

Two-Dimensional Color Uncorrelated Principal Component Analysis for Feature Extraction with Application to Face Recognition

Cairong Zhao[1,2,3] and Duoqian Miao[1,2]

[1] Department of Computer Science and Technology, Tongji University,
Shanghai 201804, China
[2] The Key Laboratory of "Embedded System and Service Computing", Ministry of Education,
Shanghai, 7201804, China
[3] The Key Laboratory of " Intelligent Perception and Systems for High-Dimensional
Information " (NJUST), Ministry of Education, Nanjing, 210094, China
zhaocairong@tongji.edu.cn

Abstract. This paper proposes a two-dimensional color uncorrelated principal component analysis algorithm(2DCUPCA) for unsupervised subspace learning directly from color face images. The 2DCUPCA can be used to explore uncorrelated properties among color-based features, which contain minimum redundancy and ensure linear independence among features. Furthermore, the proposed 2DCUPCA provided the theoretical foundations analysis and proved the uncorrelated property between color-based features in theory. This makes it sure that the extracted features directly from three color image matrices will be uncorrelated. Finally, experimental results on the AR and FRGC-2 color face databases show that 2DCUPCA achieves better recognition performance than other color face recognition methods.

Keywords: Pattern recognition; face recognition; uncorrelated principal component analysis; feature extraction.

1 Introduction

Face recognition has growing interests in the field of pattern recognition and computer vision [1]. In the last decades, large amounts of methods for face recognition were presented [2-7]. Traditional face recognition methods, such as the classical linear data representation technique, principal component analysis (PCA) [2] and linear discrimiant analysis (LDA) [3] were widely used in the areas of pattern recognition and computer vision. Furthermore, two-dimensional principal component analysis (2DPCA) [4] was brought forward. Extending this idea, Li and Yuan proposed the two-dimensional linear discriminant analysis (2DLDA) [5] for feature extraction. All these methods were used to deal with gray face images rather than color face images. Recent research efforts, however, revealed that the color could provide useful and important information for face recognition [8-18].

Z. Sun et al. (Eds.): CCBR 2013, LNCS 8232, pp. 138–145, 2013.

In [8], Yip et al. discovered that color cues did play a role in face recognition and their contribution became evident when shape cues are degraded. To cope with low-resolution faces, the work in [9] presented a new metric called "Variation ratio gain" (VRG). Dong et al. [10] defined a color prototype to represent a spherical region in color space. These color prototypes provided a good estimate for object colors. In [11], this work proposed a spatial color descriptor involving a color adjacency histogram and color vector angle histogram. Uncorrelated features contain minimum redundancy and ensure independence of features [12-13]. Therefore, reducing the correlation among features should contribute to enhance the complementation and further improve the recognition performance. Color Space Normalization (CSN) [14] technique could greatly reduce the correlation among the three color components. The aforementioned researches [10-15] also reduced the correlation among three color components of the original images to some extent. Lu et al. [16] proposed an uncorrelated multi-linear principal component analysis (UMPCA) for unsupervised subspace learning. Man et al. [17] proposed a statistically orthogonal analysis method (SOA) to obtain statistically orthogonal color-based features, but SOA lost color face spatial structure information. Nonetheless, color uncorrelated properties among the features of the original images have not been systematically explored in the current color face recognition investigations.

Motivated by the discussions above, this paper aims to develop the two-dimensional color uncorrelated principal component analysis algorithm (2DCUPCA) that extracts color space uncorrelated features.

2   Two-Dimensional Color Uncorrelated Principal Component Analysis (2D CUPCA)

2.1   The Basic Idea of the Proposed 2DCUPCA

2DPCA [4] can extract the 2D spatial features of gray images but it cannot eliminate the correlation among features. ULDA [13] and UMPCA [16] can extract uncorrelated features. However, 2DPCA, ULDA and UMPCA are not directly proposed for color face images. Research results [8-14] suggest that the color can provide important information for pattern recognition. Therefore, how to effectively exploit color information to enhance recognition performance becomes an important task in color image recognition.

Based on the aforementioned analysis and borrowing the idea of 2DPCA [4] and UMPCA [16], we propose the 2DCUPCA to obtain three mutually statistically uncorrelated two-dimensional principal component features. More details can be seen in the subsection 2.2.

2.2   Theoretical Foundation of the Proposed 2DCUPCA

In this subsection, we describe the theoretical foundation of the proposed 2DCUPCA algorithm and present the analytical solution.

Supposed there are M labeled color image samples $\mathbf{A}_j^c$ in the training set of each class, where $j = 1,2,...,M$, $c = 1,2,...,C$ and $\mathbf{C}$ denotes the number of classes, and M denotes the size of the training set.

Let $\mathbf{A}_R, \mathbf{A}_G, \mathbf{A}_B$ be $\mathbf{R,G,B}$ color component image sets of the color image samples and $\mathbf{S}_{TR}, \mathbf{S}_{TG}, \mathbf{S}_{TB}$ be the corresponding total image scatter matrices respectively. $\mathbf{S}_{BR}, \mathbf{S}_{BG}, \mathbf{S}_{BB}$ denote between-class image scatter matrices of $\mathbf{A}_R, \mathbf{A}_G, \mathbf{A}_B$ and $\mathbf{S}_{WR}, \mathbf{S}_{WG}, \mathbf{S}_{WB}$ denote within-class image scatter matrices of $\mathbf{A}_R, \mathbf{A}_G, \mathbf{A}_B$ respectively. Let $\mathbf{X}_R, \mathbf{X}_G, \mathbf{X}_B$ represent the projection matrix consisting projective vectors for $\mathbf{A}_R, \mathbf{A}_G, \mathbf{A}_B$ respectively.

Based on the 2DPCA criterion, the discriminant projection matrix $\mathbf{X}_R$ for $\mathbf{A}_R$ can be calculated by

$$\mathbf{X}_R = \arg\max \mathbf{X}_R^T \mathbf{S}_{TR} \mathbf{X}_R \tag{1}$$

Following the projection matrix $\mathbf{X}_R$, we attempt to find the projection matrix $\mathbf{X}_G$ for $\mathbf{A}_G$ in the principle of assuring completely uncorrelation between features of $\mathbf{X}_R$ and $\mathbf{X}_G$. Guided by this principle, we design the algorithm to calculate $\mathbf{X}_G$ as follows. Suppose two color component images $\mathbf{A}_{jr} \in \mathbf{A}_R$ and $\mathbf{A}_{jg} \in \mathbf{A}_G$, let $\mathbf{Y}_{jr} = \mathbf{A}_{jr}\mathbf{X}_R$ and $\mathbf{Y}_{jg} = \mathbf{A}_{jg}\mathbf{X}_G$ separately denote the corresponding projected features .The covariance between $\mathbf{Y}_{jr}$ and $\mathbf{Y}_{jg}$ is

$$\begin{aligned} Cov(\mathbf{Y}_{jr}, \mathbf{Y}_{jg}) &= E[\mathbf{Y}_{jr} - E(\mathbf{Y}_{jr})][\mathbf{Y}_{jg} - E(\mathbf{Y}_{jg})]^T \\ &= \mathbf{X}_G^T \left(\sqrt{\mathbf{S}_{TG}}\right)^T \sqrt{\mathbf{S}_{TR}} \mathbf{X}_R \end{aligned} \tag{2}$$

where M denotes the size of the training set, $\overline{\mathbf{A}_R}$ denotes the mean image of R color component image sets, $\overline{\mathbf{A}_G}$ denotes the mean image of G color component image sets, $\sqrt{\mathbf{S}_{TR}} = E\left[\mathbf{A}_{jr} - E(\mathbf{A}_{jr})\right]$ and $\sqrt{\mathbf{S}_{TG}} = E\left[\mathbf{A}_{jg} - E(\mathbf{A}_{jg})\right]$. The auto variances of $\mathbf{Y}_{jr}$ and $\mathbf{Y}_{jg}$ are defined as

$$Var(\mathbf{Y}_{jr}, \mathbf{Y}_{jr}) = E[\mathbf{Y}_{jr} - E(\mathbf{Y}_{jr})][\mathbf{Y}_{jr} - E(\mathbf{Y}_{jr})]^T = \mathbf{X}_R^T \mathbf{S}_{TG} \mathbf{X}_R \tag{3}$$

and

$$Var(\mathbf{Y}_{jg}, \mathbf{Y}_{jg}) = E[\mathbf{Y}_{jg} - E(\mathbf{Y}_{jg})][\mathbf{Y}_{jg} - E(\mathbf{Y}_{jg})]^T = \mathbf{X}_G^T \mathbf{S}_{TG} \mathbf{X}_G \tag{4}$$

The correlation between Y_{jr} and Y_{jg} can be defined as

$$\begin{aligned} Corr\left(\mathbf{Y}_{jr}, \mathbf{Y}_{jg}\right) &= \frac{Cov(\mathbf{Y}_{jr}, \mathbf{Y}_{jg})}{\sqrt{Var(\mathbf{Y}_{jg}, \mathbf{Y}_{jg})}\sqrt{Var(\mathbf{Y}_{jr}, \mathbf{Y}_{jr})}} \\ &= \frac{\mathbf{X}_G^T \left(\sqrt{\mathbf{S}_{TG}}\right)^T \sqrt{\mathbf{S}_{TR}} \mathbf{X}_R}{\sqrt{\mathbf{X}_R^T \mathbf{S}_{TR} \mathbf{X}_R} \sqrt{\mathbf{X}_G^T \mathbf{S}_{TG} \mathbf{X}_G}} \end{aligned} \tag{5}$$

To remove the statistical correlation, we set $Corr\left(Y_{jr}, Y_{jg}\right) = 0$, which is equivalent to $\mathbf{X}_G^T \left(\sqrt{\mathbf{S}_{TG}}\right)^T \sqrt{\mathbf{S}_{TR}} \mathbf{X}_R = 0$. Note that $\mathbf{X}_R$ and $\mathbf{X}_G$ are statistically orthogonal if $Corr\left(Y_{jr}, Y_{jg}\right) = 0$.

Then, we can obtain $\mathbf{X}_G$ by solving the following problem:

$$\mathbf{X}_G = \arg\max_{\mathbf{X}_G} \mathbf{X}_G^T \mathbf{S}_{TG} \mathbf{X}_G$$

$$s.t. \quad \mathbf{X}_G^T \left(\sqrt{\mathbf{S}_{TG}}\right)^T \sqrt{\mathbf{S}_{TR}} \mathbf{X}_R = 0 \tag{6}$$

For solving Formula (6), we present a theorem as follows:

Theorem 1. The optimal solution $\mathbf{X}_G$ in model (6) can be achieved by solving the eigenequation:

$$\mathbf{S}_{TG} \mathbf{X}_G = \frac{1}{2} \lambda W \Rightarrow \mathbf{X}_G = \frac{\lambda}{2} \mathbf{S}_{TG}^{-1} W \tag{7}$$

where $\mathbf{W} = \left(\sqrt{\mathbf{S}_{TG}}\right)^T \sqrt{\mathbf{S}_{TR}} \mathbf{X}_R$.

Proof: Given $\mathbf{W} = \left(\sqrt{\mathbf{S}_{TG}}\right)^T \sqrt{\mathbf{S}_{TR}} \mathbf{X}_R$. We construct the Lagrange function:

$$L(\mathbf{X}_G) = \mathbf{X}_G^T \mathbf{S}_{TG} \mathbf{X}_G - \lambda \left(\mathbf{X}_G^T \mathbf{W} - \mathbf{C}_1\right) \tag{8}$$

where λ is the Lagrange multipliers, and $\mathbf{C}_1$ is constant matrices. We set the derivative of $L(\mathbf{X}_G)$ on $\mathbf{X}_G$ to be zero:

$$\frac{\partial L(\mathbf{X}_G)}{\partial \mathbf{X}_G} = 2\mathbf{S}_{TG} \mathbf{X}_G - \lambda \mathbf{W} = 0 \tag{9}$$

That is,

$$\mathbf{X}_G = \frac{\lambda}{2} \mathbf{S}_{TG}^{-1} W \tag{10}$$

Eq.(10) is equivalent to Formula (7). Proof is over.

Furthermore, similar to $\mathbf{X}_G$, we can calculate the projection matrix $\mathbf{X}_B$. So, we calculate $\mathbf{X}_B$ by

$$\mathbf{X}_B = \arg\max_{\mathbf{X}_B} \mathbf{X}_B^T \mathbf{S}_{TB} \mathbf{X}_B$$

$$s.t. \quad \mathbf{X}_B^T \left(\sqrt{\mathbf{S}_{TB}}\right)^T \sqrt{\mathbf{S}_{TR}} \mathbf{X}_R = 0 \tag{11}$$

$$\mathbf{X}_B^T \left(\sqrt{\mathbf{S}_{TB}}\right)^T \sqrt{\mathbf{S}_{TG}} \mathbf{X}_G = 0$$

For solving Formula (11), we present a theorem as follows:

Theorem 2. X_B in Formula (11) can be achieved by solving the eigenequation:

$$X_B = \frac{S_{TB}^{-1}(\lambda W_1 + \beta W_2)}{2},$$ (12)

where $W_1 = \left(\sqrt{S_{TB}}\right)^T \sqrt{S_{TR}} X_R, W_2 = \left(\sqrt{S_{TB}}\right)^T \sqrt{S_{TG}} X_G$.

The proof of Theorem 2 is similar to the one in Theorem 1. So, it is omitted for saving space.

3   Experimental Evaluation and Analysis

In this section, we compare the classification performance of the proposed 2DCUPCA with other representative color face recognition methods through the experiments on AR and FRGC-2color face image databases. The sample images for one individual of the AR database are shown in Fig. 1(a). The images of Fig. 1(a). (a)–(g) from the first session are used as the training set, and Fig. 1(n)–(t) from the second session as the testing set.

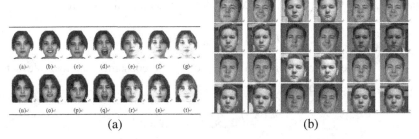

(a)   (b)

Fig. 1. (a). Sample images for one people of the AR database

The FRGC-2 color face database is a standard testing database for color face recognition. In the experiments, we selected 100 peoples, each 24 images. We cropped every image to the size of 60x60, and show images of one people from FRGC-2 in Fig. 1(b).

3.1   Experiments on the AR Database

In this experiment, the images from the first session (i.e., Fig.1(a). a, b, c, d, e, f, and g) were used for training, and the images from the second session (i.e., Fig.1(a). n, o, p, q, r, s, and t) were used for testing. Fig.2(a) shows the recognition rates vs. the variations of the dimensions (In Fig.2(a), for one-dimensional methods, the dimensions is equal to five times the numbers marked on the axes). The maximal recognition rates of each method are listed in the Table 1. As can be seen from Table 1 and Fig.2(a), 2DCUPCA obtains the best recognition rates in the experiment under variations over time, which shows the effectiveness and robustness of the proposed 2DCUPCA under variations over time. Why do 2DCUPCA perform better than other methods in this experiment? From the view of feature correlations, 2DCUPCA outperforms the other methods, indicating that the uncorrelated features extracted directly from the color face image are effective in recognition. In contrast, the features extracted by other methods are correlated, with those extracted by CPCA and CFLMME having much highly correlation. The CSN [14] and CICCA [19] methods can reduce the correlation between color-based features, but they cannot eliminate the correlation completely. However, the proposed 2DCUPCA not only eliminate the correlations between color-based features but also simultaneously retain the face spatial structure information, which helps improve the color face recognition. All of these could be partly reason of the superior recognition performance of 2DCUPCA than that of other methods in the experiment under variations over time.

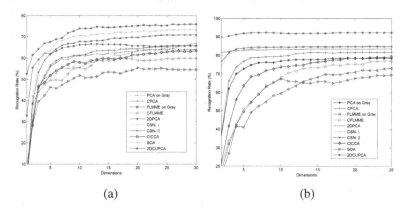

(a)   (b)

Fig. 2. (a). The recognition rates (%) versus the dimension on the AR face database;(b) The recognition rates (%) versus the dimension on the FRGC-2 face database

Table 1. The maximal recognition rates (%) and the corresponding dimensions on the AR database

Method	PCA on Gray	CPCA	FLMME on Gray	CFLMME	2DPCA
Recognition rate	64.07	65.97	55.71	59.88	66.54
Dimension	116	118	134	120	50x12

Method	CSN- I	CSN- II	CICCA	SOA	2DCUPCA
Recognition rate	73.33	70.83	63.45	66.90	75.90
Dimension	120	100	119	119	50x38

3.2   Experiments on the FRGC-2 Database

In this section, we evaluate the performance of 2DCUPCA compared with that of other methods on the FRGC-2 database. In this experiment, 12 images of each individual were selected and used for training, and the rest images were used for test. Table 2 lists the maximal recognition rates of each method and Fig.2(b) shows the recognition rates vs. the variations of the dimensions (In Fig. 2(b), for one-dimensional methods, the dimensions is equal to five times the number of dimensions axes). Once more, the experimental results show that 2DCUPCA performs better than the other methods. It is mainly reason that the proposed 2DCUPCA overcomes the limitation of redundancy among features and ensure independence of color-based features.

From Fig.2(b), we can further observe that 2DCUPCA performs better on FRGC-2 color face database than on AR color face database compared with the other gray-based methods. It is because that color cues play a more important role in uncontrolled image recognition than in controlled image recognition.

Table 2. The maximal recognition rates (%) and the corresponding dimensions on the FRGC-2 database

Method	PCA on Gray	CPCA	FLMME on Gray	CFLMME	2DPCA
Recognition rate	78.50	81.67	73.17	77.25	83.50
Dimension	84	92	156	140	60x24

Method	CSN I	CSN-II	CICCA	SOA	2DCUPCA
Recognition rate	84.67	85	79.25	69.58	92.25
Dimension	134	124	97	99	60x18

4   Conclusions

In this paper, we proposed a two-dimensional color uncorrelated principal component analysis for face recognition, which is capable of extracting uncorrelated features directly from color face images. Experimental results on the AR and FRGC-2 color face databases show that 2DCUPCA achieves better recognition performance than other color face recognition methods.

Acknowledgments. The authors would like to thank the anonymous reviewers for their critical and constructive comments and suggestions. This work is partially supported by China National Natural Science Foundation under grant No. 61203247, 61273304, 61203376, 61202170. It is also partially supported by The Project Supported by Fujian and Guangdong Natural Science Foundation under grant No. 2012J01281 and S2012040007289, respectively. It is also partially supported by the Key Laboratory of Intelligent Perception and Systems for High-Dimensional Information (NJUST) , Ministry of Education Foundation under grant No. 30920130122005.

References

1. Jain, A.K., Ross, A., Prabhaker, S.: An introduction to biometric recognition. IEEE Trans. on Circuits and System for Video Technology 14(1), 4–20 (2004)
2. Turk, M., Pentland, A.: Eigenfaces for recognition. Journal of Cognitive Neuroscience 3(1), 71–86 (1991)
3. Belhumeur, P.N., Hespanha, J.P., Krigman, D.J.: Eigenfaces vs. Fisherfaces: Recognition using class specific linear projection. IEEE Trans. on Pattern Analysis and Machine Intelligence 19(7), 711–720 (1997)

4. Yang, J., Zhang, D., Frangi, A.F., Yang, J.Y.: Two-dimensional PCA: A new approach to appearance-based face representation and recognition. IEEE Trans. on Pattern Analysis and Machine Intelligence 26(1), 131–137 (2004)
5. Li, M., Yuan, B.Z.: 2D-LDA: A statistical linear discriminant analysis for image matrix. Pattern Recognition Letters 26(5), 527–532 (2005)
6. Zhao, C.R., Lai, Z.H., Liu, C.C., Gu, X.J., Qian, J.J.: Fuzzy local maximal marginal embedding for feature extraction. Soft. Computing 16(1), 77–87 (2012)
7. Miao, D.Q., Gao, C., Zhang, N., Zhang, Z.F.: Diverse reduct subspaces based co-training for partially labeled data. International Journal of Approximate Reasoning 52(8), 1103–1117 (2011)
8. Yip, A., Sinha, P.: Role of color in face recognition, MIT technical reports, AIM-2001-035 CBCL-212 (2001)
9. Choi, J.Y., Ro, Y.M., Plataniotis, K.N.: Color face recognition for degraded face images. IEEE Trans. on Systems, Man, and Cybernetics-part b: Cybernetics 39(5), 1217–1230 (2009)
10. Dong, G., Xie, M.: Color clustering and learning for image segmentation based on neural networks. IEEE Trans. on Neural Networks 16(4), 925–936 (2005)
11. Lee, H.Y., Lee, H.K., Ha, Y.H.: Spatial color descriptor for image retrieval and video segmentation. IEEE Trans. on Multimedia 5(3), 358–367 (2003)
12. Ye, J., Janardan, R., Li, Q., Park, H.: Feature reduction via generalized uncorrelated linear discriminant analysis. IEEE Trans. Knowledge Data Engineering 18(10), 1312–1322 (2006)
13. Jin, Z., Yang, J.Y., Hu, Z.S., Lou, Z.: Face recognition based on the uncorrelated discriminant transformation. Pattern Recognition 34, 1405–1416 (2001)
14. Yang, J., Liu, C.J., Zhang, L.: Color space normalization: Enhancing the discriminating power of color spaces for face recognition. Pattern Recognition 43, 1454–1466 (2010)
15. Zhao, C.R., Liu, C.C., Lai, Z.H.: Multi-scale gist feature manifold for building recognition. Neurocomputing 74(17), 2929–2940 (2011)
16. Lu, H.P., Plataniotis, K.N., Venetsanopoulos, A.N.: Uncorrelated multilinear principal component analysis for unsupervised multilinear subspace learning. IEEE Trans. on Neural Networks 20(11), 1820–1836 (2009)
17. Man, J., Jing, X., Liu, Q., Yao, Y., Li, K., Yang, J.: Color face recognition based on statistically orthogonal analysis of projection transforms. In: Sun, Z., Lai, J., Chen, X., Tan, T. (eds.) CCBR 2011. LNCS, vol. 7098, pp. 58–65. Springer, Heidelberg (2011)
18. Zhao, C.R., Miao, D.Q., Lai, Z.H., Gao, C., Liu, C.C., Yang, J.Y.: Two-Dimensional color uncorrelated discriminant analysis for face recognition. Neurocomputing 113, 251–261 (2013)
19. Jing, X.Y., Li, S., Lan, C., Zhang, D., Yang, J.Y., Liu, Q.: Color image canonical correlation analysis for face feature extraction and recognition. Signal Processing 91, 2132–2140 (2011)

3D Face Recognition Based on Intrinsic Features

Yujie Liu[1], Feng Li[2], Weiqing Gong[3], and Zongmin Li[1]

[1] College of Computer & Communication Engineering
China University of Petroleum(east China), Qingdao City, Shandong Province, 266580
{liuyujie,lizongmin}@upc.edu.cn
[2] SIPPR Engineering Group Co., Ltd No.191,Zhongyuan Road, Zhengzhou, China, 450007
lifeng9472@gmail.com
[3] Sinopec Exploration & Production Research Institute (PEPRIS), Beijing, China, 100083
gongwq.syky@sinopec.com

Abstract. Changes in human expression cause non-rigid deformation of face models, this is a great challenge for 3D Face Recognition. To tackle this problem, there has been lots of excellent research work in recent years. In this paper, we propose a face recognition algorithm based on intrinsic features. Firstly face models are preprocessed and adjusted to standard pose for extracting nose tip, then we compute several geodesic stripes based on detected nose tip, make sampling in each stripe, and extract isometric-invariant features on each feature point. Because facial expression makes different levels of impact on different parts of face surface, we use SVM to train the matching results between stripes, getting optimal weight for each stripe. Finally, similarities are computed by weighed sum of different stripes matching results. Our experiments use the Gavab Database and the results are better than other 3D face recognition algorithms such as MDS method, showing effectiveness of our method.

Keywords: 3D face recognition, feature extraction, face expression, SVM.

1 Introduction

Nowadays, 2D face recognition methods have reached prefect recognition accuracy under certain restrained conditions. But it is susceptible to light, pose, expression, makeup and many other effects. With the invention of 3D data acquisition devices, it is easier to obtain 3D face data. Researchers began to shift the focus to 3D face recognition. 3D data contains shape and depth information which is expected to solve the current difficulties 2D face recognition is faced with.

Although 3D face data has more informations compared to face images, but it also has lots of difficulties. Besides complex preprocessing and pose adjustment procedure, non-rigid deformation of face models brought about by changes in expressions is the greatest challenge for 3D face recognition. Different expressions of the same person causes severe divergence of face shape, this makes directly intra-class shape matching similarity become very low. How to deal with impact of changes in expressions is a research problems for 3D face recognition.

Z. Sun et al. (Eds.): CCBR 2013, LNCS 8232, pp. 146–153, 2013.
© Springer International Publishing Switzerland 2013

According to different kinds of method to deal with expression problem, the present methods can be divided into four categories: 1) methods based on rigid regions; 2) methods based on local features; 3) methods based on expression invariant model.

Firstly, rigid regions-based methods select rigid regions of face surface for recognition. Wang [1] proposes partial-ICP algorithm to handle expression changes. After each iteration of ICP algorithms, points are sorted by distance, and only the nearest n% points are selected for the next iteration. The algorithm can automatically select rigid regions of face surface, decreasing impact of expression changes to recognition performance. Based on the facts that nose region is less affected by expression changes, Chang [2] extracts nose area to use ICP algorithms for registration, and get a good recognition.

Local features-based methods extracts local features such as curves, curvatures and other geometric features for representing human face. Chua [3] proposes a local feature named Point Signature. Firstly they extract significant feature points of face surface, and use curve fitting methods to describe the neighborhood shape information of each feature point. Rough alignment of model can be obtained by curve matching and finally they use ICP algorithms for fine alignment. Inspired by SIFT algorithms used in image processing field, Dirk [4] proposed the meshSIFT algorithm which is adapted to 3D model. It firstly detects scale-invariant key points of face model, followed by counting the shape index and slant angle histograms around each key points, which are regarded as local features of face model.

Expression invariant based methods are based on the facts that facial expression changes can be regarded as isometric transformation of neutral face. Based on this assumptions, Brostein [5] use Multi-Dimensional Scaling algorithm to embedded 3D face model into Euclidean space, this makes different expressions of the same person have similar representation. Rigid geometric invariant moment feature is then extracted to represent whole face. Dirk [6] downsamples the face model and extracts its' geodesic distance matrix. Then results of singular value decomposition is regarded as isometric invariant representation of face model.

This paper combines characteristics of the above methods. Based on isometry invariant characteristics of face model, we use isometry invariant local features to represent the whole face. According to the different contribution of face regions for recognition, we use machine learning method to train best matching weights of stripes. Figure 1 shows a flowchart of our algorithm.

Rest of this paper is divided into the following sections: Chapter 2 and chapter 3 introduces our algorithm implementation process; chapter 4 shows the experiments and results; finally chapter 5 makes conclusions and outlook of this paper.

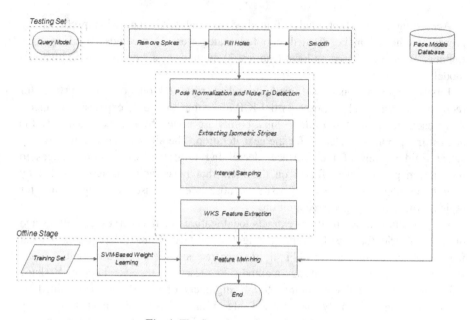

Fig. 1. The flowchart of our algorithms

2   Preprocessing and Nose Tip Detection

In this section we introduce preprocessing and nose tip detection process. 3D face scanning data often contain hair, ears and other interferences. Furthermore, since the algorithm involves calculation of geodesic stripes, it demands accurate nose tip detection results.

2.1   Preprocessing

Typically raw data preprocessing contains extracting region of interest,removing spikes, smoothing and several other procedure.

Region of interest extraction removes interference parts from original face data. Inspired by region growth algorithms used in image processing field, we think the whole face model as a number of independent undirected graph. Then region grow algorithm is easily extended to triangle mesh domain, separating undirected graphs from each other. After getting many independent connected regions. We select the region containing most points as face area.

There are still some preprocessing operations to be done. We apply Gaussian filtering algorithm to remove spikes and bilateral filtering algorithms proposed by Fleishman[7] to smooth mesh. Then we obtain satisfying face mesh data.

2.2   Nose Tip Detection

Our algorithm requires accurate detecting results of nose tip. When Face model is in a positive attitude, nose tip is the highest vertices of face mesh. However, face scanning process may have some changes in pose which can not satisfy above conditions. Therefore, shifting human face to a positive attitude is necessary. In this paper, we firstly use principal component analysis method for attitude correction, then the least squares plane fitting method is used to detect nose tip.

Face models consists of a series of mesh vertices, each vertex can be expressed as the triples <x,y,z>. Through analysis on face models, it is easy to know that maximum divergence of all vertices can be obtained by Y-axis direction, followed by the X-axis direction, and Z axis direction has the minimum. If we perform principal component analysis method on all vertices, we can extracts three axis directions. They correspond to three directions namely from the bottom up, from left to right, from back to front. Thus axes transformation can be used to adjust face model to standard pose.

After adjusting face model to standard pose, we use the least squares fitting algorithm to detect nose tip. Through fitting the plane with all vertices we can obtain a plane intersecting with the face model [8]. Among them the vertex with minimum distance to the plane is regarded as nose tip.

3   Feature Extraction and Weight Learning

3.1   Feature Extraction

After getting nose tip, we extract geodesic stripes of face model. This involves calculation of the geodesic distance. Geodesic distance on face model is the shortest curve length along face surface. Geodesic distance computation methods contains Dijkstra algorithm and Fast marching method. Since the latter can be computed along the path inside the triangle and has higher accuracy, thus we choose it to compute geodesic distance.

Regarding nose tip as the source point, we can get geodesic distance results for each vertex. In order to describe the whole face, we divided face model into a number of geodesic-spaced stripes, so that face matching problem is converted to corresponding stripe matching. Because most existing non-rigid registration algorithms need ICP algorithm to reach pre-alignment, which requires multiple iterations to achieve better results. so we make sampling in each strip and extract local features around feature points.

We sampled each stripe based on geodesic distance and the angle with nose tip. The method is as follows: Firstly, we divide face surface into N strips spaced geodesic stripes, then compute the equation $AVG_i = (Edge_i + Edge_{i+1})/2$ for the i-th stripe edges $Edge_i$, $Edge_{i+1}$. $Edge_i$ represent face regions whose geodesic distances is $Edge_i$. We sample M vertices in each stripe, that means sampling once in each $\frac{2\pi}{M}$ angle. Suppose vertex v, its geodesic distance is $geodesic_v$, and angle with nose tip is $Angle_v$. If it satisfy the following conditions:

$$\|Angle_v - \frac{2\pi j}{M}\| < thres1 \ , \quad j = 1,2,\ldots,M \tag{1}$$

$$\|geodesic_v - AVG_i\| < thres2, \quad i = 1,2,...,N \tag{2}$$

Then it is added to the collection P_{ij}. Eventually we select a sampling point from each collection, obtaining totally M×N sampling points.In experiments, we Empirically choose $thres1 = \pi/36$, $thres2 = 0.03$.

We choose isometry invariant features to describe the local surface information. Wave feature known as the wave kernel signature is proposed by Mathieu Aubry [9] As WKS features have good details description ability and isometry invariant characteristic, we chose it to describe local face shape.With all WKS features extracted for sampling points, finally we obtain full representation of the entire face.

3.2   Weight Learning

For face models M_1 and M_2 , after matching feature points on corresponding level stripe $S_i(i = 1, 2, ..., N)$, we get their similarities Sim_i. Then take the reciprocal of each dimension of the vector, we get N-dimensional feature vector $(1/Sim_1, 1/Sim_2, ..., 1/Sim_N)$. Because different regions of human face are affected differently by expression changes , they should also have different contributions to recognition. If we use weighted summations of similarity in different levels of stripes as the evaluation metric, their weights should be differentiated.

The difference between two face models are very slight. Thus the contribution of face regions has characteristic of homogeneity. That is to say , if a region is largely affected by expression changes, the intra-class matching results should be larger,decreasing its' separating capacity. So it should have lower weight . On the contrary, regions less affected by expression changes should be assigned a higher weight.

Take this characteristic into consideration, we use feature vectors combined with support vector machine method to train the optimal hyperplane, making that different hyperplane coefficients is corresponding to different region weights of human face, and finally achieve the goal to distinguish whether the face matching is intra-class or not. So we turn the recognition problem into a two-class classification problem.

After getting the similarity vector, we use trained weight coefficients to compute weighed summation,then chose the subject with the maximum weight as final recognition result. The formulation is defined in Equation 3:

$$Identity = \arg\max_{i \in C}(\vec{w} \cdot \vec{x}_i) \tag{3}$$

Vector x_i is matching similarity vector, between probe P and gallery face G . i $\in$ C represents the i-th subject in face database.

4   Results

We choose Gavab database for experiments. All subjects belong to the Caucasians, range from18 to 40 years old. Each subject has four neutral faces, including two standard pose, a looking-down pose, a looking-up pose and three expression faces, namely smiling, laughing, and a random expression.

4.1   Some Experiment Results

We firstly preprocess face models, followed by pose correction and nose tip detection. After obtaining the geodesic stripes, we sample feature points in each stripe and extract their WKS features. Finally we use the learned weight of stripes for face matching. Figure 2 shows some models after preprocessing.

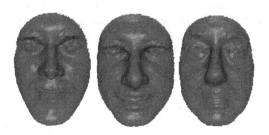

Fig. 2. Some models after preprocessing

In order to ensure consistency of each stripe, we normalized all geodesic distances. The geodesic distances are divided into five parts,with each interval between 0.2, so that there are five geodesic stripes totally.

In order to study stripe weights ,we divide the database into two sets: training set and test set. 30 subjects are chosen to be training set,the rest belongs to test set. Since each subject contains seven models, if taking combination of every two models from the same subject as positive samples, we can totally get 630 positive samples; Negative samples are chosen by combining samples from different subjects, we get 42,630 negative samples. We randomly choose 1000 as negative samples. Besides, we use LibSVM software package for SVM training. The kernel function is RBF kernel.

4.2   Results and Analysis

In order to verify different contributions of regions for recognition, we firstly use each stripe for recognition test. Each model from test set is chosen to be a probe and the nearest neighbor is regarded as a recognition result. The results are shown in table 1.

Table 1. Accuracy of Face recognition using single level stripes

Stripe Level	Level 1	Level 2	Level 3	Level 4	Level 5
Recognition rate	28.11%	37.79%	34.56%	31.79%	33.64%

As it can be seen from table 1, recognition rate using single stripe is very low. Level 1 stripe corresponding to the nose region is less affected by expression changes, but it contains limited information to distinguish between different subjects , resulting in low recognition rate. Level 2 stripe has the highest recognition rate int all stripes, it is close to nose bridge, where is not only less affected by expression changes, but also has enough information to distinguish between different subjects. Level 3 and level 4 stripes are larger affected by expression changes, so their recognition rate are not as good as level 2 stripe.

Then we combine all stripes for experiments. In order to verify the importance of choosing appropriate matching weights for stripes, we compared weighted summation trained from SVM with arithmetic mean summation. In this experiment, we choose the first K highest similarity results for each test model. If there is a model belonging to the same subject with the probe, then the recognition is considered success. The experimental results are shown in Figure 3.

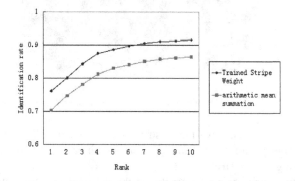

Fig. 3. Rank curve of different similarity measures in our paper

As can be seen from Figure 3, the weighted summation method reach 73.27% recognition rate when the rank value K = 1;When the rank value K = 10, the accuracy reach up to 88.48%, both higher than arithmetic mean methods. This proves the importance of learning stripe weights.

We compare our algorithm with MDS embedding method[5]. Figure 4 shows the PR curve comparison of two algorithms.

From Figure 4,we can see that our proposed algorithm is superior to MDS embedding method,which proves th effectiveness of our algorithm.

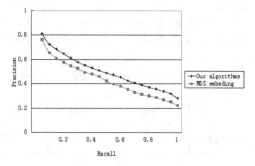

Fig. 4. Comparison of PR curve between our algorithm and MDS method

5   Conclusions

We propose an method to solve expression problems.The contribution is as follows:

Firstly we extract geodesic stripes based on nose tip, followed by spaced sampling and WKS feature extraction.This we turn surface matching problem into a local feature matching problem, then introduce SVM training method into 3D face recognition, turning face recognition into a two-class classification problem.

Because WKS feature only has limited detail description ability, it certainly lost some information of human face.If combined with other features having better detail description ability, the recognition rate can be further improved.This is our next work.

Acknowledgment. This work is partly supported by National Natural Science Foundation of China(61379106),the Scientific Research Foundation for the Excellent Middle-Aged and Youth Scientists of Shandong Province of China (Grant No.BS2010DX037), the Shandong Provincial Natural Science Foundation (Grant No.ZR2009GL014) , the Open Project Program of the State Key Lab of CAD&CG (Grant No. A1315), Zhejiang University ,the Fundamental Research Funds for the Central Universities(Grant No. 10CX04043A, 10CX04014B, 11CX04053A, 11CX06086A, 12CX06083A, 12CX06086A, 13CX06007A, 14CX06010A, 14CX06012A).

References

1. Wang, Y., Pan, G., Wu, Z., Wang, Y.: Exploring Facial Expression Effects in 3D Face Recognition Using Partial ICP. In: Narayanan, P.J., Nayar, S.K., Shum, H.-Y. (eds.) ACCV 2006. LNCS, vol. 3851, pp. 581–590. Springer, Heidelberg (2006)
2. Chang, K.J., Bowyer, K.W., Flynn, P.J.: Effects on facial expression in 3D face recognition. In: Proceedings of SPIE, pp. 100–105 (2005)
3. Chua, C.S., Han, F., Ho, Y.-K.: 3D human face recognition using point signature. In: Proceedings Fourth IEEE International Conference on Automatic Face and Gesture Recognition Cat, pp. 233–238 (2000)
4. Smeets, D., Keustermans, J., Vandermeulen, D., Suetens, P.: meshSIFT: Local surface features for 3D face recognition under expression variations and partial data. Computer Vision and Image Understanding, 158–169 (2013)
5. Bronstein, A.M., Bronstein, M.M., Kimmel, R.: Three-dimensional face recognition. International Journal of Computer Vision 64, 5–30 (2005)
6. Smeets, D., Fabry, T., Hermans, J., Vandermeulen, D., Suetens, P.: Isometric deformation modeling using singular value decomposition for 3D expression-invariant face recognition. In: Biometrics: Theory, Applications, and Systems (BTAS 2009), pp. 28–30 (2009)
7. Fleishman, S., Drori, I., Cohen, D.: Bilateral mesh denoising. ACM Transactions on Graphics 22, 950–955 (2003)
8. Wang, Y., Liu, J., Tang, X.: Robust 3D Face Recognition by Local Shape Difference Boosting. IEEE Transactions on Pattern Analysis and Machine Intelligence 32, 1–15 (2009)
9. Aubry, M., Schlickewei, U., Cremers, D.: The wave kernel signature: A quantum mechanical approach to shape analysis. In: 2011 IEEE International Conference on Computer Vision Workshops (ICCV Workshops), pp. 6–13 (2009)

A Novel Coupled Metric Learning Method and Its Application in Degraded Face Recognition

Guofeng Zou[1,*], Shuming Jiang[1], Yuanyuan Zhang[1], Guixia Fu[2], and Kejun Wang[2]

[1] Information Research Institute of Shandong Academy of Sciences, Jinan, China
zgf841122@163.com, {jsm,zhangyy}@sdas.org
[2] College of Automation, Harbin Engineering University, Harbin, China
fgx45101@163.com, wangkejun@hrbeu.edu.cn

Abstract. The coupled metric learning is a novel metric method to solve the matching problem of the elements in different data sets. In this paper, we improved the supervised locality preserving projection algorithm, and added within-class and between-class information of this algorithm to coupled metric learning, so a novel coupled metric learning method is proposed. This method can effectively extract the nonlinear feature information, and the operation is simple. The experiments based on two face databases are performed. The results show that, the proposed method can get higher recognition rate in low-resolution and fuzzy face recognition, and can reduce the computing time; it is an effective metric method.

Keywords: Metric learning, Coupled metric, SLPP, Face recognition.

1   Introduction

The metric is a function which gives the scalar distance between two patterns. Distance metric is an important basis for similarity measure between samples, and the essence of distance metric learning is to obtain another representation method with better class separability by linear or nonlinear transformation.

In recent years, some researches about distance metric have been done by researchers[1-7]. They learn a distance metric by introducing sample similarity constraint or category information, the distance metric is used to improve the data clustering or classification. These researches can be concluded to two categories: linear distance metric learning and nonlinear distance metric learning. The linear distance metric learning is equivalent to learning a linear transformation in sample space, including a variety of common linear dimensionality reduction method, such as principal component analysis [8], linear discriminant analysis [9], and independent component analysis method [10]. The nonlinear distance metric learning is equivalent to learning a nonlinear transformation in sample space, such as locally linear embedding [11], isometric mapping [12], Laplace mapping [13], in addition, there is a more flexible distance metric learning algorithm, which is based on kernel matrix [7].

Traditional distance metric learning is defined on the set of single attribute, which are incapable for the metric of elements in different set with different attribute.

---

[*] Corresponding author.

Z. Sun et al. (Eds.): CCBR 2013, LNCS 8232, pp. 154–161, 2013.

Traditional distance metric will not be able to calculate the distance of two images with different resolution. Normalized operation is performed before recognition, but the interpolation inevitably introduced false information, and sampling may miss some useful information, so it is difficult to get high recognition rate.

Aiming at the shortage of traditional distance metric, Li Bo and Ben Xianye et al proposed the coupled metric learning (CML) [14-16]. The goal of coupled metric learning is to find a coupled distance function to meet the specific requirement of the given task. Firstly, the data in different set is projected to same coupled space, and the elements with correlation should be as close as possible in new space after projection, and then metric learning is performed in this coupled space.

Based on the idea of coupled metric, we improved the supervised locality preserving projection algorithm and added supervised locality preserving information to coupled metric learning. Then the supervised locality preserving projection coupled metric learning (SLPP-CML) is proposed. This method can solve the matching problem of different faces and extract the nonlinear feature, the operation is simple and the training speed is fast. To verify the effectiveness of the proposed method, the experiments based on two face databases are performed. The experimental results show that, a higher recognition rate can be achieved in the proposed algorithm.

2   SLPP-CML

The coupled distance metric learning must be used under the constraints of supervised information. In this paper, we improved the supervised locality preserving projection (SLPP) algorithm [17]. Based on the improved SLPP algorithm, we proposed the supervised locality preserving projection coupled metric learning (SLPP-CML) method. The SLPP-CML includes the following steps:

Step1: Building the neighborhood relation in same collection. We use the k nearest neighbor method. First, building within-class adjacency graph in same collection: if the data point x_i (y_i) is one of the k within-class nearest neighbors of data point x_j (y_j), we connect these two data points; then, building between-class adjacency graph in the same collection: if the data point x_i (y_i) is one of the k between-class nearest neighbors of data point x_j (y_j), these two data points are connected.

Setp2: Building the connected relation between two collections. If the data points x_i and y_j in two different collections belong to the same class, then these two points are connected, otherwise not connected.

Step3: Constructing the relation matrix in same collection. According to the neighborhood relation collections, the relation matrixes (similarity matrixes) of within-class and between-class are constructed respectively in same collection.

Within-class similarity matrix is W corresponding to within-class adjacency graph and the within-class similarity value is W_{ij}. The definition is as follows:

$$W_{ij} = \begin{cases} \exp(-\|x_i - x_j\|^2 / t) & \text{if } x_i \text{ connected } x_j \\ 0 & \text{otherwise} \end{cases} \tag{1}$$

Between-class similarity matrix is B corresponding to between-class adjacency graph and the between-class similarity value is B_{ij}. It can be defined as follows:

$$B_{ij} = \begin{cases} \exp(-\|x_i - x_j\|^2 / t) & \text{if } x_i \text{ connected } x_j \\ 0 & \text{otherwise} \end{cases} \tag{2}$$

Where parameter t is the average distance between all sample points.

Step4: Constructing relation matrix S between two collections as follows:

$$S_{ij} = \begin{cases} 1 & \text{if } x_i \text{ connected } y_j \\ 0 & \text{otherwise} \end{cases} \tag{3}$$

Step5: Calculating the final similarity matrix C between two collections. As shown in figure 1, the similarity relations between element $x_1 \in X$ and elements of collection Y include the following several situations.

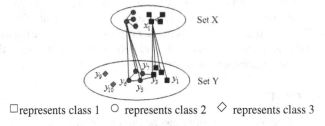

□ represents class 1   ○ represents class 2   ◇ represents class 3

Fig. 1. The relationship between elements

(A) The similarity between x_1 and y_1. These two data points in different collections belong to the same class and they are connected to each other, so the similarity of which is $C_{11} = S_{11} = 1$.

(B) The similarity between x_1 and y_5. These two data points belong to different class, but the relationship between y_5 and y_3 is the between-class neighborhood relation in the same collection, and the similarity B_{35} is the maximum similarity value, so similarity between x_1 and y_5 is $C_{15} = B_{35}$.

(C) The similarity between x_1 and y_6. The y_6 does not have between-class neighborhood relation with any element in collection Y of class 1. But there is a between-class neighborhood relation of same collection between y_5 and y_3, and within-class neighborhood relation between y_5 and y_6. So the similarity between x_1 and y_6 is defined as the product of similarity B_{35} and similarity W_{56}, which is the maximum similarity between y_6 and y_3, that is $C_{16} = B_{35} \cdot W_{56}$.

(D) The similarity between x_1 and y_9. These two data points belong to different class, there are not any between-class neighborhood relations between the elements of class 1 and class 3 in collection Y, namely $C_{19} = 0$.

Step6: Constructing the optimal objective function:

$$J = \sum_{(i,j)\in C} \left\| W_a^T (f_x(x_i) - f_y(y_j)) \right\|^2 = \sum_i \sum_j \left\| W_a^T (f_x(x_i) - f_y(y_j)) \right\|^2 \cdot C_{ij} \tag{4}$$

Where the functions f_x and f_y are considered to be linear, that is $f_x(x) = W_x^T x$, $f_y(y) = W_y^T y$. The optimal objective function can be rewritten as follow:

$$J = \sum_i \sum_j \left\| W_a^T (f_x(x_i) - f_y(y_j)) \right\|^2 \cdot C_{ij} = \sum_i \sum_j \left\| W_a^T W_x^T x_i - W_a^T W_y^T y_j \right\|^2 \cdot C_{ij} \quad (5)$$

Letting $P_x = W_x W_a$, $P_y = W_y W_a$, we can get:

$$J = \sum_i \sum_j \left\| W_a^T W_x^T x_i - W_a^T W_y^T y_j \right\|^2 \cdot C_{ij} = \sum_i \sum_j \left\| P_x^T x_i - P_y^T y_j \right\|^2 \cdot C_{ij} \quad (6)$$

Therefore, our method aims to learn two linear transformations P_x and P_y. Eq.(7) is an alternate matrix expression of Eq.(6) :

$$
\begin{aligned}
J &= Tr[P_x^T XF_1(C)X^T P_x + P_y^T YF_2(C)Y^T P_y - P_x^T XCY^T P_y - P_y^T YC^T X^T P_x] \\
&= Tr\left(\begin{bmatrix} P_x \\ P_y \end{bmatrix}^T \begin{bmatrix} X \\ & Y \end{bmatrix} \begin{bmatrix} F_1(C) & -C \\ -C^T & F_2(C) \end{bmatrix} \begin{bmatrix} X \\ & Y \end{bmatrix}^T \begin{bmatrix} P_x \\ P_y \end{bmatrix} \right)
\end{aligned}
\quad (7)
$$

Where $Tr(X)$ represent computing the trace of matrix X, $F_1(C)$ and $F_2(C)$ are diagonal matrixes, their diagonal elements are the row or column sums of similarity matrix C respectively.

Assuming that $P = \begin{bmatrix} P_x \\ P_y \end{bmatrix}$, $Z = \begin{bmatrix} X \\ & Y \end{bmatrix}$, $\Gamma = \begin{bmatrix} F_1(C) & -C \\ -C^T & F_2(C) \end{bmatrix}$, Eq.(7) can be rewritten as follow:

$$J(P) = Tr[P^T Z\Gamma Z^T P] \quad (8)$$

The solution to make Eq.(8) minimized is obtained by generalized eigen- decomposition of $(Z\Gamma Z^T)p = \lambda (ZZ^T)p$ and taking the eigenvectors $p_2, p_3, \cdots p_{m+1}$ corresponding to the second to $(m+1)$ th smallest eigenvalues $\lambda_2, \lambda_3, \cdots \lambda_{m+1}$, and $P = [p_2, p_3, \cdots p_{m+1}]$, its dimension is $(D_x + D_y) \times m$. D_x and D_y are the dimensions of samples in collection X and Y, so the transformation matrix P_x corresponds to the 1st to D_x th rows of P and P_y corresponds to the $(D_x + 1)$ th to D_y th rows.

Step7: Bringing the matrix P_x and P_y to the Eq.(6), the distance metric of the elements belonging to different collections can be realized.

3   Experiment and Analysis

The proposed coupled metric learning method is tested on Yale face database and CAS-PEAL-R1 face database. The Yale face database contains 165 pictures of 15 people with the size of 100×100 and 256 gray levels. These images were taken in different expression and illumination. In experiment, we used 6 images per person for training, a total of 90, and the other images were used as test sample, a total of 75 .

The CAS-PEAL-R1 face database contains 30863 face images, and we used the accessory data set of frontal face image subsets. The face images per person in this set include 6 different appendages; there are 3 images with different glasses and 3 images with different hats. We selected 300 images corresponding to 50 people in experiment, the odd-numbered images were used as training samples and even-numbered images were used as test samples.

(1) Experiment 1: The low-resolution face recognition

Traditional measure method will not be able to calculate the distance between two images with different resolution. So the general handling method is interpolation operation for the low-resolution image, but it is easy to introduce false information. With the increase of false information, the distortion degree increases, as shown in figure 2. Aiming at the problem of recognition rate declining because of image distortion, the researchers realized the low-resolution image compensation by restoration preprocessing, but the image restoration algorithm is often more complex, and the quality of restoration has great impact on final recognition results. However, the proposed coupled metric learning method can directly realize the feature extraction and measurement of two different resolution images, which do not need to do image restoration. So this method not only saves computing time, and avoids the negative impact of image restoration on recognition performance.

Fig. 2. The normal face image, low-resolution image and the result after restoration

In the experiment, the normal face is clear image with the size of 64×64 pixel, the low-resolution face image can be obtained through blurring and sampling, which is corresponded to normal resolution face image. The size of low-resolution face image is 16×16. The training set is consisted of normal training face image and corresponding low-resolution face image. The test set is the low-resolution face image generated by the normal test face image.

Through the theoretical analysis, the SLPP-CML algorithm has two influence factors: (1) the neighbor number k of SLPP; (2) the reserved dimensions D_c of the feature. Therefore, the recognition results based on different parameters should be discussed and analyzed, as shown in Figure 3. Figure 3 gives the recognition rate curve in two different face databases. The curve has a general change law, with the increase of feature dimensions, the recognition rate kept a decreasing trend after increasing, and the best recognition results can be achieved only in the optimal feature dimensions. In Yale face database, the recognition rate kept a higher trend when feature dimensions remain 10-20. The optimal recognition rate is 86.67% when feature dimension is 10 and neighbor number is 5. In CAS-PEAL-R1 face database, the recognition rate can reach the maximum value 86.67%, when feature dimension is 40 and neighbor number is 2.

Obviously, the neighbor number affects the recognition rate, but does not change the overall trend. The training sample number is 6 in Yale face database, and the recognition effect is optimal when the neighbor number is 5; In CAS-PEAL-R1 face database, the training sample number is 3, the neighbor number $k = 2$.

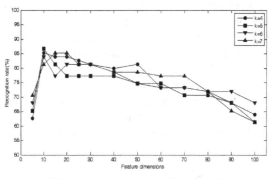

(a) The experiment result in Yale face database

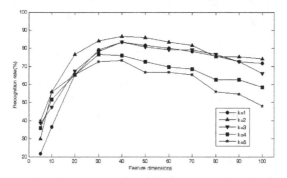

(b) The experiment result in CAS-PEAL-R1 face database

Fig. 3. The recognition rate under different dimensions and different nearest neighbor numbers

In addition, in order to illustrate the effectiveness of SLPP-CML. Based on the face after image restoration, we used the principal component analysis for feature extraction and recognition. And then the comparative experiments were carried out with Ref. [14] [16] respectively. The experiment results are shown in table 1.

Table 1. Experimental comparison of our proposed method with other methods

Method	Yale face database	CAS-PEAL-R1 face database
Image restoration[18] + PCA	61.33	55.33
CML[14]	77.33	74.67
CLPM[16]	82.67	80.67
Our method	86.67	86.67

The experiment illustrated that the results of feature extraction after restoration is not satisfactory. The method in Ref.[14] can not overcome the influences of within- class multiple modes, so the identification effect is not good. The coupled metric in Ref.[16] is conducive to resolving within-class multiple modes; the recognition effects have been greatly improved, but it does not fully consider the between-class relationships of training samples. The SLPP-CML takes advantage of the supervisory of category information, while the within-class and between-class relationship information of training samples have been considered into the metric learning, so we can get better recognition results.

Considering the recognition time, The SLPP-CML algorithm does not need to do image recovery, so it effectively reduces the face recognition time. The recognition time of SLPP-CML is about 0.0225 seconds.

(2) Experiment 2: fuzzy face recognition

Besides the low-resolution face image, figure 4 gives the fuzzy face image. Obviously, it is difficult to identify the fuzzy face image, although a part of face details can be restored by deblurring algorithm, but it still can not provide enough information in identification.

Fig. 4. The normal face image, blurred face image and deblurring result

The normal face image is clear image with size of 64×64, the blurred face image is generated through convolution based on the normal face images. Training set is composed of normal training face images and generated fuzzy face image, the test set consists of the test blurred face images. The results are shown in Table 2.

Table 2. Experimental comparison of our proposed method with other methods

Method	Yale face database	CAS-PEAL-R1 face database
Deblurring[19] + PCA	64.00	68.67
CML[14]	77.33	79.33
CLPM[16]	85.67	83.33
Our method	86.67	88.67

The neighbor number of SLPP-CML algorithm is $T-1$, where T is the number of training sample of each class. The feature dimensions of training samples in Yale and CAS-PEAL-R1 face database are 15 and 39 respectively.

4   Conclusions

Aiming at the problem that the traditional metric methods can not calculate the distance of the elements in different data sets, we proposed the coupled metric learning method based on supervised locality preserving projection. The elements of different sets are mapped to the same space combined with the within-class and between-class information, and then the metric matrix learning is performed. This algorithm can effectively extract the face nonlinear features, and the operation is simple. Low-resolution and fuzzy face recognition experiments show that the proposed method can obtain a higher recognition rate, and has a high computational efficiency.

Acknowledgements. This research is supported by National Research Foundation for the Doctoral Program of Higher Education of China (20102304110004).

References

1. Davis, J.V., Kulis, B., Jain, P., et al.: Information-theoretic metric learning. In: The 24th International Conference on Machine Learning, pp. 209–216. ACM Press, Oregon (2007)
2. Shiming, X., Feiping, N., Changshui, Z.: Learning a Mahalanobis distance metric for data clustering and classification. Pattern Recognition 41(12), 3600–3612 (2008)
3. Weinberger, K.Q., Saul, L.K.: Distance metric learning for large margin nearest neighbor classification. The Journal of Machine Learning Research 10, 207–244 (2009)
4. Kulis, B., Jain, P., Grauman, K.: Fast similarity search for learned metrics. IEEE Transactions on Pattern Analysis and Machine Intelligence 31(12), 2143–2157 (2009)
5. Zhengping, H., Liang, L., Chengqian, X., et al.: Sparse Distance Metric Learning with L1-Norm Constraint for One-Class Samples in High-Dimensional Space and Its Application. Mathematics in Practice and Theory 41(6), 116–124 (2011)
6. Lei, W., Tie, L., Huading, J.: Chunk Incremental Distance Metric Learning Algorithm Based on Manifold Regularization. Acta Electronic Sinica 39(5), 1131–1135 (2011)
7. Mahdieh, S.B., Saeed, B.S.: Kernel-based metric learning for semi-supervised clustering. Neurocomputing 73, 1352–1361 (2010)
8. Hotelling, H.: Analysis of A Complex of Statistical Variables into Principal Components. Journal of Educational Psychology 24, 417–441 (1933)
9. Fisher, R.A.: The Use of Multiple Measurements in Taxonomic Problems. Annals of Eugenics 7, 179–188 (1936)
10. Comon, P., et al.: Independent Components Analysis, a New Concept. Signal Procssing 36(3), 287–314 (1994)
11. Roweis, S.T., Saul, L.K.: Nonlinear Dimensionality Reduction by Locally Linear Embedding. Science 290, 2323–2326 (2000)
12. Tenenbaum, J., Silva, V., Langford, J.: A Global Geometric Framework for Nonlinear Dimensionality Reduction. Science 290, 2319–2323 (2000)
13. Belkin, M., Niyogi, P.: Laplacian Eigenmaps and Spectral Techniques for Embedding and Clustering. Advances in Neural Information Processing System 14, 585–591 (2002)
14. Li, B., Chang, H., Shan, S., Chen, X.: Coupled Metric Learning for Face Recognition with Degraded Images. In: Zhou, Z.-H., Washio, T. (eds.) ACML 2009. LNCS, vol. 5828, pp. 220–233. Springer, Heidelberg (2009)
15. Xianye, B., Weixiao, M., Rui, Y., et al.: An improved biometrics technique based on metric learning approach. Neurocomputing 79(11), 44–51 (2012)
16. Li, B., Chang, H., Shan, S., et al.: Low-Resolution Face Recognition via Coupled Locality Preserving Mappings. IEEE Signal Processing Letters 17(1), 20–23 (2010)
17. Zhonghua, S., Yonghui, P., et al.: A Supervised Locality Preserving Projection Algorithm for Dimensionality Reduction. Pattern Recognition and Artificial Intelligence 21(2), 233–239 (2008)
18. Yuanyuan, W., Zhimin, S., Zheng, C., et al.: Super-resolution image restoration based on maximum likelihood estimation. Chinese Journal of Scientific Instrument 29(5), 949–953 (2008)
19. Xiaofei, Y., Fujie, C., Xuejun, Y.: Template matching by wiener filtering. Journal of Computer Research & Development 37(12), 1499–1503 (2000)

Learning Symmetry Features for Face Detection Based on Sparse Group Lasso

Qi Li, Zhenan Sun, Ran He, and Tieniu Tan

Center for Research on Intelligent Perception and Computing,
National Laboratory of Pattern Recognition, Institute of Automation,
Chinese Academy of Sciences, Beijing, China
{qli,znsun,rhe,tnt}@nlpr.ia.ac.cn

Abstract. Face detection is of fundamental importance in face recognition, facial expression recognition and other face biometrics related applications. The core problem of face detection is to select a subset of features from massive local appearance descriptors such as Haar features and LBP. This paper proposes a two stage feature selection method for face detection. Firstly, feature representation of the symmetric characteristics of face pattern is formulated as a structured sparsity problem and sparse group lasso is used to select the most effective local features for face detection. Secondly, minimal redundancy maximal relevance is used to remove the redundant features in group sparsity learning. Experimental results demonstrate that the proposed feature selection method has better generalization ability than Adaboost and Lasso based feature selection methods for face detection problems.

Keywords: Face detection, sparse group lasso, minimal redundancy maximal relevance.

1 Introduction

Face detection is a key problem and a necessary step to many facial analysis algorithms, eg, face recognition, facial expression analysis, head pose estimation. How to efficiently compute and express the difference between faces and nonfaces is still a challenging task. Feature selection and appropriate classifier are needed to solve this problem. While the classification step is widely explored and quite standard, the feature selection process needs to be further researched for face detection. In this paper, we focus on feature selection method in face detection which is also a fundamental and important problem in pattern recognition and computer vision [1,6].

In the past decades, hundreds of approaches to face detection have been proposed. One of the most successful appearance-based methods is proposed by Viola and Jones [2]. The success of this method comes from a powerful feature selection method based on a well-known cascaded Boosting framework. Since then a large number of methods have been proposed following the general face detection architecture. Recently, Destrero et al. [1] proposed a sparsity enforcing

Z. Sun et al. (Eds.): CCBR 2013, LNCS 8232, pp. 162–169, 2013.

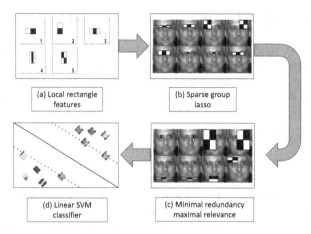

Fig. 1. Flowchart of the proposed framework. (a) Five different types of rectangle features. (b) Symmetry features selection via sparse group lasso. (c) Reducing the redundant features via minimal redundancy maximal relevance. (d) The final classification results using a linear SVM classifier.

method for learning face features. Lasso regression model was adopted to produce a sparse solution of a linear model which can be seen as a feature selection process. The sparsity based feature selection method is proved to be more effective than Viola and Jones feature selection method especially for the training set of limited size. However, there are still two unsolved problems in sparsity enforcing method: the first one is how to select discriminating features while preserving the internal symmetry structure of faces, and the second one is how to reduce the redundant features when using the sparsity enforcing method for feature selection.

To solve the first problem, we consider using sparse group lasso to select symmetry features which play important roles in object detection, recognition and matching [3,8]. Compared with lasso for feature selection, sparse group lasso not only has the property of performing feature selection but preserving the internal symmetry characteristics of faces. To solve the second problem, we choose minimal-redundancy-maximal-relevance (mRMR) to reduce the redundant features selected by the sparse group lasso algorithm. Figure 1 shows the proposed two-stage framework.

The contributions of this paper are summarized as two points. First, we combine knowledge-based methods and appearance-based methods for face detection. As to knowledge-based method, we make use of symmetry characteristics of faces. As to appearance-based method, we use sparsity enforcing method and mRMR to choose the features which are meaningful and representative. Second, the proposed framework has a better generalization ability than other feature selection methods. Besides, the number of training examples we used is usually less than Viola and Jones face detection method. So it can be easily applied to other types of less common objects.

2   The Proposed Framework for Face Detection

In this section, we discuss symmetry features and propose a two stage feature selection framework for face detection. In the first stage, we use sparse group lasso to select groups of symmetry rectangle features. In the second stage, the mRMR method is used to further reduce the selected symmetry features.

2.1   Symmetry Features

We use the rectangle features proposed by [2], which have a strong discriminating power and can be efficiently computed by integral images. Figure 1(a) shows five different kinds of used rectangle features, which are computed over different locations, sizes and aspect ratios. For each image patch will generate tens of thousands of features. So it is necessary to select a small set of compact and meaningful features.

We propose a new concept called symmetry features which reflect the mirror characteristics of faces. In a cropped face image, we use the middle column of that image as the symmetry axis. Then each feature at the right side of the symmetry axis corresponds to the same size, same aspect ratio feature at the left side of the symmetry axis. We put these two features as one group. If the center of a feature just locates at the symmetry axis, then it doesn't have a mirror feature. We put this single feature as one group. So each group of features at most has two features. Those groups of features are called symmetry features.

2.2   Feature Selection Using Sparse Group Lasso

As mentioned in Section 1, if we use the l_1 based methods for feature selection directly, we will lose symmetry characteristics of faces. Sparse group lasso proposed by [4] has a nice property of selecting features at the group and individual predictor levels. The standard form of sparse group lasso is as follows:

$$\beta = \arg \min_{\beta \in R^p} \left(\left\| Y - \sum_{l=1}^{L} X_l \beta_l \right\|_2^2 + \lambda_1 \sum_{l=1}^{L} \sqrt{\rho_l} \|\beta_l\|_2 + \lambda_2 \|\beta\|_1 \right) \tag{1}$$

where $X \in R^{n \times p}$ represents the training set of n elements with a dictionary of p features, $Y \in R^{n \times 1}$ is the output labels, $\beta \in R^{p \times 1}$ is the parameter vector. X is divided into L non-overlapping groups of features $(X_1, ..., X_L)$. The element of $X_l (l = 1, ..., L)$ is composed by symmetry features. $\beta = (\beta_1, \beta_2, ..., \beta_l)$ is the group parameter vector. $\sqrt{\rho_l}$ terms accounts for the varying group sizes. λ_1 controls the sparsity of features within a group and λ_2 controls the sparsity of the selected groups features. Depending on λ_1 and λ_2, the sparse group lasso yields sparsity at both the individual and group feature levels.

2.3   Reducing Redundant Features

More variables than needed are usually selected by the sparse group lasso when using cross validation to yield parameters λ_1 and λ_2. Compared with [2], a large number of Haar-like rectangle features will be selected by sparse group lasso. Although those features have high correlation with the detection results, lots of the same sizes and aspect ratios features almost in the same position are chosen twice or even more. In order to overcome the drawback of sparse group lasso, we choose mRMR [5] in the second stage. The features selected by mRMR can capture the face information in a broader scope by reducing the mutual redundant feature set.

Given two variables x and y, their correlation coefficient is defined as:

$$\rho(x;y) = \frac{cov(x,y)}{\sigma_x\sigma_y} = \frac{E[(x-\mu_x)(y-\mu_y)]}{\sigma_x\sigma_y} \tag{2}$$

Minimal redundancy is defined as:

$$\min R(S), R = \frac{1}{|S|^2} \sum_{x_i,x_j \in S} \rho(x_i,x_j) \tag{3}$$

Maximal relevance is defined as:

$$\max D(S,c), D = \frac{1}{|S|} \sum_{x_i \in S} \rho(x_i;c) \tag{4}$$

where S is the set of features, c is the corresponding target class of feature set S, $\rho(x_i,x_j)$ is the correlation between feature i and j, $\rho(x_i,c)$ is the correlation between feature i and c. Eq. (3) aims to select the subset of features such that the correlation between themselves are minimal. Eq. (4) aims to ensure that the selected subset features have the discriminating power when they represent different classes.

The criterion combining Eq. (3) and Eq. (4) is called minimal-redundancy-maximal-relevance (mRMR). Optimization both of them requires combining them into a single criterion function as follows:

$$max(D(S,c)/R(S)) \tag{5}$$

Incremental search methods proposed by [5] can be used to solve the optimization problem (5). Although we enforce group penalties in Eq. (1), those features selected by the first stage is not necessarily the symmetry features. First we analyze the features selected by sparse group lasso. If the groups of features are composed by two rectangle features, one of them who represents the entire group is sent to the second stage. The final output of rectangle features contains the whole groups of rectangle features that mRMR selected.

3 Experiments

The Jensen database [7] is used to evaluate different feature selection methods for face detection. All of the positive examples of Jensen database are taken from FERET database [9] and LFW database [10]. 5,000 training images and 5,000 testing images are selected sequentially where the positive and negative examples are evenly distributed between training and testing images. We resize all of the images to a base resolution of 19 by 19. Five different kinds of local rectangle features are used to generate about 64,000 rectangle features for each of the training and testing images.

3.1 Settings

Before using sparse group lasso to select symmetry features, we use l_2 norm to normalize the dataset so that each column of the training and testing dataset has unit l_2 norm. A subset of features are selected according to our proposed two stage framework. These features are used to represent the whole dataset. Considering the computational advantage, a linear SVM classifier is used. The linear SVM model is obtained based on the training set and 5-fold cross validation is used to tune the parameters. Finally we analyze the generalization ability of our method over the testing set. ROC curves are used to evaluate the performance of different feature selection methods for face detection.

The First Stage. How to determine the values of λ_1 and λ_2 is an important problem when sparse group lasso is used to select the symmetry features. In practice, the parameters λ_1 and λ_2 are set to an equal and small value because of two reasons. (1) If λ_1 and λ_2 are set to be large values, the large penalty terms will make the number of selected symmetry features relatively small. These symmetry features cannot be used for classification because of the low performance. (2) A large number of symmetry features are available to preserve the internal symmetry characteristics of faces if identical value is given to λ_1 and λ_2. These large number of symmetry features not only have meaningful representation but also can achieve a high level classification performance.

Figure 2(a) shows ROC curves with different values of λ_1, λ_2. We choose $\lambda_1 = 0.10, \lambda_2 = 0.10$ as the final parameters in the first stage of our method. This procedure leaves us with a set of 1087 groups of features (totally 2054 features). A large number of symmetry features appear around eyes, noses and mouths. Although the size of these representative symmetry features is much less than that of the original set, it is still higher than we actually need.

The Second Stage. After the selection procedure of the first stage, mRMR is used to further choose a small subset of features. At each step, mRMR choose one group of features which maximize the optimization problem (5). Finally we choose 39 groups of features (totally 67 features) which achieve the best detection accuracy after the second stage. Figure 2(b) compares the performance of our method with and without the second stage. We can see that the procedure

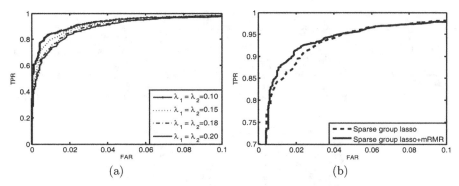

Fig. 2. Different ROC curves with the horizontal line representing the false accept rate and the vertical line representing the true positive rate. (a) ROC curves with different λ_1, λ_2 using sparse group lasso method in the first stage, (b) ROC curves of our method with and without the second stage.

of the second stage not only reduces the number of features significantly, but actually has a small gain (about 5%) at low false accept rate in terms of the detection result. This observation indicates that mRMR can select a small subset of compact and meaningful features. Figure 3(a) shows the top 40 features selected by our method. We can see that the order of the the features is changed after the second stage, and the symmetry features selected by our method are salient features appearing at different locations and sizes of faces.

3.2   Comparison with Other Methods

We also compare our method with other feature selection methods, such as Adaboost and conventional Lasso method without considering the symmetry characteristics of faces. Different features are selected by the three methods respectively and then these selected features are used to represent the whole training dataset to train different linear SVM models. Then we evaluate the effectiveness of the selected features over the testing set by the ROC curves.

The same number of features (totally 67 features) are selected using Adaboost algorithm [2] and the top 40 features are shown in Figure 3(b). Conventional Lasso method without considering the symmetry characteristics of faces is also compared with our method. Different number of features can be selected by tuning the parameter λ. Notice that when tuning the parameter λ, the number of selected features is not consistent. In order to have a fair comparison, a little higher number of features (103 features) are selected during the process. Figure 3(c) shows the top 40 features selected by conventional Lasso method. From Figure 3(c) we can see that most of the selected features seem to appear around the salient parts of faces.

The comparison of the proposed method with Adaboost and conventional Lasso method is shown in Figure 4(a). From Figure 4(a), we observe that the true positive rate (TPR) of all methods increases quickly when false accept rate (FAR) is smaller than 0.01, and TPR of all methods tends to be similar

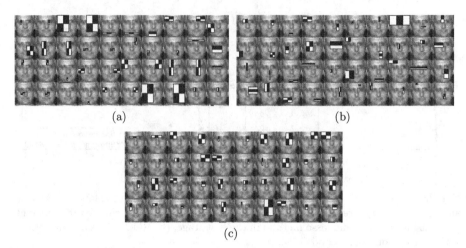

(a)   (b)

(c)

Fig. 3. Top 40 rectangle features selected by different methods: (a) our method, (b) Adabooost method, (c) conventional Lasso method

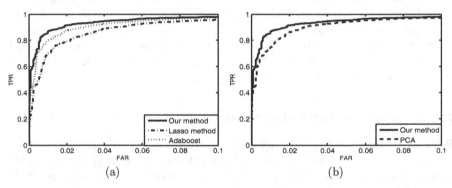

(a)   (b)

Fig. 4. Comparison of different feature selection methods for face detection: (a) ROC curves of our method, Adaboost method and conventional Lasso method with the same linear SVM classifier, (b) ROC curves of our method and PCA with the same linear SVM classifier

when FAR is larger than 0.06. We also observe that our method outperforms the other two methods. The improvement of our method against Adaboost and conventional Lasso method is nearly 5% and 10% at a relatively low FAR.

Similar to [1], we also compare our method with the classic dimensionality reduction method PCA. The projection matrix which contains the eigenvectors of the training dataset is used as the projection matrix to project the training and testing dataset to a 67 dimensional matrix. Then the training dataset is used to train a linear SVM classifier and the final classification result over testing dataset is showed in Figure 4(b). We can see that TPR of our method is about 5% higher than PCA at a relatively low FAR.

4   Conclusions

In this paper we have presented a novel two stage framework to learn symmetry features for face detection. Sparse group lasso and mRMR are used to reduce the redundant features while at the same time preserving the symmetry characteristics of faces. Experimental results have shown that our method outperforms other traditional feature selection methods under the same conditions. As parts of our future work, we will further research on implementing a robust face detection system.

Acknowledgments. This work is funded by the National Natural Science Foundation of China (Grant No. 61273272,61103155), the International S&T Cooperation Program of China (Grant No. 2010DFB14110) and the Instrument Developing Project of the Chinese Academy of Sciences (Grant No. YZ201266).

References

1. Destrero, A., De Mol, C., Odone, F., Verri, A.: A regularized framework for feature selection in face detection and authentication. International Journal of Computer Vision 83, 164–177 (2009)
2. Viola, P., Jones, M.J.: Robust real-time face detection. International Journal of Computer Vision 57, 137–154 (2004)
3. Levi, K., Weiss, Y.: Learning object detection from a small number of examples: the importance of good features. In: IEEE Computer Society Conference on Computer Vision and Pattern Recognition, pp. 53–60 (2004)
4. Friedman, J., Hastie, T., Tibshirani, R.: A note on the group lasso and a sparse group lasso, arXiv:1001.0736, 164–177 (2010)
5. Peng, H., Long, F., Ding, C.: Feature selection based on mutual information criteria of max-dependency, max-relevance, and min-redundancy. IEEE Transactions on Pattern Analysis and Machine Intelligence 27, 1226–1238 (2005)
6. He, R., Tan, T., Wang, L., Zheng, W.S.: l2, 1 Regularized correntropy for robust feature selection. In: IEEE Conference on Computer Vision and Pattern Recognition, pp. 2504–2511 (2012)
7. Jensen, O.H.: Implementing the Viola-Jones face detection algorithm. PHD thesis, Technical University of Denmark, Denmark (2008)
8. Hauagge, D.C., Snavely, N.: Image matching using local symmetry features. In: IEEE Conference on Computer Vision and Pattern Recognition, pp. 206–213 (2012)
9. Phillips, P.J.: Moon: The Facial Recognition Technology (FERET) Database, http://www.itl.nist.gov/isd/humanid/feret/feret_master.html
10. Huang, G.B., Mattar, M., Berg, T., Learned-Miller, E.: Labeled faces in the wild: A database for studying face recognition in unconstrained environments. In: Workshop on Faces in 'Real-Life' Images: Detection, Alignment, and Recognition (2008)

Analysis on Features and Metrics
in Face Image Retrieval System

Pengjun Ji, Yuchun Fang[*], and Yujie Ma

School of Computer Engineering and Science, Shanghai University,
200444 Shanghai, China
ycfang@shu.edu.cn

Abstract. In the field of face recognition (FR) and face image retrieval (FIR), features and metrics have received great attention in recent years due to their direct influence on the performance of a FR/FIR system. In this paper, we analyze the two factors for FIR in following steps. First, the face images are aligned to the same size, moreover, their illumination is balanced. Second, we extract classic features widely used in face recognition and retrieval, then utilize them in feature matching with different metrics. At last, face retrieval is performed based on the distances calculated with multiple metrics. We evaluate the efficiency of features and metrics by face retrieval in Face Recognition Grand Challenge (FRGC) database. Experimental results not only serves to select features and metrics for FIR, they also demonstrate that the two variables affect FR and FIR in different ways.

Keywords: Face retrieval, preprocessing, feature, metric.

1 Introduction

Due to its properties of visual unification, non-contact and easy-described, face image is applied in different domains such as security monitoring and criminal investigation. At the same time, following the pace of fast developing multimedia technique, large-scale digital images are widely used in daily life. Especially on popular social websites such as Weibo and Facebook, where people are more inclined to take photos with family members and friends, and upload them to their personal sites, action like this has profound impact on the application prospect of FIR, which can help people readily find the exact face images he/she wants in reasonable time.

Research on FIR lasts for a decade, approaches on different aspects of the whole retrieval process have been proposed. Smith et al. applied shape model to compute shape feature vectors for aligned face in FIR [1]. Relevance feedback was adopted by Nitta et al. to enhance FIR performance across age variation [2]. Galoogahi and Sim [3] proposed Gabor Shape descriptor to retrieval face images based on a probe sketch. Lee et al. achieved effective and robust results choosing Gabor-LBP histogram for image representation and sparse representation classifier for FIR system [4]. Ruiz-del-Solar and Navarrete [5] used a self-organization maps in interactive FIR

---

[*] Corresponding author.

Z. Sun et al. (Eds.): CCBR 2013, LNCS 8232, pp. 170–177, 2013.

system to break the gap between high-level descriptors and low-level features. Wu et al. retrieved face images by demographic classification, where the demographic information contains gender, age and ethnicity [6]. Fuzzy clustering and inference methods were developed by Conilione and Wang to derive membership degree for each semantic label to a new image, which served to better annotate face images [7]. Fang et al. [8] utilized Bayesian inference and relevance feedback to retrieval mental image from large scale database. Vikram et al. [9] proposed to preserve spatial scattering of relevant dominant points on faces, moreover, this information was put into kd-tree index structure for efficient FIR.

Most of automatic face recognition concerns matching a detected face against a database of known faces with associated identities, while Arandjelovic and Zisserman [10] solved the problem following the content-based image retrieval (CBIR) setup. To locate the specific actors, they retrieved detected face images through ranking by confidence. As a special case of CBIR, FIR not only relies on CBIR techniques, but also adjusts to special features and metrics that are more advantageous to improve the efficiency of FIR system. A typical FIR system mainly contains four parts: face image preprocessing, feature extraction, feature matching and retrieval. In this paper, we are concerned more about how much the second and third parts affect retrieval process.

This paper is organized as follows. In Section 2, face image preprocessing is introduced. Section 3 gives details of features and metrics we use. Experimental results and analysis on FRGC [11] are listed in Section 4. Section 5 draws conclusions to the experimental results.

1.1 Preprocessing

The structure of FIR is shown in Figure 1, to maintain a reasonable retrieval accuracy, face image preprocessing is critical. We have constructed our preprocessing procedure with two criteria in mind. First, all images must be aligned to a standard pose and the same size to better accommodate features to be extracted. Second, to further improve the retrieval performance, illumination interference should be eliminated as far as possible.

Fig. 1. An overview of a FIR system. It takes four steps to accomplish the retrieval procedure.

As the ground truth information can be obtained from FRGC database, to align the face images to the same size and frontal pose, we apply bicubic interpolation with 4 pairs of coordinates including centre of two eyes, nose and mouth which are provided by the database owner in advance. In mathematical theory, bicubic interpolation is an extension of cubic interpolation for interpolating data points on a two dimensional regular grid. The interpolated surface is smoother than corresponding surfaces obtained by bilinear interpolation or nearest-neighbor interpolation [12]. We change the original color images into gray-scale images simultaneously to guarantee that they are in the same format.

To eliminate the illumination interference from uncontrolled environment on face images, we rectify the illumination of them after alignment, where we employ edge-preserving filters [13] to do the illumination transfer. Illumination rectification in preprocessing process is crucial for FIR, compared with the face retrieval results without illumination rectification, the average retrieval precision increases nearly 20 percent on FRGC Experiment 4. For each target face to be preprocessed, it needs a reference face which offers the ideal illumination condition, this method divides the illumination procedure into three layers artificially and cast the illumination situation of reference face to the target face, which is less affected by geometry differences and can better preserve identification structure of the target face. Figure 2 shows preprocessing procedure.

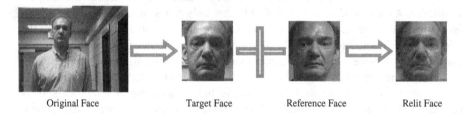

Original Face   Target Face   Reference Face   Relit Face

Fig. 2. Face image preprocessing procedure. As the ground truth information can be obtained, we are able to get a more accurate alignment results with traditional mathematical interpolation method, here the bicubic interpolation method is chosen. For a target face, reference face providing its own illumination is required, the edge-preserving method projects the illumination condition to target face and outputs the relit face handled.

2   Feature Extraction and Matching

Our primary goal is to find out how much the features and metrics impact on the FIR system. In the field of FR and FIR, there are features and metrics widely used, we select 3 features and 6 metrics to perform the matching.

Two of the selected features are based on the popular Local Binary Pattern (LBP), the Uniform LBP (ULBP) [14] and Local Gabor Binary Pattern (LGBP) [15] features. For LGBP feature, we select 1,000 dimensions of features according to their variance in descending order, it's named LGBP1000 feature in our experiments. We adopt the LGBP1000 feature in consideration of two factors: much lower computational complexity and which dimension should be selected. The source database training the index of dimensions to be selected is our self-collected face database, which contains 500 images with 50 persons, 10 images each, in order to testify whether feature selection across databases can be effective as well. The third one is the Local Difference (LD) feature [16] proposed by us, which extracts directional information of both first-order and second-order difference, compared with classic LBP operators, the LD feature reduces the computational complexity with much less dimension while maintains the accuracy.

Table 1 shows the attributes of three features we use, dimension of each feature mainly depends on block number, they increase or decrease to the same degree.

Table 1. Attributes of the three features used in the experiments

Feature	ULBP	LGBP1000	LD
Parameter	7*8 blocks, 8 sample points	7*8 blocks, 5 scales, 8 orientations	7*8 blocks, 17 orientations
Dimension	3304	1000	952

We make use of 6 different metric in the feature matching phase: the L_1 distance measure, the L_2 distance measure, the cosine distance measure, the SCD distance measure, the χ^2 distance measure and the correntropy distance measure [17].

The definition of last three distance measures are listed below,

$$D_{SCD}(X,Y) = \sum_{i=1}^{n} \frac{|x_i - y_i|}{x_i + y_i} \tag{2}$$

$$D_{\chi^2}(X,Y) = \sum_{i=1}^{n} \frac{(x_i - y_i)^2}{x_i + y_i} \tag{3}$$

$$D_{correntropy}(X,Y) = \frac{1}{n}\sum_{i=1}^{n} k_\sigma(x_i - y_i) \tag{4}$$

where $X = \{x_1, x_2, ... x_i, x_n\}$, $Y = \{y_1, y_2, ..., y_i, ... y_n\}$, $D(X,Y)$ is the distance between two vectors X and Y. In Eqn.(4), $k_\sigma(x)$ is the Gaussian kernel with kernel size σ, for a given kernel size σ, $k_\sigma(0)$ is constant. Compared to L_1 and L_2 distance measures separately, SCD and χ^2 distance measures divide the same term $x_i + y_i$, though adding complexity, the term is remarkable in helping improve the FIR precision.

3   Experimental Results and Analysis

In the case of face retrieval, we expect to explore how features and metrics affect the retrieval accuracy. It's well known that in pattern recognition and information retrieval, precision is the fraction of retrieved instances that are relevant, while recall is the fraction of relevant instances that are retrieved. To validate our results, we use the classic precision-recall curve to measure the FIR accuracy.

3.1   Experimental Settings

We assess the FIR accuracy using FRGC Version 2 database. In this database, Experiment 1 and 4 are the two databases with still face images. To evaluate the robustness of features and metrics, we choose the uncontrolled Query Set of Experiment 4 as our experiment dataset, it contains 8014 face images.

The FIR is performed on frontal face dataset of Query Set, the preprocessing procedure is described in detail in Section 2. All the face images have been aligned to the size of 140*160, examples of the experiment dataset after preprocessing are shown in Figure 3.

Fig. 3. Examples of the experiment dataset after preprocessing

There are 466 subjects in total in the Query Set, pictures each subject owns vary in the interval [2, 44]. Statistical histogram on the entire dataset is illustrated in Figure 4, our retrieval experiment is also performed on it. However, to obtain enough feedback face images during each retrieval process, we choose those persons who possess no less than 30 images as the source of query images, where there are 95 persons with 3386 face images. Thus when we carry out a FIR process, the query face images only come from the subset which contains 3386 face images, it insures enough feedback face images belong to the same class of the query image.

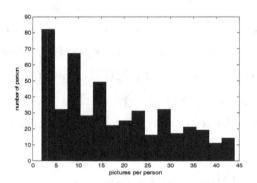

Fig. 4. Statistical histogram of Query Set on Experiment 4, FRGC Version 2

3.2   Comparative Results

To evaluate the effectiveness of features and metrics on FIR procedure, the precision-recall curve is brought as the assessment criteria. For each feature or metric itself, we perform 1,000 times random retrieval, and precision-recall curve is drawn according to the average result of the 1,000 random retrieval tests.

We compare the impact of features and metrics on FIR system in two ways. On the one hand, we compare the performance of metrics across features, on the other hand, we compare the performance of features across metrics.

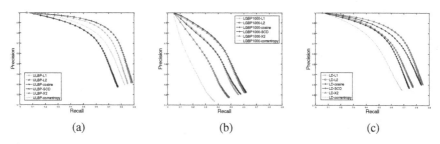

Fig. 5. Comparison between metrics on the same feature: (a) ULBP (b) LGBP1000 (c) LD

Table 2. Comparison of different metrics' precision on fixed recall points

Feature	Recall	L_1	L_2	cosine	SCD	χ^2	correntropy
ULBP	0.15	0.991	0.981	**0.979**	0.990	**0.993**	0.988
	0.30	0.972	0.936	**0.934**	0.974	**0.977**	0.956
LGBP1000	0.15	0.896	0.840	0.885	**0.936**	0.926	**0.603**
	0.30	0.730	0.571	0.722	**0.825**	0.815	**0.238**
LD	0.15	0.985	0.979	0.983	0.969	**0.986**	0.957
	0.30	0.962	0.927	0.951	0.918	**0.963**	0.879

As can be observed from Figure 5 and Table 2, for single feature, χ^2 performs best synthetically, SCD achieve relative better results on ULBP and LGBP1000 features, but not good enough in LD feature. Considering their definition equations, Eqn.(2) and Eqn.(3), under the same circumstance of dividing term $x_i + y_i$, the stability of the two metrics mainly relies on α of the numerator term $|x_i - y_i|^\alpha$, a large α will result in a better FIR performance. Thus χ^2 is more stable than SCD, which is also more suitable for FIR system requiring higher accuracy. L_1 ranks only second to χ^2, for the reason that it's of a simple expression, the computational complexity is rather low, so it goes especially well with real-time FIR system. Compared with χ^2, L_2 has a low efficiency due to the difference of not having divided term $x_i + y_i$, we believe that the role of $x_i + y_i$ is remarkable in constructing a metric. Cosine and correntropy measures perform the worst, they are unsuitable for FIR system.

It's illustrated in Figure 6 that on the overall situation, ULBP is of better performance compared with LD, and LGBP1000 comes the last. The merit of LGBP1000 is low complexity, whose dimension is far below original LGBP feature. However, it does not reach our expectation with feature selection method based on variance, the reason is that the training set is not on the FRGC database, crossing database may leads to the drop of FIR accuracy. The performance of LGBP1000 can be improved utilizing other more valid feature selection methods. ULBP which is suitable for FR is also fit for FIR, but its complexity drawback can't be ignored. LD has a dimensional advantage over the other two features, therefore, it's more suitable for FIR system with time restriction.

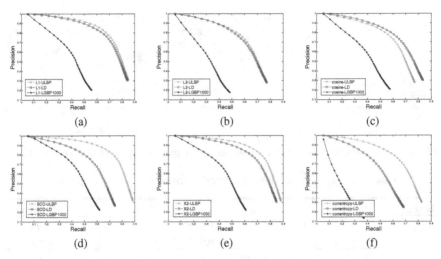

Fig. 6. Comparison between features on the same metric: (a) L_1 (b) L_2 (c) cosine (d) SCD (e) χ^2 (f) correntropy

In our previous work [17], we mainly focus on analyzing multiple metrics in LBP feature spaces for FR problem, the block-wise correntropy metric and kernel-size selection strategy proposed show advantages over other frequently adopted metrics. However, when it switches to FIR issue, the performance of correntropy distance measure drops significantly, while classic prominent χ^2 and L_1 distance measures perform consistently in the two conditions. Further, we evaluate the FIR system on different feature spaces, it proves that ULBP feature provides as high accuracy as FR condition, and the lower dimensional LD feature ensures relatively low computational complexity yet maintains precision.

4   Conclusions

In this paper, we test the overall impacts of features and metrics on FIR following the whole procedure of a FIR system. The experimental results demonstrate that the term $x_i + y_i$ is remarkable in constructing metrics, which helps to enhance FIR performance. Compared with metrics utilized in FR domain, efficiency of correntropy distance measure drops drastically in FIR procedure, while χ^2 and L_1 distance measures maintain their advantages over L_2 and cosine distance measures, SCD distance measure is unstable comparatively. Moreover, the performance of FIR system is assessed in different feature spaces, the ULBP feature achieves good results in both FR and FIR domains. In comparison with it, LD feature with lower dimensions attains high accuracy within reasonable time consumption.

Acknowledgments. The work is funded by the National Natural Science Foundation of China (No.61170155) and the Shanghai Leading Academic Discipline Project (No.J50103).

References

1. Smith, B.M., Zhu, S., Zhang, L.: Face image retrieval by shape manipulation. In: 2011 IEEE Conference on Computer Vision and Pattern Recognition (CVPR), pp. 769–776 (2011)
2. Nitta, N., Usui, A., Babaguchi, N.: Face image retrieval across age variation using relevance feedback. In: Boll, S., Tian, Q., Zhang, L., Zhang, Z., Chen, Y.-P.P. (eds.) MMM 2010. LNCS, vol. 5916, pp. 152–162. Springer, Heidelberg (2010)
3. Kiani Galoogahi, H., Sim, T.: Face photo retrieval by sketch example. In: Proceedings of the 20th ACM International Conference on Multimedia, pp. 949–952 (2012)
4. Lee, H., Chung, Y., Kim, J., Park, D.: Face image retrieval using sparse representation classifier with gabor-LBP histogram. In: Chung, Y., Yung, M. (eds.) WISA 2010. LNCS, vol. 6513, pp. 273–280. Springer, Heidelberg (2011)
5. Ruiz-del-Solar, J., Navarrete, P.: FACERET: An interactive face retrieval system based on self-organizing maps. In: Lew, M., Sebe, N., Eakins, J.P. (eds.) CIVR 2002. LNCS, vol. 2383, pp. 157–164. Springer, Heidelberg (2002)
6. Wu, B., Ai, H., Huang, C.: Facial image retrieval based on demographic classification. In: Proceedings of the 17th International Conference on Pattern Recognition, ICPR 2004, pp. 914–917 (2004)
7. Conilione, P., Wang, D.: Fuzzy Approach for Semantic Face Image Retrieval. The Computer Journal 55, 1130–1145 (2012)
8. Fang, Y., Geman, D., Boujemaa, N.: An interactive system for mental face retrieval. In: International Multimedia Conference: Proceedings of the 7th ACM SIGMM International Workshop on Multimedia Information Retrieval, pp. 193–200 (2005)
9. Vikram, T., Chidananda Gowda, K., Guru, D., Urs, S.R.: Face indexing and retrieval by spatial similarity. In: Congress on Image and Signal Processing, CISP 2008, pp. 543–547 (2008)
10. Arandjelovic, O., Zisserman, A.: Automatic face recognition for film character retrieval in feature-length films. In: IEEE Computer Society Conference on Computer Vision and Pattern Recognition, CVPR 2005, pp. 860–867 (2005)
11. Phillips, P.J., Flynn, P.J., Scruggs, T., Bowyer, K.W., Chang, J., Hoffman, K., et al.: Overview of the face recognition grand challenge. In: IEEE Computer Society Conference on Computer Vision and Pattern Recognition, CVPR 2005, pp. 947–954 (2005)
12. Bicubic interpolation in wikipedia, http://en.wikipedia.org/wiki/Bicubic_interpolation
13. Chen, X., Chen, M., Jin, X., Zhao, Q.: Face illumination transfer through edge-preserving filters. In: 2011 IEEE Conference on Computer Vision and Pattern Recognition (CVPR), pp. 281–287 (2011)
14. Ojala, T., Pietikainen, M., Maenpaa, T.: Multiresolution gray-scale and rotation invariant texture classification with local binary patterns. IEEE Transactions on Pattern Analysis and Machine Intelligence 24, 971–987 (2002)
15. Zhang, W., Shan, S., Gao, W., Chen, X., Zhang, H.: Local gabor binary pattern histogram sequence (lgbphs): A novel non-statistical model for face representation and recognition. In: Tenth IEEE International Conference on Computer Vision, ICCV 2005., pp. 786–791 (2005)
16. Cheng, G., Fang, Y., Tan, Y., Dai, W., Cai, Q.: A Local Difference coding algorithm for face recognition. In: 2011 4th International Congress on Image and Signal Processing (CISP), pp. 828–832 (2011)
17. Tan, Y., Fang, Y., Li, Y., Dai, W.: Adaptive kernel size selection for correntropy based metric. In: Park, J.-I., Kim, J. (eds.) ACCV Workshops 2012, Part I. LNCS, vol. 7728, pp. 50–60. Springer, Heidelberg (2013)

Supervised Slow Feature Analysis for Face Recognition

Xingjian Gu[*], Chuancai Liu, and Sheng Wang

School of computer science and Engineering, Nanjing University of Science and Technology
Nanjing, Jiangsu 210094, People's Republic of China
{guxingjian163,chcailiu}@163.com, 365449361@qq.com

Abstract. Slow feature analysis (SFA) is a new method based on the slowness principle and extracts slowly varying signals out of the input data. However, traditional SFA cannot be directly performed on those dataset without an obvious temporal structure. In this paper, a novel supervised slow feature analysis (SSFA) is proposed, which constructs pseudo-time series by taking advantage of the consensus information. Extensive experiments on AR and PIE face databases demonstrate superiority of our proposed method.

Keywords: slow feature analysis, consensus information, face recognition.

1 Introduction

Slow feature analysis is a new method based on slowness principle and extracts slow varying signals from times series[1].SFA was originally designed to learn invariant feature to frequent transformations. Such invariant representation of patterns would of course be ideal to cope with classification in pattern recognition problem. However, in real application many such problems do not always have a temporal structure. Thus it is necessary to reformulate the algorithm. The basic idea such as presented in[2] is to construct a large set of small pseudo-time series with only two elements chosen from patterns that belongs to the same class. The aim of the slow feature analysis[3] is to preserve the distance between nearby points in the feature space to as small as possible. It is obviously that in the ideal case the output for patterns belonging to same class is constant, thus the same class will cluster in the feature space resulting in a well performance of classification with simple techniques such as nearest-neighborhood classifier.

In many applications such as face recognition, the most common way to construct pseudo-time series has been to use the k-nearest neighborhood (k-NN) selection criterion. However, it has the tendency to include noisy pseudo-time series since a suitable parameter k is difficult to be chosen. In this paper, we propose a novel way to construct pseudo-time series using consensus information which can effectively build strong time series. Experimental results on AR face database and PIE face database show that our method is comparable.

The remaining part of this paper is arranged as follows: Section 2 provides the slow feature analysis applied on the data without an obvious temporal structure. We describe the detail of our method in section 3. Experiment and analysis are demonstrated in section 4. Conclusions are made in section 5.

---

[*] Corresponding author.

Z. Sun et al. (Eds.): CCBR 2013, LNCS 8232, pp. 178–184, 2013.
© Springer International Publishing Switzerland 2013

2   Slow Feature Analysis for Discrete Data

In this section, we describe the slow feature analysis (SFA)[2] for discrete data that does not have obvious temporal structure. Given a data set $X = \{x_1, x_2, \cdots, x_n\} \in R^{D \times n}$, and set $X_i = \{x_{ij} \mid j = 1, 2, \cdots, k\}$ is the k nearest neighbor points of x_i, the object of SFA is to find a linear transformation

$$y = W^T x, \ W \in R^{D \times d} \tag{1}$$

Such that

$$\min \Delta y = \sum_{i=1}^{n} \sum_{j=1}^{k} \left(y_i - y_{ij} \right)^2 \tag{2}$$

under the constraint $YY^T = I$, where $y_i = W^T x_i$, $Y = W^T X$ $y_{ij} = W^T x_{ij}$ and d is the dimension of feature space.

In order to solve the above objective function, it should firstly constructs a large set of short times series with only two nearby points

$$S = \{x_i, x_{ij}\}, i = 1, 2, \cdots, n \ j = 1, 2, \cdots, k \tag{3}$$

where x_{ij} is one of the k nearest neighbor points of x_i.

For the time series, the temporal variation ΔS is approximated by the time difference, where Δs_i $s_{2i} - s_{2i-1}$, $i = 1, 2, \cdots, n \times k$.

The objection function (2) can be rewritten as

$$\Delta y = \sum_{i=1}^{n} \sum_{j=1}^{k} \left(y_i - y_{ij} \right)^2 = \sum_{i=1}^{n} \sum_{j=1}^{k} \left(W^T x_i - W^T x_{ij} \right)^2 = tr \left(W^T \Delta S \Delta S^T W \right) \tag{4}$$

The minimization problem is equal to

$$\arg \min_{w} \frac{W^T A W}{W^T B W} \tag{5}$$

where $A = \Delta S \Delta S^T$ and $B = XX^T$.

3   The Details of Supervised Slow Feature Analysis (SSFA)

As it is presented in[4], the k-NN criterion graph will easily include noisy edge in the neighbor of a node, and it also has a tendency to produce noise pseudo-time series which may not in a really local neighborhood.   Inspired by the success of consensus information in clustering[5],[6] and manifold learning[7], we propose a new way to construct pseudo-time series by taking advantage of consensus information.

3.1   Consensus Matrix

In order to capture stronger relations between pairs of nodes, we define a consensus matrix in a static manner. Each item of consensus matrix, such as $C(p,q)$, indicates the probability of pairwise nodes (x_p, x_q) appear together in a local neighborhood. The process of calculating consensus matrix is summarized in algorithm 1. Such a consensus allows us to obtain a set of credible pseudo-time series, and prune out the noisy pseudo-time series even those pairwise nodes belongs to the same class (see Fig. 1). The second advantage of consensus matrix is that we could use the items of consensus as a weight to the corresponding time series, since it could favor to reveal the underlying structure of the data.

Algorithm 1. The process of producing consensus matrix
1. Initialize $C \in R^{n \times n}$ as a zero matrix
2. For $i, j - 1, 2, \cdots, n$
   (1) Compute $S_i = Knn(x_i)$ and $S_j = Knn(x_j)$
   (2) $C(i,j) = \dfrac{|S_i \cap S_j|}{K}$
3. Output consensus matrix C

Fig. 1. There are six different faces from the same individual. (a)(b) samples without any Occlusion. (c)(d)(d)(f) samples have scarf and glasses occlusion. It is obvious that it is reasonable to construct time series by ((a) (b)), ((c) (d)) and ((e) (f)). But the pairwise time series ((b) (c)) or ((d) (f)) may be noise time series even they belong to the same individual.

3.2   Our Proposed Supervised Slow Feature Analysis

Construction of Pseudo-time Series. Assume that the training samples' labels are known. We calculate consensus matrix for each class, i.e. $C_i, i = 1, 2, \cdots, K$, where K is the number of classes. The items of C_i can reflect the relationships of all pairwise points that have the same class label. For the class we set all possible combinations of two points as an initial pseudo-time series S_i^0. We sparse the pseudo-time series S_i^0 according to the consensus matrix C_i, the pairwise series (x_p, x_q) could be left only if $C_i(p,q) > \delta$, where δ is a small positive number.

Approximation of Temporal Variation. Given the pseudo-time series $S_i, i = 1, 2, \cdots, K$, where K is the number of class. As we all know the items of consensus matrix can also reveal the similarity of pairwise points. Thus we could use the items as weight to approximate the temporal variation. For any series $\left(x_p, x_q \right)$ in S_i, the Δs_{pq} is approximated by the time difference, i.e. $\Delta s_{pq} = C_i \left(p, q \right) \left(x_p - x_q \right)$. In this case, $\Delta S_i = \left\{ \Delta s_{pq} \right\}$, where x_p and x_q belong to ith class, $\Delta S = \left\{ \Delta S_i \right\}, i = 1, 2, \cdots, K$.

Alogoithm2 gives the whole algorithm, which is called supervised slow feature analysis.

Algorithm 2. Supervised slow feature analysis

1. Input: $\mathbf{X} = \left\{ \mathbf{x}_i^j \in R^D \mid i = 1, \cdots, K, j = 1, 2, \cdots, n_i \right\}$
2. Calculate consensus matrix C_i
3. Construct pseudo-time series S_i and temporal variation ΔS_i for each class according to C_i
4. Calculate A and B
5. Estimate W whose columns are the eigenvectors of $AW = \Lambda BW$ and order the columns according to the eigenvalues
6. Choose d small non-zeros eigenvalues and associated eigenvectors $U = \left(w_1, w_2, \cdots, w_d \right)$, and obtain the d-dimensional coordinates by $Y = U^T X$

---

4   Experiments and Analysis

We compare our proposed SSFA to the classic manifold learning method called Neighborhood preserving embedding (NPE)[8] and SFA using different parameter $k = 10, 15, 19$ to construct pseudo-time series. In computing consensus matrix, we set parameter k as 12 and the threshold σ as 0.5. In order to make the comparison fairly, those methods are all performed in a supervised case and a preprocessing step by PCA remaining 90% energy. The parameter k which determines the local neighborhood in NPE is set as $n_{\text{train}} - 1$, where n_{train} is the number of training samples. At last, the nearest neighbor classifier with Euclidean distance is employed to do classification task.

4.1   Experiments on the AR Database

The AR face database consists of 126 subjects with 4000 color face images as a whole. These face images were taken under varying illumination, expression and occlusions. In our experiments, we used about 3120 face images corresponding to 120 persons (60 male and 60 female), each person has 26 face images. Before implement of dimensional reduction methods, we cropped the face portion of the image into the resolution of 32×32. We perform 20 times the experiments by randomly select 20 images of each individual for training, and the rest of samples used for testing.

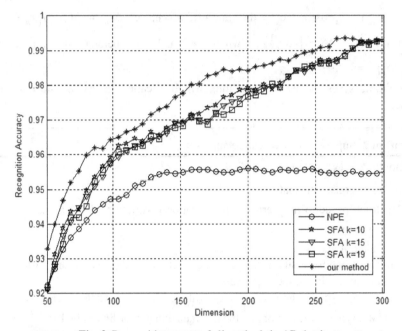

Fig. 2. Recognition curve of all methods in AR database

4.2   Experiments on the PIE Database

The CUM PIE face database contains 41,368 images from 68 individual. These images of each individual were taken under 13 different poses, 43 different illumination conditions, and with 4 different expressions. In our experiment, we select a subset contains 11,554 images of 68 individuals. Before implement our experiment, we cropped the face portion of the image into the resolution of 32×32. 20 images per person are randomly selected for training and the rest are used for testing. And we randomly repeat the experiments 20 times to obtain a static recognition rate.

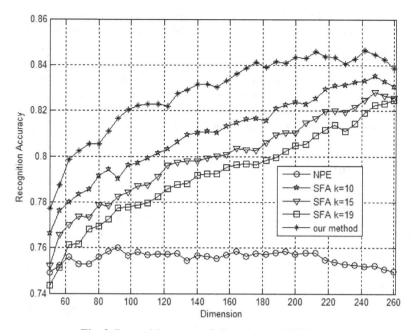

Fig. 3. Recognition curve of all methods in PIE database

4.3   Statistical Analysis

Based on random 20 times experiment as shown in Fig.2 and Fig.3, the statistical result is given in Table.1. Bold figure demonstrate the best average recognition on both AR and PIE database. By taking advantage of consensus information, some noisy pseudo-time series can be pruned out, thus SSFA (Supervised Slow Feature Analysis) proposed in our paper have a good performance in dimensionality reduction.

Table 1. The maximal average recognition rate with the standard devistion

	AR data	PIE data
NPE	95.63±0.98	76.01±1.92
SFA $k=10$	99.44±0.35	83.52±2.91
SFA $k=15$	99.44±0.35	83.03±2.95
SFA $k=19$	99.38±0.35	82.78±2.83
Our method	**99.44±0.34**	**84.63±2.46**

4.4   Experimental Observation and Discussion

Based on the two experiments presented above, a significant advantage of our method could be highlighted, i.e. the recognition rate of our method is highest. According to the result shown in fig.2, fig.3 and table 1, we can draw some conclusions: a) our method is less sensitive to the parameter k comparing to the k-nearest neighborhood selection criterion, it maybe that consensus information could help to find real time series; b) SSFA is outperform some classic manifold method, i.e. NPE. The reason maybe that our method can find "true" time series, in other words, it means that it could also explore the real local structure of the data; c)From table1, we can see that the recognition rate of our method has a relative small covariance at highest recognition rate. It demonstrates that our SSFA is more stable. In summary, the SSFA by taking advantage of consensus information is effective and robust to parameter k.

5   Conclusion

In this paper, a novel supervised slow feature analysis (SSFA) is proposed. We have identified the problem of the k-nearest neighborhood (k-NN) selection criterion to construct pseudo-time series. Consensus matrix is introduced to construct pseudo-time series to avoid some noisy time series. Experimental results show that our method is robust to parameter k, and could obtain a good recognition rate in face recognition.

Acknowledgment. This project was partially supported by National Natural Science Foundation of China (No. 61373062, No.61373063).

References

1. Wiskott, L., Sejnowski, T.J.: Slow feature analysis: unsupervised learning of invariances. Neural Computation 14, 715–770 (2002)
2. Huang, Y., Zhao, J., Tian, M., Zou, Q., Luo, S.: Slow Feature Discriminant Analysis and its application on handwritten digit recognition. In: 2009 International Joint Conference on Neural Networks, pp. 1294–1297. IEEE (2009)
3. YaPing, H., JiaLi, Z., YunHui, L., SiWei, L., Zou, Q., Tian, M.: Nonlinear dimensionality reduction using a temporal coherence principle. Information Sciences 181, 3284–3307 (2011)
4. Yang, X., Latecki, L.J.: Affinity learning on a tensor product graph with applications to shape and image retrieval. In: CVPR 2011, pp. 2369–2376. IEEE (2011)
5. Lancichinetti, A., Fortunato, S.: Consensus clustering in complex networks. Scientific reports. 2, 336 (2012)
6. Monti, S., Tamayo, P., Mesirov, J., Golub, T.: Consensus Clustering: A Resampling-Based Method for Class Discovery and Visualization of Gene Expression Microarray Data. Machine Learning 52, 91–118 (2003)
7. Premachandran, V., Kakarala, R.: Consensus of k-NNs for Robust Neighborhood Selection on Graph-Based Manifolds. In: CVPR (2013)
8. He, X., Cai, D., Yan, S., Zhang, H.-J.: Neighborhood preserving embedding. In: Tenth IEEE International Conference on Computer Vision, pp. 1208–1213. IEEE Computer Society, Washington, DC (2005)

Weight Competitive Coding
for Finger-Knuckle-Print Verification

Guangwei Gao and Jian Yang[*]

School of Computer Science and Engineering,
Nanjing University of Science and Technology,
Nanjing, P.R. China
csggao@gmail.com, csjyang@mail.njust.edu.cn

Abstract. Previous work such as Competitive coding (CompCode) has achieved promising results for online personal authentication based on Finger-knuckle-print (FKP). However, CompCode assigns the same weights for all positions when matching, which will not be stable and will be sensitive to noise, decreasing the performance of matching. In this paper, we propose a new Weighted Competitive coding (W-CompCode) scheme for effective feature matching. In feature extraction stage, we first design a weight matrix for each FKP image based on the Gabor filter response variations at each location. The locations which may have bigger variations will have bigger weights. When matching, the designed weight matrix is incorporated into the angular matching function to measure the similarity between two CompCodes. Furthermore, the weight matrix is also coded and fused with the modified Hamming distance. Experimental results on the PolyU FKP database demonstrate the effectiveness of the proposed method.

Keywords: biometrics, finger-knuckle-print, weight matrix, CompCode.

1 Introduction

Recently, the Finger-knuckle-print (FKP), as a new branch of biometric technology, has attracted increasing attention by researchers. FKP represents the inherent skin pattern of the outer surface around the phalangeal joint of one's finger, and is highly unique and rich between individuals. It can serve as a distinctive biometric identifier for online personal verification. Fig. 1(a) shows the FKP image acquisition device and the use of the system. After an FKP image is captured (as shown in Fig. 1(b)), the region of interest (ROI) is extracted from it for feature extraction and matching. Fig. 1(c) and (d) shows the ROIs of two FKP images from different fingers.

In [2], Zhang et.al applied the Gabor filtering based competitive coding (CompCode) scheme, which was first designed for palmprint verification [1], to extract and code the local orientation information as FKP features. Later, this method was extended by combining the magnitude information [3]. In [4], the Fourier

---

[*] Corresponding author.

Z. Sun et al. (Eds.): CCBR 2013, LNCS 8232, pp. 185–192, 2013.
© Springer International Publishing Switzerland 2013

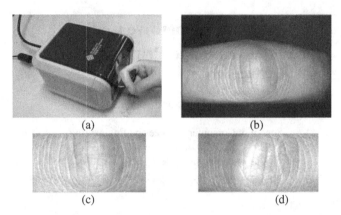

Fig. 1. (a) Outlook of The FKP image acquisition device; (b) a typical captured FKP image; (c) and (d) are two FKP ROI images extracted from different fingers

transform based band-limited phase only correlation (BLPOC) was adopted to extract the global features of FKP images. In the local-global information combination (LGIC) scheme [5], the local orientation is taken as the local feature while the Fourier transform coefficients are taken as the global features, which achieve very promising accuracy for FKP verification. In their most recent study [6], local phase and local phase congruency are integrated for more accurate recognition.

In [7], Yin et.al proposed a subspace based approach called weighted linear embedding (WLE) to extract the FKP features for recognition. In [8], a real Gabor filter was used to enhance the FKP image and the scale invariant feature transform (SIFT) was adopted to extract features. An adaptive steerable orientation coding scheme was proposed in [9], where high order steerable filters [10] was first employed to extract continuous orientation feature map, then the multilevel histogram thresholding method [11] was used to code the feature map.

The widely used CompCode is fast and effective. When matching, all positions on an image are considered as having the same importance, i.e., the same weight is assigned for each position. However, often on an FKP image, there are some pixels lying on relatively "plane" areas, i.e. these locations do not have a dominated orientation. Consequently, it is not reasonable to assign the same weight as those locations having relatively "dominated" orientation. In this paper, we propose a weighted competitive coding (W-CompCode) scheme to solve the aforementioned problem. Before feature matching, we first design a weight matrix based on the Gabor filter responses variation at each position. For those positions having dominated orientation, a relatively bigger weight is assigned and vice versa. When matching, the designed weight matrix is incorporated into the angular matching function. Thus, the difference of the importance can be well reflected. Furthermore, we also code the weight matrix, and it is fused with the modified angular matching distance. Experimental results on the PolyU FKP database show the effectiveness of the proposed method.

The rest of the paper is organized as follows. Section 2 introduces the competitive coding scheme. Section 3 describes the proposed W-CompCode method. Experiments are conducted in Section 4. Section 5 concludes the whole paper.

2   Competitive Coding (CompCode) Scheme

Gabor filters has been widely used for extracting orientation and edge information in biometric recognition systems. A 2D Gabor filter is usually defined as

$$G(x, y) = \exp\left(-\frac{1}{2}\left(\frac{x'^2}{\sigma_x^2} + \frac{y'^2}{\sigma_y^2}\right)\right) \cdot \exp\left(i2\pi f x'\right) \tag{1}$$

where $x'=x\cdot\cos\theta+y\cdot\sin\theta$, $y'=-x\cdot\sin\theta+y\cdot\cos\theta$, f is the frequency of the sinusoid factor, θ is the orientation of the normal to the parallel stripes, and σ_x and σ_y are the stand deviations of the 2D Gaussian envelop.

Denote G_R as the real part of a Gabor filter, and I_{ROI} as an FKP ROI image. With a bank of Gabor filters sharing the same parameters, except the parameter orientation, at each pixel $I_{ROI}(x,y)$, the dominant orientation feature can be extracted and coded as follows:

$$CompCode(x, y) = \arg\min_{j}\left\{I_{ROI}(x, y) * G_R(x, y, \theta_j)\right\} \tag{2}$$

where symbol * represents the convolution operation, $\theta_j=j\pi/J$, $j=\{0,...,J-1\}$, and J represents the number of different orientations.

For matching two CompCode maps P and Q, the normalized Hamming distance based angular distance is commonly used [12]:

$$HD = \frac{\sum_{x=1}^{Rows}\sum_{y=1}^{Cols}h\left(P(x, y), Q(x, y)\right)}{(J/2)S} \tag{3}$$

where S is the area of the code map, and

$$h(\alpha, \beta) = \min\left(|\alpha - \beta|, J - |\alpha - \beta|\right), \quad \alpha, \beta \in \{0,...,J-1\} \tag{4}$$

3   Weighted Competitive Coding (W-CompCode) Scheme

From the matching scheme in Eq. (3), we can observe that all positions on an image are considered as having the same importance, i.e. the same weight (1 in CompCode) is assigned to each position..

3.1   Weight Construction

Often on an FKP image, there are some pixels lying on relatively "plane" areas, i.e. these pixels do not reside on any lines and consequently do not have a dominate orientation. According, the J Gabor filter responses at such pixels do not have much variation. In such case, it is unfair to assign the same weight for each position. For robust feature matching, it is wanted that the positions having bigger filter response variation should be assigned bigger weight and vice versa.

Denote by $R=\{R_j=I_{ROI}(x,y) *G_R(x,y,\,\theta_j)\},\,j=\{0,\dots,\,J\text{-}1\}$ the Gabor filter responses at pixel (x,y). We define the "orientation magnitude" at this pixel as

$$oriMag(x,y) = \frac{abs\big(\max(R)-\min(R)\big)}{\max\big(abs\big(\max(R)\big),abs\big(\min(R)\big)\big)} \tag{5}$$

The "orientation magnitude" $oriMag(x, y)$ can measure how likely the pixel (x, y) has a dominant orientation. If it is small, we can reckon that this pixel has no dominant orientation and vice versa. Thus, $oriMag(x, y)$ can be used as a weight to measure the importance of pixel (x, y).

The "orientation magnitude" $oriMag(x, y)$ usually beyond the range [0,1]. As a weight, we expect that they are within the range [0,1]. The weight at pixel (x, y) is defined as follows:

$$W(x,y) = \frac{oriMag(x,y)-l\min}{l\max-l\min} \tag{6}$$

where $l\min = \min\limits_{(x,y)\in(Rows,Cols)}\big(oriMag(x,y)\big)$, $l\max = \max\limits_{(x,y)\in(Rows,Cols)}\big(oriMag(x,y)\big)$.

Some examples are shown in Fig. 2(c).

3.2   Matching with Weight

The original CompCode scheme adopts the normalized Hamming distance to match two CompCode code maps. In the following text, we will use HD to represent the conventional normalized Hamming distance. HD weights all positions in a code map equally. However, as discussed in Section 3.1, it is unreasonable to weights all positions equally. Instead, the code assigned to those positions having no dominant orientation will not be stable and will be sensitive to noise, decreasing the performance of matching.

According to this consideration, we propose to weight the CompCode when computing the normalized Hamming distance. With this modification, the pixel with dominant orientation can be well reflected. The modified Hamming distance can be computed as the following. Suppose that P and Q are two CompCode maps, as introduced in Section 2. Their weight matrices are W_p and W_q, respectively. Then, the modified Hamming distance, denoted by HD_M, is defined as

$$W(x,y) = \max\big(W_p(x,y),W_q(x,y)\big) \tag{7}$$

$$HD_M = \frac{\sum_{x=1}^{Rows}\sum_{y=1}^{Cols}W(x,y)\cdot h\big(P(x,y),Q(x,y)\big)}{(J/2)\sum_{x=1}^{Rows}\sum_{y=1}^{Cols}W(x,y)} \tag{8}$$

The function h has the same definition as that in Section 2. Based on our experimental results, using 6 Gabor filters of different orientations are enough. Thus, we choose 6 orientations, $\theta_j=j\pi/6,\,j=\{0,\dots,5\}$ for the competition.

Actually, the conventional CompCode matching scheme (see Eq. (3)) is a special issue of our proposed weighted matching strategy (see Eq. (8)). If we set $W(x,y)=1$, then Eq. (8) is degraded to Eq. (3). Our proposed matching scheme has accessible meanings and is more effective than Eq. (3) based on our experimental results. In addition, the process of weight construction can be accomplished together with the coding procedure. Thus, the speed of our weighted matching can be well guaranteed.

3.3   Weight Pattern Distance

From observation we find that the weight maps tend to be consistent across different code maps of the same FKP image while they different from each other in code maps from different FKP images as illustrated by examples shown in Fig. 2. This implies that further useful information can be extracted from weight maps. To this end, we propose to code the weight map and then to quantitatively measure the dissimilarity of two coded maps.

Denote by $oriMag(x, y)$ the "orientation magnitude" defined in Eq. (5), a quantization method is applied to $oriMag(x, y)$ to get the weight code. The process can be expressed as

$$wCode(x, y) = ceil\left((oriMag(x, y) - l\min) \Big/ \left(\frac{l\max - l\min}{N} \right) \right) \tag{9}$$

where $l\min$ and $l\max$ has the same definition as Eq. (6), N is the number of quantization levels. The resulting weight code is an integer within $0\sim N$. Some examples are shown in Fig. 2(d). N can be tuned by experiments on a sub-dataset and it is experimentally set as 7 in this paper.

Consider two weight codes P_w and Q_w, their weight pattern distance (WPD) is defined as

$$WPD = \frac{\sum_{x=1}^{Rows} \sum_{y=1}^{Cols} abs\left(P_w(x, y) - Q_w(x, y) \right)}{N \cdot S} \tag{10}$$

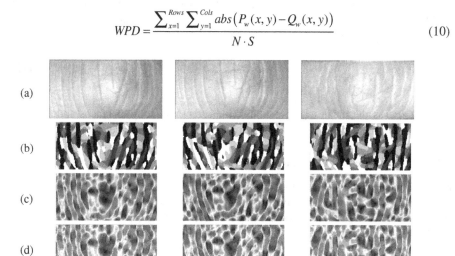

(a)

(b)

(c)

(d)

Fig. 2. (a) Sample ROI images. The first two are from the same class; (b) CompCode maps for (a); (c) weight matrices for (a); (d) weight codes for (a)

Even though *WPD* is not as powerful as HD_M, it can provide complementary information for the final decision. We can combine them together in order to create a better performance. We adopt a simple yet powerful weighted-average fusion rule to fuse HD_M and *WPD* together as

$$D = (1 - \lambda)HD_M + \lambda WPD \qquad (11)$$

where λ is a parameter to control the contribution of *WPD* to *D* and it is experimentally set as 0.15 in this paper. In the following, we refer the method using *D* to calculate the final matching distance as Weighted-CompCoce, or W-CompCode for short.

4   Experimental Results and Analysis

4.1   Database and Test Protocol

In the previous work [2-6], an FKP database was established. This database consists of the FKP region of interest (ROI) images of 4 fingers (the left index, the left middle, the right index and the right middle) from 165 volunteers. Each finger was provided 12 samples from two separated sessions with 6 samples per session, giving total of 165×4×12=7920 samples from 660 fingers. We take the images from the first session as gallery set and the images from the second session as probe set. To obtain statistical results, each image from the probe set was matched with all the images in the gallery set. A genuine matching was counted if the two images come from the same finger; otherwise, an imposter matching was counted.

The Equal Error Rate (EER), which is the point when the false accept rate (FAR) is equal to the false reject rate (FRR), is applied to evaluate the verification accuracy. A decidability index d' [13] is used to measure how well the genuine and the imposter distance are separated. d' is defined as

$$d' = \frac{|\mu_1 - \mu_2|}{\sqrt{(\sigma_1^2 + \sigma_2^2)/2}} \qquad (12)$$

where μ_1 (μ_2) is the mean of the genuine (imposter) matching distances and σ_1 (σ_2) is the standard deviation of the genuine (imposter) matching distance.

4.2   Effectiveness of Constructed Weight

In this section, we will compare the verification accuracies using *HD* and HD_M respectively to verify the effectiveness of the constructed weight matrix. Experiments are conducted on a sub-dataset containing the first 165 fingers.

The EER and d' are listed in Table 1. From the results we can see that with the constructed weight, the verification accuracy can be further improved. The drop of EER is 5.67% ((1.694-1.598)/1.694), which verify the effectiveness of the constructed weight matrix. Based on the Gabor filter responses variation, the importance of each pixel can be well reflected by the constructed weight.

Table 1. EER (%) and d' by different schemes

Method	EER	d'
HD	1.694	4.1151
HD_M	1.598	4.3573
CompCode	1.386	4.4302
W-CompCode	1.203	4.6521

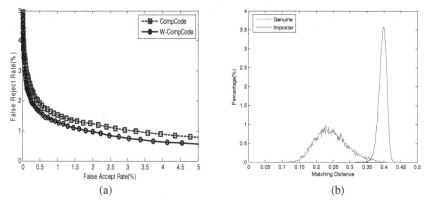

(a)   (b)

Fig. 3. (a) DET curves obtained by using CompCode and W-CompCOde; (b) distance distribution of genuine matchings and imposter matchings obtained by W-CompCOde

4.3   Performance Evaluation of W-CompCode

Compared with the original CompCode scheme, the novelty of W-CompCode lies in the matching method it adopts. In addition, it fuses the modified Hamming distance and the weight pattern distance to compute the final dissimilarity of two code maps.

In this experiment, all the classes were involved to evaluate the performance of the proposed method. Therefore, there were 3,960 images in the gallery and probe set each. The numbers of genuine matchings and imposter matchings were 23,760 and 15,657,840, respectively. The results in terms of EER and d' are summarized in Table 1. Furthermore, by adjusting the matching threshold, a DET (Detection Error Tradeoff) curve [14], which is a plot of FRR against FAR for all possible thresholds, can be created. The DET curve can reflect the overall verification accuracy of a biometric system. Fig. 3(a) shows the DET curves generated by CompCode and W-CompCode. Distance distributions of genuine matchings and imposter matchings obtained by the proposed W-CompCode are plotted in Fig. 3(b).

From the results listed in Table 1 and the DET curves shown in Fig. 3(a), we can see that W-CompCode performs better than the original ComCode. With our experimental settings, compared with the original CompCode, the drop of EER is 13.20% ((1.386-1.203)/1.386). Therefore, the experimental results clearly verify our claim that by weighting the CompCode maps and fused with the weight pattern distance, the performance of a FKP coding scheme can be largely improved.

5   Conclusions

In this paper, we develop a Weighted CompCode (W-CompCode) scheme for feature matching. Before performing angular matching, we design a weight matrix for each FKP ROI image based on the Gabor filter responses variation at each position. The positions which have bigger variations will have bigger weights. When matching, the designed weight is incorporated into the angular matching function. Furthermore, the weight is coded by a quantization method, and the Weight Pattern Distance is fused with the modified Hamming distance to form the final distance. The effectiveness of the proposed method was corroborated by experiments conducted on the benchmark PolyU FKP database.

References

1. Kong, W., Zhang, D.: Competitive coding scheme for palmprint verification. In: Proceeding of Seventeenth IEEE International Conference on Image Processing, vol. 1, pp. 520–523 (2004)
2. Zhang, L., Zhang, L., Zhang, D.: Finger-knuckle-print: a new biometric identifier. In: Proceeding of Sixteenth IEEE International Conference on Image Processing, pp. 1981–1984 (2009)
3. Zhang, L., Zhang, L., Zhang, D., Zhu, H.: Online finger-knuckle-print verification for personal authentication. Pattern Recognition 43(7), 2560–2571 (2010)
4. Zhang, L., Zhang, L., Zhang, D.: Finger-knuckle-print verification based on band-limited phase-only correlation. In: Jiang, X., Petkov, N. (eds.) CAIP 2009. LNCS, vol. 5702, pp. 141–148. Springer, Heidelberg (2009)
5. Zhang, L., Zhang, L., Zhang, D., Zhu, H.: Ensemble of local and global information for finger-knuckle-print recognition. Pattern Recognition 44(9), 1990–1998 (2011)
6. Zhang, L., Zhang, L., Zhang, D., Guo, Z.: Phase congruency induced local features for finger-knuckle-print recognition. Pattern Recognition 45(7), 2522–2531 (2012)
7. Yin, J., Zhou, J., Jin, Z., Yang, J.: Weighted linear embedding and its applications to finger-knuckle-print and palmprint recognition. In: Proceeding of International Workshop on Emerging Techniques and Challenges for Hand-Based Biometrics, pp. 1–4 (2010)
8. Morales, A., Travieso, C., Ferrer, M., Alonso, J.: Improved finger-knuckle-print authentication based on orientation enhancement. Electronics Letters 47(6), 380–381 (2011)
9. Li, Z., Wang, K., Zuo, W.: Finger-Knuckle-Print Recognition Using Local Orientation Feature Based on Steerable Filter. In: Huang, D.-S., Gupta, P., Zhang, X., Premaratne, P. (eds.) ICIC 2012. CCIS, vol. 304, pp. 224–230. Springer, Heidelberg (2012)
10. Freeman, W., Adelson, E.: The design and use of steerable filters. IEEE Transactions on Pattern Analysis and Machine Intelligence 13(9), 891–906 (1991)
11. Luessi, M., Eichmann, M., Schuster, G., Katsaggelos, A.: Framework for efficient optimal multilevel image thresholding. Journal of Electronic Imaging 18(1) (2009)
12. Zhang, D., Kong, W., You, J., Wong, M.: On-line palmprint identification. IEEE Transactions on Pattern Analysis and Machine Intelligence 25(9), 1041–1050 (2003)
13. Daugman, J.: The importance of being random: statistical principles of iris recognition. Pattern Recognition 36(2), 279–291 (2003)
14. Martin, A., Doddington, G., Kamm, T., Ordowski, M., Przybocki, M.: The DET curve in assessment of detection task performance. In: Proceeding of the Eurospeech, pp. 1895–1898 (1997)

Fingerprint Enhancement
via Sparse Representation

Xiaoduan Wang and Manhua Liu*

Department of Instrument Science and Engineering, School of EIEE, Shanghai Jiao
Tong University, Shanghai 200240, China
mhliu@sjtu.edu.cn

Abstract. Although fingerprint recognition has been widely studied for
personnel recognition in the past decades, it is still challenging problem
to achieve reliable feature extraction and recognition for poor quality
fingerprints. Fingerprint enhancement is often incorporated prior to feature extraction to improve the quality of fingerprint and achieve higher
recognition accuracy. Motivated by the recent success of sparse representation in image denoising, this paper proposes a fingerprint enhancement
method by using sparse representation. First, a set of Gabor basis functions with various orientations and frequencies are used to build a redundant dictionary for fingerprint representation. Then, the fingerprint
enhancement problem is modeled as an iterative sparse representation of
the local patch fingerprint, which can be solved by L_1-norm regularized
minimization. Experimental results and comparison on FVC fingerprint
databases are presented to show the effectiveness of the proposed method
on fingerprint enhancement, especially for poor quality fingerprints.

Keywords: Fingerprint enhancement, Sparse representation, Gabor
basis function.

1 Introduction

With the increasing demand of information security, fingerprint recognition has
been widely investigated for personnel recognition, because of its advantages
such as the convenience of data collection and high level of user acceptabil-
ity [10]. Fingerprint is a kind of human biometrics on finger tips composed of
interleaved parallel ridge and valley flows. In developing automatic fingerprint
identification system (AFIS), much efforts have been made on developing new
feature extraction and classification approaches to improve fingerprint recognition accuracy. However, the performance of fingerprint feature extraction and
recognition critically depends on the image quality. An ideal fingerprint image
usually has high contrast and well-defined ridge and valley as shown in Fig. 1a.

In practice, due to various skin conditions (e.g., wet or dry, cuts and bruises),
sensor noise and incorrect finger pressure etc., a significant number of fingerprint
images are of poor quality with blurred and corrupted ridge structure as shown

---

* Corresponding author.

Z. Sun et al. (Eds.): CCBR 2013, LNCS 8232, pp. 193–200, 2013.

in Fig. 1 b and c [10]. The degradations make the extraction of the friction ridge details extremely difficult. In extraction of minutiae features, the fingerprint degradations often results in generation and extraction of spurious minutiae points, missing genuine minutiae points, and also introducing large errors in the locations (positions and orientations) of minutiae points [10,7]. The spurious feature extraction will change the individuality of input fingerprint during the recognition process. Thus, image enhancement is necessary to remove the noise and improve the clarity of ridge and valley structure for more reliable subsequent feature extraction and matching [7,3,4].

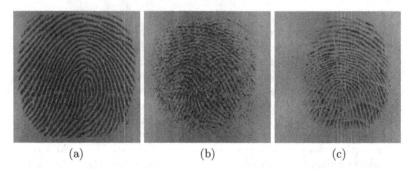

     (a)   (b)   (c)

Fig. 1. (a) Good-quality fingerprint, (b) overlapped poor-quality fingerprint and (c) poor-quality fingerprint with creases and scars

    The interleaved ridges and valleys in a gray-level fingerprint image form a sinusoidal-shaped plane wave in a local neighborhood, which has a well-defined frequency and orientation. A number of methods have been proposed to take advantage of this information to enhance fingerprint image [7,3,4,11]. Gabor filters, which have both frequency and orientation selective properties and optimal joint space frequency resolution, are the most commonly used filtering technique for fingerprint enhancement [7,3]. A Gabor filter is defined by a sinusoidal plane wave tapered by a Gaussian which can capture the periodic, yet non-stationary nature of fingerprint regions and form a very intuitive representation of fingerprint images. In this method, the dominant ridge orientation and the average ridge frequency are first estimated at each pixel based on its local neighborhood. Then a Gabor filter tuned to the local ridge orientation and frequency is applied at the pixel. This method can successfully suppress the noise on the ridges and remove the creases if the Gabor filter is tuned to the correct local orientation and frequency. However, there are several limitations in this method. First, it is still a challenging problem to reliably estimate the local ridge orientation and frequency in the poor-quality fingerprint region. Second, in the singular regions, the assumption of a single dominant ridge orientation is not valid. As a result, the filters with fixed orientation will be likely to destroy the ridge structure and lead to spurious ridge artifacts. Third, since the ridge orientation and frequency are usually estimated at block wise, there is block effect on the enhanced fingerprint image.

Another interesting technique has been proposed to perform fingerprint enhancement based on short Fourier transform (STFT) analysis in the Fourier domain which did not require to explicitly compute the local ridge orientation and ridge frequency [4]. The traditional one dimensional time-frequency analysis is extended to two dimensional fingerprint images to perform short (time/space)-frequency analysis. The Fourier spectrum of a local small region is analyzed and probabilistic estimates of the ridge orientation and frequency are computed. In addition, an energy map can be generated to distinguish between the fingerprint and the background regions.

The main challenging problem for fingerprint enhancement is to remove the image noise while reliably representing the ridge details especially in singular region. Redundant and sparse representation is a promising method for image reconstruction especially from noisy image. The study of sparse representations has become a major field of research in signal processing [2,5]. As a powerful statistical image modeling technique, sparse representation has been successfully used in denoising of signals [5]. In this paper, we propose a fingerprint enhancement approach through using sparse and redundant representation. First, Gabor basis functions with various parameters are used to build a redundant dictionary. Then, L_1-norm regularized optimization is applied to find the sparse representation of a local image patch. Finally, fingerprint image is reconstructed by a linear combination of the Gabor basis atoms and sparse coefficients.

2   Fingerprint Enhancement via Sparse Representation

We assume that all fingerprint images have been scanned with 256 gray scales at a resolution of 500 *dpi*. The objective of fingerprint enhancement algorithm is to remove the image noise and improve the clarity of ridge structures of fingerprint images. Thus, fingerprint enhancement can be considered as an image denoising or restoration problem. The fingerprint image in a local neighborhood can be considered as 2D signals which have well-defined ridge orientation and frequency. Mathematically speaking, an real valued signal $y \in \Re^N$ can be represented by a linear combination of a set of N-dimensional basis atoms:

$$y = \sum_i \alpha_i \psi_i + e = \Phi\alpha + e, \tag{1}$$

where $\Phi = [\psi_1, \psi_2, ..., \psi_M] \in R^{N \times M}$ is a dictionary composed of a collection of basis vectors; $\alpha = [\alpha_1, \alpha_2, ..., \alpha_M]$ denotes the basis coefficient vector; e denotes the additive noise imposed on the signal. The dictionary Φ can be built with a set of analytical basis functions such as curvelet, wavelets and sinusoids, or learned from example image patches. To achieve good representation, dictionary should characterize the image structures.

Given a dictionary Φ and an image patch $y \in \Re^N$, the convolution method is usually used to calculate the coefficients, but it suffers from nonorthogonality and crosstalk among the basis filters. As a local image patch generally has a specific orientation and frequency, the coefficients are thus expected to be sparse, i.e., with only few nonzero values. Inspired by recent progress and success in sparse representation, we model the fingerprint enhancement as a sparse representation problem. In sparse representation, the dictionary is redundant with $N < M$ and most entries of the coefficient vector α are zero or close to zero. If the sparsity is measured as the L_0-norm of α, which counts the non-zero coefficients, the sparse representation can be formulated as the l_0-norm regularized minimization:

$$\widehat{\alpha} = arg \min_{\alpha} \|y - \Phi\alpha\|_2 + \lambda\|\alpha\|_0 \qquad (2)$$

where λ is a regularization parameter which balances the sparsity of solution and fidelity of the approximation to y. Generally speaking, the fingerprint enhancement via sparse representation involves two steps, i.e., dictionary construction and sparse representation, which will be detailed in the following sections.

2.1   Gabor Dictionary Construction

The sinusoidal-shaped waves of ridges and valleys in fingerprint image vary slowly in a local constant orientation. Gabor filters have both frequency and orientation selective properties and have optimal joint resolution in both spatial and frequency domains [7]. Gabor basis functions form a very intuitive representation of fingerprint images since they capture the periodic, yet non-stationary nature of fingerprint regions. Therefore, it is appropriate to use Gabor basis functions to model the local patch of fingerprint images. The even-symmetric Gabor filter has the general form as:

$$h(x, y, \theta, f) = exp\{-\frac{1}{2}[\frac{x_\theta^2}{\delta_x^2} + \frac{y_\theta^2}{\delta_y^2}]\} \cos(2\pi f x_\theta + \varphi_0), \qquad (3)$$

$$x_\theta = x \cos\theta + y \sin\theta, \qquad (4)$$

$$y_\theta = -x \sin\theta + y \cos\theta, \qquad (5)$$

where θ is the orientation of Gabor filter; f is the frequency of a sinusoidal plane wave; δ_x and δ_y are the space constants of the Gaussian envelope along x and y axes, respectively; φ_0 is the initial phase angle of Gabor filter. To build the basis atoms of the dictionary, we set $\delta_x = \delta_y$ equal to the patch size. f varies from 5 to 15 at a step of 2 and θ varies from 0 to $15\pi/16$ at a step of $\pi/16$. φ_0 varies from 0 to $4\pi/5$ at a step of $\pi/5$. Each filter is preprocessed to have a zero mean and L_2 norm of 1. Finally, all the filters are used to construct the dictionary Φ for sparse fingerprint representation. Fig. 2 shows the Gabor dictionary elements.

2.2   Fingerprint Enhancement

In a local patch of fingerprint image, the configurations of parallel ridges and valleys with well-defined frequency and orientation provide useful information which helps in removing undesired noise and restore the high-quality fingerprint. Inspired by recent progress and success in sparse representation, we model the

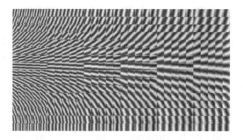

Fig. 2. The redundant dictionary used for sparse fingerprint representation, which consists of 480 Gaussian filters at 16 orientations, 6 frequencies and 5 φ_0

fingerprint enhancement as a sparse representation problem with the Gabor dictionary. Given the dictionary Φ described above, for each patch of fingerprint image, a sparse representation can be obtained by solving the optimization problem in Equation 2. However, this is a nonconvex problem and cannot be efficiently solved. In practice, convex relaxation is usually adopted to change the Equation 2 into a convex optimization problem by replacing the L_0-norm regularization with the L_1-norm regularization as:

$$\widehat{\alpha} = arg \min_{\alpha} \|y - \Phi\alpha\|_2 + \lambda \cdot \|\alpha\|_1 \qquad (6)$$

There are a wide variety of methods proposed for the above least squares optimization [5,8]. In this work, the efficient method in [8] is employed to solve this convex optimization problem. A sparse coefficient vector will be obtained and the local patch of fingerprint image can be reconstructed by $y = \Phi\alpha$. The patches are processed in raster-scan order in the fingerprint, from left to right and top to down, to generate an enhanced fingerprint image.

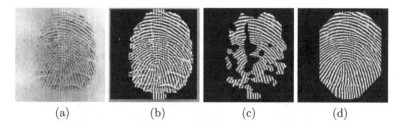

| (a) | (b) | (c) | (d) |

Fig. 3. The enhancement of a poor quality fingerprint (a) original image; (b) enhanced fingerprint in the first round of reconstruction; (c) good-quality fingerprint region separated by the consistency measure; (d) the final enhanced fingerprint

Solving the above minimization problem does not guarantee the consistency of the reconstructed fingerprint image. In addition, patch-based processing approaches are associated with spurious artifacts caused by discontinuities at the block boundaries. The consistency of the squared gradients was introduced to give a good measure of how well the gradients over a neighborhood are pointing in the same direction [1]. In our enhancement scheme, we utilize a consistency measure to measure the image quality of the reconstructed fingerprint. For the poor-quality regions, we will further iteratively and gradually to restore the image patches with the sufficient neighboring good quality image. The processing steps of the proposed fingerprint enhancement method are outlined in Algorithm 1. Fig. 3 shows the original fingerprint image, the intermediate results and the final enhancement result of the proposed method. It can be seen that the poor-quality fingerprint regions are enhanced while the quality of image reconstruction around the singularities is not affected.

Algorithm 1. Fingerprint Enhancement via Sparse Representation

---

1: **Input:** Φ: Gabor dictionary; Y: the original fingerprint image.
2: **For** each 16×16 image patch y of Y, starting from the upper-left corner with 4 pixel forward image step.

  - Normalize the image patch y to to have unit L_2-norm.
  - Solve the minimization problem in Equation (6) with Φ and y.
  - Generate the good-quality image patch $\widehat{y} = \Phi\alpha$.

3: **End**
4: Compute the consistency of the squared gradients as in [1] denoted as *cons*. Separate the image regions with *cons* < 0.8 as the poor-quality regions S_p.
5: **while** $S_p \neq \emptyset$ **do**
6:   For the image patch with the portion of good-quality image pixels larger than 50%, normalize the image patch y to have unit L_2-norm.
7:   Solve the minimization problem in Equation (6) with Φ and y.
8:   Generate the good-quality image patch $\widehat{y} = \Phi\alpha$.
9: **end while**
10: **Output:** The enhanced fingerprint image $\widehat{Y}$.

---

3   Experimental Results

To evaluate the performance, we conduct the experiments on fingerprint verification competition (FVC) databases and compare our proposed method to some state-of-arts. First, some poor-quality fingerprint samples are tested with the proposed fingerprint enhancement method. The enhancement results of the poor-quality images from FVC database are shown in Fig. 3. In comparison, the proposed method perform better to remove the noise and improve the clarity of ridge structures of fingerprint images than other methods.

While the effect of fingerprint enhancement may be gauged visually, the final objective of the enhancement process is to increase the fingerprint recognition accuracy. Thus, we conduct the verification experiments with the enhanced fingerprints on FVC2004 DB3_a [9] to test the performance improvement. This database consists of 800 fingerprint images of 500 *dpi* with 8 impressions for each finger. The NIST fingerprint software [6] is used for feature extraction

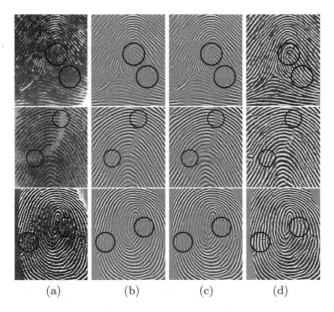

| (a) | (b) | (c) | (d) |

Fig. 4. Comparison of the enhancement results on some poor-quality fingerprints (a) original image; (b) by Gabor filter; (c) by STFT method; (d) by our proposed method

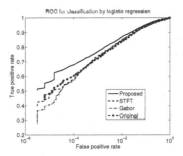

Fig. 5. ROCs comparison by different enhancement methods on FVC2004 DB3_a

and matching. The FVC protocol is adopted to evaluate the verification performance, which involves 2800 ($800 \times 7/2$) genuine trials and 4950 ($100 \times 99/2$) imposter trials for the database. The verification performance is evaluated with the plot of receiver operating characteristics (ROC) curve, which is a plot of the false positive rate (FPR) against the true positive rate (TPR). FPR determines how many incorrect positive results occur among all available negative samples whereas TPR defines how many instances are correctly matched among all available positive samples. Fig. 5 shows the comparison of ROCs with the enhanced fingerprints by the Gabor filter, STFT method and our proposed method, as well as with the original fingerprints. Comparing the ROCs, we can see that our proposed method achieves better verification performance than other methods.

4   Conclusion

In this paper, we have proposed a fingerprint enhancement method via sparse representation. First, a set of Gabor basis functions with various orientations and frequencies are used to build a redundant dictionary for sparse fingerprint representation. Then, L_1-norm based sparse representation is used to reconstruct the local fingerprint patch. Finally, experimental results and comparison on FVC fingerprint database have been presented to show the effectiveness of the proposed method, especially for enhancement of poor quality fingerprints, in comparison with some existing methods.

Acknowledgment. This work was partially supported by National Natural Science Foundation of China under the grant No. 61005024, 61105022, 61375112.

References

1. Bazen, A.M., Gerez, S.H.: Systematic methods for the computation of the directional fields and singular points of fingerprints. IEEE Trans. on Pattern Analysis and Machine Intelligence 24(7), 905–919 (2002)
2. Cands, E.J., Tao, T.: Near optimal signal recovery from random projections: Universal encoding strategies? IEEE Trans. on Information Theory 52(12), 5406–5425 (2006)
3. Cappelli, R., Maio, D., Maltoni, D.: Semi-automatic enhancement of very low quality fingerprints. In: Proceedings of 6th International Symposium on Image and Signal Processing and Analysis, Salzburg (2009)
4. Chikkerur, S., Cartwright, A.N., Govindaraju, V.: Fingerprint enhancement using stft analysis. Pattern Recognition 40(1), 198–211 (2007)
5. Elad, M., Aharon, M.: Image denoising via sparse and redundant representations over learned dictionaries. IEEE Trans. Image Processing 15(12), 3736–3745 (2006)
6. Garris, M.D., Watson, C.I., McCabe, R.M., Wilson, C.L.: User's guide to nist fingerprint image software. National Institute of Science and Technology (2001)
7. Hong, L., Wan, Y., Jain, A.K.: Fingerprint image enhancement: Algorithm and performance evaluation. IEEE Trans. on Pattern Analysis and Machine Intelligence 20(8), 777–789 (1998)
8. Lee, H., Battle, A., Raina, R., Ng, A.: Efficient sparse coding algorithms. In: Advances in Neural Information Processing Systems (NIPS), pp. 801–808 (2007)
9. Maio, D., Davide Maltoni, R., Cappelli, R., Wayman, J.L., Jain, A.K.: FVC 2004: Third fingerprint verification competition. In: Proceedings of International Conference on Biometric Authentication, Hong Kong, pp. 1–7 (July 2004)
10. Maltoni, D., Maio, D., Jain, A.K., Prabhakar, A.: Handbook of Fingerprint Recognition. Springer, New York (2003)
11. Zhao, Q., Zhang, L., Zhang, D., Huang, W., Bai, J.: Curvature and singularity driven diffusion for oriented pattern enhancement with singular points. In: CVPR, Florida, USA, pp. 2129–2135 (2009)

Real-Time Rolled Fingerprint Construction Based on Key-Column Extraction

Yongliang Zhang, Shanshan Fang, Yingjie Bian, and Yuanhong Li

Department of Computer Science and Technology, Zhejiang University of Technology,
No.288, Liuhe Road, Hangzhou, Zhejiang, China
titanzhang@zjut.edu.cn

Abstract. Fingerprint identification is an important biometric method for personal authentication. Rolled fingerprint can provide much more information than flat fingerprint, so the method is needed for construct a rolled fingerprint from a plain fingerprint sequence. Based on Key-column extraction, a real-time image mosaicking algorithm is proposed for rolled fingerprint construction. Compared to other construction methods, experimental results show that the proposed algorithm leads to a better performance, especially when the finger is rolling with a fast speed.

Keywords: Rolled fingerprint, Image mosaic, Key-column extraction.

1 Introduction

Fingerprint is one of the most important features for automated personal authentication [1][2]. A rolled fingerprint is often used in automated fingerprint identification systems (AFIS) for law enforcement agencies during enrollment while a flat fingerprint is commonly used in civil fingerprint applications, as the rolled fingerprint contains almost all the surface information of the finger, and it provides a higher degree of certainty for identification purposes compared to a flat fingerprint[3].

To compose the sequence of images of the rolling finger into a single unwrapped impression, some algorithms for rolled fingerprint construction have been proposed in the literature [4][5][6]. In [4], five image-compositing schemes are used to synthesize rolled fingerprint image sequences. The method consists of several steps including foreground estimation of the fingerprint, pixel-wise confidence estimation using the foreground of each image, and image composition using a confidence measure. In [5], the local affine transformations between two neighboring image sequences are estimated. The method has several steps including computation of the spatial shift, detection of the mosaicking point, partitioning of the tip part, and removal of the seams on the tip. In [6], MRF-based nonrigid image registration is used to find dense correspondences between images from a rolled fingerprint sequence. This method is significantly superior in various aspects compared to the two previous methods, because this method can generate conceptually more accurate rolled fingerprints by preserving the geometric properties of the finger surface. However, it does not work

Z. Sun et al. (Eds.): CCBR 2013, LNCS 8232, pp. 201–207, 2013.

in real-time manner, as this method finds dense correspondences between image frames from rolled sequences and registers every image frame to the reference image, which is defined as a frame containing a fingerprint positioned at the center. Motivated by the idea of the reference frame, a real-time rolled fingerprint construction algorithm is proposed in this paper, which is based on Key-column extraction. Key-column is defined as the column with the minimum background pixels among all the frames of the rolled fingerprint sequence. Compared to previous algorithms, experiments show that the proposed algorithm is superior, especially when the finger is rolling with a fast speed.

This paper proposes a novel rolled fingerprint construction method based on Key-column extraction. Section 2 explains the overall procedure and describes the proposed algorithm in detail, which is the main part of this paper. In Section 3, various compared experiments are introduced.

2   Algorithm

Suppose the finger is rolled from nail to nail on the capture plane, an image sequence $I = \{I_1, I_2, \cdots, I_K\}$ of rolled fingerprint is captured. A typical image sequence of rolled fingerprints is shown in Fig.1. Let I_i denote the ith frame of I, and I_0 be the background frame captured when no finger is placed on the sensor. Supposing that $I_i(x, y)$ denote the gray level of the pixel (x, y) and $W \times H$ is the size of each frame, where H is the height of the frame, while W is the width. As shown in Fig.2, the main steps of this construction algorithm are finger detection, image mosaicking, quality evaluation and performance optimization.

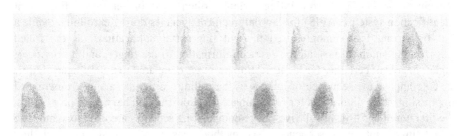

Fig. 1. Image sequence of rolled fingerprint

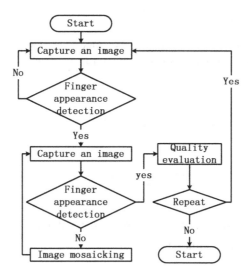

Fig. 2. The flowchart of the proposed algorithm

2.1   Finger Detection

Image capture is a process that the finger places on the sensor, rolls from nail to nail, and lifts from the sensor. It's important to detect the states of the finger, so that it can clearly certain the acquisition process. There are two different states for finger detection, finger appearance detection when the finger is firstly placed on the sensor and finger disappearance detection when the finger is firstly lifted from the sensor after rolling. Let $N(I_i)$ denotes the number that the difference of gray values between the ith frame and the background frame is larger than the given threshold T_1. And $\Gamma(h_1, h_2)$ represents the number that the gray value is between h_1 and h_2. Two control variables $N(I_i)$ and $\Gamma(h_1, h_2)$ are introduced:

$$N(I_i) = \left| \left\{ (x, y) \mid |I_i(x, y) - I_0(x, y)| > T_1 \right\}_{\substack{1 \le x \le W \\ 1 \le y \le H}} \right| .$$
(1)

$$\Gamma(h_1, h_2) = \sum_{h_1 \le h \le h_2} H_i(h) .$$
(2)

h_1 and h_2 are two parameters, $|\{\bullet\}|$ is the number of the elements in the set, and H_i is the histogram of I_i. If $N(I_i) > \alpha HW$, the finger appears; if $\Gamma(h_1, h_2) > \beta(h_2 - h_1)$, the finger disappear. Here, α and β are two given coefficients.

2.2   Image Mosaicking

Every column of the constructed image is extracted from one of the image sequence. This step is to describe the extraction rule. First, two parameters $C_i(j)$ and $F_i(j)$ are given as follows:

$$C_i(j) = \left| \{(x,y) \mid I_i(x,y) > T_2\}_{\substack{j-1 \le x \le j+1 \\ 1 \le y \le H}} \right| . \tag{3}$$

$$F_i(j) = \sum_{\substack{j-1 \le x \le j+1 \\ 1 \le y \le H}} I_i(x,y) . \tag{4}$$

where T_2 is a given threshold. Different to that defined in [1], the reference frame of the proposed algorithm is defined as follows:

$$\{i_o, j_0\} = \arg \min_{\substack{1 \le i < K \\ 2 \le j \le W-1}} \{C_i(j) \wedge F_i(j)\} . \tag{5}$$

where $\wedge$ denotes logical AND, I_{i_0} is extracted as the reference frame. The j_0 column of I_{i_0} is called as the reference column and extracted as the j_0 column of the constructed rolled fingerprint, noted as $\Bbbk(j_0) = i_0$. Suppose the finger is in a left-to-right rolling process, the $(j_0 - 1)$ column of I_{i_0-1} is extracted $(\Bbbk(j_0 - 1) = i_0 - 1)$, if $C_{i_0}(j_0 - 1) > C_{i_0-1}(j_0 - 1)$; otherwise, $\Bbbk(j_0 + 1) = i_0$. By the same token, the extraction results $\{\Bbbk(j_0)\}_{1 \le j \le W}$ are evaluated and each extracted column is called Key-column.

2.3   Quality Evaluation

The quality $Q(I_R)$ of the constructed image I_R is evaluated as follows:

$$Q(I_R) = \gamma A(I_R) + \delta V(I_R) . \tag{6}$$

where $A(I_R)$ is the proportion of the area of the foreground of I_R to the whole area of I_R, $V(I_R)$ is the normalized variance, γ and δ are two weight coefficients. If $Q(I_R) < T_3$, the construction will be repeated; T_3 is a given threshold.

2.4   Performance Optimization

In order to improve the calculation speed and the construction effect, the following optimization processes are done.

(1) Support finger rollback: suppose the finger is rolling from left to right, the finger is rolling back if one of the following two inequations is satisfied:

$$x_m - x_i > \varepsilon T_4 \tag{7}$$

$$x_m - x_i > T_4 \wedge x_m - x_{i-1} > T_4 \wedge x_m - x_{i-2} > T_4 \tag{8}$$

where $m = \arg\min_t \{x_t \,|\, 1 \le t \le i-1\}$ and x_i is the x-coordinate of the centroid point of I_i, ε is a given coefficient and T_4 is a given threshold. If rollback happens, a new construction is starting.

(2) Ignore redundant frames: the kth frame I_k is ignored, if $|x_i - x_k| < T_5$, where x_k is the x-coordinate of the centroid point of I_k and T_5 is a given threshold. Experiments show that about 22% frames of a rolled fingerprint sequence are ignored when the rolling speed is slow (more than 3s).

(3) Reduce construction seams: according to the y-coordinate of the centroid point, every frame I_i is divided into two parts, the upper portion I_i^U and the lower portion I_i^B. So two image sequences are yielded, $\{I_i^U\}_{1 \le i \le K}$ and $\{I_i^B\}_{1 \le i \le K}$. And the corresponding extraction results $\{\Bbbk(j)\}_{1 \le i \le K}^U$ and $\{\Bbbk(j)\}_{1 \le i \le W}^B$ are evaluated, respectively. As shown in Fig.3, this step can reduce construction seams caused by the elastic distortion when the finger is placed and rolled on the sensor.

(4) Remove remaining fingerprint: as shown in Fig.3, remaining fingerprint may have tremendous consequences for the rolled construction. When the gray difference between $I_R(x, y)$ and $I_0(x, y)$ is less than a given threshold T_6, the pixel (x, y) is considered as one remaining fingerprint pixel, that is to say, if $|I_R(x, y) - I_0(x, y)| < T_6$, then $I_R(x, y) = T_6$.

Fig. 3. Left constructed by the proposed algorithm, middle constructed without seams removal, right constructed without remaining fingerprint removal

3   Experimental Results

To evaluate the proposed construction algorithm, a HighLand PU-JY301U roll fingerprint sensor (each frame with 640×640 pixels and 500 dpi) is used [7]. For the rolled image sequences, databases of 290 independent fingers are created. For each finger, eight rolled impressions (four with fast rolling and four with proper rolling) are acquired under the following conditions: 1)a fast rolling speed (less than 2s); 2)a proper rolling speed (more than 2s). Six constructed roll databases (referred to as D_{A1}, D_{A2}, D_{B1}, D_{B2}, D_{C1}, D_{C2}) are yielded with the proposed algorithm (called algo-A), the algorithm proposed in [5] (called algo-B) and the algorithm described in [6] (called algo-C), respectively. For example, D_{A1} represents the database that acquired with a fast rolling speed and constructed by algo-A. For algo-B, the smoothed compositing method is applied, because this method has better matching performance than the other four methods (Naive, Center, Minimum and Foreground), as shown in the experiments in [3]. For algo-A, the parameters are used as shown in Table 1. As shown in Table 2, the average processing time of algo-A for one frame is less than that of the other three construction methods.

Table 1. Setting of parameters in algo-A

T_1	T_2	T_3	T_4	T_5	T_6	
20	240	70	10	10	10	
α	β	γ	δ	ε	h_1	h_2
0.05	100	0.5	0.5	3	100	200

Table 2. Average processing time for one frame

algo-A	algo-B	algo-C	the algorithm in [1]
13.66*ms*	50.80*ms*	59.80*ms*	1906.00*ms*

As the purpose of rolled fingerprint construction is to increase the accuracy of fingerprint recognition, it is important to check the matching performance [1]. In this paper, equal error rate (EER) is used to assess the recognition accuracy, which denotes the error rate when the false acceptance rate (FAR) and the false reject rate (FRR) are identical. A straightforward method is applied on the constructed roll fingerprint images, consisting of minutiae extraction and minutiae matching [8]. As shown in Table 3, the proposed construction algorithm leads to a better recognition performance than the other two, especially when the finger is rolling with a fast speed.

Table 3. Comparisons between algo-A, algo-B and algo-C

Algorithm	Database	EER	Database	EER
algo-A	D_{A1}	0.30%	D_{A2}	0.23%
algo-B	D_{B1}	0.70%	D_{B2}	0.52%
algo-C	D_{C1}	0.58%	D_{C2}	0.45%

4   Conclusions

Based on Key-column extraction, a real-time rolled fingerprint construction algorithm is proposed in this paper. Compared to two previous construction algorithms, experimental data validate that the performance of the proposed algorithm is superior, especially when the finger is rolling with a fast speed.

Acknowledgments. This work is supported by the International Cooperative Project of the Science Technology Department of Zhejiang Province (2012C24009).

References

1. Jain, A.K., Bolle, R., Pankanti, S.: Biometrics Personal Identification in Network Society. Kluwer, Boston (1999)
2. Miller, B.: Vital signs of identity. IEEE Spectrum 31(2), 22–30 (1994)
3. Kwon, D., Yun Il, D., Lee, S.U.: Rolled Fingerprint Construction Using MRF-Based Nonrigid Image Registration. IEEE Transactions on Image Processing 19(12), 3255–3270 (2010)
4. Ratha, N.K., Connell, J.H., Bolle, R.M.: Image Mosiacing for Rolled Fingerprint Construction. In: Proc. Int. Conf. Pattern Recognit., pp. 1651–1653 (1998)
5. Zhou, J., He, D., Rong, G.: Effective algorithm for rolled fingerprint construction. Electron. Lett. 37(8), 492–494 (2001)
6. Choi, K., Choi, H. s., Kim, J.H.: Fingerprint Mosaicking by Rolling and Sliding. In: Kanade, T., Jain, A., Ratha, N.K. (eds.) AVBPA 2005. LNCS, vol. 3546, pp. 260–269. Springer, Heidelberg (2005)
7. HighLand., PU-JY301U roll fingerprint sensor, http://www.bjhlxt.com
8. Jain, A., Hong, L., Bolle, R.: On-Line Fingerprint Verification. IEEE Trans. Pattern Anal. Mach. Intell. 19(4), 302–314 (1997)

Latent Fingerprint Recognition: Challenges and Advances

Wei Guo and Yunqi Tang*

School of Criminal Science and Technology,
People's Public Security University of China, Beijing, 100038, China
guowei1@ppsuc.edu.cn, yunqi.tang@gmail.com

Abstract. Latent fingerprint recognition is desirable for forensics applications such as criminal investigation and forensic detection. Compared to traditional fingerprint recognition, automatic latent fingerprint recognition is more challenging because it must be able to deal with the smudgy, fragmentary and nonlinearly deformed fingerprints lifted from crime scenes and it has high liability for following legal procedures. In latent fingerprint recognition, latent fingerprint development draws little attention from pattern recognition due to that latent fingerprint development is traditionally regarded as a topic of forensic medical. In practice, latent fingerprint development is a pre-step of latent fingerprint recognition, whose result would cause dramatic influence to the performance of latent fingerprint recognition system. In this paper, we claim that latent fingerprint development is important to automatic latent fingerprint recognition system, and regard research of the relationship between latent fingerprint development and automatic latent fingerprint recognition system as a new topic. Moreover, we summarize the challenges, and provide critical analysis of the advances of automatic latent fingerprint recognition.

Keywords: Latent fingerprint recognition, Challenges, Latent fingerprint development, Latent-to-full fingerprint matching.

1 Introduction

Fingerprint recognition is one of the most well-known biometrics, which has been widely applied in access control, population management, criminal investigation, immigration, etc.. And it is considered that fingerprint recognition is a well analyzed problem due to many successful methods achieving low equal error rate even on challenging databases like the FVC2004 [1] and FVC2006 [2] which includes non-ideal or perturbed prints. However, there also some challenges within fingerprint recognition. Automatic latent fingerprint recognition is one of the most challenging problems.

Latent fingerprint refers to the fingerprint found at crime scenes. In forensic[3], the fingerprints found at crime scenes are categorized as patent, latent, and

---

* Corresponding author.

Z. Sun et al. (Eds.): CCBR 2013, LNCS 8232, pp. 208–215, 2013.

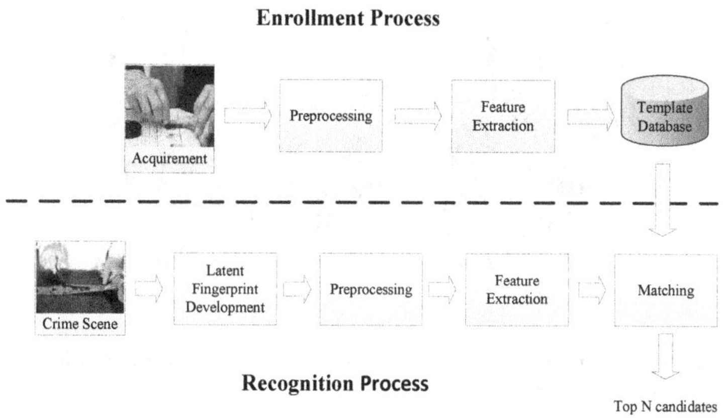

Enrollment Process

Recognition Process

Top N candidates

Fig. 1. Latent fingerprint recognition process

plastic impressions. A patent print is simply a visible print, a latent print is undetectable until brought out with a physical or chemical process designed to enhance latent print residue, and a plastic print is created when the substrate is pliable enough at the time of contact to record the three-dimensional aspects of the friction skin. Routinely, all three types are associated with the term latent print.

Latent fingerprint recognition is the ability to establish a suspect's identity based on his or her latent fingerprints. Fig.1 shows the basic processes of a latent fingerprint recognition system. In enrollment process, the rolled or plain fingerprints, which are captured from prisoners or suspects, are enrolled into the system. A rolled fingerprint image, shown as Fig.2(a), is obtained by rolling a finger from one side of the fingernail to the other in order to record all of the ridge details. And a plain image, shown as Fig.2(b), is obtained by placing the finger flat on a paper or the platen of a scanner without rolling. Both plain and rolled images are of good quality and are rich in information content. By contrast, in recognition process, a latent fingerprint image is used as input, shown in Fig.1. Latent fingerprints are extracted from surfaces of objects that are inadvertently touched or handled by a person typically at crime scenes. Generally, latent fingerprints are smudgy, blurred, fragmentary and nonlinearly deformed, which makes the qualities of latent fingerprint images are absolutely poor, shown as Fig.2(c).

Latent fingerprint recognition has become one of the most reliable and available identification methods in forensic science. Driven by its importance, automatic latent fingerprint recognition has drawn great attention from academia. Researchers dedicate to study a fully automatic latent fingerprint recognition method, and a variety of techniques have been reported in the literature. Unfortunately, the progress is not satisfactory. According to the report of National Institute of Standards and Technology (NIST) latent fingerprint testing [5], the rank-1 accuracy of an automatic latent matcher is as low as 54% on a large database of more than 40 million subjects.

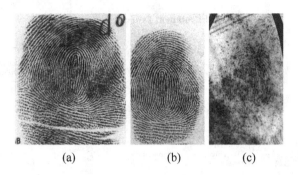

(a)   (b)   (c)

Fig. 2. Rolled, plain and latent fingerprint images[4].(a) Rolled fingerprint; (b) Plain fingerprint; (c) Latent fingerprint

In order to achieve a high latent fingerprint recognition accuracy, a semi-lights-out system[5], which requires human intervention, was proposed. In this system, features are manually extracted from a latent fingerprint, the system then performs the matching operates between probe and gallery images. The semi-lights-out system provides a feasible solution for accurate latent fingerprint recognition, but it is a type of semi-automatic method. Automatic latent fingerprint recognition is still a challenging problem.

This paper is presented due to two purposes. The first purpose is to increase the awareness and understanding of the challenges in automatic latent fingerprint recognition. To achieving this purpose, we summarize the latest research advances of automatic latent fingerprint recognition during solving the challenging problems. The second purpose is to claim the importance of latent fingerprint development. Different fingerprint development methods can result in different quality levels fingerprint images, which further cause dramatic influence to the accuracy of latent fingerprint recognition algorithms. We regard that latent fingerprint development is a important pre-step of latent fingerprint recognition. Research of the relationship between latent fingerprint development and automatic latent fingerprint recognition system is a new topic in the field of latent fingerprint recognition.

The rest of this paper is organized as follows. In section 2, we summarize the challenges and advances of latent fingerprint recognition. Section 3 discusses the future work, and section 4 concludes this paper.

2   Challenges and Advances

This section will summarize the challenges and discuss about the advances of automatic latent fingerprint recognition.

The challenges of automatic latent fingerprint recognition are mainly two-fold. Firstly, it is difficult to automatically extract features from latent fingerprints. The latent fingerprint lifted at crime scenes is mostly smudgy, blurred and fragmentary. Thus, there would be lots of noises within a latent fingerprint image, which causes that automatic feature extraction from latent fingerprints image is a challenging task. Secondly, accurate matching of a latent fingerprint to a rolled or plain fingerprint is also very challenging. In latent fingerprint recognition, the probe is a latent fingerprint image, whose quality is poor, while the gallery is a set of good quality images, which are plain or rolled images. Due to the grand gap between latent fingerprints and plain or rolled fingerprints, it is difficult to automatically perform an accurate latent-to-plain or latent-to-rolled matching.

2.1 Feature Extraction

Feature extraction is one of the most important steps in biometric recognition system. Generally speaking, feature extraction includes feature design and feature extraction. Feature design refers to design the model for uniquely representing a sample. Feature extraction refers to the operation of extracting features from a sample. Theoretically, once the feature model is defined, the feature extraction operation is easy to implement. However there are usually lots of noises within a sample, which will decrease the purity of features extracted from the sample. Therefore, a preprocess step is necessary for removing noises before executing feature extraction operation. Due to the low quality of latent fingerprint, it is difficult to remove all noises and extract pure features from fingerprint samples.

In practice, segmentation of fingerprints from fingerprint images is a feasible solution for removing noises. Many latent fingerprint segmentation methods have been presented in the literature. Feng et al. [6] proposed a novel fingerprint orientation field estimation algorithm, which can accurately segment fingerprints from background. In [6], prior knowledge of orientation field is utilized dictionary learning. Firstly, a set of orientation field dictionaries are learned from good quality fingerprints off-line. Secondly, the orientation field of a latent fingerprint is estimated using the learned dictionaries. Previously, a orientation-field-based latent fingerprint segmentation method has been presented by in [7,8]. It is a semiautomatic method, which requires manually marked region of interest and singular points. In contrast, [6] is an automatic method. Besides ridge orientation, there is also other information can be used for latent fingerprint segmentation, such as frequency features. In [9], Choi et al. utilized both ridge orientation and frequency features to achieve latent fingerprint segmentation. Total variation model is another useful model for latent fingerprint segmentation. Zhang et al. introduced this model, and proposed an adaptive total variation model and a directional total variation model respectively in [10] and [11] for latent fingerprint segmentation.

Among these latent fingerprint segmentation methods, orientation-field-based method achieves the most successful performance. The reason is that orientation field, which represents the ridge flow of a fingerprint at each location, is the remarkable characteristics of fingerprint. It is not only used for latent fingerprint segmentation, but also utilized as level-1 features for recognition [12].

Currently, fingerprint features can be categorized into three different levels: level-1, level-2 and level-3 features. Level-1 features refer to the macro details of a fingerprint, including ridge flow and pattern type. Level-2 features refer to the Galton characteristics or minutiae, such as ridge bifurcations and endings. Level-3 features are the microscopic information of a fingerprint, including pores [13], ridge contours [13], dots, and incipient ridges [14]. Research of level-1 and level-2 features has been lasted for dozen years, and has been widely utilized in commercial automatic fingerprint identification system (AFIS) due to their grand success. In contrast, level-3 features are rarely utilized in AFIS with the limitation of capture sensor. Actually, due to the microscopic information contained in level-3 features, it can increase the recognition accuracy, especially, in the scenario of large scale database matching. They have played important roles in forensic fingerprint exporter examination. While in practice, level-3 features contained in a fingerprint are not stable. Their appearance is dramatically affected by the pressure when imaging. In order to get stable level-3 features, grand efforts should be taken to research on fingerprint capture sensor and preprocess algorithm.

2.2   Latent-to-Full Matching

Latent-to-full matching is the second challenging problem of latent fingerprint recognition. Generally speaking, latent-to-full matching refers to the matching of a latent fingerprint image to a plain or rolled fingerprint image, which includes image preprocessing, feature extraction, and feature matching. In this paper, latent-to-full matching represents matching of the features extracted from a latent fingerprint to a plain or rolled fingerprint, namely feature matching.

The reasons that lead to the difficulties of latent-to-full matching mainly lie in two fold. Firstly, the ridge information of a latent fingerprint is usually blurred, discontinuous, and fragmentary. Blur and discontinuity of fingerprint ridge will cause failure of feature extraction. And fragmentation of fingerprint can decrease the information contained in a latent fingerprint. For example, a typical rolled fingerprint has around 80 minutiae, while a typical latent fingerprint may have only average 15 usable minutiae. Secondly, large nonlinear deformation is a common phenomena with a latent fingerprint. Nonlinear deformation can cause dramatic variation to the representation of the same fingerprint.

To address the problem of latent-to-full matching, many methods have been proposed in the literature. Jain et al. [4] integrated extended features including singularity, ridge quality map, ridge flow map, ridge wavelength map, and skeleton, to propose a system for matching latent fingerprints to rolled fingerprints. Paulino et al. [15,17] presented a semi-automatic algorithm to perform robust latent-to-full matching. Firstly, descriptor-based hough transform is used to align fingerprints. Manually marked minutiae and orientation field information are then integrated to measure the similarity between fingerprints. In [16], Paulino et al. also fused manually marked minutiae and derived minutiae to perform latent-to-full matching. Compared with [16] which fuses different features extracted from the same sample, Feng et al. [18] proposed a method by fusing the same features from different samples (rolled fingerprints and plain fingerprints) at three different levels. In [19], Dvornychenko also presented a fusion-based method, which fuses the results from five different latent fingerprint matchers.

3 Future Work

Although great efforts have been contributed, latent fingerprint recognition is still a open and challenging problem. In my opinion, besides the problems of feature extraction and latent-to-full matching, research of the relationship between latent fingerprint development and latent fingerprint recognition system deserves the attention from researchers.

Traditionally, latent fingerprint development, which involves a wide array of optical, physical, and chemical processes, is regarded as a topic of forensic medical. It is not introduced in the literature of automatic latent fingerprint recognition. However, the output of latent fingerprint development is took as the input of latent fingerprint recognition system, shown in Fig.1. The performance of latent fingerprint development would cause dramatic influence to the performance of latent fingerprint recognition system. Therefore, latent fingerprint development can be considered as a pre-step of latent fingerprint recognition.

Research of the relationship between latent fingerprint development and latent fingerprint recognition system can make great contribution to recognition accuracy. The reasons are concluded as following. Firstly, different latent fingerprint development methods would cause huge variation to the appearance of the same latent fingerprint. Fig.3 shows five different latent fingerprints, each of which is developed using ninhydrin and DFO. The left half part of each fingerprint is developed using ninhydrin, and the rest is developed using DFO. In this figure, we can see that the appearance of fingerprints developed using ninhydrin is absolutely different with the fingerprints developed using DFO. Secondly, different latent fingerprint development methods may introduce different noises into fingerprint images. Latent fingerprints are always left on the surface of certain materials in crime scenes, and their background is always complicate. Thus, the image quality of a latent fingerprint image is dramatically affected by development methods.

Due to the two facts described above, different latent fingerprint development methods may result in different quality levels of fingerprint images. Currently, there does not exist a preprocessing method that can handle all quality levels of fingerprint images. Design of different preprocessing algorithms for different quality levels is a practical strategy for investigating the relationship between latent fingerprint development and latent fingerprint recognition.

To construct a large scale latent fingerprint database is another work that needs further contribution in the future. A sample database is the basis for resolving a pattern recognition problem. With a sample database, we can firstly use it to train a classifier for predicting new comers, and can secondly use it to assess the performance of a given algorithm. Currently, there are only one latent fingerprint image database, which is NIST SD27 database [20], with only 258 latent fingerprint images. Thus, to construct a large scale fingerprint database,

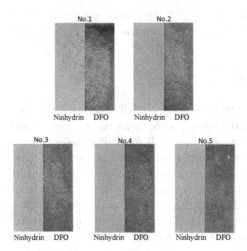

Fig. 3. Five latent fingerprints, half of each fingerprint is developed using ninhydrin, and the other half is developed using DFO

including latent, rolled and plain fingerprint images, is a urgent task within the field of latent fingerprint recognition.

4   Conclusion

Contrary to standard automated fingerprint recognition, latent fingerprint recognition processes the fingerprint images developed from the crime scenes. This paper highlights some of the challenges and advances in the field of latent fingerprint recognition, and claim that research of the relationship between latent fingerprint development and automatic latent fingerprint recognition system is a new research topic in the field of latent fingerprint recognition.

Acknowledgments. This work is funded by the Key Research Projects of Ministry of Public Security (Grant No. 2011ZDYJGADX007), the Project Supported by The Academician Funds of Ministry of Public Security, and the Fund of Beijing Municipal Commission of Education.

References

1. Maio, D., Maltoni, D., Cappelli, R., Wayman, J.L., Jain, A.K.: FVC 2004: Third fingerprint verification competition. In: ICBA 2004. LNCS, vol. 3072, pp. 1–7. Springer, Heidelberg (2004)
2. Cappelli, R., Ferrara, M., Franco, A., et al.: Fingerprint verification competition 2006. Biometric Technology Today 15(7), 7–9 (2007)
3. Lee, H.C., Gaensslen, R.E.: Advances in fingerprint technology, p. 106. CRC Press LLC, New York (2001)

4. Jain, A.K., Feng, J.: Latent fingerprint matching. IEEE Transactions on Pattern Analysis and Machine Intelligence 31(1), 88–100 (2011)
5. Dvornychenko, V.N., Garris, M.D.: Summary of NIST Latent Fingerprint Testing Workshop. NISTIR 7377 (2006), http://fingerprint.nist.gov/latent/ir_7377.pdf
6. Feng, J., Zhou, J., Jain, A.: Orientation field estimation for latent fingerprint enhancement. IEEE Transactions on Pattern Analysis and Machine Intelligence 35(4), 303–310 (2013)
7. Yoon, S., Feng, J., Jain, A.K.: Latent fingerprint enhancement via robust orientation field estimation. In: IEEE International Joint Conference on Biometrics (IJCB), pp. 1–8 (2011)
8. Yoon, S., Feng, J., Jain, A. K.: On latent fingerprint enhancement, SPIE Defense, Security, and Sensing. International Society for Optics and Photonics, (2010).
9. Choi, H., Boaventura, M., Boaventura, I.A.G., Jain, A.K.: Automatic segmentation of latent fingerprints. In: IEEE Fifth International Conference on Biometrics: Theory, Applications and Systems (BTAS), pp. 303–310 (2012)
10. Zhang, J., Lai, R., Kuo, C.C.J.: Latent fingerprint segmentation with adaptive total variation model. In: IEEE 5th IAPR International Conference on Biometrics (ICB), pp. 189–195 (2012)
11. Zhang, J., Lai, R., Kuo, C.C.J.: Latent fingerprint detection and segmentation with a directional total variation model. In: IEEE 19th IEEE International Conference on Image Processing (ICIP), pp. 1145–1148 (2012)
12. Tico, M., Kuosmanen, P.: Fingerprint matching using an orientation-based minutia descriptor. IEEE Transactions on Pattern Analysis and Machine Intelligence 25(8), 1009–1014 (2003)
13. Jain, A.K., Chen, Y., Demirkus, M.: Pores and ridges: High-resolution fingerprint matching using level 3 features. IEEE Transactions on Pattern Analysis and Machine Intelligence 29(1), 15–27 (2007)
14. Chen, Y., Jain, A.K.: Dots and incipients: extended features for partial fingerprint matching. In: IEEE Biometrics Symposium, pp. 1–6 (2007)
15. Paulino, A.A., Feng, J., Jain, A.K.: Latent Fingerprint Matching Using Descriptor-Based Hough Transform. IEEE Transactions on Information Forensics and Security 8(1), 31–45 (2013)
16. Paulino, A.A., Jain, A.K., Feng, J.: Latent Fingerprint Matching: Fusion of Manually Marked and Derived Minutiae. In: 23rd SIBGRAPI Conference on Graphics, Patterns and Images (2010)
17. Paulino, A.A., Feng, J., Jain, A.K.: Latent fingerprint matching using descriptor-based hough transform. In: 2011 International Joint Conference on Biometrics (IJCB), pp. 1–7 (2011)
18. Feng, J., Yoon, S., Jain, A.K.: Latent fingerprint matching: Fusion of rolled and plain fingerprints. In: Tistarelli, M., Nixon, M.S. (eds.) ICB 2009. LNCS, vol. 5558, pp. 695–704. Springer, Heidelberg (2009)
19. Dvornychenko, V.N.: Evaluation of fusion methods for latent fingerprint matchers. In: IEEE 5th IAPR International Conference on Biometrics (ICB), pp. 182–188 (2012)
20. Fingerprint Minutiae from Latent and Matching Tenprint Images, NIST Special Database 27 (2010), http://www.nist.gov/srd/nistsd27.htm

Feature-Level Fusion of Finger Biometrics Based on Multi-set Canonical Correlation Analysis

Jialiang Peng[1,2], Qiong Li[1,*], Qi Han[1], and Xiamu Niu[1]

[1] School of Computer Science and Technology,
Harbin Institute of Technology, Harbin 150080, China
qiong.li@hit.edu.cn
[2] Information and Network Administration Center,
Heilongjiang University, Harbin 150080, China

Abstract. Feature fusion-based multimodal biometrics has become an increasing interest to many researchers in recent years, particularly for finger biometrics. In this paper, a novel multimodal finger biometric method based on Multi-set Canonical Correlation Analysis (MCCA) is proposed. It combines finger vein, fingerprint, finger shape and finger knuckle print features of a single human finger. The proposed approach transforms multiple unimodal feature vectors into sets of canonical correlation variables, which represent fused features more efficiently in few dimensions. The experimental results on a merged multimodal finger biometric database show that the proposed approach has significant improvements over the existing approaches. It is beneficial to fuse multiple features as well as achieves lower error rates.

Keywords: Multimodal, Finger, Feature fusion, Multi-set Canonical Correlation Analysis.

1 Introduction

In recent years, various research efforts have been made on unimodal finger-based biometrics such as fingerprint, finger vein, and finger knuckle print traits [1,2,3]. However, unimodal finger-based biometric systems for personal identification suffer from challenges such as the conditions of the users health, illumination, type of sensor, and spoofing attacks [4], and not perfect in many real applications. Multimodal finger biometrics [5,6] are, therefore, attracting the attention of researchers to effectively overcome most of the above weaknesses in unimodal finger biometric systems. Multimodal finger biometrics usually contains two or more finger sources and combines them together for personal identification. It has several merits such as higher accuracy, noise resistance, universality, anti-spoof attacks, and is more robust than unimodal ones.

Feature-level fusion of finger biometrics is to utilize complementary information on all biometric modalities for representation and classification. Conventional feature fusion methods simply concatenate or integrate several kinds of features together, namely, serial feature fusion or parallel feature fusion [7][8]. Serial feature fusion is to concatenate two sets of feature vectors into one union-vector, and extracts features in the

---

* Corresponding author.

Z. Sun et al. (Eds.): CCBR 2013, LNCS 8232, pp. 216–224, 2013.
© Springer International Publishing Switzerland 2013

higher-dimension vector space. Parallel feature fusion is to integrate two sets of feature vectors into a complex vector, and extracts features in the complex vector space. Despite of the simplicity of such methods, the systems adopting such feature fusions suffer from the curse of dimensionality and small sample size (SSS) problem caused by high dimensions in the process of serial feature fusion or parallel feature fusion. Thus, the serial feature fusion or parallel feature fusion is not efficient in complicated biometric applications. There is another effective way to perform fusion at the feature level with preserving the correlation between different feature pairs. Canonical Correlation Analysis (CCA) [9], the classical statistical method and its variations have been proposed for feature-level fusion in [6,10]. CCA-based fusion methods utilize the correlation criterion function to extract canonical correlation features from the two unimodal feature vectors to form the fused feature vectors for personal identification. These methods are able to generate new combined features by analyzing the correlation relationship between two kinds of original features. Nielsen [11] proposes a Multi-set Canonical Correlation Analysis (MCCA) between multiple (more than two) sets of variables extending CCA with some constraints, and applies it to analyze remote sensing images. To fuse multiple finger traits at feature level reasonably and effectively, we are motivated to design a novel feature fusion approach based on MCCA to exploit multiple biometric features complementally and reliably.

In this paper, we propose an effective fusion method for finger multimodal biometrics, which combines feature information from four unimodal biometric systems, including finger vein, fingerprint, finger knuckle print and finger shape. The main aim is to avoid the weaknesses of previous works on feature fusion and improve the overall recognition performance of finger-based multimodal biometrics. Moreover, the proposed approach eliminates the redundant information between the features with the help of correlation information from original multiple finger features.

The remainder of this paper is organized as follows. Section 2 provides the theoretical analysis of MCCA and proposed feature fusion strategy. Section 3 is devoted to the experimental results and discussions including comparisons with other feature fusion methods in detail. Finally, conclusion is drawn in Section 4.

2   The Proposed Multimodal Feature Fusion Approach

2.1   Basic Theory of Multi-set Canonical Correlation Analysis (MCCA)

Multi-set Canonical Correlation Analysis (MCCA) [11] is an extension of CCA for analyzing linear relationships more than two sets of variables. Compared with the correlation between two canonical variables is maximized in CCA, MCCA applies an objective function of the covariance matrixes from multiple random vectors to achieve maximum overall correlation of their canonical variables.

Assume that n zero-mean random vectors $x_i \in R^{p_i} (i = 1, 2, \ldots, n)$ and $E(x_i) = 0$, where E denotes the expectation operator and p_i denotes the dimension of x_i. The objective of MCCA is to search for linear combinations $U^T = [u_1, u_2, \ldots, u_n]$ of $X^T = [x_1^T, x_2^T, \cdots, x_n^T]$ given by:

$$u_1 = \alpha_1^T x_1 \;,\; Var\{u_1\} = \alpha_1^T S_{11} \alpha_1$$
$$u_2 = \alpha_2^T x_2 \;,\; Var\{u_2\} = \alpha_2^T S_{22} \alpha_2$$
$$\vdots \qquad \vdots \qquad \qquad \vdots \qquad\qquad (1)$$
$$u_n = \alpha_n^T x_n \;,\; Var\{u_n\} = \alpha_n^T S_{nn} \alpha_n$$

where Var denotes the variance operator. With dispersion matrix:

$$\Sigma_U = \begin{bmatrix} \alpha_1^T S_{11} \alpha_1 & \alpha_1^T S_{12} \alpha_2 & \cdots & \alpha_1^T S_{1n} \alpha_n \\ \alpha_2^T S_{21} \alpha_1 & \alpha_2^T S_{22} \alpha_2 & \cdots & \alpha_2^T S_{2n} \alpha_n \\ \vdots & \vdots & \ddots & \vdots \\ \alpha_n^T S_{n1} \alpha_1 & \alpha_n^T S_{n2} \alpha_2 & \cdots & \alpha_n^T S_{nn} \alpha_n \end{bmatrix} \qquad (2)$$

where S_{ij} is the cross-covariance matrix between $x_i(i = 1, 2, \ldots, n)$ and $x_j(j = 1, 2, \ldots, n)$, S_{ii} is the covariance matrix of vector x_i and $\alpha_i \in R^{p_i}$. MCCA aims to find projective vectors $\alpha_1, \alpha_2, \ldots, \alpha_n$ that can maximize all correlations between the canonical variables $u_1, u_2, \ldots, u_n$. By doing so, the measures of Σ_U can be optimized by several criteria under some constraints [11]. The well known criterion is given by Eq.(3), namely SUMCOR [11].

$$(\alpha_1, \alpha_1, \cdots \alpha_n) = \max_{\alpha_1, \alpha_1, \cdots \alpha_n} \sum_{i=1}^n \sum_{j=1}^n \alpha_i^T S_{ij} \alpha_j$$
$$s.t. \sum_{i=1}^n \alpha_i^T S_{ii} \alpha_i = 1 \qquad (3)$$

Eq.(3) can be rewritten as the solving generalized eigenvalue problem by Eq.(4) [11].

$$\begin{bmatrix} S_{11} & S_{12} & \cdots & S_{1n} \\ S_{21} & S_{22} & \cdots & S_{2n} \\ \vdots & \vdots & \ddots & \vdots \\ S_{n1} & S_{n2} & \cdots & S_{nn} \end{bmatrix} \begin{bmatrix} \alpha_1 \\ \alpha_2 \\ \vdots \\ \alpha_n \end{bmatrix} = \lambda \begin{bmatrix} S_{11} & 0 & \cdots & 0 \\ 0 & S_{22} & \cdots & 0 \\ \vdots & \vdots & \ddots & \vdots \\ 0 & 0 & \cdots & S_{nn} \end{bmatrix} \begin{bmatrix} \alpha_1 \\ \alpha_2 \\ \vdots \\ \alpha_n \end{bmatrix} \qquad (4)$$

The desired projective vectors for x_i are computed by the conjugate eigenvectors α_{i1}, $\alpha_{i2}, \cdots \alpha_{id}$ corresponding to the first $d = \min(p_1, p_2, \cdots, p_n)$ eigenvalues $\lambda_{i1} \geq \lambda_{i2} \geq \cdots \geq \lambda_{id}$ of the Eq.(4) in [11]. The multi-set canonical correlation vectors are obtained by Eq.(5):

$$u_i = \left(\alpha_{i1}^T x_i, \alpha_{i2}^T x_i, \ldots, \alpha_{id}^T x_i\right)^T = (\alpha_{i1}, \alpha_{i2}, \ldots, \alpha_{id})^T x_i = W_i^T x_i \qquad (5)$$

where the matrix of projective vectors is $W_i = [\alpha_{i1}, \alpha_{i2}, \cdots, \alpha_{id}]_{p_i \times d}$ and $i = 1, 2, \ldots, n$.

2.2   Multimodal Finger Feature Fusion Strategy Based on MCCA

Due to the variation of the finger modalities and feature extraction methods, the features have a certain amount of redundancy that will affect the recognition performance of feature fusion. Firstly, we use the PCA method for dimensional reduction on each original feature space. Without losing of generality, in the paper, we assume that the feature vectors of finger vein (FV), fingerprint (FP), finger shape (FS) and finger knuckle print (FK) in Fig.1 are all reduced to the same dimension by PCA method. Secondly, to eliminate the disadvantaged influences on the unbalanced data distributions of above unimodal features, the data distributions of these features should be normalized into zero mean and unit variance before fusion.

Here, we further modify the selection of original conjugate eigenvectors in MCCA. As we known, the magnitude of eigenvalue always reflects the correlation between the original vectors. The larger magnitude of eigenvalue is, and the more correlative between the original vectors. As the desired canonical correlation vector for x_i , u_i is computed by the conjugate eigenvectors $\alpha_{i1}, \alpha_{i2}, \ldots, \alpha_{it}$ corresponding to the first large t absolute eigenvalues $abs(\lambda_{i1}) \geq abs(\lambda_{i2}) \geq \cdots \geq abs(\lambda_{it}) \geq 0, (1 \leq t \leq p_i)$ of Eq.(5). We can easily obtain

$$u_i = \left(\alpha_{i1}^T x_i, \alpha_{i2}^T x_i, \ldots, \alpha_{it}^T x_i\right) = (\alpha_{i1}, \alpha_{i2}, \ldots, \alpha_{it})^T x_i = W_i^T x_i \qquad (6)$$

where the projective matrix is $W_i = (\alpha_{i1}, \alpha_{i2}, \ldots, \alpha_{it})$ and $i = 1, 2, \ldots, m$. So the choice of t's value needs to satisfy Eq.(7):

$$\frac{\sum_{k=1}^{t} abs(\lambda_{ik})}{\sum_{j=1}^{p_i} abs(\lambda_{ij})} \geq \varepsilon, \ 0 \leq \varepsilon \leq 1 \qquad (7)$$

where the value of ε is chosen by 0.9 in our experiments. As a result, we can further reduce the dimension of vector U_i in multimodal feature fusion.

For the final dimension of each projected vector $u_i, i = 1, 2, \ldots, m$ from m modalities is different by computing the Eq.(7), it is difficult to apply the strategy of parallel feature fusion directly. Therefore, this paper adopts serial feature fusion strategy as shown in Eq.(8).

$$U = \begin{bmatrix} u_1 \\ u_2 \\ \vdots \\ u_m \end{bmatrix} = \begin{bmatrix} W_1^T x_1 \\ W_2^T x_2 \\ \vdots \\ W_m^T x_m \end{bmatrix} = \begin{bmatrix} W_1^T & 0 & \cdots & 0 \\ 0 & W_2^T & \cdots & 0 \\ \vdots & \vdots & \ddots & \vdots \\ 0 & 0 & \cdots & W_m^T \end{bmatrix} \begin{bmatrix} x_1 \\ x_2 \\ \vdots \\ x_m \end{bmatrix} = WX \qquad (8)$$

As a matter of fact, U is finally applied as the final fused feature vector for multimodal biometrics.

Fig.1 shows a block diagram illustrating the overall procedure of a multimodal biometric authentication that combines features from multiple finger biometric sources. The finger vein, fingerprint, finger shape and finger knuckle print are merged as a multimodal biometric system and the procedure of the authentication are listed as follows:

- Finger vein images are obtained from a capturing device consisting of near-infrared illuminators. The fingerprint images and the finger knuckle print images are captured under a visible light environment. We have done image preprocessing in order to extract biometric features accurately [12].
- The finger geometry are obtained by detecting edge lines between the finger region and the background region from the finger vein images by our pervious work [12]. The finger shape features are obtained by the Fourier descriptors (FD) method [5].

- The finger vein features in our pervious work [2] are extracted by Gabor wavelet and Local Binary Pattern (GLBP). GLBP feature representation of finger vein can enhance the finger vein recognition performance.
- The fingerprint features are extracted as fixed length FingerCodes by a bank of Gabor filters-based algorithm [1], and the finger knuckle print features are extracted by the log-Gabor phase congruency (PC) model [3].
- All the values of above four extracted features are normalized into zero mean and unit variance within the same 128-dimension vector by PCA method, as shown in Table. 1.
- In the enrollment phase, we train the multimodal finger samples to obtain the fused feature vectors U and the projective matrix W using MCCA, and then store U and W as template into the database. During the verification phase, the projective matrix W is taken out for the testing samples to extract testing feature vectors U'. Finally, the testing vectors U' are compared with the reference templates U for matching based on the nearest neighbor classifier.

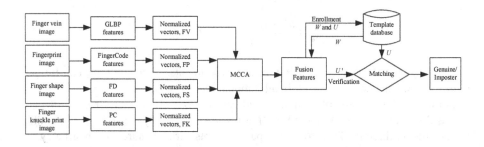

Fig. 1. The finger multimodal biometrics scheme using the proposed MCCA

3   Experimental Results and Discussions

3.1   Database

The proposed feature fusion method is evaluated based on a merged multimodal finger biometric database. This database is a virtual database, which contains finger vein, fingerprint, and finger knuckle images from three unimodal biometric databases, as shown in Fig.2. Meanwhile, the features for finger shape recognition are derived from finger vein images. For our performance evaluation with the same scale, each unimodal biometric database consists of 100 subjects, 6 samples per-subject, out of which 3 samples are used to generate the enrolled template and 3 samples for testing. The finger vein image sub-database employed in this paper is Hong Kong Polytechnic University Finger Image Database Version 1.0 [13]. There are randomly selected 100 fingers with six vein images per-subject employed for our performance evaluation. The fingerprint image sub-database contains 100 fingers with randomly selected six impressions per-subject from FVC2002 database Db1 set A [14]. The finger knuckle print image sub-database consists of randomly selected 100 fingers with six knuckles images per-subject from PolyU Finger-Knuckle-Print database [15].

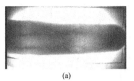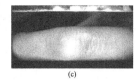

(a)   (b)   (c)   (d)

Fig. 2. (a) finger vein image sample (b) fingerprint image sample (c) finger knuckle image sample (d) finger shape image sample

Table 1. Four unimodal features on the merged multimodal finger database

Abbrev	Description
FV	The normalized 128-dimension GLBP feature of finger vein
FP	The normalized 128-dimension FingerCode feature of fingerprint
FK	The normalized 128-dimension PC feature of finger knuckle print
FS	The normalized 128-dimension FD feature of finger shape

3.2 The Comparisons and Analysis

The evaluation protocols of False Match Rate (FMR), False Non-Match Rate (FNMR), and Receiver Operator Characteristic (ROC) curve are used in this paper. Herin, we use Equal Error Rate (EER) to evaluate the performance in our experiments. Note that the lower value of EER shows the better recognition performance in biometrics. We firstly give the accuracy of finger unimodal biometric recognition in Fig. 3(a). The EER performance of finger vein, fingerprint, finger shape and finger knuckle is 0.36e-02, 1.55e-02, 2.73e-02, 2.55e-02, respectively.

To show the advantages of the proposed MCCA-based fusion method, we compare it with the existing feature fusion methods such as serial feature fusion [7], parallel feature fusion[7] and CCA-based methods [10]. All these methods still use the nearest neighbor classifier for recognition. We give abbreviations for different feature fusion approaches on finger modalities. Each abbreviation is described as in Table.2.

Table.3 shows the EER performance of fusion methods based on serial feature fusion, parallel feature fusion, CCA, and MCCA. All of them achieve higher accuracies compared with the single feature type before feature fusion. It is shown that there are $C_4^2 = 12$ means of any two unimodal feature fusion. Parallel feature fusion method utilizes Complex Fisher Discriminate Analysis (CFDA) [8] and achieves higher recognition accuracies than serial feature fusion. It turns out that CCA and MCCA have the similar recognition results due to the same computing process in both of them when only fusing two modal features by the Eq.(4). However, MCCA can give a meaningful fusing result with lower dimensions. According to Eq.(7), MCCA corresponding to the dimension of optimal fused feature vectors are shown in parentheses of Table.3. Clearly, the best recognition performance, EER=0.0013, is in favor of FVP based on the proposed approach. It is noted that there are $C_4^3 = 4$ means of any three modalities feature fusion. Feature fusion methods using serial feature fusion or MCCA can directly fuse three or all unimodal features. However, parallel feature fusion and CCA

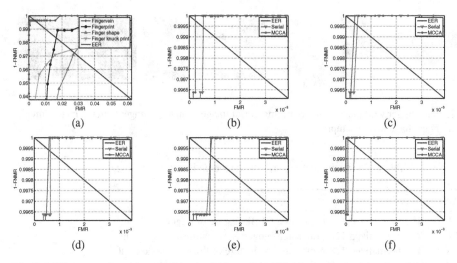

Fig. 3. ROC curves of multimodal features fusion using different methods: (a) unimodal features (b) FVPS (c) FVPK (d) FVSK (e) FPSK (f) FVPSK

Table 2. The abbreviations of different finger feature fusion approaches

Abbrev.	Description
FVP	The feature fusion of finger vein and fingerprint
FVK	The feature fusion of finger vein and finger knuckle print
FVS	The feature fusion of finger vein and finger shape
FPK	The feature fusion of fingerprint and finger knuckle print
FPS	The feature fusion of fingerprint and finger shape
FSK	The feature fusion of finger shape and finger knuckle print
FVPK	The feature fusion of finger vein, fingerprint and finger knuckle print
FVPS	The feature fusion of finger vein, fingerprint and finger shape
FVSK	The feature fusion of finger vein, finger shape and finger knuckle print
FPKS	The feature fusion of fingerprint, finger knuckle print and finger shape
FVPKS	The feature fusion of finger vein, fingerprint, finger knuckle print and finger shape

methods fail to fuse more than two modalities feature fusion. As can be seen from Table.3, the EERs become lower and the consequent performances of the multimodal finger biometrics improve in general with the number of fused feature modalities increasing. According to Eq.(7), MCCA corresponding to the dimension of optimal fused feature vectors are also shown in parentheses when different multiple feature fusions are used in Table.3. The feature fusion based on MCCA also achieve the best recognition performance by the means of FVPSK, EER=2.3900e-04. The proposed approach not only brings the effect of dimensional reduction for fusing multiple unimodal features, but also achieves higher recognition accuracies when the performance of one unimodal feature is much worse than others, such as finger shape, and finger knuckle print. This implies that MCCA indeed increases the discriminability of fused features with reducing all features to fewer dimensions after feature fusion. In fact, the feature fusion using MCCA needs less space and memory requirement compared with serial feature fusion. In other words, our method is more suited in real-world applications. Due to the page limitation, Fig.3 (b)-(f) only show ROC curves of different feature fusion approaches on FVPS, FVPK, FVSK,FPSK and FVPSK, respectively.

Table 3. The EER results of multimodal features fusion using different methods and its corresponding optimal dimensions (shown in parentheses)

Feature-level fusions	Serial [7]	Parallel [8]	CCA [10]	MCCA
FVP	0.0058 (256)	0.0023 (128)	0.0013 (256)	**0.0013 (108)**
FVS	0.0191 (256)	0.0097(128)	0.0072 (256)	**0.0072 (70)**
FVK	0.0145 (256)	0.0109 (128)	0.0097 (256)	**0.0097 (96)**
FPS	0.0217 (256)	0.0207 (128)	0.0182 (256)	**0.0182 (60)**
FPK	0.0233 (256)	0.0169 (128)	0.0102 (256)	**0.0102 (94)**
FSK	0.0253 (256)	0.0220 (128)	0.0210 (256)	**0.0210 (51)**
FVPS	5.1760e-04 (384)	NA	NA	**3.9815e-04 (144)**
FVPK	4.3797e-04 (384)	NA	NA	**3.1852e-04 (179)**
FVSK	6.3704e-04 (384)	NA	NA	**5.9769e-04 (173)**
FPSK	8.5612e-04 (384)	NA	NA	**8.3649e-04 (169)**
FVPSK	3.5834e-04 (512)	NA	NA	**2.3900e-04 (208)**

4 Conclusion

In this paper, we have presented a novel method for feature fusion of multimodal finger biometrics, in which Multi-set Canonical Correlation Analysis (MCCA) is adopted to fuse multiple feature sets efficiently. The proposed approach based on MCCA can preserve intrinsic correlation relationship among multimodal features. In addition, it has an explicit criterion for dimensional reduction, which can further reduce the dimension of fused features. The proposed approach has been evaluated on a merged multimodal finger biometric database. Results show that MCCA-based feature fusion approach has made significant improvements over the existing feature-level fusion approaches.

Acknowledgments. This work is supported by the National Natural Science Foundation of China (Grant Number: 61100187) and the China Postdoctoral Science Foundation (2011M500666).

References

1. Jain, A.K., Prabhakar, S., Hong, L., Pankanti, S.: Filterbank-based fingerprint matching. Trans. Img. Proc. 9(5), 846–859 (2000)
2. Peng, J., Li, Q., El-Latif, A.A.A., Wang, N., Niu, X.: Finger vein recognition with gabor wavelets and local binary patterns. IEICE Trans. Inf. Syst. E96-D(8), 1886–1889 (2013)
3. Zhang, L., Zhang, L., Zhang, D., Guo, Z.: Phase congruency induced local features for finger-knuckle-print recognition. Pattern Recogn 45(7), 2522–2531 (2012)

4. Ross, A., Nandakumar, K., Jain, A.K.: Handbook of Multibiometrics. Springer-Verlag, New York, Inc., Secaucus (2006)
5. Kang, B., Park, K.: Multimodal biometric method that combines veins, prints, and shape of a finger. Optical Engineering 50(1) (2011)
6. Yang, J., Zhang, X.: Feature-level fusion of fingerprint and finger-vein for personal identification. Pattern Recogn. Lett. 33(5), 623–628 (2012)
7. Yang, J., Yang, J.Y., Zhang, D., Lu, J.: Feature fusion: parallel strategy vs. serial strategy. Pattern Recognition 36(6), 1369–1381 (2003)
8. Wang, Z., Han, Q., Niu, X., Busch, C.: Feature-level fusion of iris and face for personal identification. In: Yu, W., He, H., Zhang, N. (eds.) ISNN 2009, Part III. LNCS, vol. 5553, pp. 356–364. Springer, Heidelberg (2009)
9. Hotelling, H.: Relations between two sets of variates. Biometrika 28(3/4), 321–377 (1936)
10. Yu, P., Xu, D., Zhou, H.: Feature level fusion using palmprint and finger geometry based on canonical correlation analysis. In: 2010 3rd International Conference on Advanced Computer Theory and Engineering (ICACTE), vol. 5, pp. 5–260 (2010)
11. Nielsen, A.A.: Multiset canonical correlations analysis and multispectral, truly multitemporal remote sensing data. Trans. Img. Proc. 11(3), 293–305 (2002)
12. Peng, J., Li, Q., Wang, N., El-Latif, A.A.A., Niu, X.: An effective preprocessing method for finger vein recognition. In: Fifth International Conference on Digital Image Processing, Beijing, China (2013)
13. Website: The Hong Kong Polytechnic University Finger Image Database Version 1.0 (2010), http://www.comp.polyu.edu.hk/~csajaykr/fvtdatabase.htm
14. Maio, D., Maltoni, D., Cappelli, R., Wayman, J., Jain, A.K.: Fvc 2002: Second fingerprint verification competition. In: Proceedings of 16th International Conference on Pattern Recognition, pp. 811–814 (2002)
15. Website: PolyU Finger-Knuckle-PrintDatabase (2010), http://www.comp.polyu.edu.hk/~biometrics

Discriminant Spectral Hashing
for Compact Palmprint Representation

Ying-Cong Chen[1], Meng-Hui Lim[2], Pong-Chi Yuen[2], and Jian-Huang Lai[1,*]

[1] School of Information Science and Technology, Sun-Yat-Sen University, China
chyingc@mail2.sysu.edu.cn, stsljh@mail.sysu.edu.cn
[2] Department of Computer Science, Hong Kong Baptist University, Hong Kong
{menghuilim,pcyuen}@comp.hkbu.edu.hk

Abstract. When palmprint recognition needs to be run in the device with low processing and small storage capacities, binary representation with low storage overhead, high matching speed and high discrimination power is preferred. However, existing feature extraction methods focus more on matching accuracy than representation compactness, which would result in high storage and operation cost. Inspired by Spectral Hashing that is known for compact-binary-representation extraction in the image retrieval domain, we propose a compact binary feature extraction method called Discriminant Spectral Hashing (DSH). DSH projects the feature to a discriminative subspace and then performs Spectral Hashing to obtain discriminative and compact code. Experiment results on a benchmark palmprint database show that our algorithm outperforms the existing coding-based methods in recognition accuracy with shorter code.

Keywords: Palmprint Recognition, Discriminant Spectral Hashing, Compact palmprint representation.

1   Introduction

With rapid development of information technology, palmprint recognition has been widely used for identification or authorization. In practical cases where computational and storage capacity is of high concern, compact feature representation is needed for fast matching and light storage. Palmprint representation extracted by coding-based methods relatively fits this requirement for its fast matching speed and light storage requirement. However, existing coding-based methods for palmprint recognition typically adopt filter to the palmprint images and then quantize the filtered image to extract binary code, which doesn't involve any constraint for compactness and thus the code may include some redundancy.

Zhang et al. introduced a coding method for palmprint recognition for the first time called PalmCode [1], which extracts phase feature using a 2D Gabor filter. This algorithm is very simple and fast, but the accuracy degrades as the number of enrolled users increase. Kong and Zhang proposed CompCode [2] to extract orientation feature from

---

* Corresponding author.

Z. Sun et al. (Eds.): CCBR 2013, LNCS 8232, pp. 225–232, 2013.

palmprint images and this discriminative representation enables promising recognition. Since then, the orientation feature attracts much attention. Jia et al. proposed another orientation-based algorithm named RLOC [3] as well as the pixel-to-area matching strategy, which increases the recognition performance. However, CompCode and RLOC do not make use of the information of the region with cross line or cross wrinkle, which can also be very discriminative. In order to utilize the information of such region, Guo et al. proposed BOCV algorithm [4], representing all six orientations for each region and thus the accuracy and robustness is improved. However, in BOCV, there are some so-called fragile bits that are sensitive to the external conditions. Therefore, Zhang et al. proposed E-BOCV algorithm [5], which eliminates fragile bits with a mask and achieves promising performance. These algorithms focus more on accuracy but tend to neglect efficiency. For example, RLOC [3] uses more complicated matching strategy to improve matching accuracy at the cost of lower matching speed. BOCV utilize the information of the region with cross line or cross wrinkle at the cost of higher redundancy. If recognition is needed on devices with limited processing and storage capacities, such algorithm clearly would not work well.

In recent years, quite a few advancements have been made on improving the efficiency of coding methods in the image retrieval community. It would be interesting to find out whether these methods can be adopted in biometric recognition. A very inspiring algorithm called Spectral Hashing [6] relates binary code extraction with graph partitioning. The input feature of this algorithm should meet the following 3 criteria: 1. the feature dimensions should be made uncorrelated to one another (i.e., using PCA) so that bits can be extracted dimension by dimension; 2. the input features should be embedded in the Euclidean space so that Euclidean distance can be adopted for similarity measurement; 3. the intra-user samples should have small Euclidean distance. In Spectral Hashing [6], Weiss et al. extract GIST descriptor [7] from the pixel-level features so that the GIST features are embedded in the Euclidean space. To preserve maximum global information, PCA is employed for alignment so that the feature dimensions are uncorrelated among one another after alignment. However, the third criterion is overlooked. As a result, Spectral Hashing with PCA alignment does not approximate distance between any far-separated points very well when the points are mapped from the input Euclidean space to the output Hamming space [8]. When the intra-user variation is large, genuine feature representation by Spectral Hashing with PCA alignment may not be distinguished effectively from the representations of other users because the resulting Hamming distance could be similar. This implies a potential drop in performance accuracy when large intra-user variation occurs.

To avoid imprecise mapping, discriminative projection is desirable for minimizing intra-user variation of the input features. However, seeking a discriminative projection that produces uncorrelated feature components is non-trivial. In this paper, we propose to extract binary bits from user-specific projection basis and prove that the extracted feature components are uncorrelated. Our new code extraction algorithm called Discriminant Spectral Hashing (DSH) encompasses two stages: discriminative subspace projection and binary code extraction. In the first stage, the GIST features are projected to a subspace where the projected features are uncorrelated among one another, embedded in the Euclidean space and have small intra-user variation. In the second stage, compact binary code is extracted from the projected features via employing the standard Spectral Hashing algorithm [6].

2   An Overview of Spectral Hashing

Assume that the input GIST features $x \in R^d$ are sampled from the probability distribution $p(x)$ and let $y(x)$ denote the binary code corresponding to x. In order to extract a compact code from the samples, the code extraction problem can be formulated as follows [6]:

$$\min_y \int ||y(x_1) - y(x_2)||^2 W(x_1, x_2) p(x_1) p(x_2)\, dx_1 dx_2 \qquad (2.1)$$

$$subject\ to:\ y(x) \in \{-1,1\}^k$$

$$\int y(x) p(x) dx = 0$$

$$\int y(x) y(x)^T p(x) dx = I$$

where $W(x_1, x_2) = \exp\left(-\left|\frac{|x_1 - x_2||^2}{\epsilon^2}\right)\right.$. If the constraint $y(x) \in \{-1,1\}^k$ is relaxed, then the problem (2.1) is equivalent to the following problem:

$$L_p f = \lambda f \qquad (2.2)$$

where L_p is an operator that maps f to g by $\frac{g(x)}{p(x)} = D(x) f(x) p(x) - \int W(s,x) f(s) p(s) ds$ with $D(x) = \int W(x,s) ds$. Assuming that $p(x)$ is uniformly distributed, the analytical solution is given by:

$$f(x_i) = \cos\left(\frac{j\pi}{b_i - a_i} x_i\right) \qquad (2.3)$$

$$\lambda_{i,j} = 1 - e^{-\frac{\epsilon^2}{2}\left|\frac{j\pi}{b_i - a_i}\right|^2}$$

where b_i and a_i are the maximum and minimum feature values of the i-th dimension, respectively; x_i is the i-th dimensional GIST feature of a sample; $\lambda_{i,j}$ is the i-th dimensional eigenvalue of Spectral Hashing corresponding to the j-th bit and f is the eigenfunction. In order to extract a k-bit binary code, Weiss Y. et al. first apply PCA on the GIST features for alignment, and then perform Spectral Hashing as follows: 1. calculate k spectral eigenvalues $\lambda_{i,j}$ for each of the d dimensions, such that $1 \le i \le d$ and $1 \le j \le k$; 2. calculate the eigenfunctions corresponding to the k smallest eigenvalues; 3. quantize the k eigenfunctions to obtain the final binary code.

3   Discriminant Spectral Hashing (DSH)

Input Feature of DSH. The quality of input feature of DSH is essential for reliable recognition. As discussed in [9], pixel-level feature is often embedded in nonlinear manifold. Therefore, feeding pixel-level feature directly into the DSH algorithm will not lead to discriminative representation. Weiss et al. computes the GIST feature [7] using an oriented filter at different scales and embed orientations in the Euclidean space [6]. We follow the same strategy in extracting GIST feature before applying our DSH algorithm.

In this section, we describe our DSH algorithm, where the system framework is shown in Fig.1. During training, GIST features are extracted from the preprocessed images and then subspace training and Spectral-Hashing training are performed to extract the DSH parameters. During query, GIST features of a query image are extracted and then the DSH code is extracted via subspace projection and bit extraction stages. Finally, similarity between images is evaluated using the Hamming distance.

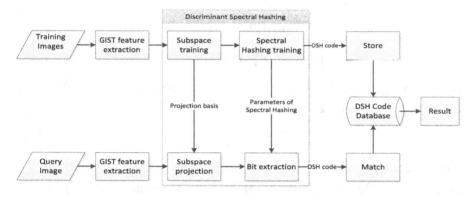

Fig. 1. An overview of our DSH algorithm

3.1   Subspace Projection

We formulate an optimization problem to find the proper projection basis of the discriminative subspace by minimizing intra-user variation. We impose a constraint such that the single-dimensional output feature dimensions are uncorrelated among one another:

$$\min_{y_a, y_b} \quad \Sigma_{a,b} W_{ab} ||y_a - y_b||^2 \tag{3.1}$$

$$\text{Subject to:} \sum_a y_a y_a^T = I$$

where $W_{ab} = \begin{cases} 1 & \text{if sample } i \text{ and } j \text{ come from class } c \\ 0 & \text{if sample } i \text{ and } j \text{ come from different class} \end{cases}$ with $1 \leq a, b \leq N$,

N is the number of samples, y_a and y_b are column vectors containing k projected feature elements of the i-th sample, $||y_a - y_b||^2$ represents the Euclidean distance between y_a and y_b, and I is a $k \times k$ identity matrix.

Problem (3.1) can be rewritten as:

$$\min_{Y} \quad trace(Y(D - W)Y^T) \tag{3.2}$$

$$Subject\ to: YY^T = I$$

where $Y \in R^{k \times N}$; $W \in R^{N \times N}$ whose elements are defined as W_{ab} in (3.1). D is a diagonal matrix where $D(i, i) = \sum_{j=1}^{N} W_{ij}$

Note that in (3.1) and (3.2), no mapping is involved to map an input feature set X $\in R^{d \times N}$ (d is the number of input feature) to an output feature set $Y \in R^{k \times N}$. To address the out-of-sample data problem, a mapping function is defined to map X to Y, such that $Y = F(X)$. In this paper, we demonstrate the simplest case by letting $F(X)$ to be linear, i.e., $Y = U^T X$:

$$\min_{U} \quad trace(U^T RU) \tag{3.3}$$

$$subject\ to: U^T CU = I$$

where $R = X(D - W)X^T$, $C = XX^T$ and X is the input feature where each column represents a sample and each row represents a single-dimensional feature.

To solve (3.3), we formulate the generalized eigen-decomposition problem as follows:

$$Ru = \lambda' Cu \tag{3.4}$$

Solving (3.4) yields a series of eigenvalue-eigenvector pairs, i.e., $(\lambda'_1 u_1), (\lambda'_2 u_2), (\lambda'_3 u_3)...(\lambda'_N u_N)$, where $\lambda'_1 < \lambda'_2 < \lambda'_3 < \cdots < \lambda'_N$. In fact, the projection matrix $U = [u_1 u_2 u_3 ... u_d]$ consists of elements corresponding to d smallest eigenvalues λ'. To prove this, we multiply u at both sides of (3.4):

$$\lambda' = \frac{u^t Ru}{u^T Cu} = u^T Ru \tag{3.5}$$

where $u^T Cu$ is normalized to 1. Since the objective function $trace(U^T RU)$ can be rewritten as $\sum_{i=1}^{d} u_i^T Ru_i$, from (3.5), we have

$$trace(U^T RU) = \sum_{i=1}^{d} u_i^T Ru_i = \sum_{i=1}^{d} \lambda'_i \tag{3.6}$$

Equation (3.6) suggests taking d smallest eigenvalues λ'_i to minimize the objective function. It is also worth noting that the projected single-dimensional feature components $u_1^T X, u_2^T X, ..., u_k^T X$ are uncorrelated among one another, i.e., $u_p^T XX^T u_q = u_p^T Cu_q = 0$ with $p \neq q$. Since R and C are symmetric due to symmetric D and W, given two eigenvalue-eigenvector pairs, $(\lambda'_p u_q)$ and $(\lambda'_p u_q)$ with $p \neq q$ and the results from (3.4), we notice

$$u_p^T Cu_q = \frac{1}{\lambda'_q} u_p^T Ru_q = \frac{1}{\lambda'_q} (R^T u_p)^T u_q = \frac{1}{\lambda'_q} (Ru_p)^T u_q \tag{3.7}$$

From (3.4), equation (3.7) can further be expressed by:

$$\frac{1}{\lambda_q'}\left(Ru_p\right)^T u_q = \frac{\lambda_p'}{\lambda_q'}u_p^T C^T u_q = \frac{\lambda_p'}{\lambda_q'}u_p^T C u_q \tag{3.8}$$

Since $\lambda_p' \neq \lambda_q'$ and $u_p^T C u_q = \frac{\lambda_p'}{\lambda_q'}u_p^T C u_q$, we have

$$u_p^T C u_q = 0 \quad for\ p \neq q \tag{3.9}$$

which implies the non-correlation constraint in (3.1). This completes the proof.

In summary, to learn the subspace, we solve the eigen-decomposition problem in (3.5) for obtaining a series of eigenvalue-eigenvector pairs. The projection basis U is then obtained by choosing d eigenvectors corresponding to the smallest eigenvalues.

3.2   Bit Extraction

After projecting the feature to the trained subspace, we apply the original Spectral Hashing algorithm detailed in Section 2 to extract the binary code. Given an input GIST feature x (column vector), we project it to the subspace as $U^T x$, then the binary code can be extracted as follows: (1) Identify the maximum (a_i) and minimum (b_i) values for all d dimensions (input parameters of Spectral Hashing); (2) calculate $f(u_i^T x)$ and $\lambda_{i,j}$ for $i,j \in \{1,2,3 \dots k\}$ using (3.10); and (3) extract bits from quantizing $f(u_i^T x)$ with k smallest eigenvalues $\lambda_{i,j}$.

$$f(u_i^T x) = cos\left(\frac{j\pi}{b_i - a_i}u_i^T x\right) \tag{3.10}$$

$$\lambda_{i,j} = 1 - e^{-\frac{\epsilon^2}{2}\left|\frac{j\pi}{b_i - a_i}\right|^2}$$

4   Experiment

The PolyU database [11] is employed for experimental justification of our DSH algorithm, where this database contains palmprint images belonging to 400 users with 20 per user. We randomly choose 3 palmprints for each user for training, and use the rest for testing. The number of genuine and imposter matching are 20400 and 8139600, respectively. Since we are targeting devices with low computation and storage capacity, we do not enlarge the training set [3], i.e., by creating additional training images via rotation or translation.

4.1   Code Length Analysis

Fig.2 shows the total-error-rate (FAR+FRR) performance of DSH with respect to a collection of code lengths. . It is noticed that the error rate decreases rapidly at first as code length increases, and the performance stabilizes at about 0.008 at 150 bits. When the code length exceeds 300 bits, slight performance degradation is observed. This could be explained by that the additional bases adopted for generating longer binary representation are eigenvectors with smaller eigenvalues that may be less discriminative in the subspace projection. The best performance is achieved at 220 bits. Compared with existing schemes in Table 1, the best performance of DSH occurs at bit length that is 14 times and 28 times shorter than CompCode and BOCV, respectively.

4.2   Performance Analysis

Fig. 3 illustrates the ROC performance of our DSH algorithm with respect to the existing bit extraction algorithms: Spectral Hashing [6], CompCode [2] and BOCV [4]. It is observed that our DSH algorithm outperforms the other methods significantly. Table.1 shows that Discriminant Spectral Hashing achieves the best performance with the lowest TER, apart from being the most compact code.

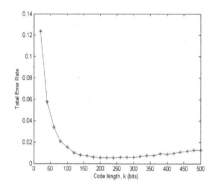

Fig. 2. Code length vs Total Error Rate

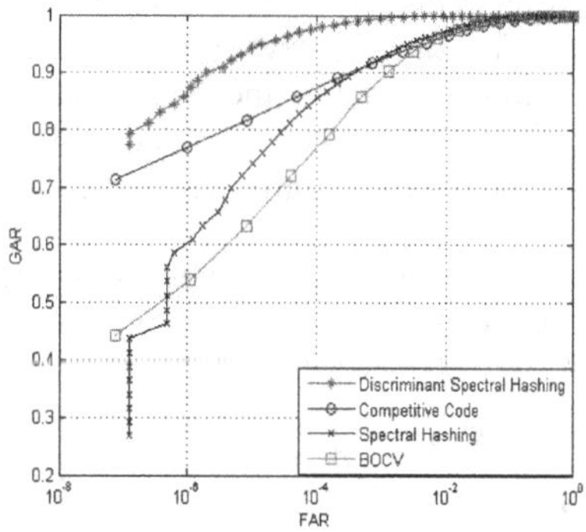

Fig. 3. Performance of DSH with respect to SH, CompCode and BOCV

Table 1. Total Error Rate

	DSH	CompCode [2]	SH [6]	BOCV [4]
Total Error Rate	0.0054	0.0452	0.0353	0.0391
Code length (bits)	220	3072	220	6144

4.2   Memory Cost, Bit Extraction Speed and Matching Speed

Our system is implemented using Matlab 2012 on a Intel(R) Core(TM) i3-2130 CPU @ 3.40GHZ 3.40GHZ. We compare the memory cost, bit extraction speed and matching speed of DSH with BOCV and CompCode in Table 2. Due to the compactness of DSH code, DSH requires shorter matching time and smaller storage capacity than BOCV and CompCode at the cost of longer bit extraction time (particularly due to time-consuming GIST feature extraction - nearly 177 ms per image).

Table 2. Memory cost and Matching speed

	Template Storage (MB)	Matching Time (us)	Bit Extraction Time (ms)
DSH	0.22	34.16	179
BOCV [4]	3.57	502.80	14
CompCode [2]	2.20	208.45	21

5   Conclusion

In this paper, we propose a Discriminant Spectral Hashing algorithm to extract compact palmprint representation. In the first stage, a discriminative subspace is learned using user-specific information to fulfill the three requirements on the input of Spectral Hashing. In the second stage, Spectral Hashing is applied for binary code extraction. To the best of our knowledge, such hashing algorithm has never been applied in palmprint representation before and surprisingly it leads to promising result. The compact palmprint representation drastically reduces the demand on processing speed and storage capacity, therefore enabling palmprint recognition on cheap devices. Compared to the state-of-art coding-based palmprint recognition methods, DSH code achieves higher recognition accuracy with much more compact representation.

Acknowledgments. This work was supported by NSFC (61173084 and 61128009). National Science & Technology Pillar Program (No. 2012BAK16B06).

References

1. Zhang, D., Kong, W.K., You, J., Wong, M.: Online palmprint identification. IEEE Transactions on Pattern Analysis and Machine Intelligence 25(9), 1041–1050 (2003)
2. Kong, A.K., Zhang, D.: Competitive coding scheme for palmprint verification. In: Proceedings of the 17th International Conference on Pattern Recognition, vol. 1, pp. 520–523. IEEE (2004)
3. Jia, W., Huang, D.S., Zhang, D.: Palmprint verification based on robust line orientation code. Pattern Recognition 41(5), 1504–1513 (2008)
4. Guo, Z., Zhang, D., Zhang, L., Zuo, W.: Palmprint verification using binary orientation co-occurrence vector. Pattern Recognition Letters 30(13), 1219–1227 (2009)
5. Zhang, L., Li, H., Niu, J.: Fragile Bits in Palmprint Recognition. IEEE Signal Processing Letters 19(10), 663–666 (2012)
6. Weiss, Y., Torralba, A., Fergus, R.: Spectral hashing. Neural Information Processing Systems (2008)
7. Oliva, A., Torralba, A.: Modeling the shape of the scene: A holistic representation of the spatial envelope. International Journal of Computer Vision 42(3), 145–175 (2001)
8. Weiss, Y., Fergus, R., Torralba, A.: Multidimensional spectral hashing. In: Fitzgibbon, A., Lazebnik, S., Perona, P., Sato, Y., Schmid, C. (eds.) ECCV 2012, Part V. LNCS, vol. 7576, pp. 340–353. Springer, Heidelberg (2012)
9. Verbeek, J.: Learning nonlinear image manifolds by global alignment of local linear models. IEEE Transactions on Pattern Analysis and Machine Intelligence 28(8), 1236–1250 (2006)
10. Torralba, A., Fergus, R., Weiss, Y.: Small codes and large image databases for recognition. Computer Vision and Pattern Recognition (2008)
11. http://www4.comp.polyu.edu.hk/~biometrics/2D_3D_Palmprint.files/ROI.zip

A Boosted Cascade of Directional Local Binary Patterns for Multispectral Palmprint Recognition

Linlin Shen, Bojie Liu and Jinwen He

School of Computer Science and Software Engineering, Shenzhen University
Shenzhen, China
llshen@szu.edu.cn

Abstract. In this paper, a recently developed local feature descriptor, namely directional local binary patterns (DLBP), was first proposed for palmprint recognition. Compared with local binary patterns (LBP) and directional binary code (DBC), DLBP contains more information on both edge and texture. A cascade structure using AdaBoost algorithm is then used to reduce the feature dimension of DLBP and computational costs of classification. The proposed approach was applied to fuse multispectral palmprint images captured under red, green, blue and near-infrared (NIR) lighting sources for personal identification. Experimental results suggest that the proposed algorithm performs much better than DBC, LBP and PalmCode in identifying palmprint images captured using different illuminations. When fusing the multispectral images, the proposed approach has also been shown to achieve higher accuracy than other methods in literature such as QPCA (Quaternion PCA) and QDWT (Quaternion Discrete Wavelet Transform).

Keywords: Palmprint Recognition, Directional Local Binary Patterns, Fusion.

1 Introduction

The biometrics technologies have been increasingly used for automated and accurate person authentication and recognition. As one of the key biometric modalities, palm offers many advantages in terms of natural integration into different application environments, ease of use, social acceptance, availability of cheap and reliable sensors, and so on.

Palmprint based personal authentication system was first developed by Zhang's group in [20]. In this system, a tuned Gabor wavelet was designed to extract local texture features, which was then coded as PalmCode for efficient matching and storage. Since then, a number of similar approaches have been developed. Kong proposed to use a number of wavelets for local feature representation and code these features by so called Competitive Code [5] and Fusion Code [6]. Improvements on system performance have been reported. As PalmCode, Competitive Code and Fusion Code are actually trying to extract the orientation and frequency information of local pixel variances, other mathematical tools like directional wavelet and line orientation code have also been applied to this problem [2, 4, 21]. Instead of extracting local

Z. Sun et al. (Eds.): CCBR 2013, LNCS 8232, pp. 233–240, 2013.

features, another category of methods transform the palmrprint image to the learned subspace for better discrimination. For example, both Principal Component Analysis (PCA) [8] and Linear Discriminant Analysis (LDA) [15] have been adopted for such purpose. Research results published show that palmprint recognition system is quite robust and efficient [11].

Though attracted lots of attention for civilian and forensic usage, palmprint itself is also prone to sensor level spoof attacks. One way to improve anti-spoofing capability is to introduce intrinsic characteristics such as the veins of the palm. Located beneath the skin, the inner vessel structures of palm can be easily captured by near-infrared (NIR) light [23]. Similar to palmprint, both local features and holistic approaches have been applied to the NIR images for personal authentication. Local feature based methods mainly apply Gabor filters [19], cutoff Gaussian filters [12], matched filters [1, 22], Neighborhood Matching Radon Transform (NMRT) [24] and Scale Invariant Feature Transform (SIFT) [7] for feature extraction. Holistic approaches use subspaces like PCA and Locality Preserving Projection (LPP) to project the palm vein images for better discrimination [14]. Two separate cameras were used in [14] to obtain palmprint and palmvein images, which are then registered before fusion. A device capable of acquiring multispectral palmprint images simultaneously has been implemented in [19]. Score level fusion was then used to fuse features extracted using six Gabor filters from different palm traits. In [18], when competitive code was extracted to represent palmprint images, the binarized responses of matched filters were used as features of palmvein images. Recently, quaternion matrix has also been used to fuse red, green, blue and NIR palmprint images for personal identification [16].

In this work, we first propose to use a recently proposed efficient descriptor, namely Directional Local Binary Patterns (DLBP) [25], to capture both texture and directional edge information for palmprint representation. Though containing rich texture and spatial information, dimension of the extracted DLBP feature is very large, which require large computational costs. We first use AdaBoost algorithm to select discriminative DLBP features for classification and then further applied a cascade structure to significantly speed up the palm recognition process. The efficient classifier was finally applied to fuse multispectral palmprint images (red, green, blue and NIR) for personal identification. When tested using the public PolyU multispectral palmprint database, experimental results show that DLBP achieves much better performances than LBP, DBC and PalmCode. The proposed cascade can substantially improve the system efficiency, with similar performance. Fusion tests on the database also suggest that the developed system achieves better results than the work using quaternion matrix [16].

2   The Proposed Method

2.1   Directional Local Binary Pattern

Given an image I, the DLBP at a pixel $z_{x,y}$ is defined as:

$$DLBP_{a,d}(z_{x,y}) = f(I'_{a,d}(z_{x,y}), I'_{a,d}(z_{x-1,y-1})) * 2^0 + f(I'_{a,d}(z_{x,y}), I'_{a,d}(z_{x,y-1})) * 2^1$$
$$+ f(I'_{a,d}(z_{x,y}), I'_{a,d}(z_{x+1,y-1})) * 2^2 + f(I'_{a,d}(z_{x,y}), I'_{a,d}(z_{x+1,y})) * 2^3 \quad (1)$$
$$+ f(I'_{a,d}(z_{x,y}), I'_{a,d}(z_{x+1,y+1})) * 2^4 + f(I'_{a,d}(z_{x,y}), I'_{a,d}(z_{x,y+1})) * 2^5$$
$$+ f(I'_{a,d}(z_{x,y}), I'_{a,d}(z_{x-1,y+1})) * 2^6 + f(I'_{a,d}(z_{x,y}), I'_{a,d}(z_{x-1,y})) * 2^7$$

where d is the distance between $z_{x,y}$ and its neighbors, a is the direction such as $0^0, 45^0, 90^0$ or 135^0. $f( )$ is a thresholding function Figure 1 shows the calculation of DLBP with distance 1 along 0 degree direction. Based on the horizontal differences, the edge strength computed at each pixel is compared with its central pixel and coded as a bit string '00101101'.

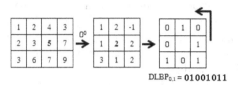

$DLBP_{0,1} = $ **01001011**

Fig. 1. Calculation of DLBP with distance 1 along 0 degree direction

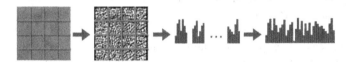

Fig. 2. DLBP images and the generated histograms

Once the DLBP images of different directions were extracted from a palmprint image, they can be further divided into a number of non-overlapping windows and a number of histograms can be generated from these regions. When the image with size 64×64 was divided into 256 sub regions, a concatenated histogram with 256×256×4 = 262,144 bins could be generated. Though containing rich texture and spatial information, the dimension of extracted DLBP feature is huge, which could bring large computational costs to the following classification process. Some feature selection strategy has to be applied to remove redundant information.

2.2   Boosted Cascade of DLBP

As boosting algorithms have been successfully applied to build efficient classification system [22], we also choose to use AdaBoost algorithm for this purpose. In this paper, we mainly aim to select the subset of regions whose histogram contains more discriminative information for classification.

As a two-class oriented algorithm, intra-personal and inter-personal spaces have to be used to convert palmprint recognition into a two-class problem. Dissimilarities between palmprints of the same person (intra-personal space) and dissimilarities between palmprints of the different people (extra-personal space) are defined as below:

$$CI = \{d(Hist_1(I_p), Hist_1(I_q)), \cdots, d(Hist_k(I_p), Hist_k(I_q)), \cdots d(Hist_N(I_p), Hist_N(I_q)), p = q\} \qquad (3)$$
$$CE = \{d(Hist_1(I_p), Hist_1(I_q)), \cdots, d(Hist_k(I_p), Hist_k(I_q)), \cdots d(Hist_N(I_p), Hist_N(I_q)), p \neq q\}$$

where I_p and I_q are the palmprint images from people p and q respectively, $Hist_k(I)$ represent the kth DLBP histogram extracted from the palmprint image I (see equation (2)), and $d(Hist_k(I_p), Hist_k(I_q))$ calculates the χ^2 distance between histograms $Hist_k(I_p)$ and $Hist_k(I_q)$.

When an unknown palmprint image was matched with each gallery image, it was in most cases compared with other person's palmprints, i.e. the difference is in the extra-personal space. Cascade structure has been shown to be very effective in fast rejecting these negative samples in face detection [23]. Following that work, we also build a boosted cascade of DBLP classifier for efficient palmprint recognition. A number of stage classifiers are first learned using AdaBoost algorithms and then cascaded to build a final classifier.

Three sets of samples, i.e. positive set P, negative set N and validation set V were used to train the set of stage classifiers. When P and V are kept unchanged, negative set N is updated each iteration as the false alarms of current cascade. Using the positive training set P and updated negative set N, a stage classifier with preset detection and false alarm rate could be successfully learned and added to current cascade. The cascading process continues until the cascaded classifier achieves desired accuracy on the validation set. The process could be summarized as below:

1.   t=0;
2.   Generate positive set P, negative set N_t and validation set V from training samples using intra and extra person difference spaces
3.   Decide the desirable detection rate d and false alarm rate f for each stage classifier and the targets for cascade D, F
4.   While performance of the cascade do not meet target
     1) Set $d_t = 0$, $f_t = 1$
     2) While $d_t < d$ or $f_t > f$
          a) Train a new boosted stage classifier A_t with n_t features using P and N_t
          b)   Validate the detection rate d_t, false alarm rate f_t of A_t on set V
          c) Adjust the threshold of A_t until $d_t \geq d$
          d)   Verify f_t
          e) $n_t = n_t + 1$
     3) Update the cascade by adding A_t
     4) t = t+1
     5) Update negative set N_t
     6) Validate the performance of current cascade on set V

2.3   Fusion

As presented in the introduction, there is much complementary information between palmprint images acquired using different visible and NIR lights. When variant palmprint images such as red and NIR, are captured at the same time and matched with registered person, the differences of red and NIR palmprints are passed to two cascades of stage classifiers and two scores (S_P and S_V) representing the similarities with the matched person are calculated. The distance between subjects P and Q can be calculated using weighted combination of S_P and S_V:

$$d(P,Q) = \alpha \times S_P' + (1-\alpha) \times S_V' \qquad (4)$$

where S_{NRI}' and S_{VI}' are the normalized scores of S_{NRI} and S_{VI}, respectively. The Min-Max normalization rule [24] are used in the paper to calculate the normalized score S' from S .

3   Experimental Results

3.1   The Multispectral Palmprint Database

The public PolyU multispectral palmprint database was used in this paper for testing. The database consists of palmprint images captured from 500 different palms, with each palm sampled 12 times in two sessions. In each session, six groups of images were acquired for a palm. Each group contained four images lighted using red, green, blue and NIR sources. In total there are 6,000 groups of images available. The time interval between two sessions is about 5-15 days. While the 3,000 groups of images captured in the first session were used as training, the remaining samples were used for testing. Fig. 3 shows an example palmprint image captured from different bands.

Fig. 3. Example palmprint images captured from red, green, blue and NIR channels

3.2   Results

We first test the performance of the proposed approach using palmrpint images captured with different lighting sources. Recognition accuracy is obtained by matching each testing palmprint with all the samples in the training set. When 3000 samples captured in the first session are available for training, 3000 samples captured in the second session are used for testing. The recognition accuracy for different number of samples in gallery per palm was shown in Table 1. One can observe from the table that the palmprint captured using red lighting source achieves the best accuracy, as high as 100% accuracy was achieved when only 3 samples per palm were available. Following red light source, the palmprint captured using NIR lighting gives the best performance.

Table 1. Performances of the proposed method for different palmprint images

No. of samples/subject in gallery	NIR	Red	Green	Blue
1	99.30	99.80	99.17	99.37
2	99.80	99.93	99.57	99.80
3	99.87	100.00	99.70	99.80
4	99.97	100.00	99.70	99.87
5	100.00	100.00	99.80	99.87
6	100.00	100.00	99.80	99.87

We also compared the proposed DLBP approach with that of DBC, LBP and PalmCode using different palmprint images. The results suggest that DLBP perform consistently better than DBC, LBP and PalmCode. Figure 4 shows the performances of different methods on both NIR and red palmprint images.

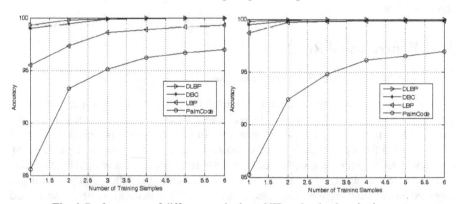

Fig. 4. Performances of different methods on NIR and red palmprint images

Table 2. Performances of the proposed method for different palmprint images

NIR	Red	Green	Blue	Accuracy (%)
1	1	0	0	99.87
1	0	1	0	99.87
1	0	0	1	99.90
0	1	1	0	99.87
0	1	0	1	99.90
0	0	1	1	99.67
1	1	1	0	99.93
1	1	0	1	99.90
1	0	1	1	99.87
0	1	1	1	99.93
1	1	1	1	99.93

Palmprint images captured using different lighting sources shall contain complementary information, so further improvement would be achieved when these images are fused for recognition. Table 2 summarizes the accuracy of the boosted cascade of DLBP fusing different plamprint images. Since 100% accuracy has been achieved for red and NIR palmprint images when six samples per palm are available in gallery, we reduce the number of the samples to one to make the problem more challenging. When '1' represents the inclusion of the spectrum, '0' represents the exclusion of the spectrum for fusion. As high as 99.93% accuracy was achieved when red and green images were fused with NIR, blue images, or both.

To compare with other approaches available in literature, we list in Table 3 the results reported in [19] using the same database. In this work, red, green blue and NIR palmprint images were represented by a quaternion matrix, PCA (Principal Component Analysis) and DWT (Discrete Wavelet Transform) were then applied on the matrix for feature extraction. When QPCA (Quaternion PCA) mainly captures global appearance of palmprint images, QDWT (Quaternion Discrete Wavelet Transform) represents local texture information. One can observe from Table 3 that the proposed DLBP approach achieves better results than QPCA, QDWT and the fusion of QPCA and QDWT.

Table 3. Comparison with other methods in literature

Methods	Accuracy (%)
QPCA	98.13%
QDWT	98.50%
QPCA + QDWT	98.83%
The proposed approach	**99.93%**

4   Conclusions

A DLBP based method for multispectral palmprint recognition has been proposed. To reduce the huge dimension of extracted DLBP feature, AdaBoost algorithm and the cascade structure are applied. As each stage classifier uses tens of DLBP features only, the system can efficiently reject inter-personal differences. To fuse palmprint images captured using different illumination, the output of different learned cascades are simply weighted for final decision. The proposed method was successfully applied to palmprint identification and extensively tested using the publicly available databases, i.e. PolyU multispectral palmprint database. The experimental results show that DLBP perform much better than DBC, LBP and PalmCode.

Acknowledgments. Research supported by National Natural Science Foundation of China (61272050), the Science Foundation of Shenzhen City (JC201104210035A), the Science Foundation of Guangdong Province (S2011010003890) and the Open Research Fund of the State Key Laboratory of Information Engineering in Surveying, Mapping and Remote Sensing (11R02).

References

1. Chen, H., Lu, G., Wang, R.: A new palm vein matching method based on ICP algorithm. In: Proceedings of International Conference on Image Processing, Seoul, pp. 1207–1211 (2011)
2. Guo, Z., Zuo, W., Zhang, L., Zhang, D.: A unified distance measurement for orientation coding in palmprint verification. Neural Computing 73(4-6), 944–950 (2010)

3. Jain, A., Nandakumar, K., Ross, A.: Score normalization in multimodal biometric systems. Pattern Recognition 38(12), 2270–2285 (2005)
4. Jia, W., Huang, D.S., Zhang, D.: Palmprint verification based on robust line orientation code. Pattern Recognition 41(5), 1521–1530 (2008)
5. Kong, A., Zhang, D.: Competitive coding scheme for palmprint verification. In: Proceedings of the 17th International Conference on Pattern Recognition, Cambridge, pp. 520–523 (2004)
6. Kong, A., Zhang, D.: Palmprint identification using feature-level fusion. Pattern Recognition 39(3), 478–487 (2006)
7. Ladoux, P.-O., Rosenberger, C., Dorizzi, B.: Palm vein verification system based on SIFT matching. In: Tistarelli, M., Nixon, M.S. (eds.) ICB 2009. LNCS, vol. 5558, pp. 1290–1298. Springer, Heidelberg (2009)
8. Lu, G., Zhang, D., Wang, K.: Palmprint recognition using eigenpalm features. Pattern Recognition Letters 24(9), 1463–1467 (2003)
9. Ojala, T., Pietikainen, M., Maenpaa, T.: Multiresolution gray-scale and rotation invariant texture classification with local binary patterns. IEEE Transactions on Pattern Analysis and Machine Intelligence 24(7), 971–987 (2002)
10. Shen, L., Bai, L.: MutualBoost learning for selecting Gabor features for face recognition. Pattern Recognition Letters 27(15), 1758–1767 (2006)
11. Shen, L., Wu, S., Zheng, S., Ji, Z.: Embedded palmprint recognition system using OMAP 3530. Sensors 12(2), 1482–1493 (2012)
12. Toh, K.-A., Eng, H.-L., Choo, Y.-S., Cha, Y.-L., Yau, W.-Y., Low, K.-S.: Identity verification through palm vein and crease texture. In: Zhang, D., Jain, A.K. (eds.) ICB 2005. LNCS, vol. 3832, pp. 546–553. Springer, Heidelberg (2005)
13. Viola, P., Jones, M.: Robust real-time face detection. International Journal of Computer Vision 57(2), 137–154 (2004)
14. Wang, J.G., Yau, W.Y., Sunwandy, A., Sung, E.: Person recognition by fusing palmprint and palm vein images based on "Laplacianpalm" representation. Pattern Recognition 41(5), 1531–1544 (2008)
15. Wu, X., Zhang, D., Wang, K.: Fisherpalm based palmprint recognition. Pattern Recognition Letters 24(15), 2819–2938 (2003)
16. Xu, X., Guo, Z., Song, C., Li, Y.: Multispectral palmprint recognition using a quaternion matrix. Sensors 12(4), 4633–4647 (2012)
17. Zhang, B., Zhang, L., Zhang, D., Shen, L.: Directional binary code with application to PolyU near-infrared face database. Pattern Recognition Letters 31(14), 2337–2344 (2010a)
18. Zhang, D., Guo, Z., Lu, G., Zhang, L., Liu, Y., Zuo, W.: Online joint palmprint and palmvein verification. Expert System with Applications 38(3), 2621–2631 (2011)
19. Zhang, D., Guo, Z., Lu, G., Zhang, L., Zuo, W.: An online system of multispectral palmprint verification. IEEE Transactions on Instrument and Measurements 59(2), 480–490 (2010b)
20. Zhang, D., Kong, A., You, J., Wong, M.: Online palmprint identification. IEEE Transactions on Pattern Analysis and Machine Intelligence 25(9), 1041–1050 (2003)
21. Zhang, L., Zhang, D.: Characterization of palmprints by wavelet signatures via directional context modeling. IEEE Transactions on Systems, Man and Cybernetics, Part B 34(3), 1335–1347 (2004)
22. Zhang, Y.-B., Li, Q., You, J., Bhattacharya, P.: Palm vein extraction and matching for personal authentication. In: Qiu, G., Leung, C., Xue, X.-Y., Laurini, R. (eds.) VISUAL 2007. LNCS, vol. 4781, pp. 154–164. Springer, Heidelberg (2007)
23. Zharov, V.P., Ferguson, S., Eidt, J.F., Howard, P.C., Fink, L.M., Waner, M.: Infrared imaging of subcutaneous veins. Lasers in Surgery and Medicine 34, 56–61 (2004)
24. Zhou, Y., Kumar, A.: Human identification using palm-vein images. IEEE Transactions on Information Forensics and Security 6(4), 1259–1274 (2011)
25. Shen, L., He, J.: Face recognition with directional local binary patterns. In: Sun, Z., Lai, J., Chen, X., Tan, T. (eds.) CCBR 2011. LNCS, vol. 7098, pp. 10–16. Springer, Heidelberg (2011)

A Robust Approach for Palm ROI Extraction
Based on Real-Time Region Learning[*]

Meng Yan, Dongmei Sun, Shouguo Zhao, and Jiajia Zhou

Laboratory of Biometric Authentication Institute of Information Science, the Key Laboratory
of Advanced Information Science and Network Technology of Beijing School of Computer
and Information Technology , Beijing Jiaotong University,China
{dmsun,09120432}@bjtu.edu.cn

Abstract. A palmprint based authentication system that can work with a
popular webcam in non-contact acquisition mode is potentially a good choice
for biometric applications.However,this camera based imaging acquisition
mode causes the difficulty for the location of palmprint due to the unstable palm
position and variable illumination condition and effects the extraction of palm
region of interest(ROI).In particular,changes in illumination of the system effect
its performance heavily. The process of extract palm ROI has been discussed in
different papers, but hardly does very well under variable light conditions and
pose changes.In this paper,we propose a robust approach for localizing the palm
and extracting the ROI based on real-time region learning.A dynamical region
is learned to binarize the image and get the hand contour to extract the palm
ROI. In a database of 1000 video clips of hand under different illumination and
poses,the accurate extraction rate reaches 92%.

Keywords: Biometrecs,Camera based palmprint identification,Region learning,
Palm ROI.

1   Introduction

The cameras in mobile devices such as cell phones and laptops can effectively double
as a biometric sensor,providing security and ease of use for access to the devices as
well as of the services.The cameras in such devices are fixed and the user presents the
biometric modality in an unrestricted and intuitive manner. The obtained images vary
considerably due to changes in illumination ,background ,poses and false views.This
adversely affects the palm extraction rate.If the recognition systems employ a
capturing setup that constrains poses and distance,and provides uniform lighting
condition and background,the freedom of users will be severly limited and hinder the
wide application of biometric authentication systems based on video imaging.In the
purpose of more user-friendly to the video imaging palmprint system,we propose a
robust approach for localizing the palm and extracting the ROI based on real-time

[*] This work is supported by NSFC (No 61201158), PCSIRT (No. IRT201206) and the Key
Laboratory of Advanced Information Science and Network Technology of Beijing.

Z. Sun et al. (Eds.): CCBR 2013, LNCS 8232, pp. 241–248, 2013.

region learning and a dynamical region is learned to binarize the current frame and get the hand contour to extract the stable palm ROI.

The rest of the paper is organized as follows.Section 2 gives a short survey of related work.Section 3 describes system framework of the proposed scheme and gives the details about the acquisition of hand images and pre-processing course. Section 4,5 reports our experimental results and conclusions with our plan.

2   Related Work

Methods of dealing with changes in illumination ,poses and complex backgrounds have been studyed extensively,for example the face alignment recognition under pose and illumination invariance[1],gait of view invariance recognition[2],and dealing with different poses for hand geometry based authentication[3].Most of the palmprint recognition schemes proposed in recent years used to extract a region on palm for personal authentication use geometrical techniques[4,5] and spectral approach by han [6].They have played wavelet-based segmentation to find the locations of finger tip and four finger roots in[6].For attaining this,they have found the boundary of palm image and then transformed palm boundary coordinates to a profile of curvature.Then they use wavelet transform to convert the curvature into multi resolution signal.In the final,they separated the sub-bands and detected corner points of palm boundary through local minimums of transformed profile.Although this method shows successful in extracting ROI,it suffers from high demands of processing and well suitable environments.On the other hand,geometrical techniques used in other researches cannot promise high accuracy in extracting ROI in unstable environment and most of them state their approach is an approximate solution [5].Histogram analysis and inner boundary tracking algorithm is used for extracting palm ROI in[7].This paper performs some geometrical operations to generate ROI. One of the advantages of the proposed method is that it is not sensitive to rotation and translation.

They propose a novel way of contact less hand recognition in[8].This method of hand detection is based on a combination of skin color modeling and shape models. This approach assumes that the hand is being held parallel to the plane of imaging system.

In this paper ,we extend their projects to apply in more natural imaging system under variable lighting conditions and pose changes. A novel approach for addressing the positon of the palm ROI by real-time learning some certain zone of current frame dynamically to get the contour of hand under the modified Ycrcb color space[9]is proposed.

3   Palm ROI Extraction

The whole extraction system includes hand image frames acquisition from nat-ura l imaging system like webcam,pre-processing to modified Ycrcb color space,hand contour extraction based on real-time region learning, palm ROI obtained with the finger valley point position proposal(see fig.1).

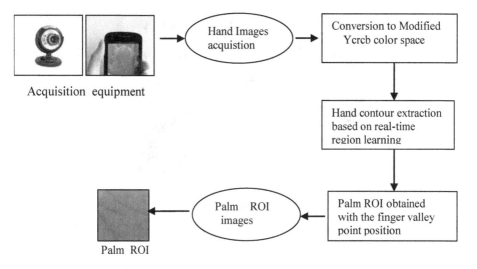

Fig. 1. Diagram of the proposed palm Roi extraction

3.1 Modified YCrCb Color Space

Ycrcb color space is a widely used model in a digital video,It separates the luminance Y form the chrominace component Cb and Cr.The existing traditional convertation from RGB to Ycrcb color space algorithms described in equation 1 have many deficiencies in bright lights.when the enhancement of light Y value byond two hundred ,the Cb and Cr cluster become terrible.

$$\left\{ \begin{array}{l} Y = 0.299R + 0.587G + 0.114B \\ Cr = -0.147R - 0.289G + 0.436B \\ Cb = 0.615R - 0.515G - 0.100B \end{array} \right. \tag{1}$$

An improved RGB color space conversion setps to Ycrcb color space listed in the follow formula 2,as specified in paper[9].

$$\left\{ \begin{array}{l} Y = 0.299R + 0.587G + 0.114B \\ Cr = \left\{ \begin{array}{ll} (R-Y)0.713...Y < 200 \\ [(R-Y)^2 0.713][-(5000/91)(Y-200)^{-2}+7].........Y >= 200 \end{array} \right\} \\ Cb = \left\{ \begin{array}{ll} (B-Y)0.564...Y < 200 \\ [(B-Y)^2 0.564][125(Y-200)^{-2}-3].........................Y >= 200 \end{array} \right\} \end{array} \right. \tag{2}$$

As follows are pictures of experimental comparison results(see fig.2).

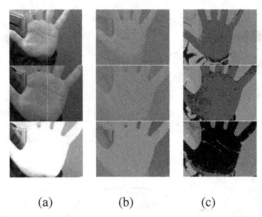

(a)   (b)   (c)

Fig. 2. Followed by the original image are the traditional Ycrcb color space picture and the improved color space picture

    (a) The original image samples from video frames under different lights.
    (b) Ycrcb images of the traditional Ycrcb color space with the formula 1.
    (c) Modified Ycrcb pictures of improved RGB color space to Ycrcb color space with the formula 2.

It obviously that the hands of c column pictures has better contrast with the background than the b column images. The Cr,Cb value of the modified Ycrcb color space pictures has better clustering stability to light intesnsity and more robust to the environment,and make the extraction of the skin area more easy.

3.2 Palm ROI Position Based on Valleys

The common preprocessing step used in[10]computes the two valley points A and B as shown in Fig 3.

Fig. 3. Extraciton of palm Roi based on finger valleys

We find the A and B from the inflection points of the outer hand contour line. The region of interest in the hand image is defined with respect to the two vally points A and B.We assume the middle valley point C.In the vertical bisected direction of line joining A and B(denoted by len-AB) ,the seclected distance is 0.25*(len-AB). Then we try to find a square of side length as len-AB and the square is aligned to the vertical bisected direction of line AB ,we think of it as ROI(white area in fig.3).

3.3   The Apporach Based on Real-Time Region Learning

This part we describe the whole process of original video hand frame pictures to get the bianry hand contour and capture the palm ROI based on real-time region learning.

Step 1) Given a video stream of hand frames $X_1, X_2 \dots, X_n$ of size M×N(M,N>>10 pixel) for one person.

Step 2) Process the frames with the improved Ycrcb color space algorithm to reduce the influence of lighting effect.

Step 3) Create a dynamic learning region.Specially,we change the size of re-gion from 10×10 to M×N by increasing 10 pixels one time andthe position of region respectively from left to right and top to bottom of the X_i frame by the step of the width of region.An exampleis shown in figure 4.The learning region moves from small to large in order on the frame flow.

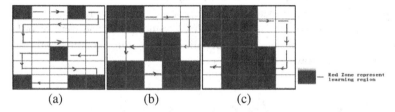

(a)   (b)   (c)

Fig. 4. Example of simple schenmatic for learning region changes

(a) A 10×10 size region box (red area)moves from left to right and top to bottom by the step of 10 pixels in the X_i frame;

(b) A 20×20 size region box moves by the step of 20 pixels as the same as the step of (a);

(c) A 30×30 size region box moves as the same as the previous step;

(d) 40×40......50×50..;

(e) The process stops until the size of region box is M×N.

Step 4) Calculate the maximum and minimum value of Cr,Cb in the every real -time learning region and use Ti initialized as zero as a thresh-old for binarizing the image in the formula 3.

$$\begin{cases} Cr_{\min} - Ti \le Frame[Cr] \le Cr_{\max} + Ti \\ Cb_{\min} - Ti \le Frame[Cb] \le Cb_{\max} + Ti \end{cases} \tag{3}$$

The value of Ti increases by the step of $(Cr_{\max} - Cr_{\min})/10(var\,ible)$ or $(Cb_{\max} - Cb_{\min})/10$ to the restriction $Cr_{\min}, Cb_{\min}(Ti \le Cr_{\min}, Cb_{\min})$.

Step 5) Successively with obtained hand contours we carry the valley point position algorithm to get palm Roi. In those binary images ,some hardly has hand contour and some has more than one hand contour,but there must be several pictures containing relatively complete hand contour due to the thereshold of binarizing the image dynamically up-to-date.It is variable.When the extraction become stable and relatively accurate,the process of Step 4 is terminated.Those pictures are the last necessary palm ROI.

Step 6) To receive next frame and follows the step 1 to 5 to get the palm RO I.In our plan,we assume the sequential extraction of three effecti-ve im ages is successful.Then we can call next person.

4   Experiment and Results

In our test,we use Logitech HD c270 webcam,vs 2010 programming environment and opencv 2.4.3 package to develop this palmprint extraction system.We present results of proposed approach on collecting palms of one hundred people under different lights and pose changes.For each subject,both the left and right hands are taken into account and 5 videos clips with 40 frames persecond were recorded for the hand.Some source hand images under different lighting conditions(fig.5)and pose change(fig.6) are shown as follows.

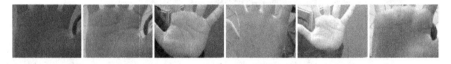

Fig. 5. Palm images variations under different lighting conditions

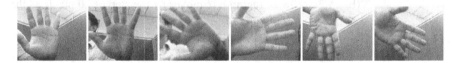

Fig. 6. Hand images variations in pose

After the images acquisition,they are transformed to modified Ycrcb color space(fig.7) and then they are carried with the region based learning algorithm(fig.8).

Fig. 7. Images to modified Ycrcb color space

Fig. 8. Dynamical changes of hand binary pictures based on the region learning and the red square is the learning region

When the learning region moves to the position as shown in fig.8,we get the entire hand contour gradually.Then we get the relatively clear binary images of hand to the application of the finger point position issue to gain the stable palm ROI(fig.9).

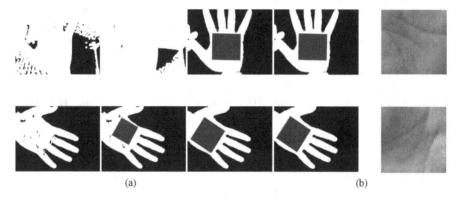

(a)   (b)

Fig. 9. To get the stable palm gradually.(a) The capture of the maxium square in the dynamical binary pictures;(b) Palm of ROI obtained finally.

In the test of one hundred subjects ,the rate of extraction reachs 95% and the corresponding precisely rate is 92% which can meet the basic requirements and this means the extraction of finger valleys position is right.The erroneous results(fig.10) analysis:when there are a lot area of near-skin color by the finger root points and particulary uneven illumination on the hands,the results will be affected to some certain extent.

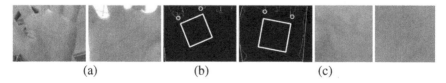

(a)   (b)   (c)

Fig. 10. The inaccrutate extract pictures.(a) The source images;(b) The main hand contour lines drawn to capture the maximum squre;(c) Pam ROI inaccrute region

5   Conclusions

In this paper,we present a novel method for the palm Roi extraction based on the learning region.The proposed method adopts modified Ycrcb color space and the palm ROI position based on finger valleys.According to the experiments results,the proposed method achieves encouraging correct classification rate,and Our future work includes following issues: when there are a lot area of near-skincolor by the finger root points and particulary uneven illumination on the hands,how we can slove the situation.In the subsequent tests, we can optimize this algorithm to reduce the computation time to meet more users.

References

1. Kahraman, F., Kurt, B., Gokmen, M.: Robust face alignment for illumination and pose invariant face recognition. In: CVPR (November 2007)
2. Kale, A., Chowdhury, A.R.: Towards a view invariant gait recognition algorithm. In: IEEE Conference on AVSS, pp. 143–150 (2003)
3. Zheng, G., Wang, C.J., Boult, T.E.: Application of projective invariants in hand geometry biometrics. IEEE Transactions on Information Forensics and Security 2(4), 758–768 (2007)
4. Zhang, D., Kong, W.K., You, J., Wong, M.: Online palmprint identification. IEEE Trans. Pattern Anal. Mach. Intell. 25(9), 1041–1050 (2003)
5. Lin, C.L., Chuang, T.C., Fan, H.C.: palmprint identification using Hierarchical Decomposition. Patter. Recogn. 38, 2639–2652 (2005)
6. Han, C.C., Cheng, H.L., Lin, C.L., Fan, K.C.: Personal Authetication, Using palmprint Features. Patter. Recogn. 36, 371–381 (2003)
7. Kashiha, M.A., Faez, K.: Developing a Method for Segmenting Palmprint into Region-Of-Interest. In: Proceedings of Fourth International Conference on Sciences of Electronic, Technologies of Information and Telecommunications, SETIT (March 2007)
8. Poon, C., Wong, D.C.M., Shen, H.C.: A New Method in locating and segmenting Palmprint into Region-of-Interest. In: Proceedings of the 17th International Conference on Pattern Recognition 2004, ICPR 2004 (2004)
9. Jian-qiu, C., Hua-qing, W., Zhang-li, L.: Skin Color Division Base on Modified Ycrcb Color Space. Journal of Chongqing Jiaotong University Natrural Science 3 (2010)
10. Di, L., Dongmei, S., Zhengding, Q.: A Novel Image Enhancement Mthod for SIFT Feature Extraction of Low Resolution Palmprint Images. Neural Comput. & Applic. 21, 1835–1844 (2012)

Measuring Biometric Feature Information in Palmprint Images

Weiqian Shi, Dongmei Sun*, and Shenghui Wang

The Key Laboratory of Advanced Information Science
and Network Technology of Beijing,
Institute of Information Science,
Beijing Jiaotong University, Beijing, China
{dmsun,12120385}@bjtu.edu.cn

Abstract. The measurement of biometric feature information is important for biometric technology, as for it can determine the uniqueness of biometric features, compare the performance of several feature extraction methods and quantify whether combination of features or biometric fusion offers any advantage. In this paper, we study the measurement of palmprint feature information using relative entropy between intra-person and inter-population. We compute the biometric feature information in which the feature extracted by three different methods, including: Principal Component Analysis (PCA), Linear Discriminant Analysis(LDA) and Locality Preserving Projections(LPP). The average biometric feature information is calculated to be approximately 280 bits for PCA, 246 bits for LDA features and 460 bits for LPP.

Keywords: Biometric, Palmprint images, Feature information, Relative entropy.

1 Introduction

Measuring the information in biometric, such as face, iris, fingerprint or palmprint, is an issue gradually gaining more attention because it can answer a number of questions related to security strength. First of all, there has always been an interest in finding out how unique different biometric types are, which ones are more reliable than others and under what conditions. Secondly, performance of different methods and technologies may be evaluated based on knowledge of information content of biometric samples and templates they produce. Finally, it becomes possible to say whether creating fusion biometric systems results in higher information.

Biometric information (BI) is defined as "the discriminating extra bits needed to represent an intraclass distribution with respect to the interclass feature distribution or, from the biometric recognition system point of the view, the decrease in uncertainty about the identity of a person due to a set of biometric

* This work is supported by NSFC (No 61201158), PCSIRT (No. IRT201206) and the Key Laboratory of Advanced Information Science and Network Technology of Beijing.

Z. Sun et al. (Eds.): CCBR 2013, LNCS 8232, pp. 249–257, 2013.

measurements"[1]. In other words, initially, the person is a part of the population and can be anybody. However, after biometric measurements are acquired, the information for identification is available and the uncertainty decreases.

Compared with other biometrics technologies, palmprint has several advantages: low resolution, low cost, non-intrusiveness, stable structure features and high user acceptance[2]. It is for these reasons that palmprint has recently attracted an increasing amount of attention from researchers.

Several approaches were developed about biometric information. Daugman[3] suggested using discrimination entropy to calculate the information content of the iris by analyzing distributions of matching scores. Arakala et al. [4] proposed a preliminary theoretical model to predict the entropy of a retina template. Yagiz et al.[5] estimated the KL-Divergence as biometric information through nearest neighbor(NN) distance. The recently developed method by Adler[6] measuring the iris images of biometric information by using the concept of relative entropy, which is a measure of the distance between two probability distributions.

In this paper, we calculate the information through relative entropy in palmprint images. The database we use is from Palmprint Database of Beijing Jiaotong University.

2 Method

The diagram of our method is shown in Fig.1.

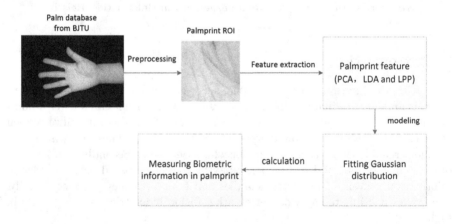

Fig. 1. Method diagram

Our effort contain four steps:

Step 1: Palmprint images preprocess: we transform original RGB mode images to grayscale mode, apply a Gaussian low-pass filter to the grayscale image, and then extract the hand contour by applying a contour following algorithm to a binarized image, locate the fingertips and the valleys between the fingers, finally palmprint ROI is normalized to 128×128 pixels [7].

Step 2: Palmprint feature extraction: we make use of three palmprint feature extraction algorithms, i.e. Principal Component Analysis (PCA), Linear Discriminant Analysis(LDA) and Locality Preserving Projections(LPP) algorithms, we extract three different set of the palmprint features.

Step 3: Gaussian modelling of palmprint feature: as Gaussian distribution is the most widely used model and it is a good reflection of the real world distributions, we modeled the features as Gaussian distributions.

Step 4: Calculation of Palmprint biometric information: we measure the palmprint image information based on an information theoretic concept of relative entropy. We calculate the biometric feature information three algorithms and find the difference and analysis.

2.1 Relative Entropy

The relative entropy, (also called information divergence, information gain, or Kullback-Leibler divergence), D(p∥q) is a measure of distance from a true probability distribution p to an assumed distribution q, it defined as:

$$D(p \parallel q) = \int_{\chi} p(x) \log_2 \frac{p(x)}{q(x)} dx \tag{1}$$

where χ is a set of all feature dimensions, p(x) is the feature distribution for one individual, or intra-person distribution, and q(x) is the feature distribution in the whole population, or inter-person distribution. In the above definition,relative entropy is always nonnegative and is zero if and only if p = q. It is often useful to think of relative entropy as a "distance" between distributions [8].

The relative entropy D(p∥q) was preferred over the shannon entropy H(p) since it allows to determine the amount of information distinguishing one person, discribed by the distribution p(x) based on the assume total population distribution q(x).

2.2 Feature Extraction

There are numerous approaches proposed for palmprint feature extraction. Principal component analysis (PCA) [9], also known as "eigenpalm", as the most fundamental dimensionality reduction methods, has been widely used in face recognition and palmprint identification[10]. The key idea is to project the high dimensional features to an orthogonal subspace for their compact representations.

PCA seeks a projection that best represents the data in a least-squares sense. The matrix ww^T is a projection onto the principal component space spanned by w which minimizes the following objective function,

$$min \sum_{i=1}^{n} \left| x_i - ww^T x_i \right|^2 \tag{2}$$

The second method we use to extract palmprint features is Linear Discriminant Analysis (LDA), also known as Fisherpalms [11]. In this method, LDA is used to project palmprints from this high-dimensional original palmprint space to a significantly lower dimensional feature space (Fisherpalm space), seeks the projection directions that are advantageous for discrimination. In other words, the ratio of the determinant of the between-class scatter to that of the within-class scatter is maximized. Suppose we have a set of n-dimensional samples x_1, $x_2, x_3, ..., x_n$, belonging to l classes of palms. The objective function is as follows,

$$max \frac{w^T S_B w}{w^T S_W w} \tag{3}$$

$$S_B = \sum_{i=1}^{l} |C_i| (m^i - m)(m^i - m)^T \tag{4}$$

$$S_W = \sum_{i=1}^{l} |C_i| E\left[(x^i - m^i)(x^i - m^i)^T\right]^T \tag{5}$$

where m is the total sample mean vector, $|C_i|$ is the number of samples in class C_i, m^i are the average vectors of C_i, x^i are the sample vectors associated to C_i, S_W is the within-class scatter matrix and S_B the between-class scatter matrix.

However, both of them effectively only the Euclidean structure of feature space. LPP [12] has been proposed in palmprint recently, which takes into account the space structure of the samples, and in the process of dimension reduction, it can thus find a good linear embedding that preserves local structural information and intrisinc geometry of the data space. In this way, the unwanted variations resulting from changes in lighting, expression, and pose may be eliminated or reduced. [13] The objective function of LPP is as follows:

$$min \sum (y_i - y_j)^2 S_{ij} \tag{6}$$

The objective function with our choice of symmetric weights $S_{ij}(S_{ij} = S_{ji})$ incurs a heavy penalty if neighboring points x_i and x_j are mapped far apart. Therefore, minimizing it is an attempt to ensure that if x_i and x_j are close then y_i and y_j are close as well. S_{ij} can be thought of as a similarity measure between objects.

2.3 Distribution Modeling

Considering of the Gaussian model is the most common and good reflection of the real world distributions[6], we can write person distribution as:

$$p(x) = \frac{1}{\sqrt{|2\pi \Sigma_p|}} exp(-\frac{1}{2}(x - \mu_p)^t \Sigma_p^{-1}(x - \mu_p)) \tag{7}$$

whereas the population distribution q(x) is defined similarily, replacing q by p. The number of samples of all the palm images in the system is denoted as

N_q. Defining the samples of the palmprint images be x_1, $x_2, x_3, ..., x_N$, then the population feature mean value is defined as a vector:

$$\mu_q = E(x) = \frac{1}{N_q} \sum_{i=1}^{N_q} x_i \qquad (8)$$

the individual person mean is replacing q by p. The population feature co-variance is defined:

$$\Sigma_q = E[(X - \mu_q)^t (X - \mu_q)] = \frac{1}{N_q - 1} \sum_{i=1}^{N_q} (X - \mu_q)^t (X - \mu_q) \qquad (9)$$

also, the person feature covariance, Σ_p, is defined analogously. μ_q and μ_p are feature vector with the size of $N \times 1$, feature covariances are matrices of size $N \times N$.

Based on the Gaussian distribution, the relative entropy will be easy to cac-ulate, $D(p \parallel q)$ as follows [1]:

$$D(P \parallel Q) = K \left(\ln \frac{|2\pi \Sigma_q|}{|2\pi \Sigma_p|} + trace \left((\Sigma_p + T) \Sigma_1^{-1} \right) - I \right) \qquad (10)$$

where $T = (\mu_p - \mu_q)^t (\mu_p - \mu_q)$, and $k = log_2 \sqrt{e}$

Generate a mapping form the biometric features to the new space. Accord-ing to the Singular Value Decomposition (SVD), within the feature covariance matrix,

$$U S_q V^t = svd(\Sigma_q) = svd(cov(x)) \qquad (11)$$

So the individual's is

$$S_p = V^t \Sigma_p U \qquad (12)$$

$$S_t = V^t (U_p - U_q)^t (U_p - U_q) U \qquad (13)$$

The Σ_p in the most occation is singular and it may lead some troubles. $|\Sigma_p|$ will decrease to zero and the relative entropy we measured will turn to infinity. To solve this problem, multiplying the mask M [1] ,

$$M \begin{cases} 1, & if \ i = j \ or \ (i < L \bigcup j < L) \\ 0, & if \ otherwise \end{cases} \qquad (14)$$

which we choose L=4 for the recommended of L is better when $L = \frac{3}{4} N_q$ this will regularizes the Σ_p, then $D(p \parallel q)$ will not diverge.

Based on above, the equation (5) can be written as:

$$D(P \parallel Q) = K \left(\ln(\frac{|S_q|}{|S_p|}) + trace \left((S_p + S_t) S_q^{-1} - I \right) V^t \right) \qquad (15)$$

3 Experiments and Results

To evaluate the effectiveness of proposed method, a hand image database is set up. 980 right hand images from 98 individuals are captured using CCD camera based device, 10 images for each individuals.

After preprocessing, palmprint derived from the original database. palm database normalized to 128×128 pixels . The image in the palmprint database were also cropped in 64×64 pixels for the contrast test.

3.1 The Effect of Dimensions on Biometric Information

The biometric information were calculated using the features extracted by the methods of PCA(eigenpalm) features, LDA features(fisherpalm) and LPP features(Laplacianpalm).

As we expect, the dimension we choose has effect on the PCA feature information. We changed the dimension from 50 to 200 to observe the changes of relative entropy. The results shown in Table 1.

Table 1. PCA Feature Information and Dimensions

Dimensions BI(bits)	50	100	150	200
Average BI	186.42	285.26	386.85	474.91

With the increase of dimension, a trend showing a steady growth of the biometric feature information. But we also can conclude that the relative entropy grow faster in low dimensional feature than high dimensional feature. Although the high-dimensional feature contains more biometric information , it also related to the increase of computational complexity. High dimensionality is critical to high performance, we should trade off the biometric information and computational complexity.

3.2 The Effect of Palmprint Image Size on Biometric Information

The size of the palmprint image also have influence in the information. So we cropped the pixels from 128×128 pixels to 64×64 pixels, and experiment them both in PCA,LDA and LPP features.

Table 2. Three methods' average biometric information and image size

Methods Size	PCA	LDA	LPP
128 × 128	280.05	246.35	460.54
64 × 64	186.56	129.21	209.90

With the size of 128×128 pixels, the mean of PCA, LDA, LPP feature biomtric information is 280, 246, 460 respectively. When the size change to 64×64 pixels, PCA, LDA, LPP feature calculate the relative entropy is 186, 129 and 209 for each. The detailed data presented in the following.

3.3   BI of different Feature Extraction Methods

The following Figure 2,3 illustrate the biometric information calculated for each PCA, LDA and LPP features, respectively.

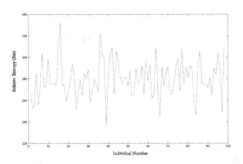

Fig. 2. PCA features biometric information, x axis present the individual's number and the y axis is relative entropy in bits

From Fig.2, we find that PCA features were measure the relative entropy with the dimension of 97, for the sake of the same dimension with LDA. From the experiment result, the mean of overall features is 280.0449 bits with the size of 128×128 pixels, higher than the LDA features

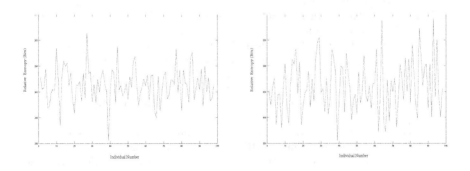

Fig. 3. The left side is LDA features biometric information,the right side LPP features biometric information. X axis present the individual's number, y axis is relative entropy in bits.

Fig.3. Left side shows that the detail information of the LDA feature. The avearage information is 246.3485 bits, with the size of 128×128 pixels.

The right one illustrates that comapare all the three experiments, the LPP approach provides a best representation and it contains the highest information. It may because the palm images probably reside on a nonlinear manifold, the unwanted variations resulting from changes in lighting and pose may be eliminated or reduced.

4   Conclusions

In this paper, we measure biometric feature information in the palmprint image using relative entropy. Based on three different feature extraction methods, contains: Principal Component Analysis (PCA), Linear Discriminant Analysis(LDA) and Locality Preserving Projections(LPP), we fitted the features to the Gussian distributions and calculated the biometric feature information. The effect of dimensions and image size on biometric information in PCA is presented, we also analysis the average information of the three kinds of feature extraction methods.

Acknowledgment. This work is supported by NSFC (No 61201158), PCSIRT (No. IRT201206) and the Key Laboratory of Advanced Information Science and Network Technology of Beijing.

References

1. Adler, A., Youmaran, R., Loyka, S.: Towards a measure of biometric information. In: Canadian Conference on Electrical and Computer Engineering, CCECE 2006, pp. 210–213 (2006)
2. Duta, N., Jain, A.K., Mardia, K.V.: Matching of palmprints. Pattern Recogn. Lett. 23(4), 477–485 (2002)
3. Daugman, J.: The importance of being random: statistical principles of iris recognition. Pattern Recognition 36(2), 279–291 (2003)
4. Arakala, A., Culpepper, J.S., Jeffers, J., Turpin, A., Boztaş, S., Horadam, K.J., McKendrick, A.M.: Entropy of the retina template. In: Tistarelli, M., Nixon, M.S. (eds.) ICB 2009. LNCS, vol. 5558, pp. 1250–1259. Springer, Heidelberg (2009)
5. Sutcu, Y., Sencar, H.T., Memon, N.: How to measure biometric information? In: 2010 20th International Conference on Pattern Recognition (ICPR), pp. 1469–1472 (2010)
6. Youmaran, R., Adler, A.: Measuring biometric sample quality in terms of biometric feature information in iris images. JECE, 22:22 (January 2012)
7. Zhang, Y., Sun, D., Qiu, Z.: Hand-based single sample biometrics recognition. Neural Computing and Applications 21(8), 1835–1844 (2012)
8. Cover, T.M., Thomas, J.A.: Elements of information theory. Wiley-Interscience, New York (1991)
9. Turk, M., Pentland, A.: Eigenfaces for recognition. J. Cognitive Neuroscience 3(1), 71–86 (1991)
10. Lu, G., Zhang, D., Wang, K.: Palmprint recognition using eigenpalms features. Pattern Recogn. Lett. 24(9-10), 1463–1467 (2003)

11. Wu, X., Zhang, D., Wang, K.: Fisherpalms based palmprint recognition. Pattern Recognition Letters, 2829–2838 (2003)
12. He, X., Niyogi, P.: Locality preserving projections. In: Thrun, S., Saul, L., Schölkopf, B. (eds.) Advances in Neural Information Processing Systems, vol. 16. MIT Press, Cambridge (2004)
13. He, X., Yan, S., Hu, Y., Zhang, H.-J.: Learning a locality preserving subspace for visual recognition. In: Proceedings of the Ninth IEEE International Conference on Computer Vision, ICCV 2003, vol. 2. IEEE Computer Society Press, Washington, DC (2003)

Modified Binary Pattern for Finger Vein Recognition

Rongyang Xiao, Gongping Yang[*], Yilong Yin, and Lu Yang

School of Computer Science and Technology, Shandong University,
Jinan, 250101, P.R. China
canyueyang@126.com, {gpyang,ylyin}@sdu.edu.cn,
yangluhi@163.com

Abstract. In this paper, the Center-Symmetric local binary pattern (CSLBP) operator is firstly used as a feature extraction method for finger vein recognition. The CSLBP feature can be viewed as a combination of the texture-based feature and the gradient-based feature. Moreover, CSLBP is easy-to-implement and computational simplicity. However, due to its small spatial support area, the bit-wise comparison therein made between two single pixel values is much affected by noise and sensitive to image translation and rotation. To address this problem, we further present a modified feature, termed Multi-scale Block Center-Symmetric local binary pattern (MB-CSLBP). Instead of individual pixel, in MB-CSLBP we perform the comparison based on average values of block sub- regions. It encodes not only microstructures but also macrostructures of image patterns, and hence provides a more complete image representation than the basic LBP and CSLBP operator. Experiments show that better performances are gained by the proposed method.

Keywords: Finger Vein Recognition, CSLBP, MB-CSLBP.

1   Introduction

Biometric recognition refers to the use of distinctive physiological and behavioral characteristics (e.g., fingerprints, face, hand geometry, iris, gait, signature), called biometric identifiers or simply biometrics, for automatically recognizing a person [1]. Since it is difficult to misplace, forge or share biometric identifiers, biometric recognition is more reliable than traditional token-based methods (e.g., keys or ID cards) and knowledge-based methods (e.g., passwords or PINs). Besides, biometric recognition also promises better security, higher efficiency, and better user experience in many cases. Among various kinds of biometric identifiers, finger vein recognition is a newly emerging biometrics technology. Medical research proves that each finger has a unique vein pattern that can be used for personal verification [2]. Generally, the finger vein recognition demonstrates some advantages over other biometrics methods [3]: (1) non-contact: finger vein patterns are not influenced by surface conditions, and it is more acceptable for the users; (2) live body identification: finger vein patterns

---

[*] Corresponding Author.

Z. Sun et al. (Eds.): CCBR 2013, LNCS 8232, pp. 258–265, 2013.

can only be identified on a live body without fake finger attacks in fingerprint recognition; (3) higher security: finger vein patterns are internal features that are difficult to forge; (4) smaller device size: most finger vein capturing devices are smaller in size as compared to palm vein based verification devices.

Local binary pattern (LBP) is a popular technique used for image representation and classification [4]. Due to its high discriminative power and invariant against any monotonic transformation of the gray scale, LBP has been widely applied in various applications such as texture analysis and object recognition. In [5] a LBP based finger vein recognition method was proposed. Heikkila et al. [6] proposed a modified version of the LBP feature to describe the surroundings of a key-point, called the center-symmetric local binary pattern (CSLBP). The CSLBP descriptor inherits the desirable properties of both the SIFT descriptor and the LBP feature, and is computationally simple. So in this paper, we propose the CSLBP as a new feature extraction method for finger vein recognition. However, the original CSLBP operator has the following drawback in its application to finger vein recognition. The comparison based on pixel-level is much affected by noise and sensitive to image translation and rotation. Moreover, features calculated in the local 3×3 neighborhood cannot capture larger scale structure (macrostructure) that may be dominant features of finger vein image. Inspired by [7], we propose a novel representation, called Multiscale Block CSLBP (MB-CSLBP), to overcome the limitations of CSLBP and apply it to finger vein recognition. In MB-CSLBP, we compare average values of subregions Instead of individual pixels. MB-CSLBP code presents several advantages: (1) It is less sensitive to noise and more robust than CSLBP; (2) it encodes not only microstructures but also macrostructures of image patterns, and hence integrates more information for image representation.

The rest of this paper is organized as follows: In Section 2, we first give a brief review of the LBP and CSLBP methods and then introduce the MB-CSLBP representation. In section 3, experiments and analysis will be presented and in the last section conclusions will be given.

2   The Proposed Method

2.1   Center-Symmetric Local Binary Pattern (CSLBP)

The basic LBP operator can be defined as an ordered set of binary values determined by comparing the gray values of a center pixel and its neighboring pixels. Let g_c and g_n in (1) denote the gray value of the center pixel (x_c, y_c) and its eight neighboring pixels, respectively. If g_n is smaller than g_c, the binary result of the pixel is set to 0, otherwise to 1. All the results are combined to an 8-bit binary string. The binary values can be expressed in decimal form as shown in (1):

$$LBP(x_c, y_c) = \sum_{n=0}^{n=7} s(g_n - g_c)2^n$$

$$s(x) = \begin{cases} 1, & x \geq 0 \\ 0, & otherwise \end{cases}$$

(1)

The CSLBP is a modified version of LBP. In CSLBP, instead of comparing the neighboring pixels with the center pixel, the center-symmetric pairs of pixels are compared, such as (g_0, g_4), (g_1, g_5) in Fig. 1. The CSLBP features can be computed by Equation (2):

$$CSLBP = \sum_{n=0}^{n=3} s(g_n - g_{n+4})2^n$$

$$s(x) = \begin{cases} 1, & x \geq T \\ 0, & otherwise \end{cases}$$

(2)

Here g_n and g_{n+4} correspond to the gray-level of center-symmetric pairs of pixels of the 3X3 descriptor. T is a user-specified small value, and which is used to increase the robustness of CSLBP feature on flat image regions by thresholding the graylevel differences [6]. In our experiments, T was given a value of 0.5. From the computation of CSLBP, we can see that the CSLBP is closely related to the gradient operator, because, like some gradient operators, it considers graylevel differences between pairs of opposite pixels in a neighborhood. This way the CSLBP feature take advantage of both the properties of the LBP and the gradient based features. The LBP and CSLBP encoding procedure is illustrated in Fig. 1.

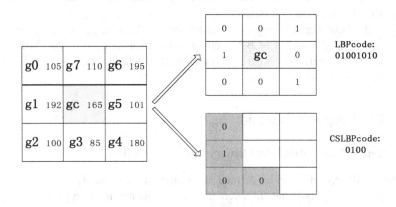

Fig. 1. LBP and CSLBP operator

2.2   Multi-scale Block CSLBP (MB-CSLBP)

As mentioned above the comparison based on pixel-level is much affected by noise and sensitive to image translation and rotation, In MB-CSLBP, the comparison between single pixels in CSLBP is replaced with comparison between average gray-values of sub-regions, Each sub-region is a square block containing neighboring pixels. The whole filter is composed of 9 blocks. We take the side length L of the block as a parameter, and $9\,L\,L$ denoting the scale of the MB-CSLBP operator (particularly, $9\ 1\ 1$ MB-CSLBP is in fact the original CSLBP). The computational process can be expressed in Equation (3):

$$MB\text{-}CSLBP = \sum_{n=0}^{n=3} s(B_n - B_{n+4})2^n$$

$$B = \sum_{k=0}^{L^2} g_k \tag{3}$$

$$s(x) = \begin{cases} 1, & x \geq T \\ 0, & otherwise \end{cases}$$

In (3) g is the gray-value of individual pixel and B is the sum of gray-values of the nth block. In order to simplify the computation, we use the sum instead of the average gray-value of each sub-region. A $3\ 3$ MB-CSLBP encoding procedure is illustrated in the following Fig. 2.

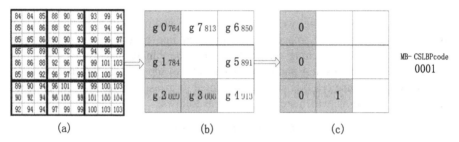

(a)   (b)   (c)

Fig. 2. The MB-CSLBP operator. (a) the 3×3 gray values of original. (b) compute the sum gray values of each block. (c) comparison of center-symmetric pairs of pixels and get the MB-CSLBPcode.

2.3   Finger Vein Recognition System

A typical finger vein recognition system mainly includes four stages: image capturing, image preprocessing, feature extraction and matching. The captured raw finger vein images usually have problems such as rotation, low contrast, non-uniform illumination and background noise, thus preprocessing is necessary for feature extraction and matching. The original spatial resolution of the finger vein image is 320×240.After rotation correction, ROI (region of interesting) extraction and size normalization, the size of the region used for feature extraction is reduced to 240×80. The procedure are shown in Fig. 3(a) ~ (d).

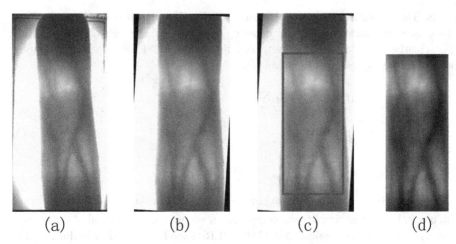

(a)   (b)   (c)   (d)

Fig. 3. Image capturing and preprocessing. (a) the original finger vein image. (b) image rotation correction. (3) ROI extraction. (4) image size and gray normalization.

After image preprocessing, we use the aforementioned methods to perform feature extraction, and then every image will be encoded into an exclusive binary string theoretically. In the matching stage, Denoting the binary feature of image in the database by BinaryCodeA and the binary feature of input image by BinaryCodeB, the Hamming Distance (HD) is generally adopted to measure dissimilarities between the two binary patterns, which are represented as follows:

$$HD = \frac{\|BinaryCodeA \otimes BinaryCodeB\|}{LengthofBinaryCode} \tag{4}$$

In (4), $\otimes$ is a Boolean exclusive-OR operator between two binary patterns.

3   Experiments and Analysis

3.1   Database and Experiment Setting

We conduct the experiments using our finger vein database which collects 136 fingers, where each finger contributes 20 finger vein images. In this work, we evaluate the performance of the proposed method in verification mode and identification mode respectively, and the measurement of our proposed method is evaluated by the EER (equal error rate). EER is the error rate when the FRR (false rejection rate) equals the FAR (false acceptance rate) and which is suited for measuring the overall performance of biometrics systems because the FRR and FAR are treated equally.

3.2   Verification Mode

In order to diminish the influence of class imbalances, in the verification mode, we use all the 20 vein images in intra-class matching meanwhile the first 6 vein images in interclass matching. Consequently, there are 25,840 (136×19×20/2) intra-class matching and 330,480 (6 ×135 ×6 ×136/2) interclass matching in total. Here we test the performance of the proposed method with the block size 3×3, 5×5, 7×7, 9×9. The EERs of proposed method and LBP are listed in Table 1, and the ROC curves are shown in Fig. 4. From Table 1 and Fig. 4, we can see that the CSLBP method can get a lower EER than the LBP, and a much better performance are gained by the proposed MS-CSLBP method.

Table 1. Verificaion performance with different methods

methods	EER
LBP	0.0440
CSLBP	0.0314
MB-CSLBP(3x3)	0.0261
MB-CSLBP(5x5)	0.0218
MB-CSLBP(7x7)	0.0211
MB-CSLBP(9x9)	0.0242

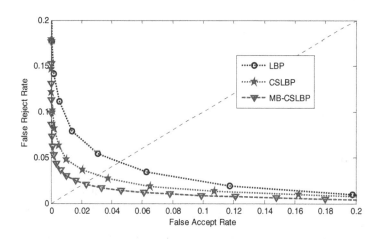

Fig. 4. ROC curves by different methods

3.3   Identification Mode

In the identification mode, we conduct experiments in the close-set database (all the samples are in the enrollment database). We do not know the class of input finger vein image and attempt to identify which class it belongs to. We randomly select one sample in each class as template and use other nineteen samples in each class as test samples (probes). Therefore, we get 136 templates and 136*19 probes totally. Each probe will be matched with all the templates. For each probe, the matching result will be ranked based on the matching score. The CMC (cumulative match curves) is shown in Fig. 5, and the rank-one recognition rate and lowest rank of perfect recognition is given in Table 2. From the experimental results we can see the proposed method is better than LBP and CSLBP based method.

Table 2. Identification performance by different methods

methods	rank-one recognition rate	lowest rank of perfect recognition
LBP	93.4%	118
CSLBP	96.1%	83
MB-CSLBP	97.4%	45

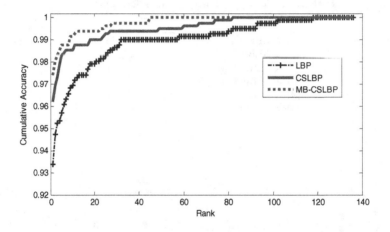

Fig. 5. The Cumulative match curves by different methods

4   Conclusion

In this paper, the Center-Symmetric local binary operator is firstly used as a feature extraction method for finger vein recognition. A better performance is gained by this method, but it is too local to be robust. In order to address the limitation of the CSLBP operator, we present a novel and efficient feature, termed Multi-scale Block Center-Symmetric local binary pattern (MB-CSLBP), within which sub-region average gray-values are used for comparison instead of single pixels. Experiments show that the proposed method can achieve a better performance than the basic LBP and CSLBP operator.

Acknowledgments. This work is supported by National Natural Science Foundation of China under Grant No. 61173069, 61070097, Program for New Century Excellent Talents in University of Ministry of Education of China under Grant No. NCET-11-0315 and Shandong Natural Science Funds for Distinguished Young Scholar. The authors would particularly like to thank the anonymous reviewers for their helpful suggestions.

References

1. Ross, A.A., Nandakumar, K., Jain, A.K.: Handbook of Multibiometrics, 1st edn. Springer, Berlin (2006)
2. Yanagawa, T., Aoki, S., Ohyama, T.: Human finger vein images are diverse and its patterns are useful for personal identification. MHF Prepr. Ser. 12, 1–7 (2007)
3. Liu, Z., Yin, Y.L., Wang, H.J., Song, S.L., Li, Q.L.: Finger vein recognition with manifold learning. J. Netw. Comput. Appl. 33, 275–282 (2010)
4. Ojala, T., Pietikainen, M., Maenpaa, T.: Multiresolution gray-scale and rotation invariant texture classification with local binary patterns. IEEE Trans. Pattern Anal. Mach. Intell. 24, 429–436 (2002)
5. Lee, E.C., Jung, H., Kim, D.: New finger biometric method using near infrared imaging. Sensors 11, 2319–2333 (2011)
6. Heikkila, M., Schmid, C.: Description of interest regions with local binary patterns. Pattern Recogn. 42, 425–436 (2009)
7. Liao, S., Zhu, X., Lei, Z., Zhang, L., Li, S.Z.: Learning Multi-scale Block Local Binary Patterns for Face Recognition. In: Lee, S.-W., Li, S.Z. (eds.) ICB 2007. LNCS, vol. 4642, pp. 828–837. Springer, Heidelberg (2007)

Novel Hierarchical Structure
Based Finger Vein Image Quality Assessment

Shan Juan Xie[1,*], Bin Zhou[1], Jucheng Yang[2], Yu Lu[3], and Yuliang Pan[1]

[1] Institute of Remote Sensing and Earth Science, Hangzhou Normal University, China
shanj_x@hotmail.com, hznu_bzhou@126.com, ylpan001@126.com
[2] College of Computer Science & Information Engineering,
Tianjin University of Science and Technology, China
juchengyang@hotmail.com
[3] College of Electronic & Information Engineering, Chonbuk National University, South Korea
luyu0311@gmail.com

Abstract. Instead of existing image based and geometry based quality estimation method for finger vein image, this paper proposed a novel quality metrics from the hierarchical structure of finger vein. The thick major vessels and short minor vessels construct the hierarchical structure of finger vein, and lead to the hierarchical energy distribution. A Gaussian Energy Model is simulated to assess the hierarchical quality of the major vessel and the minor vessel respectively using Gabor filter. The efficient of matching performance and the accuracy of quality assessment are evaluated in the experimental parts.

Keywords: Finger vein, Quality assessment, Hierarchical structure, Gaussian.

1 Introduction

Finger vein is applied as a new highlight technology for personal identification, which is exploiting the differences in the light absorption properties of the hemoglobin in blood vessels and the surrounding tissues. Veins become visible and perform the darker intensity than other tissues. Finger vein patterns are sufficiently unique of persons to promise the safe verification. Moreover, compared with fingerprints, finger vein pattern is not exposed to the outside and enjoys the advantage of being resistant to forgery. In addition, the small size of device and contactless operation enhance its widely applications.

However, since the vein exists inside the finger, the captured finger vein images are always not high quality due to the varying tissues and bones, the uneven illuminations or, furthermore, changes in the physical conditions and blood flow make the same vein appear different in each acquisition in thickness and brightness. It is well-known that reliable and accurate recognition is a challenging task and heavily dependent on the quality of the finger vein image. If a poor quality image as shown in Fig.1(a) is inputted into the matching system, it will reflect back on the uniqueness and security.

Currently, the International Standard Organization (ISO) has only defined the quality standard for fingerprint, face and iris recognition [1-3]. Quality assessment for

---

* Corresponding author.

Z. Sun et al. (Eds.): CCBR 2013, LNCS 8232, pp. 266–273, 2013.

vascular pattern image has been conducted. Pascual et al. measured the vein quality using the contrast, variance and light distribution between vein and skin vessels [4]. Michael.et al built a metric called the Grey level Co-Occurrence matrix [5]. Hartung et al. combined the Grey level Co-Occurrence matrix and optionally available metadata to estimate the vascular pattern quality [6].

However, these quality metrics only focus on the image intensity quality, the environment or the sensor effects. No quality assessment method is based on the vein pattern itself. Nevertheless, all the existing vein recognition systems are based on vein features, including the precise minutiae information or global and local features of vein pattern [7-11]. This motivates us to explore an efficient method to assess the quality of the vein pattern. The Gabor filter with eight directions is used to analyze finger vein energy distribution in each direction. Then, a Gaussian Energy Model is computed and accessed for the vein pattern quality.

The remainder of this paper is organized as follows: Sec.2 proposes the state-of -art about the hierarchical structure based quality assessment method. Sec.3 reports the experimental results, and Sec.4 concludes the paper.

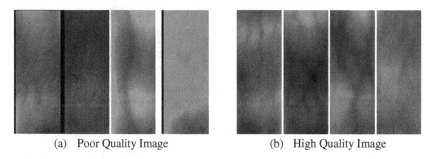

(a)   Poor Quality Image   (b)   High Quality Image

Fig. 1. Finger vein images with poor and high quality

2   Novel Hierarchical Structure Based Quality Assessment

2.1   Unique Hierarchical Structure of Finger Vein

A good analogy is to imagine the fingerprint as the tree ring, which is constructed by the series of oriental ridges and valleys as shown in Fig.2. Since the high quality fingerprint image has the well-organized orientation property, quality assessments are explored for fingerprint images based on the orientation consistency, ridge-valley contrast or orientation flow [20]. Although the finger vein and fingerprint have in common with the ridge construction, the vein ridges look disorganized, with random thicknesses, lengths, orientation flows or connections. In the worse, it is completely mystified if we use the same quality assessment method as fingerprint, since all these properties are independent with the vein quality.

If anything, a tree branch is the best image of choice to describe the vein property. Those minor branches are connected with the clear main branches, and formed lots of bifurcation points as shown in Fig.2. Intuitively, the hierarchy constructer property of finger vein is contributed for the vein quality standards, a high quality vein image should both contain the clear main branches to sustain the main structure and abundant minor branches to provide the sufficiently unique of personal verification.

Assume a fingerprint and finger vein image are convoluted with an eight-direction filter like Gabor filter. The fingerprint energy will spread almost equally for each direction and distribute approximately as the Uniform distribution. On the contrary, instead of the uniform distribution, the finger vein energy of the eight components will perform more like the Gaussian distribution. The main blood vessels like the main branches flow from one side to another side on the vertical direction and form an energy peak. The minor vessels have the energy degeneration than the main vessels, which are connected to the main vessels randomly and then less energy are focused.

Moreover, the geometry property of the finger contour, in the other words, the two straight lines can be contributed for the finger appearance detection and finger rotation correlation.

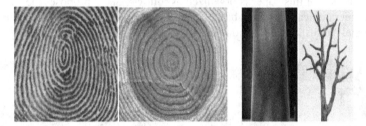

Fig. 2. Analogy comparisons of the fingerprint and the finger vein image

2.2   Hierarchical Structure Assessment

The random tree structure of vein results that the vein energy has the hierarchical energy distribution. Specifically, the main vessels like the main branches flow from one side to another side and perform as the thicker vein, which focus most of the energy. On the contrary, the minor vessels are connected to the main vessels randomly with energy degeneration. To make the hierarchical energy distribution property prominent, the vein image is segmented by the Hough transform [12] and enhanced by the guided filter [13] is filtered by the Gabor filter with eight directions [14] as shown in Fig.3, which is defined in Eq.1.

$$G(I, f_0, \theta_k, \delta) = \exp\left\{-\frac{1}{2}\left(\frac{x_{\theta_k}^2 + y_{\theta_k}^2}{\delta^2}\right)\right\}\cos(2\pi f_0 x_{\theta_k})$$

$$\text{Where} \quad \begin{bmatrix} x_{\theta_k} \\ y_{\theta_k} \end{bmatrix} = \begin{bmatrix} \cos\theta_k & \sin\theta_k \\ -\sin\theta_k & \cos\theta_k \end{bmatrix}\begin{bmatrix} x \\ y \end{bmatrix} \tag{1}$$

Where $\theta_k = k\pi/8, k = (1,2,...,8)$ and f_0 respectively denote the orientation and the center frequency of the Gabor filter. Thus eight filtered components are generated by the bank of Gabor filters as shown in Fig. 3.

A novel model is built based on the distribution of eight direction components of Gabor filter, which called Gaussian Energy Model. Energy of the eight direction filtered components are computed and analyzed for High/Poor quality images as shown in Fig. 4. We can find the image which is recovered by the guided filter [13] showed clear major vessels on the horizontal direction and abundant minor vessels on the other directions.

Fig. 3. Eight components from the bank of Gabor filter

The tested image shown in the 3rd row of Fig.4, which is a predefined as a poor quality image, shows the clear vein pattern by the proposed method that is different with the normal gray value or image contrast based quality assessment method.

The Gaussian Energy Models is built for the high/poor quality images by analyzing their energy distributions as shown in Fig.5. Two quality metrics are concluded for quality assessment:

- Major vessels quality (*Q_major*): A high quality vein image should qualify the clear and thick major vessels and focus the dominant energy of the image more than $\overline{Major}$, which is the expected energy value for high quality image.

- Minor vessels quality (*Q_minor*): A high quality vein image should have the abundant minor branches, which are contributed for the safety and uniqueness, the energy proportion on the minor branches should not less than the expected average level $\overline{Minor}$.

The expected value of $\overline{Major}$ and $\overline{Minor}$ are computed in the experimental part by simulating huge of high/poor quality sample images.

Then, the vein pattern quality can be defined as:

$$PQ = Q\_major \times Q\_minor \tag{2}$$

$$Q\_major = \begin{cases} 1 - \dfrac{\left|\arg\max_{i=1,2,\ldots8}(D_i) - \overline{Major}\right|}{\alpha_0 \cdot \overline{Major}} & \arg\max_{i=1,2,\ldots8}(D_i) > \overline{Major} \\[4ex] \dfrac{\overline{Major} - \arg\max_{i=1,2,\ldots8}(D_i)}{\alpha_1 \cdot \overline{Major}} & \arg\max_{i=1,2,\ldots8}(D_i) \le \overline{Major} \end{cases} \tag{3}$$

$$Q\_minor = \begin{cases} 1 - \beta_0 \cdot Diff & Diff \le 0.1 \\[2ex] 1 - \dfrac{Diff}{\beta_1 \cdot \overline{Minor}} & Diff > 0.1 \end{cases} \qquad \text{Where,} \qquad Diff = \left|\dfrac{\sum\limits_{i=1,2,3,7,8} D_i}{\sum\limits_{i=1,2,\ldots,8} D_i} - \overline{Minor}\right| \tag{4}$$

(α_0, α_1) and (β_0, β_1) are specified as the impact factor, which represents the quality influence degree and also contributed for the quality score normalization.

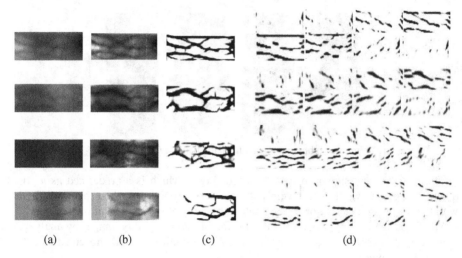

(a)   (b)   (c)   (d)

Fig. 4. Eight direction component analysis for High/Poor quality images.(a) the detected ROI, (b) the enhanced image, (c) the composit vein pattern from eight direction components,(d) the extracted direction components by Gabor filter.

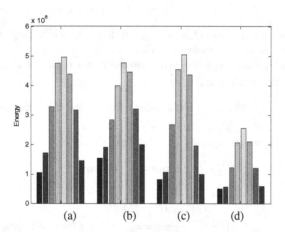

Fig. 5. Gaussian Energy Map for the images in Fig.4

2.3   Quality Metrics Computation

Three quality metrics are simulated based on the manually selected 1000 high quality images and 200 poor quality images. Fig.6 shows the average Gaussian Energy Map of the high quality and poor quality finger vein image. The expected $\overline{Major}$ =3.22e+08, and $\overline{Minor}$ =0.3977.

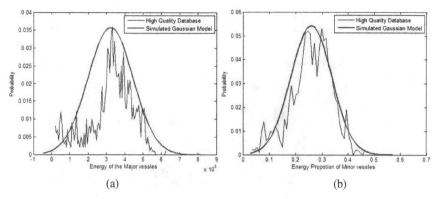

(a)   (b)

Fig. 6. Vessels energy distributions of the selected high quality database of (a) Energy distributions of major vessels, (b) Energy distributions of minor vessels

3   Experimental Results

3.1   Database

The database used here is a public finger vein database, including 106 individuals. The Group of Machine Learning and Applications, Shandong University (SDUMLA) set up the Homologous Multi-modal Traits Database [19], which consists of face images, finger vein images, gait videos, iris images and fingerprint images. Each individual was asked to provide images of his/her index finger, middle finger and ring finger of both hands, and the collection for each finger is repeated by six times. Therefore, the finger vein database is composed of 3,816 images.

3.2   Quality Assessment Performance

As shown in Table.1, eight predefined high/poor quality images are evaluated using the proposed system. The high quality image (a)-(d) are assigned a high quality score, and the predefined poor quality image (g) which is recovered by Guided filter also show a high quality score. The images (f)-(h) which contains less major vessels and minor vessels perform a low quality score. The tested image (e) and (g) are the predefined poor quality images by the normal gray value or image contrast based quality assessment method. . However, they show the clear vein pattern, and are easy for matching. The hierarchical feature based method can estimate the finger vein quality more accuracy than the intensity based or geometry based methods. The matching performance of the ranked images is shown in Table.2. Images with low vein pattern qualities seriously affect the matching performance. Estimating the image quality and rejecting those low quality images will improve the matching performance.

3.3   Throughout

Throughout is an important parameter to evaluate the quality assessment performance. From the tested 3816 images, the proposed quality assessment method is fast and the average processing time for quality assessment is 150-200ms per sample. These experiments are performed on an Intel Core 2 Quad processor and the MATLAB.

Table 1. Quality assessment results for the predefined high/poor quality images

	High quality				Predefined poor quality			
Original Image								
	(a)	(b)	(c)	(d)	(e)	(f)	(g)	(h)
Pattern Quality	0.87	0.81	0.84	0.89	0.78	0.14	0.64	0.003

Table 2. Matching Evaluations for the quality ranked images using the method [19]

Quality Value	PQ<0.3	0.3 < PQ < 0.5	0.5 < PQ < 0.8	PQ<0.8
Amount of images	50	151	525	3078
Matching Accuracy	30%	90.35%	98.86%	99.06%

4   Conclusions and Future Work

In the paper, a new quality metrics is proposed for the finger vein quality estimation based on the hierarchical vein feature itself, including the major vein pattern quality and minor vein quality. The vein pattern quality denotes both the vein uniqueness quality to promise the false accept rate and false reject rate for the matching performance. The proposed assessment system is also appropriate for other vascular images. In the future work, the larger public finger vein database is expected for the threshold training, and the novel hierarchical feature will be combined with other proper features to improve the accuracy of quality assessment.

References

1. International Organization for Standardization (ISO), ISO/IEC TR 29794-4:2010 Biometric Sample Quality - Part 4: Finger Image (ISO/IEC TC JTC1/SC37), ISO Std
2. International Organization for Standardization (ISO), ISO/IEC WD 29794-6 Biometric Sample Quality - Part 6: Iris Image (ISO/IEC TC JTC1/SC37), ISO Std
3. International Organization for Standardization (ISO), ISO/IEC TR 29794-5:2010 Biometric sample quality – Part 5:Face image data (ISO/IEC TC JTC1/SC 37), ISO Std
4. Pascual, J.E.S., Uriarte-Antonio, J., Sanchez-Reillo, R., Lorenz, M.G.: Capturing hand or wrist vein images for biometric authentication using low-cost devices. In: IIH-MSP, pp. 318–322 (2010)

5. Michael, G.K.O., Connie, T., Hoe, L.S., Jin, A.T.B.:. Design and implementation of a contactless palm vein recognition system. In: 2010 Symposium on Information and Communication Technology, pp. 92–99 (2010)
6. Hartung, D., Martin, S., Busch, C.: Quality Estimation for Vascular Pattern Recognition. In: Proceedings of the IEEE International Conference on Hand-based Biometrics, pp. 1–6 (2011)
7. Wang, L., Leedham, G., Cho, S.-Y.: Minutiae feature analysis for infrared hand vein pattern biometrics. Pattern Recognit. 41(3), 920–929 (2008)
8. Yang, J.F., Shi, Y.H., Yang, J.L.: Personal identification based on finger-vein features. Computers in Human Behavior (5), 1565–1570 (2011)
9. Yang, J., Shi, Y., Yang, J.: Finger-vein recognition based on a bank of gabor filters. In: Zha, H., Taniguchi, R.-i., Maybank, S. (eds.) ACCV 2009, Part I. LNCS, vol. 5994, pp. 374–383. Springer, Heidelberg (2010)
10. Mirmohamadsadeghi, L., Drygajlo, A.: Palm vein recognition with local binary patterns and local derivative patterns. In: 2011 International Joint Conference on Biometrics (IJCB), pp. 1–6 (2011)
11. Hartung, D., Olsen, M.A., Xu, H., Busch, C.: Spectral minutiae for vein pattern recognition. In: The IEEE International Joint Conference on Biometrics, IJCB (2011)
12. Duda, R.O., Hart, P.E.: Use of the Hough Transform to Detect Lines and Curves in Pictures. Communications of the Association Computing Machinery 15(1), 11–15 (1972)
13. Xie, S.J., Yang, J.C., Yoon, S., Lu, Y., Park, D.S.: Guided Gabor filter for finger vein pattern extraction. In: 2012 Eighth International Conference on Signal Image Technology and Internet Based Systems, pp. 118–123 (2012)
14. Lee, T.: Image Representation Using 2D Gabor Wavelets. IEEE Trans. Pattern Analysis and Machine Intelligence 18(10), 959–971 (1996)
15. Maltoni, D., Maio, D., Jain, A.K., Prabhakar, S.: Handbook of Fingerprint Recognition, pp. 164–165. Springer (2003)
16. Afsar, F.A., Arif, M., Hussain, M.: Fingerprint identification and verification system using minutiae matching. In: Proc. National Conf. Emerging Technologies, pp. 141–146 (2003)
17. He, X.C., Yung, N.H.C.: Corner detector based on global and local curvature properties. Optical Engineering 47(5), 057008–1–12 (2008)
18. Draper, N., Smith, H.: Applied Regression Analysis, 2nd edn. John Wiley, Chichester (1981)
19. Yin, Y., Liu, L., Sun, X.: SDUMLA-HMT: A Multimodal Biometric Database. In: Sun, Z., Lai, J., Chen, X., Tan, T. (eds.) CCBR 2011. LNCS, vol. 7098, pp. 260–268. Springer, Heidelberg (2011)
20. Xie, S.J., Yang, J.C., Yoon, S., Park, D.S.: Intelligent Fingerprint Quality Analysis using Online Sequential Extreme Learning Machine. Soft. Computing 16(9), 1555–1568 (2012)

Finger-Vein Recognition Based on Fusion of Pixel Level Feature and Super-Pixel Level Feature

Fei Liu, Gongping Yang[*], Yilong Yin, and Xiaoming Xi

School of Computer Science and Technology, Shandong University,
Jinan, 250101, P.R. China
lf_ff@sina.com, {gpyang,ylyin}@sdu.edu.cn, fyzq10@126.com

Abstract. Finger-vein is a promising biometric technique for the identity authentication. However, the finger displacement or the illumination variation in image capturing may cause bad recognition performance. To overcome these limitations, multi-biometric system, an effective method to improve the performance, is proposed. In this paper, a new multimodal biometric system based on pixel level feature and super-pixel level feature is proposed. First, the pixel level feature and the super-pixel level feature are extracted and matched by the Euclidean distance respectively. Then, pixel-super-pixel fusing score (PSPFS) is generated by the weighted fusion strategy. At last, the PSPFS is used to make the decision. Experimental results show that the proposed fusion method not only has better performance than the methods using single level feature, but also outperforms the fusion methods based on the fusion of two pixel level features.

Keywords: finger-vein recognition, pixel level feature, super-pixel level feature, score-level fusion.

1 Introduction

Biometrics, which makes use of biometric traits like faces [1], irises [2], gaits [3], fingerprints [4], and veins to identify individuals, has attracted more and more attention. Finger-vein recognition [5] is one of the new emerging biometrics and has been well studied recently. Compared with other biometric traits, finger-vein has higher degree of concealment and security in the identification. Furthermore, compared with other vein recognitions, such as, dorsal vein recognition [6], palm vein recognition [7], the size of imaging device in finger vein recognition is smaller and the credibility is higher. Currently, researchers have developed many kinds of algorithms to improve the recognition accuracy. In [8], local binary pattern (LBP) is proposed and applied to the finger-vein recognition [9]. In [10], the authors extract the finger-vein pattern from the image and take the pattern structure as feature to identify. In [11], the minutiae features, including bifurcation points and ending points, which can be used for geometric representation of the vein patterns shape, are extracted from these vein patterns.

However, for finger-vein recognition using single feature, when we capture the finger-vein image, the finger displacement variation may cause the large change within

---

[*] Corresponding author.

Z. Sun et al. (Eds.): CCBR 2013, LNCS 8232, pp. 274–281, 2013.
© Springer International Publishing Switzerland 2013

class, and the illumination variation result in lower image quality, the large change within class and the lower image quality may cause failure to recognition finally. In order to enhance the performance of finger-vein recognition, multi-biometric systems are employed, [12] exploits finger vein features in local moments, topological structure and statistics respectively, and a fusion scheme is adopted for decision making, obtaining a good performance rate. Wang and Liu extract the phase and direction texture features for combination in feature level fusion, finally a modified Hamming distance is used for matching in [13]. Although multi-biometric systems above can achieve high accuracy, the actual effects are all subjected to the characteristics of the pixels, which are sensitive to the pixel noise. Furthermore, because the complementarity of the pixel level features is inadequate, so the fusion effect is not perfect.

Due to the limitations mentioned above, super-pixel level feature has been proposed to overcome the existing problems. The SLIC method [14] clusters pixels into perceptually meaningful atomic regions firstly, which can be used to replace the rigid structure of the pixel grid, and then the features are computed at the small blob-based super-pixels. Super-pixel level features are the rough description of the finger-vein image and can overcome shortcoming of the pixel features as well as robust to the noise in pixel level. In addition, the super-pixel has its unique advantages, such as, high efficiency, homogeneity, and local image consistency, which can improve the recognition performance.

These advantages motivate us to fuse the pixel and the super-pixel level features together to make finger-vein more efficient for personal identification. In this paper, we propose a new finger-vein recognition method based on the fusion of pixel level and super-pixel level features. Extensive experiments show that the proposed method can significantly improve recognition performance as well as the universality.

The rest of this paper is organized as follows: Section 2, the proposed fusion method for finger-vein recognition is described. Section 3 presents the experimental result and analyses. Finally, Section 4 concludes the paper.

2   The Proposed Method

In this section, we describe the proposed fusion method in detail. We first describe the preprocessing of finger vein image. Then, different level features are extracted, including pixel level features and super-pixel level feature, and each matching score are computed. After these steps, the scores are fused by the weighted average strategy. Finally, the fused scores are used to make the final decision. Fig.1. shows the block diagram of our proposed method.

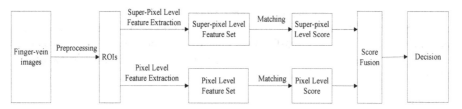

Fig. 1. The block diagram of the proposed finger vein recognition method

2.1   Preprocessing

Usually, the captured finger-vein images have many problems such as low contrast, non-uniformed illumination and background clutter, thus preprocessing is necessary for feature extraction and matching. The preprocessing we used mainly includes image gray processing, ROI extraction, size and gray normalization.

Image gray processing: we transform the original 24-bit color image with a size of 320×240 (as shown in Figure 2(a)) to an 8-bit gray image to reduce the computational complexity based on the gray-scale equation.

ROI extraction: the width and height of the finger region can be obtained based on the maximum and minimum abscissa values of the finger profile. A rectangle region can be captured based on the width and height (as shown in Figure 2(b)).

Size and gray normalization: we use the bilinear interpolation for size normalization, and the size of the normalized ROI is set to be 96 × 64. In order to extract efficient features, gray normalization is used to obtain a uniform gray distribution (as shown in Figure 2(c)).

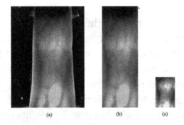

(a)   (b)   (c)

Fig. 2. Example of processing

2.2   Feature Extraction and Matching

A.   Pixel Level Features Extraction
In order to prove that the super-pixel level feature is general, we respectively fuse it with three kinds of pixel-level features, including LBP feature representing the whole image information, pattern structure (PS) feature denoting the vein pattern and minutiae (M) feature with the minutiae information.

LBP Feature
The LBP operator is an ordered set of binary values determined by comparing a pixel value and values of its neighboring pixels. We use LBP operator [14] to extract a finger vein binary codes. And then transform the binary codes into decimal number as LBP feature. Lastly we adopt the Euclidean distance to measure dissimilarities between two LBP features.

PS Feature
The PS feature can be defined as a topology structure of the binary finger vein pattern image, as shown in Fig. 3.

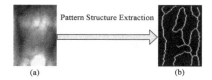

Fig. 3. Extracted PS feature

We adopt the following matching method to measure the similarity of two PS features, as shown in Equation (1-2).

$$D(L, K) = \frac{2}{N_L + N_k} \times \sum_{i=1}^{M} \sum_{j=1}^{N} [L(i,j) \cap K(i,j)] \qquad (1)$$

$$PS_{Score} = max_{0<s<p1, 0<t<p2} D_n(s,t) \qquad (2)$$

where, $\cap$ is a Boolean exclusive-AND operator, M × N is the size of the image. N_L and N_k denote the number of points in finger-vein image L and K respectively.

M Feature

The minutiae consist of cross points and extreme points. For a 3 × 3 block shown in Fig.4, if the value of p_0 is 1, and N_{trans} is greater or equal to 6, which demotes the alternate switching frequency from 0 to 1, the point p_0 is seen as the cross point, and if the N_{trans} is equal to 2, the point p_0 is regarded as the extreme point. A modified Hausdorff distance (MIID) [11] is adopted to get the M-Score between two point sets.

p_8	p_2	p_3
p_7	p_0	p_4
p_6	p_6	p_5

Fig. 4. Example of a 3×3 block

B. Super-pixel (SP) Feature Extraction

We introduce the effective algorithm SLIC proposed by [13], to produce super-pixels, which clusters pixels in the combined five-dimensional color and image plane space to efficiently generate compact, nearly uniform super-pixels. SLIC method produces super-pixels at a lower computational cost while achieving a good segmentation quality, as shown in Fig. 5.

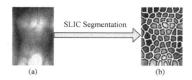

Fig. 5. Image segmented using SLIC into super-pixels of (approximate) size 65

SP feature is extracted from the super-pixel image, as shown in Fig. 4(b). In this paper, we extract three super-pixel level features to constitute a three dimensional feature vector, which are histogram feature, gradient feature and entropy feature. The extractions of these features are as follows:

Histogram feature: we extract the histograms of each super-pixel block firstly, then, a histogram feature vector is generated by these histograms, which will be the first dimension of the SP feature.

Gradient feature: in the first place, the gradient values of each super-pixel block are extracted, next a gradient feature vector is generated by these values, that is the second dimension of the SP feature.

Entropy feature: we first extract the entropies of each super-pixel block, next an entropy feature vector is generated, which is the third dimension of the SP feature.

2.3   Score-Level Fusion

A number of matching scores had been produced in Section 2.2. Since the scores are heterogeneous, score normalization is needed to transform these scores into a common domain [0,1] to combining them. The different features extracted from the same pattern have different effects on recognition, so the scores are fused by the weighted average strategy based on the equation *(3)* and the EER is minimized to obtain the optimum weights W_i. The equation *(3)* is defined as follow.

$$Matching\ Score = \sum_{i=1}^{2} Score(Feature_i) \times W_i \tag{3}$$

3   Experimental Results and Analysis

3.1   Database

The experiments were conducted using the self-built finger vein database which was collected from 34 individuals. Each individual is asked to provide 30 images for each of the index and middle fingers on the both hands. So our database includes 4,080 ($34 \times 4 \times 30$) finger vein images.

3.2   The Experiment Settings

In this work, two experiments are designed to evaluate the proposed method: (a) Experiment 1 is performed to evaluate the performance of the fusion of super-pixel level features with LBP feature, PS feature and M feature respectively. (b) Experiment 2 compares the fusion of pixel level features and the fusion of super-pixel level and pixel level features.

We perform the experiments in verification and identification mode respectively. In verification mode, we get 59,160 ($136 \times C_{30}^2$) intra-class matching results and 82,620

(68×3×135× 3) interclass matching results. The EER (equal error rate) is used to evaluate the verification performance .Closed-set identification experiments were also conducted. We use the first 10 finger vein images of each class as test samples and randomly select one image from the remaining 20 samples as templates. So, there are 136 templates and 1,360 (130 × 10) probes in total. We use the recognition rate to evaluate the identification performance.

3.3   Experiment 1

Firstly, we compare the fusion method of the SP feature and the LBP feature with the single SP feature and the single LBP feature separately. The ROC curves are shown in Fig. 6(a).The rank one recognition rate and the lowest rank of perfect recognition (i.e., the lowest rank when the recognition rate reaches 100%) are listed in Table 1(n.1).From the ROC and the Table1 we can see that the fusion method performs better than the single LBP-based method and the SP-based method.

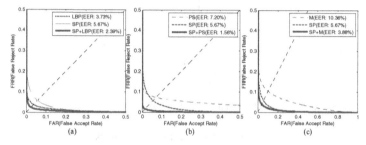

Fig. 6. The ROC curves in the verification mode

Table 1. Identification performance by different methods

n.1	Recognition Rate	n.2	Recognition Rate	n.3	Recognition Rate
LBP	96.91%	PS	92.21%	M	87.72%
SP	89.78%	SP	89.78%	SP	89.78%
Fusion	98.01%	Fusion	95.66%	Fusion	95.29%

Secondly, we compare the fusion method of the SP feature and the PS feature with the single SP feature and the single LBP feature separately. Their ROC curves are shown in Fig. 6 (b). And the rank one recognition rate and the lowest rank of perfect recognition are listed in Table 1(n.2). From the experimental results we can see that the performance of the fusion method is much better than that of the single PS-based method and the SP-based method.

Thirdly, we compare the fusion method of the SP level feature and the M feature with the single minutiae feature and the single SP feature. The ROC curves are shown in Fig. 6 (c). The rank one recognition rate and the lowest rank of perfect recognition are listed in Table 1(n.3). From the experimental results we can see that the fusion method is much better than that of the single M-based method and the SP-based method.

3.4   Experiment 2

In this experiment, we evaluate the performance of the fusions of two random pixel level features, and compare the proposed fusion method and the fusion in pixel level. Fig.6 shows the comparison between pixel level fusion method and single pixel level feature base on the EER conditions. The verification performance by different methods is listed in Table 2. From Fig.7 and Table 2, we can see that among these methods, the first two fusion methods give higher performance result in recognition, however, the third is lower than the single feature and it is apparent that the fusion method based on the pixel feature and the super-pixel level features, not only has good performance than methods based single feature, but also outperforms the pixel-pixel fusion methods.

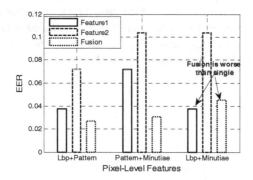

Fig. 7. Comparison of EER between fusion methods and the single-feature methods

Table 2. EER of different fusion methods

LBP(0.0373)+		PS(0.0720)+		M(0.1036)+	
LBP+M	0.0453	PS+M	0.0354	M+LBP	0.0453
LBP+PS	0.0270	PS+ LBP	0.0270	M+PS	0.0354
LBP+SP	0.0239	PS+SP	0.0156	M+SP	0.0348

4   Conclusions and Future Work

In this paper, we propose a novel finger-vein recognition method based on the score-level fusion of pixel and super-pixel level feature. The experimental results show the superior performance of our method in comparison with the methods based single feature as well as the fusions in pixel level. The advantages of our method can be summarized as follows: (1) Pixel level feature can describe the details of the finger-vein image. (2) Super-pixel level feature can descript the rough feature of the image and it is highly robust to the pixel noise. (3) The features in two level have great complementary, so their fusion can improve the recognition performance greatly.

In the future, the research is planned to focus on two aspects: one is the exploration of the super-pixel segmentation algorithm that is most suitable for the finger-vein; the other is the choice of the effective and complementary super-pixel level features of finger-vein image.

Acknowledgments. This work is supported by National Natural Science Foundation of China under Grant No.61173069 and 61070097, Program for New Century Excellent Talents in University of Ministry of Education of China and Shandong Natural Science Funds for Distinguished Young Scholar. The authors would like to thank the anonymous reviewers for their helpful suggestions.

References

1. Jiang, X., Mandal, B., Kot, A.: Eigenfeature Regularization and Extraction in Face Recognition. In: IEEE Transaction on Pattern Analysis and Machine Intelligence, pp. 383–393 (2008)
2. Daugman, J.: How Iris recognition works. IEEE Trans. Circuits Syst. Video Technol. 14(1), 21–30 (2004)
3. Wang, L., Tan, T., Ning, H., Hu, W.: Silhouette Analysis-Based Gait Recognition for Human Identification. IEEE Trans. Pattern Analysis and Machine Intelligence, 1505–1518 (2003)
4. Ito, K., Nakajima, H., Kobayashi, K., Aoki, T., Higuchi, T.: A fingerprint matching algorithm using phase-only correlation. IEICE Transactions on Fundamentals of Electronics, Communications and Computer Sciences, 682–691 (2004)
5. Yanagawa, T., Aoki, S., Ohyama, T.: Human finger vein images are diverse and its patterns are useful for personal identification. MHF Preprint Series, pp. 1–7 (2007)
6. Heenaye-mamode Khan, M., Subramanian, R.K., Mamode Khan, N.A.: Low dimensional representation of dorsal hand vein features using Principle Component Analysis. In: The Proceedings of World Academy of Science, Engineering and Technology, pp. 1091–1097 (2009)
7. Ladoux, P.-O., Rosenberger, C., Dorizzi, B.: Palm vein verification system based on SIFT matching. In: Tistarelli, M., Nixon, M.S. (eds.) ICB 2009. LNCS, vol. 5558, pp. 1290–1298. Springer, Heidelberg (2009)
8. Zhang, B., Gao, Y., Zhao, S., Liu, J.: Local derivative pattern versus local binary pattern: Face recognition with high-order local pattern descriptor. In: IEEE Trans. Image Process, pp. 533–544 (2010)
9. Rosdi, B.A., Shing, C.W., Suandi, S.A.: Finger vein recognition using local line binary pattern. Sensors, 11357–11371 (2011)
10. Kono, M., Ueki, H., Umemura, S.: A new method for identification of individuals by using of vein pattern of a finger. In: Processing of the 5th Symposium on Measurement, pp. 9–12 (2000)
11. Yu, C.B., Qin, H.F., Zhang, L., Cui, Y.Z.: Finger-vein image recognition combining modified hausdorff distance with minutiae feature matching. Biomed. Sci. Eng., 261–272 (2009)
12. Yang, J.F., Shi, Y.H., Yang, J.L., Jiang, L.H.: A novel finger-vein recognition method with feature combination. In: Proceedings of the 16th IEEE International Conference on Image Processing, Cairo, pp. 2709–2712 (2009)
13. Wang, K.J., Liu, J.Y., Popoola, O.P., Feng, W.X.: Finger vein identification based on 2-D gabor filter. In: Proceedings of the 2nd International Conference on Industrial Mechatronics and Automation, pp. 10–13 (2010)
14. Shaji, A., Smith, K., Lucchi, A., Fua, P., Süsstrunk, S.: SLIC Superpixels Compared to State-of-the-art Superpixel Methods. IEEE Transactions on Pattern Analysis and Machine Intelligence 34(11), 2274–2282 (2012)
15. Lee, E.C., Jung, H., Kim, D.: New finger biometric method using near infrared imaging. Sensors, 2319–2333 (2011)

The CFVD Reflection-Type Finger-Vein Image Database with Evaluation Baseline

Congcong Zhang[1], Xiaomei Li[2], Zhi Liu[1,*], Qijun Zhao[3],
Hui Xu[1], and Fangqi Su[1]

[1] School of Information Science and Engineering,
Shandong University, Jinan, 250100, PRC
`liuzhi@sdu.edu.cn`
[2] The Second Hospital of Shandong University
[3] National Key Laboratory of Fundamental Science on Synthetic Vision,
School of Computer Science, Sichuan University,
Chengdu, 610065, PRC

Abstract. In this paper, we describe the reflection-type finger-vein image database named by CFVD for biometrics research, including its acquisition, contents and evaluation baseline. The main contributions of this work include the following points: providing the worldwide researchers with reflection-type finger-vein recognition uniform database and ground-truth evaluation baseline. Currently, the CFVD database contains 1345 images of 130 fingers from 13 individuals (10 males and 3 females). Based on this database, the researchers can evaluate the performance of their algorithms for reflection-type finger-vein recognition. As the first reflection-type finger-vein image database available in the public domain, we believe that it will promote the development of finger-vein recognition techniques. We are keeping enlarging this database by including the finger-vein data of additional people.

Keywords: Reflection-type finger-vein recognition, biometrics, performance evaluation.

1 Introduction

Personal identification technology is becoming more and more important in everyday life. Traditionally, the authentication mode such as key, password, IC card are not safe enough because they could be lost or easily forgotten. To ensure higher security, biometric technology has been applied to a wide range of systems including door control systems, attendance systems and PC login.

Biometrics relies on the automated identification or verification of an individual based on unique physiological or behavioral characteristics. Physiological characteristics refer to inherited traits that are formed in the early embryonic stages of human development. It has high security and reliability because biometric features are hard to replicate and stolen. As well as security, the convenience of biometric verification system is becoming more and more popular [1].

---

* Corresponding author.

Z. Sun et al. (Eds.): CCBR 2013, LNCS 8232, pp. 282–287, 2013.

Biometric characteristics include fingerprint, face, iris, retina, signature, gait, voice, hand vein, hand or finger geometry and DNA information, while fingerprint, face, iris and signature are considered as traditional ones. Vein pattern is the network of blood vessels beneath person's skin. The idea using vein patterns as a form of biometric technology was first proposed in 1992, while researchers only paid attentions to vein authentication in last ten years [2]. Finger vein recognition [3] is a new biometric identification technology using the fact that different person has a different finger vein pattern.

Finger veins are subcutaneous structures that randomly construct a network and spread along a finger. Finger vein patterns are sufficiently different across individuals, and they are stable unaffected by ageing and no significant change in adults by observing. It is believed that the patterns of blood vein are unique to every individual, even among twins [3].

Contrasting with other biometric traits, such as face or fingerprint, finger vein patterns provide a really specific that they are hidden inside of human body distinguishing them from other forms which are captured externally. On the other hand, finger veins are internal, thus this characteristic makes the systems highly secure, and they are not affected by the situation of the outer skin and easy to be captured.

Much progress on finger-vein biometrics has been made in the past few years. There are mainly two approaches for acquiring the finger-vein images, transmission-type and reflection-type. The transmission-type finger-vein image capturing device uses the transmission light for imaging and the reflection-type device captures the images by reflection light, which can be illustrated in Fig. 1. However, this field remains a research area far from maturity, and its applications are still limited in controllable environments. Especially, the current research mainly focus on transmission-type [4,5,6]. Actually, many applications requires the reflection-type finger-vein recognition which has a smaller size and can be easily integrated in embedded systems. Therefore, it is becoming more and more significant to discover the bottleneck and the valuable future research topics by evaluating and comparing the potential finger-vein recognition technologies exhaustively and objectively.

Aiming at these goals, large-scale and diverse finger-vein image databases are obviously one of the basic requirements. However, to our best knowledge, although some transmission-type finger-vein image databases have been published, so far there is no public reflection-type finger-vein image databases with common evaluation baselines for this biometric researching. To complement the existing resource finger-vein research, we design and construct a large-scale reflection-type finger-vein image database — the CFVD finger-vein image database which covers subjects various in age, sex and work, under the different ambient lighting, different backgrounds. Currently, it contains 1345 images of 13 individuals (10 males and 3 females).

CFVD database has advantages both in the quality of finger-vein images and in a number of controlled variations of the recording conditions, which facilitate the training and evaluating all kinds of finger-vein recognition algorithms, particularly those statistical-based learning techniques.

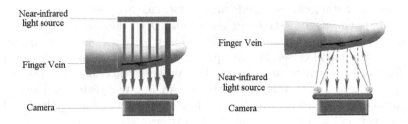

Fig. 1. Acquiring finger-vein images by Transmission-type (left) and reflection-type (right)

This paper describes the design, collection, and characters of the CFVD database in detail. In addition, the evaluation protocols for finger-vein recognition based on CFVD are presented to regulate the potential future evaluation among different finger-vein recognition algorithms in combination with the different preprocessing methods.

2   Image Acquisition

A special device with reflection light was developed to obtain near-infrared (NIR) finger-vein images. This device is illustrated in Fig. 2.

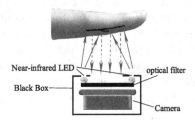

Fig. 2. The structure of our reflection-type finger-vein image capturing system

The device includes the following modules: camera with a resolution of 640 pixels × 480 pixels, optical filters (maintains the wavelength more than $850nm$), and an NIR light source with its wavelength at $850nm$. Fig. 3 shows the captured image.

3   Design of the CFVD

We constructed the reflection-type finger-vein image database for the performance evaluation of the recognition algorithm with a limited rotation degree (less than or equal to 30°), which accounts for light finger curl, and uses unfixed scale by using our capturing device introduced in Section 2.

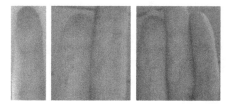

Fig. 3. The finger-vein images captured by our acquisition device

Two collection sessions were arranged, with a break of 30 days between the first and second sessions. A total of 12 subjects enrolled in the first collection session, of which 6 returned for the second session. Subjects mainly came from Shandong University, primarily undergraduate students and a small number of faculty and staff members. The demographic information of participating subjects in terms of gender, ethnicity, and age are summarized in Table 1.

Table 1. The demographic information of participating subjects

Gender		Ethnicity		Age			
Male	Female	Native	Foreign	20 − 30	30 − 40	40 − 50	> 50
10	3	13	0	12	1	0	0

In both collection sessions, male subjects accounted for about two-thirds of the total number of subjects, partially because that the majority of subjects were students from engineering and science departments. The distribution of gender groups is similar to that of the overall Shandong University enrollment. The age demographics are dominated by the younger groups, which is typical for a college population.

The current database contains the reflection-type finger-vein images of the forefinger, middle finger, little finger, two fingers including forefinger and middle finger, and three fingers including forefinger middle finger and ring finger of both hands from 13 subjects. For each partition, many images were captured at different times. A total of 1345 samples were collected for the database. Fig. 4 presents some examples of reflection-type finger vein images from different subjects that can be found in the database. Given that every finger is suitable for personal identification, the finger vein images from various fingers can be considered to be from different individuals in the experiments.

In the CFVD database, the name of each image folder indicates the identity of the subject and the filename of each image show the majority of the personal information of that image such as individual identifier, gender and finger identifier. Its format is *JPEG*. The image resolution is 640 × 480.

Fig. 4. Samples of reflection-type finger vein images from different subjects in the database

4   Evaluation Protocol

Even based on the same finger-vein image database, there are many possible methods to evaluate a specific recognition method. To facilitate the comparisons among the results of different methods, a standard evaluation protocol accompanying with the database is proposed in this paper.

Commonly, the tasks of finger-vein recognition can be classified as two models, identification and verification. According to applications, CFVD evaluation protocol focus on verification. For a verification task, the system needs to tell whether the claimed identity is that of the input finger-vein image by matching it against the prototypes of the claimed identity.

So firstly, the gallery set, the training set and the testing set are defined. The gallery set contains the images of known individuals that will be used for matching with the probe images. In the evaluation protocol, the gallery set consists of 390 images of the 130 fingers, with each subject having thirty images. Then, the training set is formed from the images from gallery set, which is used for those statistic learning methods training procedure. We construct a training set containing 130 images of 13 subjects in the CFVD database.

At last, the testing set is a collection of probe images of unknown individuals that need to be recognized, which is constructed by the residual images expect those of gallery set.

In our evaluation protocol, for the verification task, each image in a testing set is matched against all the images in the gallery set. By accumulating the false positives and false negatives for a specific threshold, the false-reject and false-accept rates can be estimated for that testing set. By moving the threshold over all possible values, the receiver operating characteristic curve for each probe set will be generated.

The CFVD database will be public for all research groups soon. Now the CFVD database is not perfect enough, and there is still much work to do, for example the sample size is still small and there is not much diversity in age. We will continue to enrich the CFVD database next. Everyone can acquire the CFVD database through our website soon.

5   Conclusions

In this paper, we describe the reflection-type finger-vein image capturing device setup, the contents of the CFVD reflection-type finger-vein image database and the evaluation protocol based on this database.

The main characteristics of the CFVD reflection-type finger-vein database lie in three aspects: 1) the reflection-type finger-vein images, consisting of 1345 images of 13 subjects with different ages and different sexes; 2) the captured images are with the same light source and same imaging sensor, but different capture conditions; and 3) In image capturing scenario, the fingers are allowed to be located with different degrees, so that the reflection-type finger-vein images contained in this database have varying positions.

With the proposed evaluation protocol, some experimental results according to the two common recognition methods have been reported on the database, which demonstrate the usefulness of CFVD on showing the strengths and weaknesses of different algorithms.

The size of the database is still relatively small. We are keeping expanding it by collecting the finger-vein data of additional people. We believe that this database, as the first reflection-type finger-vein image database available in the public domain, will promote the literature of finger-vein recognition.

Acknowledgments. This work was supported in part by the National Natural Science Foundation of China (No. 60977058 and 61202161), Independent Innovation Foundation of Shandong University (IIFSDU) (No.2012JC015 and 2012DX001), Development plan of science and technology in Shandong Province (No.2012GGE27073).

References

1. Marqués, I., Graña, M.: Image Security and Biometrics: A Review. In: Corchado, E., Snášel, V., Abraham, A., Woźniak, M., Graña, M., Cho, S.-B. (eds.) HAIS 2012, Part II. LNCS, vol. 7209, pp. 436–447. Springer, Heidelberg (2012)
2. Aboalsamh, H.: Recent advancements in biometrics: vein and fingerprint authentication. In: 14th WSEAS International Conference on Computers (Part of the 14th WSEAS CSCC Multiconference), pp. 459–462 (2010)
3. Luo, H., Yu, F., Pan, J., Chu, S., Tsai, P.: A survey of vein recognition techniques. Information Technology Journal 9, 1142–1149 (2010)
4. Nguyen, D.T., Park, Y.H., Shin, K.Y., Park, K.R.: New Finger-vein Recognition Method Based on Image Quality Assessment. KSII Transactions on Internet and Information Systems (TIIS) 7, 347–365 (2013)
5. Meng, X., Yang, G., Yin, Y., Xiao, R.: Finger Vein Recognition Based on Local Directional Code. Sensors 12, 14937–14952 (2012)
6. Park, Y.H., Park, K.R.: Image Quality Enhancement Using the Direction and Thickness of Vein Lines for Finger-Vein Recognition. International Journal of Advanced Robotic Systems 9 (2012)

A New ROI Extraction Method
of Non-contact Finger Vein Images

Chunting Zuo[1], Kejun Wang[1,*], and Xinjing Song[2]

[1] College of Automation, Harbin Engineering University, Harbin, China
zuochunting11@163.com, wangkejun@hrbeu.edu.cn
[2] China Electronics Technology Group Corporation No.38 Research Institute, Hefei, China
lucksxj@163.com

Abstract. This paper proposes a new rotation correction based method to extract regions of interest (ROI) from non-contact finger vein images. Firstly, finger median lines and image center points are used to make rotation correction. Then the arc diameter of fingertips is introduced to locate and determine sizes of ROI .Finally, do the size normalization. It is proved by experiments that the algorithm can effectively eliminate the finger vein image rotation and translation to some extent, and it is still efficient when the light is uneven to a certain degree or images are not clear enough. That is to say, this algorithm has high accuracy and is robust at the same time.

Keywords. image processing, finger-vein images, regions of interest (ROI), rotation correction.

1 Introduction

In a finger vein recognition system for non-contact acquisition, people tested will not have to touch the collecting device with their fingers. So, it can protect people from data legacy and produces no discomfort, which makes it quite acceptable.

There is less research on the ROI extraction for non-contact finger-vein images. In [1-2] the ROI of finger-vein images were efficiently extracted, but nonlinear factors, for example, rotation, which would probably happen when fingers are naturally placed, were not taken into account in these two methods ,so the extracting accuracy wouldn't be stable. And extraction methods of palmprint [3] , palm vein [4] and hand vein [5] images mostly rely on auxiliary locating device. Although Han et al [6] proposed a non-contact expanded method to extract the ROI of palmprint samples, then Li Qiang [7] successfully applied it to the non-contact expanded ROI extraction for hand veins, it was expected that samples should be obviously webbed. However, fingers are too slender and straight to meet the prerequisite of this method, that is to say, it is not proper to introduced this technique to determining the ROI of finger-vein images.

In this regard, in [8] it proposed to make rotation correction on the base of the finger centre of mass and the midpoint of the line segment which is formed by the last column

---

* Corresponding author.

Z. Sun et al. (Eds.): CCBR 2013, LNCS 8232, pp. 288–297, 2013.
© Springer International Publishing Switzerland 2013

pixels of the finger contour. Then with the help of the projection values of each column pixels in the vertical direction, it located the first knuckle to determine the ROI of finger-vein images. This algorithm is effective to extract the ROI of non-contact finger-vein samples, and it can overcome rotation and translation to a certain extent. However, when illumination is uneven or images are not clear enough, it can only get inaccurate ROI images. For this consideration, the paper made some improvements and put up with a new extracting method in which the finger median and the middle center of images were exploited to make rotation and transformation correction, and the diameter of fingertip arc was used to acquire positioning point to determine ROI.

Experiments have proven that the new technique performs very well, which is reflected in the following three aspects: 1) This non-contact finger-vein ROI extraction method can effectively eliminate a certain degree's rotation and translation transformation. 2) This non-contact finger-vein ROI extraction method has good robustness for uneven illumination and poor image quality to some extent. 3) The ROI positioning accuracy can meet the requirements in Identification tasks.

2   Rotation Correction

Non-contact acquisition for finger veins results in no fixed bolt constraints , so fingers are naturally placed, in other words, different samples of the same finger vary from each other in the horizontal offset and the rotational angle. Therefore, we need to rotate finger images to the horizontal before positioning ROI steps.

Fig.1 shows the complete finger regions according to literature [8] and [9]. The following steps of this paper were conducted in images of this type.

(a). Finger upward sloping   (b). Finger downward sloping   (c). Basically horizontal finger

Fig. 1. Random deflection of fingers

As can be seen in Fig.1, non-contact finger images are randomly deflected, so rotation correction is indispensable. Rotation angles of the finger-vein samples can be obtained by the slope of the finger medians. In binary finger images, the finger contour is made up with edge points, and the finger median is made up with midpoints of the upper and the lower points in finger contour, which can be connected and approximately fit a straight line . So the slope sign of this line determines the rotation direction and the slope value determines the rotation angle.

Finger median can be obtained by least square fitting, figure 2 shows the distribution of median points and the fitting line. As a mathematical optimization algorithm, the least square method is adopted to find the best solution by minimizing the square error sum between the obtained data and the actual data. As for the linear equation fitting, it means to acquire the best value of the Intercept , a , and the slope, b , when the square error sum function reached a minimum value, in which the square error is between the indeterminate equation and a set of data elements which are supposed to fit the linear equation.

Fig. 2. Line fitting of finger median

An assumed linear equation is expressed as:

$$y = a + bx \tag{1}$$

a and b can be calculated by the Equation (2):

$$a = \overline{y} - b\overline{x}, \quad b = \frac{\overline{xy} - \overline{x}\,\overline{y}}{\overline{x^2} - \overline{x}^2} \tag{2}$$

Among them,

$$\overline{x} = \frac{1}{n}\sum_{i=1}^{n} x_i, \qquad \overline{y} = \frac{1}{n}\sum_{i=1}^{n} y_i$$

$$\overline{x^2} = \frac{1}{n}\sum_{i=1}^{n} x_i^2, \qquad \overline{xy} = \frac{1}{n}\sum_{i=1}^{n} x_i y_i \tag{3}$$

a is the intercept and b is the slope of the line, so the direction and the value of rotation angle needed can be obtained by calculating the sign and value of b, that is, the lockwise rotation angle should be $\theta = \tan^{-1} b$.

The next step is to adjust fingers to the horizontal direction in accordance with image rotation algorithms. To rotate the image is to make all points roll around a reference point about a fixed angle, and usually the center position is selected as the reference point. The image rotation has a fundamental property as follows---- relatively to the reference point, every point is in the same distance as before rotating. Stick to this, then we can seek out the corresponding relationship of coordinate points.

The first step of image rotation is to moving the origin of the image coordinate system from the lower left corner to the image center, that's because the image center is taken as the reference point of rotation. If there is an image whose width is w and height is h, and a point in it which is expressed as (x_0, y_0) in the original coordinate system X'O'Y' and expressed as (x_1, y_1) in the new coordinate system XOY, then there are:

$$x_1 = x_0 - w/2; \; y_1 = y_0 - h/2 \qquad (4)$$

We assume that the image needs rotating clockwise. When point $A(x_1, y_1)$ rolls clockwise around the origin to point $B(x_2, y_2)$, c_2 is the clockwise rotation angle and $c_2 = \theta$. According to the fundamental property of rotation, the distance from B to the origin is the same as that from A which equals to r (Fig.3).

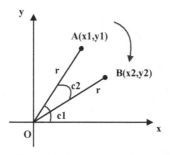

Fig. 3. Description of image rotation

Before rotation, there are $x_1 = r \cos c_1; \; y_1 = r \sin c_1$, after rotating the angle of c_2:

$$x_2 = r \cos(c_1 - c_2) = r \cos c_1 \cos c_2 + r \sin c_1 \sin c_2 = x_1 \cos c_2 + y_1 \sin c_2 \quad (5)$$

$$y_2 = r \sin(c_1 - c_2) = r \sin c_1 \cos c_2 - r \cos c_1 \sin c_2 = -x_1 \sin c_2 + y_1 \cos c_2 \quad (6)$$

But the new coordinates (x_2, y_2) are in the new coordinate system, they should be converted to the original:

$$x_3 = x_2 + w/2; \; y_3 = y_2 + h/2 \qquad (7)$$

After image rotation the size changes, set the excess pixels to black, so we get the rotation corrected finger region of Fig. 4.

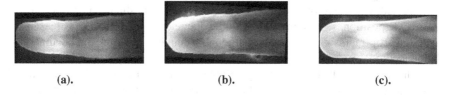

(a).   (b).   (c).

Fig. 4. Finger region after rotation correction

3   Determination of the ROI of Finger-Vein Images

Compared to fingertip and finger root, fingers veins are relatively clear and distinguishable in the middle part, so it would help to classify if we take this region as ROI and extract features from it.

Literature [8] located the first knuckle to determine the ROI through seeking the maximum value of the sum of column pixels. This is due to more infrared light gets through joints than muscles, and the muscles at the first knuckle are thinner than those at the second one.

Figure 5 shows the projection curves in the column direction of different finger-vein images, it can be seen that when the light is well-distributed and the image is of high quality, the projection curve will have two distinct peaks and the second peak is not as tall as the first one (the first case), only in this circumstance the method in [8] can ideally locate the first knuckle point; when light is uneven and pixels of fingertip are very bright which may form another peak higher than the first knuckle (the second case) or the projection curve of low-quality image has none or more than two peaks curve (the third case), the method in [8] will locate ROI with great inaccuracy.

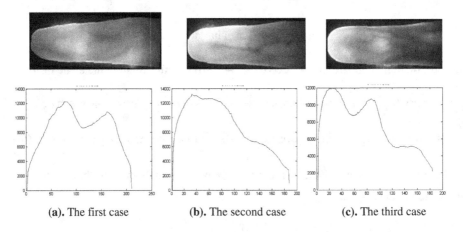

(a). The first case   (b). The second case   (c). The third case

Fig. 5. Finger-vein images and projection curves in column direction

In this regard, this paper promoted to determine the ROI through the fingertip arc diameters. Fingers are of different thickness, so the arc diameter of fingertips is different. In addition, fingertips approximate arcs and the arc diameter is close to the first knuckle position, so locating ROI with the diameter of fingertip arcs is feasible.

The fingertip radius can be obtained through a rough estimation and accurate calculation method.

Rough estimation: In the finger region after rotation correction, the left point of finger median is taken as the start and the circle centre is laid on the finger median, so the distance between the start and the center of the circle is the radius. From the start, move the centre along the finger median, and the radius will increase. When the circle is exceeding the finger contour, we can get the maximum estimated value of the radius.

Accurate calculation: From rough estimation, we can get the points of the roughly estimated arc, then the arc radius can be exactly calculated through circle fitting. Fig.6 is a schematic view of the calculating process.

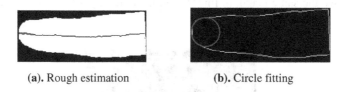

(a). Rough estimation   **(b).** Circle fitting

Fig. 6. Tthe calculation of fingertip radius

Circle fitting of the fingertip arc is solved in the least squares optimization algorithm, too. Assuming a point on the arc, (X,Y), satisfies the circle equation:

$$R^2 = (X - A)^2 + (Y - B)^2 \tag{8}$$

A, B, R can be calculated by the following formula:

$$A = -\frac{a}{2} \,,\; B = -\frac{b}{2} \,,\; R = \frac{1}{2}\sqrt{a^2 + b^2 - 4c} \tag{9}$$

In the formula above, there are:

$$a = \frac{HD - EG}{CG - D^2} \,,\; b = \frac{HC - ED}{D^2 - GC} \,,$$

$$c = -\frac{\sum(X_i^2 + Y_i^2) + a\sum X_i + b\sum Y_i}{N} \tag{10}$$

C, D, E, G, H are shown in formula as follows:

$$C = (N\sum X_i^2 - \sum X_i \sum X_i)$$
$$D = (N\sum X_i Y_i - \sum X_i \sum Y_i)$$
$$E = N\sum X_i^3 + N\sum X_i Y_i^2 - \sum(X_i^2 + Y_i^2)\sum X_i \tag{11}$$
$$G = \left(N\sum Y_i^2 - \sum Y_i \sum Y_i\right)$$
$$H = N\sum X_i^2 Y_i + N\sum Y_i^3 - \sum(X_i^2 + Y_i^2)\sum Y_i$$

In the finger region after rotation correction, the left point of finger median is taken as the start and the left dividing line of the ROI can be represented as $L1 : x = 2 * R$.

So the right dividing line is $L2 : x = 2 * R + d$, Where d represents the horizontal length of the extracted ROI. According to statistics, the finger region after rotation correction is about 200 pixels in length and the fingertip diameter is about 50. Assuming to remove the same length in finger root, then the finger left would be about 100, so here d is taken as 100.

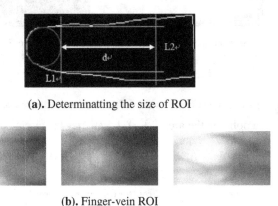

(a). Determinatting the size of ROI

(b). Finger-vein ROI

Fig. 7. The ROI of finger-vein images

In the contour image, considering the region between $L1$ and $L2$, the vertical width of ROI region is determinate by the minimum and the maximum vertical value of the finger contour. As shown in Fig.7, that rectangle surrounded by the four lines is the ROI.

The analysis of finger-vein images indicates that the height of finger-vein ROI images is about 60 pixels, therefore, the ROI are height normalizd to 60.

4   Experimental Results and Analysis

All the experiments were taken on the finger-vein database of our laboratory, which contains 105×5 images (105 people, each person's index finger has been taken photos of for 5 times). Extract complete finger images according to the literature [8] and [9], and use the method in this paper to extract ROI and normalize them to 100×60 . Then we did experiments and comparative analysis as follows.

4.1   Experimental Analysis of Rotation and Translation Transformation

There is an obvious relationship of rotation and translation between vein images of the same finger image. Due to the paper's space limit, we only select three pairs to specify the performance against rotation and translation of our technique, which are described in Fig.8: The first pair has obvious rotation transformation, the second has apparent rotation and translation, and the third one has significant rotation with a little translation.

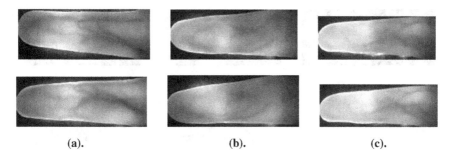

(a).   (b).   (c).

Fig. 8. Samples of rotation and translation

Fig.9 shows their extracted ROI according to this paper's method, it can be seen that there is little difference between ROI of the same finger in spite of rotation or translation transformation. This indicates that using this extracting method, the rotation and translation to a certain degree will not cause great difference in ROI, that is, this extracting method can greatly reduce the possibility of rejection or misrecognition caused by rotation and translation transformation—It has great robustness to rotation and translation.

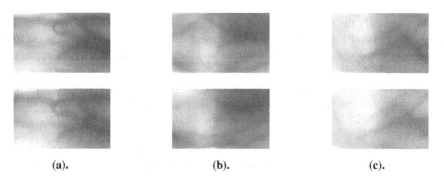

(a).   (b).   (c).

Fig. 9. ROI of rotation and translation samples

4.2   Experimental Analysis of Uneven Illumination and Poor- Quality Images

Section 2 describes if the literature [8] method was used in the situation of illumination unevenness and poor- quality images, we could not get accurate ROI. Do the same experiments as Fig.5 with method in this paper, and Fig.10 shows the results.

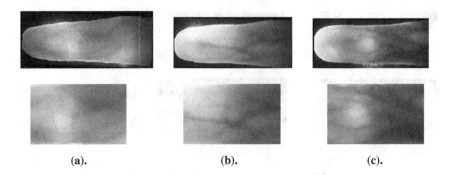

(a).   (b).   (c).

Fig. 10. Samples in Fig.5 and ROI with method in this paper

Fig.10 shows that the proposed method performs very well not only when the illumination is well-distributed and the quality of images is fine (the first case) but also in the situation of uneven illumination (the second case) or poor quality images (the third case). The application has been improved by this method.

4.3   Experimental Analysis of the Identification Precision

In order to verify the ROI extraction accuracy can meet the recognition requirements, 1: 1 validation and 1: N identification experiments were respectively done on the ROI regions extracted with method of this paper and the whole finger regions. Four of the five images of every finger were randomly chosen to constitute a training base, and the image left was the test object. Based on traditional NMF feature extraction method and the nearest neighbor classifier, we did experiments when the dimension of features was 16, 25 or 36, whose results are shown in Table 1.

Table 1. Comparison of recognition accuracy between the whole finger and the ROI

	Image of the whole finger			Image of the ROI		
Dimension of features	16	25	36	16	25	36
Validation Accuracy %	89.52	93.42	94.30	89.91	94.30	94.88
Classification Accuracy %	83.81	88.57	90.48	86.67	91.43	94.29

As can be seen from Table 1, in the same dimension, the validation experiment accuracy of ROI is about one percent more than that of the whole finger, and the classification experiment accuracy of ROI is nearly 4 percent higher. This obviously shows that the proposed method has a great advantage in extracting ROI and it can meet the requirements of the subsequent recognition task. In addition, tests using the ROI need less time and memory capacity than using a full finger region.

So we conclude that this method can effectively eliminate the finger vein image rotation and translation to some extent, and it is still efficient when the light is uneven to a certain degree or images are not clear enough. That is to say, this algorithm has high accuracy and is robust at the same time.

References

1. Chengbo, Y.U., Huafeng, Q.I.N.: Biometric Identification Technology: The Finger Vein Recognition Technology, pp. 117–119. Tsinghua University Press, Beijing (2009)
2. Shangling, S.: Nose pore recognition and finger vein recognition, pp. 62–64. Shandong University, Ji'nan (2009)
3. Kumar, A., Wong, D.C.M., Shen, H.C., et al.: Personal Verification Using Palmprint and Hand Geometry Biometric. In: Kittler, J., Nixon, M.S. (eds.) AVBPA 2003. LNCS, vol. 2688, pp. 668–678. Springer, Heidelberg (2003)
4. Xiuyan, L., Tiegen, L., Shichao, D., et al.: Fast recognition of hand vein with SURF descriptors. Chinese Journal of Scientific Instrument 32(4), 831–836 (2011)
5. Wang, J.G., Yau, W.Y., Suwandy, A., et al.: Person recognition by fusing palmprint and palm vein images based on "Laplacian palm" representation. Pattern Recognition 41(5), 1514–1527 (2008)
6. Han, C., Cheng, H., Lin, C., et al.: Personal authentication using palm-print features. Pattern Recognition 36, 371–381 (2003)
7. Qiang, L.I.: Research on hand feature recognition and feature level fusion, pp. 22–24. Beijing Jiaotong University, Beijing (2006)
8. Hui, M., Kejun, W.: A ROI Extraction Method of Finger Vein Based on Rotation Correction. Journal of intelligent systems 7(3), 1–6 (2012)
9. Hui, M.A.: Research on Decision-Level Fusion Methods Based on the to the Dual Mode Recognition of Fingerprint. Harbin Engineering University, Harbin (2012)
10. Guorong, W., Yimin, W., Sanzheng, Q.: Generalized Inverses: Theory and Computations. Science Press, Beijing (2004)
11. Hongtao, H.: Digital image processing. Beijing institute of technology press, Beijing (2002)

Categorizing Finger-Vein Images Using a Hierarchal Approach

Dun Tan[1], Jinfeng Yang[1], and Chenghua Xu[2]

[1] Tianjin Key Lab for Advanced Signal Processing,
Civil Aviation University of China
[2] Institute of Electronics, Chinese Academy of Science
jfyang@cauc.edu.cn

Abstract. To improve the efficiency of finger-vein recognition system over a large database, this paper proposed a level-based framework for automatically categorizing finger-vein images. The proposed framework consists of two layers. The first is based on appearance features, and the second is based on content features. In each layer, an improved k-means algorithm is employed for clustering finger-vein images. Finally,the POC (Phase-Only-Correction) algorithm is applied for image matching. Experimental results demonstrate that the proposed method exhibits an exciting performance in recognition efficiency improvement.

Keywords: Finger-vein image, clustering, hierarchal method, classification.

1 Introduction

As a new biometric trait for personal verification in security, the finger-vein trait exhibits some excellent advantages in liveness, anti-counterfeiting and friendliness apart from uniqueness, universality, permanence and measurability. So finger-vein recognition has been viewed as a promising technology in personal identification [1], [2], [3], [4], [8], [10], [11].

The matching efficiency, besides the accuracy, always should be addressed for any biometric system in the real situation, especially for some real applications (e.g., airport security, the national borders or criminal investigation). To improve the matching efficiency, categorizing the enrolled biometric images often is a desirable strategy in practice. In this paper, a meaningful attempt is made for automatic finger-vein image categorization. Compared with traditional finger-vein recognition system, a test finger-vein image will be matched with the finger-vein images in its category, which is helpful for greatly reducing the matching cost in the recognition process.

To improve the efficiency of a recognition system, many previous works that can automatically classify some traditional biometric traits have been done(e.g., fingerprint, iris, palmprint, etc.). Fadzilah [5] gives a review in this aspect (i.e. heuristic approach, syntactic approach, neural approach, statistical approach), which have been applied to the fingerprint classification. Arun and Manisha [6]

Z. Sun et al. (Eds.): CCBR 2013, LNCS 8232, pp. 298–305, 2013.

use the anatomical structures of iris for iris categorization. Xiang [7] reports a method that using palm print lines for palmprint image classification. Unfortunately, no attentions have been paid to categorize finger-vein images in the current literature. To achieve finger-vein image classification, two main issues should be addressed.

1. Unlike fingerprint which can be classified into five categories: whorl, right loop, left loop, arch, and tented arch by its ridge line feature, the finger-vein images are difficult in categorization based on their visual information.
2. It is difficult to find a statistic feature which can easily divide the finger-vein images into several classes with large interclass variation and small intraclass variation.

To solve the problems mentioned above, a novel finger-vein classification algorithm is introduced in this paper which can improve the efficiency of a finger-vein recognition system. Before describing the proposed method in detail, some finger-vein image samples are listed in Fig. 1. These ROI images are extracted from their original images which are captured using a homemade finger-vein acquisition system, which is detailed in [8], [9].

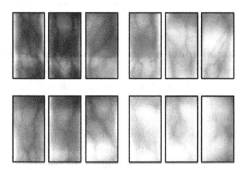

Fig. 1. ROIs of some finger-vein image samples

From Fig. 1, we can clearly see that the finger-vein images vary in their appearance and content. Moreover, whether the images look bright or dark in their appearance, the finger-vein image contents, which are determined by vein structures, also vary in vessel network complexity. Therefore, for finger-vein images, the appearance property is independent of the content property. Inspired by this observation, a hierarchal framework is proposed here for finger-vein image categorization, as shown in Fig. 2.

In this framework, the appearance and content features of finger-vein images are respectively used for the first and second level classification. In this way, m categorizations can be achieved for a finger-vein image database. Unlike fingerprint classification, the supervised methods are obviously undesirable for finger-vein image clustering. An unsupervised method based on an improved k-means clustering algorithm is therefore used here in finger-vein image categorization process.

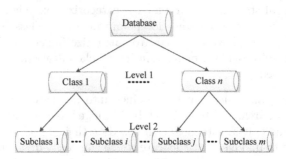

Fig. 2. A hierarchal framework for finger-vein image categorization

The rest of the paper is organized as follows, Section 2 describes the features used for image clustering. The experiment results are reported in Section 3, and some conclusions are described in Section 4.

2   Feature Analysis

Feature extraction is an important step for a biometric recognition system. Finding appropriate features of the finger-vein images (e.g. Luminance, texture, geometry, networks etc.) also is an essential part for finger-vein image clustering. For multiple level finger-vein image categorization, two important issues should be considered: 1) The dimension of feature vector should not be very large for reducing the computation and memory cost in training and classifying; 2) The features should be robustly to noise, rotation and translation.

Currently, many methods have been proposed for finger-vein feature extraction [2], [3], These methods are useful in finger-vein feature analysis. But for finger-vein image clustering, we should extract some features considering their clustering properties in multiple level, as shown in Fig. 2. So, the following appearance and content features are used here for finger-vein image cluster analysis.

2.1   Appearance-Based Feature

Due to the differences of fingers in fat, thickness, vein distribution and shape, the appearances of finger-vein images are different in practice, as shown in Fig. 1. So the image appearance features are chosen as the first level feature for finger-vein image clustering. Some finger-vein image quality evaluation methods have been proposed [10], [11]. Here, three image features, the gradient, image contrast and information entropy, are used for finger-vein image quality evaluation. The image clarity is described as

$$G = \frac{1}{(M-1)*(N-1)} \sum_{i=1}^{M} \sum_{j=1}^{N} \sqrt{\nabla f_x^2(i,j) + \nabla f_y^2(i,j)} \qquad (1)$$

where M is the number of row and N is the number of column, $\bigtriangledown f_x^2(i,j)$ represents the horizontal gradient and $\bigtriangledown f_y^2(i,j)$ is the vertical gradient.

The image contrast is given by

$$C = \frac{1}{(M)*(N)} \sqrt{\sum_{i=1}^{M}\sum_{j=1}^{N}(f(i,j)-\overline{f})^2} \qquad (2)$$

where $f(i,j)$ represents grey value of a pixel and $\overline{f}$ is the average value of the whole image.

The information entropy is described as

$$S = -\sum_{k=0}^{255} P(k)\log_2 P(k) \qquad (3)$$

where $P(k)$ represents the probability that pixels in the kth grey-level in an image.

2.2 Content-Based Feature

The specific ridge texture is one of the main content-based features in finger-vein image. Gabor filter is powerful in capturing specific texture information in images. Since the finger-vein appear ridges in images, the even-symmetric Gabor filter is used to exploit the content features determined by the finger-vein networks. The even-symmetric Gabor filter is represented as

$$G_k^e(x,y,\theta_k,f) = \frac{1}{2\pi\sigma_x^2\sigma_y^2}\exp\left\{-\frac{1}{2}\left(\frac{x_{\theta_k}^2}{\sigma_x^2}+\frac{y_{\theta_k}^2}{\sigma_y^2}\right)\right\}\cos(2\pi f x_{\theta_k}) \qquad (4)$$

where

$$\begin{bmatrix} x_{\theta_k} \\ y_{\theta_k} \end{bmatrix} = \begin{bmatrix} \sin\theta_k & \cos\theta_k \\ -\cos\theta_k & \sin\theta_k \end{bmatrix}\begin{bmatrix} x \\ y \end{bmatrix}, \quad \hat{j} = \sqrt{-1} \qquad (5)$$

where $k(=1,2,\cdots,8)$ is the orientation index, $\theta_k(=k\pi/8$ denotes the kth orientation, and f is the center frequency. Here, a bank of even-symmetric Gabor filter with eight orientations is used to filter finger-vein images. Assuming that $I(x,y)$ denote a finger-vein image, $F_k(x,y)$ denote a filtered $I(x,y)$ in the kth orientation, we can obtain

$$F_k(x,y) = G_k^e(x,y,\theta_k,f)*I(x,y) \qquad (6)$$

where $*$ denotes convolution operation in tow dimensions. Thus, for a finger-vein image, eight filtered images are generated by Gabor filters.

Some results are shown in Fig.3, we can see from Fig.3 that the filtered images vary with orientations. So, an 8-dimensional vector based on the statistical information of the filtered images is constructed for finger-vein image roughly classification,

$$\boldsymbol{E} = [e_1,\cdots,e_k,\cdots,e_8]^T, \qquad (7)$$

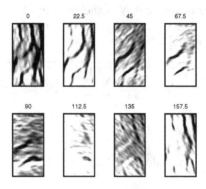

Fig. 3. The filtered images with eight orientations

where

$$e_k = \frac{1}{M * N} \sum_{i=1}^{M} \sum_{j=1}^{N} F_k(i,j)^2 \tag{8}$$

where M is the number of row and N is number of column.

3   Experiments

In this section, the used image database contains 4000 finger-vein images from 400 individuals. Each individual contributes 10 finger-vein images of the right forefinger. The captured finger-vein images are 8-bit gray images with a resolution of 320×240, and all segmented ROIs are resized to 80×160 considering finger variations in profile and size.

3.1   Clustering Number Selection

Due to no prior categorization information, the finger-vein images should be automatically clustered under an unsupervised learning scheme. Here, an improved k-means algorithm [12] is used to implement clustering procedure, and the silhouette index is selected to test the validity of clustering. The silhouette index can report the variability of clusters in interclass and intraclass level. The higher values of the silhouette indexes are, the better the clustering results are. The silhouette index is defined as

$$Sil(i) = \frac{b(i) - a(i)}{max\{a(i), b(i)\}} \tag{9}$$

where $a(i)$ represents the average distance between ith pattern and its intraclass patterns, and $b(i)$ represents the average distance of between ith pattern and its all interclass patterns. The Silhouette indexes of clustering results on the

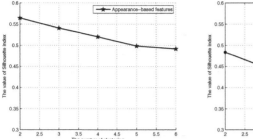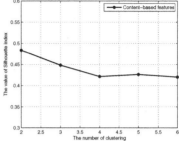

Fig. 4. The variations of the silhouette indexes with different class number for different features. (a) Appearance-based features. (b) Content-based features.

Table 1. The correct classification rates on the appearance-based and content-based features

	CCRs	
class number	appearance-based features	content-based features
2	99.5%	99%
3	97.54%	97.92%
4	95.42%	78.92%

appearance-based features and the content-based features are respectively shown in Fig. 4(a) and Fig. 4(b).

From Fig. 4(a) and Fig. 4(b), we can see that the silhouette index values of the appearance-based features and the content-based features are the biggest when the clustering number is two. To evaluate the correct rate of classification whether will be affected by increasing the class number or not, we first use k-means to cluster 400 different finger-vein images from 400 individuals into two, three and four classes respectively based on the appearance-based and content-based features. Then, a nonlinear kernel SVM classifier [13] is used to evaluate the classification results. The correct classification rates (CCRs) of SVM is listed in Table 1. From Table 1, we can see that the CCRs obviously decrease with increasing the cluster numbers. So the accuracy of a finger-vein based system will reduce with increasing the number of categories in this manner.

3.2   The Valuation of the Proposed Hierarchical Model

Considering the appearance-based features and the content-based features are independent, two layer hierarchical model, as shown in Fig. 2, is desirable to increase the class number as well as reduce matching cost in practice. According to the results from Fig. 4(a) and Fig. 4(b), the final categorization number m is four, where the appearance-based features are used as the first layer classification, and the content-based features are used as the second layer classification.

Table 2. The correct classification rates of the proposed framework

Training samples	CCRs		
	level 1	level 2	The proposed framwork
200*6	100%	99%	99%
400*6	99.5%	98.75%	98.75%

Table 3. Results from the different matching plane

Method	T(s)	EER
POC	3.299	0.211
POC+proposed	1.6731	0.191

To evaluate the performance of the proposed hierarchical model in finger-vein classification, we respectively extract three images from 200, 400 individual fingers as training samples and six images as testing samples. Using different SVMs as classifiers, the CCRs of each level classifier and our classify systems based hierarchal framework are listed in Table 2.

Using the proposed framework for classification, the error rates of each level will accumulate. From Table 2, we can see that the CCR of the proposed hierarchal framework system is lower than that of each level. But, compared Table 2 with Table 1, we can clearly see that the CCRs of the proposed framework are obviously higher than those of the appearance-based features and the content-based features when the cluster number is four. So, the experimental results show that the proposed method has a good performance in classifying finger-vein images.

To evaluate the efficiency of the proposed method in finger-vein matching, the Phase Only Correlation (POC) measure [14] is applied here for image matching. The proposed algorithm is implemented using MATLAB R2010a on a standard desktop PC which is equipped with a Core i3, CPU 2.7 GHz and 2 GB RAM.

For the proposed framework, the matching time is computed by averaging the matching time in each sample categorization because the sample numbers of different classes are different. The time costs for implementing a matching using the proposed method and the traditional matching method are listed in Table 3. Table 3 shows that the proposed method can reduce the matching time to 49.28% compared with traditional POC matching scheme. Hence, the proposed method has a good performance in reducing the matching cost.

4   Conclusion

In this paper, the proposed method could effectively classify the finger-vein images with high CCRs and improve the recognition efficiency. In future, more reliable finger-vein features will be explored for better categorizing finger-vein images. Besides, the performance of algorithm in large scale finger-vein database is still to be proved.

Acknowledgment. This work is jointly supported by National Natural Science Foundation of China (No. 61073143, No.61379102, No.61001176), Tianjin Municipal Science and Technology Support Key Project (No. 07ZCKFGX03700).

References

1. Xu, M., Sun, Q.: Vasculature Development in Embryos and Its Regulatory Mechanisms. Chinese Journal of Comparative Medicine 13(1), 45–49 (2003)
2. Miura, N., Nagasaka, A., Miyatake, T.: Feature extraction of finger-vein patterns based on repeated line tracking and its application to personal identification. Mach. Vis. Appl. 15(4), 194–203 (2004)
3. Da, W.J., Huan, Y.S.: Driver identification using finger-vein patterns with radon transform and neural network. Expert Systems with Applications 36, 5793–5799 (2009)
4. Sun, D.M., Liu, D., Liu, H.: Two modality-based bi-finger vein verification system. In: Proc. of Int'l Conf. on Signal Processing, pp. 1690–1693 (2010)
5. Ahmad, F., Mohamad, D.: A Review on Fingerprint Classification Techniques. In: International Conference on Computer Technology and Development, pp. 411–415 (2009)
6. Ross, A., Sunder, M.S.: Block Based Texture Analysis for iris classification and matching. Computer Vision and Pattern Recognition Conference (2010)
7. Wu, X., Zhang, D., Wang, K., et al.: Palmprint Classification Using Principal Lines. Pattern Recognition 37(10), 1987–1998 (2004)
8. Yang, J.F., Li, X.: Efficient finger-vein localization and recognition. In: Proc. International Conference on Pattern Recognition, pp. 1148–1151 (2010)
9. Yang, J.F., Shi, Y.H.: Finger-vein ROI localization and vein ridge enhancement. Pattern Recognition Letters 33(12), 1569–1579 (2012)
10. Ma, H., Wang, K., Fan, L., Cui, F.: A finger-vein Image Quality Assessment Method Using Object and Human Visual System Index. In: Yang, J., Fang, F., Sun, C. (eds.) IScIDE 2012. LNCS, vol. 7751, pp. 498–506. Springer, Heidelberg (2013)
11. Yang, L., Yang, G., Yin, Y.: Finger vein image quality evaluation using support vector machines. Optical Engineering 52(2), 027003-1-027003-9 (2013)
12. Zhou, S.B., Xu, Z.Y.: New Method for Determining Optimal Number of Cluster in K-means Clustering Algorithm. Computer Engineering and Application of China 46(16), 27–31 (2010)
13. Gunn, S.R.: Support Vector Machines for Classification and Regression. University of Southampton (1998)
14. Lee, E.C., Jung, H., Kim, D.: New finger biometric method using near infrared imaging. Sensors 11, 2319–2333 (2011)

Exploring User-Specific Threshold
in Finger Vein Authentication

Lu Yang, Gongping Yang[*], Yilong Yin, and Rongyang Xiao

School of Computer Science and Technology, Shandong University,
Jinan, 250101, P.R. China
yangluhi@163.com, {gpyang,ylyin}@sdu.edu.cn,
canyueyang@126.com

Abstract. One major factor of finger vein authentication performance variability is the difference in the recognizability of different users. It may be effective to enhance the authentication performance by improving the recognizability of each user. In this paper, we determine a specific threshold for each user to carry out identity authentication, comparing to the traditional common threshold. The user-specific threshold is calculated according to user's impostor matching scores. We compare the authentication performances of the common threshold and the user-specific threshold respectively in the verification mode and the recognition mode. The experiments perform on our self-built finger vein database, and experimental results show that the user-specific threshold possesses promising advantage in finger vein authentication.

Keywords: Finger vein authentication, user-specific threshold.

1 Introduction

Biometrics makes use of personal physiological and/or behavioral characteristics to automatically recognize individual. In recent years, a new physiological characteristics-based biometrics technique finger vein, which uses vein patterns in human finger to authenticate, attracts increasing attentions from the biometrics research communities. Compared with other biometric authentication techniques, e.g., faces, irises, fingerprints, voices and etc., finger vein has obvious advantages in living-body identification, noninvasive and noncontact image capture, and high security [9].

Robustness of algorithm and recognizability of user are two main factors of finger vein authentication performance variability. Lots of works have been done for enhancing the robustness of finger vein authentication algorithms. Miura *et al.* firstly proposed two classical finger vein feature extraction methods [1], [2], i.e., the repeated line tracking method and the maximum curvature point method, which are both based on the segmentation of vein texture. Then, Lee *et al.* [8] and Yang *et al.* [4] respectively proposed the local binary pattern (LBP) and the personalized best bit map (PBBM) to extract the finger vein feature, which are both based on the binary codes. Yang *et al.* [5]

---

[*] Corresponding author.

Z. Sun et al. (Eds.): CCBR 2013, LNCS 8232, pp. 306–313, 2013.

also employed two-directional and two-dimensional principal component analysis $(2D)^2$PCA with metric learning in finger vein authentication. Recently, Kumar *et al.* [3] and Yang *et al.* [10] applied Gabor filter in finger vein authentication. The Gabor filter family with different sizes and different orientations can effectively extract the shape feature of finger vein. Although these attempts have been done and achieved better authentication performance, there are few literatures exploring the recognizability of user in finger vein authentication system.

In this paper, we will enhance the authentication performance through improving the recognizability of each user in authentication system. The recognizability of user represents the inherent vein pattern recognizability in certain degree, but it is generally affected by the quality of finger vein image. The different recognizability manifest as the disproportionate contribution to the genuine accept rate (GAR) and false accept rate (FAR) in the benchmark level. In other words, different users are prone to different type of errors. When a common threshold is used for a finger vein authentication system, the GAR of users with large intra-class variations may be low. Similarity, the FAR associated with users having small inter-class variations may be high. Therefore, for each user, how to improve the GAR and at same time limit the FAR is the key problem in enhancing the overall authentication performance. Inspired by the literature [6], we explore the user-specific threshold to solve this problem. We provide different thresholds for different users according to their own matching score distributions. For users with large intra-class variations, we will assign a relatively big threshold to increase the GAR, and for users with small inter-class variations, we will give a relatively small threshold to reduce the FAR. Experimental results in the verification mode and the recognition mode both show that the user-specific threshold can effectively improve finger vein authentication performance.

In the remainder of this paper, we introduce the framework of finger vein authentication system and the user-specific threshold algorithm in Section 2. We present the experimental database and settings in Section 3. Section 4 shows the experimental results and our analyses. Finally, we summarize our work in Section 5.

2   Related Technology

In this section, we will introduce the algorithms of the finger vein authentication system in detail, and the user-specific threshold algorithm we used is also presented.

2.1   Framework of Finger Vein Authentication

A typical finger vein authentication system covers image acquisition, preprocessing, feature extraction and matching. The finger vein images used in this paper are from our self-built database, which will be introduced in detail in Section 3. Our work about image preprocessing [7] is used, which mainly includes skewed image detection and correction, region of interest (ROI) segmentation and image size normalization. Besides, the local feature extraction method LBP technique and the global feature extraction method $(2D)^2PCA$ technique [5, 11] are respectively employed for feature extraction. The LBP operator can effectively represent the spatial structure of local image texture based on the image gray scale, by which a binary pattern was extracted from a stretched rectangular finger vein region. $(2D)^2PCA$ is a popular feature extraction technology, which will transform the image matrix to a two-dimensional feature matrix reflecting the global information of the image. Correspondingly the Hamming distance and the Euclidean distance are used to estimate the similarities between the input vein features and the enrolled vein feature in matching.

2.2   Algorithm of User-Specific Threshold

The matching threshold for each user is calculated using her cumulative histogram of impostor scores. The detail procedure of algorithm is described as follows:

1) Calculate the cumulative histogram of the impostor scores for every user in the database.

2) Use $t_i(p)$ as the threshold for the *ith* user in the database, which retains p fraction of impostor scores in the cumulative histogram, $0 : p : 1$.

3) Calculate $FAR_i(p)$ and $GAR_i(p)$ based on the specific threshold $t_i(p)$.

4) Obtain the total FAR and GAR of all users in the database using Eq. (1) and (2).

$$FAR(p) = \Sigma_i FAR_i(p) \tag{1}$$

$$GAR(p) = \Sigma_i GAR_i(p) \tag{2}$$

5) Generate the ROC curve using $FAR(p)$ and $GAR(p)$.

The p corresponding to a appointed FAR will be used to invoke the set of user-specific thresholds (i.e., $t_i(p)$).

3   Experimental Database and Settings

3.1   The Experimental Database

The finger vein images in our database are captured by a device manufactured by the Joint Lab for Intelligent Computing and Intelligent System of Wuhan University, China, which is shown in Fig. 1. Our finger vein database is collected from 34 individuals, including 20 males and 14 females, in two separate sessions separated by 20 days. In each session, the subject is asked to provide 30 images for each of the index and middle fingers on the both hands. Therefore, there are 4,080 finger vein images. Some typical original images and their corresponding normalized ROI images are separately shown in Fig. 2.

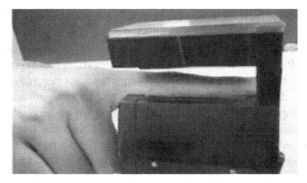

Fig. 1. The imaging device

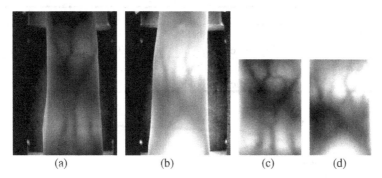

(a)   (b)   (c)   (d)

Fig. 2. (a) and (b) are typical finger vein images; (c) and (d) are the corresponding ROI images

3.2   The Experimental Settings

In order to comprehensively ascertain the effectiveness of user-specific threshold, we perform two types of experiments on the aforementioned database: the verification mode experiment and the recognition mode experiment. The first 20 finger vein images per finger are used in the experiments. In the verification mode, there are including 51,680 ($136 \times 20 \times 19$) intra-class matchings and 7344,000 ($136 \times 20 \times 135 \times 20$) inter-class matchings. In the recognition mode, the first 10 images per finger are used in training set to generate the common threshold and user-specific thresholds, and the rest images per finger are used in testing set, in which the 11th image is seen as the class template, and the other images are used as the probes. All probes will be matched with all class templates, totally including 166,464 ($136 \times 9 \times 136$) matchings.

4   Experimental Results

4.1   The Verification Mode Experiments

In verification mode, we will compare the GAR values under the same FAR value to evaluate the performance of the common threshold and the user-specific threshold.

The experimental results from these two methods are summarized in Table 1, and the corresponding ROC curves are given in Fig. 3. From Table 1 and Fig. 3, we can see that the user-specific threshold outperforms the common threshold whether using the local feature LBP or the global feature $(2D)^2PCA$ to extract the finger vein patterns. The user-specific threshold is calculated according to user's matching scores, so it is more effective than the common threshold in user verification. With the recognizability improvement of each user, the system performance will be enhanced. Besides, the superiority of the user-specific threshold with the 0.1% FAR is more obvious than it with the 1% FAR. We have reason to believe that in the environment with high demand for security the user-specific threshold will play a better role.

Table 1. Compare of GAR values

GAR		LBP	$(2D)^2PCA$
FAR=0.1%	Common threshold	0.8895	0.8714
	Specific threshold	0.955	0.9157
FAR=1%	Common threshold	0.9571	0.921
	Specific threshold	0.9737	0.9446

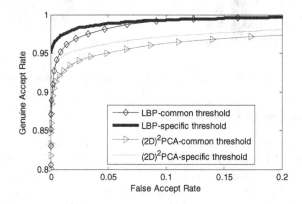

Fig. 3. The ROC curves of common threshold and user-specific threshold

4.2   The Recognition Mode Experiments

In recognition mode, firstly the matching scores between one probe and all class templates are sorted in ascending order. And then we separately detect the matching scores less than the common threshold and the user-specific threshold obtained from the training set. If there is no such matching score, the probe cannot be recognized. For the detected matching scores, further confirmation is executed to determine whether these scores are generated by the probe and its class template. If there is a score generated by the probe and its class template, the probe will be recognized.

We determine the common threshold and user-specific threshold when the FAR is 0.1% and 1% from the training set, which are suggested in Table 2. We can see that the user-specific thresholds are not only different from the common threshold, but also different from each other.

Based on these thresholds, the cumulative matching performance is shown in Fig. 4 and Fig. 5, and the recognition rates are listed in Table 3. It is important to note that the cumulative rates in Fig. 4 and Fig. 5 are the recognition rates, not the rank-one recognition rates. From the experimental results, we can see that the performance of the user-specific threshold is better than that of the common threshold, which indicates that the user-specific threshold work well in the recognition mode as in the verification mode. Our results also consistently suggest that the smaller FAR, the bigger superiority of the user-specific threshold. In addition, the recognition rate does not reach upward of 100%, and there are two reasons: one is that there is no matching score which is less than threshold for some images; the other is that there is matching score less than threshold, but it does not generated by the image and its class template.

Table 2. The thresholds with FAR=0.1% and 1%

Threshold	Common threshold		Specific threshold (first five users)	
	LBP	$(2D)^2$PCA	LBP	$(2D)^2$PCA
FAR=0.1%	0.43	0.29	0.43	0.32
			0.48	0.31
			0.49	0.38
			0.47	0.41
			0.47	0.37
FAR=1%	0.48	0.34	0.47	0.35
			0.54	0.34
			0.51	0.42
			0.48	0.45
			0.51	0.41

Table 3. The recognition rates on testing set

Recognition rate		LBP	$(2D)^2$PCA
FAR=0.1%	Common threshold	0.8386	0.8278
	Specific threshold	0.9284	0.8862
FAR=1%	Common threshold	0.9110	0.8974
	Specific threshold	0.9508	0.9272

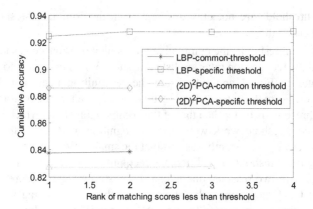

Fig. 4. The cumulative match curves (FAR=0.1%)

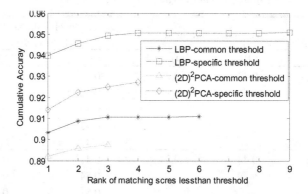

Fig. 5. The cumulative match curves (FAR=1%)

5   Conclusions

In consideration of user's disproportionate contribution to the performance of finger vein authentication, we enhance the authentication performance through improving recognizability of each user by the user-specific threshold. From the experimental results, compared with the common threshold, the user-specific threshold performs promising advantages both in the verification mode and the recognition mode. However, although we can use the user-specific threshold to improve GAR and at same time control FAR for each user, the reasons of the phenomenon that different users are prone to different type of errors are complicated, and we will explore this work in the future.

Acknowledgments. This work is supported by National Natural Science Foundation of China under Grant No. 61173069, 61070097, Program for New Century Excellent Talents in University of Ministry of Education of China under Grant No.

NCET-11-0315 and Shandong Natural Science Funds for Distinguished Young Scholar. The authors would particularly like to thank the anonymous reviewers for their helpful suggestions.

References

1. Miura, N., Nagasaka, A., Miyatake, T.: Feature extraction of finger vein patterns based on repeated line tracking and its application to personal identification. Mach. Vis. Appl. 15(4), 194–203 (2004)
2. Miura, N., Nagasaka, A., Miyatake, T.: Extraction of finger-vein patterns using maximum curvature points in image profiles. IEICE. T. Inf. Syst. E90-D(8), 1185–1194 (2007)
3. Kumar, A., Zhou, Y.B.: Human identification using finger images. IEEE Trans. Image Process. 21(4), 2228–2244 (2012)
4. Yang, G.P., Xi, X.M., Yin, Y.L.: Finger vein recognition based on a personalized best bit map. Sensors 12(2), 1738–1757 (2012)
5. Yang, G.P., Xi, X.M., Yin, Y.L.: Finger vein recognition based on $(2D)^2$PCA and metric learning. J. Biomed. Biotechnol., 1–9 (2012)
6. Jain, A.K., Ross, A.A.: Learning user-specific parameters in a multibiometric system. In: Proceeding of International Conference on Image Processing (2002)
7. Yang, L., Yang, G.P., Yin, Y.L., Xiao, R.Y.: Sliding window-based region of interest extraction for finger vein images. Sensors 13(3), 3799–3815 (2013)
8. Lee, E.C., Jung, H., Kim, D.: New finger biometric method using near infrared imaging. Sensors 11(3), 2319–2333 (2011)
9. Hashimoto, J.: Finger vein authentication technology and its future. In: Symposium on VLSI Circuits (2006)
10. Yang, J.F., Shi, Y.H.: Finger-vein ROI localization and vein ridge enhancement. Patt. Recogn. Lett. 33(12), 1569–1579 (2012)
11. Zhang, D., Zhou, Z.H. $(2D)^2$PCA: two-directional two-dimensional PCA for efficient face representation and recognition. Neurocomputing 69(1-3), 224–231 (2005)

Palm Vein Recognition by Combining Curvelet Transform and Gabor Filter

Junwen Sun and Waleed Abdulla

Department of Electrical and Comuter Engineering, Univeristy of Auckland
38 Princes Street, Auckland, New Zealand
{junwen.sun,w.abdulla}@auckland.ac.nz

Abstract. Biometrics research based on palm vein recognition has been developed rapidly in recently years. However, due to the poor palm vein image quality, the performance of the recognition is not good enough. Recently, coding algorithms, such as Curvelet transform and Gabor Filter have been proposed and have been attracting much research attention. While the Curvelet Transform is good at extracting the linear features from the palm vein images, the Gabor Filter excels in extracting the orientation features. By investigating these two different coding schemes, we propose in this paper a score-level fusion scheme for palm print/vein verification. The proposed method was applied on the HK PolyU Database and an EER of 0.1023% was achieved, which outperforms using the Curvelet Transform or Gabor Filter alone.

Keywords: Palm vein recognition, Curvelet Transform, Gabor Filter.

1 Introduction

Hand-based biometrics, including fingerprint recognition, finger knuckle print recognition and palm recognition, have been used in many areas such as national ID cards and e-passports due to its efficiency and high security. Similar with these biometrics, the palm vein pattern provides a significant uniqueness since vein patterns of individuals are different, even between identical twins[1]. In addition, the palm veins are only visible under infrared light. Thus it's hard to copy or forge fake palm vein patterns. The palm veins are thick and quite sparse. The availability of such complementary features (palm lines and veins) allows for increased discrimination between individuals [2-4]. Moreover, the palm vein features are also useful for liveness detection for the prevention of spoof attacks[5].

Feature extraction is important for palm vein recognition and many of them have been applied in palm print recognition before. However, the palm veins, which are only visible in near-infrared light, are dim and obscure. According to the survey of palm print recognition[6], the palm print feature extraction methods can be divided into three main categories: line-based approaches, sub-space approaches and statistical approaches. However, the thick and unclear veins images are not suitable for the edge detectors. Gabor Filter[7], Wavelet Transform[8, 9], Curvelet Transform[10, 11] are applied to

Z. Sun et al. (Eds.): CCBR 2013, LNCS 8232, pp. 314–321, 2013.
© Springer International Publishing Switzerland 2013

extract the statistical information in other domains. These statistical approaches extract the stable information of the palm images and have high recognition accuracy.

In order to improve the performance of palm print/vein recognition system, several combination methods have been proposed [12, 13]. However, instead of using several images in different spectral light, we propose a combining approach to utilize the palm print and palm vein information at the same time with single near-infrared palm image. The rest of the paper is arranged as follows. Algorithms for feature extraction based on Curvelet Transform and Gabor Filter is described in Section 2. The score combination algorithm is described in Section 3. In Section 4, some experiments are carried out to test the performance of the proposed method. Finally, our conclusion is given in Section 5.

2 Feature Extraction

2.1 Curvelet Transform

The features of the palm print/vein images can be extracted in frequency domain, i.e. Fourier Transform[14], Wavelet Transform [8, 15, 16]. However, Curvelet Transform is more suitable for palm feature extraction than wavelets to extract curvilinear features. Curvelet transform directly takes the edge as the basic representation element; it also provides optimal sparse representations of objects along the edges. Such representations are sparser than the wavelet decomposition of the object. The second generation of Curvelet Transform is introduced in 2006[17] which is simpler, faster, and less redundant compared with the first-generation Curvelet Transform.

The mother curvelet φ_j of second generation Curvelet Transform is defined at scale 2^{-j}, orientation θ_l and position $X_K^{j,l}$ as

$$\varphi_{j,l,k(X)} = \varphi_j(R_{\theta_l}(X - X_K^{j,l})) . \tag{1}$$

Where R_{θ_l} is the rotation by θ_l radians. θ_l is the equi-spaced sequence of rotation angles $\theta_l = 2\pi * 2^{-\lfloor j/2 \rfloor} l$, with integer l such that $0 \leq \theta_l \leq 2\pi$. $K = (k_1, k_2) \in Z^2$ is the sequence of translation parameters.

In continuous frequency v, the Curvelet Transform of function f can be expressed as:

$$c(j, l, k) = < f, \varphi_{j,k,l} > = \int_{R^2} \hat{f}(v) \hat{\varphi}_j(R_{\theta_l}) e^{iX_K^{j,l} \cdot v} dv . \tag{2}$$

Where $\varphi_{j,k,l}$ is the curvelet, f is the image function in frequency domain, j, k, l is the scale, direction and position parameter respectively.

The Curvelet Transform is implemented in frequency domain. The discrete transform takes as input data defined on a Cartesian grid and outputs a collection of coefficients. The coefficient $c(j, l, k)$ is a set of multi-scale pyramid intensities as shown in the Fig.1.

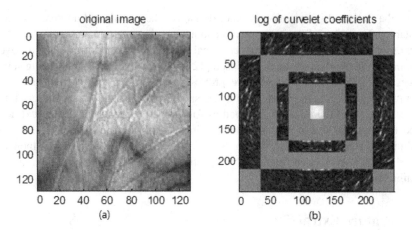

Fig. 1. (a) Original image and (b) its Curvelet coefficients[11]. The x, y axes represent image pixels.

The coefficient $c(j, l, k)$ can represent the curvilinear features of the palm print/vein image. However, only a small portion of the coefficients is needed to reconstruct the original image and generate good recognition rate[11]. Thus only 10% of the coefficients are used to reduce the data storage and computation load for matching, and are denoted as CurveMap in this paper.

2.2   Gabor Filter

The Gabor Filter Method, also called competitive coding scheme in palm print recognition, was proposed in [3] and developed in [18, 19]. 2-D Gabor Filter is applied to the palm vein image with six different orientations: $0, {}^{\pi}/_6, {}^{\pi}/_3, {}^{\pi}/_2, {}^{2\pi}/_3, {}^{5\pi}/_6$. After the filter, each pixel in the original image will be represented as a winning-orientation[3] which is then coded into 3-bit. Due to its 'competitive' scheme, it can extract the comparatively stable orientation information of the palm.

An example of the Gabor Filter palm image (GaborMap) is shown in Fig. 2.

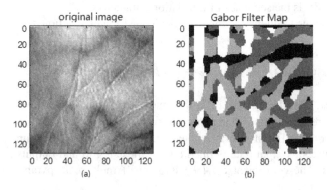

Fig. 2. (a) Original image and (b) its Gabor Filter Map. The x, y axes represent image pixels.

3   Score Combination

The similarity, or hamming distance, of two CurveMaps (only 0 and 1 in the CurveMaps), can be calculated by template matching. Let T_C denote a prepared CurveMap template in the database and I_C denote the CurveMap of a new input palm, we match T_C and I_C through logical "exclusive or" operation. The matching score is calculated as

$$S_C(T_C, I_C) = \frac{1}{M*N} \sum_{i=1}^{M} \sum_{j=1}^{N} \overline{[T_C(\iota, j) \oplus I_C(\iota, j)]}. \tag{3}$$

Where M × N is the size of T_C or I_C (T_C and I_C must be the same size), $\oplus$ is the logical "exclusive or" operation, and − is the logical "not" operation.

Similarly, the matching score of two GaborMaps is calculated as:

$$S_G(T_G, I_G) = \frac{1}{M*N} \sum_{i=1}^{M} \sum_{j=1}^{N} \overline{[T_G(\iota, j) \oplus I_G(\iota, j)]}. \tag{4}$$

The two different classifiers, Curvelet Transform and Gabor Filter, extract different information from the palm vein image, i.e. curvilinear features and orientations. The curvilinear features, including palm prints on the surface of the palm, provide details for the palm, while orientations represent more robust features in different ambient illumination and palm positions.

The combination of these two methods would increase the recognition rate. The strategy of combing the two different matching scores is as follows:

$$S = \lambda * S_G' + (1 - \lambda) * S_G'. \tag{5}$$

Where S_C' and S_G' are the re-scaled matching scores S_C and S_G to the same range [0 1].

4   Experiments and Results

4.1   Image Database

The Hong Kong PolyU multispectral palm print database[16] consists of 500 different palms. Six samples were collected for every palm in two sessions with an average time interval of nine days. So there are 500*12=6000 groups of palm print images in the database. The ROI Database is extracted from the multispectral palm print database using the key points between fingers described in [20]. Each palm image in the ROI database is an 8-bit depth 128*128 grayscale image.

4.2   Features Extraction and Matching

In the feature extraction stage, both Curvelet Transform and Gabor Filter were performed on the ROI palm vein database. Each of the method would generate a comparing score of likelihood. A total of 14340 comparisons are performed, in which 7500 comparisons are intra-class matching. Equal error rate (EER), the rate when false acceptance rate (FAR) is equal to false rejection rate (FRR) is used to evaluate the performance.

The Curvelet Transform is applied to extract the linear features first. For each 128*128 input image, a set of Curvelet Transform coefficients was generated. The EER for Curvelet Transform method is 0.41%. The Gabor Filter is applied to extract the orientation features from the palm vein image. The matching score distribution is shown in the following figure. The EER for Gabor Filter method is 0.25%.

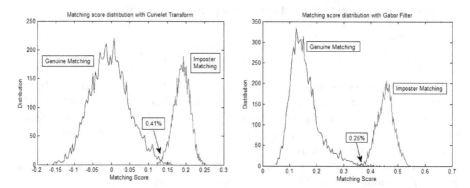

Fig. 3. Matching score distribution with Curvelet Transform (Left) and Gabor Filter (Right), respectively

By application of equation (4), the EER changes with different combination coefficients, as shown in Fig. 4.

When score combination coefficient $\lambda = 0$, the recognition system solely operates with Gabor Filter and have an EER of 0.25%; when $\lambda = 1$, the system operates only with Curvelet Transform with an EER of 0.41%. If we choose $\lambda \subset \{0,1\}$, the system combines the two methods together and achieves the best result of 0.1023% at several points. It can be noticed that the EER reaches a platform below 0.1170% when $\lambda \subset \{0.45,0.67\}$. Thus, score combination coefficient λ can be set without much prior knowledge about the palm vein database. The system will work at peak performance when score combination coefficient λ is set around 0.55.

Compared with the state-of-art Matched-Filter algorithm which claims EER of 0.3091%[21], multispectral palm image recognition with an EER of 0.50%[12], our combination method achieves better performance. The other combination methods, for example, combination of palm print (in white light) and palm vein, can achieve higher EER of 0.0158%[21], but have to take two palm images in two different lights (white and near-infrared).

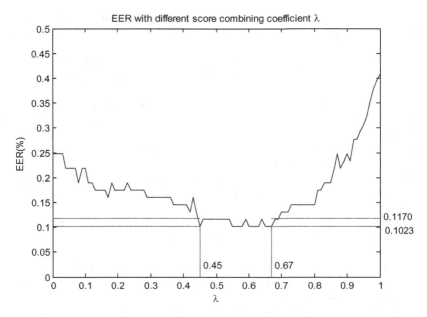

Fig. 4. EER with different score combining coefficient λ

5 Conclusion and Discussion

This paper has presented a combining approach for reliable personal recognition using two palm vein representations methods. The CurveMap provides details for the palm, while GaborMap represents a more robust orientation feature in different ambient illumination and palm positions. The combination of these two methods has increased the recognition accuracy to an EER of 0.1023%.

More palm print/vein recognition methods will be considered to join the fusion scheme to achieve better performance. For example, the line extraction method [22, 23] and local patterns[24] can be combined to utilize other palm vein image features.

Acknowledgments. Authors thankfully acknowledge Biometrics Research Centre (BRC) of Hong Kong Polytechnic University for providing Multi-Spectral palm print database used in this work.

References

1. Kumar, A., Hanmandlu, M., Gupta, H.M.: Online biometric authentication using hand vein patterns. In: IEEE Symposium on Computational Intelligence for Security and Defense Applications, CISDA 2009, pp. 1–7 (2009)
2. Jian-Gang, W., Wei-Yun, Y., Suwandy, A., Sung, E.: Fusion of Palmprint and Palm Vein Images for Person Recognition Based on "Laplacianpalm" Feature. In: IEEE Conference on Computer Vision and Pattern Recognition, CVPR 2007, pp. 1–8 (2007)

3. Kong, A.W.K., Zhang, D.: Competitive coding scheme for palmprint verification. In: Proceedings of the 17th International Conference on Pattern Recognition, ICPR 2004, vol. 1, pp. 520–523 (2004)
4. Watanabe, M., Endoh, T., Shiohara, M., Sasaki, S.: Palm vein authentication technology and its applications. In: Proceedings of the Biometric Consortium Coference, Hyatt Regency Crystal City, Arlington, VA, USA (2005)
5. Qin, B., Pan, J.-F., Cao, G.-Z., Du, G.-G.: The Anti-spoofing Study of Vein Identification System. In: International Conference on Computational Intelligence and Security, CIS 2009, pp. 357–360 (2009)
6. Kong, A., Zhang, D., Kamel, M.: A survey of palmprint recognition. Pattern Recognition 42, 1408–1418 (2009)
7. Ghandehari, A., Safabakhsh, R.: Palmprint Verification Using Circular Gabor Filter. In: Tistarelli, M., Nixon, M.S. (eds.) ICB 2009. LNCS, vol. 5558, pp. 675–684. Springer, Heidelberg (2009)
8. Xiang-Qian, W., Kuan-Quan, W., David, Z.: Wavelet based palm print recognition. In: Proceedings of the 2002 International Conference on Machine Learning and Cybernetics, vol. 3, pp. 1253–1257 (2002)
9. Tamrakar, D., Khanna, P.: Analysis of Palmprint Verification Using Wavelet Filter and Competitive Code. In: 2010 International Conference on Computational Intelligence and Communication Networks (CICN), pp. 20–25 (2010)
10. Li, Q., Zeng, Y., Peng, X., Yang, K.: Curvelet-based palm vein biometric recognition. Chinese Optics Letters 8, 577–579 (2010)
11. Sun, J., Abdulla, W.: Palm vein recognition using curvelet transform. Presented at the Proceedings of the 27th Conference on Image and Vision Computing New Zealand, Dunedin, New Zealand (2012)
12. Ying, H., Zhenan, S., Tieniu, T., Chao, R.: Multispectral palm image fusion for accurate contact-free palmprint recognition. In: 15th IEEE International Conference on Image Processing, ICIP 2008, pp. 281–284 (2008)
13. Dong, H., Zhenhua, G., Zhang, D.: Multispectral palmprint recognition using wavelet-based image fusion. In: 9th International Conference on Signal Processing, ICSP 2008, pp. 2074–2077 (2008)
14. Li, W.-X., Zhang, D., Xu, Z.-Q.: Palmprint Recognition Based on Fourier Transform. Journal of Software 13 (2002)
15. Hsieh, C.-T., Lai, E., Wang, Y.-C.: An effective algorithm for fingerprint image enhancement based on wavelet transform. Pattern Recognition 36, 303–312 (2003)
16. Zhang, L.: The Hong Kong Polytechnic University (PolyU) Multispectral Palmprint Database, http://www.comp.polyu.edu.hk/~biometrics/MultispectralPalmprint/MSP.htm
17. Candès, E., Demanet, L., Donoho, D., Ying, L.: Fast Discrete Curvelet Transforms. Multiscale Modeling and Simulation 5, 861–899 (2006)
18. Zhenan, S., Tieniu, T., Yunhong, W., Li, S.Z.: Ordinal palmprint represention for personal identification. In: IEEE Computer Society Conference on Computer Vision and Pattern Recognition, CVPR 2005, vol. 1, pp. 279–284 (2005)
19. Zhenhua, G., Wangmeng, Z., Lei, Z., Zhang, D.: Palmprint verification using consistent orientation coding. In: 2009 16th IEEE International Conference on Image Processing (ICIP), pp. 1985–1988 (2009)
20. Zhang, D., Zhenhua, G., Guangming, L., Lei, Z., Wangmeng, Z.: An Online System of Multispectral Palmprint Verification. IEEE Transactions on Instrumentation and Measurement 59, 480–490 (2010)

21. Zhang, D., Guo, Z., Lu, G., Zhang, L., Liu, Y., Zuo, W.: Online joint palmprint and palmvein verification. Expert Systems with Applications 38, 2621–2631 (2011)
22. Zhang, Y.-B., Li, Q., You, J., Bhattacharya, P.: Palm Vein Extraction and Matching for Personal Authentication. In: Qiu, G., Leung, C., Xue, X., Laurini, R. (eds.) VISUAL 2007. LNCS, vol. 4781, pp. 154–164. Springer, Heidelberg (2007)
23. Jia, W., Huang, D.-S., Zhang, D.: Palmprint verification based on robust line orientation code. Pattern Recognition 41, 1504–1513 (2008)
24. Mirmohamadsadeghi, L., Drygajlo, A.: Palm vein recognition with Local Binary Patterns and Local Derivative Patterns. In: 2011 International Joint Conference on Biometrics (IJCB), pp. 1–6 (2011)

Liveness Detection of Dorsal Hand Vein Based on the Analysis of Fourier Spectral

Yiding Wang and Zhanyong Zhao[*]

College of Information Engineering, North China University of Technology
Beijing, China
wangyd@ncut.edu.cn, sunue_zzy@163.com

Abstract. Liveness detection of dorsal hand vein is a necessary step towards higher reliability of identification and is attracting increasing attention of researchers. However, there's only few published research in this area. This paper proposes a novel method for liveness detection of dorsal hand vein. First, by applying the Fourier Transform, a feature is extracted as a statistical value of spectral energy derived from every blocked spectrum of single wavelength infrared images. Second, regarding the principle of blocking, massive experiments have been performed to find the optimum feature with the maxmin criterion. Furthermore, an SVM classifier is employed for clustering. The experimental results have verified the effectiveness of our proposed method.

Keywords: Dorsal hand vein, Fourier Transform, Liveness, Spectral energy.

1   Introduction

Since the original idea of personal identification from near-infrared image of human hand vein has been proposed by Joseph Rice [1] and supported by MacGregor [2], vein identification has attracted more and more attentions as a biometric identification method. However, a typical near-infrared dorsal hand vein recognition (NIRDHVR) system is vulnerable to spoofing by printed vein pictures or rubber gloves which contain drawn or printed dorsal hand vein structures from live people. Fig. 1 shows some typical examples of fake dorsal hand vein and the corresponding image.

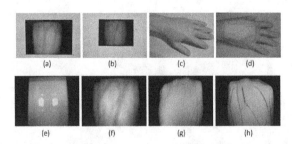

Fig. 1. Some fake dorsal hand vein resources and corresponding captured images. Types from left column to right are: (a) photographic paper, (b) normal paper, (c) thick rubber glove and (d) thin rubber glove; (e), (f), (g) and (h) corresponding vein images above.

---

[*] Corresponding author.

Z. Sun et al. (Eds.): CCBR 2013, LNCS 8232, pp. 322–329, 2013.
© Springer International Publishing Switzerland 2013

To ensure that only live dorsal hand vein is allowed to be used for enrollment and identification in an authentication system based dorsal hand vein, we propose a novel liveness detection method using energy spectrum named block spectral energy. First of all, the resources obtained by a near-infrared camera are pre-processed and the region of interest (ROI) is extracted. Subsequently, features of block spectral energy are calculated in the frequency domain. To evaluate the efficacy of the extracted features in dorsal hand vein liveness detection, the Support Vector Machine (SVM) is used to analyze the discrimination between live and fake data.

The rest of this paper is organized as follows: section 2 introduces the database. Section 3 analyzes the principle of hand vein liveness detection. Our kernel strategy of block spectral energy is detailed in section 4. Section 5 specifies the selection of optimum features based on the maxmin criterion. In section 6, the experiments show the effectiveness of our method. In section 7, we give the conclusion of our work and discuss the future work.

2   Dataset

To test the distinction of the live and fake dorsal hand vein, we established a new dataset named NCUT-LFDHV database which contains both the live and fake data. 20 live dorsal hand vein images from NCUT-DHV database are selected and printed as photos, among which 10 are printed on Kodak photographic paper and other 10 images are printed on normal paper. Meanwhile, images of 10 pairs of live hand wearing thick rubber gloves as well as wearing thin rubber gloves are both captured as the other two types of fake data. In order to avoid the distinction caused by using different devices, we selected 10 persons to obtain live hand vein images to form the live data part of NCUT-LFDHV instead of data from NCUT-DHV database. From Fig.1(e) we can spot the captured images from samples printed on photographic paper show no vein structure because of specular reflection. Even if we draw the vein texture on the surface of the photo, it also contains significant bright spots. Therefore this type is removed from the test. For each object we measured 10 times with slight changes of position and rotation (the size of image is 381*381 pixels after pre-processing), thus a database containing 300 negative samples (100 for printed on normal paper, 100 for thick rubber gloves and 100 for thin rubber gloves) and 200 positive samples is built.

3   Principle of Hand Vein Liveness Detection

For face recognition [3] and fingerprint identification [4], the effectiveness of multispectral liveness detection under invisible light has been proved. To some extent, it implies that the difference between the fake and the live samples under invisible light is much more obvious than under visible light. Fig.2 shows the different absorption curves of different materials for the incident light of various wavelength bands. The difference of absorption equaling reflection is also the basis of multispectral liveness detection.

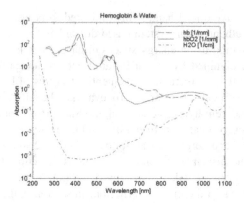

Fig. 2. Absorption curves of different materials as the wavelength of light varies [5]

Since our dorsal hand vein images depend on diffuse reflection of the near-infrared light, the Lambertian reflectance model is used in this case [6].The reflection light intensity I at a location (x, y) is written as:

$$I(x, y) = A_0(x, y) * r(x, y) * \cos\theta(x, y) \,. \tag{1}$$

Where $A_0(x, y)$ is the incident light intensity at the target location (x, y), $r(x, y)$ is the object reflectance, and $\theta(x, y)$ is the angle between the surface norm and the receiver's view point. In our case, both $A_0(x, y)$ and $\theta(x, y)$ are fixed, which means $r(x, y)$ is the only factor leads to different reflectance. Based on this principle, the multispectral method for hand vein liveness detection is theoretically feasible under different wavelengths of infrared light. Considering this method needs additional equipment and several images as data, it increases the complexity of system and the error rate in operation. Thus, we try to give a solution of this problem on images captured from near-infrared light at a single wavelength.

4 Block Spectral Energy Strategy

4.1 Fourier Transform

Although the Fourier transform has been widely used in image processing [7], to the best of our knowledge, no published works use this transformation to distinguish live and fake dorsal hand vein. Considering both the effectiveness and the cost of adding additional hardware components, we choose to analyze the infrared dorsal hand vein images captured at a single wavelength in frequency domain. For image processing, two-dimensional discrete Fourier Transform and its inverse Transform are defined as:

$$F(\mu, v) = 1 / (M * N) * \sum_{m=0}^{M-1} \sum_{n=0}^{N-1} f(m, n) \exp[-j2\pi(m * \mu / M + n * v / N)]. \tag{2}$$

$$f(x, y) = \sum_{m=0}^{M-1} \sum_{n=0}^{N-1} F(\mu, v) \exp[j2\pi(m * x / M + n * y / N)]. \tag{3}$$

where $f(x, y)$ and $F(\mu, v)$ are an image and its two-dimensional Fourier Transform with size of $M * N$, $j = \sqrt{-1}$, x, y and μ, v represent coordinates of pixels in the spatial domain and the frequency domain, respectively. Some spectrograms of live and fake dorsal hand vein images after Fourier Transform are shown in Fig.3.

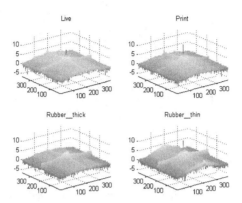

Fig. 3. The Fourier transform of four types of data: live, normal paper, thick rubber and thin rubber

As observed in Fig.3, it is obvious that there are differences between the live sample and other three types of fake samples. We analyze that the differences in the low frequency region are caused by the diverse absorption rates of infrared light for different materials while the differences in the high frequency region are derived from the inconsistent properties between drawn strokes and textures of real vein. Therefore, we present to distinguish them with a single wavelength infrared light rather than multi-spectral. In order to quantify these differences, a feature named "energy spectrum", which computing the spectral energy of related Fourier Transform, is proposed.

4.2   Feature Extraction

Let $X(x, y)$ and E_s represent amplitude values located on (x, y) and spectral energy of region S in the related spectrogram, respectively. According to the Parseval theorem [8], we have:

$$E_s = \sum_{x \in H} \sum_{y \in V} |X(x, y)|^2 \Delta x \Delta y, H, V \in F \qquad (4)$$

where H, V represent horizontal and vertical frequency axis of spectrogram F, respectively. We named this strategy as block spectral energy.

First, we divide the whole spectrogram, using a low-pass filter and a high-pass filter, into two parts which can be seemed as dorsal hand vein outline and texture respectively. Secondly, we calculate the spectral energy of each part from both all live data and all types of fake samples, and save this two-dimension feature. As demonstrated in Fig.4, although most of thick and thin rubber samples are separated from live human, there is still no stable and obvious dividing line to identify live and fake samples due to a large overlapping between live and printed samples, which means the accurate cut-off frequency value is hard to obtain.

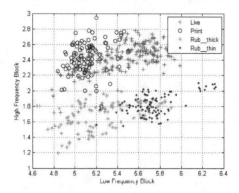

Fig. 4. The distribution of two-dimension block spectral energy

However, on the other hand, it can be seen from Fig.3 that the differences show regional characteristics corresponding to different frequency bands. Thus, in order to increase the distance between the two classes, we propose to segment the whole spectrogram to three regions (S_1, S_2, S_3) with the (Seg_1, Seg_2) which all are centered on the null frequencies along both horizontal and vertical axes (as shown in Fig.5).

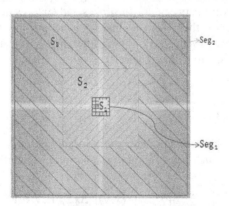

Fig. 5. The schematic diagram of spectrum blocks strategy

Through this design, we induct an intermediate zone between the original two regions (low and high frequency). On the other hand, the divisibility of a series of nonlinear distribution of data in low-dimension could increase after been mapped into a high-dimension. In the following processing, we compute the energy of each block $(or_i, i = 1,2,3)$ and integrate them into a coordinate (like $[or_1, or_2, or_3]$) as the feature for classification. The 3D distribution is showed in Fig.6.

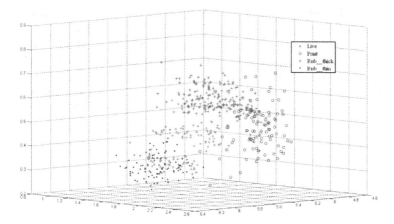

Fig. 6. The distribution of three-dimension block spectral energy

5   Selection Criterion of Best Feature

As mentioned above, the feature representing samples for the liveness detection is achieved. Then we need to determine the size of every region to obtain the optimum feature. In this stage the maxmin criterion is employed as the solution. Fig.7 shows the key steps of this process utilizing the maxmin criterion [9].

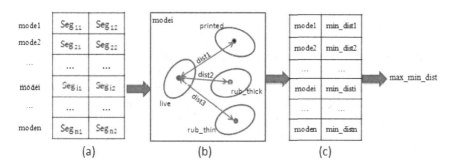

Fig. 7. The flow chart of determination of best feature

Firstly, according to the size of our data (380*380 pixels) and the rule of Seg_1 and Seg_2 (from 10 to 150 pixels, step size 20 pixels and $Seg_1 < Seg_2$) we defined, 28 types of modes are obtained. As demonstrated in Fig.7(a), n is 28 and each $mode_i$ corresponds a pair of (Seg_{i1}, Seg_{i2}) which divides the whole spectrogram into three parts with Seg_{i1} and Seg_{i2}. In Fig.7(b), secondly, each ellipse represents coordinate $[or_1, or_2, or_3]$ (calculating with the equation 4) distribution area of each type of samples. And the colored dot at the center of each ellipse represents the mean coordinate of this type. For each mode, three distances $[dist_1, dist_2, dist_3]$ between the mean coordinate of live and each fake sample can be obtained. Then we just keep the minimum Euclidean distance of $[dist_1, dist_2, dist_3]$ in each mode as the min_dist showed in Fig.7(c). With the gradual growth of Seg_1 and Seg_2, we obtain a series of minimum distance values. After finishing the all 28 types of modes, there will be 28 min_dist for comparison. According to the maxmin criterion, we choose the (Seg_1, Seg_2) corresponding to the maximum value among 28 min_dist as our optimal classification mode. The segment values, which mean that in all types of modes it possesses a maximum between-class distance, are 10 pixels and 90 pixels in our case (as shown in Fig.8).

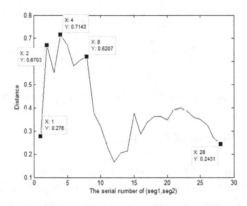

Fig. 8. The Euclidean distance of coordinate corresponding to different segment boundary: No.4 corresponding to (10, 90)

6   Experiments

Due to the nonlinear distribution of block spectral energy features, SVM is chosen to train the live-or-fake classifier. The test result is shown in Table 1. Based on n-fold cross validation and repeated verification we adopted, it is easy to see from Table.1 that the accuracy of recognition rate is stable. The range of error rate whether False Accept Rate (FAR) or False Reject Rate (FRR) is not large with a good verification. Consequently, it can be declared that this block spectral energy feature has a notable capability for distinguishing live and fake dorsal hand vein samples in our dataset and the measure is convenient. After all, our method can be considered as an effective candidate for dorsal hand vein liveness detection in a NIRDHVR system.

Table 1. The minimum, average and maximum values of detection accuracy, FRR and FAR of live samples VS fake samples

Rate(%)	Minimum	Average	Maximum
Accuracy	93.0	96.31	99.0
FAR	0	2.14	4.5
FRR	0	1.54	4.5

7   Conclusions

In this paper, we propose a novel feature for dorsal hand vein liveness detection based on block spectral energy. Three types of typical fake attempts are designed and corresponding samples are collected. A database including 500 images is established which contains both with live samples and three types of fake samples. The main contributions of this presented work include analyzing the difference between live and fake samples in frequency domain, presenting a strategy of block spectral energy and determining the related parameters using the maxmin criterion. After the feature is presented, the SVM is used to train and predict the distribution. Experiment results have showed the high discrimination ability of this feature and verified the effectiveness of our block strategy. And our further work will focus on enlarge the type of the fake dorsal hand vein and the capacity of both the live and fake database. In additional, evaluating the practical use of our proposed method is also an important topic.

Acknowledgement. This work is supported by the National Natural Science Fund Committee of China (NSFC No.61271368). The authors would also like to thanks for Hong Wei, Amario and Chen Li for their constructive advices and grateful for comments from the anonymous associate editor and reviewers.

References

1. Sweeney, E.: Veincheck—A technical perspective. J. Information Security Technical Report 3, 47–51 (1998)
2. MacGregor, P., Welford, R.: Veincheck: imaging for security and personnel identification. J. Adv. Imaging 6, 52–56 (1991)
3. Zhang, Z., Yi, D., Lei, Z., et al.: Face liveness detection by learning multispectral reflectance distributions. In: 2011 IEEE International Conference on Automatic Face & Gesture Recognition and Workshops (FG 2011), pp. 436–441. IEEE (2011)
4. Rowe, R.K.: Multispectral liveness determination, U.S. Patent. 7,539,330 (2009)
5. Biomedical Optics in Portland, http://omlc.ogi.edu/spectra/hemoglobin/index.html
6. Basri, R., Jacobs, D.W.: Lambertian reflectance and linear subspaces. IEEE Transactions on J. Pattern Analysis and Machine Intelligence 25, 218–233 (2003)
7. Maio, D., Jain, A.K.: Handbook of fingerprint recognition. Springer (2009)
8. Agrawal, R., Faloutsos, C., Swami, A.: Efficient similarity search in sequence databases. In: Lomet, D.B. (ed.) FODO 1993. LNCS, vol. 730, pp. 69–94. Springer, Heidelberg (1993)
9. Shen, C.C., Tsai, W.H.: A graph matching approach to optimal task assignment in distributed computing systems using a minimax criterion. IEEE Transactions on J. Computers 100, 197–203 (1985)

The Affection of Gabor Parameters
to Iris Recognition and Their Optimization

Fei He[1], Yuanning Liu[1], Xiaodong Zhu[1,*], Weijie Deng[1], Xiaoxu Zhang[1],
and Guang Huo[1,2]

[1] Jilin University, College of Computer Science and Technology,
Qianjin Road 2699, 130012, Changchun, China
[2] Northeast Dianli University, Informatization Office,
Changchun Road 169, 132012, Jilin, China
hefei10@mails.jlu.edu.cn, {liuyn,zhuxd,xiaoxu}@jlu.edu.cn,
465006620@qq.com, yanhuo1860@126.com
http://www.springer.com/lncs

Abstract. In this paper, a Gabor filter optimization method based on
real-coded genetic algorithm is presented for iris recognition. First, we
list Gabor filter parameters and analyzed the validity of the expression
for texture features. Then, since Gabor parameters has a great influence
in Correct Recognition Rate, we took Gabor kernel parameters as chro-
mosomes and Discriminative Index as fitness to on the CASIA V3 and
JLUBR-IRIS for optimization. Moreover, the optimized Gabor filters are
adopted to extract features for corresponding iris databases, which can
obtain excellent results.

Keywords: iris recognition, texture information, Gabor filters, feature
extraction.

1 Introduction

Biometric recognition technology plays an important role in information security got more and more attention recently. Especially, iris recognition has the
advantages of high accuracy, uniqueness and invariability [1]. Feature extraction
as a core issue is related to the performance and robustness of iris recognition.
In iris recognition, using Gabor filters to texture feature extraction has become
one of the main methods [2] [3] [4]. And different Gabor filter may directly affect the efficiency to feature extraction. Looking for parameters of Gabor filter
can significantly improve the effectiveness of the features [5]. Hongguang Sun
used Particle Swarm Optimization (PSO) to optimize Gabor wavelet parameters, but PSO may fall into local optimization [6]. Kumar used the Ant Colony
Optimization (ACO) algorithm to find the optimal parameters [7], but the ACO
has the problem of over more computation. In this paper, we first discuss the
influence of 2D-Gabor parameters on the recognition rate. Then the real-coded

---

* Corresponding author.

Z. Sun et al. (Eds.): CCBR 2013, LNCS 8232, pp. 330–337, 2013.
© Springer International Publishing Switzerland 2013

genetic algorithm (GA) is adopted to Gabor filter parameter optimization [8], the entire populations tend to be optimized, at the same time consume. In the experiments,optimized Gabor filters can achieve distinctive correct recognition rate (CRR) and false reject rate (FRR) on CASIA V3 and JLUBR-IRIS iris database.

The rest of the article is organized follows, the section 2 briefly introduces the Gabor filters and the feature extraction process; These section 3 details the process of the real-coded genetic algorithm optimization and the significance of each parameter; Experimental results and comparisons are reported in section 4; Section 5 summarizes the work of this paper.

2 Gabor Filters

2.1 Gabor Kernels

2D-Gabor filters can decompose the scales and directions of the input signal. By adjusting the filter center frequency, it can achieve simultaneously space and frequency domain of joint optimum resolution [2].

Generally, (1) formulas can be used to represent the 2D Gabor function:

$$g(x, y) = \exp\{-\pi[\frac{(x-x_0)^2}{\alpha^2} + \frac{(y-y_0)^2}{\beta^2}]\} \\ \times \exp\{-2\pi i[\omega(x - x_0)\cos\varphi + \omega(y - y_0)\sin\varphi]\} \tag{1}$$

Where(x_0, y_0) is the center of the receptive field in the spatial domain, α and β are standard deviations of the Gaussian envelope along x and y axis and determine the filter bandwidth.ω is the frequency of the filter, the size of theω is representing iris information in the frequency domain[9], it can be defined as $\omega = \sqrt{(\mu_0)^2 + (\nu_0)^2}$.$\varphi$ is the direction of modulation for the filter, the size of the φ is characterized iris information based on a direction, it can be defined as $\varphi = \arctan(\mu_0/\nu_0)$, where (μ_0, ν_0) respectively define frequency in the x and y axis.

2.2 Gabor Feature Extraction and Matching

We adopted multiple directions and scales Gabor filters to extract iris features. As shown in figure1,Which $\overline{M}$ is average of amplitude matrix after filteringm and n respectively represent the number of directions and scales of Gabor filters. The $m \times n$ dimensional features vector can be denoted as:

$$Vector_{mag} = [\overline{M}_1, \overline{M}_2, \cdots\cdots, \overline{M}_{m \times n}] \tag{2}$$

For the features vector extracted from samples, we normalized them before alignment by Euclidean distance [10],the Euclidean distance formula is shown as:

$$Dis = \sqrt{\sum_{i=1}^{M \times N} \sum_{j=1}^{b} (m_i^j(input) - m_i^j(enrolled))^2} \tag{3}$$

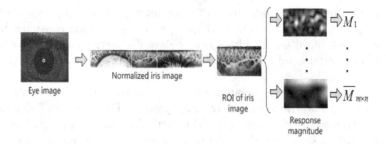

Eye image

Normalized iris image

ROI of iris image

Response magnitude

Fig. 1. The process of feature extraction

3 Gabor Filter Optimization

3.1 Genetic Algorithm

Genetic algorithms will encode units as chromosome with features. New units will be produced by mutating and crossing in the process of evolution. Units with high quality were selected by the value of the fitness function. These new units will form a new population. We use GA to Gabor filters optimization and get the optimal solution by the unit with the highest fitness in the final generation as optimized Gabor parameters[11].

3.2 Algorithm Setup

(1)Encoding mode schema
We have four Gabor parameters in this paper, including two continuous parameters ω, φ, and sampling values of directions and scales, which are discrete parameters. Some of these parameters have a wide range, which request a continuous searching space. In the purpose of reducing the complexity of the algorithm, real-coded schema was chosen in this paper.
(2)Fitness function schema
We judge the discrimination by the Discriminative Index (DI) value in the Formula (4)

$$d = \frac{|\mu_1 - \mu_2|}{\sqrt{\frac{\sigma_1^2 + \sigma_2^2}{2}}} \tag{4}$$

In Formula (4), is the average of the intra-class matching scoresis the standard deviation of the intra-class matching scores.
(3)Selection operator schema
A probabilistic selection is performed based upon the individuals fitness such that the better individuals have an increased chance of being selected. The simplest selection scheme Roulette wheel algorithm [12] is chosen as the schema of the selection operator.

(4)Crossover operator
Due to the real values of Gabor parameters, Randomized cross-over schema was chosen as the crossover operator. Real valued simple crossover is identical to the binary version presented above in equations (5). Arithmetic crossover produces two complimentary linear combinations of the parents. Suppose we have two training samples α and β, then the way to cross them is as follows:

$$\begin{cases} \alpha' = \alpha^* p + \beta^* (1 - p) \\ \beta' = \beta^* p + \alpha^* (1 - p) \end{cases} \tag{5}$$

In that p is a random number between 0 and 1. Here we set p = 0.5, according to the independence among Gabor filters.
(5)Mutation operator
The mutation operator is $\theta \times (Y - X)$, where θ is a randomly generated number between 0 and 1. X and Y are the highest value and the lowest value of a certain Gabor parameter respectively.

4   Experimental Results

4.1   Iris Databases

In this paper, we adopt JLUBR-IRIS database which is independently developed by Jilin University staffs. Captured device uses $8mm$ lens, and the image size is $640 * 480$. We selected 90 images from 9 classes to extract feature. 7 images of each class were chosen as templates, the left 3 images as test sample. And then, we use threshold method to make a decision of identification.

In addition, we also do the experiment on the public database CASIA V3, developed by Chinese Academy of Sciences.

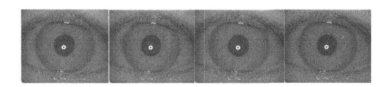

Fig. 2. Images in JLUBR-IRIS database

4.2   Gabor Filter Selection

(1)Direction parameter selection
Physiological experiments show that human has only 5 degrees in direction distinguishing [13]. Meanwhile, we only consider symmetrical Gabor filters. Therefore, can be determined by m ($m < 36$), which is the amount of the direction between$[0°, 180°]$. The octave of the fixed filter bank is 0.459, while maximum

frequency is 76.9, which has various degrees to generate Gabor filters, the results shown as follows:

Table 1. The impact of the direction parameters to the recognition rate in JLUBR-IRIS

θ	0°	60°	120°	140°	160°
FRR(%)	1.5	1.6	2	14	1.3
CRR(%)	97	96.8	96	82	86

If the octave of the fixed filter bank is 0.471007, while maximum frequency is 17.52424, which has various degrees to generate Gabor filters. The results are shown as follows:

Table 2. The impact of the direction parameters to the recognition rate in CASIA V3

θ	0°	20°	40°	60°	80°	100°	120°	140°	160°
FRR(%)	4.5	5	5	4.2	5	9.2	15	14	1.3
CRR(%)	91	90	90	91	90	82	70	82	86

This experimental results show that, the Gabor features have direction selectivity. If the direction we select is closer to the direction which contains more texture information, we can extract more effective features.

(2) Frequency parameter selection

If the octave of the fixed filter bank is 0.459, while maximum frequency is 76.9, which has various frequency to generate Gabor filters. the results are shown as follows:

Table 3. The impact of the frequency parameters to the recognition rate in JLUBR-IRIS

ω	8.28	11.38	15.66	21.5	40.7	55.97	76.95
FRR(%)	2.2	2.2	2.7	1.7	3.3	2.5	1.9
CRR(%)	95.6	95.6	94.6	96.6	93.4	95	96

If the octave of the fixed filter bank is 0.471007, while maximum frequency is 17.524247, which has various frequency to generate Gabor filters. The results are shown as follows:

Table 4. The impact of the frequency parameters to the recognition rate in CASIA V3

frequency ω	FRR(%)	CRR(%)
12.64	3.7	93.6
17.52	4.5	91

This experimental results show that if the frequency band we select is closer to the frequency range of the iris images, we can extract more effective features.
(3)The combination of optimal 2-D Gabor filters parameters

From the above we can give a conclusion that four parameters were optimized by genetic algorithm: the range of direction number m [0,36], which is discrete value; the range of max frequency F [1.4 ,128], which is continuous value; the range of octave $\mu[0.2, 1]$, which is continuous value; the range of scale $\sigma[1, 50]$, which is discrete value.

When we studied the genetic algorithm of real-coded, the filter parameters for extracting feature by genetic algorithm, and the parameters of genetic process were set for 30 individuals as the population size, 0.8 as the crossover rate selection, 0.06 as the mutation rate selection and 200 generation as the termination of algebra selection. We used that pattern to optimize parameters of Gabor filters corresponding to the CASIA V3 and JLUBR-IRIS iris database, and got the optimal parameters combination of two iris database values finally.

The optimized parameters values we obtained were $(9, 2, 14.135216, 0.41326)$ and$(3, 8, 34.572628, 0.372319)$ on JLUBR-IRIS and CASIA V3 database respectively. The ROC curves in Fig.3 is drawn from the experimental data obtained from the experiment in JLUBR-IRIS and CASIA V3.

We conducted some comparative experiments of our optimized Gabor parameters and other solutions, which were intended for CASIA-V1 in existing literatures [14][15], by the same experimental protocol on CASIA-V3. From Table 6 shown, our trained Gabor filters outperformed other predefine Gabor parameters on CASIA-V3. Here we appropriated them for CASIA-V3 to show their

Table 5. The details in Equal Error Rate

Dataset	Threshold	FRR(%)	FAR(%)	CRR(%)
JLUBR-IRIS	0.022	1.35	1.35	97.3
CASIA V3	0.058	3.6	3.6	92.8

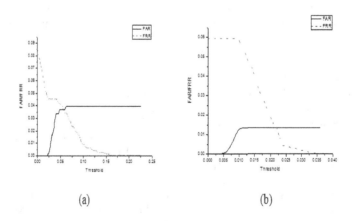

(a)   (b)

Fig. 3. (a)ROC curves of CASIA V3, (b) JLUBR-IRIS datasets

Table 6. The performance comparisons of different Gabor filters on CASIA-V3

Reference	f_{max}	df	scales	orientations	Overall accuracy	$EER(\%)$
Yu[14]	32	2	4	4	88.1	11.7
Ma[15]	64	2	6	4	90.3	9.5
Proposed	34.572628	0.372319	3	8	92.8	3.6

non-university for different datasets. That proves the inevitability of Gabor parameter optimization.

5   Conclusions

2D-Gabor transform parameters and their influence to the iris recognition rate were studied in this paper. Based on the study of the occurrence development process and application of 2D-Gabor functions and specific meaning of the parameters were explained. Through lots of experiment, we verified the reasonable value range of each parameter in iris recognition. In Gabor parameters optimization for JLUBR-IRIS and CASIA V3 iris database, proper Gabor parameters are optimized based on real-coded genetic algorithm to get a better reliability and usability of iris recognition system.

References

1. Lee, H., Lee, S.H., Kim, T., et al.: Secure user identification for consumer electronics devices. IEEE Transactions on Consumer Electronics 54(4), 1798–1802 (2008)
2. Daugman, J.: How iris recognition works. IEEE Transactions on Circuits and Systems for Video Technology 14(1), 21–30 (2004)
3. Kamarainen, J.K., Kyrki, V., Kalviainen, H.: Invariance properties of Gabor filter-based features-overview and applications. IEEE Transactions on Image Processing 15(5), 1088–1099 (2006)
4. Nabti, M., Bouridane, A.: An effective and fast iris recognition system based on a combined multiscale feature extraction technique. Pattern Recognition 41(3), 868–879 (2008)
5. Lin, Z., Lu, B.: Iris recognition method based on the optimized Gabor filters. In: 2010 3rd International Congress on Image and Signal Processing (CISP), 4th edn., pp. 1868–1872. IEEE (2010)
6. Tsai, C.C., Taur, J.S., Tao, C.W.: Iris recognition using gabor filters optimized by the particle swarm technique. In: IEEE International Conference on Systems, Man and Cybernetics SMC, 2008, pp. 921–926. IEEE (2008)
7. Kumar, A., Hanmandlu, M., Sanghvi, H., et al.: Decision level biometric fusion using Ant Colony Optimization. In: 2010 17th IEEE International Conference on Image Processing (ICIP), pp. 3105–3108. IEEE (2010)
8. Blanco, A., Delgado, M., Pegalajar, M.C.: A real-coded genetic algorithm for training recurrent neural networks. Neural networks 14(1), 93–105 (2001)
9. Daugman, J.G.: Uncertainty relation for resolution in space, spatial frequency, and orientation optimized by two-dimensional visual cortical filters. Optical Society of America, Journal, A: Optics and Image Science 2(7), 1160–1169 (1985)

10. Ma, L., Tan, T., Wang, Y., et al.: Efficient iris recognition by characterizing key local variations. IEEE Transactions on Image Processing 13(6), 739–750 (2004)
11. Goldberg, D.E., Holland, J.H.: Genetic algorithms and machine learning. Machine Learning 3(2), 95–99 (1988)
12. Houck, C.R., Joines, J.A., Kay, M.G.: A genetic algorithm for function optimization: a Matlab implementation. NCSU-IE TR, 95(09) (1995)
13. Webster, M.A., De Valois, R.L.: Relationship between spatial-frequency and orientation tuning of striate-cortex cells. Journal of Optical Society of America 7(11), 1124–1132 (1985)
14. Ma, L., Wang, Y., Tan, T.: Iris recognition based on multichannel gabor filtering. In: The 5th Asian Conference on Computer Vision, pp. 23–25 (2002)
15. Nabti, M., Bouridane, A.: An effective and fast iris recognition system based on a combined multi-scale feature extraction technique. Pattern Recognition 41(3), 868–879 (2008)

Defocused Iris Image Restoration
Based on Spectral Curve Fitting

Huiying Ren, Yuqing He[*], Siyuan Wang, Chunquan Gan, and Jixing Wang

Key Laboratory of Photoelectronic Imaging Technology and System,
Ministry of Education of China, School of Optoelectronics,
Beijing Institute of Technology, Beijing 10081, China
yuqinghe@bit.edu.cn

Abstract. Despite the rapid development of iris image capturing system and recognition algorithms, defocused iris images occurs a lot due to the restriction of optical system's depth of field. To take advantage of the useful texture information for iris recognition in more unconstrained environment, we proposed a scheme for iris image deblurring based on fitting ellipse curve in the frequency spectral image. To get the parameters for Point Spread Function(PSF) initialization, we first calculate the frequency spectral image of defocused iris images, and then fit the ellipse with Hough Transform to get the defocus estimation. Blind deconvolution is chosen as the restoration method in which the PSF is refined through iteration. Experiments with both artificial data and real data are conducted and the results demonstrated the effectiveness of our method to restore defocused iris images.

Keywords: iris recognition, image restoration, curve fitting, defocus estimation.

1   Introduction

Iris recognition in restricted environment has developed rapidly in recent years. Most researches focused on iris localization and feature extraction methods for iris images in users' cooperation mode. In authentication of people in unconstrained environment such as mobile phones and surveillance equipments, the performance of iris recognition decreases because of the degraded images. Defocused iris images owing to restricts of Depth of Field (DOF) appear a lot in these situations. Restoring the defocused images is a proper way to enhance the system's robustness.

Researches have been done on deblurring of defocused iris images. David S. Stokeret al [1] proposed a deblurring and denoising approach to restore both single images and multiframes. They determine the point spread function (PSF) through the specular corneal reflection of illumination source. Byung Jun Kang[2] et al take both motion and optical blur into consideration and proposed a restoration method in terms of recognition rather than visibility. Bo Liu et al[3] introduce an approach in which the stable bits of an iris image are selected to do recognition. Results show that the

---

[*] Corresponding author.

Z. Sun et al. (Eds.): CCBR 2013, LNCS 8232, pp. 338–344, 2013.

selected bits which are robustness to noise achieve a good performance especially in power sensitive solutions. Nadezhda Sazonova et al[4] and Nguyen K. et al[5] adopted the idea that quantifies the out-of-focus iris images to some blur levels. The above study on defocused iris images have all elevated the recognition performance. But they didn't give the defocus amount precisely or approximately. Jing Liu et al [6] proposed a scheme to deblur both motion and defocused iris images by a region-selected refining method. In [7], Byung Jun Kang and Kang Ryoung Park proposed a real-time deblurring method in terms of focus scores and a CLS restoration filter. They gave a way to evaluate the amount of image blurring, but most of the past methods are effective when the parameters of the optical system is known. In cases that the optical properties are not given, focus value based methods didn't show their accuracy. In our approach, we estimate the defocus radius of every iris image without parameters of capturing devices by means of elliptic curve fitting of spectral image and restore it with the blind deconvolution.

The rest of paper is organized as follows. In Section 2 the defocus amount estimation algorithm based on the elliptic curve fitting is proposed. We illustrate the restoration in Section 3 and give the experimental results in Section 4. Conclusions are made in Section 5.

2 Deblurring Iris Images: PSF Initialization

Image degradation model[8] can be described as $g = hf + n$, in which g , h, f and n represent the degraded image, the degradation function, the original image and the noise respectively. Restoration is the process of figuring out a best estimation of f with the prior knowledge of h and n. The expression of the degradation in frequency domain is shown as Equation (1).

$$G(u,v) = F(u,v)H(u,v) + N(u,v) \tag{1}$$

The framework we proposed for defocused iris image restoration is shown in Fig.1.

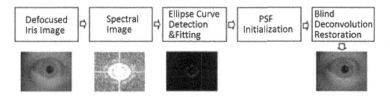

Fig. 1. The framework of our proposed restoration method

The most important step is to find the PSF of the defocused iris image to determine h in the image degradation process. This can be achieved through the defocus estimation and elliptic curve fitting.

2.1 Estimation of Defocus Amount

A image quality assessment procedure is essential before deblurring iris images to divide captured iris images into seriously blurred images, clear images and blurred images that can be restored. Seriously blurred images should be given up while the clear images should be applied immediately in iris recognition. The proposed method aims at restore iris images in the third situation.

A point in object space is mapped into a small round spot in image space when the optical system is out of focus due to the limited DOF. The corresponding PSF of this kind defocusing can be simplified to a disc function as follows:

$$h(x,y) = \begin{cases} \dfrac{1}{\pi r^2} & , \text{ when } x^2 + y^2 \le r^2 \\ 0 & , \qquad \text{other} \end{cases} \tag{2}$$

while r is the blur radius. The Fourier transform of $h(x, y)$ is as Equation (3):

$$H(u,v) = \frac{2J_1\left[r\sqrt{\left(\dfrac{2\pi}{M}u\right)^2 + \left(\dfrac{2\pi}{N}v\right)^2} \right]}{\sqrt{\left(\dfrac{2\pi}{M}u\right)^2 + \left(\dfrac{2\pi}{N}v\right)^2}} \tag{3}$$

J_1 is the first order Bessel function of first kind. $M \times N$ is the scale of Fourier transform and u, v represent the spatial frequency. Then the first dark elliptical ring orbit in spectral image can be described as Equation (4):

$$2\pi r \sqrt{\left(\frac{u}{M}\right)^2 + \left(\frac{v}{N}\right)^2} = 3.83 \tag{4}$$

If the noise is little enough, the blur radius can be obtained by the first dark ring of $G(u,v)$, which determines the blur kernel and the initial PSF.

2.2   Elliptic Curve Fitting

In Section 2.1, we first calculate the spectral of the defocused image and do morphological processing. Then the edge of the processed spectral image is extracted by Canny Operator. A refined elliptic boundary curve is obtained after the above steps. We utilized an ellipse detection algorithm based on Hough Transform to determine the parameters of the ellipse[9]. Let the points in the boundary image be (x_i, y_i), the long and short axes of the ellipse be a and b. Point (x_0, y_0) denotes the center of the ellipse. The principle of Hough Transform in parameter space is described as follows:

$$H(x_0, y_0, a, b, c) = \sum^n h(x_i, y_i, x_0, y_0, a, b, c) \tag{5}$$

In which

$$h(x_i, y_i, x_0, y_0, a, b, c) = \begin{cases} 1, g(x_i, y_i, x_0, y_0, a, b, c) = 0 \\ 0, g(x_i, y_i, x_0, y_0, a, b, c) \ne 0 \end{cases} \tag{6}$$

$$g(x_i, y_i, x_0, y_0, a, b, c) = \frac{(x - x_0)^2}{a^2} + \frac{(y - y_0)^2}{b^2} - c = 0 \tag{7}$$

For each point of the boundary image, if it satisfies $g(x_i, y_i, x_0, y_0, a, b, c) = 0$, the correspond 5-dimensional parameters represent the ellipse that pass through this point. To fit the ellipse curve in the boundary image, the parameter set maximizing H needs to be calculated. In our experiment, the spectral images of the blurred iris images are centrosymmetric, so that x_0 and y_0 are both defined as the central of the image, which simplifies the calculation. After the other three parameters a, b and c are determined through the Hough Transform, r is defined according to comparison of (4) and (7).

Once the blur radius r is determined, the degradation function $h(x, y)$ of the system can be immediately obtained by Equation (2), then we initialize the PSF by $h(x, y)$.

3   Deblurring Iris Images by Blind Deconvolution

The blind deconvolution[10] is applied in our approach to restore the defocused iris images. For a single defocused iris image, an iterative process is implemented:

(1) Set the maximum iteration time k. When the iteration time is greater, the time-consuming raises a lot while the precision doesn't increase much; otherwise the precision decreases. In our experiment, we set it as 10.

(2) Calculate the Fourier Transform of $g(x, y)$, $f(x, y)$ and $h(x, y)$. Initialize the data as $F^{(0)}(u, v)=G(u, v)$, $H^{(0)}(u, v)=H(u, v)$.

(3) Calculate the power spectrum of noise as α. In the iteration process, the power spectrum of noise α is determined on basis of its uniformity and floats in the iteration in a certain range of $(1\pm5\%)\alpha_0$, α_0 is defined by the average variance of several small flat regions in the image. We choose several 24×24 pixels regions.

(4) Update the data by following equations:

$$F^{(k+1)}(u,v)=\left[\frac{H^{(k)*}(u,v)}{\left|H^{(k)}(u,v)\right|^2+\alpha\Big/\left|F^{(k)}(u,v)\right|^2}\right]G(u,v) \qquad (8)$$

$$H^{(k+1)}(u,v)=\left[\frac{F^{(k)*}(u,v)}{1\Big/\left|H^{(k)}(u,v)\right|^2+\left|F^{(k)}(u,v)\right|^2}\right]G(u,v) \qquad (9)$$

$$k=k+1 \qquad (10)$$

(5) If iteration time achieves the set value, applying inverse Fourier Transform to $F^{(k+1)}(u, v)$ and get original image $f(x, y)$. Otherwise return to (4).

4   Experiments and Results

4.1   Dataset

To examine the effectiveness of our proposed framework for iris image deblurring, we build both an artificial dataset which contains 750 artificial defocused iris images based on a CASIA 3.0 and a real dataset which contains defocused iris images of unknown defocus amount captured in the laboratory.

4.2   Artificial Data

Each original well-focused iris image is blurred by blur kernels built by different blur radius in a range of 2 to 6 pixels. Fig.2 shows some examples in our dataset.

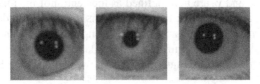

Fig. 2. Examples of Artificial iris images

After the deblurring, iris images are preprocessing by localization, segmentation and normalization. 2-D Gabor filters [11] [12] are built for texture extraction and encoding. The average PSNRs and Equal Error Rates (EERs) of previous method proposed by Byung Jun Kang et al [7] and our method are compared in Table 1.The proposed method outperforms that in [7] in terms of PSNR and EER. We achieve an EER of 0.883% which is 0.0602% descend from the original defocused iris images.

Table 1. PSNRs and EERs on artificial images

	PSNR	EER
Defocused iris images	26.4309	1.485%
Deblurring Method in [7]	26.9112	1.020%
The proposed method	26.9821	0.883%

4.3   Real Data

We also captured defocused iris images with our capturing device with random defocus amount and carried on experiments by method in [7] and our method. Fig.3 shows an example of images we collected and the restored image we obtained. A number of 104 images from 26 individuals are collected. Part of the intra-class and inter-class Hamming Distance (HD) distribution is shown in Fig.4.

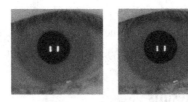

Fig. 3. Deblurring result of real image. The left is a segmented example of captured defocused iris image. The right is the restored one by proposed method.

In Fig.3, the high-frequency information and sharpness increases visually after image restoration. From Fig.4 we can see that intra-class HD decreases obviously in the case that the proposed method is implemented on the defocused iris images we collected in laboratory. We got an average of intra-class HD dropped from 0.2542 to

0.2095 and inter-class raised from 0.4727 to 0.4855 using our method while an average of intra-class and inter-class HD is 0.2493 and 0.4785 using method in [7]. This gives a conclusion that the restoration makes the recognition more reliable and usable.

The results show that our proposed framework outperforms previous method in not only image quality but also recognition performance. Due to the accuracy in curve fitting by Hough Transform, our method gives a respectively reliable estimation of blur radius. An important aspect of our research is that due to the independence of blur amount calculating with the optical property of image capturing device, the proposed method offers a way to do defocused iris recognition in cross-platforms.

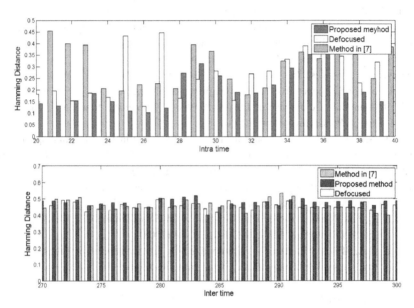

Fig. 4. Part of intra-class and inter-class Hamming Distance distribution

5   Conclusion

In this article we introduced a new framework for iris image restoration in which blur amount is estimated by spectral curve fitting with the unknown parameters of the optical system. Experimental results show the effectiveness for improving the recognition performance. But the proposed method is relatively complex which leads to higher time consumption. Future work should be done to fasten the processing such as optimizing the curve fitting algorithm.

Acknowledgement. This project is supported by National Science Foundation of China (No. 60905012, 60572058) and Open Fund of Beijing Institute of Technology. We would like to thank Institute of Automation, Chinese Academy of Sciences for allowing us to use the CASIA database in this research.

References

1. Stoker, D., Wedd, J., Lavelle, E., Laan, J.: Restoration and recognition of distant, blurry irises. Applied Optics 52(9), 1864–1875 (2013)
2. Kang, B., Park, R.: A Study on Restoration of Iris Images with Motion-and-Optical Blur on Mobile Iris Recognition Devices. J. International Journal of Imaging Systems and Technology 19, 323–331 (2009)
3. Liu, B., Lam, S., Srikanthan, T., Yuan, W.: Iris Recognition of Defocused Images for Mobile Phones. J. International Journal of Pattern Recognition and Artificial Intelligence 26(8), 1260010-1–1260010-23 (2012)
4. Sazonova, N., Schuckers, S., Johnson, P., Lopez, P., Sazonov, E.: Impact of out-of-focus blur on iris recognition. In: Proceedings of the SPIE-The International Society for Optical Engineering, p. 80291S. SPIE Press, Florida (2011)
5. Nguyen, K., Fookes, C., Sridharan, S., Denman, S.: Focus-score Weighted Super-resolution for Uncooperative Iris Recognition at a Distance and on The Move. In: 2010 25th International Conference of Image and Vision Computing New Zealand (IVCNZ), pp. 1–8. IEEE Press, Queenstown (2010)
6. Liu, J., Sun, Z., Tan, T.: Iris image deblurring based on refinement of point spread function. In: Zheng, W.-S., Sun, Z., Wang, Y., Chen, X., Yuen, P.C., Lai, J. (eds.) CCBR 2012. LNCS, vol. 7701, pp. 184–192. Springer, Heidelberg (2012)
7. Kang, B., Park, K.: Real-time image restoration for iris recognition systems. IEEE Trans. on Systems, Man, and Cybernetics, Part B 37, 1555–1566 (2007)
8. Kang, B., Park, K.: Restoration of motion-blurred iris image on mobile iris recognition devices. Optical Engineering 47, 117202-1–117202-8 (2008)
9. Basca, C.A., Talos, M., Brad, R.: Randomized Hough Transform for Ellipse Detection with Result Clustering, Computer as a Tool. In: EUROCON 2005, vol. 2, pp. 1397–1400 (2005)
10. Levin, A., Weiss, Y., Durand, F., Freeman, W.: Understanding and evaluating blind deconvolution algorithms. In: IEEE Conf. on Computer Vision and Pattern Recognition, pp. 1964–1971. IEEE (2009)
11. Daugman, J.: How iris recognition works. IEEE Trans. on Circuits and Systems for Video Technology 14, 21–30 (2004)
12. Ma, L., Wang, Y., Tan, T.: Iris Recognition Based on Multichannel Gabor Filtering. In: Asian Conference on Computer Vision, pp. 279–283. ACCV Press, Melbourne (2002)

Light Field Photography for Iris Image Acquisition

Chi Zhang[1,2], Guangqi Hou[1], Zhenan Sun[1], Tieniu Tan[1,2], and Zhiliang Zhou[3]

[1] Center for Research on Intelligent Perception and Computing,
National Laboratory of Pattern Recognition,
Institute of Automation, Chinese Academy of Sciences
[2] College of Engineering and Information Technology
University of Chinese Academy of Sciences
[3] Laboratory of Computational Optical Imaging Technology,
Academy of Opto-Electronics, Chinese Academy of Sciences
{chi.zhang,gqhou,znsun,tnt}@nlpr.ia.ac.cn, zhouzl@aoe.ac.cn

Abstract. Conventional iris sensors usually have limited depth of field (DoF) so that it is difficult to capture focused iris images for personal identification. This paper introduces the first attempt to extend DoF of iris image acquisition based on light field photography. There are mainly three contributions of our work. Firstly, a novel iris sensor is developed based on light field photography. Secondly, the first light field iris image database is constructed using the sensor. Thirdly, a number of experiments are conducted to demonstrate the advantages of the developed light field iris sensor over conventional iris sensors in terms of DoF and its influence on iris recognition performance. The experimental results show that refocused iris images can be reconstructed from the light field imaging data with comparable quality to the optically well-focused iris images. Therefore the light field iris sensor can achieve much higher accuracy of iris recognition than conventional iris sensors in the range of defocused imaging.

Keywords: iris sensor, light field photography, depth of field, refocus.

1 Introduction

Iris pattern is unique for extremely accurate personal identification [1] but it is difficult to capture high quality iris images. A bottle neck of iris imaging system is the trade-off between the DoF and the size of the aperture in conventional camera. Therefore conventional iris sensors usually have limited DoF which causes constraints of position and motion on human subjects during iris recognition.

A number of studies have been investigated to extend DoF of iris imaging. Matey et al. tried to extend the DoF of the iris-on-the-move (IOM) system by decreasing the aperture and increasing the strength of NIR illumination [2]. But the strong NIR illumination has the risk to the safety of human eyes. Guo et al. [3] and Dong et al. [4][5] used the pan-tilt-zoom (PTZ) iris cameras to actively capture iris images using adaptive optical lens, which can greatly extend the DoF of iris imaging. However, PTZ unit usually involves heavy mechanical devices and it is difficult to meet practical requirements of iris image acquisition.

Z. Sun et al. (Eds.): CCBR 2013, LNCS 8232, pp. 345–352, 2013.

It is desirable to capture iris images with a large DoF camera in a short exposure period. However, there is a trade-off between DoF and the size of the aperture in conventional camera. Therefore we turn to novel camera concepts such as light field photography for possible breakthrough of DoF problem in iris imaging.

A new hand-held light-field camera was introduced in 2006 by Ng [6], which offers an extended DoF free of balance the trade-off as the conventional cameras. A microlens array is inserted between photon sensor and main lens in light-field cameras. So a light field camera is capable to record both position and direction of rays from visual scenes simultaneously. Thus, the light-field camera can extend the depth of field exceeding that of the conventional camera up to 6 times practically [8]. It offers an opportunity for the iris imaging.

In this paper, a preliminary study of the possibility of light field photography for iris image acquisition is investigated. The main contributions of this paper include:

1) A novel iris sensor is developed based on light field photography.

2) The first light field iris image database is constructed using the sensor.

3) A number of experiments are conducted to demonstrate the advantages of the developed light field iris sensor over conventional iris sensors in terms of DoF and its influence on iris recognition performance.

2   Related Work

Although auto-focus iris cameras may fail to capture qualified iris images from walking subjects, it remains a valuable attempt to equivalently extend the DoF of iris imaging system [3][5][4] without decreasing aperture size, since it dynamically adjusts lens to focus at an interested object plane. The only drawback is the lens-motor movement is too slow to adapt to the change of human positions.

Ren Ng [6] introduced the first hand held light-field camera produced by inserting a microlens array in front of photo sensor of a traditional camera. It can digitally refocus the light-field image at different object planes after it was captured. Light-field camera is also capable to extend the DoF of iris imaging as the auto-focus camera, while it avoids slow mechanics because of its shoot and refocusing scheme.

Raghavendra et al. [7] introduced light-field camera to face recognition recently. Our work on light field iris image acquisition is inspired and encouraged by the success of light field face recognition. Compared with the light-field imaging for face recognition, iris recognition with the light-field camera is a more challenging task. Since the detailed texture of iris is the principal features used in iris recognition, the iris imaging system needs a joint design of optics, illumination, sensor, lens, algorithms and so on.

3   Light-Field Iris Image Acquisition, Processing and Comparison

To verify that the iris imaging by light-field camera outperforms conventional camera in the extended DoF, a complete process is designed to measure the improvement in a given depth range, which includes three steps: 1. light-field iris image acquisition; 2. image processing; 3. comparison.

3.1   Light-Field Iris Image Acquisition

We build a light-field iris imaging system, as shown in Fig. 1, which includes an optical table, a scaled sliding rail, a light-field camera and an illumination system.

The photo sensor for iris imaging should be sensitive to NIR illumination, which is absent in commercial light-field cameras, Lytro [9] and Raytrix [8]. Fortunately, we find a special designed industry light-field camera [10] that has a monochrome CCD sensor, which provides the adequate NIR response for iris imaging. A light-field iris raw image is shown in Fig. 3(a)

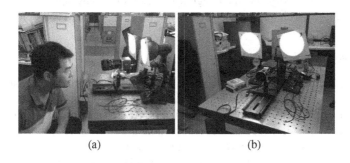

(a)   (b)

Fig. 1. The platform of imaging the iris by the light-field camera

3.2   Light-Field Image Processing

We develop software to process the raw light-field iris images. It includes three modules: 1) A calibration module, which calibrates the light-field camera using a set of reference raw light-field images and physical parameters of the light-field camera; 2) A decoding module, which decodes the raw light-field iris image to the 4D light field function; and 3) A refocusing module, which generates a stack of refocused iris images at a sequence of synthetic image planes.

It is necessary to develop a digital refocusing algorithm for the generation of high-quality iris images. As shown in Fig. 2, the rays that defocused at the optical image plane

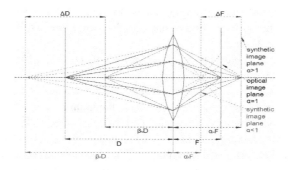

Fig. 2. The light field photography generates the image at a synthetic image plane

(the microlens array plane in the light-field camera) may be refocused at a synthetic image plane by computing the integrating function [11] shown in Eq. (1) where F denotes the image length, α denotes the ratio of optical image length to refocused image length and $E_{(\alpha \cdot F)}(x', y')$ is the refocused image. L_F is the light field function [12].

$$E_{(\alpha F)}(x', y') = \frac{1}{\alpha^2 F^2} \iint L_F((u(1 - \frac{1}{\alpha}) + \frac{x'}{\alpha}), v(1 - \frac{1}{\alpha}) + \frac{y'}{\alpha}), u, v) du dv \quad (1)$$

Ng [11] also proposed a Fourier slicing refocusing algorithm, which has a lower computational complexity than the integration based refocusing algorithm. The Fourier slice refocusing algorithm is advantageous when a larger angular resolution is available.

3.3 Comparison

We need to explicitly compare the reported iris recognition performance based on the iris images captured from the conventional camera and the light-field camera with the same lens, aperture, sensor and other parameters. At the same time, since the detailed texture in iris images is critical to iris recognition, the two cameras should maintain a strict synchronism in both temporal and spatial dimensions.

A difficulty in implementing this comparison is how to capture the iris images by the conventional camera which satisfies the requirements mentioned above. Inspired by Ng [11], a desirable method is to compare the iris images captured by a light-field camera with a hypothetical conventional camera that has an output by summarizing all the pixels in each microlens image.

We compare iris recognition performance of the refocused iris images captured by the light-field camera in a given depth range with the corresponding iris images by the conventional camera. Equal error rate (EER) and discriminating index (DI)[13] are used to evaluate the performance of the conventional camera versus the light-field camera.

4 Experiments

4.1 The Light-Field Iris Image Database

We constructed a light-field iris image database to verify the performance of iris imaging by light field camera. To the best of our knowledge, it is the first iris image database captured by light-field camera.

In this database, 14 subjects participated in the collection of light-field iris images. The distance between the iris and the light-field camera can be accurately adjusted via moving the sliding rail. We represent the DoF by the refocusing ratio α, as explained in Appendix. Such representation is independent of the main lens and thus more suitable in this paper, since we discuss the extended DoF by refocusing only.

Consequently, we captured a sequence of iris images for each class in a given depth range approximately from $\alpha = 0.8$ to $\alpha = 1.2$. The sequence of iris images is captured with continuously varying distance between the iris and the camera. Each sequence includes approximately 80 to 100 raw light field images.

4.2 Preprocessing

The raw light-field iris image cannot be used for recognition directly, as shown in Fig 3(a). The raw light-field image consists of microlens-images. The preprocessing has three steps: decoding, refocusing and quality-based selection.

Firstly, the raw light-field image can be decoded to form a 4D light field function. Secondly, the 4D light-field function is processed by interpolating and refocusing simultaneously to produce a stack of images focused on a sequence of synthetic image planes with a spatial resolution of 640×480. Finally, the best refocused iris image can be selected from the stack of refocused images.

4.3 Experimental Settings

The captured iris images are classified into three sets. The first set denoted by F includes the well-focused iris images by the hypothetical conventional camera ($\alpha = 1$), as shown in Fig. 3 (d). The second set denoted by D includes the defocused iris images by the hypothetical conventional camera ($\alpha < 1$) or ($\alpha > 1$), as shown in Fig. 3 (b) and (c). The images in the third set denoted by R are refocused iris images from the corresponding images of D, as shown in Fig. 3 (e) and (f).

All of the iris images are localized and segmented by the algorithm introduced by Li et al. [14]. We apply the ordinal features introduced by Sun et al. [13] as the texture features of the iris and then use the Hamming distance to measure the dissimilarity between two iris codes.

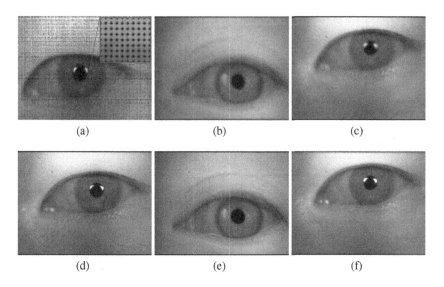

(a) (b) (c)

(d) (e) (f)

Fig. 3. Example iris images. (a) is the raw data of the light-field iris image that consists of microlens-images. (d) is a sample from F that includes well focused iris images from the hypothetic conventional camera. (b) and (c) are samples from D that includes defocused iris images from the hypothetic conventional camera captured at a given depth range. (e) and (f) are samples from R that are refocused images captured at same position with the images in D.

4.4   Experiment Results

The iris image datasets of F, D and R contain 922, 1072 and 1072 iris images respectively. For each set, all possible intra-class comparisons are used to estimate the genuine distribution. The number of intra-class comparisons of three datasets is shown in Table 1. To measure the imposter distribution, each image of one class is used to match all iris images in other classes. The number of inter-class comparisons is shown in Table 1.

According to Table 1, the iris recognition performance measures on F and R obtain comparable results, while the performance on D gains significantly worse results, which is consistent to the quality of images shown in Fig. 3.

The Hamming distance distributions on datasets of F, D and R are shown in Fig. 4 (a), (b) and (c) respectively. Apparently, F has a similar distribution with R. Compared with F and R, however, the distribution of genuine and imposter distance of D indicates a weaker discrimination, since it has a smaller distance between the mean intra class Hamming distance and the mean inter class Hamming distance and a larger overlap region of the distribution of genuine and imposter distance.

Table 1. The comparison among three sets of iris images

Datasets	EER	DI	Number of intraclass comparisons	Number of interclass comparisons
F	0.50%	4.37	18052	406529
R	0.71%	4.32	27098	546148
D	1.97%	3.31	27098	546148

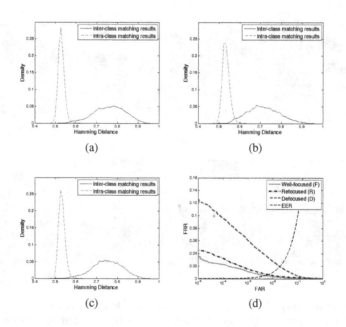

(a)

(b)

(c)

(d)

Fig. 4. Performance curves of iris recognition. (a),(b) and (c) show the distributions of intra- and inter-class iris matchings from well-focused (F), defocused (D) and refocused (R) respectively. (d) ROC curves of F,D and R.

The similar results are shown in ROC curve on datasets F, D and R as shown in Fig. 4(d). With the FAR decreasing to 10^{-5}, the FRR on D fast increases over 0.12 while the FRRs of F and R are still lower than 0.05.

5   Conclusions

In this paper, we introduced a light-field iris imaging system. It is the first iris imaging system using the light-field camera. Based on the refocusing ability of the light-field camera, the depth of field is extended free of constraining by the trading-off between DoF and aperture size. To verify the ability of extending the DOF, we compared the recognition performance on the iris sets captured by the light-field camera and the hypothetic conventional camera respectively in the depth range from $\alpha = 0.8$ to $\alpha = 1.2$. Experiments show that the refocused iris images has an approximately equally recognition performance with the well-focused images. While the corresponding defocused iris images gain a remarkably worse performance as they are imaged out of the allowed DoF of the conventional camera.

Acknowledgement. This work is funded by the National Natural Science Foundation of China (Grant No. 61273272, 61075024, 61302184), the International S&T Cooperation Program of China (Grant No. 2010DFB14110) and the Instrument Developing Project of the Chinese Academy of Sciences (Grant No. YZ201266).

References

1. Daugman, J.G.: High confidence visual recognition of persons by a test of statistical independence. IEEE Transactions on Pattern Analysis and Machine Intelligence 15(11), 1148–1161 (1993)
2. Matey, J.R., Naroditsky, O., Hanna, K., Kolczynski, R., Loiacono, D.J., Mangru, S., Tinker, M., Zappia, T.M., Zhao, W.Y.: Iris on the move: Acquisition of images for iris recognition in less constrained environments. Proceedings of the IEEE 94(11), 1936–1947 (2006)
3. Guo, G., Jones, M.J.: A system for automatic iris capturing. Mitsubishi Electric Research Laboratories, TR2005-044 (2005)
4. Dong, W., Sun, Z., Tan, T.: Self-adaptive iris image acquisition system. In: Proc. of SPIE, vol. 6944 (2008)
5. Dong, W., Sun, Z., Tan, T.: A Design of Iris Recognition System at a Distance. In: Chinese Conference on Pattern Recognition, CCPR 2009, pp. 1–5. IEEE (2009)
6. Ng, R., Levoy, M., Bredif, M., Duval, G., Horowitz, M., Hanrahan, P.: Light Field Photography with A Hand-held Plenoptic Camera. Technical Report CSTR. 2(11), 7–55 (2005)
7. Raghavendra, R., Bian, Y., Kiran, B.R., Christoph, B.: A new perspective - face recognition with light field camera. In: 2013 6th IAPR International Conference on Biometrics (ICB). IEEE (2013)
8. Raytrix, Inc., http://www.raytrix.com/
9. Lytro, Inc., http://www.lytro.com/
10. Zhou, Z.: Research on Light Field Imaging Technology. PhD thesis, University of Science and Technology of China (2011)
11. Ng, R.: Digital Light Field Photography. PhD thesis, Stanford University (2006)

12. Levoy, M., Hanrahan, P.: Light Field Rendering. In: Proceedings of the 23rd Annual Conference on Computer Graphics and Interactive Techniques, pp. 31–42. ACM (1996)
13. Sun, Z., Tan, T.: Ordinal Measures for Iris Recognition. IEEE Transactions on Pattern Analysis and Machine Intelligence 31(12), 2211–2226 (2009)
14. Li, H., Sun, Z., Tan, T.: Robust iris segmentation based on learned boundary detectors. In: 2012 5th IAPR International Conference on Biometrics (ICB), pp. 317–322. IEEE (2012)

Appendix:

The definition of the DoF in conventional camera is the distance between the nearest and farthest objects in a scene that appear acceptably sharp in an image. The DoF is commonly calculated by Eq. (2) :

$$DoF = D_F - D_N \tag{2}$$

where D_N is the distance from the camera to the near limit of DOF and D_F is the distance D_F from the camera to the far limit of DOF. They can be represented as shown in (3) :

$$D_F = \beta_F D, D_N = \beta_N D \tag{3}$$

where D is the optic object distance. β_N and β_F are ratios of D to D_N and D_F. According to optical fundamental formulation, β has a monotonous map to α, in the following form:

$$\frac{1}{\beta \cdot D} + \frac{1}{\alpha \cdot F} = \frac{1}{f} \tag{4}$$

where F is the optic image length and f is the focal length of the lens. Thus, we can use α_F and α_N to represent the DoF.

A Novel Iris Image Quality Evaluation Based on Coarse-to-Fine Method

Ying Chen[1,2], Yuanning Liu[1], Xiaodong Zhu[1,*], Xiaoxu Zhang[1], Haiying Xu[1],
Guang Huo[1,3], and Ning Deng[1]

[1] Jilin University, College of Computer Science and Technology,
Qianjin Street 2699, 130012, Changchun, China
[2] Nanchang Hangkong University, College of Software,
FengHe Nan Road 696, 330063, Nanchang, China
[3] Northeast Dianli University, Informatization Office,
Changchun Road 169, 132012, Jilin, China
c_y2008@163.com, {liuyn,zhuxd,xiaoxu}@jlu.edu.cn, 490933395@qq.com,
yanhuo1860@126.com, dylantengjlu@yahoo.com
http://www.springer.com/lncs

Abstract. An effective image evaluation algorithm is vital for iris recognition system. This paper proposes a coarse-to-fine quality evaluation method to iris image. Five criterions are adopted in this paper, which are variance, gradient, edge strength, fuzzy entropy, information entropy, for iris image coarse evaluation. In fine quality evaluation phase, which mainly focus on evaluation of spatial location and effective regional. The experimental results show that our proposed method are able to meet the need of practical iris recognition system.

Keywords: Biometrics, Iris image quality evaluation, Coarse-to-fine method.

1 Introduction

The performance of iris recognition system depends on the iris image quality. Therefore, it is crucial to design algorithms to evaluate iris image's quality to further meet the requirements of iris recognition system. At present, there are many researchers focus on iris image evaluation [1-5]. Chaskar et al. [1] evaluated individual iris image by assessing image own prominent factors, which including dilation measure, ideal iris resolution, actual iris resolution, processable iris resolution, signal to noise ratio, occlusion measure, specular reflection, eccentric distance measure, angular assessment. Proenca [2] proposed a method to assess the quality of visible wavelength light iris samples captured in unconstrained conditions; evaluation factors including occlusions, area, papillary dilation, focus, motion, angle, and levels of iris pigmentation. Lee et al. [3] firstly distinguished blurred images from the in-focus images, and then discriminated occluded image

---

* Corresponding author.

Z. Sun et al. (Eds.): CCBR 2013, LNCS 8232, pp. 353–360, 2013.

and useful images based on region of interest. Ma et al. [4] assessed the quality of each image in the input sequence and selected a clear iris images, they firstly constructed two local quality descriptors and then adopted SVM method to distinguish whether the corresponding iris image is clear.

The major drawback of most traditional iris image quality evaluation methods is that they have not take into account time cost, in other words, most of them did not consider the trade-off between time and precision. To solve this problem, this paper divides iris image quality evaluation into two stages, which are coarse evaluation and fine evaluation. Coarse evaluation stage mainly focuses on pre-evaluation, select the images with clear texture for subsequent processing. Fine evaluation stage uses position and effective regions to do the further quality evaluation.

2   Coarse Evaluations

Practical iris recognition system captures a large number of iris images for subsequent feature extraction and recognition, which increase throughput as well as burden of the system, reduce the efficiency of the system, increase processing time, affects the system performance. In order to overcome the above problems, the rapid screening for fast batch capture iris images becomes a crucial task.

2.1   Five Criterions

Five criterions are adopted in this paper, which are the standard deviation, gradient, edge strength, fuzzy entropy, information entropy, for iris image coarse evaluation.

(1)Variance. It reflects the uniformity of the image gray level distribution. The smaller the variance is, the lower the image resolution. Let the size of a digital image I be $H \times W$, and $f(i,j)\|i \in [0, H-1], j \in [0, W-1]$ be the gray value of the pixel located at the point (i,j), set $mean$ and $variance$ denote the mean and variance of gray value, then $mean$ and $variance$ can be calculated via equation (1).

$$variance = \sum_{i=0}^{H-1}\sum_{k=0}^{W-1}(f(i,j) - mean)^2 = \sum_{i=0}^{H-1}\sum_{j=0}^{W-1}(f(i,j) - \frac{\sum_{i=0}^{H-1}\sum_{j=0}^{W-1}f(i,j)}{H \times W})^2.$$

(1)

(2) Gradient Number. It reflects the clarity and the distinctness degree of the image texture. The process of computing gradient number of image I is comprised of three steps as follows. Step 1. Compute horizontal gradient d_x and vertical gradient d_y of each point. Step 2. Compute gradient of each point via equation (2).

$$Gradient(i,j) = \sqrt{d_x(i,j)^2 + d_y(i,j)^2}.$$

(2)

Step 3. Calculate the number of points whose gradient value over 150. Value of 150 is the gradient evaluation criteria, which is empirical value through a large number of the experiments. Set *gradient* denotes the number of gradient points, and then *gradient* can be calculated via equation (3).

$$gradient = 1, \; if \; Gradient(i,j) > 150. \tag{3}$$

(3) Edge Strength. It reflects the distinction of image edge, which combined with the gradient is able to reflect the availability of iris texture more effectively. Step 1. Image filtering is done on both horizontal and vertical direction using Sobel filter and we will get two filtered images named as $VerticalImage$ and $HorizontalImage$, whose sizes are $H \times W$. Step 2. Set *edge* denotes the number of gradient points, and then *edge* can be calculated via equation (4), where $P_V(i,j)$ and $P_H(i,j)$ are represent pixel the value of $VerticalImage$ and $HorizontalImage$ of the point (i,j), respectively.

$$edge = \frac{\sum\limits_{i=0}^{H-1}\sum\limits_{j=0}^{W-1} matrix(i,j)}{H \times W} = \frac{\sum\limits_{i=0}^{H-1}\sum\limits_{j=0}^{W-1} \sqrt{P_V(i,j)^2 + P_H(i,j)^2}}{H \times W}. \tag{4}$$

(4) Fuzzy Entropy. It reflects the image blur, fuzzy set A should clarify the nature of the change, that is, more closer to $1/2$, the greater the A's ambiguity; the farther from $1/2$, the smaller the ambiguity. Step 1. Compute fuzzy number P of each pixel. Step 2. Fuzzy number S can be computed by equation (5).

$$S(i,j) = -P(i,j) \times \log(P(i,j)) - (1 - P(i,j)) \times \log(1 - P(i,j)). \tag{5}$$

Step 3. Set *fuzzy* denotes fuzzy entropy of a image, and then *fuzzy* can be calculated via equation (6).

$$fuzzy = \frac{\sum\limits_{i=0}^{H-1}\sum\limits_{j=0}^{W-1} S(i,j)}{H \times W \times \log(2)}. \tag{6}$$

(5) Information Entropy. The image information entropy reflects the amount of information. The calculation process is shown in equation (7), where $P(i)$ is probability of pixels.

$$entropy = -\sum_{i=0}^{255} P(i) \times \log(P(i)). \tag{7}$$

2.2   Weighted Coarse Evaluation Criterion

Weighted coarse evaluation *coarse_val* can be computed via equation (8). the larger the *coarse_val* is, the better the image is.

$$coarse\_val = \alpha \times variance + \beta \times gradient + \lambda \times edge + \gamma \times fuzzy + \mu \times entropy. \tag{8}$$

In order to get the weighted coefficient, we select 300 images from 50 classes on CASIA-V4 Interval, JLUBRIRIS-V1 and JLUBRIRIS-V2 iris image databases as experimental samples to do the corresponding weights training, the training process is as follows:Step 1. Obtain 300 eigenvalues for each feature $Feature(i)$. Step 2. Compute coefficients for each feature.

$$coff(i)[j] = \frac{Feature(i)[j+1] - Feature(i)[j]}{\sum\limits_{i=0}^{4}(Feature(i)[j+1] - Feature(i)[j])}, \quad j = 0, \cdots, 299. \quad (9)$$

According to the above formula, 300 coefficients obtained for each sample. Step 3. Compute the resulting coefficient corresponding to each feature.

$$coff_i = \frac{\sum\limits_{j=0}^{299} coff(i)[j]}{300}, \quad i = 0, 1, \cdots, 4. \quad (10)$$

After the above training, the values of α, β, λ, γ and μ are 0.2318, 0.0974, 0.1710, 0.2553 and 0.2445, respectively.

3   Fine Evaluations

3.1   Spatial Location Evaluate Algorithm

Usually, human eye iris images are required in the center of the image as much as possible, which means the center coordinates of the image should be as close to the center coordinates of the iris circle as possible, hence the measure of the spatial position of the iris image parameters can be defined as equation (11).

$$SpaceR = 1 - \frac{\sqrt{(x_{ROI} - x_{im})^2 + (y_{ROI} - y_{im})^2}}{MaxDis}. \quad (11)$$

where $MaxDis$ represents the maximum distance from all points to center coordinate,(x_{im}, y_{im}) represents the coordinates of the center position of the image, (x_{ROI}, y_{ROI}) represents the coordinates of the center of the iris. According to the equation (11), parameter $SpaceR$ values in $[0,1]$.

3.2   Effective Regional Evaluate Algorithm

The circular iris region is affected by pupil zoom, as well as by eyelash and eyelid occlusion. When the light is too strong, the pupil would instantly enlarged 2-3 times, then the iris region reduced severely, resulting in the unavailable iris or extracted information is not comprehensive. Similarly, the human eyelid and eyelashes usually cover the upper and lower portions of the iris, serious coverage leads to the unavailable image. The purpose of this section is to evaluate the effective area of the iris image.

Step 1. Loading iris image, and locate the image. In this paper, we adopt segmentation method based on region of interest for JLUBRIRIS-V1 (V2) databases, and adopt segmentation method based on voting mechanism for CASIA-V4 Interval databases, for more details about these two segmentation methods, one can refer to [6] [7]. Iris segmentation result is shown in Figure 1 (b).

Step 2. Image enhancement. This study utilize morphological operations to enhance iris image, the process operation is shown in Figure 1 (c). Morphology is conducted on the image to get the image $tempImage1$ (result of the white top) and $tempImage2$ (result of the black top). The final enhanced iris image can be computed by $enhanceImage = src + tempImage1 - tempImage2$, where src represents the source image. Set the target pixel information as zero, and set the other pixels surrounding the target pixels into 255, the process result as shown in Figure 1 (d).

Step 3. Remove pupil from the binarized image. According to the histogram of the enhanced image, since the left pixels of the first peak represents the black pixels of image which are the pupil and eyelashes area, so binarizate image after the first peak, the binarized iris image is shown in Figure 1 (e). Using the iris pupil radius obtained in step 1 to remove the pupil part, the result as shown in Figure 1 (f).

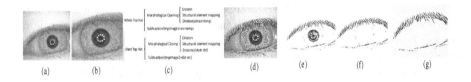

Fig. 1. Illustration of an iris image preprocessing(a) original iris image, (b) iris region location, (c)enhancement method, (d) result of enhancement image, (e) binarization image, (f) remove pupil area, (g) remove salt and pepper noises

Step 4. Iris image filtering by Sobel filter. Using above vertical Sobel filtering to remove part of the binarized iris points interference.

Step 5. Remove salt and pepper noise using region growing method.

Step 6. Detect and record horizontal and vertical coordinates of the above image eyelashes pixel.

Step 7. Calculate the effective area of iris images. (1) Calculate the total number of pixels of iris annular region $TotalNum$. (2) Calculate the eyelid occlusion of the iris ring pixel points $EyelidNum$. (3) Calculate the eyelash occlusions of the iris ring points pixel $EyelashesNum$. (4) Calculate the number of pupil region pixels $PupilNum$. Measure the effective area as follows:

$$Validity = \frac{TotalNum - EyelidNum - EyelahesNum - PupilNum}{TotalNum}. \quad (12)$$

This measurement not only reflects the iris image obscured situation, but also reflects the impact of the pupil illumination conditions on the iris area stretching effects, hence it can objectively reflect the size of the effective area of the iris. The value range is [0,1], the closer the value of 1 indicates that the less block and the larger effective area of iris; and the closer the value of 0 indicates that the larger block, the smaller the effective area of the iris.

3.3   Weighted Fine Evaluation Criterion

Weighted coarse evaluation $fine\_val$ can be computed via equation (13).

$$fine\_val = w_1 \times SpaceR + w_2 \times Validity. \tag{13}$$

In following experiments, w_1 and w_2 are set at 0.15 and 0.85 according to previous experiments.

4   Experimental Result and Discussions

4.1   Description of Iris Image Databases

The JLUBRIRIS iris image database were established by Jilin University iris biometric and information security lab, which have four versions, namely JLUBRIRIS-V1 (V2, V3, and V4). JLUBRIRIS iris image were collected under different light conditions, at different times, in different periods, left and right eyes were collected. The diversity of samples is fully guarantee for scientific research. Public and free iris image database includes CASIA (four versions) [8]. CASIA database contains near infrared images and is by far the most widely used on iris biometric experiments. CASIA-V4 contains a total of 54,601 iris images from more than 1,800 genuine subjects and 1,000 virtual subjects. All iris images are 8 bit gray-level JPEG files, collected under near infrared illumination or synthesized. In following experiments, we randomly select 500 images, 600 images and 300 images from JLUBRIRIS-V1, JLUBRIRIS-V2, and CASIA-V4 Interval, as experimental samples, respectively.

4.2   Experimental Result for Coarse Evaluation

In most cases, ground truth is essential for performing a quantitative analysis of an algorithms' results, in this paper, 20 qualified teachers and doctors to subjective evaluation on these experimental images and their evaluation results as ground truth. Table 1 shows the accurate evaluation rate (AER) and computational complexity for three iris image databases.

In order to show coarse evaluation intuitively, set iris image of Fig. 2 as experimental samples, the evaluation results are shown in Table 2. Form Table 2, it is can be seen that the proposed method can effectively distinguish the effective texture clear images form the textures invalid image, and the average execution time of the algorithm is less than 0.1s, which meets for the real-time requirements, which can effectively filter out a large part of the low-quality images and improve the overall efficiency of the iris recognition system.

Table 1. Performance of coarse evaluation

Databases	AER	Fastest Time	Slowest Time	Average Time
JLUBRIRIS-V1	98.3%	0.067s	0.126s	0.095s
JLUBRIRIS-V2	98.1%	0.069s	0.132s	0.098s
CASIA-V4 Interval	97.8%	0.078s	0.147s	0.102s

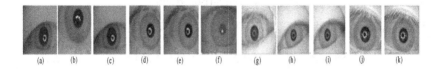

Fig. 2. Samples of iris images

Table 2. Coarse evaluation results

Sample	Variance	Gradient	Edge	Fuzzy Entropy	Information Entropy	coarse_val
Fig. 2(a)	38.2296	0	7.3352	-0.7312	-4.7423	8.7698
Fig. 2(b)	34.4895	15	6.6255	-0.7970	-4.5881	9.2634
Fig. 2(c)	37.6055	0	7.1104	-0.7298	-4.7253	8.5912
Fig. 2(d)	29.4669	0	8.8562	-0.8068	-4.5914	7.0163
Fig. 2(e)	29.2460	0	8.7101	-0.8109	-4.5835	6.9410
Fig. 2(f)	19.2650	47	8.2186	-0.6029	-4.2654	9.2520
Fig. 2(g)	41.4149	283	11.1017	-0.5751	-4.8594	37.7276
Fig. 2(h)	44.4887	248	8.1154	-0.5909	-4.9778	34.4875
Fig. 2(i)	44.7447	270	8.3588	-0.6005	-4.9813	36.7279
Fig. 2(j)	42.5154	113	26.0674	-0.7356	-4.9326	23.9250
Fig. 2(k)	43.5191	120	24.9964	-0.7306	-4.9714	24.6481

4.3 Experimental Result for Fine Evaluation

Table 3 shows the result of random image spatial location and effective regional evaluation. Table 4 shows the AER and computational complexity for three iris image databases. In order to further exhibit the efficiency of our proposed approach, we carry out experiments to provide a comparative analysis of our proposed method with some state-of-the-art methods on JLURBIRIR-V3 databases. Table 5 summarizes the best results obtained by each method.

Table 3. Spatial location and effective region for three databases

Iris databases	JLUBRIRIS-V2	CASIA-V4 Interval	JLUBRIRIS-V1
Spatial location	0.925270	0.947174	0.917730
Effective area	0.56729	0.592118	0.814092

Table 4. Performance of fine evaluation

Databases	AER	Fastest Time	Slowest Time	Average Time
JLUBRIRIS-V1	98.0%	0.093s	0.159s	0.112s
JLUBRIRIS-V2	98.2%	0.105s	0.168s	0.121s
CASIA-V4 Interval	97.2%	0.130s	0.172s	0.134s

Table 5. Comparison results

Algorithm	AER	Fastest Time	Slowest Time	Average Time
Ma et al. [4]	90.17%	1.425s	2.046s	1.736s
Proenca [2]	88.50%	2.003s	2.710s	2.175s
Proposed	89%	0.179s	0.214s	0.190s

From Table 3, Table 4 and Table 5, it is can be seen that our proposed algorithm achieved good experimental results in terms of speed and accuracy rate compared to other literatures. The proposed algorithm achieves trade-off between accuracy and evaluation accuracy.

5 Conclusions

In this paper, we proposed a coarse-to-fine iris image quality evaluation algorithm, the experimental results show that the proposed quality evaluation method has high performance. In coarse stage, it can accurately filter out unqualified images for subsequent processing to save time. Fine evaluation stage further evaluate image to meet expectations for the overall performance of iris recognition system.

References

1. Chaskar, U.M., Sutaone, M.S., Shan, N.S.: Iris image quality assessment for biometric application. International Journal of Computer Science Issues 9, 474–4478 (2012)
2. Proenca, H.: Quality Assessment of Degraded Iris Images Acquired in the Visible Wavelength. IEEE T. Inf. Foren. Sec. 6, 82–95 (2011)
3. Lee, J.C., Su, Y., Tu, T.M.: A novel approach to image quality assessment in iris recognition systems. Imaging Sci. J. 58, 136–145 (2010)
4. Ma, L., Tan, T.N., Wang, Y.H., Zhang, D.X.: Personal identification based on iris texture analysis. IEEE T. Pattern Anal. 25, 1519–1533 (2003)
5. Kang, B.J., Park, K.R.: A new multi-unit iris authentication based on quality assessment and score level fusion for mobile phones. Mach. Vision Appl. 21, 541–553 (2010)
6. Liu, H., Chen, Y., Zhu, X.D.: Iris location algorithm based on region of interest. Computer Applications and Software 25(10), 255–257 (2008)
7. Hu, Z.X.: Research and Implement about Key Problems in Iris Acquisition, JiLin University (2006)
8. CASIA Iris Image Database,
   http://www.cbsr.ia.ac.cn/english/IrisDatabase.asp

An Embedded Self-adaptive Iris Image Acquisition System in a Large Working Volume

Chunquan Gan, Yuqing He, Jiaqi Li, Huiying Ren, and Jixing Wang

Key Laboratory of Photoelectronic Imaging Technology and System,
Ministry of Education of China, School of Optoelectronics,
Beijing Institute of Technology, Beijing 100081, China
yuqinghe@bit.edu.cn

Abstract. Iris image acquisition is a key step in the iris recognition. Usually most of current systems have a short working volume and users need to cooperate in the specific range, which limits the system application. In this paper, we designed an embedded self-adaptive iris image acquisition system using a single camera with a large working volume. It can capture the user's iris in the distance from 0.3 meter to 1.1 meter. A variable zoom camera is co-located in a pan-tilt-unit (PTU) for face detection and iris image acquisition. Combining the face detection and eye location, the system can center and zoom the camera for eyes. The micro controller unit (MCU) controls the peripheral components including PTU, camera, distance sensor, etc. The DSP is used to realize the algorithm and communicate with MCU. Experimental results show the proposed system can capture high-quality iris images efficiently.

Keywords: iris recognition, image acquisition, embedded system, face detection, eye location.

1 Introduction

Iris recognition is an excellent biometrics method with non-invasiveness, uniqueness, stability and low false recognition rate. Iris image acquisition is the fundamental step of the iris recognition [1]. Nowadays lots of practical iris products have been developed such as BM-ET series, ACCESS series, IrisPass series, IKEMB series and so on. However, most of productions have short working volume, which is about 10cm to 30cm [1]. In this mode, the iris image acquisition needs user to cooperate highly with the machine and stand in specific range.

In order to make the iris recognition system easier to use, we expect the system could capture iris image automatically at a distance. Self-adaptive iris image acquisition system has been proposed and people have turned their sight on designing such kind of iris image acquisition system. W. Dong et al. [2] use an iris camera on the PTU self-adaptive to people with different heights and use another wide-angle USB camera to detect human's face. It only captures the iris image in the distance of 3 meters with working volume of 10cm. So it limits the users' position and needs users' cooperation. H. Jung et al. [3] developed an iris acquisition system using PTU-based system, which includes a PTU, an iris camera and a scene camera. The two cameras

Z. Sun et al. (Eds.): CCBR 2013, LNCS 8232, pp. 361–369, 2013.
© Springer International Publishing Switzerland 2013

are combined in a coaxial optical structure, and a cold mirror is inserted between the cameras. Due to the coaxial optical structure, the system does not need the optical axis displacement related compensation required in parallel type systems. J. Villar et al [4] introduce an iris acquisition system with working distance as long as 30 meters. The system uses a wide-field-of-view camera to locate a subject for face and eyes. A narrow-field-of-view camera attached to an 8-inch telescope to capture the iris image. Maybe it has the longest working distance in the published iris recognition systems. But with the disadvantages of illumination, face tracking, image stabilization etc, it is not practical. W. Dong et al [5], F.Wheeler et al [6] and P. Smith et al [7] also developed long-distance iris recognition systems. Both of them use the wide-angle camera to detect human's face while narrow-angle camera capture iris image, and then the videos are transmitted into computer to perform the following recognition. These systems cannot work at fully automatic self-adaptive mode, and combining the computer, some of them may have big size and be heavy. So it is not useful in practice applications. Is it essential to use at least two cameras to capture iris image at a distance in large working volume, and is the computer necessary in iris recognition system? If a single camera is able to detect human's face and capture iris image and then transmits the image to an embedded board to recognition, the size of the system maybe much smaller, which would be interesting and easy to use.

In this paper, we present a self-adaptive iris image acquisition system using a single camera based on DSP. It can capture iris image automatically without user's interaction at a distance from 0.3 meter to 1.1 meter. The rest of paper is organized as follow. In Section 2, the design of the hardware's key components is described. Then the system working flow and algorithms are analyzed in Section 3. Section 4 shows the experimental results. Finally, some conclusions are given.

2   Design of the Hardware's Key Components

In this paper, we use a variable zoom camera and PTU to detect face and capture iris image. The block diagram of the system is shown in Fig.1. When starting acquisition, the light source is opened and the camera uses the minimum focus with a wide field of view to detect human's face. The DSP analyzes the video, draws the location of the face and finds out the position of the eyes. Ultrasound distance unit measures the distance between the camera and eyes. Combining the distance and the eye's position, PTU moves the camera staring at one of the eyes. Then system sets the camera's zoom to corresponding number and focuses to get proper iris images. At last, DSP captures the iris images and stores them in the flash.

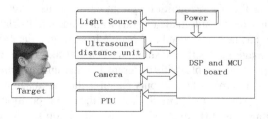

Fig. 1. The block diagram of the prototype

On hardware part, particular attention should be paid on the following issues:

1) Safe illumination. The illumination should not harm human's eyes.
2) Camera and lens design. The camera should has a large working volume.
3) Hardware design of the embedded module. The module uses DSP and MCU to detect the face and eyes, control the camera, PTU, ultrasound unit and so on.

Now, we describe the three issues above in details.

2.1   Safe Illumination

The iris is very small. Without illumination, the captured image may be very dark, which will affect the recognition rate. Near infrared(NIR) illumination can enhance the iris image texture and bring users without uncomfortable feeling, so NIR illumination is often used as light source in iris recognition systems. However, strong illumination may result in permanent vision impairment due to obscuration or a non-functioning of the cornea, the lens, and the retina. When designing the light source, the threshold of radiant magnitude should not greater than the published exposure limits [8]. A small spot light source is much more harmful than a large source size with the same illumination, so we chose two arrays of near infrared LED as the light source.

According to CIE eye's safety standard, the limit of the Irradiance is no large than $10mW/cm^2$. The NIR LED's parameter is as follows. The center wavelength $\lambda = 850nm$, its maximum luminescent intensity $I_e = 200mw/sr$, luminous angle $\Omega = 30$ degree. When the current is 100mA, the irradiance of one LED $\Phi_e = I_e \times \Omega = 161.56mW$. If the distance $l = 30$ cm, the luminous area $S= (tan\Omega \times l)^2 \times \pi = 954.48$ cm^2. So the maximum irradiance value of one LED $E_e = \Phi_e / S = 0.16mW/cm^2$. Compared to the exposure limit ($10 \ mW/cm^2$), the maximum number of the LED is $10/0.17 = 62.5$. In this system, we use 60 LED lights on 2 PCB board (each for 30). According the analysis above, measurement at the LED arrays resulted in irradiance is always below $10mW/cm^2$ in the distance from 0.3 meter to 1.1meter.

2.2   Camera and Lens Design

In this paper, we need to design a zoom camera with the feature of wide-angle and narrow-angle modes. When the system needs to detect the human face, the camera should be used in wide-angle mode to achieve a large field of view; when system is used to capture the iris image, the camera should be used in narrow-angle mode to achieve a high magnification. That means the camera needs a large variable focal length.

The camera's focal length is related with the image sensor's size and the working distance. We suppose the camera focus is f, l is the object distance and l' is the image distance, diameter of the iris is D, iris image on CCD sensor is d, the image's magnification β can be got as $\beta = -\dfrac{d}{D} = \dfrac{l'}{l}$. According Newton Imaging Formula $\dfrac{1}{l'} - \dfrac{1}{l} = \dfrac{1}{f}$, we get the following equation:

$$f = \frac{-l}{D/d + 1} \tag{1}$$

Usually, the diameter of human's iris is 10mm; d is 0.9mm, so the focal length needed for the distance from 0.3 to 1.1 meter is shown in Table 1.

Table 1. The focus needed corresponding with the working distance

Distance(cm)	30	40	50	60	70	80	90	100	110
Focal length(mm)	24.8	33.1	41.3	49.6	57.9	66.1	74.4	82.6	90.9

According to Table 1, if the focus of the lens is between 5mm to 90mm, it can meet the system's demands. Based on the discussion above, we designed a kind of variable zoom camera. Its image sensor is 1/4 inch, 752×582 pixels CCD. The focal length is 3.84 to 94.4mm. It can export a channel of analog video with 30 frames/second. It could zoom and focus in command of the MCU with the communication of RS232 serial communication protocol. We test the performance of the camera at different distance. The magnification of the camera is shown in Table 2.

Table 2. The magnification of the camera at different distance

Distance(cm)	30	40	50	60	70	80	90	100	110
Minimum Magnification(pixel/cm)	27	21	15	11	10	9	7	6	6
Maximum Magnification(pixel/cm)	177	378	349	360	343	328	280	229	216

In common, the diameter of the iris is 1cm, so according to the Table 2, we could get the proper size of the iris image at different distance from 30cm to 110cm.

2.3   Hardware Design of the Embedded Module

The embedded module includes one piece of DSP and MCU respectively. The DSP is used to receive the video from the camera, detect the human face, locate the positions of eyes, communicate with the MCU and store the iris image and so on. The MCU is used to control the PTU, send command to camera, read the distance message from the ultrasound unit. The system's diagram is shown in Fig. 2.

The main signal processing chip is TI TMS320DM642. The integrated DSP processor is mainly used to load the video from the camera, process algorithm for image processing, communicate with the MCU and store the images. Those involve one channel video input, one channel serial port and memory chip such as FLASH or SDRAM. The DSP could not read the analog video directly. It needs A/D convert chip to convert the analog video into digital video. The communication between DSP and A/D chip is I^2C. All of those have integrated on a DSP Core Board.

The MCU chip is an ATMEL ATMEGA128 whose CPU is a 16/32 bit RISC processor. It has very rich peripheral. We mainly use it to control the peripheral components, such as the PTU, ultrasound unit and camera. The PTU is controlled by RS-485 cable using the standard protocol Pelco-D. The camera is controlled by RS-232 cable which can achieve zoom, focus automatically or manually. The ultrasound distance unit is controlled by the common I/O pin. Another task of the MCU is receiving the command from DSP and sending the responding signal to DSP by UART.

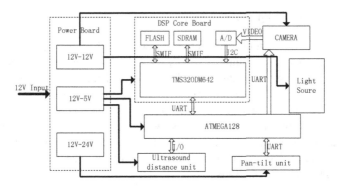

Fig. 2. Sketch of the embedded self-adaptive iris image acquisition system

The whole system is powered by 12V voltage. Light source can be powered by 12V directly, the same as the camera. But the DSP and MCU being powered by 5V and the PTU is powered by 24V. So in addition to the embedded module, a step-down circuit and a step-up circuit are needed.

3   The System Working Flow and Algorithms

In the previous section, we described the important components for the iris capturing system. Now, we will explain the algorithms and service software needed to run the system. The system's working flow chart is shown in Fig. 3.

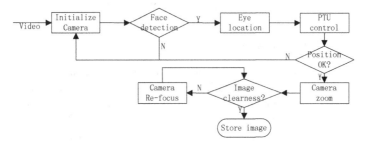

Fig. 3. The system's working flow chart

When starting the capture, the camera will initialize its focal length to minimum, then DSP looks for a face in the camera video image until one is found. Following crops a bounding box around the face, DSP try to locate the eyes and crop two bounding box around the eyes. Then the PTU is used to move camera so that the eye region gets closer to the center of camera. Ultrasound unit calculates the distance between the camera and eyes. Next the camera sets zoom to corresponding focus and autofocus. DSP will estimate the quality of the image. If the image is not clear enough, DSP will refocus the camera unless the image is clearness. At last, DSP captures the iris image and stores it in the flash.

3.1   Face Detection and Eye Location

To capture the iris, the system first has to know whether there is a person in the scene. We use the face detect algorithm that simply use Haar-like features originally selected using AdaBoost learning algorithm [9]. After a face is detected, we need to detect the location of eyes. We use Gray Integral Projection [10] to locate the eyes. We take gray-level projection of the face on horizontal and vertical direction. For the gray value of eyes is below than skin's, there has two valleys on the integral graphs, which can be used to determine the eyes' vertical coordinates roughly. After image binarization by the OTSU method, the horizontal ordinate can also be located. The whole process takes less than 30ms.

3.2   PTU Control

After the eyes' positions are detected in the video image frame, we could get three points of the image, the center point of the image and the center points of the two eyes. In order to make the eye's center point in the center of the image, we need pan and tilt the PTU. The angle of the PTU need to move is related to the minimum magnification of the camera which is shown in Tab.2. According to that table, we can get the real distance we should move by using the formula $d = D/\mu$, where D is the pixels need to move, μ is the minimum magnification of the camera at the certain distance from the face to camera. By using $\tan\theta = d/s$, we can get the angle need to move. Where s is the distance from the face to camera, it could be measured by the ultrasound distance unit. The moving speed of the PTU is fixed. So if we run the PTU for a certain time, the angle which the PTU moved is fixed.

3.3   Camera Zoom and Autofocus

After positioning the eye in the center of the camera, the next step is zooming up the image to appropriate size. But at different distance, the zoom number is different, which is related to focal length. In order to solve this problem, we look up the "zoom number - distance" mapping table. We image the iris at different distance with different zoom number. If the image is in focus and the diameter of the iris area is larger than 150 pixels, we record the zoom number and get the mapping table. Part of the mapping relationship is shown in Table 3.

Table 3. "Zoom number - Distance" mapping table

Distance(cm)	30-35	36-45	46-55	56-65	66-75	76-85	86-95	96-110
Zoom number(x)	6-7	8-23	10-23	11-23	12-22	14-19	15-18	16-18

According to this table, we can look up the zoom number after the ultrasound distance unit getting the distance of the camera and the eye. For example, if the distance is 70cm, so we just zoom up the camera to 12 times to 22 times. The gap between the zoom numbers is in favor of improving the robust of the system.

The camera can focus automatically or manually. We set the camera in autofocus mode. After zooming, the camera focuses the iris image automatically. The whole process takes about 0.5 to 2 seconds.

3.4 Image Quality Evaluation

While zoom up the camera, the autofocus is also should be done. But we found the image could not in focus sometimes. So, we need to judge whether the image is clear enough. We calculate the Square Plane Sum Modulus Difference (SPSMD) [11] of the image to reflect the energy of image high frequency component. The larger the calculation of SPSMD is, the more accurate the image focusing will be. After the autofocus, system starts to focus near. If the value of SPSMD is getting lower, it means the image is defocusing. So we need to focus far then calculate the SPSMD, unless SPSMD becomes the maximum. The maximum value of the SPSMD is measured in the experiment before. More details could be found in [11].

4   Experimental Results

In our system, we used a single camera to capture the iris image automatically based on the DSP in the distance from 0.3 meter to 1.1 meter. As an image acquisition system, we mainly concern about capture volume, operation time and image quality.

4.1   Capture Volume

The capture depth is about 0.3m to 1.1m. But it is a conservative data. For if people move nearer, and we decrease the illumination, the minimum distance can be 0.1m.

The capture angle is limited by the visual field of the camera, because the face must appear in the image. The maximum angle field of view of the camera is 55.5° at horizontal direction and 42.5° at vertical direction. So the camera's view is about 1.16×0.84 m^2 and 0.32×0.23 m^2 in the distance of 1.1m and 0.3m respectively.

Summing up the capture depth and angle, the still capture volume is about 0.35m^3. If we pan and tilt the camera at first, the capture range will be much huger.

4.2   Operation Time

We recorded the operation time on each step. Face detection and eye location need less than 30ms. Considering the stably of the system, we use the low speed PTU. The pan and tilt time is about 2s to 4s. Ultrasound unit needs 100ms to measure the distance. The camera zooms and autofocus use 0.5s to 2s. Combining some delays between each step, the total operation time is about 3.5s to 7s. We compare the operation time with other systems. For example, W. Dong's system [5] needs 2.7 to 5.1s, the other one[2] needs 3s; H. Jung's system[3] needs 4.5s etc. Our system's processing time is acceptable in iris recognition system. If we use a high speed PTU and optimize the performance, the operation time will be less.

4.3   Image Quality

We used the system to capture a series of images in different distance. Fig. 4 shows the iris images taken in different working distance.

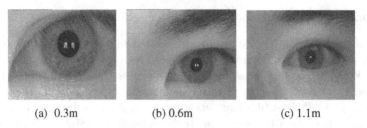

(a) 0.3m   (b) 0.6m   (c) 1.1m

Fig. 4. Iris images taken in different working distance

From the images above we can see that all the images captured in different working distance present clear texture. The iris diameter in Fig.4(a)(b)(c) is 362, 200 and 157 pixels respectively, which is big enough for identification. The difference between the images is the longer of the distance, the image will be darker. If we increase the illumination of long working distance, the iris image will be much clear.

Besides the long acquisition rang, this system also has a long rang of focal length in a certain distance. This may reduce the difficult of camera zoom and autofocus, which improves the robust of the system. Fig. 5 shows the iris images taken in 70cm at different zoom number. The iris diameter is 153, 207, 245, 340 pixels respectively.

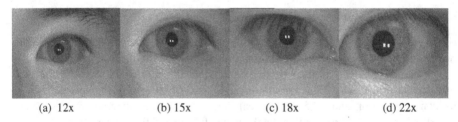

(a) 12x   (b) 15x   (c) 18x   (d) 22x

Fig. 5. The iris images taken in 70cm at12x, 15x, 18x, 22x focal length

5   Conclusions

In this paper, we designed an embedded self-adaptive iris image acquisition system using a single camera in a large working volume. If the user stand front of the camera and stare on it, the system will acquire the proper iris image automatically. The system integrates techniques of optical imaging, electronic control, face and eye detection algorithms, imaging processing and so on. We believe this work is a good attempt to make the iris recognition more convenient and practical.

Acknowledgements. This work is supported by National Science Foundation of China (No. 60905012, 60572058) and International Fund of Beijing Institute of Technology.

References

1. Liu, Y., He, Y., Gan, C., Zhu, J., Li, L.: A Review of Advances in Iris image Acquisition System. In: Zheng, W.-S., Sun, Z., Wang, Y., Chen, X., Yuen, P.C., Lai, J. (eds.) CCBR 2012. LNCS, vol. 7701, pp. 210–218. Springer, Heidelberg (2012)
2. Dong, W., Sun, Z., Tan, T.: A design of iris recognition system at a distance. In: Pattern Recognition, CCPR 2009 (2009)
3. Jung, H., Hyun, J., Park, K., Kim, J.: Coaxial optical structure for iris recognition from a distance. Optical Engineering 50(5), 1–8 (2011)
4. Villar, J., Ives, R., Matey, J.: Design and Implementation of a Long Range Iris Recognition System. IEEE (2010)
5. Dong, W., Sun, Z., Tan, T., Qiu, X.: Self-adaptive iris image acquisition system. In: Proceedings of the SPIE, Orlando, FL, vol. 6944, pp. 6–14 (2008)
6. Wheeler, F., Perera, A., Abramovich, G., Yu, B., Tu, P.: Stand-off Iris Recognition System. In: 2nd IEEE International Conference, BTAS 2008 (2008)
7. Smith, P., Rickman, J., Hartsell, J.: Relaxing the constraints on image capture for iris recognition systems. In: Proc. of SPIE, vol. 8371. SPIE (2012)
8. Abramovich, G., Wheeler, F.W.: LED eye safety considerations in the design of iris capture systems. In: Proc. SPIE, vol. 8029 (2011)
9. Villa, P., Jones, M.: Rapid object detection using a boosted cascade of simple features. In: IEEE Conference on Computer Vision and Pattern Recognition, pp. 1:511–1:518 (2001)
10. Brunelli, R., Poggio, T.: Face recognition: Features versus templates. IEEE Transaction on Pattern Analysis and Machine Intelligence 15(10), 1042–1052 (1993)
11. Zheng, Y., Wu, Y., Ni, X.: Resear on automatic focusing in real time. Opto-Electronic Engineering (April 2004)

A New Method for Sclera Vessel Recognition Using OLBP

Abhijit Das[1,*], Umapada Pal[2], Miguel A. Ferrer Ballester[3], and Michael Blumenstein[1]

[1] Institute for Integrated and Intelligent Systems, Griffith University, Queensland, Australia
[2] Computer Vision and Pattern Recognition Unit, Indian Statistical Institute, Kolkata, India
[3] IDeTIC, University of Las Palmas de Gran Canaria, Las Palmas, Spain
abhijit.das@griffithuni.edu.au, umapada@isical.ac.in,
mferrer@dsc.ulpgc.es, m.blumenstein@griffith.edu.au

Abstract. This paper proposes a new sclera vessel recognition technique. The vessel patterns of sclera are unique for each individual and this can be utilized to identify a person uniquely. In this research we have used a time adaptive active contour-based region growing technique for sclera segmentation. Prior to that, we have made some tonal and illumination correction to get a clearer sclera area without the distributing vessel structure. This is because the presence of complex vessel structures occasionally affects the region-growing process. The sclera vessels are not prominent in the images, so in order to make them clearly visible, a local image enhancement process using a Haar high pass filter is incorporated. To get the total orientation of the vessels, we have used Orientated Local Binary Pattern (OLBP). The OLBP images of each class are used for template matching for classification by calculating the minimum Hamming Distance. We have used the UBIRIS version 1 dataset for the experimentation of our research. The proposed approach has achieved high recognition accuracy employing the above-mentioned dataset.

Keywords: Sclera Biometric, Sclera vessels, Patterns, OLBP, LBP, Haar filter.

1 Introduction

Biometrics refers to automatic authentication of individuals based on their physiological and behavioral characteristics. A large number of research works have been performed in the field of biometrics over the last few decades. But no single biometric technique can be applied universally. So, further research on biometric traits is required. Sclera recognition is considered to be a good trait to complement traditional traits, as sclera is a highly-protected portions of the eye. Personal identification by the vessel pattern of the sclera is possible because these patterns possess a high degree of randomness and this makes it ideal for personal identification.

The various steps involves in sclera recognition are accurate segmentation of the sclera area, sclera vessel enhancement and the extraction of discriminative features of

---

* Corresponding author.

Z. Sun et al. (Eds.): CCBR 2013, LNCS 8232, pp. 370–377, 2013.

the sclera vessel pattern for authentication and identification purposes. Objective also focuses that the authentication system should work in real-time so that extraction, representation and comparison of texture images should not consume large computational resources.

This paper proposes a whole biometric scheme for personal identification based on sclera trait. We propose a new preprocessing technique for vein highlighting which makes it possible to apply region growing based algorithm for sclera segmentation. Otherwise the vein inside the sclera creates hindrance to standard region growing. The sclera parameterization based on OLBP is also new in the literature. The OLBP texture measure is judged appropriate for sclera segmentation because it is able to improve the vein structure representation by the vein trajectory orientation statistic. The hamming distance is used as sclera identification score here.

The organization of the paper is as follows: Section 2 explains the proposed approach of segmentation, preprocessing of the sclera images, followed by the sclera vessel enhancement process, feature extraction and classification. In Section 3 the experimental details are given, and Section 4 draws the overall conclusions.

2   Proposed Approach

Several approaches are proposed on sclera biometric in the literature. To our knowledge, first recognized work on sclera biometric is recorded in [1]. Automatic segmentation processes of sclera are proposed in [4], [6] and many features like LBP [9], GLCM [8] are used for recognition. Pieces of work on multi-angled sclera recognition [2, 7] well as multimodal eye recognition techniques [3, 5, 10] are also proposed using sclera and iris. In this section we explain a new sclera recognition technique. The content of this section includes a sclera segmentation process, a sclera vein enhancement technique, feature extraction of sclera texture patterns and sclera image registration. This is finally followed by the classification technique.

2.1   Sclera Segmentation

Generally the portion of blood vessels inside the sclera region is randomly-oriented which creates a pattern. As they are oriented in different layers, the intensity of the vessels varies highly. Some of them are quite bright and bundled. And this creates a hindrance to standard region growing. So we have considered the red channel of the image for segmentation, as the blood vessels are less prominent here as shown in figure 1(b). A representation for each color channel is indicated in Figure 1.

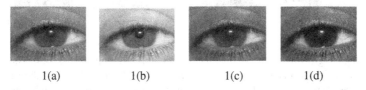

| 1(a) | 1(b) | 1(c) | 1(d) |

Fig. 1. (a) The image of the original RGB image, (b) The red channel component of 1(a), (c) The Green channel component of 1(a), and 1(d) blue channel component of 1(a)

Adaptive histogram equalization is performed with a small window of 2x2 to reduce the vessel content. Next to which we use a bank of low pass Haar reconstruction filters to get a clear white sclera without the vessel. The filter is used with a high cut off. Analyzing different results, the cut off value that produces the best result is determined and used for experimentation. The figure 2(a) is the histogram equalized image and 2(b) the Haar filtered image of 2(a).

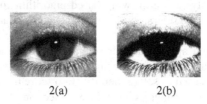

2(a)   2(b)

Fig. 2. (a) Is the histogram equalized image and (b) the Haar filtered image of 2(a)

This preprocessed image can be used for segmentation by a time adaptive active contour-based region growing segmentation method in [11]. The right and the left sclera are segmented separately. For region growing-based segmentation, we need a seed point. In order to get the seed point we use Daugmans integro–differential method [12], which is used to calculate the center of the iris. From the center of the iris at a distance of 1.1 of the radius length of the iris and a deviation of 45 degrees with the horizontal, the seed point for region growing is set in both sides of the sclera as explained in Figure 3.

Fig. 3. Seed point for sclera segmentation

Now the seed point grows to provide the total sclera region as explained in Figure 4.

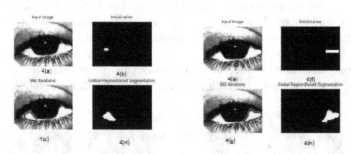

Fig. 4. Region growing segmentation method of left and right sclera. 4(a) The Histogram equalized and filtered image of red component of 1(a),,4(b) Initial size of the seed for right sclera,4(c) Segmented image of 4(a),4(d) Segmented mask developed for right sclera, 4(e)The Histogram equalized and filtered image of red component of 1(a),4(f) Initial size of the seed for left sclera,4(g) Segmented image of 4(e), 4(h) Segmented mask developed for left sclera.

The green channel images of the RGB are masked by the segmented mask to get the region of interest as shown in Figure 5. The green channel image is used because here the vessel patterns look most prominent as shown in Figure 1(c).

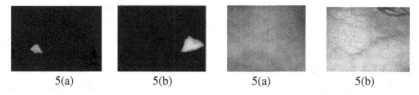

5(a)	5(b)	5(a)	5(b)

Fig. 5. (a) & (b) Segmented region of interest. (c) & (d) a microscopic view of the ROI

2.2   Sclera Vein Structure Enhancement

The vessels in the sclera are not prominent, so in order to make them clearly visible, image enhancement is required. Adaptive histogram equalization is performed with a large window size of 42 x 42 to make the vessel structure more prominent as shown in Figure 6.

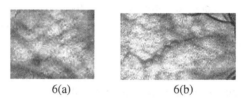

6(a)	6(b)

Fig. 6. The adaptive histogram images of the vessels in 5(c) & 5(d)

Then a bank of high pass decomposition Haar wavelet multi-resolution filters is used for obtaining the final enhanced vessel structure. The filter is used with a high cut off. The cut off value is determined empirically; the cut off value that produced the best result was used for experimentation. A Median filter is used to reduce some noise that is present in the surrounding area of the vessel. The images of the enhanced vessels following Haar filtering are provided in Figure 7.

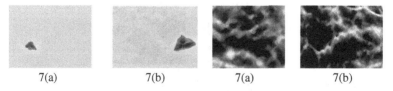

7(a)	7(b)	7(a)	7(b)

Fig. 7. 7(a) & 7(b) The images of enhanced vessel 7(c) & 7(d), a microscopic view of 7(a) & 7(b)

2.3   Feature Extraction Method

Local patterns, such as LBP (Local Binary Patterns), can be seen as a unifying approach to the traditionally statistical and structural approaches of texture analysis. Applied to black and white images, an LBP can be considered as the concatenation of the binary gradient directions. This contains micro-pattern information of the distribution of the edges, spots, and other local figures in an image which can be used as features for sclera recognition. Local patterns used for sclera features and the classifier used for sclera identification are discussed as follows. The original LBP operator labels the pixel of an image by thresholding the 3×3 neighbourhood of each pixel and concatenating the results binomially to form a number. Assume that a given image is defined as $I(Z) = I(x, y)$. The LBP operator transforms the input image to (Z) as follows:

$$LBP(Z_c) = \sum_{p=0}^{7} s\left(I(Z_p) - I(Z_c)\right) \cdot 2^p,$$

Where $s(l) = \begin{cases} 1 & l \geq 0 \\ 0 & l < 0 \end{cases}$ is the unit step function and $I(Z_p)$ is the 8-neighborhood around $I(Z_c)$. The feature representation method called Orientated Local Binary Pattern (OLBP) [13] is an extension of the local binary pattern (LBP). OLBP can represent more explicitly the orientation information of the strokes which is an important characteristic of scripts. The $OLBP$ of a given pixel Z_c is computed as follows:

1.   Compute the sequence $s\left(I(Z_p) - I(Z_c)\right), p = 0, \dots, 7.$

2.   Find the starting index ($Start$) and ending index (End) of the longest continuous 0 substring looking cyclically in the sequence of the previous step. $Start$ =argmax(($StringLength$)), End= $Start + StringLength(StartOri)$-1,

3. The index of the zeros substring center is the $OLBP$, i.e.
$OLBP(Z_c) = round((Start + End)/2)mod8,$

Where $round()$ rounds a number to the nearest integer, and mod is the arithmetic complement operation. An example of OLBP images of the vessel structure are presented in Figure 8.

Fig. 8. OLBP of the vein images

2.4   Image Registration

In order to make image translation independent, we have registered the iris centre to the centre of the image for each of the OLBP images produced in the earlier section. Registration is performed by using the following equations.

$$rowdiff = Imgx - Ix \qquad (1)$$

$$columndiff = Imgy - Iy \qquad (2)$$

where (Ix, Iy) represents the iris centre location, $(Imgx, Imgy)$ is the image centre, and $(rowdiff, columndiff)$ denotes the relative distance of the iris centre from the image centre. Now the relative amount of shift in row direction and column direction is applied to the OLBP image to register it against the image centre.

2.5   Classification

Template-based matching is used for classification. The gallery of query images is overlapped over the template of each class. The OLBP regions are binarized to get a binary template. Subsequently, identification is performed by template matching over the OLBP region as the Hamming Distance between the query image and templates, the matching which creates the minimum Hamming Distance is considered as the class of the query image. The Hamming Distance is calculated as below.

$$HD = \sum \frac{(\text{template} \oplus \text{query}) \cap (\text{mask} \cup \text{query mask})}{\text{template} - \sim(\text{mask} \cup \text{query mask})} \qquad (3)$$

Mask and query mask are the masks of the template and query image. The symbol $\oplus$ signifies the XOR operation, the symbol $\cap$ signifies the AND operation, the symbol $\cup$ signifies the OR operation, - signifies subtraction operator and the symbol $\sim$ signifies the NOT operation.

3   Experiments and Results

The experimental setup and the results of our proposed work are explained in this section.

3.1   Data Set

In order to evaluate the performance of our proposed method, the UBIRIS v1 database [14] is utilized for our experiments. This database consists of 1877 RGB images taken in two distinct sessions (1205 images in session 1 and 672 images in session 2) from 241 identities where each channel of RGB color space is represented in grey-scale. The database contains blurred images and images with blinking eyes. Both high resolution images (800×600) and low resolution images (200×150) are provided in the database. All the images are in JPEG format. We have used different quality of images. Some of them are not occluded having good quality of sclera regions visible, some of them are of medium quality and the third type is of poor quality with respect to sclera region visibility.

For our experimentation we have considered the images of session 1. One image from the session is randomly chosen and utilized for template generation and the other four were used as query images. So we have 241*4 scores for FRR and 242*241 score for FAR statistics. Among this 54 images were discarded because of failures during acquire. All the stimulation experiments performed here were developed in Matlab

3.2   Experimental Results

The experiments have been conducted to work out the sclera identification capability of the proposed features and classifier. As it is a classical identification or verification problem, the results will be given in terms of Cumulative Matching Curves (CMC) and Equal Error Rate (EER) curve. The CMC & EER curve is displayed in Figure 9. Along the X- axis we have the rank of the CMC and along the Y- axis the identification rate. Based on the interpretation of the graph it can be noted that faithful accuracy is achieved. Along the X- axis we have the matching score and along the Y-axis the density.

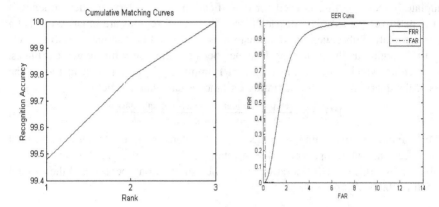

Fig. 9. CMC curve for recognition & EER curve for recognition

Table 1 provides the numerical data of Equal Error Rate and the Cumulative Matching Curves of the verification experiment.

Table 1. Equal Error Rate and the Cumulative Matching of the verification

Dataset	EER(%)	Cumulative Matching
UBIRIS version 1	0.52	99.48%

The results of the proposed work is put in perspective with the state-of-the-art by analyzing it with the most similar work on UBIRIS version 1, we could find in the literature. Table 2 reflects a state-of-the-art analysis of the most similar work on UBIRIS version 1.

Table 2. The state-of-the-art analysis the most similar work on UBIRIS version 1

Work	Equal Error Rate (in %)
Zhou et al. [4]	1.34
Oh et al. [9]	0.47(manual segmentation for some images)
Proposed System	0.52

4   Conclusions

This paper deals with a novel method of sclera recognition. We have proposed a sclera preprocessing algorithm to whiten the sclera eye portion, which improves the accuracy of the active contour procedure proposed for sclera segmentation. The vessel pattern has been enhanced with adaptive histogram equalization and a high pass Haar filter for establishing appropriate features. The OLBP provides information about the different pattern structures of sclera. Identification is accomplished by template matching over the OLBP region as minimum hamming distance matching. The proposed approach has achieved high recognition accuracy employing the UBRIS version1 dataset.

References

1. Derakhshani, R., Ross, A., Crihalmeanu, S.: A new biometric modality based on conjunctival vasculature. In: Proc. of Artificial Neural Networks in Engineering, pp. 1–8 (2006)
2. Zhou, Z., Du, Y., Thomas, N.L., Delp, E.J.: Multi-angled sclera recognition. In: IEEE Workshop on Computational Intelligence in Biometrics and Identity Management, pp. 103–108 (2011)
3. Zhou, Z., Du, Y., Thomas, N.L., Delp, E.J.: Multimodal eye recognition. In: Proceedings of the International Society for Optical Engineering, vol. 7708(770806), pp. 1–10 (2010)
4. Zhou, Z., Du, Y., Thomas, N.L., Delp, E.J.: A new biometric sclera recognition. IEEE Transaction on System, Man And Cybernatics –PART A: System And Human 42(3), 571–583 (2012)
5. Zhou, Z., Du, Y., Thomas, N.L., Delp, E.J.: Quality Fusion Based Multimodal Eye Recognition. In: IEEE International Conference on Systems, Man, and Cybernetics, pp. 1297–1302 (2012)
6. Khosravi, M.H., Safabakhsh, R.: Human eye sclera detection and tracking using a modified time-adaptive self-organizing map. Pattern Recognition 41, 2571–2593 (2008)
7. Crihalmeanu, S., Ross, A.: Multispectral sclera patterns for ocular biometric recognition. Pattern Recognition Letters 33, 1860–1869 (2012)
8. Tankasala, S.P., Doynov, P., Derakhshani, R.R., Ross, A., Crihalmeanu, S.: Biometric Recognition of Conjunctival Vasculature using GLCM Features. In: International Conference on Image Information Processing, pp. 1–6 (2011)
9. Oh, K., Toh, K.: Extracting Sclera Features for Cancelable Identity Verification. In: 5th IAPR International Conference on Biometric, pp. 245–250 (2012)
10. Gottemukkula, V., Saripalle, S.K., Tankasala, S.P., Derakhshani, R., Pasula, R., Ross, A.: Fusing Iris and Conjunctival Vasculature: Ocular Biometrics in the Visible Spectrum. In: IEEE Conference on Technologies for Homeland Security, pp. 150–155 (2012)
11. Chan, T.F., Luminita, A.V.: Active Contours Without Edges. IEEE Transaction on Image Proccessing 10(2), 266–277 (2001)
12. Daugman, J.G.: High confidence visual recognition of persons by a test of statistical independence. IEEE Transactions on Pattern Analysis and Machine Intelligence 15(11), 1148–1161 (1993)
13. Bu, W., Wub, X., Gaob, E.: Hand Vein Recognition Based on Orientation of LBP. In: Proc. of SPIE, vol. 8371(83711), pp. 1–12 (2012)
14. UBIRIS version 1 dataset for eye, http://iris.di.ubi.pt/

Venous Congestion Detection Method
Based on HSI Color Space

Wei Qi Yuan[1], Le Chang[1,2], Xiao Sun[3], and Hai Teng[3]

[1] Computer Vision Group, Shenyang University of Technology No.111, ShenLiao West Road, Economic & Technological Development Zone, Shenyang 110087, P. R. China
Changle1105@163.com
[2] Liaoning Guidaojiaotong Polytechnic Institute   No.170, Nujiang Street , Huang GU Zone, Shenyang 110036, P. R. China
[3] Feng Tian Hospital Affiliated To Shenyang Medical College No.7 South Road, Tie Xi Zone, Shenyang 110021, P. R. China

Abstract. The venous congestion is a very important kind of feature in iridology. How to detect and analyze the venous congestion is crucial to the automatic iris diagnosis system. Based on the HSI color space, this paper presents an effective method to extract the venous congestion. The iris image will be located and segmented at first, then fuse the H components and S components to quantitate the venous congestion. Experimental results show the validity of this approach.

Keywords: Iridology, venous congestion, HSI.

1   Introduction

Eyes as the only visual organ of the human body, not only can help people to see the external world, but also can help people understand their health situation. As early as one thousand of years ago, China's traditional medicine—Chinese medicine, found that human health condition might be verified through observing the abnormal change of human eyes. Now it is applied to clinical practice and known as " Five round and eight profile theory" . In other countries, iridology has more than a hundred years of history to analyze the relationship between the iris and the health of the human body.

Iridology mainly uses some unusual feature of iris to analyze the health condition of the human body. It is harmless, non-invasive, painless and inexpensive. Blue Ring is one of the most important signs to reveal the diseases and also called Venous Congestion [1]. It appeared in the outer ring of iris and surrounded by blue. According to the iridology, Venous Congestion means that toxic substances are deposited in tissues, susceptible to joint stiffness, loss of arterial elasticity, etc. Fengming Li mentioned in the book "The Department of Ophthalmology", when the human body in hepatolenticular degeneration (Wilson disease), the iris will be surrounded by a blue ring [2]. The etiology and pathogenesis of this disease is abnormal human copper metabolism, and it makes large amounts of copper deposited in tissue. Venous congestion has important value in the diagnosis of Wilson's disease [3].

In the field of iris diagnosis and medicine, observation and analysis of the venous congestion mainly relies on manual work, this method has disadvantages of strong

Z. Sun et al. (Eds.): CCBR 2013, LNCS 8232, pp. 378–385, 2013.
© Springer International Publishing Switzerland 2013

subjectivity, inaccuracy and impossible for a quantitative analysis. The main purpose of this study gives a quantitative detection method of venous congestion by image processing algorithm. At present, has not yet been retrieved related articles in venous congestion detection research.

2   Image Acquisition and Preprocessing

2.1   Image Acquisition

Because the eyes are sensitive to the outside environment especially the changes of light, it has brought difficulties to the image acquisition. There are many kinds of image acquisition equipment shown on the market, these devices capable of acquiring iris image clearly, but the intensity of light make people feel discomfort. We used the light guide plate to reduce the intensity of light and collected more than 884 iris images by the cooperation with the Fen Tian Hospital affiliated to ShenYange medical college,the size of each image is 600*800 pixels. The database contains 42 different degrees of venous congestion images.

2.2   Iris Preprocessing

Compared with the color of other parts in iris image, The color of venous congestion is different from the others, so we used the color information to detect the venous congestion. By analyzing the iris image in our database, we found that some people have the same color with venous congestion for cosmetic reasons. In order to avoid eyelid interference we selected the fix area by iris location, as shown in Fig 1 right.

To locate the inner and outer boundary of iris accurately, we need to detect three edge point of each boundary and determine a circle. Here is the detailed instruction:

(1) As shown in Fig1, determine a point P in the pupil by the gray projection operator   mentioned in reference [4].

(2) Making P as a starting point , using the 2×20 gradient template to locate the three inner boundary points A, B, C along the horizontal and straight directions, determining the pupil center O.

(3) Starting from the point O, using the method mentioned in the procedure (2) to locate other two outer boundary points E, F.

Suppose R1 is the distance of EO, R2 is the distance of FO, R is the radius of the pupil. The area is selected to detect the venous congestion is: Point O is the center, 2*R is high, 2*Max （R1，R2） is width. The area is shown in Fig.2.

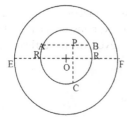

Fig. 1. Iris location

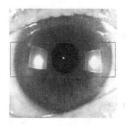

Fig. 2. Iris segmentation

3   Detection of Venous Congestion

3.1   Selection of Color Space

In order to detect the venous congestion in the iris image effectively, we process the iris image in HSI color space. HSI model is proposed in 1915 by H. A. Munseu, this color space reflects the perception way of the human visual system. The HSI model includes three basic components: hue, saturation and intensity [5]. The hue is relate to the wavelength of light,it means the different colors experience of the human senses, Such as red, green, blue etc. The saturation reflects the purity of color, pure spectral color is fully saturated, join white light will dilute the saturation. Saturation is bigger, color will look brighter, and vice versa. The intensity reflects the image brightness and gray. Select the HSI color space to detect the venous congestion is mainly because : intensity has nothing to do with the color of the image, Hue and saturation is closely related to the way of color sense. These features make the HSI model is suitable for the detection and analysis of color characteristics.

3.2   Extaction of the Color Information

Through the above analysis, we use the hue to segment the venous congestion area. In order to locate the venous congestion area accurately, this paper chose a color template image shown in Fig.3 to analysis the hue distribution. The color template image shows the relation between the hue value and the corresponding color. Starting from the three o'clock position, along the clockwise direction, the hue value gradually increased from 0 to 1. At the six o'clock position hue value is 0.25, at the nine o'clock position hue value is 0.5, at the twelve o'clock position hue value is 0.75. The No.2 and No.4 image of Fig.3 shows the detection results when the Hue value is between 0.547 to 0.708.

Fig. 3. Color template and the results of using H values to extract the color information

Different degrees of venous congestion represent the different health situation, so we not only detect it accurately, but also need to analyze the severity of venous congestion. We choose an experimental region which includes the different degree of venous congestion, as shown in Fig.4.As can be seen from the chart, the color of venous congestion changing from shallow to deep, the S value is changing from small to big and H values are distributed around 0.5.I values is mainly showing the gray feature of iris. So we used the H and S values to detect the venous congestion.

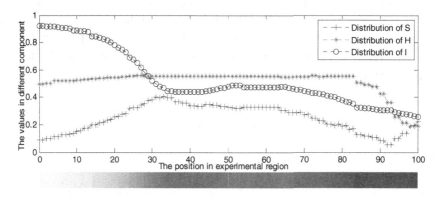

Fig. 4. H, S, I distribution in different degrees of venous congestion

According to iridology conclusion and the iris image we collected, the venous congestion mainly distributed in 1/3 area of iris from outside to inside. We select the gray area shown as Fig.5 to detect the venous congestion, this area is usually not to be blocked or interference. Supposed this area is Ω ,the number of pixels is K, x,y satisfy the following formula:

$$\sqrt{(x-\frac{M}{2})^2+(y-\frac{N}{2})^2} > r+\frac{1}{3}(R-r)$$ (1)

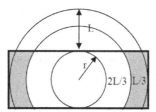

Fig. 5. The area we selected to detect the venous congestion

The detection result R can be calculated by formula (2):

$$R=\frac{\sum_{x,y\in\Omega}(a*H(x,y)*f(x,y)+b*S(x,y))}{K}$$ (2)

$$f(x, y) = \begin{cases} 1 & h_{min} < H(x, y) < h_{max} \\ 0 & other \end{cases} \tag{3}$$

The function $H(x, y)$ is the H values of selected iris area, $S(x, y)$ is the S values of selected iris area, function $f(x, y)$ is used to detect the color information. h_{min}, h_{max} is the minimum and maximum values of the venous congestion color information. Because the color of venous congestion is mainly distribute from seven o'clock to eleven o'clock in color template, so $h_{min} = 0.547$, $h_{max} = 0.708$. Experiment results shown this values can locate the venous congestion area effectively. a, b are the weights of $H(x, y)$ and $S(x, y)$, $a + b = 1$.

4   Experiment Results and Analysis

4.1   Experiment Result about the Effect of Light

In the process of iris image acquisition, natural light will influence the accuracy of venous congestion extraction. In order to analyze the effect of light on this algorithm, we collect two images about the same sample in different light environment. The procedures are shown as follows:

(1) Iris image normalization, changing two original iris images into rectangular.

(2) Select the $M \times N$ sub area in both two normalized images and named F, F'.

(3) Changing the F, F' into HSI color space and calculate the illumination variation E. Taking the H channel as an example, the formula is as follows:

$$E_H = \left| \frac{1}{M * N} \sum_{x=1}^{M} \sum_{y=1}^{N} F_H(x, y) - \frac{1}{M * N} \sum_{x=1}^{M} \sum_{y=1}^{N} F'_H(x, y) \right| \tag{4}$$

(4) Calculate the proportion of illumination variation P, Takeing the H channel as an example, the formula is as follows:

$$P_H = \frac{E_H}{(E_H + E_S + E_I)} \times 100\% \tag{5}$$

The table below shows the illumination variation and proportion in different color channel.

Table 1. Result of illumination variation E and proportion P in H,S,I

Color channel	Illumination variation E	Proportion P
H	0.05231	11.22%
S	0.07728	16.57%
I	0.33684	72.21%

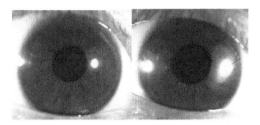

Fig. 6. Two iris image collected in different illumination

From the above experiment results, the influence of light to H channel and S channel is smaller than I, the proportion of I reached 72.21%. By using H channel and S channel to extract the venous congestion can reduce the effect of illumination effectiveness.

4.2   Venous Congestion Detection Experiment Results

In order to verify the effectiveness of the proposed method, Four types of samples are selected and named normal, mild, moderate, severe(shown in Fig.7). These four images are used to select the appropriate parameters for the method we proposed.   Supposed detection results of four images are Ra, Rb, Rc, Rd (calculated by formula 2), we need to select the appropriate parameter a and b to make value P as big as possible. P is calculated by:

$$p = \frac{\overline{M}}{|\overline{M} - R_a| * |\overline{M} - R_b| * |\overline{M} - R_c| * |\overline{M} - R_d| * 10^3} \tag{6}$$

$$\overline{M} = \frac{R_d - R_a}{3} \tag{7}$$

From the experiment shown in Fig.8, when b=0. 8 and a=0. 2, our method can get the best detection results, and Ra=0.0359,Rb=0.3218,Rc=0.5584,Rd=0.6977.

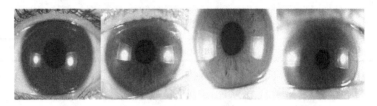

Fig. 7. Four kinds of iris image we selected in experiments

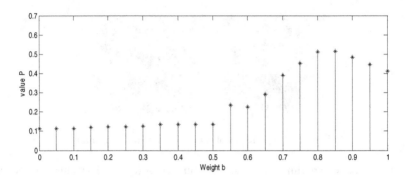

Fig. 8. Parameter selection of b and the value of P

By analysing the result Ra,Rb,Rc,Rd, we get the effective range of different degree of venous congestion.The rang of Normal iris is: $[0, \dfrac{R_b + R_a}{2}]$. The range of mild iris is: $(\dfrac{R_b + R_a}{2}, \dfrac{R_b + R_c}{2}]$. The range of moderate is: $(\dfrac{R_b + R_c}{2}, \dfrac{R_d + R_c}{2}]$. The range of severe is: $(\dfrac{R_d + R_c}{2}, 1]$. The final range and detection results as shown in Tab.2.

From the Tab.2 we get the high accuracy in normal and milt iris image. The main reason for failure detection is the influence of lighte position. we still need to do some improvement in how to avoid the light positon in iris images.

Table 2. The range selection and the results of detection

	Distribution range	Sample number	Accuracy rate
Normal	0-0.1789	400	98%
Milt	0.1789-0.4401	8	100%
Moderate	0.4401-0.6281	22	90.1%
Severe	0.6281-1	6	83.3%

5   Conclusions

In this paper, we propose a venous congestion detection method aimed at eliminating the subjective and the qualitative characteristic of the traditional iridology. The experimental results reasonably demonstrate the effectiveness of the method we described in this paper. Venous congestion is a typical kind of iridology features, but the prevalence rate is still very low. From all 884 iris images only 42 iris images have venous congestion feature, the scale of the database still needs to increase.

Acknowledgement. This work is supported by the National Natural Science Foundation of China(No.61271365).

References

1. Navratil, F.: Iridology - For your eyes only, pp. 81–107. C.V.Mosby (2001)
2. Li, F.: The Department of Ophthalmology, Beijing (2011)
3. Zhang, X.: The analysis of K-F Ring and hepatolenticular degeneration. J. Clinical Ophthalmology 9, 11–13 (2001)
4. Yuan, W., Lin, Z., Xu, L.: A new Iris location algorith based on eyes structure. Opto-Electronic Engineering 34, 112–116 (2007)
5. Welch, E., Moorhead, R., Owens, J.K.: Image processing using the HSI color space. In: Conference Proceedings-IEEE Southeastcon, Williamsburg, USA, vol. 2, pp. 722–725 (1991)

Mobile Authentication through Touch-Behavior Features

Zhongmin Cai, Chao Shen, Miao Wang, Yunpeng Song, and Jialin Wang

MOEKey Lab For Intelligent Networks and Network Security
Xi'an Jiaotong University
No.28 Xianning West Road,
Xi'an, Shaanxi, 710049
{zmcai,cshen,mwang,ypsong,jlwang}@sei.xjtu.edu.cn

Abstract. The increasing use of touchscreen mobile phones to access sensitive and personal data has given rise to the need of secure and usable authentication technique. This paper presents a novel approach to authentication on touch-screen mobile devices. The basic idea was to exploit user interaction data of touchscreen mobile phone to authenticate users based on the way they perform touch operations. A filed study was conducted to design typical touch-operation scenarios and gather users' data. Behavioral features were extracted to accurately characterize users' behavior. Diverse classification methods were employed to perform the authentication task. Experiments are included to demonstrate the effectiveness of the proposed approach, which achieves a false-acceptance rate of 4.05%, and a false-rejection rate of 3.27%. This level of accuracy shows that these are indeed identity information in touch behavior that can be used as a mobile authentication mechanism.

Keywords: Mobile Authentication, Biometric, Touch-Behavior Features.

1   Introduction

With the fast development of mobile computation, smartphones have become an inseparable part of people's daily lives and work. More and more personal and sensitive data has been stored on smartphones. Not surprisingly, the security of these mobile devices has become a very important problem. Effective user authentication is a fundamental security requirement in protection of computing systems. For touchscreen smartphones, current authentication mechanisms usually use passwords. Although password authentication is simple and easy to implement, it is subject to the problems of being forgotten and stolen. Thus, alternative authentication mechanisms which are reliable and convenient on mobile devices should be developed.

This paper explores the feasibility of using behavioral features in touch operations on touchscreen smartphones as a behavioral biometric to authenticate a user. We designed a user interface consisting of typical touch-operation scenarios and captured users' touch-behavior data. We extracted behavioral features to characterize users' touch behavior and performed experiments to see whether they provide enough discriminatory power to identify users. Empirical results are encouraging, which achieves a false-acceptance rate of 4.05% and a false-rejection rate of 3.27%.

Z. Sun et al. (Eds.): CCBR 2013, LNCS 8232, pp. 386–393, 2013.

This level of accuracy shows that there is indeed identity information in touch behavior that can be used for mobile authentication.

Section 2 discusses the related work. Section 3 designs touch-operation scenarios and introduces the dataset. Section 4 defines and extracts the touch-behavior features. Section 5 and 6 explains the classifiers, evaluation procedural and performance metrics. Section 7 presents the experimental design and analyzes the results. Section 8 concludes this paper and pinpoints directions for future research.

2   Related Work

Mobile authentication using touch-behavior features is a new research area. There are only a few pieces of related work. Saevane and Bhatarakosol [1] proposed an authentication mechanism using keystroke dynamics on touchscreen mobile devices. Users were asked to input 10-digit phone number using a simulated keyboard on the touchscreen. The features used included the pressure of the finger tip, hold time and transition time. A *kNN* classifier was employed to perform user classifications. They reported 99% of accuracy if the pressure feature was included and 90% without the pressure feature. Luca *et al.* [2] proposed to use behavioral features in unlock and graphical password operations on touchscreen mobile phones to authenticate a user. The touch operations were largely single touches which involves only one finger. They reported average accuracies of 50% for unlock operation and of 77% for graphical passwords. Sae-Bae *et al.* [3] performed user authentication experiments on iPad using behavioral features in multi-touch operations. 34 volunteers were involved. They reported equal-error rates of 7%-15% for one mode of multi-touch and EERs of 2.6%-3.9% if two multi-touch modes are combined. Frank *et al.* [4] proposed to use behavioral features of left-right sliding and up-down sliding on touchscreen mobile phones for continuous authentication. They employed *kNN* and SVM to perform user classification and reported EER of 0%-4%.

These efforts showed a promising direction of using touch-behavior features in authentication. But the technique is still in its infancy, and only a small portion of touch gestures were explored and no serious efforts have been made on behavioral features in multi-touch operations. In this paper, we analyzed behavioral features in both single-touch and multi-touch operations. We also performed an in-depth investigation of the feasibility of mobile authentication through touch-behavior characteristics.

3   Touch-Behavior Data

In this study we built a controlled environment to collect touch-behavior data, so as to insulate intrinsic behavior characteristics as the principle factor in behavior analysis.

3.1   Supporting Apparatus

We set up a smartphone and developed an application as a uniform platform for touch-behavior data acquisition. The smartphone was a Samsung Galaxy Note with a dual-core 1.4 GHz processor and 1 GB of RAM, running Android 2.3.5 operating system. It was equipped with a 5.29-inch display and the resolution was set as 800×1280. The application, written in Java, was developed for providing subjects the scenarios to perform typical touch operations. During the data acquisition, the application recorded (1) the corresponding touch event, (2) the position at which the event occurred, (3) the timestamp of the event, (4) the pressure of the touch finger.

3.2   Touch-Operation Scenarios

We designed touch-operation scenarios that could represent typical and diverse touch operations in users' daily interactions. Figure 1 shows four different touch-operation scenarios that we developed, including simple one-finger operation (single-touch) and various two-finger operations (multi-touches). Figure 1.a shows the single-touch scenario, which consists of four times one-finger drag-and-drop operation, and requires subjects to drag one solid cube and then drop it on the position of hollow cube. Figure 1.b-d show different multi-touch scenarios, which contain two-finger drag-and-drop operations, two-finger zoom-in and zoom-out operations, and two-finger rotation operations. The numbers in these scenarios represent the order of operations. It is worthy of note that designs of touch-operation scenarios may not be unique. However, our scenarios cover all typical and common operations in users' daily interactions with touchscreens.

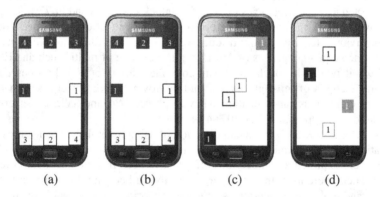

(a)   (b)   (c)   (d)

Fig. 1. Four designed touch-behavior operation scenarios

3.3   Instruction to Subjects

One touch-behavior sample was collected by asking a subject to perform all four touch-operation scenarios one time. Subjects were required to focus on the experiment, and to avoid distractions while the experiment was in progress. Each sample corresponds to one error-free repetition of the four touch-operation scenarios.

3.4   Subjects

We recruited 20 subjects from the university, and all but two subjects reported using touchscreen mobile phones. The subjects consisted of 13 males and 7 females, and all were right-handed. Subjects were asked to take one round of data acquisition per day, and repeat all four touch-operation scenarios 10 times per round. Subjects took between 10 and 30 days to complete the data acquisition. Each subject provided touch-behavior samples, i.e., performed 100 repetitions of the four touch-behavior operation scenarios. Finally, we obtained a dataset with 2,000 samples from 20 subjects.

4   Features

In this section, we extracted a set of touch-behavior features, and used distance-measure method to obtain feature-distance vector for reducing influence of variability.

4.1   Feature Extraction

The acquired data are sequences of touch-behavior operations, such as drag-and-drop and zooming-in actions. These actions cannot be used directly by a classifier. Thus touch-behavior features were extracted from these actions, and then were organized into a vector for representing one touch-behavior sample. We characterized touch-behavior actions based on two measures: position and pressure. Each measure was then analyzed individually, and converted into several features, to form the feature vector. In this study, we categorized them into single-touch features and multi-touch features. Table 1 summarized the derived features, which formed a 44-dimensional feature vector to represent each touch-behavior sample.

Table 1. Touch-Behavior Features

Category	Touch-Behavior Features	Definitions	#
Single-touch	Sliding speed curve	The speed sequences for each of 4 single-touch sliding movements	4
	Sliding offset	The distance between practical and ideal trajectory for each of 4 single-touch sliding movements	4
	Variance of finger pressure	The variance of pressures for the touch events consisting of the 4 single-touch sliding movements	4
Multi-touch	Distance curve between two fingers	The distance sequences between two fingertips for each of 8 two-finger multi-touch sliding movements	8
	Angle curve between two fingers	The angle sequences between two fingertips for each of 8 two-finger multi-touch sliding movements	8
	Variance of finger pressure	The variance of pressures for each of 2 fingers in touching events consisting of the 8 two-finger sliding movements in the 3 multi-touch scenarios	16

4.2   Distance Measure

The touch-behavior features represented by curves cannot be directly used to a classifier due to high dimensionality and behavioral variability. Thus we developed a distance-measure method to transform the raw feature vector to feature-distance vector as the input for classifiers. We first employed the Dynamic Time Warping (DTW) distance [5] to compute the distance vector of curve-style features. The reasons are that (1) touch-behavior features (e.g., sliding speed curve) of two data samples are not likely to be consisted of the exactly same number of points (touch events); (2) DTW distance can be applied to measure the distance between the features of two samples without deforming either or both of the two sequences in order to get an equal number of points. We next applied Manhattan distance to compute the distance vector of other features. The reason is that this distance is the absolute value of cumulative difference between features thus it is independent between dimensions, and could preserve physical interpretation of the features.

5   Classifier Implementation

By ensuring the diversity in a set of classifier, we could examine whether an observed effect is specific to one type of classifier or more generalized to a range of classifiers.

5.1   Neural Network

Neural network is a prevalent classification method of identifying patterns [6]. Here we employed a single hidden layer neural network. During training, we built the network with m input nodes, $(2m+1)$ hidden nodes, and one output node. The network was trained to produce ± 1.0 on the output score on training samples. During testing, testing samples were run through the network, and the output of the network was recorded as the classification score.

5.2   MCMC-Based Bayesian Network

Bayesian network is a multi-layer network implementing a naïve Bayesian classifier [7]. Here we used a three-layer Bayesian neural network. During training, the parametric network was trained by using the Markov Chain Monte Carlo (MCMC) technique to draw posterior samples of the parameters involved (network weights and Bayesian parameters). During testing, the parameter samples, derived from the testing samples via MCMC, were used to compute the probability that a testing sample is genuine. This probability value was then considered as the classification score.

5.3   Support Vector Machine

Support vector machine generalized the ideas of finding an optimal hyper-plane for performing binary classification [8]. During training, the SVM was trained on training samples with a RBF kernel function. The SVM parameter v and kernel parameter γ were set to 0.03 and 0.07 respectively. During testing, the testing samples were projected on a high-dimensional space, and the distance between the samples and the hyper-plane is computed as the classification score.

6   Evaluation Procedure

6.1   Training and Testing

We started by designating one of our 20 subjects as the legitimate user, and the rest as impostors. In training phase, we trained the classifier on randomly-selected half of behavioral samples from the legitimate user and the same number of behavioral samples from impostors. In testing phase, we measured ability of the classifier to discriminate between the legitimate user and impostors. We first computed the classification scores on the remaining samples from the legitimate user. We then computed the classification scores on the remaining behavioral samples from all the impostors.

We next repeated the above process, by designating each of the rest subjects as legitimate user in turn. Additionally, since we randomly selected the samples for training and testing, and we wanted to account for this randomness, we repeated the above procedure ten times, each time with an independent draw from the entire dataset.

6.2   Calculating Classifier Performance

To convert these classification scores into aggregate measures of classifier performance, we calculated the false-acceptance rate (FAR) and false-rejection rate (FRR). We also brought FAR and FRR together to generate a graphical summary of performance known as ROC curve by varying the threshold on classification score [9].

7   Results and Analysis

Figure 2 and Table 2 show the ROC curves and average FAR and FRR of the mobile authentication task for each of three classifiers. As a result, the effectiveness of our approach can be assessed on a comparison of classifier performance.

Our first observation is that the error rates of all three classifiers are below 10%, which shows that these is indeed identity information in touch behavior that can be used for mobile authentication. The best performance obtained by SVM achieves a FAR of 4.05% and a FRR of 3.27% at the median threshold. This result is very promising, and can be competitive with the best results (an authentication accuracy of 96%) and better than the average accuracies of 77% reported in [2] which also investigated the authentication technique using touch-behavior features. The reason is perhaps the newly proposed multi-touch behavioral features in our work.

Our second observation is that the SVM classifier has a much better performance than other two classifiers. We can observe that the ROC curve of SVM is much lower than others. This may be the fact that SVM can convert the problem of classification into quadratic optimization in the context of insufficiency of prior knowledge, and still maintain high accuracy and stability. We also note that the standard deviations of error rates for SVM are smaller than the other two. This indicates that it may be robust to the variability of touch behavior and various parameter selection procedures.

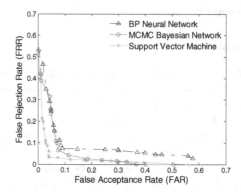

Fig. 2. ROC curves for the three different classifiers used in this study

Table 2. FARs and FRRs of authentication (with standard deviations in parentheses)

Classifier	FAR (%)	FRR (%)
BP Neural Network	9.16 (3.51)	8.27 (5.49)
MCMC Bayesian Network	7.40 (4.55)	6.36 (5.01)
Support Vector Machine	4.05 (3.12)	3.27 (3.18)

Table 3. HTER performance and Confidence Interval at different confidence levels

Classifier	HTER (%)	Confidential Interval (%) around HTER for		
		90%	95%	99%
BP Neural Network	8.72	±2.19	±2.61	±3.43
MCMC Bayesian Network	6.88	±2.06	±2.46	±3.23
Support Vector Machine	3.66	±1.51	±1.80	±2.36

Additionally, we implemented a statistical test by computing the *half total error rate* (HTER) and confidence interval (CI) [11], to statistically assess the performance of our approach. The results show that the approach using SVM classifier provides the lowest HTER and CI compared to the other two classifiers, with the 95% confidence interval laying at 3.66% ± 1.80%.

8   Conclusion and Future Work

Using smartphones to access sensitive and personal data raises the question of secure and convenient authentication methods whether touch behaviors reflect users' identify information. This paper presented a novel approach to authentication on touchscreen mobile devices, by analyzing users' touch-behavior features in their interactive operations with touchscreen smartphones. We conducted a filed study that designed typical touch-operation scenarios and collected users' data. We extracted behavioral features to accurately characterize users' touch behavior. We then employed diverse classification techniques to perform the authentication task. Experimental results demonstrated the efficacy of the proposed approach, and showed these are indeed identity information in touch behavior that can be used for mobile authentication.

Acknowledgements. The research is supported by NFSC (61175039, 61221063), 863 High Tech Development Plan (2007AA01Z464, 2012AA011003), Research Fund for Doctoral Program of Higher Education of China (20090201120032), International Research Collaboration Project of Shaanxi Province (2013KW11) and Fundamental Research Funds for Central Universities (2012jdhz08).

References

1. Saevanee, H., Bhatarakosol, P.: User Authentication using Combination of Behavioral Biometrics over the Touchpad acting like Touch screen of Mobile Device. In: Proc. Int'l Conf. Comp. Elect. Engineer, pp. 82–86 (2008)
2. Luca, A.D., Hang, A., Brudy, F., Lindner, C., Hussmann, H.: Touch Me Once and I Know It's You!: Implicit Authentication based on Touchscreen Patterns. In: Proc. ACM Annu. Conf. Human Factors in Computing Systems, pp. 987–996 (2012)
3. Sae-Bae, N., Ahmed, K., Isbister, K., Memon, N.: Biometric-Rich Gestures: a Novel Approach to Authentication on Multi-Touch Devices. In: Proc. ACM Annu. Conf. Human Factors in Computing Systems, pp. 977–986 (2012)
4. Frank, M., Biederty, R., Ma, E., Martinovic, I., Song, D.: Touchalytics: On the Applicability of Touchscreen Input as a Behavioral Biometric for Continuous Authentication. IEEE Trans. Info. Forensics and Security 8(1), 136–148 (2013)
5. Marzal, A., Vidal, E.: Computation of Normalized Edit Distance and Applications. IEEE Trans. Pattern Analysis and machine intelligence 15(9), 926–932 (1993)
6. Duda, R., Hart, P., Stork, D.: Pattern Classification, 2nd edn. John Wiley and Sons, New York (2001)
7. Neal, R.M.: Bayesian Learning for Neural Networks. Springer, New York (1996)
8. Cortes, C., Vapnik, V.: Support Vector Networks. Machine Learning 20(3), 273–297 (1995)
9. Swets, J.A., Pickett, R.M.: Evaluation of Diagnostic Systems: Methods From Signal Detection Theory. Academic, New York (1982)
10. Bengio, S., Mariethoz, J.: A statistical Significance Test for Person Authentication. In: Proc. Speaker and Language Recognition Workshop, pp. 237–244 (2004)

Emotional Speaker Recognition Based on Model Space Migration through Translated Learning*

Li Chen and Yingchun Yang

Zhejiang University
{stchenli,yyc}@zju.edu.cn

Abstract. Speaker-emotion variability is one of the major factors causing the degradation of the performance of speaker recognition system. The difficulty is mainly induced by the shift of the acoustic space, thus the emotional model could not be generated only by neutral utterances. This paper presents a translated learning method which utilizes both the neutral and emotional speech in the development data as translators to build "bridges" between neutral model space and emotional model space. With the help of these translators, GMM emotional model can be produced through its neutral model. The experiments carried on MASC show an IR increase of 2.81% over the GMM-UBM system.

Keywords: Emotional speaker recognition, neighbor similarity effect, corresponding component GMM.

1 Introduction

There are many challenges in applying speaker recognition system into practice, such as background noise, channel effect and speaker-emotion variability. Emotional speaker recognition, which means the emotion states of training speech and testing speech are different, is devoted to solving the problem of speaker-emotion variability.

In recent years, many efforts have been made to solve the problem of unmatched emotion states, and most of them can be categorized into two groups: normalization technique and enrich technique. The main idea of normalization is to remove emotional information from speeches. Bao et al proposed a method named Emotion Attribute Projection (EAP) to remove subspace that may cause emotion variability [1]. Huang et al proposed Pitch-dependent Difference Detection and Modification (PDDM) to modify segments with high difference to neutral speech using scaling and pruning strategy [2]. Enrich technique is learning the transformation rules from developing corpus, and applying them into evaluation process to expand the speaker's neutral model to his/her emotional model. Shan et al proposed two Neutral-Emotion GMM Transformation (NEGT) methods. NEGT-1 [3] and NEGT-2 [4] works on model layer and score layer respectively, and each GMM component in emotional model is a linear combination of the 32 GMM components in neutral

---
* Thanks to 973 Program 2013CB329504, the Fundamental Research Funds for the Central Universities 2013 and National Natural Science Foundation of China (NSFC60970080) for funding.

Z. Sun et al. (Eds.): CCBR 2013, LNCS 8232, pp. 394–401, 2013.

model. However, the complexity of the new model becomes dramatically high, which is usually more than 10,000 GMM components, and the linear combination is a rough assumption without phonetic knowledge. Dai [5][6] proposed a novel transfer learning method named translated learning to solve the problem that the source and target feature space are totally different, and the idea can also be used to figure out our feature space mismatch problem.

In this paper, we aim to find out the methods to transform neutral model to emotional model using the translated learning. The translators are chosen from the development data, and the "bridges" are the corresponding GMM component under the same phonetic event of different emotion states because fine grain "bridges" brings more precise transformation rules. When train utterance comes, the k-nearest neighbors of its neutral component are selected from all the "bridges" mentioned above. Using these "bridges" as transformation rules, its corresponding emotional component could be constructed.   The new emotional model is employed to recognize the speaker of emotional speech.

The rest of the paper is organized as follows. Section 2 introduces the translated learning algorithm and how the "bridges" we select – GMM component of the same phonetic event. Section 3 presents the framework of our algorithm and the detailed description. In section 4, experiment results of our algorithm on MASC are reported. Finally, section 5 gives a summary and conclusion.

2   Translated Learning Algorithm

2.1   Translated Learning

Translated learning is known as solving the problem that training data and test data are in totally different space. The strategy is to make use of available data that have both features of the source and the target domains to construct a translator. In the emotional speaker recognition context, acoustic space can be seemed as the known "source space" and the emotional acoustic space is the unknown "target space". And these two are of different space. Thus, the performance of emotional speaker recognition is unsatisfied.   We must construct the translator mentioned before to link these two spaces, the development data is selected to serve as this role because it contains both a speaker's neutral and emotional utterance. Selecting the "Bridges" which links the source space and the target space in a translator is one of the most important aspects of translated learning.

We consider two grains of the "bridges". First is the coarse grain. We select the emotional model and the neutral model of one speaker, but it's too rough to explain the transformation rule. Thus, we consider the more fine "bridge" – GMM component of the same phonetic event.

2.2   Similar Neighbors of GMM Component of the Same Phonetic Event

Since Reynolds [7] firstly proposed Gaussian Mixture Model (GMM) in 1995, it has been recognized as the robust model representing the distribution of speakers' acoustic space. A GMM is a weighted sum of Gaussian components and is given by equation (1):

$$p(x \mid \lambda) = \sum_{c=1}^{Nc} w_c N(u_c, \Sigma_c, x).$$ (1)

Each GMM component is an acoustic class representing special broad phonetic event, such as vowels, nasals or fricatives [7]. The mean u_c is the average of the features of the acoustic class, and the covariance matrix Σ_c represents the variability of features within the acoustic class. Under the framework of GMM-UBM, each model is adapted from the Universal Background Model. Thus, we assume that the same GMM component of each model represents the same phonetic event.

In K-nearest neighbors (KNN) method, adjacent samples are clustered within a class, the same class means that the samples in this class have similar attribute. Same idea is adopted here, and Kullback-Leibler divergence (KL divergence) [8] is selected as the criterion to judge whether two samples are neighbors. KL divergence is used in measuring the distance of two models, especially probabilistic models.

There are many factors causing the shift of acoustic space. For the same speaker, different emotional states and phonetic events are the major reasons. If these two factors are considered simultaneously, the rule is not obvious. The correlation between $KL(N_{i,j_1}, N_{k,j_2})$ and $KL(E_{i,j_1}, E_{k,j_2})$ is calculated as equation (2). $KL(N_{i,j_1}, N_{k,j_2})$ means KL divergence between $j_1 th$ GMM component of ith person's and $j_2 th$ GMM component of kth person's neutral model, while $KL(E_{i,j_1}, E_{k,j_2})$ means that of the emotional model.

$$\rho_{\alpha\beta} = \frac{Cov(\alpha, \beta)}{\sqrt{D(\alpha)}\sqrt{D(\beta)}}.$$ (2)

α represents the variable $KL(N_{i,j_1}, N_{k,j_2})$ and β represents the variable $KL(E_{i,j_1}, E_{k,j_2})$. The correlation is just 0.204. Now, we consider when the phonetic event is fixed, how the emotional state affect the shift of the acoustic space.

Fig.1 depicts KL divergence of a GMM component and that of other people. Meaning of the parameters is the same as before (i and j are randomly selected). It can be observed that under the same phonetic event, $KL(N_{i,j}, N_{k,j})$ and $KL(E_{i,j}, E_{k,j})$ are almost the same. If we treat $KL(N_{i,j}, N_{k,j})$ as variable α and $KL(E_{i,j}, E_{k,j})$ as another variable β, the correlation of these two variables is computed as equation (2).

According to computing on the development data, the correlation is 0.734. Therefore, we can draw out that $KL(N_{i,j}, N_{k,j})$ and $KL(E_{i,j}, E_{k,j})$ is highly correlated.

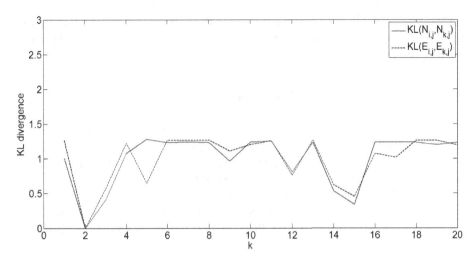

Fig. 1. KL divergence of the same phonetic event between speaker and other 20 speakers in both neutral and emotional state

For each $N_{i,j}$, we select m person $k_1, k_2, ..., k_m$, so that they are ith speakers' neutral neighbors. Supposing k_0 is the person satisfying equation (3).

$$k_0 = \min \arg KL(E_{i,j}, E_{k,j})$$ (3)

The percentage of k_0 falling into the set of neutral neighbors $\{k_1, k_2, ..., k_m\}$ is drawn in Fig.2.

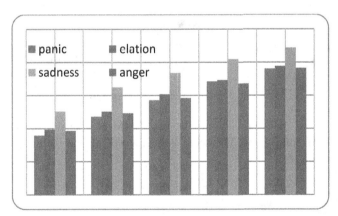

Fig. 2. Percentage of the 1-nearest neighbor of emotional GMM component falling into the m-nearest neighbors of neutral GMM component

The closest emotional GMM component can almost be covered when m reaches 5. Based on these phenomena, we can conclude that although the acoustic space under emotional state will shift from neutral state, the neighbors of neutral and emotion

GMM component are similar. If we can obtain the neutral-emotional model with the same phonetic order in the development data, we can construct a speaker's emotional model in the evaluation corpus.

3   Description of the Algorithm

The framework of our system is shown in Fig. 3. Firstly, on the development data, neutral and emotional model with corresponding GMM components are built. All these pairs compose the translators. The bridge between the neutral component and emotional component is the transform rule. Secondly, when a speaker comes, his/her neutral model is trained from his neutral utterances. Among all neutral components in the translators, we select k neighbors of each GMM component. By utilizing the k bridges, we can construct his/her emotional model. Finally the score is computed on the new emotional model.

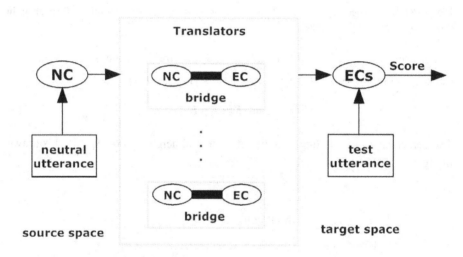

Fig. 3. Framework of our algorithm

In Fig. 3, NC is the abbreviation of neutral GMM component, and EC is that of emotional GMM component. The score is average of all the likelihood score, just shown in equation (4).

$$Score = \frac{\sum_{t}\sum_{j}\min(p(x_t, E(k_x, j)))}{T} \tag{4}$$

$x_t (t = 1, 2, \cdots, T)$ is the feature of the total utterance. $x = 1, 2, ..., m$ represents the neighbor index.

4   Experiment

Mandarin Affective Speech Corpus (MASC) [9], an emotional speech database, is used in our experiments. The corpus contains recordings of 68 Chinese speakers (23 female and 45 male). All speeches are expressed under five emotional states: neutral, anger, elation, sadness and panic. 20 sentences are spoken for three times under each emotional state, and 2 extra paragraphs for neutral. Each sentence is short and the length is between 5s and 10s. Each paragraph is longer relatively, with lasting about 40s length. All speeches are recorded with the same microphone. Only the male's data are used in our experiments. These sentences cover most of the phonemes in mandarin speech. The first 20 speakers' data are used as the developing data, and the other 25 speakers are used as evaluation data. Among them, the 2 paragraphs are used to train neutral model, and the sentences are used to test.

All the features mentioned in our experiments are 13-order MFCC with 32ms window length and 16ms frame rate. We applied voicebox[10] to extract features.

For training UBM, all data in the development set is applied, and the total length is about 2 hours. A single GMM with 1024 mixtures is trained using the Expectation-Maximization (EM) algorithm. All speaker models are trained by Bayesian adaptation from the UBM with the speaker's 2 neutral paragraphs.We apply netlab[11] to train UBM-GMM system.

The Identification Rate(IR) result of our method is shown in Table 1.

Table 1. Baseline Reslut

	IR(%)
neutral	96.47
Anger	34.87
sadness	60.80
elation	38.07
panic	36.60
average	53.36

In the experiment, we select k neighbors to verify the effectiveness of our system. The purpose of this experiment is to verify how k (number of neighbors) affects the performance of our algorithm. The IR of selecting different value of $k(k = 1, 2, \cdots, 6)$ is shown in Table 2.

In Table 2, the column means the value of m ranges from 1 to 5. The row means when selecting k neighbors, the IR of all test segments under each emotion.

It is observed that IR increases with the value of m until meeting a certain value. IR reaches the maximum at $m \leq 5$ for neutral, sadness and elation, and $m \geq 6$ for anger and elation. Total IR reaches the maximum at $m = 5$. This is coincide with the theory that at $k = 5$, most neighbors can be covered.

When our algorithm is applied, it is observed that the effects are profound, with an IR increase of 2.81% over the GMM-UBM system. And the improvement is more obvious under anger, elation and panic emotion state. These states are known as high-different emotion state mentioned in [2]. It means when the feature space changed dramatically, the effect of our algorithm is more profound.

Table 2. Result of our algorithm

	neutral	anger	sadness	elation	panic	Average
1	94.73	34.53	57.60	38.20	35.40	52.09
2	95.07	36.27	59.47	41.93	37.13	53.97
3	95.40	36.87	60.13	43.60	38.80	54.96
4	95.37	37.73	61.27	44.33	39.73	55.69
5	95.37	38.40	61.80	45.20	40.07	56.17
6	94.80	38.73	60.33	45.20	39.20	55.65

Compared to the method in [3], our method is much faster than NEGT, and it can be used to generate UBM-GMM model other than the simplified GMM model. Besides, the improvement of IR is more obvious.

Because of the data of female is scarce, the translators can't be built because it can't cover most speakers in female, thus many speakers' neighbors are missed. Thus, the experiment results of female are not reported here.

5   Conclusion

This paper proposes a novel method to build emotional model. Based on the translated learning, our method is proposed to build neutral-emotional translator as the hidden mapping function, then each neutral GMM component is mapped into emotional one. Only neutral speech is required to build speaker model and the emotional information of the test utterance isn't needed. This method brings a promising result with 2.81% increase of IR over the GMM-UBM system. The future work is to construct more precise rule such as risk minimization mentioned in [5] to make the transformed rule more robust.

References

1. Bao, H., Xu, M., Zheng, T.F.: Emotion Attribute Projection for Speaker Recognition on Emotional Speech. In: Interspeech, pp. 758–761 (2007)
2. Huang, T., Yang, Y.: Applying pitch-dependent difference detection and modification to emotional speaker recognition. In: Interspeech, pp. 2751-2754 (2008)
3. Shan, Z., Yang, Y.: Natural-Emotion GMM Transformation Algorithm for Emotional Speaker Recognition. In: Interspeech, pp.782-785 (2007)

4. Shan, Z., Yang, Y.: Learning Polynomial Function Based Neutral-Emotion GMM Transformation for Emotional Speaker Recognition. In: ICPR 2008, vol. 1(4), pp. 8–11 (December 2008)
5. Dai, W., Chen, Y., Xue, G., Yang, Q., Yu, Y.: Translated Learning: Transfer Learning across Different Feature Space. In: Proc. Of NIPS (2008)
6. Dai, W., Yang, Q., Xue, G.-R., Yu, Y.: Boosting for transfer learning. In: Proceedings of the 24th International Conference on Machine Learning, Corvalis, Oregon, June 20-24, pp. 193–200 (2007)
7. Reynolds, D.A., Rose, R.C.: Robust Text-Independent Speaker Identification Using Gaussian Mixture Speaker Models. IEEE Transactions on Speech and Audio Processing 3(1), 72–83 (1995)
8. Moreno, P., Ho, P., Vasconcelos, N.: A Kullback-Leibler Divergence Based Kernel for SVM Classification in Multimedia Applications. In: NIPS, Vancouver (December 2003)
9. Wu, T., Yang, Y., Wu, Z., Li, D.: MASC:A Speech Corpus in Mandarin for Emotion Analysis and Affective Speaker Recognition. In: ODYSSEY 2006, pp. 1–5 (June 2006)
10. http://www.ee.ic.ac.uk/hp/staff/dmb/voicebox/voicebox.html
11. http://www1.aston.ac.uk/ncrg/

Identification of People
at a Distance Using Effective Block List

Dongdong Nie[1] and Qinyong Ma[2,*]

[1] College of Science, Yanshan University, Qinhuangdao 066004, China
[2] College of Information Science and Engineering,
Yanshan University, Qinhuangdao 066004, China
{niedd,mqyray}@163.com

Abstract. Gait energy image is an efficient gait descriptor for human gait recognition, but gait information in gait energy image is redundant and susceptible to shape scaling and drifting. To solve the problem, effective block list is proposed to express gait more effectively in this paper. For each row in the steady part of gait energy image, two blocks with max variation are selected to construct an effective block list. The same subject's difference sequence of effective block lists generally has a lower mean value, so it is used to measure the similarity between two subjects. Experimental results show that, the proposed effective block list is more efficient than gait energy image, and has a good ability to derive more effective feature extraction and expression methods.

Keywords: biometrics, gait expression, gait recognition, gait energy image, effective block list.

1 Introduction

Gait recognition identifies individuals in image sequences by their walking styles. Human gait is a special biometric feature for human identification since gait is the only perceivable biometric for personal identification at a distance. For other biometrics such as fingerprints and face, valid data can't be obtained at a distance, while human gait can be distinguished obviously.

Gait recognition works have focused on analyzing video sequences of human walks directly. In a complete gait recognition processing, subjects are segmented from video sequences firstly, then features are extracted from the silhouette sequences, and subjects are classified based on the extracted gait features. The step of extracting effective gait features from quality-limited silhouettes is especially important in gait recognition, while some works utilize complex classification methods to improve recognition rates [1], [2].

Gait recognition techniques can be divided roughly into two categories: model-based [3], [4] and appearance-based approaches [5], [6]. Model-based approaches fit a

---

* Corresponding author.

Z. Sun et al. (Eds.): CCBR 2013, LNCS 8232, pp. 402–408, 2013.
© Springer International Publishing Switzerland 2013

model to the image data and then analyze the variation of its parameters, while appearance-based approaches extract statistical features from a subject's silhouette to distinguish different walkers.

For the gait recognition at a distance, gait model is hard to be established precisely, so many appearance-based approaches are proposed in this case. To overcome the noisy silhouettes resulted from complex outdoor background and relatively far distance, silhouettes over one gait cycle can be averaged such that each gait video is represented by gait energy images (GEIs): a set of gray-level average silhouette images [7]. GEI based approaches exhibited good adaptability to the noisy silhouettes, and achieve high recognition rates in the gait recognition at a distance [8], [9].

A point's intensity value in a GEI shows the estimated possibility of human body shows up at corresponding position. But the error introduced in the silhouette extracting stage may lead to drifted or scaled shape [10], [11]. GEI classification by direct template matching can't overcome the GEI variation. Scaled GEI [7] or special distance calculation method [2] can achieve better results with increased computational complexity. Besides, intensity values of the GEI inner foreground region are near 255, and intensity values of the background region are 0. Altogether, gait information in GEI is redundant and susceptible to shape scaling and drifting. To solve this problem, this paper proposes to use intensity distribution to extract effective block list (EBL) from GEI to represent gait subject.

Various classification techniques have been applied to gait recognition. Han et al. [7] utilized (Principal Component Analysis) PCA and Multiple Discriminant Analysis (MDA) to reduce the dimensions of GEI. Huang et al. [2] proposed an image-to-class distance for human gait recognition. Xu et al. [1] have recently proposed to classify gait objects by a kind of sparse representation. To facilitate the comparison with other algorithms, many gait recognition researches experiment with nearest neighbor classifier. This paper also adopts the nearest neighbor classifier in the experiments.

2   Effective Block List (EBL)

In this section, we give specific details about the proposed EBL.

Let GEI be denoted by $G(x, y)$. For each row in the steady part of a GEI, two points are selected to construct the EBL. Steady part means the row number is fixed to the range from forehead to knee approximately. The range is fixed based on the size of GEI. In the paper, the size of GEI is 128×88, so the row number is fixed to the range from 3 to 93. The coordinates of the two points in the i-th row of the GEI steady part are respectively defined as:

$$C_{i,1} = (i, j_1) \tag{1}$$

$$C_{i,2} = (i, j_2) \tag{2}$$

where j_1 and j_2 are respectively calculated as:

$$j_1 = \arg \max_{j \in [1, n/2]} \sum_{k=-w}^{w} (G(i, j+k) - \mu_{i,j})^2 \tag{3}$$

$$j_2 = \arg \max_{j \in [n/2+1,n]} \sum_{k=-w}^{w} (G(i, j+k) - \mu_{i,j})^2 \tag{4}$$

where w is the parameter of local range, n is the width of the GEI, $\mu_{i,j}$ is the mean intensity of a $w \times 1$ block centered at point (i, j).

Let the steady part height of GEI be represented by m, and a $w_1 \times w_1$ block centered at point (i, j) be represented by $R_{i,j}$, the EBL can be described by:

$$R = \left\{ R_{1,C_{1,1}}, R_{2,C_{2,1}}, ..., R_{i,C_{i,1}}, ..., R_{m,C_{m,1}}, R_{1,C_{1,2}}, R_{2,C_{2,2}}, ..., R_{i,C_{i,2}}, ..., R_{m,C_{m,2}} \right\} \tag{5}$$

Fig. 1(a) and Fig. 1(c) show two subjects' GEIs with EBL center points marked, corresponding EBLs are showed in figure 1(b) and figure 1(d) respectively. It can be seen from the figure that compared with GEI, EBL composed of the characteristic blocks greatly reducing the redundant data and refine the valid information.

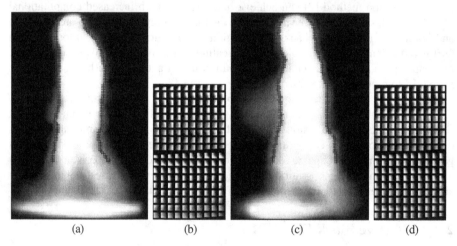

| (a) | (b) | (c) | (d) |

Fig. 1. Examples of GEI and EBL

Let the EBL of a probe GEI be denoted by $R^p = \left\{ R^p_{i,C_{i,h}} \mid i = 1, ..., m; h = 1, 2 \right\}$, the EBL of a gallery GEI be denoted by $R^g = \left\{ R^g_{i,C_{i,h}} \mid i = 1, ..., m; h = 1, 2 \right\}$. The intensity distance sequence is defines as:

$$R_D = \left\{ \left\| R^p_{i,C_{i,h}} - R^g_{i,C_{i,h}} \right\| \mid i = 1, ..., m; h = 1, 2 \right\} \tag{6}$$

Fig. 2(a) shows a filtered intensity distance sequence of two GEIs belong to a same subject, and Fig. 2(b) shows a filtered intensity distance sequence of two GEIs belong to different subjects. It can be seen from the figure that same subject's distance sequence has a lower mean value. The mean distance is used as the measuring standard to calculate the similarity between two GEIs.

Let the EBL's coordinates sequence of a probe GEI be denoted by $C^p = \left\{ C^p_{i,h} \mid i = 1, ..., m; h = 1, 2 \right\}$, and let the EBL's coordinates sequence of a gallery

GEI be denoted by $C^g = \{C^g_{i,h} \mid i = 1,...,m; h = 1,2\}$. The position distance sequence is defines as:

$$C_D = \{ \left| C^g_{i,h} - C^p_{i,h} \right| \mid i = 1,...,m; h = 1,2 \} \qquad (7)$$

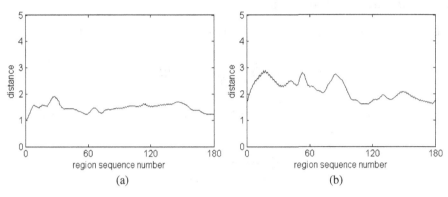

Fig. 2. Examples of intensity distance sequence

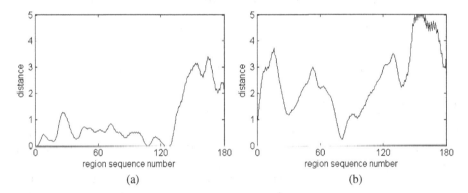

Fig. 3. Examples of position distance sequence

Instinctively, position distance is also a good measuring standard to calculate the similarity between two GEIs, so we verify the hypothesis in similar way. Fig. 3(a) shows a filtered position distance sequence of two GEIs belong to a same subject, and Fig. 3(b) shows a filtered position distance sequence of two GEIs belong to different subjects. Although same subject's distance sequence has a lower mean value, the two sequences show large variability. So we don't take position distance as the measuring standard to calculate the similarity between two GEIs.

The Gabor feature has been demonstrated to be an effective feature for face recognition and gait recognition [1], [6]. In order to validate the extension ability of EBL, Gabor feature is calculated in this paper. For each GEI, we use 40 Gabor kernel functions from five scales and eight orientations to filter the image, so each point in the GEI is represented by a 40 dimensional Gabor feature vector. For each block in the

EBL, we use corresponding Gabor features to represent each point in the block. Similar to EBL defined by Equation (5), the Gabor EBL is denoted as follows:

$$G = \left\{ G_{1,C_{1,1}}, G_{2,C_{2,1}}, ..., G_{i,C_{i,1}}, ..., G_{m,C_{m,1}}, G_{1,C_{1,2}}, G_{2,C_{2,2}}, ..., G_{i,C_{i,2}}, ..., G_{m,C_{m,2}} \right\} \tag{8}$$

3   Similarity Computation

The distance between a probe's EBL R^p and a gallery's EBL R^g is calculated as:

$$D(R^p, R^g) = \sum_{h=1}^{2} \sum_{i=1}^{m} \left\| R^p_{i,C_{i,h}} - R^g_{i,C_{i,h}} \right\| \tag{9}$$

Similarly, the distance between a probe's Gabor EBL G^p and a gallery's Gabor EBL G^g is calculated as:

$$D(G^p, G^g) = \sum_{d=1}^{40} \sum_{h=1}^{2} \sum_{i=1}^{m} \left\| G^p_{i,C_{i,h},d} - G^g_{i,C_{i,h},d} \right\| \tag{10}$$

where $G^p_{i,C_{i,h},d}$ and $G^g_{i,C_{i,h},d}$ are the block matrix compose of the d-th component of $G_{i,C_{i,h}}$ Gabor vectors of probe and gallery respectively.

To facilitate the comparison with relevant algorithms, we adopt the nearest neighbor classifier. Current subject is classified as the known subject with shortest distance to it.

4   Experimental Results

The proposed algorithm was implemented by Matlab R2011a, and evaluated using the USF HumanID outdoor gait database [12]. The USF gait database was collected with complex background at a relatively far distance. It consists of 1,870 sequences from 122 subjects. There are five covariates for each subject: change in viewpoints (Left or Right), change in walking surface (Grass or Concrete), change in shoe type (A or B), change in carrying condition (carrying a Briefcase or No Briefcase), and change in time (May or November) and clothing. Sarkar et al. [12] specify one gallery set containing the videos of all the 122 subjects and twelve probe sets (A-L) consisting of different numbers of subjects.

GEI was experimentally demonstrated by many works to be an effective and efficient gait descriptor for human gait recognition [1], [7], [8], [9]. The proposed EBL extract effective information from GEI. So GEI is experimentally compared with EBL firstly. We implement the GEI [7] with the silhouettes of all cycles in a gait sequence, and classify subjects (represented by GEI) using the nearest neighbor classifier. The results are listed in Table 1. In the table, rank n means the percentage of the correct subjects appearing in any of the first n places of the retrieved rank list. EBL is calculated with $w = w_1 = 6$, and the recognition rates with EBL as gait features using the same classifier are also listed in Table 1.

Table 1. Recognition rates of GEI and EBL

Probe	GEI		EBL	
	Rank 1	Rank 5	Rank 1	Rank 5
A	83	93	63	85
B	87	94	94	98
C	74	91	44	80
D	22	46	36	53
E	22	55	38	58
F	10	32	14	35
G	17	40	22	42
H	53	78	63	82
I	53	78	62	85
J	38	68	36	63
K	9	12	18	36
L	6	12	12	30
Mean	**41**	**62**	**43**	**64**

It can be seen from Table 1 that compared with GEI, the proposed EBL has a higher mean recognition rate. EBL is extracted from GEI to reduce redundant data and refine valid information. The results confirm the effectiveness of EBL.

As a gait representation method, EBL can be used as the basic of other feature extraction methods. In order to demonstrate the ability, Gabor features generated from EBL are used to classify subjects with Equation (10) with $w=w_1=5$, the recognition rates are listed in Table 2 as Gabor EBL. Table 2 also lists the recognition rates with Gabor features generated from GEI as gait features, the recognition rates are quoted from [1].

It can be seen from Table 2 that Gabor EBL has a higher mean recognition rate than Gabor GEI, it means EBL has a good ability to derive more effective feature extraction and expression method.

Table 2. Recognition rates of Gabor GEI and Gabor EBL

Probe	Gabor GEI [1]		Gabor EBL	
	Rank 1	Rank 5	Rank 1	Rank 5
A	87	95	85	95
B	85	94	94	96
C	74	91	67	87
D	26	55	34	60
E	33	47	38	57
F	14	31	15	45
G	19	38	18	45
H	81	93	88	97
I	69	91	87	98
J	62	81	58	83
K	3	24	15	39
L	6	24	9	36
Mean	**51**	**68**	**54**	**73**

5   Conclusion

This paper proposes EBL as a new gait expression method for human gait recognition. EBL is extracted from GEI to reduce redundant data and refine valid information. Besides, EBL can be used as the basic of other feature extraction methods.

Since EBL contains effective gait information, more EBL based algorithms can be developed to achieve higher recognition rates in the future.

Acknowledgement. The research is supported jointly by the Hebei Province Natural Sciences Foundation (Grant No. A2011203053), and the Qinhuangdao Research & Development Program of Science & Technology (Grant No. 2012021A044).

References

1. Xu, D., Huang, Y., Zeng, Z., et al.: Human Gait Recognition Using Patch Distribution Feature and Locality-Constrained Group Sparse Representation. IEEE Transactions on Image Processing 21(1), 316–326 (2012)
2. Huang, X., Xu, D., Cham, T.J.: Face and Human Gait Recognition Using Image-to-Class Distance. IEEE Transactions on Circuits and Systems for Video Technology 20(3), 431–438 (2010)
3. Gu, J., Ding, X., Wang, S., et al.: Action and Gait Recognition From Recovered 3D Human Joints. IEEE Transactions on Systems, Man, and Cybernetics 40(4), 1021–1033 (2010)
4. Sharma, S., Tiwari, R., Shukla, A., et al.: Identification of People Using Gait Biometrics. International Journal of Machine Learning and Computing 1(4), 409–415 (2011)
5. Wang, C., Zhang, J., Wang, L., et al.: Human Identification Using Temporal Information Preserving Gait Template. IEEE Transactions on Pattern Analysis and Machine Intelligence 34(11), 2164–2176 (2012)
6. Hu, H.: Enhanced Gabor Feature Based Classification Using a Regularized Locally Tensor Discriminant Model. IEEE Transactions on Circuits and Systems for Video Technology 23(7), 1274–1286 (2013)
7. Han, J., Bhanu, B.: Individual Recognition Using Gait Energy Image. IEEE Transactions on Pattern Analysis and Machine Intelligence 28(2), 316–322 (2006)
8. Hong, S., Lee, H., Kim, E.: Probabilistic gait modelling and recognition. IET Computer Vision 7(1), 56–70 (2013)
9. Kusakunniran, W., Wu, Q., Zhang, J., et al.: Gait Recognition Under Various Viewing Angles Based on Correlated Motion Regression. IEEE Transactions on Circuits and Systems for Video Technology 22(6), 966–980 (2012)
10. Kim, D., Kim, D., Paik, J.: Gait Recognition Using Active Shape Model and Motion Prediction. IET Computer Vision 4(1), 25–36 (2010)
11. Huang, X., Boulgouris, N.V.: Gait Recognition with Shifted Energy Image and Structural Feature Extraction. IEEE Transactions on Image Processing 21(4), 2256–2268 (2012)
12. Sarkar, S., Phillips, P.J., Liu, Z., et al.: The humanID gait challenge problem: data sets, performance, and analysis. IEEE Transactions on Pattern Analysis and Machine Intelligence 27(2), 162–177 (2005)

A Study of the Consistency in Keystroke Dynamics

Chao Shen[1], Roy A. Maxion[2], and Zhongmin Cai[1]

[1] MOE KLINNS Lab, Xi'an Jiaotong University, Xi'an, Shaanxi, China
[2] Computer Science Department, Carnegie Mellon University, Pittsburgh, PA, USA
{cshen,zmcai}@sei.xjtu.edu.cn, maxion@cs.cmu.edu

Abstract. Keystroke dynamics is the process of identifying individual users on the basis of their distinctive typing rhythms. Most current approaches implicitly assume that individual typing behavior has high consistency as well as high discriminatory ability, both of which underpin the power of the technique. However, no earlier work has been done to quantify or measure the consistency of typing behavior. This study aims to investigate the consistency of users' typing behavior in keystroke dynamics. We obtain a keystroke benchmark dataset, propose a consistency measurement model, develop an evaluation methodology, and conduct three studies. We first quantify the consistency of users' behavior in repeatedly typing a password, observing that a typical user's typing behavior would become consistent over time, and changes in her typing would diminish. We then measure the consistency of keystroke timing features, finding that the combination of all features has the best consistency and smallest fluctuation. We finally examine the effect of consistency on keystroke-biometric systems, observing that the authentication performance gets better as the user's typing behavior becomes more consistent.

Keywords: Keystroke dynamics, Evaluation and benchmarking, Consistency.

1 Introduction

Keystroke dynamics is the analysis of individual typing behavior for use as a biometric identifier. Current research largely uses the timing latencies, which are extracted from typing behavior between key-down and key-up events, to discriminate legitimate users from impostors. Its prerequisite is the high discriminability and consistency of users' typing behavior.

It has been established that users' typing behavior is a form of perceptual-motor skill acquisition, and the gradual improvement of a repeated activity [1]. Most computer users have the experience of being required to use a new password or type a certain paragraph repeatedly. At the beginning, the typing behavior for the new text (either a password or a paragraph) appears to be clumsy, but by time it becomes easy and quick, and to the end it would become consistent and fluent [15].

In the field of keystroke biometrics, the typing behavior is used to discriminate users, so the influence of gradual skill acquisition may be an issue. However, most current approaches implicitly assume the timing latencies have high consistency as well

Z. Sun et al. (Eds.): CCBR 2013, LNCS 8232, pp. 409–416, 2013.
© Springer International Publishing Switzerland 2013

as high discriminatory power. Moreover, due to lack of consistency measure and benchmark dataset, no earlier studies have been done to investigate the consistency of users' typing behavior.

2   Background and Related Work

Keystroke dynamics is the procedure of measuring and assessing users' typing behavior. Since Forsen *et al.* [3] first investigated in 1977 whether the way of users typing their names could be used to distinguish a legitimate user from an impostor, several usages for keystroke dynamics have been proposed. There are really two usages of interest for this biometric: static analysis (e.g., verification at login time) and continuous analysis (e.g., verification throughout the use of a computer). Most static analysis approaches use fixed-text models [4], [5], [6], [7], [8], in which they use the same static piece of text (e.g., password), to identify users. In these approaches, the length of the required text varies between different studies, and usually the use of a long text [5], [6] could lead to a better performance. Recent work has explored free-text models for continuous verification [9], [10], in which users' keystroke activities are monitored and analyzed during their routine computing activities, and have shown good potential if observing sufficient period of data.

In terms of consistency considerations, there are only few efforts of implicitly exploring consistency in keystroke dynamics, by investigating the effect of enrollment sample size on detection results or the use of updating strategies for performance improvement. Bartmann *et al.* [13] examined the authentication results at different amount of enrollment data, and they observed that the results get better with more amounts of enrolment data. Kang *et al.* [14] showed that the authentication results get improved when they continually retrain the classifier with recent typing data.

3   Problem and Approach

In this work, our goal is to investigate the consistency of users' typing behavior in keystroke dynamics, in part to assess the effect of the consistency on keystroke-biometric systems. To achieve this goal, we obtain a benchmark dataset, propose a consistency measurement model, develop evaluation methodology, and conduct three studies. Specifically, we lay out a set of three questions to guide our investigation:

1. How is the consistency of a user's behavior in typing a password?
2. How is the consistency of the keystroke timing features?
3. Does the consistency affect the accuracy of keystroke-biometric system?

Each question concerns a different facet of the consistency of users' typing behavior in keystroke dynamics. We conduct three studies to answer these questions. In Sections 4–6, we describe the three studies in more detail.

4 Study1: Consistency and Tying a Password

In this study, we measure and quantify the consistency of a user's behavior and its change in repeatedly typing a password. The purpose of Study 1 is to answer the question: *how is the consistency of a user's behavior in typing a password?*

4.1 Study 1: Method

4.1.1 Collecting Data

We used an existing dataset that has been published and shared in our previous study [12]. The data were obtained when 51 users typed the same 10-character password 400 times each. The 400 passwords were typed in 8 sessions of 50 passwords each, with the sessions all occurring on different days. The password was **.tie5Roanl**.

The reasons for the dataset enabling our study of the consistency of keystroke dynamics are that (a) the data set is generated by 51 users, (b) the password is novel, and (c) it is typed many times by each user.

4.1.2 Extracting Features

We extracted keystroke timing features from key-down and key-up events. Usually three types of features are used: (1) the latency between keydown events in a digram (keydown-keydown time); (2) the latency between keyup and keydown events in a digram (keyup-keydown time), and (3) the length of time that a key is pressed (hold time). For each repetition of the password, we extracted 31 timing features: 10 keydown-keydown times, 10 keyup-keydown times, and 11 hold times.

4.1.3 Proposing a Consistency Measurement Model

We developed a simple and effective consistency measure, based on Gini Mean Difference (GMD) [2]. Since direct use of timing features could not accurately reflect the overall picture of a user's typing behavior, here we employed distance-based metric to compute the consistency. We used cosine distance to calculate the distance between each feature sample and a reference sample, and then used this distance to represent the feature sample. We chose cosine distance instead of commonly used Euclidean distance due to its generalized applicability of measuring the similarity of two samples with result between 0 and 1. We next calculated the mean of the absolute difference between all possible pairs of the distances as the consistency measurement. We defined the consistency measurement of the typing behavior for user k as:

$$GMD_{cons}(k) = \frac{1}{n(n-1)} \sum_{i=1}^{n} \sum_{j=1}^{n} |DM_i - DM_j|$$

where the DM_i is the distance measure associated with timing features, and n is the number of feature samples of that user. This measurement is a real value which is zero if the data are identical, and increases as the data become more diverse.

4.1.4   Measuring the Consistency

For a given user, we first computed the distance measurement between each of her feature samples and a reference sample. The procedure is as follow:

Step 1: Generate the reference sample using a one vector due to its simplicity.
Step 2: Compute the pairwise distance between each feature sample and the reference sample by using cosine distance.

Then given the distance metrics from a reference sample, we could easily obtain the consistency measurements across difference sessions. The procedure is as follow:
Step 1: Compute the consistency measurement of all distance samples in one session from a user by using the proposed consistency model.
Step 2: Repeat *Step 1* for all reaming sessions of that user.
Step 3: Repeat the above procedure and calculate the average consistency measurements for all 51 users in each of 8 sessions.

4.2   Study 1: Results

Figure 1 shows a plot of the average consistency measurements and the standard deviations of users' typing behavior in different sessions over all 51 users. The figure reveals that the consistency measurement improves greatly within first three sessions, but after the fourth session, only small fluctuations with error range are apparent. These results suggest a typical user would become consistent when repeatedly typing a password, and the changes in her typing diminish after a number of repetitions.

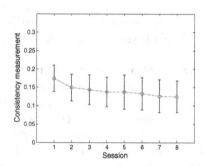

Fig. 1. Consistency measurement over different sessions. Error bars represent the standard deviation in the consistency measurements of all 51 users.

The above results show a user would provide better consistency on her typing with more repetitions in an average manner. But in many evaluations, an individual user may also provide poor consistency in her typing behavior. This poor consistency may have an effect on keystroke timing features, as will be explored in Study 2.

5   Study 2: Consistency and Keystroke Timing Features

When users' typing behavior becomes consistent, the keystroke timing features must change. Here we conduct a study to answer the question: *how is the consistency of the keystroke timing features?*

5.1   Study 2: Method

We generated all combinations of keystroke timing features, and used the consistency measurement model to evaluate the consistency of each feature combination.

5.1.1   Deriving Feature Combinations

Current researchers typically used three kinds of time interval as keystroke features: keydown-keydown time (KDD), keyup-keydown time (KUD), and hold time (KH). Here we derived seven combinations of the individual timing features. They are: (1) three individual keystroke features (KDD, KUD, and KH); (2) three two-component feature combination (KDD and KUD, KDD and KH, KUD and KH); (3) one three-component feature combination.

5.1.2   Measuring Consistency of Each Feature Combination

We employed the consistency measurement model to calculate the consistency on each of seven feature combinations in different data sessions. We first computed the consistency measurement of each feature combination in one session overall all users. Then we calculated the metric for all other sessions.

5.2   Study 2: Results

Figure 2 depicts the consistency measurements of different feature combinations over different data sessions.

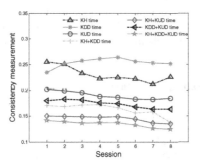

Fig. 2. Consistency measurements of seven feature combinations across different data sessions. This figure shows the change and comparison of consistency for three individual features, three two-component feature combinations, and one three-component feature combination.

   The results from Figure 2 show that nearly the consistency of all the feature combinations (with the exception of KDD feature) gets better when the users type more repetitions of the password. Specifically, the combination of all three individual features holds best consistency and smallest fluctuation. Moreover, we observe that the consistency of the KUD time and its change are much better and more stable than other two individual features. These results confirm the earlier logic [4], [5] that using multiple features would lead to better overall performance, and are consistent with the previous results [5] which showed the discriminability of each feature combination.

The above results show the consistency of keystroke timing features will improve with more repetitions. But if a biometric system is trained with inconsistent feature samples, it may lead to a poor performance. Thus the consistency may have an influence on the accuracy of keystroke-biometric systems, as will be explored in Study 3.

6   Study 3: Consistency and Biometric-System Accuracy

Having shown that the keystroke timing features get more consistent with more repetitions of password, it is natural to investigate whether the consistency manifests in the error rates of keystroke-biometric systems. The purpose of Study 3 is to answer the question: *does the consistency affect the accuracy of keystroke-biometric systems?*

6.1   Study 3: Method

We first develop a keystroke-authentication system. We then examine the authentication accuracy at different levels of consistency.

6.1.1   Keystroke-Authentication System

We implemented the keystroke-authentication system which was proposed by Araujo *et al.* [11]. The reason is that this approach had the top performance in a field of approaches evaluated in our previous work [12]. The system was divided into two phase: an enrollment phase and an authentication phase. In the enrollment phase, a training dataset composed by several repetitions of the password from a legitimate user is used to build a profile of the user. Then, the mean vector and mean absolute deviation of each feature are calculated. In the authentication phase, a test sample is presented to the system and compared with the profile. The system produces a classification score indicating whether the test sample is similar to the profile or different from the profile.

6.1.2   Training and Testing Procedure

We started by designating one of 51 users as the legitimate user, and the rest as impostors. We trained and tested the authentication system as follows:

Step 1: we run the enrollment phase of the system on the feature vectors from one session's password data (50 repetitions) typed by the legitimate user.

Step 2: we run the authentication phase of the system on the feature vectors from another session's password data (50 repetitions) typed by the legitimate user, to test its ability to classify the legitimate user.

Step 3: the evaluation procedures of above two steps (*Step 1* and *Step 2*) can be performed by any two of the eight sessions' data. To examine the effect of consistency on performance, we first used Session 1 as the training session and Session 2 as the testing session for the legitimate user. We then used Session 2 and session 3 as the training and testing sessions respectively. We continued in this way until Session 7 and Session 8 were used as the training and testing sessions for the legitimate user.

Step 4: we run the authentication phase of the system on the feature vectors from the first session's password data typed by each of the 50 impostors, to test its ability to classify the impostors.

This process was then repeated, designating each of the other users as the legitimate user in turn.

6.1.3   Calculating Authentication Performance

To convert the classification scores of legitimate users and impostors into aggregate measures of classifier performance, we computed false-acceptance rate (FAR) and false-rejection rate (FRR). We brought FAR and FRR together to generate an ROC curve, and we also set the threshold for the classification scores to make the FAR equal with FRR, for presenting the equal-error rate (EER).

6.2   Study 3: Results

Figure 3 show the ROC curves for different training and testing data sessions from legitimate user, which represents different levels of consistency.

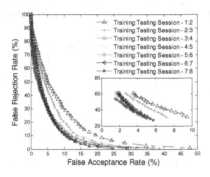

Fig. 3. ROC curves for different training and testing data sessions from legitimate user. The inside panel details the points of ROC curves at the left corner.

We can obtain that the EER of the evaluation, which uses the training and testing sessions of Session 1 and 2 from the legitimate user, is 14.27%, and the corresponding ROC curve is worse than other 6 evaluations. When using the training and testing sessions from the legitimate user with more repetitions (like Session 3 and 4), the EER reduces to 10.29% and the corresponding ROC curve obviously gets improved. Along with the results (obtained in Study 1 and Study 2) that users' typing behavior would become more consistent with more repetitions of the password, we could draw a conclusion that the authentication accuracy gets better as the user's typing becomes more consistent with more repetitions of the password.

7   Conclusion and Future Work

The goal of this work is to investigate the consistency of users' typing behavior in keystroke dynamics, in part to assess the effect of the consistency on keystroke-biometric systems. Experimental results show: (1) a typical user's typing behavior would become consistent over time and the changes in her typing would diminish; (2)

the use of all features has the best consistency and smallest fluctuation; (3) the authentication accuracy gets better as users' typing behavior becomes more consistent.

Acknowledgements. The research is supported by NFSC (61175039, 61221063), 863 High Tech Development Plan (2007AA01Z464, 2012AA011003), Research Fund for Doctoral Pro-gram of Higher Education of China (20090201120032), International Research Collaboration Project of Shaanxi Province (2013KW11) and Fundamental Research Funds for Central Universities (2012jdhz08). This work was also partially supported by the US National Science Foundation, grant number CNS-0716677.

References

1. Rosenbaum, D.A., Carlson, R.A., Gilmore, R.O.: Acquisition of Intellectual and Percep-tual-Motor Skills. Annual Review of Psychology 52, 453–470 (2001)
2. Yitzhaki, S.: Gini's Mean Difference: a Superior Measure of Variability for Non-Normal Distributions. METRON-Int'l J. Statistics 285–316 (2003)
3. Forsen, G., Nelson, M., Staron, R.: Personal Attributes Authentication Techniques., Tech. Report RADC-TR-77-1033, Griffis Air Force Base (1977)
4. Bergadano, F., Gunetti, D., Picardi, C.: Identity Verification through Dynamic Keystroke Analysis. Intell. Data Anal. 7(5), 469–496 (2003)
5. Bergadano, F., Gunetti, D., Picardi, C.: User Authentication through Keystroke Dynamics. ACM Trans. Inf. Syst. Secur. 5(4), 367–397 (2002)
6. Gaines, R., Lisowski, W., Press, S., Shapiro, N.: Authentication by Keystroke Timing: Some Preliminary Results (1980)
7. Joyce, R., Gupta, G.: Identity Authentication based on Keystroke Latencies. Commun. ACM 33(2), 168–176 (1990)
8. Monrose, F., Rubin, A.D.: Keystroke Dynamics as a Biometric for Authentication. Future Gener. Comput. Syst. 16(4), 351–359 (2000)
9. Dowland, P., Furnell, S.A.: A Long-term Trial of Keystroke Profiling using Digraph, Tri-graph, and Keyword Latencies. In: Deswarte, Y., Cuppens, F., Jajodia, S., Wang, L. (eds.) Security and Protection in Information Processing Systems. IFIP International Federation for Information Processing, vol. 147, pp. 275–289. Springer, Heidelberg (2004)
10. Gunetti, D., Picardi, C.: Keystroke Analysis of Free Text. ACM Trans. Inf. Syst. Se-cur. 8(3), 312–347 (2005)
11. Araujo, L.C.F., Sucupira, L.H.R., Lizarraga, M.G., Ling, L.L., Yabu-Uti, J.B.T.: User Au-thentication through Typing Biometrics Features. IEEE Trans. Signal Process. 53(2), 851–855 (2005)
12. Killourhy, K.S., Maxion, R.A.: Comparing Anomaly Detectors for Keystroke Dynamics. In: Proc. Annual Int'l Conf. Dependable Systems and Networks, pp. 125–134 (2009)
13. Bartmann, D., Bakdi, I., Achatz, M.: On the Design of an Authentication System Based on Keystroke Dynamics Using a Predefined Input Text. Int'l J. Infor. Secur. Priva. 1(2), 1–12 (2007)
14. Kang, P., Hwang, S.-s., Cho, S.: Continual Retraining of Keystroke Dynamics based Au-thenticator. In: Lee, S.-W., Li, S.Z. (eds.) ICB 2007. LNCS, vol. 4642, pp. 1203–1211. Springer, Heidelberg (2007)
15. Cialdini, R.B.: Influence: Science and practice. Needham Heights (2001)

A Large RGB-D Gait Dataset
and the Baseline Algorithm

Shiqi Yu[1], Qing Wang[1], and Yongzhen Huang[2]

[1] College of Computer Science and Software Engineering,
Shenzhen University, Shenzhen, 518060, China
[2] National Laboratory of Pattern Recognition, Institute of Automation,
Chinese Academy of Sciences, Beijing, 100190, China
shiqi.yu@szu.edu.cn, 1017963733@qq.com, yzhuang@nlpr.ia.ac.cn

Abstract. With the development of depth sensors, images with high quality depth can be obtained easily. Using depth information, some challenging problems in gait recognition can be reconsidered and better solutions can be developed. To prompt gait recognition with depth information, a large RGB-D gait dataset is introduced. It contains 99 subjects, with 8 sequences for each subjects in two different views. A baseline algorithm, namely Gait Energy Surface (GES), is proposed for researchers to evaluate their own algorithms. Even it is a baseline algorithm, encouraging experimental results have been achieved.

Keywords: Gait recognition, depth image, RGB-D dataset.

1 Introduction

Vision-based gait recognition is identifying an individual from videos by the manner in which he or she walks. Gait recognition has recently received an increasing interest from researchers because gait has many unique advantages. Gait has been considered as a suitable biometric and has great potential for human identification in visual surveillance. In recent years, many gait recognition methods have been developed [1–3]. But there are still many challenging problems in gait recognition. Such problems include robustness to the variations of view, illumination, clothing, carrying condition, shoes, etc. It is difficult to solve these problems using 2D color images.

Exciting depth sensors have been developed constantly in these years, such as TOF cameras [4] from MESA Imaging, Kinect [5] from Microsoft, Xtion PRO LIVE [6] from ASUS, Leap Motion Controller [7] from Leap Motion, etc. These kind of sensors can provide useful depth information of a scenery. Using the shape cue in depth images, we can develop better gait recognition algorithms which are robust to the variations mentioned above.

To develop gait recognition algorithms using depth images, a large dataset is needed. Some researchers have created some RGB-D datasets to explore the potential of depth images. The dataset used in [8] includes 15 subjects. There are 20 subjects in the experiments in [9] and [10]. The dataset described in [11]

Z. Sun et al. (Eds.): CCBR 2013, LNCS 8232, pp. 417–424, 2013.

is a little larger, which contains 30 subjects. To the best of our knowledge, the largest publicly available one is DGait Dataset [12] which contains videos from 53 subjects. The number of subject is still not enough for effective evaluation. A larger dataset as well as proper a baseline algorithm is needed for the development of gait recognition with depth information, which is the main task of this paper.

The organization of this paper is as follows. Section 2 describes the gait database. The baseline algorithm is presented in Section 3, and experimental results are shown in Section 4. Section 5 concludes this paper.

2   SZU RGB-D Gait Dataset

We created a large RGB-D gait dataset, namely SZU RGB-D Gait Dataset [1], using ASUS Xtion PRO LIVE [6]. ASUS Xtion PRO LIVE is a kind of Kinect-like sensor. It is lightweight without motor in it. So it can be powered by USB (do not need an AC adapter). We can capture color and depth images using OpenNI SDK [13].

The sensor is fixed to a tripod, about 80cm high from the ground. Subjects walk in the scene, and are demanded to walk in two directions. So gait data can be captured from two views. The first one is the side view (90 degrees), the second is about 30 degrees from the side view (60 degrees). For each view, there were 4 video sequences captured. Two sequences are right walking ones, and two are left walking. When subjects walk, synthesized color images (RGB image) and depth images are captured. The depth images have been calibrated, and pixels from the same position of a color image and the synthesized depth image represent the same object in the real world.

The dataset contains 99 subjects. Gait data from 99 subjects stored in 792 ($99 \times 4 \times 2views$) sequences. The color and depth image resolutions are all 640×480. Some image samples are shown in Fig. 1.

2.1   Depth to XYZ

The pixel values in depth images represent the distances (in Z direction) from the camera to the objects. The depth values are stored in two bytes (16 bits), measured with the unit of millimeter. The pixels in a depth image can be regarded as a point cloud. Many methods need the X, Y and Z values of the points, but depth images can only provide Z values. X and Y values can be recovered according to the relationship shown in Fig. 2.

The field of view (FOV) in X direction is show in Fig. 2. Suppose O is the camera. The view angle is α. P is the object in the real world. Line segment $\overline{LR}$ is on the image plane, and represents a horizontal line in a depth image. The length of $\overline{OZ}$ is equal to P's depth value. We can get point P's X value $\overline{ZP}$ as follows.

$$\overline{ZP} = \overline{OZ} \tan \theta \tag{1}$$

---

[1] The dataset will be publicly available at http://yushiqi.cn/dataset/.

Fig. 1. Image samples from SZU RGB-D Gait Dataset. The first row contains color images, and the second contains depth ones.

$$\tan\theta = \frac{\overline{CP_p}\tan(\alpha/2)}{\overline{CL}} \tag{2}$$

Suppose Z is the depth value at (X_p, Y_p) in a depth image. X_p and Y_p are measured with the unit of pixel. From the Xtion PRO LIVE specifications, it can be found that the horizontal and vertical view angles are $58°$ and $45°$ respectively. According to Equation (1)-(2), the absolute position X and Y can be obtain as:

$$X = Z\frac{(X_p - W/2) * \tan(29°)}{W/2} \tag{3}$$

$$Y = Z\frac{(Y_p - H/2) * \tan(22.5°)}{H/2} \tag{4}$$

3   Baseline Algorithm

The shape cue in depth images is the unique advantage compared with 2D images. In most gait recognition algorithms which use 2D images, the human body silhouettes are normalized to a fixed height. If a child has a similar body shape with an adult, it will be a little difficult to distinguish their silhouettes after normalization. If depth images are used, the body heights can be measured in millimeter, and a great difference can be found.

In the dataset, color images and the synthesized depth images are all captured. There are two baseline algorithms introduced in the following subsections. For

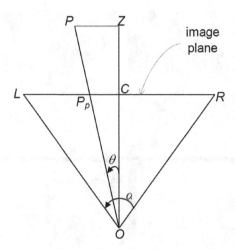

Fig. 2. The field of view (FOV) in X direction. O is the position of a camera. P is the real object. P_p is the position of point P in the image plane.

depth images, Gait Energy Surface (GES) is proposed. For color images, we use Gait Energy Image (GEI) proposed in [14].

3.1   Gait Energy Surface

In depth images, the depth of a human body is distinctly different from the depth of the background most of the time. So the human body can be relatively easy to be obtained using background substraction algorithms. The pixels on the body can be represented in an XYZ coordinate system using Equation (3) and (4). They can be regarded as a point cloud.

In our algorithm, the point cloud is put into a cuboid with 2000mm width, 2000mm height, 1000mm depth as shown in the right figure in Fig. 3. Because most people are not taller than 2000mm, all the points can be in the cuboid. The center of the gravity of the point cloud is placed on the center of the cuboid. The points in the cuboid is from the surface of a human body. The surface can be described by a mesh built from the point cloud.

The cuboid can be divided into many small cells. Suppose there are $N_x \times N_y \times N_z$ cells. Each cell is a small cuboid. When the surface crosses with a cell, the cell will be set to 1. Otherwise, it will be 0 as shown in the right figure in Fig. 3. We can use a 3D matrix with the size $N_x \times N_y \times N_z$ to represent the surface of a human body.

It is computationally high to estimate whether a surface crosses with a cell. However, since the body surface has been dense sampled, we can calculate if there are points in a cell. Our strategy is that only if there are points in a cell, the cell can be marked as 1. The complexity of this method is much lower than that of calculating if a surface crosses with a cell. With this strategy, the surface of a human body can be represented by a 3D 0-1 matrix, which is the raw

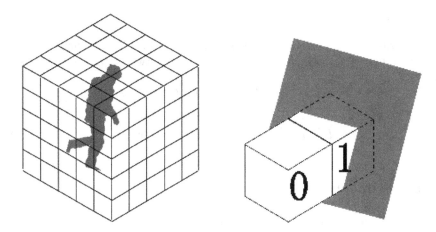

Fig. 3. The left figure shows that the human body surface is located in a cuboid. The cuboid is divided into a number of small cells. The two cells in the right figure are from the cuboid. If the surface crosses with a cell, the cell is marked to 1.

feature in our dataset. In [9], the representation is similar. But they "counting the number of points in each bin". If a subject is close to the depth camera, there will be many points in a bin/cell. So their representation is not robust to the distance between a subject to the camera.

In [8], Sivapalan *et al.* build a volume, not a surface, for a human body. Since depth cameras can only capture the surface data, we do not know the body shape cue behind the surface. So it is difficult to model the body with volumes.

Suppose V_i is extracted from the ith frame in a gait cycle. It is a 3D 0-1 matrix with a size $N_x \times N_y \times N_z$. The proposed gait energy surface is defined as follows:

$$GES(x, y, z) = \frac{1}{N} \sum_{i=1}^{N} V_i(x, y, z) \tag{5}$$

where $x \in \{1, 2, \cdots, N_x\}$, $y \in \{1, 2, \cdots, N_y\}$, $z \in \{1, 2, \cdots, N_z\}$, and N is the number of frames in a gait cycle.

3.2   Gait Energy Image

For gait recognition in color images, gait energy image proposed in [14] is considered to be the baseline algorithm. Gait energy image is defined as:

$$GEI(x, y) = \frac{1}{N} \sum_{i=1}^{N} B_i(x, y) \tag{6}$$

where $x \in \{1, 2, \cdots, N_x\}$, $y \in \{1, 2, \cdots, N_y\}$, B_i is the ith silhouette of a human body, and N is the number of frames in a gait cycle.

3.3 Classifier

Because what we proposed here is a baseline algorithm. Nearest neighbor classifier is employed for classification. The distance between two sequences is as follows:

$$D_{GES} = \sum_{x,y,z} |GES_1(x,y,z) - GES_2(x,y,z)| \tag{7}$$

$$D_{GEI} = \sum_{x,y} |GEI_1(x,y) - GEI_2(x,y)| \tag{8}$$

4 Experiments and Analysis

There are 99 subjects in SZU RGB-D Gait Dataset, and 8 sequences are captured from each subject. Four of them (Seq. No. 1-4) are captured in side view (90 degrees), and four (Seq. No. 5-8) are with 60 degrees. Four experiments shown in Table 1 are designed to evaluate an algorithm's performance. Exp. 1 and Exp. 3 are for evaluation without the change of views, and Exp. 2 and Exp 4 can be used to evaluate the robustness to the change of views.

Table 1. Four experiments designed for performance evaluation

	Exp. 1	Exp. 2	Exp. 3	Exp. 4
Gallery Set	Depth seq. #1-2	Depth seq. #1-2	Color seq. #1-2	Color seq. #1-2
Probe Set	Depth seq. #3-4	Depth seq. #5-8	Color seq. #3-4	Color seq. #5-8

In Exp. 1 and Exp. 3, GES from depth images and GEI from color images are employed respectively. For GES the matrix size is 100×100. That means the cell size in the cuboid is $20mm \times 20mm \times 20mm$. For GEI, all silhouettes in a gait cycle are normalized to 100×100. The curves of the cumulative match score are shown in Fig. 4. From the results, it can be found that both of them achieve high recognition rates. But GES achieves a higher recognition rate than GEI due to the contribution of the shape cue in depth images.

Exp. 2 and Exp. 4 evaluates the robustness to the change of views since the view angle of the probe set is different from that of the gallery set. The results are shown in Fig. 5. In this group of experiments, GEI outperforms GES. We thought that shape cue in depth images should be helpful to view changing. But in the baseline algorithm, view invariant features are not extracted. If the body surface is rotated to the same view, better performance should be obtain. How to extract view invariant feature is a valuable research topic in future.

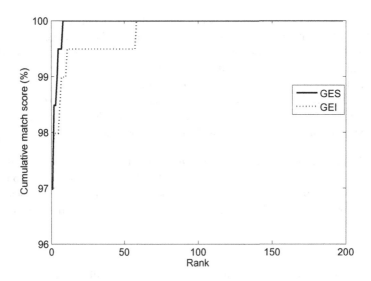

Fig. 4. The cumulative match score of Exp. 1 and Exp. 3. For Exp. 1, the GES method is used, and for Exp. 3, GEI is used

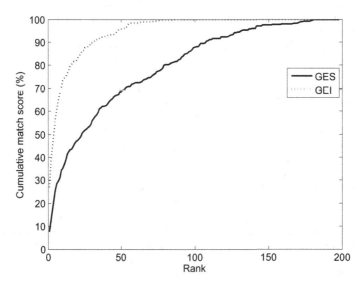

Fig. 5. The cumulative match score of Exp. 2 and Exp. 4. For Exp. 2, the GES method is used, and for Exp. 4, GEI is used

5 Conclusions

A large scale RGB-D gait dataset is described in the paper. It contains 99 subjects with 2 different views. To the best of our knowledge, it is the largest public RGB-D gait dataset. Besides, a baseline algorithm is also introduced. The dataset and the baseline algorithm can provide for researchers a platform to develop and evaluate their gait recognition algorithm.

For gait recognition using the proposed form of data, many interesting topics could be studied, such as human body matching in an XYZ space, view invariant feature extraction, human body modeling for recognition, etc.

Acknowledgments. This work is partly supported by the National Natural Science Foundation of China (Grant No. 61202158 and 61203252), Natural Science Foundation of SZU (Grant No. 201211), Tsinghua National Laboratory for Information Science and Technology Cross-discipline Foundation and Open Projects Program of NLPR, China.

References

1. Tao, D., Li, X., Wu, X., Maybank, S.J.: General tensor discriminant analysis and gabor features for gait recognition. IEEE Transactions on Pattern Analysis and Machine Intelligence 29(10), 1700–1715 (2007)
2. Wang, L., Ning, H., Tan, T., Hu, W.: Fusion of static and dynamic body biometrics for gait recognition. IEEE Transactions on Circuits and Systems for Video Technology 14(2), 149–158 (2004)
3. Wang, L., Tan, T., Ning, H., Hu, W.: Silhouette analysis-based gait recognition for human identification. IEEE Transactions on Pattern Analysis and Machine Intelligence 25(12), 1505–1518 (2003)
4. TOF cameras of MESA Imaging AG., http://www.mesa-imaging.ch
5. Microsoft Kinect for XBOX 360, http://www.xbox.com/en-US/kinect
6. ASUS Xtion PRO LIVE Sensor,
   http://www.asus.com/Multimedia/Xtion_PRO_LIVE/
7. Leap Motion Controller, https://www.leapmotion.com/
8. Sivapalan, S., Chen, D., Denman, S., Sridharan, S., Fookes, C.: Gait energy volumes and frontal gait recognition using depth images. In: Proceedings of the International Joint Conference on Biometrics, pp. 1–6 (2011)
9. Nambiar, A.M., Correia, P., Soares, L.D.: Frontal gait recognition combining 2d and 3d data. In: Proceedings of the on Multimedia and security, pp. 145–150 (2012)
10. Kumar, M.S.N., Babu, R.V.: Human gait recognition using depth camera: a covariance based approach. In: Proceedings of the Eighth Indian Conference on Computer Vision, Graphics and Image Processing, ICVGIP 2012, pp. 20:1–20:6 (2012)
11. Chattopadhyay, P., Roy, A., Sural, S., Mukhopadhyay, J.: Pose depth volume extraction from rgb-d streams for frontal gait recognition. Journal of Visual Communication and Image Representation (in press 2013)
12. Borràs, R., Lapedriza, À., Igual, L.: Depth information in human gait analysis: An experimental study on gender recognition. In: Campilho, A., Kamel, M. (eds.) ICIAR 2012, Part II. LNCS, vol. 7325, pp. 98–105. Springer, Heidelberg (2012)
13. OpenNI Web Site, http://www.openni.org/
14. Han, J., Bhanu, B.: Individual recognition using gait energy image. IEEE Transactions on Pattern Analysis and Machine Intelligence 28(2), 316–322 (2006)

Application of HMM to Online Signature Verification Based on Segment Differences

Jie Zou[1] and Zengfu Wang[1,2]

[1] Department of Automation, University of Science and Technology of China,
Hefei Anhui 230027, China
[2] Institute of Intelligent Machines, Chinese Academy of Sciences, Hefei Anhui 230031, China
qvbso@mail.ustc.edu.cn, zfwang@ustc.edu.cn

Abstract. In this paper, a novel application of Hidden Markov Model (HMM) to online signature verification is proposed, this application utilizes segment difference values obtained by segmentation Dynamic Time Warping (DTW) as observations of HMM. It combines the advantages of segmentation DTW which measures the features in local, and advantages of HMM which models the variability of observation sequences in global. Firstly, correspondences of the critical points in signatures are marked by segmentation DTW. Then, a variety of differences between corresponding segments are calculated by classical DTW. Finally, HMM is trained by utilizing these differences. In this paper, the practical meaning of the model states is clear and can be illustrated as degrees of similarity. Consequently, the HMM topology is set to ergodic. The validity of the proposed method was tested on the public SVC2004 signature database.

Keywords: Online Signature Verification, Segmentation Dynamic Time Warping, Hidden Markov Model (HMM).

1 Introduction

Signature verification is one of the oldest identity validation methods in the areas of financial transactions and document authentication. Compared with the traditional signature verification methods in which only static images of signature are utilized, online signature verification is more reliable. Because, in order to produce an imitation, an impostor has to reproduce more information than the visible signature, that is , the "gesture" of signing, which is invisible and, thus, more difficult to be imitated than the trajectory of the signature[1].

In the online signature verification field, broad and extensive researches have been done, and many novel methods have been proposed[2]. Among those existing methods, Dynamic Time Warping (DTW), which exploits dynamic programming techniques to measure the differences between signatures[3][4][5], and Hidden Markov Model (HMM), which adopts statistical methods to model the variability of discrete time-random signals, have attracted researcher's intensive attention[6][7][8].

Z. Sun et al. (Eds.): CCBR 2013, LNCS 8232, pp. 425–432, 2013.
© Springer International Publishing Switzerland 2013

There are two problems when HMM is applied to signature verification.1) Disturbances of noises in samples. The initial applications of HMM, in which sample point features are directly used to train the model, usually suffer from such noises that degrade the verification performance[6][9]. To soften the disturbances, some researchers proposed using the segment features to construct the model[10][11]. However, it is very difficult to split signatures consistently. 2) Determination of the number of states. Although the state is invisible, it has practical meaning in specific applications. For example, in character recognition, each state corresponds to a stroke[12].Therefore, the states number can be determined in advance by counting strokes number in the template. In signature verification studies, however, it is difficult to figure out the states number in advance without the templates.

DTW can be used to measure signals' differences based on the best point-to-point correspondences[3]. Over-warped problem usually occurs when the best correspondences are searched in global. Consequently, forgery signature undergoes too much warping so that it seems to be more "authentic"[13]. In order to overcome the shortcoming, segmentation DTW is proposed. The basic idea of the algorithm is to match the critical points in signatures and calculate the matched segments difference[13][14]. However, segmentation DTW may also mismatch critical points because of inconsistency and jerk of signing.

In this paper, we propose a new method of online signature verification that overcomes the above disadvantages of segmentation DTW and HMM. Firstly, segmentation DTW algorithm is employed to extract segment differences between signatures. Secondly, the observation sequences consisting of these segment differences are utilized to construct the HMM. The practical meaning of the state of the HMM is clear and can be illustrated as degree of similarity. Thus the number of states is determined according to the model fitness rather than the length of signatures. HMM topology is set to ergodic. According to the inherent nature of HMM, a small difference value generally corresponds to a high similarity state with high probability, but it's still possible for a small difference value to correspond to a low similarity state; and vice versa. So we can expect that mismatching effects produced by the segmentation DTW can be smoothed.

2   Segment Difference Extraction Based on Segmentation DTW

2.1   Signature Segmentation

Zou et al. extended the BBMDTW method to achieve consistent matches between template signature and different test signatures [14][15].The consistent correspondences between template signature and two testing signatures are presented in Fig.1. Each red "*" denotes a critical point, the number beside each "*" is the index of the critical point sequence. The critical points that have same index are matched.

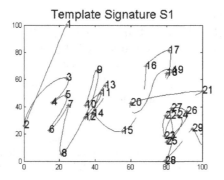

Template Signature S1

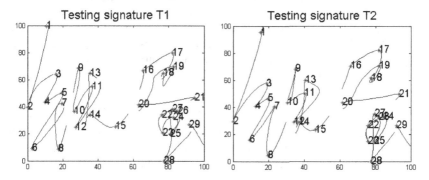

Testing signature T1   Testing signature T2

Fig. 1. Consistent correspondences between a template signature and two testing signatures

2.2   Calculation of Segment Difference Value and Feature Selection

The classical DTW are employed to calculate a variety of segment difference values(features) based on the consistent correspondences of critical points, including horizontal and vertical position trajectories, azimuth and altitude of the pen with respect to the tablet, pressure signal, and first/second order time derivative of them.

In our system, we used the above difference values as features. The inherent nature of difference value is that the smaller it is, the more similar two signatures are. Therefore, the principle of the mean and deviation minimization is employed to select out the discriminative features [15].

3   HMM Configuration

A continuous HMM was chosen to model differences between signatures. A complete HMM description can be found in the literature [16]. Formally, a description of a continuous HMM begins with hidden states $\mathbf{S} = \{S_1, \dots, S_H\}$, where H is the number of states. The state at discrete time n will be denoted as q_n.The state transition matrix is $\mathbf{A} = \{a_{ij}\}$, where $a_{ij} = P(q_{n+1} = S_j | q_n = S_i), 1 \leq i, j \leq H$ .The   observation symbol probability density function in state j is $b_j(\mathbf{O}), 1 \leq j \leq H$. The initial state distribution is $\boldsymbol{\pi} = \{\pi_i\}$, where $\pi_i = P(q_1 = S_i), 1 \leq j \leq H$.

In the proposed method, the observation symbol probabilities $b_j(\mathbf{O})$ are modeled as mixtures of M multivariate Gaussian densities, $b_j(\mathbf{O}) = \sum_{m=1}^{M} c_{jm} P(\mathbf{O}|\boldsymbol{\mu}_{jm}, \boldsymbol{\Sigma}_{jm}), 1 \leq j \leq H$, where $P(\mathbf{O}|\boldsymbol{\mu}_{jm}, \boldsymbol{\Sigma}_{jm})$ is a multivariate Gaussian distribution with mean $\boldsymbol{\mu}_{jm}$ and diagonal covariance matrix $\boldsymbol{\Sigma}_{jm}$, and the coefficients are restricted to $\sum_{m=1}^{M} c_{jm} = 1$. Thus the observation symbol density function can be parameterized as $\mathbf{B} = \{c_{jm}, \boldsymbol{\mu}_{jm}, \boldsymbol{\Sigma}_{jm}\}, 1 \leq j \leq H, \ 1 \leq m \leq M$. The symbol $\lambda = \{\boldsymbol{\pi}, \mathbf{A}, \mathbf{B}\}$ denotes the complete parameter set of the model.

To initialize $b_j(\mathbf{O}), 1 \leq j \leq H$, segment difference observations of training signatures $\mathbf{O} = \{\mathbf{O}_1, \dots \mathbf{O}_i, \dots, \mathbf{O}_N\}$ are clustered into H*M groups by using the k-means algorithm according to the maximum likelihood criterion, where $\mathbf{O}_i$ is difference observations of the ith testing signature compared with the reference signature, N is the number of testing signature, $1 \leq i \leq N$. Let $\boldsymbol{\mu}_{h,m}, \boldsymbol{\Sigma}_{h,m} 1 \leq h \leq H, 1 \leq m \leq M$ be the mean vector and covariance matrix of the h*mth group. The observation symbol probability density function in each state is initialized as the following steps.

1. Let $j = 1$, $F = \{\sum_i^k f_{h,m}(i) \mid 1 \leq h \leq H, 1 \leq m \leq M\}$, where $f_{h,m}(i) = \mu_{h,m}(i) + \Sigma_{h,m}(i,i)$, K is the number of selected features, $S = \{S_1, \dots, S_H\}$.
2. $\boldsymbol{\mu}_{h,m}$ and $\boldsymbol{\Sigma}_{h,m}$ which have the minimal $\sum_i^k f_{h,m}(i)$ inF are set to the mean vector and covariance matrix of the $b_j(\mathbf{O})$ in the state S_j which has the top degree of similarity in S.
3. Remove the minimal $\sum_i^k f_{h,m}(i)$ from F and S_j from S. Let $j = j + 1$.
4. If $j > H$, end; else jump to step 2.

The coefficient $c_{jm}, 1 \leq m \leq M$ are randomly selected and are restricted to $\sum_{m=1}^{M} c_{jm} = 1, 1 \leq j \leq H$.

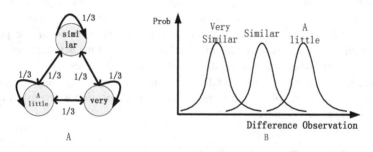

Fig. 2. (A) Topology of the HMM with three states. (B) Difference observation distribution in each state.

According to the practical meaning of states, the HMM topology is set to ergodic. Fig.2 A shows an example of ergodic topology of HMM where the states number is 3. Distributions of difference observation $b_j(\mathbf{O})$ in each state are illustrated in Fig.2B. The state transition matrix is initially set up to $a_{ij} = 1/H, 1 \leq i, j \leq H$. The initial state distribution $\boldsymbol{\pi} = \{\pi_1, \dots, \pi_H\}$ is set up as $\{1/H, \dots, 1/H\}$.

The Baum-Welch algorithm is employed to train HMM [16]. To prevent the covariance from becoming too small, we set a stopping threshold as 10^{-4}. The similarity score of an input segment difference observation $\mathbf{O}$ emitted from HMM$\lambda = \{\pi, \mathbf{A}, \mathbf{B}\}$ is calculated as $(1/K)\log P(\mathbf{O}|\lambda)$ by using the forward and backward algorithm [16], where K is the length of observation sequence.

4   Experiments

4.1   Experimental Protocol

In our experiment, we used task 2 of SVC2004 to test the validity of the proposed method[17]. The corpus consists of 40 sets. Each set contains 20 genuine signatures that were written by one signer in two sessions. Time span between two sessions was at least one week. In each session10 genuine signatures were written. And another 20 skilled forgery signatures for the signer were provided by at least four other signers.

Five signatures randomly selected from the first session compose training set for train HMM. The 10 genuine signatures in second session and 20 skilled forgery signatures   compose testing set. So we get training set $\mathbf{S} = \{s_1, s_2, \dots, s_M\}$ and testing set $\mathbf{T} = \{t_1, t_2, \dots, t_N\}$, where M and N is the number of signatures in set S and T respectively.

Since the difference is relative, each $s_i \in S, 1 \leq i \leq M$ is chosen as template signature alternately. Segment difference observations $\mathbf{O}_i^s = \{\mathbf{O}_{i1}^s, \dots \mathbf{O}_{i1-1}^s, \mathbf{O}_{i1+1}^s, \dots, \mathbf{O}_{iM}^s\}$ between s_i and $s_j \in S, 1 \leq i, j \leq M$ and $i \neq j$ are used to train HMM $\lambda_i = \{\pi_i, \mathbf{A}_i, \mathbf{B}_i\}$ $1 \leq i \leq M$ which uses s_i as template. In the process of training, the feature extraction and selection method described in Section2 are used to construct the segment difference observations. The similarity score $S(\mathbf{O}_{ij}^s)$ between training signature s_j and s_i emitted from λ_i is calculated as $(1/K_i)\log P(\mathbf{O}_{ij}^s|\lambda_i)$ by using the forward and backward algorithm, where K_i is the number of segment in signature s_i, $\mathbf{O}_{ij}^s \in \mathbf{O}_i^s$ .Let μ_i^s and σ_i^s be the mean and deviation of $\{S(\mathbf{O}_{i1}^s), \dots S(\mathbf{O}_{ii-1}^s), S(\mathbf{O}_{ii+1}^s), \dots, S(\mathbf{O}_{iM}^s)\}$, which will be used to normalize the similarity score of testing signature emitted from λ_i.

Let $\mathbf{O}_j^T = \{\mathbf{O}_{j1}^t, \dots, \mathbf{O}_{jM}^t\}$ be the segment difference observation between testing signature $t_j \in T, 1 \leq j \leq N$ and template signature $s_i \in S, 1 \leq i \leq M$. Let $S(\mathbf{O}_{ji}^t) = (1/K_i)\log P(\mathbf{O}_{ji}^t|\lambda_i)$ be the similarity score between testing signature t_j and template signature s_i emitted from λ_i.The equation $S'(\mathbf{O}_{ji}^t) = (S(\mathbf{O}_{ji}^t) - \mu_i^s)/\sigma_i^s$ is applied to normalize $S(\mathbf{O}_{ji}^t)$. Let $sim(t_j) = \sum_{i=1}^M S'(\mathbf{O}_{ji}^t), 1 \leq j \leq N$ be the similarity score between testing signature t_j and training set S. Based on $sim(t_j)$ $1 \leq j \leq N$, false rejection rates (FRR) and false acceptance rates (FAR) are computed for a specific threshold values. Then we calculated the equal error rates (EER).

The above whole procedure was repeated 20 times. The average EER is considered as a holistic performance of the system on one signer.

4.2   Experiment Setup

In this section, we evaluated the effects of the proposed method on the verification performance with different number of Gaussian mixtures per state and different number of states.

Comparison of the Number of Gaussian Mixtures. The number of HMM states were fixed as three. Then we changed the number of Gaussian mixtures from one to seven. The experiment results are presented in Fig.3.

It can be observed from Fig.3 that best average EER over 40 sets is achieved when the number of Gaussian mixture is 1, and average EER increases as the number of Gaussian mixture increases. Explanation of the degraded performance is the data scarcity. As the number of Gaussian mixture increases, the number of parameters needed to be estimated increases too. Consequently, the training for HMM become inadequate.

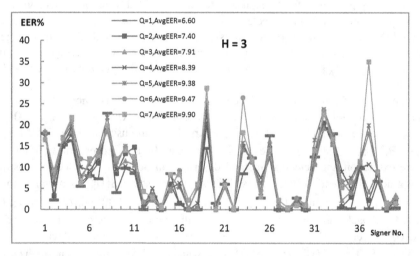

Fig. 3. Results of experiment A. H denotes the number of HMM states, Q denotes the number of Gaussian mixture, AvgEER is average EER over 40 signature sets.

Comparison of the Number of States. Based on the results from the experiment A, the initial configuration for the experiment B is as follows. We fixed the number of Gaussian mixture per states to one and changed the number of states from two to seven. The experiment results are presented in Fig.4.

We can see from Fig.4 that the best average EER over 40 sets is achieved when the number of states is 2, and the average EER increases as the number of states increases. For the signature sets which have high writing consistency, for example 16th, 40th signature sets, the verification results are always good whatever the number of states is. But for the signature sets which have low writing consistency, for example 8th, 33th signature sets, the verification results are bad and usually average EER increases as the number of states increases. As the practical meaning of state corresponds to degree of similarity, increasing the number of states will enhance the capability of the model, meanwhile, make the model more sensitive to the variation in writing. When the number of data is scare and writing consistency is low, average EER usually increases as the number of states increases.

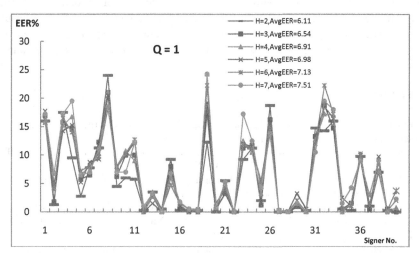

Fig. 4. Results of experiment B, H denotes the number of HMM states, Q denotes the number of Gaussian mixture, AvgEER is average EER over 40 signature sets

Comparison with the Competition Results. In Table 1, we present the best average EER achieved by our method and the best two average EERs results in the first international signature verification competition. According to experiments results presented in Table 1, we conclude that the proposed method using segment difference as observation of HMM in on-line signature verification outperform the contrast methods and thus the effectiveness of our method is verified.

Table 1. EERs of our method and the best two results in the competition for the task 2 of SVC2004 dataset

EER(%)	Average	Standard deviation	Maximum
The proposed method	6.11	6.58	24
HMM proposed by Fierrez [6]	6.90	9.45	50
DTW proposed by Kholmatov[5]	6.96	11.76	65

5   Conclusions

In this paper, a novel method which utilizes segment difference as observations of HMM was presented. The method combined the advantages of segmentation DTW and HMM:1)By exploiting the HMM to model on-line signing process, signatures are considered as random but not deterministic sequences,2)By exploiting segment features to train HMM, the effects of noise are smoothened. Our verification performance results on SVC2004 database in task 2 are 6.11% for skilled forgeries.

In experiments, we observed that for the signature sets which have bad verification results, their consistency of signing is usually not high, and corresponding difference scores are big; conversely, for the signature sets which have good verification results, their consistency of signing is usually high, corresponding difference scores are small. Thus, the difference scores can be used as mean of stability evaluation for signature.

References

1. Plamondon, R., Lorette, G.: Automatic signature verification and writer identification - the state of the art. Pattern Recogn. Lett 22(2), 107–131 (1989)
2. Impedovo, D., Pirlo, G.: Automatic Signature Verification: The State of the Art. IEEE Trans. on Sys. Man. Cybernet- Pt C. 38(5), 609–635 (2008)
3. Sakoe, H.: Dynamic Programming Optimisation for Spoken Word Recognition. IEEE Trans. on Acoustics, Speech and Signal Processing, 43–49 (1978)
4. Chang, W.D., Shin, J.: Modified Dynamic Time Warping for Stroke-based On-line Signature Verification. In: Proceedings of the Ninth International Conference on Document Analysis and Recognition, vol. 02, pp. 724–728 (2007)
5. Kholmatov, A., Yanikoglu, B.: Identity authentication using improved online signature verification method. Pattern Recog. Lett. 26(2005), 2400–2408 (2005)
6. Fierrez, J., Ortega-Garcia, J., Ramos, D.: HMM-based on-line signature verification: Feature extraction and signature modeling. Pattern Recog. Lett. 2325-2334 (2007)
7. Igarza, J.J., Goirizelaia, I., Espinosam, K.: Online handwritten signature verification using Hidden Markov Models. Progress in PRSIA, 391–399 (2003)
8. Van, B.L., Garcia-Salicetti, S., Dorizzi, B.: On Using the Veterbi Path Along with HMM Likelihood Information for Onling Signature Verification. IEEE Trans. on Sys. Man. and Cybernetics-PART B 38(5), 1237–1247 (2007)
9. Yang, L., Widjaja, B.K., Prasad, R.: Application of Hidden Markov Models for Signature Verification. Pattern Recog. 28(2), 161–170 (1995)
10. Dolfing, J.G.A., Aarts, E.H.L.: Online Signature Verification with Hidden Markov Models. In: Proc. Internat. Conf. on Pattern Recog., pp. 1309–1312 (1998)
11. Shafiei, A.: New On-line Signature Verification Algorithm Using Variable Length Segmentation and HMM. In: Proc. of Conf. on Docu. Anal. and Recog. (2003)
12. Hu, J., Brown, M.K.: HMM Based Online Handwriting Recognition. IEEE Tran. on Pattern Analysis and Machine Intelligence 18(10), 1039–1045 (2002)
13. Feng, H., Wah, C.C.: Online Signature Verification Using a New Extreme Points Warping Technique. Pattern Recog. Lett. 24(16), 2943–2951 (2003)
14. Li, B.: Improved Critical Point Correspondence for On-line Signature Verification. International Journal of Information Technology 12(7), 45–56 (2006)
15. Zou, J., Wu, Z.C.: Online Signature Verification System Based on Support Vector Data Description. Pattern Recog. and Artificial Intelligence 24(2), 284–290 (2011)
16. Rabiner, L.R.: A Tutorial on Hidden Markov Models and Selected Applications in Speech Recognition. Proceedings of the IEEE 77(2), 257–286 (1989)
17. Yeung, D.-Y., Chang, H., Xiong, Y., George, S.E., Kashi, R.S., Matsumoto, T., Rigoll, G.: SVC 2004: First International Signature Verification Competition. In: Zhang, D., Jain, A.K. (eds.) ICBA 2004. LNCS, vol. 3072, pp. 16–22. Springer, Heidelberg (2004)

Multimodal Biometrics Recognition Based on Image Latent Semantic Analysis and Extreme Learning Machine

Jucheng Yang[1], Yanbin Jiao[2], Chao Wang[1], Chao Wu[1], and Yarui Chen[1]

[1] College of Computer Science and Information Engineering,
Tianjin University of Science and Technology, Tianjin, China
jcyang@tust.edu.cn
[2] Hubei Province Toacco Corporation (Xianning Branch), Xianning, China
jiaoyanibincool@gmail.com

Abstract. Multimodal biometrics recognition system suffers from the shortcomings of large data processing and much time cost during the recognition. To overcome the shortcomings of the traditional methods, in this paper, a novel multimodal biometrics recognition method is proposed by using image latent semantic analysis and extreme learning machine method. The image latent semantic analysis for multimodal biometrics feature extraction will extract abandon information from the images and the extreme learning machine method has the merits of high accuracy and fast speed. With this new method, the latent semantic features from the multimodal biometrics images are digged out to improve the recognition accuracy. Finally, the extreme learning machine is used as the classifier. The experiments show that the proposed algorithm has get better performances both in recognition accuracy and speed.

Keywords: Multimodal bimetrics, Image Latent Semantic Analysis, Extreme Learning Machine.

1 Introduction

Reliable and practical security identity authentication system has a great market. However, the traditional identity authentication system based on password or ID card has a lot of defects. In recent years, biometric authentication has been improved in reliability and accuracy [1]. There are many biological characteristics that meet the conditions and have been studied for biometrics recognition. The examples of biometrics include human face, fingerprints, iris, plamprint, vein, voice, gait, signature, retinal pattern and DNA. However, all kinds of biometric features have the shortcomings and limitations due to their characteristics of themselves. There is no single biometric authentication system can satisfy all the identification applications. Because of the complexity of the building actual system and application, each single biometrics system is suffered the following problems in different reasons [2].

However, multimodal biometrics technology takes full advantage of the diversity and complementarily between multi-biological characteristics of human body. It will

Z. Sun et al. (Eds.): CCBR 2013, LNCS 8232, pp. 433–440, 2013.

improve the performance of system from the noise immunity, universality, reliability, security and so on [3]. There are sizeable amounts of literature proposed different approaches for multimodal biometric systems [4][5]. Usually, multi-biometrics data can be combined at different levels: fusion at the data-sensor level, fusion at the feature level, fusion at the matching level, and fusion at the decision level. Among them, fusion at matching score, rank and decision levels has their shortcomings [6]. However, comparing with these kinds of fusion levels, fusion at the feature level can obtain the most of information. It will achieve a better accuracy if it has a better fusion in the feature level.

Ross and Govindarajan [7] proposed a method for fusing hand and face at the feature level. Singh et. al. [8] proposed a method for the infrared and visible face recognition fusion. Zhou and Bhanu [9] proposed to fuse face and gait at a distance in video. Rattani et. al. [1] proposed to fuse the face and fingerprint. These algorithms achieved good performances. However, it is hard to solve the problem if the feature set of multimodal modalities is incompatible and with high dimensional data. So, it is essential to build a fast and efficient multimodal biometrics system. In this paper, a new algorithm is proposed for multimodal biometric recognition based on image latent semantic analysis and extreme learning machine. The concept of latent semantic analysis proposed by Deerwester [10] was in order to dig out the latent relationship mapping between terms and the documents. Inspired by this traditional latent semantic analysis, many scholars took this method widely used in the scene classification and target discovery.

In this paper, the algorithm of Latent Semantic Analysis (LSA) is introduced into the multi-biometric in order to dig out the latent semantic features among the several multimodal biometrics. Moreover, in recently years, Huang [11] proposed a new learning algorithm, namely Extreme Learning Machine (ELM) which based on a single-hidden layer feed-forward neural network (SLFN). It was proven that it is able to quickly solve the classification and regression problems. And ELM for face classification usually achieves better generalization performance and much less time costs[12]. So here, the ELM method is applied to multimodal biometric system in order to improve the speed and so as to achieve a real-time application. The experimental results show that the proposed method has better performances both in recognition accuracy and speed.

The rest of the paper is organized as follows. Section 2 introduces some related theories on LSA and ELM. Section 3 explains the proposed method in details. Section 4 shows the experimental results. Finally, conclusions are drawn in Section 5.

2   Theory

2.1   Image Latent Semantic Analysis (LSA)

LSA initially is used for text classification to dig out the latent relationship between the terms and documents. It uses Singular Value Decomposition (SVD) to decompose the Terms-Document matrix to establish the relative model between terms and documents [10]. Through SVD, the approximate terms-document matrix with rank R is built, and it may reduce the "noise" which exists in the original term-document matrix. And it will highlight the semantic structures between the term-document.

In recent years, the method of LSA applied on image analysis has attracted great attentions of scholars [13]. Inspired by natural language processing in bag of visual words, researchers explore to methods of representation of the document to represent the image visual information. Csurka et. al. [14] regard the local image features as the bag of visual words. Therefore, it is feasible to analyze and understand the image with the mature technique of the text analysis and retrieval.

The algorithm of the image LSA (ILSA) extraction is summarized as below: First, the image is divided into regular sub-block or rectangle region. Then, one or more type features extracted from each image piece to form the visual vocabulary, and to build the semantic concept modeling by using the bag of visual words and the model of visual language [15]. Similar to the text analysis, the Visual vocabulary-Image matrix is built. Then the constructed matrix is decomposed to dig out the semantic relationship mapping between image semantic features and images. And then the image latent semantic features are extracted, which are obtained from the Visual vocabulary–Image matrix.

The image latent semantic feature is more abundant than the traditional image semantic information, which is relative to the low-level features; it has stronger expression and the classification ability. Meanwhile, the image latent semantic features indirectly used to describe the image, so it can overcome the effects of some disadvantage factors.

2.2   Extreme Learning Machine

In recent years, Huang et. al. [11] proposed a new learning algorithm, namely ELM, which is based on the SLFN. For n samples $\{X_i, T_i\}$, $X_i = [x_{i1}, x_{i2}, ..., x_{in}]^T \in R^m$, $T_i = [t_{i1}, t_{i2}, ..., t_{im}]^T \in R^m$, a hidden layer has $\tilde{N}$ units and the excitation function $f(x)$ in the ELM. The unified model for SLFN is defined as follow:

$$\sum_{i=1}^{\tilde{N}} \beta_i f_i(X_j) = \sum_{i=1}^{\tilde{N}} \beta_i f(a_i \cdot X_j + b_i) = t_j, j = 1, 2, ..., N \tag{1}$$

Where $a_i = [a_{i1}, a_{i2}, ..., a_{in}]^T$ is the input weight with the ith unit of the hidden layer and b_i is the deviation. The weight between the ith unit of the hidden layer and the output layer is $\beta_i = [\beta_{i1}, \beta_{i2}, ..., \beta_{im}]^T$. $f(x)$ can be the any of excitation.

The above equation can be defined as follow:

$$H\beta = T \tag{2}$$

Because of the learning ability of the standard SLFN, the actual output can be nearly equal to the ideal output, as in the following formula:

$$\sum_{j=1}^{\tilde{N}} \left\| t_j - y_j \right\| = 0 \qquad (3)$$

Therefore, the above formula can be expressed as follow:

$$H\beta = Y \qquad (4)$$

Huang[11] has proved that the connection weights and the thresholds will appear as a fixed value when the training is stable once the excitation function is an infinitely differentiable function. The least squares solution of linear equations as follow:

$$\beta = H^+ Y \qquad (5)$$

Where H^+ is the Moore-Penrosefo generalized inverse matrix of the output layer matrix H.

3   Proposed Method

The proposed multimodal biometric identification system framework is as shown in Figure 1, which used face and fingerprint as the biometrics characters. The image latent semantic analysis is used for multimodal biometrics feature extraction, and the ELM is used as classifier. The system mainly includes the follow steps: preprocessing, visual vocabulary extraction, image latent semantic analysis and ELM classification.

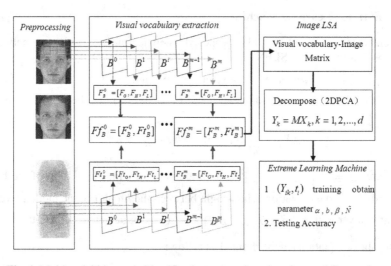

Fig. 1. Multimodal biometric identification system based on face and fingerprint

(1) Pre-processing. In order to obtain more enough visual vocabulary, first of all, the face and fingerprint image are divided into blocks. More visual vocabulary means more block numbers. So we adopt dynamic partitioning algorithm to block the image face and fingerprint. The size of the block window is set $p \times q$ predefined. Then the

block window scan the biometrics image from left to right and top to bottom according to the step length L.

(2) Visual vocabulary extraction. Low-level feature extraction is one of the key steps in biometric. So, The features are extracted from the face and fingerprint for visual vocabulary. For a face image A_{MN} whose size is $M \times N$, the visual vocabulary size is $p \times q$, and the total number of visual vocabulary is K. the features are extracted to compose a visual vocabulary with Gabor filter, LBP and invariant moment features.

A. *Gabor filters features.* Gabor filter not only has good directional selectivity and frequency selective characteristics, but also can carry on the time-frequency analysis of the image. So it is the best choice to extract image features under different direction and different frequency. The Gabor filters commonly used in face recognition have the following form:

$$\varphi_{\mu,v}(z) = \frac{\left\| k_{\mu,v} \right\|^2}{\sigma^2} e^{-\frac{\left\| k_{\mu,v} \right\|^2 \| z \|^2}{2\sigma^2}} [e^{ik_{\mu,v}z} - e^{-\frac{\sigma 2}{2}}] \tag{6}$$

In this paper, the value of scale and direction respectively are 3 and 2. So the Gabor filter feature of face is defined as $F_G = [G_{pq\,0,0}, G_{pq\,0,1}, \ldots G_{pq\,2,1}]$. Similarly, The Gabor filter feature of fingerprint is defined as $Ft_G = [G_{pq\,0,0}, G_{pq\,0,1}, \ldots G_{pq\,2,1}]$.

B. *Local binary pattern (LBP) features.* LBP has stronger robustness for illumination and expression. The LBP operator standard description as shown equation (11):

$$LBP_{P,R}(x) = \sum_{P=0}^{P-1} S(i_p - i_x)2^P, \qquad s(v) = \begin{cases} 1 & v \geq \delta \\ 0 & v \leq \delta \end{cases} \tag{7}$$

The LBP features of face are defined as F_L, the size is 59 dimensions. Similarly, the LBP features of the fingerprint are defined as Ft_L.

C. *Invariant moment features.* Invariant moment has a special strengthen in rotating, scaling and translation invariance. It has very strong ability to describe the image of regional characteristics. The Hu invariant moment is commonly used [16]. Seven Hu invariant moment features of face are defined as F_H. Similarly, the Hu invariant moment features of fingerprint are defined as Ft_H and fingerprint fusion feature Ft_B. Then, the visual vocabulary is formed by the face and fingerprint fusion $F_B = [F_G, F_H, F_L]$ and $Ft_B = [Ft_G, Ft_H, Ft_L]$, So the visual vocabulary is defined as $Ff_B = [F_B, Ft_B]$.

(3) Image Latent Semantic Analysis. Firstly, the visual vocabulary-image matrix M is built. In order to get the image latent semantic features and retain the spatial information of the visual vocabulary-image matrix, 2D-PCA is used to decompose the

matrix M [17]. Then, the proximity matrix y_k is obtained. For a given image sample matrix M, we can get $Y_k = FX_k, k = 1,2,...d$, where $X_k = (X_1, X_2,..., X_d)$ is the eigenvector corresponding biggest d Eigen values of the test images. And Y_k is the principal component.

(4) ELM for classification. For the n samples (Y_{tk}, t_j), ELM can be summarized as follows. Firstly, randomly assign input weight and bias. Second, calculate the hidden layer output matrix by the formula (8). Finally, calculate the output weight.

$$\sum_{i=1}^{\tilde{N}} \beta_i f_i(Y_{tk}) = \sum_{i=1}^{\tilde{N}} \beta_i f(a_i \cdot Y_{tk} + b_i) = O_j, j = 1,2,...,N \tag{8}$$

4   Experiments

For experiments, there are few public multimodal biometrics database includes both face and the corresponding fingerprint databases. Usually, the synthesis databases were often used [18]. In our experiments, the multimodal biometric databases of face and fingerprint image were established by selecting from the two famous public databases: the ORL face database and the FVC2002 fingerprint database. The total number of images was 640 in the database. Among them, there were 320 face images and 320 fingerprint images which were selected from the ORL database and FVC2002 DB2A database with 40 different people and each people have 8 face and fingerprint images, respectively.

Experiments were done on the established multimodal biometrics database ORL_FVC2002. Firstly, to compare with different feature extraction methods, the Support Vector Machine (SVM) was used as the classifier. The results were shown in Table 1. In Table 1, the Face-Gabor filter and Fingerprint-Gabor filter method mean experiment in a single face or fingerprint with Gabor filter. The individual face recognition experiments were tested on the ORL face database, and the individual fingerprint recognition experiments were tested on the FVC2002 database. And the Face- low-level fusion method means that the three low-level features were extracted by Gabor filter, LBP and Hu invariant moment for feature level fusion. The method of Face+Fingerprint-Fusion feature method means that fusing the one or more types low-level features of face and fingerprint. And Face+Fingerprint-ILSA feature method means that the image latent semantic features were extracted from the Visual vocabulary-Image matrix after fusing each image piece.

Table 1. Experiment results of different methods on the ORL_FVC2002 database

Algorithms\Sample(N)	N=4	N=5	N=6	N=7	Mean
Face-Gabor filter method	0.85625	0.89	0.95	0.967	0.9158
Face- low-level fusion feature method	0.925	0.925	0.95	0.95	0.9375
Fingerprint-Gabor filter method	0.600	0.683	0.85	0.875	0.752
Fingerprint- low-level fusion feature method	0.61	0.722	0.8889	0.8889	0.77745
Face+Fingerprint-Fusion feature method	0.8375	0.8583	0.8875	0.875	0.8646
Face+Fingerprint-ILSA feature method	0.925	0.933	0.9875	1.000	0.9614

From Table 1, we can see that the method of directly fusion the low-level features of the face and fingerprint, the average accuracy is lower than the single face recognition, but it is higher than the single fingerprint recognition, which reaches to 86.46%. The main reason may be the texture information of fingerprint has a certain effects on the overall recognition. However, the algorithm of the face+fingerprint LSA feature method has the best accuracy, which reaches to 96.14%.

Table 2 and Table 3 are the recognition accuracy results and time costs for three learning algorithm of BP, SVM, and ELM, respectively. From Table 2, we can see that the accuracy of ELM and SVM is almost the same. The average accuracy of ELM is 95.57%, and the SVM is 96.14%. Both of them are higher than the BP neural network learning. However, from Table 3, we can see that the learning algorithm of ELM has an obvious advantage. The time cost of the BP and SVM is dozens of times and even hundred of that of ELM. The total time is only 1.9314 seconds consists of the training time and testing time.

Table 2. Recognition Accuracy for three learning algorithms (ORL_FVC2002)

Method\Sample N	N=4	N=5	N=6	N=7	Mean
BP	0.74375	0.775	0.8125	0.825	0.7891
SVM	0.925	0.933	0.9875	1.000	0.9614
ELM	0.91875	0.9417	0.9875	0.975	0.9558

Table 3. Time costs for three learning algorithm (ORL_FVC2002)

Method\Training Time	Training Time	Testing Time	Total Time
BP	358.2365	0.3860	358.6225
SVM	67.9155	4.7130	72.6285
ELM	1.7871	0.1470	1.9314

5   Conclusion

In this paper, a novel and effective multimodal biometrics recognition system is proposed based on image latent semantic analysis and extreme learning machine. We introduce the concept of image latent semantic analysis into the multimodal biometrics recognition system, and the visual vocabulary—image matrix is used to dig out the latent relationship between the visual vocabulary and biometrics image as to further improve the performance. In the classification phase, the novel ELM learning algorithm is applied for classifier. It is not only has better classification accuracy, but also greatly improves the speed of the system.

Acknowledgement. This work is supported in part by the National Natural Science Foundation of China under Grant No. 61063035.

References

1. Rattani, A., Kisku, D.R., Bicego, M., et al.: Feature Level Fusion Face and Fingerprint biometrics. In: First IEEE International Conference on Digital Object Identifier, pp. 1–6 (2007)
2. Conti, V., Militello, C., Sorbello, F.: A frequency-based approach for feature fusion in fingerprint and iris multimodal biometric identification system. IEEE Transactions on Systems, Man, and Cybernetics-Part C: Applications and Reviews 40(4), 384–395 (2010)
3. Fernandez, F.A., Fierrez, J., Ramos, D., Rodriguez, J.G.: Quality-Based Conditional processing in Multi-biometrics: Application to Sensor Interoperability. IEEE Transaction on Systems, Man and Cybernetics, Part A: Systems and Humans 40(6), 1168–1179 (2010)
4. Ross, A., Jain, A.: Information fusion in biometric. Pattern Recognition Letters 24(13), 2115–2125 (2003)
5. Yang, F., Ma, B.F.: A new mixed-mode biometrics information fusion based-on fingerprint, hand-geometry and palm-print. In: Fourth International Conference on Image and Graphics, pp. 689–693 (2007)
6. Fierrez-Aguilar, J., Ortega-Garcia, J., Gonzalea-Rodriguez, J.: Fusion strategies in Biometric multimodal verification. In: International Conference on Multimedia and Expo., vol. 3(III), pp. 5–8 (2003)
7. Ross, A.A., Govindarajan, R.: Feature level fusion using hand and face biometrics, pp. 196–204. International Society for Optics and Photonics (2005)
8. Singh, R., Vatsa, M., Noore, A.: Integrated multilevel image fusion and match score fusion of visible and infrared face images for robust face recognition. Pattern Recognition 41(3), 880–893 (2008)
9. Zhou, X.L., Bhanu, B.: Feature fusion of face and Gait for human recognition at a distance in video. In: International Conference on Pattern Recognition, pp. 529–532 (2006)
10. Deerwester, S., Dumais, S.T., Furnas, G.W., et al.: Indexing by latent semantic analysis. Journal of the American Society for Information Science 41(6), 391–407 (1990)
11. Huang, G.B., Zhu, Q.Y., Siew, C.K.: Extreme Learning machine: Theory and Applications. Neurocomputing 70(1-3), 489–501 (2006)
12. Yang, J.C., Jiao, Y.B., Xiong, N., Park, D.S.: Fast Face Gender Recognition by Using Local Ternary Pattern and Extreme Learning Machine. KSII Transactions on Internet and Information Systems 7(7) (2013)
13. Pham, T.T., Maillot, N.E., Lim, J.H., et al.: Latent semantic fusion model for image retrieval and annotation. In: 16th ACM Conference on Conference on Information and knowledge Management, pp. 439–444 (2007)
14. Csurka, G.: Visual categorization with bags of key points Workshop on Statistical Learning in Computer Vision. In: ECCV (2004)
15. Fei-Fei, L., Fergus, R., Torralba, A.: Recognizing and learning object categories and A stochastic grammar of images
16. Yang, J.C., Park, D.S.: A fingerprint verification algorithm using tessellated invariant moment features. Neurocomputing 71(10), 1939–1946 (2008)
17. Yang, J., Zhang, D., Frang, A.F., et al.: Two-dimensional PCA: a new approach to appearance-based face representation and recognition, vol. 26(1), pp. 131–137 (2004)
18. Son, B., Lee, Y.: Biometric Authentication System Using Reduced Joint Feature Vector of Iris and Face. In: Kanade, T., Jain, A., Ratha, N.K. (eds.) AVBPA 2005. LNCS, vol. 3546, pp. 513–522. Springer, Heidelberg (2005)

Age and Gender Estimation
Using Multiple-Image Features

Chang-Ling Ku, Chun-Hsiang Chiou, Zhe-Yuan Gao, Yun-Je Tsai,
and Chiou-Shann Fuh

Department of Computer Science and Information Engineering,
National Taiwan University, Taipei 10617, Taiwan(R.O.C)
{s86032michael,krapshsa,Gaozheyuan13,jpm9ie8c}@gmail.com,
fuh@csie.ntu.edu.tw

Abstract. We proposed a real-time system based on multiple frames in this paper to estimate age and gender using facial images. Most of the previous proposed methods are basically based on using a single frame to estimation age and gender. However, limited resources and unpredictable factors on real-time systems are possible to make the result unstable and inaccurate. In order to calibrate the inaccuracy and instability of the previous systems, we decide to construct our system with multiple frames and multiple databases. The first approach we proposed is detecting faces and labeling features from the source images with Stacked Trimmed Active Shape Model (STASM). Then, we perform the alignment of the 76 feature points. Afterwards, we extract features using Speeded Up Robust Features (SURF). After that, we apply the Support Vector Machine (SVM) on the data for preliminary classification. Finally, the data will be sent to the multiple-image and multiple-database classification system to classify the final result. In our experiments, both the training and testing data are from three public available databases which are MORPH, FG-NET, and FERET databases. The experimental result of our proposed method is extremely accurate. Furthermore, the robustness of our system outperforms the previous system based on a single frame.

Keywords: Age Estimation, Gender Estimation, Stacked Trimmed Active Shape Model, Speeded Up Robust Feature, Support Vector Machine, MORPH, FG-NET, FERET.

1   Introduction

In our daily lives, the face information [4, 7] of human has been widely explored and the related applications have also been well developed by companies and government agencies. Age and gender estimation has become one of the top surveyed topics in the academicfield of computer vision. This technique is also extensively applied to various kinds of systems, such as authorization and surveillance systems in malls, customs, and banks. We can generally separate the application of age and gender estimation into two aspects. The first one will be related to the field of Human-Computer Interaction (HCI).

Z. Sun et al. (Eds.): CCBR 2013, LNCS 8232, pp. 441–448, 2013.

The estimation technique will be a positive factor that helps the computer to vary its response to different users. The other usage of age and gender estimation is surveillance systems, for instance, the authorization system and automatic surveillance system based on facial image can cover up some defects for systems only based on other information such as fingerprint which will be very helpful on preventing crimes. Moreover, this system can be used in malls and stores to automatically authorize people for buying some adult product (e.g. tobacco, alcohol) or some restricted goods. It can also be used as a recommendation system.

As the need of the application increases, the studies in age estimation do not require the accuracy to be perfect. The progress of this study has not improved rapidly in the past few years since the applications using age estimation simply need a wide range of age. For better usage, the development of the application is based on the fundamental robust techniques and strong theories. Hence, increasing the accuracy of a narrow range of age is going to be a top priority in this field of research. For achieving this goal, analyzing with both human and machine perspectives will be necessary [6]. We also notice that most researchers in this field neglect the influence of race. Since the speed of aging and other biological variation will be different between different races, it will be a major factor to affect the result of age estimation. On the other hand, the cultural difference will vary people's appearance from others. This will also be another major factor that influences the result for the estimation.

2   Background

Most previous proposed methods focus on improving the accuracy by trying different kinds of features [3] or some slight modification on the current classifier using regression methods [5]. However, the inaccuracy seems inevitable no matter how the methods of finding features are improved. Facing this situation, we will propose a method based on some basic concepts to make some improvement. Using single image on age and gender estimation is still a trend since the database with single image is easier to acquire compared with multiple image databases. Therefore, a compromising method is proposed by accepting multiple-input on a single person to improve the accuracy for this part of the system.

In fact, this approach is not the first time to be proposed in this field of research. However, the previous research [13] focused on both multi-view image and local features. Local features will sometimes be an inaccurate factor in both age and gender estimation. Therefore, some modifications have been done in our research which will make the result of the estimation more accurate.

3   Approach

Fig. 1 shows the modules of our proposed system. Before the main procedures, some pre-processing should be done in order to decrease the complexity of time and space. We accept both webcam videos and database images as our input format. This design will be helpful for the following procedures. Since color information of human faces is ignored in our current research, converting the input images into grayscale image will be necessary for time and space concern. Using the landmarks to detect faces in the entire image is a crucial step. We can easily separate the face from the image using the feedback information from the Stacked Trimmed Active Shape Model (STASM) [9]. However, this method could be vulnerable in a single-image based system since the system will crash if the STASM landmark cannot be found in that single input. It is fortunate that the problem will not occur based on multiple inputs since we can calibrate the detection by calculating the movement of the person in different frames. In this instance, we can ignore the defects this method will bring. At the end of pre-processing, we have to remove the background of the image for the accuracy of the later work.

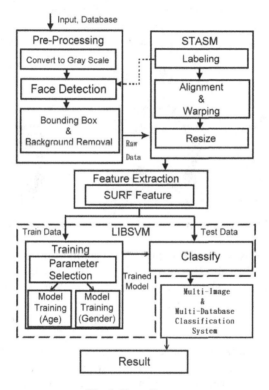

Fig. 1. Flow diagram

After the pre-processing, the image will be the raw data for the remaining system. We use a self-modified version of STASM to process our image. The first step is labeling the feature points. As Fig. 2 shows that we will generate 76 landmarks on the human facial features and outline. The landmarks here will not be used as feature points to classify our result. These landmarks are for our next step: alignment and warping. After labeling all the images in the databases, we have to choose a proper image as a standard image. Fig. 2 is also the standard image in our research. We have to align all 76 landmarks on the image to the landmarks on the standard image. After this step, we will get a new image after warping. Fig. 3 is the original image, and Fig. 4 is the image after alignment and warping. An important step before we extract features is resizing the image into a smaller size (e.g. 30x40, 45x60, 60x80, pixels). The design of the resizing step can vary for different hardware or even be ignored in some circumstances. In this research, since time is a major factor in a real-time system and limited hardware is available. The minor difference of the accuracy can be neglected. We use the size with 60 pixels of the maximum edge in our research.

In the feature extraction module, we use Speeded Up Robust Features (SURF) [1]. SURF features are typically a robust local feature detector used for 3D reconstruction and object recognition (e.g. Fig. 5), and so on. The development of SURF features are inspired by Scale-Invariant Feature Transform (SIFT) [8] which is another kind of features. SIFT feature slightly outperforms SURF feature when time is not a critical factor. The main reason we choose SURF feature instead of SIFT feature is that since our system is designed as a real-time system and SURF feature is several times faster than SIFT feature.

Fig. 2. After STASM labeling   **Fig. 3.** Original image   **Fig. 4.** After alignment and warping

The final module is for model training and classification. A library for Support Vector Machines (LIBSVM) [2] is used as our tool. This tool is based on the theory of Support Vector Machine which is a study in machine learning and often used for regression analysis and classification. The basic concept of SVM is to construct a set of hyper-plane in a high dimensional space which can be defined into a kernel function $K(x,y)$. We can measure the relative nearness of the test data to each category of datas using the information of the kernel function. The LIBSVM tool also provides a training program with different modes. A Python-based program in LIBSVM is able to select appropriate parameters for nonlinear classification training. After the input data and parameter are given to the program the training will start. We have tried three difference sizes of images with the maximum edge of 40, 60, and 80 pixels in our research. The result for 40 pixels is awful, and the results for 60 and 80 pixels are similar. In this case, we decide to use the image of 60 pixels for speed. As for the detail of training, we train age and gender into two models separately for different purposes. After the model is trained, the system will be ready for testing. The same step will be performed on all training and testing images. Then we input the model and the testing image into the SVM classifier. The basic concept of our research is based on multiple images, we will capture 3 or 7 frames from the video to vote for the final result. If we are performing gender estimation, one more step will be done before classification result is shown on the screen. Since there are three different databases (e.g. FERET [10, 12], MORPH [11], FG-NET.) available, we will have three different trained models from these three databases. The testing image will test with three models separately and we will take the majority as the final result. Fig. 6 shows the design details of our classification system.

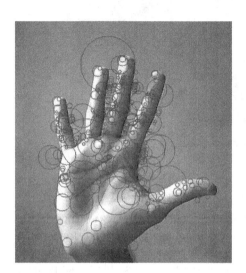

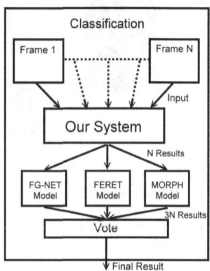

Fig. 5. SURF feature tool in OpenCV   **Fig. 6.** Classification flow diagram

4   Experiments

Our experiments run on a Windows x86/x64 platform. The input will be either videos captured by the webcam or simply any image files. As for our modified version of STASM, we reserve the part of finding landmarks yet modify it to feedback to our system for finding the bounding box of the image. We also add a damaged image removal mechanism after the process of alignment and warping. For speed concern, we resize the image. Although the result for using the original image will be obviously better, it is unreliable for a real-time system since it will take tens of seconds to generate the result. We have done the comparison using the original STASM landmark features and SURF features. SURF features always perform better in accuracy than STASM landmark features. Therefore, we replace STASM features with SURF feature. We have also done the comparison between SURF features and SIFT features. A compromising decision has been done since SIFT features perform better in accuracy, yet SURF feature is much faster than SIFT feature. The model training is a time-consuming task which usually take hours for each model to complete training. Fig. 7 is the testing interface of our system using webcam. The block in the figure shows the result of our classification.

Fig. 7. Testing interface

5 Discussion and Conclusion

Since our research focus on real-time systems, time becomes a major factor. Therefore, the design of our system makes the calculation of the result extremely fast (e.g. less than 3 seconds). However, accuracy has been sacrificed in the compromise we have done which causes the accuracy of our system is not able to out-perform other researcher's result. In this situation, using the voting system constructed by both multiple databases and multiple images is helpful for us to maintain the accuracy on a standard level. The model-training method is reliable yet a time-consuming work. Also, the quality of the databases we used can still be improved despite they are the most popular public available databases in age and gender estimation currently. Furthermore, the databases we use mostly include three particular races in, Europeans, Caucasians and African Americans. We have done some experiments of picking out the Asian from the database and simply use these data to train another model since our test data are mostly Asians. Statistics shows that it will be more accurate on both age and gender estimations for filtering the race of training data. Therefore, we consider race an important factor in this research. The result of the gender estimation for sizes of 40, 60, and 80 pixels are shown in Table 1, 2, and 3. We can tell by the chart that for gender estimation using bigger training data will obviously lead to a better result. For age estimation, however, the difference between different sizes is minor which are showed in Fig. 8. Some contradictions may even occur in some cases. Hence, we conclude that for age estimation we have to add more age-related features to help improve the accuracy.

Table 1. Result of gender estimation for size 60 pixels

	Accuracy
Set1	90.81
Set2	91.56
Set3	94.14
Set4	88.29
Set5	88.62
Average	90.68

Table 2. Result of gender estimation for size 40 pixels

	Accuracy
Set1	89.34
Set2	91.93
Set3	94.32
Set4	89.01
Set5	90.64
Average	91.05

Table 3. Result of gender estimation for size 80 pixels

	Accuracy
Set1	90.63
Set2	92.29
Set3	94.51
Set4	99.82
Set5	89.91
Average	93.43

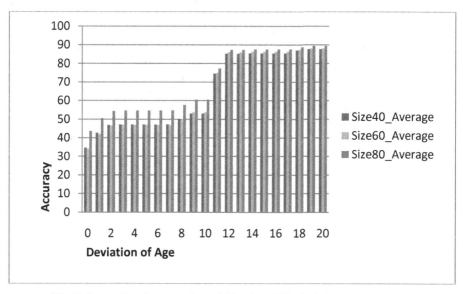

Fig. 8. Comparison between sizes of 40, 60, and 80 pixels for age estimation

References

1. Bay, H., Ess, A., Tuytelaars, T., Gool, L.V.: SURF: Speeded Up Robust Features. Computer Vision and Image Understanding 110(3), 346–359 (2008)
2. Fan, R.E., Chen, P.H., Lin, C.J.: Working Set Selection Using Second Order Information for Training SVM. Journal of Machine Learning Research 6, 1889–1918 (2005)
3. Choi, S.E., Lee, Y.J., Lee, S.J., Park, K.R., Kim, J.: Age Estimation Using a Hierarchical Classifier Based on Global and Local Facial Features. Pattern Recognition 44(6), 1262–1281 (2011)
4. Fu, Y., Guo, G., Huang, T.S.: Age Synthesis and Estimation via Faces: A Survey. IEEE Transactions on Pattern Analysis and Machine Intelligence 32(11), 1955–1976 (2010)
5. Guo, G., Fu, Y., Dyer, C.R., Huang, T.S.: Image-Based Human Age Estimation by Maniold Learning and Locally Adjusted Robust Regression. IEEE Transactions on Image Processing 17(7), 1178–1188 (2008)
6. Han, H., Otto, C., Jain, A.K.: Age Estimation from Face Images: Human vs. Machine Performance. In: Proceedings of IAPR International Conference on Biometrics, Madrid, Spain, pp. 1–8 (2013)
7. Kwon, Y.H., da Vitoria Lobo, N.: Age Classification from Facial Images. Computer Vision and Image Understanding 74(1), 1–21 (1999)
8. David, L.G.: Object Recognition from Local Scale-Invariant Features. In: Proceedings of International Conference on Computer Vision, Corfu, Greece, vol. 2, pp. 1150–1157 (1999)
9. Milborrow, S., Nicolls, F.: Locating Facial Features with an Extended Active Shape Model. In: Forsyth, D., Torr, P., Zisserman, A. (eds.) ECCV 2008, Part IV. LNCS, vol. 5305, pp. 504–513. Springer, Heidelberg (2008)
10. Phillips, P.J., Rauss, P.J., Der, S.Z.: FERET (Face Recognition Technology) Recognition Algorithm Development and Test Results. Army Research Laboratory, Technical Report 995 (1996)
11. Ricanek Jr., K., Tesafaye, T.: MORPH: A Longitudinal Image Database of Normal Adult Age-Progression. In: Proceedings of IEEE International Conference on Automatic Face and Gesture Recognition, Southampton, UK, pp. 341–345 (2006)
12. Phillips, P.J., Moon, H., Rauss, P.J., Rizvi, S.: The FERET Evaluation Methodology for Face Recognition Algorithms. IEEE Transactions on Pattern Analysis and Machine Intelligence 22(10), 1090–1104 (2000)
13. Song, Z., Ni, B., Guo, D., Sim, T., Yan, S.: Learning Universal Multi-view Age Estimator by Video Contexts. In: Proceedings of International Conference on Computer Vision, Barcelona, Spain, pp. 1–8 (2011)

Morphological Investigations of Skulls for Sex Determination Based on Sparse Principal Component Analysis

Li Luo[1], Liang Chang[1], Rong Liu[2], and Fuqing Duan[1,*]

[1] College of Information Science and Technology, Beijing Normal University, 100875, China
[2] Base Department, Beijing Institute of Clothing Technology Beijing, 100029, China
luoli@mail.bnu.edu.cn,
{changliang,fqduan}@bnu.edu.cn

Abstract. Sex determination from skeletons is a significant step in the analysis of forensic anthropology. The relationship between morphological characteristics and the gender of skull is of great importance in forensic anthropology research. This paper presents an automatic method relating the local morphological characteristics of the skull to the sex classification based on sparse principle component analysis (SPCA). Our contributions are: (1)A set of important local characteristics on the skull are obtained using sparse principal component analysis, which correspond to local areas on the skull. The importance of the local characteristics in sex classification are obtained; (2)Experiments on Chinese skulls including 127 males and 81 females are given. The results show the effectiveness of SPCA on Sex determination.

Keywords: Sex determination, Forensic anthropology, Morphology, Sparse principal component analysis, Fisher discriminant analysis.

1   Introduction

In the forensic anthropology, sex identification for unknown skeleton is an important work. According to experience and previous studies [1-3], sex classification using pelvis morphological characteristics has the highest accuracy. However, not all cases of forensic anthropology has complete skeleton, as skull is composed of hard tissue, it is easily preserved, and in most cases, we could only get the skull completely. So, sex identification through the skull becomes the core content of forensic anthropology, and it also is the first step in craniofacial reconstruction [4]. The common investigations of sex classification include morphology discriminant method and measurement discriminant method. Morphology discriminant method relies mainly on expert's understanding of the morphology characteristic differences between the male skull and the female skull. The subjectivity of the expert's understanding about the skull's morphology characteristics has an important influence in sexing identification. Measurement discriminant method is to measure some geometric quantities of the

---

* Corresponding author.

Z. Sun et al. (Eds.): CCBR 2013, LNCS 8232, pp. 449–456, 2013.

skull first, then to establish discriminant function through these quantities to identify the gender. Measurement discriminant method is realized easily by using computer, but the requirement for the measuring precision is very high, and the precise measurement of the skull is quite difficult. Moreover, as the age changes, the size of the skull will also change. All these make the difficulty of the measurement discriminant method increased.

In this article, we proposed an automatic method for relating the local characteristics of the skull to the gender classification accuracy by sparse principal component analysis. This method explains how the features of the local areas influence the classification result. Compared with the traditional methods, the innovation and the main contribution of this method are: 1) it gives a clear explanation about the importance of the skull local area for classification. 2) it proposes a promising tool for inexperienced observers to determine the gender of a skull without much human-computer interaction 3) it is without tedious manual measurement and got rid of the influence of the skull size. This article is arranged as follows: the second section is about the related work; the third part is about the materials and the methods; the fourth quarter presents the experiment and the results; the last part is conclusion.

2   Related Works

Some researchers used x-ray photograph for identification[5-8]. Another methods[3] are to use morphological traits for sex determination; Recently, people proposed to build discriminant function using some geometric quantities for identification. Chunbiao Li[9] got the frontal sagittal arc shape curve through measuring some points on the frontal median sagittal contour, Then used multivariate stepwise discriminant analysis to establish gender discriminant function for the Fourier transform coefficient of the curve, did sex identification to the adult cranial from northeast area of China, and the recognition rate is up to 84.21% for the male skull and 83.33% for the female skull. Walker[10] measured the characteristics in five regions, such as in orbital margin and glabella, and identified the gender by means of quadratic discriminant function; the accuracy reaches to 90%.Jant Z and Ousley[11] issued the computer-aided software called Fordisc® for skeleton analysis. This software got skeleton characteristics through a human-computer interactive way, utilized the American criminal investigation database to establish the gender discriminant function. Wuyang Shui[12] defined 14 geometrical quantities, utilized 94 samples in the Chinese craniofacial database to establish the statistics discriminant function by using stepwise fisher discriminant method, then used another 39 samples for test, and the accuracy can reach to 87%.

3   Materials and Methods

3.1   Materials

This study has been approved by the Institutional Review Board (IRB) of Image Center for Brain Research, National Key Laboratory of Cognitive Neuroscience and

Learning, Beijing Normal University. It is carried out on a database of 208 whole skull CT scans on voluntary persons that mostly come from Han ethnic group in North of China, age 19–75 years for females and 21-67 years for males. There are 81 females and 127 males. The CT images were obtained by a clinical multi-slice CT scanner system (Siemens Sensation 16) in the Xian yang hospital located in western China. The images of each subject are restored in DICOM format with a size of approximately $512 \times 512 \times 250$. Each 3D skull surface is extracted from the CT images and represented as a triangle mesh including about 150,000 vertices. All the skulls are substantially complete, i.e. each skull contains all the bones from calvarias to jaw, and has the full mouth of teeth.

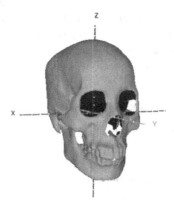

Fig. 1. One skull in the uniform coordinate system

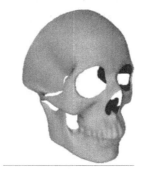

Fig. 2. The back part of the reference skull is cut away

All the samples are transformed into a uniform coordinate system, to eliminate the inconsistence in position, pose and scale caused by data acquirement. The uniform coordinate system is determined by four skull landmarks, left porion, right porion, left (or right) orbitale and glabella (denote as Lp, Rp, Lo, G). The Frankfurt plane[13] is determined from three points, Lp, Rp, Lo. The coordinate origin (denotes as O) is the intersection point of the line LpRp and the plane that contains point G and orthogonally intersects with line LpRp. We take the line ORp as x axis. The z axis is the line through the point O and with the direction being the normal of the Frankfurt plane. Then y axis is obtained by the cross product of z and x axis. Once the uniform coordinate system is defined, all the prototypic skulls are transformed into it. Finally, the scale of all the samples is standardized by setting the distance between Lp and Rp to unit, i.e. each vertex (x, y, z) of the skull is scaled by $\left(\dfrac{x}{\left|L_p - R_p\right|}, \dfrac{y}{\left|L_p - R_p\right|}, \dfrac{z}{\left|L_p - R_p\right|} \right)$. One skull in the uniform coordinate system is shown in Figure.1.

The original skull meshes have different connectivity. In statistical learning, a dense correspondence has to be established across the training set. Here we adopt the dense registration method described in [5]. Since there are too many vertices in the whole head and the face recognition mainly depends on the front part of the head, same as the ones in [5], the reference for registration is also a selected skull whose back parts are cut away. As shown in Figure.2, the reference skull has 41,059. After registration, all skulls have same connectivity with same number of vertices.

3.2   Sparse Principal Component Analysis (SPCA)

PCA is a powerful tool to build statistical shape model, which can efficiently describe the shape variance and ensure that only statistically likely shapes are represented. It has been used in many applications [14,15].PCA suffers from the fact that each principal component is a linear combination of all the original variables, thus it is often difficult to interpret the results. Zou et al.[16]take the advantage of PCA and adopt methods from Elastic Net regression[17] to put forward a new feature extraction method which is called sparse principal component analysis(SPCA).SPCA is quite useful in extracting the sparse principal component which represents the local feature of the sample. In our research, we construct a model based on SPCA and Fisher discriminant analysis to propose a promising method for determining the sex of a skull.

SPCA can be described as an extension of PCA, where a constraint of the number of nonzero loadings is added. Zou et al. take advantage of formulating PCA as a regression problem leading to the SPCA criterion[18]

$$\arg\min_{\mathbf{A},\mathbf{B}} \sum_{i=1}^{n} \left\| \mathbf{x}_i - \mathbf{A}\mathbf{B}^T \mathbf{x}_i \right\|^2 + \lambda \sum_{j=1}^{k} \left\| \mathbf{b}_j \right\|^2 + \sum_{j=1}^{k} \eta_j \left\| \mathbf{b}_j \right\|_1 \tag{1}$$
$$s.t.\ \mathbf{A}^T \mathbf{A} = \mathbf{I}$$

Here, $\mathbf{x}_i$ is the i th column of $\mathbf{X}^T$, n denotes the number of the samples, k is retained in the model. The columns of $\mathbf{B}$ represent the principal directions $\left(\mathbf{b}_j, j = 1, 2, \cdots, k \right)$ and $\mathbf{B}$ projects sample $\mathbf{x}_i$ onto those directions. The matrix $\mathbf{A}$ converts the sample back to the original space. Thus, the first part measures the reconstruction error of the model. The second part is to ensure a unique solution by including L2 penalty, and this is also applicable when $p > n$ (p denotes the number of variables, n denotes the number of samples), and the third part introduces sparsity by L1 penalty. These two latter parts are adopted from Elastic Net regression. The parameter λ should be the same for all principle components and be set beforehand. For providing good flexibility, η can be different for each principle component. Here, we use the same algorithm in [16] to solve SPCA.

3.3   Fisher Discriminant Analysis

The Fisher criterion is to find a projection vector space in which the samples of the different class are separated, while the samples of the same class are aggregated, the criterion can be represented as the following rules:

$$\max \mathbf{J}_F(\mathbf{w}) = \frac{\tilde{S}_b}{\tilde{S}_w} = \frac{(\tilde{m}_1 - \tilde{m}_2)^2}{\tilde{S}_1^{\,2} + \tilde{S}_2^{\,2}} \tag{2}$$

We define the within-class scatter matrix to be $\mathbf{S}_w$, and the between-class scatter matrix to be $\mathbf{S}_b$, $\mathbf{w}$ to be the projection vector, the fisher criterion is as follows:

$$\max_{\mathbf{w}} \mathbf{J}_F(\mathbf{w}) = \frac{\mathbf{w}^T \mathbf{S}_b \mathbf{w}}{\mathbf{w}^T \mathbf{S}_w \mathbf{w}} \tag{3}$$

Equation (3) can be solved by lagrangian multiplier method.

In our experiment, we project each skull feature vector $\mathbf{b}$ onto the Fisher vector. The classification threshold ω_0 is chosen according to prior knowledge. The decision rules are:

If $\mathbf{w}^T \mathbf{b} + \omega_0 > 0$, $\mathbf{b}$ belongs to the first class; otherwise, $\mathbf{b}$ belongs to the second class.

We project the skull vectors onto the principal directions by SPCA. For each principal direction, a Fisher discriminant score (F-score) is calculated to describe the classification ability. The larger the F-score is, the higher the classification ability will be. The F-score is defined as follows:

$$F = \frac{(\mu_1 - \mu_2)^2}{\sigma_1^2 + \sigma_2^2} \tag{4}$$

Where $\mu_i \, (i = 1, 2)$ and $\sigma_i^2 \, (i = 1, 2)$ denotes the mean and the variance of the projected skull vectors respectively.

The procedure of our algorithm is as follows:

Step1: perform sparse decomposition model by using SPCA to get several local characteristics of the skull.

Step2: sort the F-scores corresponding to the principal directions from big to small, project each of the skull vector onto the first eight directions respectively, and find a threshold to discriminate the gender of the skull. Then, find out the classification ability of these local areas of skull.

Step3: after project each of the skull vectors onto these eight directions, use Fisher discriminant analysis to find out the classification ability when all these eight local areas are taken into consideration together.

Step4: project each of the skull vectors onto all the principal directions, use Fisher discriminant analysis to find out the classification ability.

4   Results

In our experiment, we use 208 whole skull CT scans, as described in Section 2. The samples include 127 males and 81 females. The dimension of each skull is 40969*3, which is high. We set the sparsity parameter as 4000 for each principal component in the experiments. Using trial and error technique, we choose the best principal component number. As the correct rates are always the same, we determined 33 as our principal component number. Then by SPCA, we get the eight directions which represent the eight corresponding local features of a skull, and choose the four most remarkable features shown in figure.3.

Fig. 3. The four most important local areas for sex determination, the light color area denotes the local area which is surrounded by the ellipse circle

We project the skull data onto all of the principal directions with varying the principal component number from 30 to 140, and determine the gender of the skull by Fisher discriminant analysis. The variation of the correct rates are shown in Figure.4, from the figure, we find out that the more principal component we choose, the higher the classification rate will be . So we decide the number as 135, and the classification is shown in Figure.5.

No matter how the principal component number is changed, the correct rates are always the same. The cause of this result is that the local area corresponding to the feature has almost no change with the varying of the number. The four most important skull local areas for classification in our experiment are consistent with the corresponding morphological results. With the increase of the principal component number, the classification effect is getting better and better. The result shows that when we take all the local areas into consideration to classify the gender, the correct rate is close to a quite high value, which proves that SPCA is a powerful tool for sex determination, and it also can explain the result clearly.

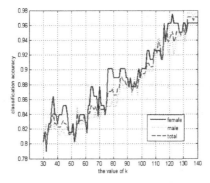

Fig. 4. Variation of classification accuracy when take all the local features into consideration

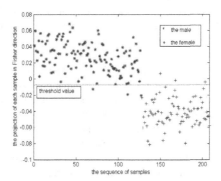

Fig. 5. Classification of samples

5   Conclusion

Traditional morphological methods depend heavily on physical anthropologists' subjective understanding of population differences in sexual dimorphism. Different observers usually have a significant difference when performing the visual assessment of the morphological traits, especially for those inexperienced observers. On the other hand, discriminant analysis for skeletal measurements depends less on the examiner's professional qualification and experience, but it requires a high measurement precision, which is not easy to realize. In this paper, instead of depending on geometric measurements or experience of observers, we use 3d point cloud data to extract features, which represent the local characteristics of the skull by SPCA. And this method can take the advantages of both morphological and metrical methods.

From our experiment, we can get the importance of each skull local area in sex determination, which is consistent with the morphological results. Moreover, experimental results show the effectiveness of SPCA in sex determination.

Acknowledgments. This work was partially supported by the National Natural Science Foundation of China (No. 61272363, 60736008).

References

1. Miller, E.: Forensic Anthropology, Department of Anthropology, California State University, Los Angeles
2. Spradley, M.K., Jantz, R.L.: Sex estimation in forensic anthropology: skull versus postcranial elements. Journal of Forensic Sciences 56(2), 289–296 (2011)
3. Williams, B.A., Rogers, T.L.: Evaluating the accuracy and precision of cranial morphological traits for sex determination. Journal of Forensic Sciences 51(4), 729–735 (2006)
4. Duan, F., Yang, S., Huang, D., et al.: Craniofacial reconstruction based on multi-linear subspace analysis. Multimedia Tools and Applications, pp. 1–15 (2013), doi:10.1007/s11042-012-1351-2
5. Hu, Y., Duan, F., Yin, B., et al.: A hierarchical dense deformable model for 3D face reconstruction from skull. Multimedia Tools and Applications 64(2), 345–364 (2013)
6. Hsiao, T.H., Chang, H.P., Liu, K.M.: Sex determination by discriminant function analysis of lateral radiographic cephalometry. Journal of Forensic Sciences 41(5), 792 (1996)
7. Veyre-Goulet, S.A., Mercier, C., Robin, O., et al.: Recent human sexual dimorphism study using cephalometric plots on lateral teleradiography and discriminant function analysis. Journal of Forensic Sciences 53(4), 786–789 (2008)
8. Inoue, M., Inoue, T., Fushimi, Y., et al.: Sex determination by discriminant function analysis of lateral cranial form. Forensic Science International 57(2), 109–117 (1992)
9. Li, C.B.: Study on sex difference of adult human skull in the northeast china by stepwise discriminant analysis. Journal of China Medical University 21(1), 28–31 (1992)
10. Walker, P.L.: Sexing skulls using discriminant function analysis of visually assessed traits. American Journal of Physical Anthropology 136(1), 39–50 (2008)
11. Jantz, R.L., Ousley, S.D.: FORDISC 3: computerized forensic discriminant functions, Version 3.0. The University of Tennessee, Knoxville (2005)
12. Shui, W.Y.: Research and application of craniofacial morphology. Dissertation. Beijing normal university (2011)
13. Wikipedia Frankfurt plane. The Wikimedia Foundation. Inc. Web (2011), http://en.wikipedia.org/wiki/Frankfurt_plane (accessed August 21, 2011)
14. Bin, J., Ali, L., Yongheng, Z.: Data Mining of Cataclysmic Variables Candidates in Massive Spectra. Spectroscopy and Spectral Analysis 31(8), 2278–2282 (2011) (in Chinese)
15. Liu, X., Sun, Y., Wu, Y.: Reduction of Hyperspectral Dimensions and Construction of Discrimination Models for Identifying Wetland Plant Species. Spectroscopy and Spectral Analysis 32(2), 459–464 (2012) (in Chinese)
16. Zou, H., Hastie, T., Tibshirani, R.: Sparse principal component analysis. Journal of Computational and Graphical Statistics 15(2), 265–286 (2006)
17. Zou, H., Hastie, T.: Regularization and variable selection via the elastic net. Journal of the Royal Statistical Society: Series B (Statistical Methodology) 67(2), 301–320 (2005)
18. Ólafsdóttir, H., Ersbøll, B.K., Larsen, R.: Analysis of craniofacial images using computational atlases and deformation fields. DTU Informatics (2007)

Head Pose Estimation with Improved Random Regression Forests

Ronghang Zhu, Gaoli Sang, Ying Cai, Jian You, and Qijun Zhao[*]

National Key Laboratory of Fundamental Science on Synthetic Vision,
Institute of Image and Graphics, School of Computer Science, Sichuan University
qjzhao@scu.edu.cn

Abstract. Head pose estimation is an important step in many face related applications. In this paper, we propose to use random regression forests to estimate head poses in 2D face images. Given a 2D face image, Gabor filters are first applied to extract raw high-dimensional features. Linear discriminant analysis (LDA) is then used to reduce the feature dimension. Random regression forests are constructed in the low dimensional feature space. Unlike traditional random forests, when generating tree predictors in the forests we weight the features according to the eigenvalues associated with their corresponding LDA axes. The proposed method has been evaluated on a set of 2D face images synthesized from the BU-3DFE database and on the CMU-PIE database. The experimental results demonstrate the effectiveness of the proposed method.

Keywords: Head pose estimation, Random regression forests, Feature weighting.

1 Introduction

Head pose estimation is usually considered as an important part of human behavior analysis. It is essentially a classification or regression problem. Accurate and robust algorithms for head pose estimation can be beneficial to many applications, such as gaze estimation, fatigue driving detection, and posture correction. Research on head pose estimation has been attracting much attention of researchers from the fields of computer vision, machine learning, pattern recognition, medical imaging, etc. During the past decades, a number of methods have been proposed [1],[2]. However, it is still a challenge problem to estimate head pose from a single 2D face image.

Random forests, proposed by Breiman [3], are an effective tool for classification and regression. Recently, Gabriele et al. [4] used random forests to estimate 3D head pose in 3D face images, and obtained impressive results. They utilized depth information as feature vectors when constructing the tree predictors in random forests. Therefore, their method can not be directly applied to 2D face images, which have limited information compared with 3D face images and are more sensitive to illumination variations.

---

[*] Corresponding author.

Z. Sun et al. (Eds.): CCBR 2013, LNCS 8232, pp. 457–465, 2013.
© Springer International Publishing Switzerland 2013

In this paper, we attempt to solve the problem of estimating 3D head pose in 2D face images by using random forests. To this end, we first extract Gabor features from 2D face images, and then use Linear Discriminant Analysis (LDA) to reduce the feature dimension and associate with each feature an importance index (i.e., a weight). Finally, we construct random forests based on the obtained features. Unlike the methods in [4], our method considers the importance of different features when constructing random forests. As a result, our constructed random forests are more effective, which has been proven by our experimental results.

The remainder of this paper is organized as follows. Section 2 briefly introduces related work. Section 3 presents the improved random regression forests based head pose estimation method. Section 4 then reports the experimental results. Finally, conclusions are drawn in Section 5.

2   Related Work

2.1   Random Regression Forests

Random forests are an ensemble of tree predictors that can cope with classification and regression problems. To construct one tree in a forest, N samples are randomly chosen with replacement from the given set of training data. Assuming each sample is represented by M features, m ($m \ll M$) of them are selected at random at each non-leaf node in the tree. The samples arriving at a non-leaf node are split into two subsets (one for the left branch and the other for the right branch) based on a binary test on the selected m features of these samples. The tree keeps growing until the number of samples arriving at the node is sufficiently small, or the samples are all of the same class, or the tree reaches the maximum number of layers. Figure 1 shows an example random regression forest.

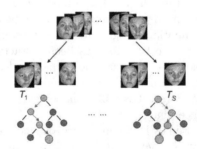

Fig. 1. An example of random regression forests. For each tree, the binary tests at the non-leaf nodes direct an input sample towards a leaf, where a real-valued, multivariate distribution of the output parameters is stored. The forest combines the results of all leaves to produce a probabilistic prediction in the real-valued output space.

2.2   Linear Discriminant Analysis

Linear discriminant analysis (LDA) is a tool for data dimension reduction. It has been widely used in face recognition [9]. The aim of LDA is to find projection axes such that samples, after being projected onto the axes, are far from each other if they are from different classes, or close to each other if they are of the same class. A complete description of LDA can be found in [5].

Given a number of N n-dimension samples $x_1, x_2, \ldots, x_N \in R^n$ belonging to K classes $c_1, c_2, \ldots, c_K$, the objective function of LDA is defined as follows:

$$\alpha_{opt} = \arg \max \frac{\alpha^T S_b \alpha}{\alpha^T S_w \alpha}, \tag{1}$$

$$S_b = \sum_{k=1}^{K} N_k (\mu^k - \mu)(\mu^k - \mu)^T, \tag{2}$$

$$S_w = \sum_{k=1}^{K} \sum_{x_i \in c_k} (x_i - \mu^k)(x_i - \mu^k)^T, \tag{3}$$

where N_k is the number of samples in the k-th class, μ is the global centroid, μ^k is the centroid of the k-th class. S_w and S_b are called, respectively, the within-class scatter matrix and the between-class scatter matrix. The projection axes α are commonly obtained by maximizing the between class covariance and simultaneously minimizing the within class covariance.

It can be mathematically shown that the optimal projection axes are the eigenvectors corresponding to the non-zero eigenvalues of the following general eigen-decomposition problem:

$$S_b \alpha = \lambda S_w \alpha. \tag{4}$$

The eigenvalue associated with an eigenvector gives a natural measure of the significance of the corresponding feature dimension.

3   The Proposed Method

Our goal is to estimate the rotation angles of the head in a 2D face image. The rest of this section introduces in detail the proposed method.

3.1   Feature Extraction

Given a training set of 2D face images with annotated head pose labels (in this paper, we consider yaw and pitch), the Gabor features are first calculated by convoluting the face images with the following Gabor filters,

$$g = \exp(-\frac{x'^2 + \gamma^2 y'^2}{2\sigma^2}) \exp(i \cdot (2\pi f x' + \psi)), \tag{5}$$

$$x' = x \cos\theta + y \sin\theta, \tag{6}$$

$$y' = -x \sin\theta + y \cos\theta, \tag{7}$$

where f represents the spatial frequency of the sinusoidal factor, θ represents the orientation of the normal to the parallel stripes of a Gabor function, ψ is the phase offset, σ is the standard deviation of the Gaussian envelope, and γ is the spatial aspect ratio specifying the ellipticity of the support of the Gabor function.

In this paper, 5 spatial frequencies (i.e., $f = 1,2,\ldots,5$) and 8 orientations (i.e., $\theta = 0°, 22.5°, 45°, \ldots, 135°, 157.5°$) were used. The resulting Gabor features are of very high dimension, and not suitable for constructing random regression forests. Hence, LDA is applied to reduce the dimension. In the lower dimensional feature space, the i-th feature is assigned with a weight, which is defined as follows,

$$w_i - \frac{\lambda_i}{\sum\limits_{j=1}^{M} \lambda_j}, \tag{8}$$

where λ_i is the eigenvalue associated with the i-th eigenvector, and M is the dimension of the reduced feature space. This weight measures the importance of the feature, and will be used to guide the selection of features in constructing tree predictors in the random regression forest.

3.2   Training Random Forests

To train a random forest of S trees $T = \{T_1, T_2, \ldots, T_S\}$, the trees are built one by one from a set of annotated samples, which are randomly chosen from the given set of training data. For each tree, N samples are randomly chosen, and then at each non-leaf node in the tree, m features are randomly chosen out of the M features to learn a binary test for the node. The tree keeps growing until the maximum depth is reached or a minimum number of samples are left, where a leaf is created. The leaf stores the mean of the pose angles of all the samples arriving at it. As proven by Breiman [3], the generalization error of a forest of tree classifiers depends on the strength of the individual trees in the forest and the correlation between them. Motivated by this fact, we choose features according to their weights. That is, the feature with larger weight has higher probability to be chosen. At each non-leaf node, we randomly generate m features from M features without repeat. Specifically, the larger the weight of a feature is, the higher the probability of choosing it. In this way, the constructed trees are more effective, and a better random forest can be obtained.

3.3   Binary Test

At each non-leaf node in a tree, a binary test, denoted as ϕ, is conducted to determine which branch the sample should be forwarded to. The binary test is defined by a chosen feature and its associated threshold. Given a sample, the binary test compares its feature with the threshold, and forwards the sample to the left branch if the evaluation result is lower than the threshold, or forwards it to the right branch otherwise. In the training phase, a pool of binary tests $\{\phi_i\}$ is generated at every non-leaf node by randomly choosing a feature from the m features and a threshold for it. In order to choose the best binary test from these randomly generated binary tests, we use the information gain to evaluate the effectiveness of each binary test. Specifically, all the training samples (denoted as X) arriving at the node are first split into the left and right branches by the binary test under evaluation. The two subsets are denoted as X_L and X_R, respectively. The information gain of this splitting is then computed as follows,

$$IG(\phi_i) = H(X) - H(X_L) - H(X_R), \tag{9}$$

where $H(\bullet)$ is information entropy. The binary test with the highest information gain is taken as the best one for the node.

3.4 Predicting Head Poses

Once the random regression forest is constructed, it can be used to predict the head pose in a new unseen 2D face image. The head poses predicted by different trees are averaged to give the final estimation of the head pose in the input 2D face image.

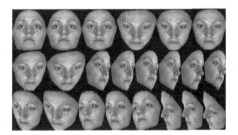

Fig. 2. Example 2D face images of a person with different poses in the synthetic database

4   Experiments

4.1   Databases and Protocols

We evaluate our proposed method using the BU-3DFE database [6] and the CMU-PIE database [7]. The BU-3DFE database contains the 3D full faces of 100 persons taken under standard illumination and various expressions. The background in these data has been removed. In order to construct ground truth data for evaluating the proposed method, we first correct the poses of these 3D faces to frontal pose. They are then rotated with known angles and projected to 2D images. We simulate the yaw angles from -60 to 60 degrees and the pitch angles from -30 to 30 degrees (both with an interval of 10 degrees). Figure 2 shows some example face images in this synthetic database. In our experiments, we use the images of 50 persons for training and the rest for testing.

The CMU-PIE database includes 2D face images of 68 persons. Each person has 13 different poses. An illustration of the pose variation in the CMU database is shown in Figure 3. In our experiments, we first crop the face regions from the original images. We randomly select the images of 34 people for training, and the rest for testing.

In order to evaluate the effectiveness of weighting features in constructing random forests, we compare the Gabor+LDA random forests without weighting features (denoted as GLRF) and with weighting features (denoted as WRF). In addition, we implement the probabilistic framework based method proposed in [8] (denoted as MBPF), and compare it with our proposed method. For each method, we do 10-fold cross validation experiments on both of the two databases, and report the average head pose estimation errors.

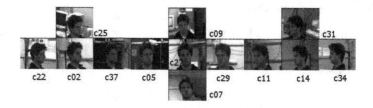

Fig. 3. An illustration of the pose variation in the CMU-PIE database

4.2   Experimental Results on the Synthetic Database

In the synthetic database, the size of face images is 16×16 pixels, and the resulting Gabor features of a face image are of 10240 ($16 \times 16 \times 40$) dimension. The features are reduced to 90 dimension by LDA. There are two important parameters in random forests: The number of trees and the number of randomly selected features at each node. We will experiment on these two parameters to see their effects on pose estimation accuracy. Figure 4 shows the estimation errors of yaw and pitch angles by different methods when different numbers of trees are used (for all cases 9 features are chosen). Table 1 summarizes the best results achieved by different methods. Obviously, the proposed method is much better than the existing method in [8]. By comparing the results of GLRF and WRF, it can be seen that (i) weighting features is effective in improving the pose estimation accuracy of random forests, and (ii) WRF is less sensitive to the number of trees and uses fewer number of trees. This proves that weighting features can help to construct more effective tree predictors. Figure 5 shows the estimation errors of yaw and pitch angles by the WRF method when 0 to 25 features are chosen (for all cases, 45 trees are used). The accuracy of the random forests is apparently improved when the features are weighted. Table 2 lists the best accuracy of different methods. Again, the proposed method with weighting features achieves the best results.

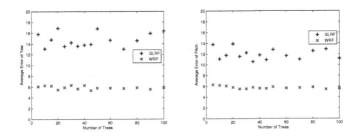

Fig. 4. Average estimation errors of yaw (left) and pitch (right) angles vs. the number of trees on the synthetic database

Table 1. The minimum pose estimation errors of different methods on the synthetic database when different numbers of trees are used

Method	Yaw (No. of Trees)	Pitch (No. of Trees)
GLRF	13.0(70)	10.5(35)
MBPF	14.0(N/A)	12.0(N/A)
WRF	5.3(45)	5.5(25)

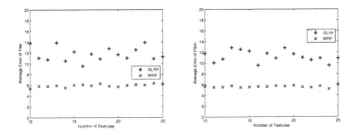

Fig. 5. Average estimation errors of yaw (left) and pitch (right) angles vs. the number of features on the synthetic database

4.3   Experimental Results on the CMU-PIE Database

Unlike the 2D face images in the synthetic database, the images in the CMU-PIE database were captured in real scenarios. The results on the CMU-PIE database are shown in Figures 6 and 7, and Tables 3 and 4, which again prove the effectiveness of our proposed method. However, compared with the accuracy

Table 2. The minimum pose estimation errors of different methods on the synthetic database when different numbers of features are chosen

Method	Yaw (No. of Chosen Features)	Pitch (No. of Chosen Features)
GLRF	9.6(17)	9.8(17)
MBPF	14.0(N/A)	12.0(N/A)
WRF	5.5(15)	5.4(22)

Table 3. The minimum estimation errors of different methods on the CMU-PIE database when different numbers of trees are used

Method	Yaw (No. of Trees)	Pitch (No. of Trees)
GLRF	8.0(90)	7.8(30)
MBPF	10.2(N/A)	10.0(N/A)
WRF	4.9(40)	4.2(50)

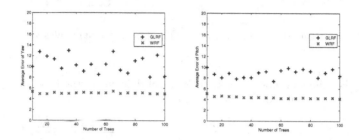

Fig. 6. Average estimation errors of yaw (left) and pitch (right) angles vs. the number of trees on the CMU-PIE database

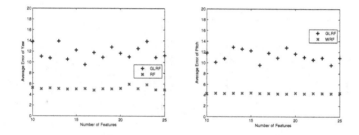

Fig. 7. Average estimation errors of yaw (left) and pitch (right) angles vs. the number of chosen features on the CMU-PIE database

Table 4. The minimum estimation errors of different methods on the CMU-PIE database when different numbers of features are chosen

Method	Yaw (No. of Chosen Features)	Pitch (No. of Chosen Features)
GLRF	9.6(16)	8.9(17)
MBPF	10.2(N/A)	10.1(N/A)
WRF	5.8(16)	5.2(19)

achieved on the synthetic database, the accuracy on the CMU-PIE database is a little bit worse. This is because of the more complicated background in the face images in the CMU-PIE database.

5   Conclusions

We have presented an improved random forest based method for estimating the head pose in 2D face images by weighting the features when constructing tree predictors in the random forest. We have conducted a series of experiments on two databases. The experimental results demonstrated that the random forests generated with our proposed method indeed improve the head pose estimation accuracy. In our future work, we are going to further improve the accuracy of the proposed method on real-world face images by incorporating into the method more advanced face image preprocessing techniques and feature extraction methods.

Acknowledgements. This work is supported by a grant from the National Natural Science Foundation of China (No. 61202161).

References

1. Murphy-Chutorian, E., Trivedi, M.M.: Head pose estimation in computer vision: A survey. IEEE Transactions on Pattern Analysis and Machine Intelligence 31(4), 607–626 (2009)
2. Havens, S., Marshall, H.P., Pielmeier, C., et al.: Automatic Grain Type Classification of Snow Micro Penetromoter Signals With Random Forests (2013)
3. Breiman, L.: Random forests. J. Machine Learning 45(1), 5–32 (2001)
4. Fanelli, G., Dantone, M., Gall, J., et al.: Random forests for real time 3d face analysis. International Journal of Computer Vision 101(3), 437–458 (2013)
5. Duda, R.O., Hart, P.E.: Pattern classification and scene analysis. Wiley, New York (1973)
6. Yin, L., Wei, X., Sun, Y., et al.: A high-resolution 3D dynamic facial expression database. In: 8th International Conference on Automatic Face and Gesture Recognition(FGR), pp. 1–6. IEEE Press, Santa Barbara (2008)
7. Sim, T., Baker, S., Bsat, M.: The CMU pose, illumination, and expression (PIE) database. In: Fifth IEEE International Conference on Automatic Face and Gesture Recognition, pp. 46–51. IEEE Press (2002)
8. Aghajanian, J., Simon, P.: Face Pose Estimation in Uncontrolled Environments. BMVC 1(2), 1–11 (2009)
9. Hu, W., Ma, B., Chai, X.: Head pose estimation using simple local gabor binary pattern. In: Sun, Z., Lai, J., Chen, X., Tan, T. (eds.) CCBR 2011. LNCS, vol. 7098, pp. 74–81. Springer, Heidelberg (2011)

Author Index